S0-BZV-212

# PREACHING THE MEMORY OF VIRTUE AND VICE

# SERMO: STUDIES ON PATRISTIC, MEDIEVAL, AND REFORMATION SERMONS AND PREACHING



Previously published volumes in this series are listed at the back of this book.

VOLUME 4

# Preaching the Memory of Virtue and Vice

## Memory, Images, and Preaching in the Late Middle Ages

by

Kimberly A. Rivers

BREPOLS

**British Library Cataloguing in Publication Data**

Rivers, Kimberly A.
Preaching the memory of virtue and vice : memory, images, and preaching in the late Middles Ages. -- (Sermo ; v. 4)
1. Sermons, Medieval--Europe. 2. Preaching--Europe--History--Middle Ages, 600-1500. 3. Mnemonics--History--To 1500. 4. Bible--Mnemonic devices--History--To 1500.
I. Title II. Series
251'.0094'0902-dc22

ISBN-13: 9782503515250





D/2010/0095/27
ISBN: 978-2-503-51525-0

Printed in the E.U. on acid-free paper

*To Kim, Quynh, and Liem*

# Contents

## Part III. The Spread of Mnemonic Exempla

# Illustrations

*Figures*



*Tables*

# Preface

Since I began the study of mnemonics and medieval preaching in the early 1990s, the topic of memory, which was just beginning to appeal to modern scholars as a subject of investigation, has continued to grow in popularity. Now there are studies on almost every aspect of memory imaginable, from its effect on the way that people envisioned saints and heros to the commemoration of important events to studies of mnemonic techniques. No single study could ever hope to include such a diversity of approaches. This book began as an examination of the *picturae* in the works of the classicizing friars. These seemed like such strange images to find in medieval biblical commentaries that I felt they needed more investigation. Once I had concluded that the *picturae* functioned as mnemonic devices, I became eager to trace the history of the use of such devices by the friars. Because this topic is so large, I have had to make many choices about what to include in my study. What I have tried to accomplish in this work is to expand the discussion of how medieval preachers incorporated mnemonic teachings into their preaching methods, and at the same time begin to lay out a chronology of the use of mnemonic techniques in the Middle Ages that previous studies have lacked. Most of the preachers and medieval scholars examined in this book, though not all, were members of the mendicant orders. I have also tried to indicate the integral role of Franciscans to the spread of mnemonic techniques in the Middle Ages, thus restoring them to their rightful place alongside the Dominicans. In no sense could I claim to have exhausted the material about either order's use of mnemonics in either their preaching roles or their religious mission, but one has to stop somewhere. I hope to explore the Franciscan contribution in greater detail in future works, and I expect other scholars will also have much to contribute.

Writing a book that grew out of a thesis project inevitably involves an author in a number of debts. My greatest debt is to my supervisor, Professor Joseph Goering, of the University of Toronto, for his enthusiasm, guidance, and ability to read long chapters at a moment's notice; he has been a model for my interactions with students. I was also greatly assisted by the advice and assistance of Professors Deborah Black, Stephen Dumont, and Brian Stock. I would like to thank the librarians at the Pontifical Institute of Mediaeval Studies, especially Nancy Kovacs, for her success in tracking down elusive Italian articles. At the University of Wisconsin Oshkosh, I have benefited greatly from the research support of the Faculty Development Board, which made possible the writing of several chapters. I also owe much to the interlibrary loan librarians, especially Erin Czech, for keeping me supplied with books and articles for the last thirteen years. Finally, I have to thank my husband, Kim, who has put up with the writing of this book from its inception as a graduate thesis to its final form. Without him, I would never have finished the degree, much less the book.

# AUTHOR'S NOTE

It is difficult to be entirely consistent in the spelling of medieval names. For the many medieval authors dealt with in this book, I have generally used the native forms. In cases when the names are quite well known, I have used the form by which they are best known among English scholars. All translations are mine unless noted otherwise.

# Abbreviations

| | |
|---|---|
| *Ad Her.* | Cicero, *De ratione dicendi Ad C. Herennium libri* IV *[M. Tulli Ciceronis Ad Herennium libri* VI*]*, ed. by Fridericus Marx (Leipzig: Teubner, 1894) |
| *AFH* | *Archivum franciscanum historicum* |
| *AFP* | *Archivum fratrum praedicatorum* |
| *Ars praed.* | Francesc Eiximenis, '*Ars praedicandi*', ed. by P. Martí de Barcelona, in *Hometage a Antoni Rubió i Lluch: Miscellània d'estudis literaris històricis i lingüistics*, 3 vols (Barcelona: [n. pub.], 1936), II, 300–40 |
| *Artif. eloq.* | John O. Ward, '*Artificiosa eloquentia* in the Middle Ages: The Study of Cicero's *De inventione*, the *Ad Herennium* and Quintilian's *De institutione oratoria* from the Early Middle Ages to the Thirteenth Century with Special Reference to the Schools of Northern France' (unpublished doctoral thesis, University of Toronto, 1972) |
| *BGTPM* | *Beiträge der Geschichte der Theologie und der Philosophie des Mittelalters* |
| BL | British Library |
| BnF | Bibliothèque nationale de France |
| *BRO* | Alfred Brotherston Emden, *A Biographical Register of the University of Oxford to A.D. 1500*, 3 vols (Oxford: Clarendon Press, 1957–59) |

CCCM — Corpus Christianorum Continuatio Mediaevalis (Turnhout: Brepols, 1966–)

CCSL — Corpus Christianorum Series Latina (Turnhout: Brepols, 1953–)

*De eruditione* — Vincent de Beauvais, *De eruditione filiorum nobilium*, ed. by Arpad Steiner (Cambridge, MA: Medieval Academy of America, 1938)

*De modo* — Guibert de Tournai, *De modo addiscendi*, ed. by Enrico Bonifacio (Turin: Società Editrice Internazionale, 1953)

*De modo comp.* — Thomas Waleys, *De modo componendi sermones*, in *Artes Praedicandi: Contribution à l'histoire de la rhétorique au moyen âge*, ed. by Thomas Marie Charland (Ottawa: Institut d'études médiévales, 1936), pp. 325–403

*Didas.* — Hugh of St Victor, *Didascalicon: De studio legendi*, ed. by Charles Henry Buttimer (Washington, DC: Catholic University of America Press, 1939)

*DNB* — *Dictionary of National Biography* (Oxford: Oxford University Press, 1909–)

EETS — Early English Text Society

*EFA* — Beryl Smalley, *English Friars and Antiquity in the Early Fourteenth Century* (Oxford: Blackwell, 1960)

*Fasc. mor.* — *Fasciculus morum: A Fourteenth-Century Preacher's Handbook*, ed. by Siegfried Wenzel (University Park: Pennsylvania State University Press, 1989)

*Fulg. meta.* — *Fulgentius metaforalis: Ein Beitrag zur Geschichte der antiken Mythologie im Mittelalter*, ed. by Hans Liebeschütz, Studien der Bibliothek Warburg, 4 (Leipzig: Teubner, 1926)

*Inst. orat.* — Quintilian, *Institutionis oratoriae libri duodecim*, ed. by Michael Winterbottom, 2 vols (Oxford: Clarendon Press, 1970)

| | |
|---|---|
| Nahum | Kimberly A. Rivers, 'Pictures, Preaching and Memory in Robert Holcot's Commentary on the Twelve Prophets' (unpublished MSL thesis, Pontifical Institute of Mediaeval Studies, 1993) |
| PL | *Patrologiae cursus completus [...] Series Latina*, ed. by Jacques-Paul Migne, 221 vols (Paris: Garnier, 1844–91) |
| *Rhet. novis.* | Boncompagnus, *Rhetorica novissima*, ed. by A. Gaudenzi, in *Scripta anecdota antiquissimorum glossatorum* (Bologna: [n. pub.], 1892), vol. II |
| *Summa de arte* | Thomas of Chobham, *Summa de arte praedicandi*, ed. by Franco Morenzoni, CCCM, 82 (Turnhout: Brepols, 1988) |
| *Summa de exemplis* | Giovanni da San Gimignano, *Summa de exemplis et rerum similitudinibus locvpletissima Verbi Dei Concionatoribus cunctisque litararum studiosis maximo usui futura* (Lyon: Simphorianum Beraud et Stehanum Michaelem, 1585) |

# INTRODUCTION

In the mid-fourteenth century, the Catalan Franciscan Francesc Eiximenis († 1409) wrote a manual explaining how to compose sermons for his fellow preachers. Most of the rules for sermon composition followed the well-laid-out schemes of medieval preaching treatises, but one section of his manual was atypical: Eiximenis included advice for memorizing a sermon. For instance, he told his readers that

> if you wish to remember many things, think of various parts of a city or village that are well-known to you, and through straight routes and continuous streets proceed by placing memorials in noteworthy places. And you can do the same thing in a large church, so that you should think of memorable places and chapels according to the sites, pictures, distances, and their invocations, and to each one attach your memorial, using some similitude. Running through these places later, you will be able to remember well the things located there. So if you have to speak about the Trinity, place that topic on the greater altar, since the Trinity is something great amid all the rest; if you have to speak about purity, place it in your imagination on the altar of the blessed Virgin; if about contemplation, on the altar of St. John, and so on with the rest of the things you need to remember, setting them in places fixed and coordinated to them by some similitude, just as we said, and you will be able to remember them.[1]

Francesc's ideas were not original to him. There were, in fact, a number of different memory schemes available to medieval thinkers, some originating in monastic meditative practice, some in pedagogical practice, and some in classical rhetorical theory. The variation best known to modern scholars is the mnemonic

[1] Francesc Eiximenis, *On Two Kinds of Order that Aid Understanding and Memory*, trans. by Kimberly A. Rivers, in *The Medieval Craft of Memory: An Anthology of Texts and Pictures*, ed. by Mary J. Carruthers and Jan M. Ziolkowski (Philadelphia: University of Pennsylvania Press, 2002), pp. 189–204 (p. 201).

scheme in the *Rhetorica ad Herennium* (first century BC): according to its anonymous author, anything could be remembered through the use of images and places. One had first to memorize an ordered set of places, such as a temple or parts of a well-known street or house. Once one had a visual memory of a series of physical locations, one could then set in these places images of the things one wished to remember. To retrieve the images, one simply revisited the memorized places in order, and the images would remind one of what one had memorized.[2] Francesc's recommendation to place imaginatively the topics from a sermon around the chapels and altars of a church probably represents a medieval adaptation of the *Ad Herennium*'s plan.

What was unusual about Francesc's preaching manual was that he chose to include mnemonic rules at all. Most of these manuals, known in the Middle Ages as *artes praedicandi* (arts of preaching), did not include memory rules, despite the fact that many, if not most, preachers spoke without a full written script in front of them (though some may have had notes — see Chapter 1, below) and despite the fact that they must have been aware of these rules. Eiximenis's treatise is invaluable because it reveals some of the practices of teaching and learning of medieval preachers.

Francesc Eiximenis was a member of the Franciscan order, which, along with the Dominican order, was created in the thirteenth century to preach the necessity of penitence, confession, and orthodox belief to the laity of Europe. Mary Carruthers, like Frances Yates and Paolo Rossi before her, credits the Dominicans Albertus Magnus and Thomas Aquinas with reviving the *Ad Herennium*'s memory system in the thirteenth century, which had fallen into disfavour from around the fourth century through the twelfth century.[3] Because of the new oratorical skills demanded by their preaching vocation, the Franciscans and Dominicans would appear to have required the mnemonic techniques

[2] Cicero, *De ratione dicendi Ad C. Herennium libri IV [M. Tulli Ciceronis Ad Herennium libri VI]*, ed. by Fridericus Marx (Leipzig: Teubner, 1894), III. 16–24, pp. 277–87. For an English translation, see *Ad C. Herennium: De ratione dicendi (Rhetorica ad Herennium)*, trans. by Harry Caplan, Loeb Classical Library (Cambridge, MA: Harvard University Press, 1954), III.16, pp. 207–19.

[3] Paolo Rossi, *Clavis Universalis: Arti Mnemoniche e logica combinatoria da Lullo a Leibniz* (Milan: Ricciardi, 1960), pp. 38–43 (see now the translation of Rossi, *Logic and the Art of Memory*, trans. by Stephen Clucas (Chicago: University of Chicago, 2000)); Frances A. Yates, *The Art of Memory* (Chicago: University of Chicago Press, 1966), pp. 60–61; Mary J. Carruthers, *The Book of Memory: A Study of Memory in Medieval Culture* (Cambridge: Cambridge University Press, 1990), pp. 70–71.

developed by ancient orators. Yates had already assumed that the Dominicans used the ancient mnemonic as an aid to their project of absorbing Aristotelian learning into Christian thought, particularly into its teachings about the virtues and vices. She also thought that the Dominicans must have used the memory technique chiefly for remembering sermons.[4] Carruthers concurs with Yates that the new forms of oratory appearing in the thirteenth century contributed to the revival of the architectural mnemonic.[5]

This view has recently been challenged by Sabine Heimann-Seelbach's work on fifteenth-century *ars memorativa* treatises. Though relatively few medieval authors addressed the subject of mnemonics directly, a new genre called the *ars memorativa* devoted solely to mnenmonics appeared at the beginning of the fifteenth century. European libraries in fact teem with copies of these treatises that describe complicated rules for remembering anything that a reader might not wish to forget, including letters, sermons, accounts, literary works, and the like. Heimann-Seelbach has meticulously catalogued these manuscripts and made an important study of them. She argues that the impetus for the sudden outpouring of mnemonic treatises in the fifteenth century did not grow out of medieval memory practice, as Yates had asserted, but instead stemmed from the humanist desire to memorize entire texts for ethical purposes and from the availability of mnemonic practices from Greek sources.[6] She sees almost no evidence for the use of the *Ad Herennium*'s memory method in the Middle Ages. Despite Heimann-Seelbach's extensive research into the fifteenth-century sources and into the ancient background of rhetorical thought, she has not examined many of the medieval sources discussed in this book. Therefore, I would argue that it is too soon to rule out the influence of the *Ad Herennium* in the Middle Ages. In English-speaking countries, relatively little attention has been given to memory's relationship to preaching and religious life, though scholars in France and Italy have taken up the topic more seriously. Their investigations have been limited mainly to Renaissance thinkers and to preachers like the fifteenth-century

[4] Yates, *Art of Memory*, pp. 77–78, 84–85.

[5] Carruthers, *Book of Memory*, p. 153. She adds to this picture the Dominicans' interest in the new psychology of Aristotle, which increased the prestige of memory as a kind of reasoning.

[6] Sabine Heimann-Seelbach, *Ars und scientia: Genese, Überlieferung und Funktionen der mnemotechnischen Traktatliteratur im 15. Jahrhundert; mit Edition und Untersuchung dreier deutscher Traktate und ihrer lateinischen Vorlagen*, Frühe Neuzeit, 58 (Tübingen: Niemeyer, 2000), pp. 477–88, 506.

Franciscan San Bernardino, though the work of Lina Bolzoni has begun to expand to late medieval Italian preachers.[7]

The aim of this volume is to demonstrate the integral role of memory and mnemonic techniques in medieval preaching across Europe from the thirteenth to the early fifteenth century. I argue that the mendicant orders, as well as other preachers and scholars, inherited from the early Middle Ages both simple mnemonic techniques of pedagogical and rhetorical practice and a tradition of monastic meditation founded on memory images. In the thirteenth century Dominican and Franciscan writers drew on these basic techniques even as they also regarded the ancient mnemonic system described by the *Ad Herennium* in a far more positive light than did previous generations. The increasing emphasis that intellectuals put on cognitive science, on ethics, and on distinctions between rhetoric and logic created a climate welcoming to an image-based memory system designed for orators. The book also delves into the Franciscan contribution to mnemonics, which has been almost entirely neglected by scholars. Yates had assumed that the Dominicans had a special role to play in promoting memory techniques in the Middle Ages, and scholars usually quote Albertus Magnus and Thomas Aquinas when they discuss medieval memory practices. The works by Francesc Eiximenis, Guibert de Tournai, and David von Augsburg examined here will show that the Franciscans were also vitally interested in memory. It is still too soon to say how different the two orders were in their overall approaches to memory. What does seem clear is that the Franciscans came to value imaginative meditation as part of their own spiritual lives. Their habit of meditating on mental images of the virtues and vices eventually spilled out into their sermons in the *picturae*. Some Dominicans seem also to have followed this practice.

Following rules like the ones described by Eiximenis above, the friars inserted verbal mnemonic 'images' into their sermons and exempla collections as a way to aid the recall of both preachers and listeners. The products of such mnemonic practices stud medieval sermons: elaborate allegories of castles, forts, and houses; careful schemas of sevens, as in the seven gifts of the Holy Spirit, the seven vices and virtues, the seven petitions of the *Pater Noster*; and verbal *picturae* and

[7] For example, Jacques Berlioz, 'La Mémoire du prédicateur: Recherches sur la mémorisation des récits exemplaires (XIII$^{e}$–XV$^{e}$ siècles)', in *Temps, mémoire, tradition au moyen âge: Actes du XIII$^{e}$ Congrès de la société des historiens médiévistes de l'enseignement supérieur public, Aix-en-Provence, 4–5 Juin 1982* (Aix-en-Provence: Université de Provence, 1983), pp. 157–83; Carlo Delcorno, 'L'ars praedicandi di Bernardino da Siena', *Lettere italiane*, 32 (1980), 441–75; and Lina Bolzoni, 'Teatralità e tecniche della memoria in Bernardino da Siena', *Intersezioni*, 4 (1984), 271–87.

*imagines*, often based on ancient or mythographical descriptions, which were then allegorized in moral terms. These techniques were especially popular in fourteenth-century England. The group of scriptural exegetes known as the English classicizing friars pioneered mnemonic images based on mythographic depictions allegorized as virtues and vices, which then circulated on the Continent in exempla collections.

It is my contention that verbal images and complicated schemas were intended to aid in the remembering of sermons by both preachers and the laity by providing ordering devices. Verbal imagery also provoked the affective response that led to devotion and penitence, much like the visual imagery ornamenting churches across medieval Europe. Finally, I suggest that allegories of the virtues and vices, among other topics, may have served as foci for simple meditation by the laity as well as the clergy. The images of Penance, Prayer, and Humility in the *Moralitates* of the English Dominican Robert Holcot were not oddities but in fact were so widely diffused in late medieval culture as to provoke debate about the proper use of both mental and visual imagery in religious life. Such imagery contributed to the increasing interest in meditation and imagery among both the clergy at large and the laity in the late Middle Ages. Though I have devoted much attention to the *picturae* of the classicizing friars, I in no way wish to de-emphasize the mnemonic function of other structuring devices in medieval preaching.[8] Certainly I deal with many of them in the book. However, because it seemed to me that the *picturae* required both more analysis of their mnemonic function and more investigation into their dispersal across Europe, I have concentrated on them in this study.

It is also my aim to contribute to the ever-expanding body of scholarship on mnemonic practices in the Middle Ages and the Early Modern period by providing a framework of the chronological development of mnemonics in the Middle Ages. The groundwork on the topic was laid by Ludwig Volkmann's 1929 article on the 'Ars memorativa', Helga Hajdú's *Das mnemotechnische Schrifttum des Mittelalters* (1936), Paolo Rossi's *Clavis Universalis* (1960), and Frances Yates's *The Art of Memory* (1966).[9] Volkmann and Hajdú provided initial forays

[8] For examples of other kinds of mnemonic structuring devices in medieval sermons, see Kirsten M. Berg, 'On the Use of Mnemonic Schemes in Sermon Composition: The Old Norwegian Homily Book', in *Constructing the Medieval Sermon*, ed. by Roger Andersson, Sermo, 6 (Turnhout: Brepols, 2007), pp. 221–36.

[9] Ludwig Volkmann, 'Ars memorativa', *Jahrbuch der Kunsthistorischen Sammlungen in Wien*, Neue Folge, 30 (1929), 111–200; Helga Hajdú, *Das mnemotechnische Schrifttum des Mittelalters* (Vienna: Leo, 1936).

into the mnemonic arts of the Middle Ages and Renaissance period but hardly exhausted the material or its implications for European culture. Yates traced the history of the ancient art of memory up through the Renaissance, when it inspired hermetic philosophers like Giordano Bruno to search for the key to universal knowledge.[10] Her approach was complemented by Rossi's *Clavis Universalis*, which documented the function of mnemonics in the development of the scientific method.[11] Because both Rossi and Yates were most interested in the Renaissance material, little work was done on the medieval period until recently. Mary Carruthers's more recent study, *The Book of Memory*, has begun to fill this gap.[12] She has purposely overturned the usual dichotomy between a popular orality, dependent on memory, and a literate elite, reliant on writing. She instead contends that 'medieval culture was fundamentally memorial, to the same degree that modern culture in the West is documentary', and that the value of memory training to a culture depends more on the importance of rhetoric than on whether texts are presented in oral or written forms.[13] Her second book, *The Craft of Thought* (1998), considers how early medieval monks created their own monastic rhetoric with a concomitant monastic *memoria* as part of their life of prayer.[14] New research has also begun to elucidate mnemonic practice at the borders of the Middle Ages. Jocelyn Penny Small's *Wax Tablets of the Mind* re-examines the memory practices of antiquity, while Heimann-Seelbach's book *Ars und Scientia*

[10] See also Frances A. Yates, 'Ciceronian Art of Memory', in *Medioevo e Rinascimento: Studi in onore di Bruno Nardi*, 2 vols (Florence: Sansoni, 1956), II, 873–903; and her 'Lodovico da Pirano's Memory Treatise', in *Cultural Aspects of the Italian Renaissance: Essays in Honor of Paul Oskar Kristeller*, ed. by Cecil A. Clough (New York: Zambelli, 1976), pp. 111–22.

[11] See also Paolo Rossi, 'La construzione delle immagini nei tratti di memoria artificiale del Rinascimento', in *Umanesimo e Simbolismo*, ed. by Enrico Castelli (Padua: CEDAM, 1958), pp. 161–78, and Paolo Rossi, 'Immagini e memoria locale nei secoli XIV e XV', *Revista critica di storia della filosofia*, 2 (1958), 149–91.

[12] Carruthers has continued her investigation into medieval attitudes toward memory in 'The Poet as Master Builder: Composition and Locational Memory in the Middle Ages', *New Literary History*, 24 (1993), 881–904, and 'Boncompagno at the Cutting-Edge of Rhetoric: Rhetorical Memoria and the Craft of Memory', *Journal of Medieval Latin*, 6 (1996), 44–64. She has also revised some of the conclusions of her earlier book in *The Book of Memory: A Study of Memory in Medieval Culture*, 2nd edn (New York: Cambridge University Press, 2008). However, I have not been able to incorporate her revised views into this book.

[13] Carruthers, *Book of Memory*, pp. 8, 11.

[14] Mary J. Carruthers, *The Craft of Thought: Meditation, Rhetoric, and the Making of Images, 400–1200* (Cambridge: Cambridge University Press, 1998).

both catalogues the extant *ars memorativa* treatises of the fifteenth century and places them in the context of early humanist thought.[15] Susan Hagen's *Allegorical Remembrance* provides a fine example of how analysing *memoria* elucidates nuances of vernacular literature, as do many of the studies in the recently published volume *Medieval Memory: Text and Image*.[16] Lina Bolzoni has written much about early modern attitudes toward memory and literary invention, as well as about late medieval Italian preachers, while I have written about the mnemonic techniques of Francesc Eiximenis.[17] It is my hope that this book will contribute to a more general understanding of memory and preaching across medieval Europe. I feel justified in including discussion of authors from many different European countries because their views are representative of the culture of Western Christendom as a whole.

## *Whose Memory?*

One issue for the reader to bear in mind is that unlike ancient mnemonic systems, whose principles were designed to aid the memories of orators alone (with perhaps a few concessions to their listeners), medieval mnemonic schemes were aimed at least as much at the listener as the speaker. This twofold emphasis was possible because most of the mnemonic devices discussed in this book affected the structure of the sermon and did not merely 'hide' in the mind of the preacher, as ancient memory devices did. The kinds of mnemonic images that will be explored in this book appeared in the text itself; indeed, their seeming incongruity with the rest of the text can be an indicator of their mnemonic function. The *picturae* of

[15] Jocelyn Penny Small, *Wax Tablets of the Mind* (London: Routledge, 1997).

[16] Susan K. Hagen, *Allegorical Remembrance: A Study of 'The Pilgrimage of the Life of Man' as a Medieval Treatise on Seeing and Remembering* (Athens: University of Georgia Press, 1990); *Medieval Memory: Image and Text*, ed by. Frank Willaert and others, Fédération internationale des Instituts d'études médiévales: Textes et études du moyen âge, 27 (Turnhout: Brepols, 2004).

[17] See, for instance, Lina Bolzoni, *The Gallery of Memory: Literary and Iconographic Models in the Age of the Printing Press*, trans. by Jeremy Parzen (Toronto: University of Toronto Press, 2001); Lina Bolzoni, *The Web of Images: Vernacular Preaching from its Origins to St Bernardino da Siena* (Aldershot: Ashgate, 2004). See also her *La stanza della memoria: Modeli letterari e iconografici nell'éta della stampa* (Turin: Einaudi, 1995). Kimberly A. Rivers, 'Memory and Medieval Preaching: Mnemonic Advice in the *Ars praedicandi* of Francesc Eiximenis (*c.*1327–1409)', *Viator*, 30 (1999), 253–84.

the classicizing friars are the best example of such images. In other cases, the image contains the 'message' of the sermon, as it were, and is clearly useful to both speaker and listener. Many examples of this kind of memory image will be found in Chapter 4, below.

## *Sources*

Because so much of medieval learned culture was international in scope, the sources used in this book originate in countries ranging from Catalonia to Germany. It is clear that many of the authors discussed knew and drew on each other's works. For instance, Johannes von Werden was familiar with Robert Holcot, and Jean de Hesdin used Pierre Bersuire's works in his biblical commentaries. Because medieval authors tended not to be as forthcoming about mnemonic techniques as early modern writers, I have tried to incorporate as many medieval examples of mnemonics as I could, especially those that have been little discussed in modern secondary literature.[18] These authors include Francesc Eiximenis, Guibert de Tournai, Johannes von Werden, and David von Augsburg. Though they are not as well known to modern audiences, each of these medieval authors was either quite influential in his time or the author of a medieval best-seller. For this reason, I will argue that their views are quite revealing of medieval culture. Each will be discussed more fully later in the book. I have also devoted much space to exegesis of these four authors' ideas, both because their mnemonic associations have not been much discussed in the secondary literature and because such careful attention to their ideas reveals how medieval mnemonics functioned. Finally, although Hugh of St Victor's ideas about memory have received attention by modern scholars, I have discussed his ideas in some detail for two reasons. First, the degree to which memory skills underlay his educational programme has not been fully recognized, and so I have tried to make this relationship clear. Second, Hugh's pedagogical and mnemonic plans greatly influenced the Franciscans and to a lesser degree the Dominicans. They therefore require treatment in this book.

[18] For collections of documents illustrating mnemonic practices in the Middle Ages, see *The Medieval Craft of Memory* and *Gedächtnislehren und Gedächtniskünste in Antike und Frühmittelalter*, ed. by Jörg Jochen Berns (Tübingen: Niemeyer, 2003).

## *Overview of Book*

Part I of the present study examines the transformation of memory techniques in the High Middle Ages. Chapter 1 examines the medieval sources of mnemonic techniques, starting with the monastic methods developed in the early Middle Ages. It then looks at the changes that the twelfth century brought to the views of memory within both the monastic and new scholastic settings. Both monks and scholars felt more pressure to memorize material quickly, but they tended to rely on memory methods that had served previous generations. However, the career of Hugh of St Victor reveals that one major change of the twelfth century was a tendency to articulate both memory methods and memory contents in writing. Chapter 2 takes up the mendicant contribution to medieval memory theory, documenting how changes within the schools' curricula in rhetoric, logic, and cognitive science allowed the mendicants, among the leading scholars of the day, to re-evaluate the ancient memory method of the *Ad Herennium* in a more favourable light than in preceding centuries. It also looks at the Franciscan attitude toward memory, which has not been examined in any great detail, showing how Guibert de Tournai folded all the memory methods of his day into one convenient place. Chapter 3 examines how David von Augsburg adopted a Cistercian view of human psychology to emphasize the importance of memory in Franciscan religious life in texts that became the foundation of Franciscan meditation methods. Memory needed to be cleansed of the recall of past sins and to learn to concentrate its attention on God, first by focusing memory's attention on the benefits of God, particularly the great gift of the Passion, and second by stripping away evil and depraved thoughts and painting one's soul with images of the virtues instead.

Part II looks specifically at how the preacher's memory was constructed in the High and late Middle Ages. Chapter 4 deals more directly with the issue of preaching by analysing what the new *ars praedicandi* had to say about memory before turning to a detailed examination of Francesc Eiximenis's *ars praedicandi* and his memory method. Chapter 5 looks at some of the ways that medieval preachers justified the use of images in churches and exempla in preaching, while Chapter 6 looks at one of the best examples of medieval mnemonic exempla, the *picturae* of the classicizing friars.

Finally, Part III treats the ways that the classicizing friars' *picturae* spread to the Continent and their fate, looking first at France in Chapter 7 and Germany in Chapter 8. Chapter 9 contrasts the use of mnemonics by Italian preachers with that of the preachers of northern Europe.

Before turning to the main narrative of the book, it may be useful for some readers to encounter a brief background of ancient mnemonic techniques. Readers already familiar with the ancient technique could skip this section of the introduction.

## *Mnemonics and the Ancient Rhetorical Tradition*

Medieval monks, writers, and scholars inherited many traditions about memory and created some of their own. In particular, they were aware of classical rhetorical techniques for improving one's memory. In antiquity, such methods were known as 'artificial memory' or 'the art of memory'. From the fifth century BC, an *ars* in Latin or *technē* in Greek consisted of 'a set of rules, system or method of making or doing, whether of the useful arts, or of the fine arts'.[19] Classical sources attributed the invention of the art for memory to the poet Simonides of Keos (*c.* 556–486 BC). Jocelyn Penny Small thinks that two things happened in the early fifth century that affected the way that Greeks saw memory and thus helped to bring about Simonides' invention: first, there were more written words than there used to be and thus people needed a new way of retrieving them; and second, the invention of writing brought the concept of a fixed text that needed to be repeated word for word. Poets such as Simonides no longer composed their works anew from stock phrases for each performance. Instead, they composed their poems once and used a greater variety of words than what was possible before. But the greater variation of words required more effort to remember what they were. Hence the need for improved memory techniques.[20]

Simonides' invention stemmed from his recall of the places of dinner guests around a table after the roof of his host's house had collapsed. According to Cicero, this incident helped him to understand the importance of order to memory: 'And so for those who would train this part of the mind, places [*locos*] must be selected and those things [*rerum*] which they want to hold in memory must be reproduced in the mind and put in those places: thus it would be that the order of the places would preserve the order of things; moreover, the likeness [*effigies*] of the things would represent the things themselves.'[21]

[19] Small, *Wax Tablets*, p. 81.

[20] Small, *Wax Tablets*, p. 83.

[21] Cicero, *De oratore*, trans. by E. W. Sutton, Loeb Classical Library (Cambridge, MA: Harvard University Press, 1979), 2. 353–54, cited in Small, *Wax Tablets*, p. 83.

The poet's insight supposedly spawned all the memory methods that came later, both Greek and Roman. The ones that have been preserved for us are available in rhetorical texts, because memory was especially useful for orators and because it eventually became enshrined as a formal part of rhetoric by the second century BC.[22] Small thinks there was a large variety of memory methods available in antiquity. What you needed to remember drove what method you chose.[23] Nonetheless, two main approaches emerge from the sources remaining to us, both from the Latin rhetorical tradition.[24] The first is the 'Ciceronian' system laid out in the *Rhetorica ad Herennium* and affirmed by Cicero's comments in *De oratore*.[25] The second is a modified version of the same system advocated by Quintilian in his *Institutio oratoria*. Because an understanding of these two systems will allow one to grasp the medieval variants more quickly, it is useful to consider them here.

### *Rhetorica ad Herennium*

The *Rhetorica ad Herennium*'s mnemonic system is the one with which modern scholars are the most familiar.[26] The *Rhetorica ad Herennium* was written *c.* 88–85 BC, within a few years of Cicero's *De inventione*, and is similar in style: medieval scholars believed Cicero to be the author of both works.[27] According to this rhetorical handbook, there are two related kinds of enhanced memory: memory for things (*res*) and for words (*verba*). *Res* could be physical items, but they could also be concepts, names, and the like. To remember things, the first step is to memorize a series of places (*loci*), connected to each other in logical order, so

[22] Small, *Wax Tablets*, p. 83.

[23] Small, *Wax Tablets*, p. 117.

[24] No sources remain for ancient Greek mnemonic practice. For what little evidence we have about the Greeks, who, according to Cicero, invented mnemonics, see Yates, *Art of Memory*, pp. 27–49, and Small, *Wax Tablets*, chap. 7. Heimann-Seelbach, *Ars und Scientia*, also makes some interesting suggestions about Greek methods, pp. 417–43. See also Herwig Blum, *Die Antike Mnemotechnik* (New York: Olms, 1969).

[25] James Jerome Murphy, *Rhetoric in the Middle Ages: A History of Rhetorical Theory from St. Augustine to the Renaissance* (Berkeley and Los Angeles: University of California Press, 1974), pp. 18–19.

[26] Though there are now many descriptions of artificial memory in the *Ad Herennium*, Yates's is still the best, *Art of Memory*, pp. 1–17.

[27] Small, *Wax Tablets*, p. 98.

that one may move through them mentally either forwards or backwards from any place. The loci can be real or imaginary (real ones are easier to visualize) and should be distinct enough from one another to avoid confusion. To reinforce this order, one can place distinguishing marks at regular intervals, such as a golden hand at the fifth locus.[28]

Once the loci are mastered, one sets images of the things to be remembered in these mental places. The *Ad Herennium* describes the kinds of images to use:

> We ought, then, to set up images of a kind that can adhere longest in memory. And we shall do so if we establish likenesses as striking as possible; if we set up images that are not many or vague, but doing something [*agentes imagines*]; if we assign to them exceptional beauty or singular ugliness; if we dress some of them with crowns or with purple cloaks, for example, so that the likeness may be more distinct to us; or if we somehow disfigure them, as by introducing one stained with blood or soiled with mud or smeared with red paint, so that its form is more striking, or by assigning certain comic effects to our images, for that, too, will ensure our remembering them more readily. The things we easily remember when they are real we likewise remember without difficulty when they are figments, if they have been carefully delineated.[29]

When one wishes to remember something, such as an idea or person, one should form a striking image associated with it and set it in the first place. Then, when one wishes to recall the item, one can return to the place and call up the image. The emphasis is on order and imagery; every writer on the topic from antiquity through the Renaissance stresses order as the key to the whole. Many sum up the process with an oft-used quotation: 'for the places are similar to wax tablets or papyrus, the images to letters, the disposition and placement of the images are like writing, and the delivery is like reading'.[30]

This plan constitutes memory for things; to learn memory for words, or verbatim memorization, the author of the *Ad Herennium* counsels an expanded version of the same system, using an image for each word or phrase and employing puns to condense the material.[31] The author considers memory for words far more difficult, because it requires many more images and places; however, he does not find it a waste of time. By practising this more intricate mnemonic, the orator strengthens 'memory for things', which is generally more useful.[32]

[28] *Ad Her.*, III.16–19, pp. 277–80.

[29] *Ad Her.*, III.32, p. 284; Caplan's translation, III.32 and 37.

[30] *Ad Her.*, III.17, p. 278; my translation.

[31] *Ad Her.*, III.21, pp. 282–83.

[32] Heimann-Seelbach, *Ars und Scientia*, pp. 437–38, suggests that memory for words may have been a feature of Greek mnemonic theory.

In fact, few ancient orators recommended this system for memorizing a speech verbatim. Cicero placed memory for words below memory for things in importance for an orator, as the latter helped a speaker in pinning down his thoughts with images and the order of topics with places.[33] This is not to claim that ancient orators never memorized speeches or other written materials, only that they probably did not attempt to match an image and place to every word.[34] Small notes that modern testing shows mnemonic strategies to be especially helpful in recall of content rather than actual words.[35] Thus, while the ancient mnemonic system might have seemed ideal for orators to memorize the exact words for their speeches, it was probably used more often to keep track of the order of the argument, the main points of one's own speech, and also of one's opponents in a legal case.[36]

Certainly, when Cicero wanted to recommend a mnemonic system in his famous work on speaking, *De oratore*, he turned to Simonides' art. He explained that his treatment was brief not because of his dislike of the system but from the fact that it was so well known.[37] It was clear that Cicero really believed that the art of memory works. His speaker in the dialogue, Antonius, expresses gratitude for Simonides' invention and chides those unskilled in the memory art who complain that one's memory will be weighed down by the extra burden of images to remember. He has seen men with almost divine memories — Charmadas of Athens and Metrodorus of Scepsis in Asia — both of whom claimed to use images and places to remember.[38]

[33] *M. Tullii Ciceronis Rhetorica*, I: *Libros De oratore tres continens*, ed. by A. S. Wilkins (Oxford: Clarendon Press, 1963), II.88, ll. 359–60: 'Sed verborum memoria, quae minus est nobis necessaria, maiore imaginum varietate distinguitur [...] rerum memoria propria est oratoris; eam singulis personis bene positis notare possumus, ut sententias imaginibus, ordinem locis comprehendamus.'

[34] Quintilian preferred to memorize a written speech if time and memory capacity allowed, but if these interfered, it was far better to have a good grasp of the facts (*Institutionis oratoriae libri duodecim*, ed. by Michael Winterbottom, 2 vols (Oxford: Clarendon Press, 1970), XI.2, §§ 45–50).

[35] Small, *Wax Tablets*, p. 114.

[36] Cicero, *De oratore*, ed. by Wilkins, II.87, l. 355.

[37] Cicero, *De oratore*, ed. by Wilkins, II.87, l. 358: 'Quare ne in re nota et pervulgata multus et insolens sim.'

[38] *Inst. orat.*, XI.2, §§ 23–26.

### *Institutio oratoria*

Cicero's favourable attitude contrasts strongly with that of the advocate of the second mnemonic system, Quintilian. Like Cicero, he recounts the story of Simonides' invention of the art of memory and elaborates the rules. As Yates points out, Quintilian's presentation surpasses the *Ad Herennium*'s in clarity, as when, for instance, he describes how the rooms of one's home may serve as loci.[39] Despite this clear exposition, however, Quintilian rejects the system's utility for orators. It may, he concedes, be useful for an auctioneer who can reel off the objects sold to their buyers, but such a mnemonic system will impede the flow of an orator's words by the sheer weight of images.[40]

Yet, though he denies the efficacy of the entire system, he sees possible benefits of each of the art of memory's elements: place, images, and order. He mentions the importance of place twice: once in relating Simonides' system and once in presenting his own method. Quintilian declares that one can test Simonides' observation of the memorial benefits of impressing places in one's head by simple experiment. When we return to a spot after some time, we recognize not only the place, but also what we did there, the people present, even what we were thinking at the time.[41]

He also seems to allow the use of places in memory when describing his own system:

> There is one thing which will be of assistance to everyone, namely, to learn a passage by heart from the same tablets on which he has committed it to writing. For he will have certain tracks to guide him in his pursuit of memory, and the mind's eye will be fixed not merely on the pages on which the words were written, but on individual lines, and at times he will speak as though he were reading aloud. Further, if the writing should be interrupted by some erasure, addition or alteration, there are certain symbols available, the sight of which will prevent us from wandering from the track. This device bears some resemblance to the mnemonic system which I mentioned above, but if my experience is worth anything, is at once more expeditious and more effective.[42]

[39] Yates, *Art of Memory*, p. 23; *Inst. orat.*, XI.2, § 20.

[40] *Inst. orat.*, XI.2, §§ 25–26.

[41] *Inst. orat.*, XI.2, § 17.

[42] *Inst. orat.*, XI.2, §§ 32–33; translation from Quintilian, *The Institutio Oratoria: With an English Translation by H. E. Butler*, Loeb Classical Library (London: Heinemann, 1921), XI.2, §§ 32–33 (henceforth, trans. by Butler).

Here the rhetorical expert seems to provide a kind of mnemonic place in the writing on the tablet. He also obviously countenances the use of images as ways of 'marking' the text.

In addition, Quintilian recommends order, which most authors called the key to the art of memory. For him, order arises from *divisio* and *compositio*, both of which provide a solid structure to the speech. He thinks that they are almost the only way of remembering what we have thought up to say:

> For correct division will be an absolute safeguard against error in the order of our speech, since there are certain points not merely in the distribution of the various questions in our speech, but also in their development [...] which naturally come first, second, and third, and so on, while the connexion will be so perfect that nothing can be omitted or inserted without the fact of the omission or insertion being obvious.[43]

The arrangement of one's ideas contributes to order and consequently preserves the memory of what one wishes to retain.

Because these terms will recur in discussions of mnemonics, it is worth taking some trouble to tease out their meaning. *Compositio* means something like 'style' or 'the orderly arrangement of ideas with style'. *Divisio* is a little harder; its functions appear closely related to *partitio*. Quintilian defines both so:

> *Division* [...] means the division of a group of things into its component parts, *partition* is the separation of an individual whole into its elements, *order* the correct disposition of things in such a way that what follows coheres with what precedes.[44]

Partition is a subset of division and is the term Quintilian uses most frequently to refer to the enumeration of points or *propositiones* that an orator intends to cover in his proof.[45] It delivers signposts to the speaker and to the audience of the material to follow and is obviously useful to memory. This function is likely what Quintilian refers to as division.[46]

[43] *Inst. orat.*, XI.2, § 37, trans. by Butler.

[44] *Inst. orat.*, VII.1, § 1, trans. by Butler.

[45] The five parts of a forensic speech, according to Quintilian, are the exordium, the statement of facts, the proof, the refutation, and the peroration, with the partition and the propositions belonging to the proof (*Inst. orat.*, III.9, § 2).

[46] In his *De nuptiis*, Martianus Capella defines division as 'that part which comprises a brief outline of all the sections in the speech', V.556. (William Stahl and Richard Johnson with E. L. Burge, *Martianus Capella and the Seven Liberal Arts*, 2 vols (New York: Columbia University Press, 1971–77), II, 209).

Thus, though Quintilian disapproves of Simonides' system, he is willing to make use of certain elements. Practise is the real key, aided by logical order and skilful composition, but there is room for places and images by always using the same wax tablets to study from and by placing a few images at problem points.

To sum up: the essential features of the 'Ciceronian' method are the creation of logically ordered mental 'places' and the fixing of mental images in them. Quintilian's simpler mnemonic system also uses order, places, and images, but in a less structured form. The 'place' is either the physical location where you first memorized something or the tablets from which you worked. Images can be either mentally or physically located on the tablets, while order arises from the logical arrangement of ideas in composition.

What was the influence of these two systems in the Middle Ages? It has commonly been supposed that only the 'Ciceronian' as laid out in the *Ad Herennium* influenced medieval mnemonic practices, because it was the only one of the three classical works that described it to be known in its entirety throughout the Middle Ages.[47] This work drew considerable respect from Cicero's supposed authorship. Incomplete copies of both *De oratore* and the *Institutio* seem also to have circulated, but complete copies became available only in 1416 for Quintilian and 1422 for Cicero.[48] The *textus mutilatus* of Quintilian, which did circulate, omitted the section on memory.[49] This picture, as it was originally presented by Yates, is overly dependent on the use of entire works, and for that matter, on texts. We should not assume that complete copies of Cicero and Quintilian offered the only forum in which medieval students could learn about memory. In fact, a variety of ways existed for the two orators to exercise their influence.

First, *florilegia* and incomplete copies of texts must not be overlooked. It is clear, for instance, that in the thirteenth century Guibert de Tournai, OFM, knew at least portions of the both *De oratore* and the *Institutio*. Significantly, in *De modo addiscendi* he quotes from the memory section of Cicero's *De oratore*: 'and

[47] Yates, *Art of Memory*, pp. 55–57. For a brief history of the medieval circulation of all three rhetorical handbooks, see Murphy, *Rhetoric in the Middle Ages*, pp. 109, 116–30.

[48] Leighton Durham Reynolds and Nigel Guy Wilson, *Scribes and Scholars: A Guide to the Transmission of Greek and Latin Literature*, 2nd edn (Oxford: Clarendon Press, 1974), pp. 89, 121, 123.

[49] Murphy, *Rhetoric in the Middle Ages*, p. 125. Murphy reproduces Francis Henry Colson's table of omissions in *textus mutilati*. Both types dropped Quintilian's *Inst. orat.*, XI.1–2, which includes the memory section.

Tully [Cicero] in the book [*De oratore*] teaches us to use places as wax and images as letters'.[50] Guibert also relates Cicero's depiction of the invention of the art of memory and a story about Simonides and Themistocles. Since he also quotes the comparison of mnemonics to wax and letters from Martianus Capella and the *Ad Herennium* in the same paragraph, it is possible that he knew the *De oratore* from excerpts in a *florilegium* or from citations in another author. Guibert's quotations indicate that at least portions of *De oratore's* treatment of memory were available to medieval authors. The same may be true for Quintilian. Although Guibert does not cite the *Institutio's* memory section, he does quote extensively from the rest of the work in *De modo*.

Second, one must consider indirect influence. A direct, medieval quotation from Quintilian on memory has yet to materialize, but his influence clearly lived on in the writings of rhetoricians whom he inspired. For this reason it is useful to consider some of the lesser known rhetoricians who composed their works in the late antique period.

In the fourth and fifth centuries, three rhetoricians clearly follow Quintilian's lead in their view of memory training. C. Iulius Victor (fourth century), whose *Ars rhetorica* is based partly on Quintilian's work,[51] disdains the use of places and simulacra, which do not seem effective to him. He recommends, as Quintilian had done, that one memorize verbatim both one's own writings and the best of other people's orations and histories. In this way, one will always have a superior exemplar in one's head as a guide for composition. He also echoes Quintilian's advice about *divisio* and *compositio* for retention of what we write and think:

> [F]or he who composes an oration correctly will never be able to err. There are certain points not only in the distribution of questions, but also in their development, and if the first and second points connect to one another successively, nothing will be able to be subtracted through forgetfulness, as the context warns of the next points.[52]

[50] Guibert de Tournai, *De modo addiscendi*, ed. by Enrico Bonifacio (Turin: Società Editrice Internazionale, 1953), pp. 215–16: 'Et Tullius in libro locis pro cera, simulacris pro litteris uti docet'. See Chapter 2, below, for an extended discussion of Guibert's memory methods.

[51] See Robert Browning, 'Oratory and Epistolography', in *Cambridge History of Classical Literature*, II: *Latin Literature*, ed. by E. J. Kenney (Cambridge: Cambridge University Press, 1982), p. 756; C. Iulius Victor, *Ars rhetorica*, in *Rhetores Latini minores*, ed. by Carolus Halm (Leipzig: Teubner, 1863), pp. 371–448; John O. Ward, '*Artificiosa eloquentia* in the Middle Ages: The Study of Cicero's *De inventione*, the *Ad Herennium* and Quintilian's *De institutione oratoria* from the Early Middle Ages to the Thirteenth Century with Special Reference to the Schools of Northern France' (unpublished doctoral thesis, University of Toronto, 1972), p. 85, n. 16.

[52] C. Iulius Victor, *Ars rhetorica*, p. 440: 'nam qui recte conpegerit orationem, numquam poterit errare. Certa sunt quaedam non solum in digerendis quaestionibus, sed etiam in persequendis.

Another fourth-century rhetorician, C. Chirius Fortunatianus, imitates Quintilian's handling of memory.[53] He, too, attributes the art of memory to Simonides, giving a very brief synopsis. Then he asks, 'what is a better and simpler scheme of memory? That, if an oration is long, it may be learned through parts'. Constant practise, the use of *notae*, and learning from the same wax tablets on which one wrote will cement the process, Fortunatianus concludes.[54]

In the early fifth century, Martianus Capella, like Quintilian, provides a synopsis of both systems of mnemonics.[55] He begins by stating that order is the chief memory precept and describes how Simonides discovered this principle:

> Simonides, who was both poet and philosopher, is said to have discovered the rules of this subject, for when a banquet hall suddenly collapsed, and the next of kin could not identify those buried, he supplied the seating order and names from memory. From this experience he learned that it is order which makes possible the rules of memory. But order must be practiced (*meditandus*) in lighted places (*loci illustres*), in which semblances of things and images of ideas should be placed; for example, you might remember a wedding by a bride veiled in saffron or a homicide by a sword and arms, which images the place gives back to memory as though deposited there. For just as what is written is contained in wax and letters, so what is commanded to memory is impressed in places as if in wax or on a written page; but the memory of things is contained in images as if in letters.[56]

After outlining this system, Martianus admits that it requires a great deal of practise, and that it has long been the custom to write out what one wishes to remember,[57] placing *notae* to mark off individual sections. These things to be

Et si prima et secunda deinceps cohaereant, nihil per oblivionem subtrahi poterit, ipso consequentium admonente contextu'.

[53] Ward notes Fortunatianus's use of Quintilian on memory (*Artif. eloq.* p. 85 n. 17); for a discussion of Fortunatianus's life and works, see 'Fortunatianus (#7)', in *Paulys Realencyclopädie der classischen Altertumswissenschaft*, 24 vols, ed. by August Friedrich von Pauly and others (Stuttgart: Druckenmüller, 1958), VII, pt I, 44–55.

[54] C. Chirius Fortunatianus, *Artis rhetoricae libri III*, in *Rhetores Latini minores*, ed. by Halm, pp. 78–134 (see III.13, p. 129): 'Quae melior et simplicior memoriae ratio est? ut si longior fuerit oratio, per partes ediscatur.'

[55] There is little certain information about Martianus's life. Most scholars place him in the early fifth century, though a few prefer the fourth century. Stahl and Johnson, *Martianus Capella*, I, 9–15.

[56] Martianus Capella, *De nuptiis Philologiae et Mercurii*, ed. by James Willis (Leipzig: Teubner, 1983), V. 538. See Stahl and Johnson, *Martianus Capella*, II, 203 n. 230. Stahl's and Johnson's translation, p. 203. I have used this translation except for the technical terms for artificial memory.

[57] Capella, *De nuptiis*, ed. by Willis, V. 539: 'sed, ut diximus, magnam exercitationem res laboremque conquirit, in qua illud observari compertum est solere, ut scribimus ipsi quae facile volumus retinere'.

memorized should not be read out loud, but rather practised in a murmur at night. He also mentions memory for words, but does not recommend it unless there is ample time for practise and if the speaker has a natural gift of memory.

Martianus imitates Quintilian by supplying first Simonides' art and then Quintilian's method. Carruthers has interpreted this entire passage as an example only of an 'elementary' mnemonic system, denying that the first section refers to the *Ad Herennium*'s system.[58] While it is certainly the case that Martianus is recommending Quintilian's simplified version here, he is just as clearly contrasting one mnemotechnic with another, just as Quintilian and Fortunatianus do.

That rhetoricians like Martianus and Fortunatianus helped transmit the artificial memory schemes, especially Quintilian's, can again be seen in Guibert de Tournai's *De modo addiscendi*, in which he quotes directly from Martianus a number of times and from a rhetorician remarkably like Fortunatianus. Quintilian's method, or one similar to it, is found in the works of Geoffroi de Vinsauf, Johannes de Garlandia, and Hugh of St Victor, as will be shown below.

Finally, one must assume that memory methods could be taught orally, without the aid of the major texts or their derivatives. After all, it is not that hard to describe any of these systems. Though this may well have been the most common way for students to learn memory methods, oral teaching is much harder for a modern scholar to track.

From the early fifth century until Thierry de Chartres struggles with the *Ad Herennium* in the twelfth, we have not yet found any extended discussions of either Simonides' system or Quintilian's modified mnemonic, as both Yates and Carruthers have already observed. The reasons for this disappearance may be many. One of the most obvious, however, is a simple matter of the textbooks used in early medieval schools. The *Ad Herennium*'s fortunes varied. Written around the time of Cicero, it fell into disuse until the fourth century and was then known but not popular until the eleventh and twelfth centuries. From around 650–850, judging by the extant manuscripts, the minor Latin rhetoricians held sway in the schools, while works like the *Ad Herennium*, Quintilian's *Institutio*, and Cicero's *De inventione* were utilized mainly in the compilation of extracts (*De oratore* was read even more rarely).[59] From the ninth century on there was a move towards recovery and correcting the more important rhetorical works.[60] The interest in all

[58] Carruthers, *Book of Memory*, p. 147.

[59] *Artif. eloq.*, pp. 84–87, 119.

[60] *Artif. eloq.*, p. 144. According to Ward, from the seventh to the ninth centuries certain sections dropped out of Quintilian's text, including most of the section on memory (XI.2); *Artif. eloq.*, p. 143 n. 44.

three major rhetorical works seems to have culminated in the twelfth century, faded in the thirteenth, and then been revived in fourteenth-century Italy.

As for Martianus Capella, his *De nuptiis* was certainly known and read. In many Carolingian schools, Martianus's book constituted the curriculum for the liberal arts, including rhetoric. In fact, the glosses and commentaries on Book V of *De nuptiis* furnish the main body of rhetorical writing in this period.[61] It is thought that several Irish scholars studying in France were responsible for promoting Martianus's revival in the schools.[62] At least three commentaries on him were completed by ninth-century scholars, including Johannes Scotus Eriugena and Remigius of Auxerre.[63] They were thus exposed to Martianus's treatment of memory and include that section in their commentaries. Remigius is laconic in his comments on memory in Book V. He interprets Martianus's recommendation that 'you might remember a wedding by a bride veiled in saffron or a homicide by a sword and arms, which images the place gives back to memory as though deposited there'[64] as '"just as", namely if you wish to remember a wedding or a murderer. Then "place", in which place, that is in the murder, you ought to make a sword, for example, the sword of Ulysses or the arms of Vulcan.'[65] He also refers to place in connection with the wedding as 'locus est ipse nuptiae', that is, 'it is the place of the wedding'. It is not clear whether Remigius sees 'locus' as a mental place or an association of a place with a homicide or wedding that occurred there. It is possible that he is interpreting Martianus's views on memory through the eyes of someone trained in Quintilian's system.

[61] Paul Oskar Kristeller, 'Philosophy and Rhetoric: The Middle Ages', in *Renaissance Thought and its Sources*, ed. by Michael Mooney (New York: Columbia University Press, 1979), pp. 228–41 (p. 230); *Artif. eloq.*, p. 162.

[62] Kristeller, 'Philosophy and Rhetoric', p. 230; Cora E. Lutz, 'Martianus Capella', in *Catalogus translationum et commentariorum: Medieval and Renaissance Latin Translations and Commentaries*, ed. by Paul Oskar Kristeller and F. Edward Cranz (Washington, DC: Catholic University of America Press, 1971), pp. 367–81 (pp. 368–69).

[63] *Artif. eloq.*, pp. 162, 171, and William Stahl, 'To a Better Understanding of Martianus Capella', *Speculum*, 40 (1965), 102–15.

[64] Capella, *De nuptiis*, ed. by Willis, V. 538: 'veluti nuptiarum velatam flammeo nubentem, aut homicidae gladium vel arma detineas, quas species locus tamquam depositas reddat'.

[65] Remigius of Auxerre, *Commentum in Martianum Capellam*, ed. by Cora E. Lutz, 2 vols (Leiden: Brill, 1965), II, V.269.7: 'VELUTI scilicet si velis habere memoriam NUPTIARUM aut HOMICIDAE. Ecce locus in quo locus, id est in homicidio, debes gladium deformare, verbi gratia, gladium Ulixis vel arma Vulcani.'

Eriugena's comments aim to define the words of Martianus's book more than to explain how a memory system worked:

> *Detineas* [you should hold in mind], you should understand images of a wedding. *Velatam nubentem* [a bride veiled], some say *Velata homicidae* is a proper name, others say that *Velatam* is the proper name of the woman who was married to her husband in saffron, others say *Velatam* means a nun. *Gladium* [sword], that is of Ulysses, who killed Ajax.[66]

His assertions do not indicate whether or not Martianus's ideas on memory were perfectly understood. It is possible that the system was so well understood that a detailed explanation of it was not necessary. However, his references to other opinions do provide clear evidence that the memory section was being discussed.

Such were the fortunes of the major textbooks discussing artificial memory that have survived from the early Middle Ages. Of course, the availability and use of rhetorical textbooks was not the only factor affecting the transmission of memory systems to the Middle Ages. The need for rhetoric and its precepts was no longer the same. In this case the conception of rhetoric began to change in the various societies scattered around Europe from the fifth to the late eleventh centuries. In Greek and Roman antiquity, rhetorical discourse had been tied firmly to the world of law and politics, when cases were tried before judges, jury, and public, and public speaking skills became a necessity and a means of livelihood. This use of rhetoric as preparation for civil discourse continued through the late antique period and into the early Middle Ages, even though changes in public life under the empire had rendered it obsolete.[67] Some of the encyclopedic works which transmitted classical rhetoric also handed down this idea: Cassiodorus held that 'the art of rhetoric is, as the masters of secular letters teach, the science of speaking well in civil questions'.[68] Clearly, since early medieval society did not conform to this picture of civil affairs, it might be argued that a dropping off of interest in this conception of rhetoric, or at least in the parts most related to

[66] *Iohannis Scotia Annotationes in Marcianum*, ed. by Cora E. Lutz (Cambridge, MA: Medieval Academy of America, 1939), p. 269: 'DETINEAS nuptiarum subaudis imagines. VELATAM NUBENTEM Quidam dicunt ut proprium nomen sit Velata homicidae, alii dicunt Velatam proprium nomen feminae quae nupsit flammeo marito suo, alii dicunt Velatam nonnam. GLADIUM id est Ulixis qui Aiacem interfecit.'

[67] See Brian Vickers, *In Defence of Rhetoric* (Oxford: Clarendon Press, 1988), chap. 1, and Richard McKeon, 'Rhetoric in the Middle Ages', *Speculum*, 17 (1942), 1–32 (pp. 13–15).

[68] Cassiodorus, *Institutes*, ed. by Roger Aubrey Baskerville Mynors (Oxford: Clarendon Press, 1937), II.2.1.97, cited in McKeon, 'Rhetoric in the Middle Ages', p. 14.

performance, such as memory and delivery, would not be surprising. Indeed, we do see some confirmation of such a trend, as John Ward notes:

> The fact [...] that the *De inventione* could become the basic text-book of Latin rhetoric until c.1150, despite its failure to deal with *pronuntiatio*, *memoria*, and *elocutio*, illustrates in general the drift from practical to intellectual that characterizes late antique and medieval rhetorical history.[69]

One might also characterize the shift as one from oral presentation to written. Even the iconography of rhetoric (as one of the components of the seven liberal arts) changes from gestures of delivery to stylus and wax.[70]

On the other hand, there is no inherent reason why such a change should nullify the importance of memory. Quintilian, in discussing the importance of memory for orators, also acknowledges its integral role in education, noting that learning is useless if everything that one hears slips away.[71] Hugh of St Victor echoes the same sentiment.[72] Certainly, education itself did not disappear in the early Middle Ages.[73] Some mnemonic principles may have been taught orally in the schools; we shall examine a twelfth-century example of a schoolboy's mnemonic in the next chapter.

Finally, Janet Coleman has recently suggested that one reason why the *Ad Herennium*'s memory system may have gone out of fashion in the fourth century was its association with pagan culture and even sorcery.[74] She observes that most

[69] John O. Ward, 'From Antiquity to the Renaissance: Glosses and Commentaries on Cicero's Rhetorica', in *Medieval Eloquence: Studies in the Theory and Practice of Medieval Rhetoric*, ed. by James Jerome Murphy (Berkeley and Los Angeles: University of California Press, 1978), pp. 26–67 (pp. 42–43), cited in Vickers, *In Defence*, p. 224.

[70] Vickers, *In Defence*, p. 227.

[71] *Inst. orat.*, XI.2, § 1: 'Nam et omnis disciplina memoria constat, frustraque docemur, si quidquid audimus praeterfluat.'

[72] William M. Green, 'Hugo of St. Victor: *De tribus maximis circumstantiis gestorum*', *Speculum*, 18 (1943), 484–93 (p. 490): 'In sola enim memoria omnis utilitas doctrinae consistit, quia sicut audisse non profuit ei qui non potuit intelligere, ita nec intellexisse valuit ei qui vel noluit vel non potuit retinere.'

[73] For extensive information on this point, see Pierre Riché, *Education and Culture in the Barbarian West from the Sixth through the Eighth Century*, trans. by John J. Contreni (Columbia: University of South Carolina Press, 1976); Pierre Riché, *Écoles et enseignement dans le haut moyen âge: Fin du V^e^ siècle–milieu du XI^e^ siècle* (Paris: Picard, 1989); Rosamond McKitterick, *The Carolingians and the Written Word* (Cambridge: Cambridge University Press, 1989).

[74] Janet Coleman, *Ancient and Medieval Memories: Studies in the Reconstruction of the Past* (Cambridge: Cambridge University Press, 1992), pp. 118–19.

of the university rhetors from the fourth century onwards were held in suspicion by Christians, especially since the great rhetoricians of the fourth through the sixth centuries remained pagans. Rhetors were sometimes accused of pagan sorcery by people who thought their memories had been damaged so that they could not remember their classical education. Peter Brown has interpreted sorcery accusations as a sign of a social conflict between up-and-coming Christians at court and a traditional pagan aristocracy. He notes that accusations of sorcery tended to be made against 'holders of ill-defined traditional status', and 'professors of rhetoric and philosophy, and poets [...] were the supreme examples of men whose status was not fixed'. Such an association between pagan rhetoric and sorcery would not be likely to foster the mnemonic tradition of ancient rhetoric.

Though the *Ad Herennium*'s memory system fell out of favour for centuries, medieval writers and scholars found other ways to preserve their memories, as we shall see in the following chapter.

# Part I. The Transformation of Memory in the High Middle Ages

Chapter 1

# The Pressures of Memory in the Twelfth Century

To discuss the history of memory and preaching in the Middle Ages is also to discuss the history of the schools, for both the subject matter of medieval preaching and its form were in large part products of the schools.[1] Medieval preachers learned the rudiments of doctrine and biblical scholarship at the cathedral schools, universities, or mendicant *studia* that they attended; they also learned how to preach. From the point of view of mnemonic teaching, perhaps the most important tip they learned in the schools was how to generate copiousness of material from their basic logical and rhetorical training, a subject that will be explored in depth in Chapter 3.

But the schools themselves were something new in the eleventh and twelfth centuries. Before then, education, as well as training in *memoria*, was largely the province of monks. Many scholars have drawn attention to a contrast in learning styles between monastic and scholastic education, a contrast that has probably been somewhat overstated.[2] The influence of monastic authors and their memorial practices never disappeared in the Middle Ages, even in the world of the

[1] Parts of this chapter previously appeared in Rivers, 'Memory and Medieval Preaching', pp. 253–84.

[2] Constant J. Mews makes this point forcefully in 'Monastic Educational Culture Revisited: The Witness of Zwiefalten and the Hirsau Reform', in *Medieval Monastic Education*, ed. by Carolyn Muessig (London: Leicester University Press, 2001), pp. 182–97. Stephen C. Ferruolo, *The Origins of the University: The Schools of Paris and their Critics, 1100–1215* (Stanford: Stanford University Press, 1985), details the contemporary debates about changes in teaching methods and subjects. M. T. Clanchy, *Abelard: A Medieval Life* (Oxford: Blackwell, 1997) describes the background of the schools in Paris during Abelard's career.

schools, partly because many of the great educators of the thirteenth century, the mendicants, were themselves products of religious life.[3] However, it is true that educational practice in the schools did come to value different qualities from monastic education, such as verbal acuity in debate, and it gave less time for the *otium*, or leisure, so valued in monastic meditation. Early developments in the schools did not cause teachers and students to abandon memorial techniques practised for centuries; in fact, they clung to them. What contemporaries in the twelfth century did comment on was the pressure some scholars, and even some monks, felt as changes occurred in the spiritual and educational norms practised for centuries. Perhaps in reaction to the changes, some writers articulated these norms in writing. Hugh of St Victor can be seen as a figure with a foot in the worlds of both monastic and scholastic education, who strove to comprehend the pedagogical learning of his time into one, relatively conservative, system. His work demonstrates the mnemonic learning of the twelfth century and indicates how some of its ideas came to reside in print. To see how this might be so, it is necessary to look briefly first at monastic education and its memory practices and then to compare it with the new methods of the schools.

## *Monastic 'Memoria'*

Much of monastic life in Western Europe before the twelfth century (and even after) was based on the Rule of St Benedict. As part of the religious life outlined in the Rule, one of the monks' main tasks was *lectio divina*, reading and meditating on Scripture.[4] As Leclercq has described it, reading meant a physical kind of exercise that involved the whole body, because of the practice of reading the text aloud, or at least moving the lips.[5] Meditation had both secular and Christian

[3] A point Mary Carruthers makes in 'Late Antique Rhetoric, Early Monasticism, and the Revival of School Rhetoric', in *Latin Grammar and Rhetoric: From Classical Theory to Medieval Practice*, ed. by Carol Dana Lanham (London: Continuum, 2002), pp. 239–57. Bert Roest also stresses the religious aspect of Franciscan training in 'Franciscan Educational Perspectives: Reworking Monastic Traditions', in *Medieval Monastic Education*, ed. by Muessig, pp. 168–81.

[4] The basic work for monastic meditation is Jean Leclercq, *The Love of Learning and the Desire for God* (New York: Fordham University Press, 1982), especially pp. 11–23.

[5] The question of whether ancient and medieval people read aloud or silently has been a vexed one. For an entry into the debate, see Paul Saenger, 'Silent Reading: Its Impact on Late Medieval Script and Society', *Viator*, 13 (1982), 367–414, and Paul Saenger, *Space Between Words: The Origins of Silent Reading* (Stanford: Stanford University Press, 1997).

connotations. In secular usage, it could mean 'to think or reflect' or 'to prepare' for something. As Leclercq puts it: 'To practice a thing by thinking of it, is to fix it in the memory, to learn it.'[6] Christian usage focused this kind of attention on the scriptural text, so that meditation came to imply reading the text, inscribing it in memory, understanding its meaning, and putting its sense into action. Monks often described meditation as *ruminatio*, literally 'chewing' over the things in one's memory. For monks, meditation on the Bible was not about abstract knowledge, but about life and experience.

This profound attention to reading and religious texts affected the way that monks composed texts of their own. The words of Scripture were so deeply em-cbedded in the minds of monks that a biblical allusion called up the whole quotation and similar phrases elsewhere in the Bible. Leclercq calls each word of Scripture a 'hook' that 'catches hold of one or several others which become linked together and make up the fabric of the exposé'.[7] Monastic writing was thus associative, moving from one verbal echo to another, rather than following a more obviously 'logical' structure. It was also an imaginative writing with a firm reliance on pictorial detail.

Recently, Mary Carruthers has recast Leclercq's picture of monastic meditation into a schema of monastic rhetoric.[8] In *The Craft of Thought*, she describes monastic life as 'an orthopraxis', 'the craft of making prayer continuously' (*sacra pagina*), and sees meditation as a craft of making thoughts about God.[9] She argues that the life of prayer for a monk was essentially a kind of rhetorical composition that required its own kind of rhetoric, one to which inventive recollection was essential. This kind of monastic rhetoric was not associated with public persuasion, as was the better known classical rhetoric, but instead was developed early in Christianity as a discipline or *via* of inventive meditation based on memorized locational inventory structures.[10] Carruthers calls this inventive recollection *sancta memoria*, and she is careful to distinguish it from the

[6] Leclercq, *Love of Learning*, p. 16.

[7] Leclercq, *Love of Learning*, p. 73.

[8] For what follows, I have relied on Carruthers, *Craft of Thought*; Carruthers, 'Poet as Master Builder'; and Carruthers, 'Reading with Attitude, Remembering the Book', in *The Book and the Body*, ed. by Dolores Warwick Frese and Katherine O'Brien O'Keefe, University of Notre Dame Ward-Philips Lectures in English Language and Literature, 14 (Notre Dame: University of Notre Dame Press, 1997), pp. 1–33.

[9] Carruthers, *Craft of Thought*, pp. 1, 2.

[10] Carruthers, *Craft of Thought*, pp. 11–12.

mnemonic practices outlined in the *Rhetorica ad Herennium*, though they shared some characteristics.[11]

Like that of the *Ad Herennium*, monastic memory practices made extensive use of images, or *picturae*, as sites of recall. Strong emotions like fear or extreme sadness began the process of prayer and meditation.[12] Such emotion was called up by 'a useful image, a recollective cue that most often takes the form of what we would call a picture'.[13] Early medieval monks created their pictures from remembered texts, mostly from Scripture or commentaries, 'vivified', as Carruthers puts it, to make a fearful or anxiety-producing impression. The pictures were not 'mnemonic' in the sense that most people would assume, in that each bit was not there to help one memorize some specific bit of information. Rather the places in a picture like the Plan of St Gall or a picture of the heavenly Jerusalem contained spots appropriate for matching with a text. So one might associate a quotation from the Psalms that reminds one of Jerusalem in one of the arches in Jerusalem. One then looked at the picture and the chosen spot and ruminated over the bit of the Psalms and any other related things in memory much like a *catena* of literary quotations. The sites acted as points for expansion of the things in one's head. The expansion was then part of the composition of prayer, or, for some, of a literary composition.[14]

What Leclercq and Carruthers describe as monastic meditation may well have been a goal that not all monks were able to reach. Others probably had a much more limited grasp of Latin and even of the liturgy. For them, rote memory probably played a greater role in their education and in their religious life than the *sancta memoria* described by Carruthers. Learning Latin at least through the twelfth century began with learning the alphabet letter by letter with much emphasis put on learning how to pronounce first the letters, then the syllables, and finally Latin texts.[15] Latin students, whether monks or not, could then read Latin texts with little understanding of their meaning.

Many monks probably remained at this level throughout their lives, knowing only how to pronounce the words, not to understand their meaning. In the

[11] Carruthers, *Craft of Thought*, p. 10.

[12] Carruthers, *Craft of Thought*, pp. 95–103.

[13] Carruthers, 'Reading with Attitude', p. 21.

[14] See Carruthers's reworking of these ideas in 'Late Antique Rhetoric', pp. 239–57.

[15] Clanchy, *Abelard*, pp. 59–60; Suzanne Reynolds, *Medieval Reading: Grammar, Rhetoric and the Classical Text*, Cambridge Studies in Medieval Literature, 27 (Cambridge: Cambridge University Press, 1996), pp. 8–9. See also Carruthers, *Book of Memory*, pp. 111–12.

eleventh century, Petrus Damianus complained about clerics who could not understand what they read, content to babble texts syllable by syllable.[16] Still, this skill would have allowed them to participate in the chant that made up much of Benedictine life. Monks learned liturgy and some Scripture, particularly the Psalms, by constant repetition. Susan Boynton has described how child oblates learned the essential skills of liturgical chant, including singing, reading, and writing, through aural repetition and imitation of their teachers.[17] In Michael Clanchy's view, 'The strong emphasis on speech and rote learning made memory an essential element in medieval literacy.'[18] Skilled though they were in chant, the monks sometimes made mistakes. Clanchy notes that in monastic choirs the demon Tutivillus was thought to collect up sackfuls of dropped syllables from the Psalms to be weighed up at the Last Judgement.[19] Evidently the missed syllables were considered faults either of memory, pronunciation, or laziness.

It is possible that the missed syllables were dropped because monks' memories were put under too great a strain in the central Middle Ages. Janet Coleman speculates that Cluny's elaboration of the liturgy between the tenth and the twelfth centuries stretched 'the natural limits of monastic remembrance'.[20] Freed from other duties, the monks at Cluny devoted themselves to the liturgical office and prayer until they took up almost the entire day. By the twelfth century, the round of liturgical prayers and offices was certainly long, requiring the recitation of at least 215 Psalms a day.[21] In Coleman's words, 'in general, by the time of abbot Peter the Venerable (1150s), the Cluniac was engaged in a near heroic practice of the liturgy in a continuous manner, whose prolixity of psalmody was

[16] Petrus Damianus, *Contra inscitiam et incuriam clericorum*, PL, CXLV, cols 497–504 (col. 497). Cited in Reynolds, *Medieval Reading*, p. 9.

[17] Susan Boynton, 'Training for the Liturgy as a Form of Monastic Education', in *Medieval Monastic Education*, ed. by Muessig, pp. 7–20.

[18] Clanchy, *Abelard*, pp. 61–62.

[19] M. T. Clanchy, *From Memory to Written Record*, 2nd edn (Oxford: Blackwell, 1993), p. 187. See also Margaret Jennings, 'Tutivillus: The Literary Career of the Recording Demon', *Studies in Philology*, 74 (1977), 1–91 (pp. 10–15).

[20] Coleman, *Ancient and Medieval Memories*, pp. 151–54.

[21] Robert Folz, 'Pierre le Vénérable et la liturgie', in *Pierre Abélard, Pierre le Vénérable: Les Courants philosophiques, littéraires et artistiques en Occident au milieu du XII^e^ siècle: [Actes et mémoires du colloque international], Abbaye de Cluny, 2 au 9 juillet 1972*, Colloques internationaux du Centre national de la recherche scientifique, 546 (Paris: Éditions du Centre national de la recherche scientifique, 1975), pp. 143–63 (p. 149).

to inspire criticism from outside as well as from Peter the Venerable himself'.[22] Coleman explains Peter the Venerable's efforts to modify the Office for his order as a way to deal with too great a burden on monastic memory and sees the changes that the Cistercians made to memorial practice, which she calls 'blanched memory', as a response to these problems.[23] The idea that Cluniac liturgical practices overloaded monastic memory is certainly an interesting one, but it has to be noted that none of the commentators at the time actually mention the taxation of memory as a reason for reducing the length of the liturgy. In fact, until the end of the eleventh century, there was no contemporary criticism about the length of the liturgy at Cluny. As Giles Constable has remarked, 'On the contrary, the almost universal admiration of Cluny, and the widespread influence of its customs, shows that its liturgy, although distasteful to many modern scholars, was on the whole well suited to the devotional needs and ideals of monks at that time.'[24]

Peter King has also emphasized the normality of monks knowing and reciting the Psalms on a daily basis, regardless of their religious affiliation. He assumes that most monks had all the Psalms memorized and quotes Petrus Damianus's comment as evidence: 'When you are going from one place to another, or on a journey, or about some necessary business, let your lips continually ruminate something from the Scriptures, grinding the psalms as in a mortar, so that they may ever give forth an odour as of aromatic plants.'[25] King does not think it would have been difficult for monks at Cluny to say all 150 Psalms around the body of a deceased brother during the watches of the night or to chant the whole Psalter on Good Friday, though he does concede that singing additional offices, such as the Little Office of Our Lady and the Office of All Saints after the daily ones did lengthen the amount of time that monks spent in choir.[26]

By the twelfth century, however, there certainly were complaints, from both inside and outside of Cluny. Peter the Venerable conceded that many monks found the tedium of the additions to the liturgy to be 'burdensome and

[22] Coleman, *Ancient and Medieval Memories*, p. 152.

[23] Coleman, *Ancient and Medieval Memories*, p. 154, and chaps 10 and 11.

[24] Giles Constable, 'The Monastic Policy of Peter the Venerable', in *Pierre Abélard, Pierre le Vénérable*, pp. 119–42 (p. 127).

[25] Peter King, *Western Monasticism: A History of the Monastic Movement in the Latin Church*, Cistercian Studies Series, 185 (Kalamazoo: Cistercian, 1999), p. 129. King notes that St Pachomius had said almost exactly the same thing.

[26] King, *Western Monasticism*, pp. 129–30.

hateful'.[27] Monks literally lost sleep because of the length of the nightly offices and could not find time for private devotions amid the tight daily schedule of prayer. As Coleman herself puts it, the competing ideas about how long the liturgy should be and how fast the chant should be performed were at least as much about time as they were about other issues, such as memory. Time for the *negotiosum otium* (labourious leisure) of the Cluniac monastery appeared to be different from the time for meditation among the Cistercians and even more different from time in the urban world of the schools. In the end, Constable's observation that Peter the Venerable wanted to adopt Cluniac monasticism to the new spirituality of the twelfth century, which desired more time and space for personal spiritual development, seems correct.[28] If one already has 150 Psalms memorized, saying 215 of them a day might not so much strain the memory as strain one's patience, particularly if there were other activities in which one might prefer to engage. The question facing monks and scholars in the twelfth century was what was the best use to which to put one's memory and one's time, for certainly the rise of the schools and their new form of education put pressure on both aspects of masters' and students' lives.

## *The Schools*

Though monastic education provided the dominant model of education in the early Middle Ages, by the eleventh century, it began to lose ground to urban schools connected to cathedrals.[29] In the ninth century as part of his reorganization of Carolingian monasticism, Benedict of Aniane had decided to bar children from outside the monastery from monastic schools, reserving them only for novices and oblates. Though that measure was quickly forgotten in the disorder of the next centuries, the monastic reformers of the eleventh and twelfth centuries went back to his ideas. They thought that it was not part of the vocation

[27] Constable, 'Monastic Policy', p. 128.

[28] Constable, 'Monastic Policy', pp. 120, 128.

[29] For the rise of the schools, especially in and around Paris, I have relied on John W. Baldwin, *Masters, Princes and Merchants: The Social Views of Peter the Chanter and his Circle*, 2 vols (Princeton: Princeton University Press, 1970); Marcia L. Colish, *Medieval Foundations of the Western Intellectual Tradition, 400–1400* (New Haven: Yale University Press, 1997), pp. 265–73; Ferruolo, *Origins of the University*; Katherine S. B. Keats-Rohan, 'John of Salisbury and Education in Twelfth Century Paris from the Account of his *Metalogicon*', *History of Universities*, 6 (1986–87), 1–45; Hastings Rashdall, *The Universities in the Middle Ages*, ed. by Frederick Maurice Powicke and Alfred Brotherston Emden, 3 vols (Oxford: Clarendon Press, 1936).

of a monk to be a teacher.[30] That provision combined with the appeal of the cities that arose with the quickening of the economy in the eleventh and twelfth centuries led to the preeminence of the new schools. Across Europe, cathedral schools with well-known masters could establish a reputation for themselves for a generation or two, such as Liège in the late tenth and eleventh centuries and Reims in the eleventh.[31] Students began to migrate to these schools for instruction in the *trivium* (grammar, logic, and rhetoric), moral education, and in Italy and southern France, medicine and Roman law. By the beginning of the twelfth century, the teaching in these new schools was perceived to be dangerous by monastic observers, putting too much emphasis on the novelties of learning, rather than on the religious experience emphasized in monasteries.[32]

## *Changes Brought about by the Schools*

The teaching and learning practices of the twelfth-century schools also brought changes in attitudes toward memory. However one may choose to portray the transition between the older monastic tradition of education and the new methods of the schools (and there is some debate),[33] there seems little reason to doubt that the new style put increased pressure on students, and perhaps on professors as well, to master material quickly. As students poured into cities like Paris to find teachers willing to impart their knowledge of logic, theology, grammar, and law, they found themselves exposed to a greater variety of teachers and subjects than could have been available in one place for centuries. Both students and masters had to remember more than they used to, and they had to learn things faster.[34]

[30] Pierre Riché, 'L'Enfant dans la société monastique', in *Pierre Abélard, Pierre le Vénérable*, pp. 689–701 (p. 692). For a clear description of Benedict of Aniane's reform, see King, *Western Monasticism*, chap. 5.

[31] C. Stephen Jaeger, *The Envy of Angels: Cathedral Schools and Social Ideals in Medieval Europe, 950–1200* (Philadelphia: University of Pennsylvania Press, 1994), chap. 3.

[32] Jaeger, *Envy of Angels*, pp. 218–20; Ferruolo, *Origins of the University*, p. 87.

[33] See, for instance, Ivan Illich, *In the Vineyard of the Text: A Commentary to Hugh's 'Didascalicon'* (Chicago: University of Chicago Press, 1993). Ferruolo, *Origins of the University*, details the contemporary debates about changes in teaching methods and subjects. Clanchy, *Abelard*, describes the background of the schools in Paris during Abelard's career.

[34] In *Craft of Thought*, Carruthers emphasizes the compositional aspect of memory over the 'storehouse' approach (see p. 68). However, in the case of university students, one has to give some credence to the idea that students needed a 'storehouse' of information to pass exams.

According to Clanchy, 'Memory-skills were valued as highly by scholastic masters like Abelard as they were by monks.'[35] Peter Abelard himself was described by an anonymous commentator as being someone 'of inestimable cleverness, unsurpassed memory and superhuman capacity', indicating that his reputation and stature depended in part on his good memory.[36] John of Salisbury also thought to mention memory as a capacity of a good teacher, commending, in the preface to his *Metalogicon*, masters of 'noble talent, subtle searching, diligent studies, excellent memories, and copious words'.[37] Though many scholars see the twelfth century as a point of transition in medieval culture between orality and literacy, it is important to realize that the dependence on writing was a gradual change and one that was still incomplete in the twelfth century, even for masters in the schools.[38] Clanchy emphasizes that books were hard to get and that writing was in many ways still the preserve of the monasteries. In fact, many of the famous early masters, such as Anselm de Laon and Guillaume de Champeaux, left little written evidence of their teaching, despite their fame in the schools. Their reputations depended on their oral teaching and what their students said to other students about their ideas.[39] The schools came to be a place where skill in lecturing, preaching, and disputation, all in large part oral activities, were highly valued.[40] Scholars like Anselm of Aosta, Archbishop of Canterbury, and Abelard may have been able to write down their ideas because they were monks with all of the resources of a monastery, including its scriptorium, at their disposal.[41]

[35] Clanchy, *Abelard*, p. 62.

[36] Clanchy, *Abelard*, p. 62; Constant J. Mews, 'In Search of a Name and its Significance: A Twelfth-Century Anecdote about Thierry and Peter Abelard', *Traditio*, 44 (1988), 171–200 (p. 172), in quotation.

[37] Cited in Ferruolo, *Origins of the University*, p. 153.

[38] Brian Stock, *The Implications of Literacy: Written Language and Models of Interpretation in the Eleventh and Twelfth Centuries* (Princeton: Princeton University Press, 1983), emphasizes that writing did not suddenly replace orality, but that 'oral discourse effectively began to function within a universe of communications governed by texts' (p. 3); Jaeger, *Envy of Angels*, pp. 190–91.

[39] Clanchy, *Abelard*, pp. 45, 62, 77, 88.

[40] As Petrus Cantor commented in his much-cited statement on the fundamentals of theological training: 'In tribus autem consistit exercitium sacre scripture: in lectione, disputatione, predicatione, cuilibet istorum inimica est prolixitas, mater oblivionis et noverca memorie.' Most scholars leave out the reference to the dangers to memory of prolixity in all three areas. Baldwin, *Masters, Princes, and Merchants*, I, 90.

[41] For Anselm of Aosta's reputation in the twelfth century, see also Constant J. Mews, 'Orality, Literacy, and Authority in the Twelfth-Century Schools', *Exemplaria*, 2 (1990), 475–500 (pp. 475–76).

Students, too, required a good memory to succeed in the schools. Some contemporary testimony records the increasing pressures in the educational world. The Benedictine monk Pierre de Celles, for instance, in a letter to John of Salisbury, bemoaned the changes that the Parisian scholastic system had brought to the life of study, preferring the monastery, where one could perceive truth, 'without the labour of reading, the aversion of seeing [*fastidio videndi*], without deception or error in understanding, without the anxiety of remembering, without the fear of forgetting'.[42] Similarly, Hugh of St Victor seems to have been put off by the methods in the other schools of Paris because there was too much haste and disorder.[43] The requirement of a superior memory to succeed in the competitive world of the schools also appears in the Cistercian Caesarius von Heisterbach's exemplum of the Abbot of Morimond, who, as a young man, had done homage to the devil in return for a sharper intellect and a stronger memory. He became the greatest scholar in Paris. After his death, God gave him the option to escape hell by renouncing the schools and becoming a Cistercian.[44] Though this story obviously served as propaganda for the Cistercian order, the fact that a good memory was worth risking the pains of hell for seems telling.

It seems that twelfth-century scholars had a particular need for a good memory. How, then, did they deal with the pressures of their situation? This is a hard question to answer, because relatively few scholars reveal their study habits. It seems likely that a variety of methods served masters and students in their desire to keep important information at their disposal, which we shall consider in turn.

We should consider first whether scholars in the twelfth century and later turned to the same memory aid that modern scholars have relied on, that is, writing, in the form of note-taking. Both Clanchy and Charles Burnett have argued that this was the case.[45] In *From Memory to Written Record*, Clanchy claimed that '[t]he practice of making memoranda, whether on wax or parchment, contradicts the common assumption that medieval people had such good

[42] Pierre de Celles, *Opera omnia*, PL, CCII, cols 519–20: 'sine labore legendi, sine fastidio videndi, sine fallacia, vel errore intelligendi, since sollicitudine retinendi, sine timore obliviscendi'. Cited in Alberto Forny, 'Giacomo da Vitry, predicatore e "sociologo"', *La Cultura*, 17 (1980), 34–89 (p. 55).

[43] Ferruolo, *Origins of the University*, pp. 35–40.

[44] Cited in Ferruolo, *Origins of the University*, p. 67.

[45] Clanchy, *From Memory to Written Record*, p. 120; Charles Burnett, 'Give him the White Cow: Notes and Note-Taking in the Universities in the Twelfth and Thirteenth Centuries', *History of Universities*, 14 (1995–96), 1–30 (p. 2).

memories that they required no notes. Once they were literate, they had the same needs as a modern writer.'[46] In his biography of Abelard, and in the second edition of *From Memory to Written Record*, Clanchy concedes more scope for the claims of memory, perhaps especially in the twelfth century.[47] Still, we must consider that note-taking may have been a more attractive option to students in class than trying to recall what they learned.

It is not easy to discover how or even whether students and masters took notes, especially in the early years of the schools. Clanchy indicates that in the twelfth century, it was difficult for scholars to get things into writing, because they lacked the formal *scriptoria* of the monasteries. Rapid note-taking was difficult with quill pens on parchment and even with wax tablets.[48] Though it may have been difficult, it evidently was not impossible. Jacques de Vitry relates that Foulques de Neuilly († 1202), a rural and dissolute priest, after undergoing a conversion experience, became convinced that he should preach to the people.[49] Ashamed that he was unlettered and had no knowledge of Scripture, he went to Paris 'in order that, in the schools of the theologians, he might collect in writing in his tablets [*in tabulis suis*] some authorities and moral examples, which he could carry with him'.[50] When Foulques got to Paris, he entered the school of Petrus Cantor 'with his tablets and stylus' (cum tabulis stylo seu grafio). Both comments indicate that Foulques both needed to and was able to write down notes of the matters he studied in the schools. Writing on wax tablets, though, was in no way a permanent form of preservation, and in fact, Jacques de Vitry also tells us that Foulques 'frequently ruminated over and commended firmly to memory certain moral and common sayings, which he was able to receive and collect from the mouth of his

[46] Clanchy, *From Memory to Written Record*, p. 120.

[47] See the discussion above, and Clancy, *From Memory to Written Record*, pp. 193–96.

[48] Clanchy, *Abelard*, p. 88.

[49] David L. d'Avray gives some account of Foulques's preaching career in *The Preaching of the Friars: Sermons Diffused from Paris before 1300* (Oxford: Oxford University Press, 1985), pp. 22–25. See also Baldwin, *Masters, Princes and Merchants*, I, 36–39, and Milton Gutsch, 'A Twelfth-Century Preacher–Fulk of Neuilly', in *The Crusades, and Other Historical Essays Presented to Dana C. Munro by his Former Students*, ed. by Louis John Paetow (New York: Crofts, 1928), pp. 183–206.

[50] *The Historia Occidentalis of Jacques de Vitry: A Critical Edition*, ed. by John Frederick Hinnebusch (Fribourg: University Press, 1972), pp. 89–90: 'Erubescens autem quod ydiota et illiteratus esset et diuinas scripturas ignoret, profectus est Parisius, ut in scolis theologorum aliquas auctoritates et moralia documenta in tabulis suis, quas secum portauerat, scribendo colligeret, uelut lapides limpidissimos ad prosternendum Goliam.'

teacher according to his own capacity'.[51] Foulques evidently needed to write down first the material that he heard in class and that he intended to memorize later. Jacques gives us no idea of what methods Foulques might have used for memorization, though the language of 'rumination' strongly suggests a monastic context. Given Foulques's educational background — he was 'unlettered', that is, ignorant of Latin — before he reached Paris, one cannot generalize much from his experience, other than to say it was possible to take wax tablets into class. It remains possible that Jacques mentioned his habit of taking notes because it was unusual.[52]

In the later Middle Ages, there is much more evidence that students relied on written notes. For instance, they may have used a stylus ('dry point') to make marginal notations in their books. Burnett indicates that when a stylus was made from lead, it left a grey mark similar to that left by a modern-day pencil.[53] Students also had access to tiny wax tablets that could fit inside one's fist and which might have been more useful in class, as well as bits of parchment, called *cedula* or *schedula*.[54] University regulations at Paris and elsewhere from the fourteenth century on often forbade the practice of masters dictating the set texts to students in class *ad pennam* (at the pace of the pen).[55]

Burnett also provides evidence of one potential system for note taking in the twelfth century, seen in a letter by a certain John of Tilbury to King Henry II of England. In this letter, John praises the wonders, not of a memory method, but rather of a note-taking method that will allow a 'notary' to take down the words of a speaker 'with the same speed as that by which the words are uttered'.[56] His

[51] *Historia Occidentalis*, chap. 8, ed. by Hinnebusch, p. 94: 'De cuius fonte limpidissimo predictus Fulco sacerdos potare desiderans, cum tabulis et stylo seu grafio scolas eius humilter est ingressus, quedam uerba moralis et uulgaria, que secundum capacitatem ingenii recipere et colligere ex ore magistri sui potuit, frequenter ruminando et firmiter memorie commendando.'

[52] Though Jacques de Vitry also says that the masters and students of Paris took notes at Foulques's sermons. See the discussion below, in Chapter 3.

[53] Burnett, 'Give him the White Cow', pp. 12–13.

[54] Burnett, 'Give him the White Cow', pp. 16–17. See the depiction of the wax tablets on p. 17.

[55] Burnett, 'Give him the White Cow', pp. 7–8; Walter J. Ong, *Ramus, Method and the Decay of Dialogue* (Cambridge, MA: Harvard University Press, 1958), also makes note of this phenomenon, p. 155. A discussion of note-taking at the University of Uppsala in the late Middle Ages, as well as examples of lecture notes, can be found in *Studium Upsalense: Specimens of the Oldest Lecture Notes Taken in the Mediaeval University of Uppsala*, ed. by Anders Piltz (Uppsala: Uppsala Universitet, 1977).

[56] Burnett, 'Give him the White Cow', p. 3.

wondrous art is aimed especially at scholars, who were of the opinion, according to John, 'that if anyone were to know the notarial art, without doubt he would be an expert (*peritus*) in things human and divine'. John implies that capturing the master's exact words on paper will eventually make the student as learned as the master:

> For when the master sitting on his professional chair (*magister in cathedra sedens*) gives seven or eight lectures (*lectiones*) and the notary sitting opposite him takes down all the words that he says in the very same order, with the same swiftness of his flying notarial hand as that by which the master pronounces them (for he will very easily be able to do this), and then, when the lectures are finished, having all the words of the master written down (*scripto recepta*) — not paraphrases or similar words, but the very same words and no others — always in front of his eyes, he can read and reread them for as long as he wishes and as much as he wishes, and by the assiduity of his reading he can reconstitute the lecture from the words and relive the lecture (*lectionem in usum duxerit*), and then, when through the words of the master the pupil becomes learned (*doctus*), in a short space of time, how does he differ from his master? Well, I leave that to *your* wise judgement not mine.[57]

The benefits of John's plan seem to lie in the possibility of having access to the master's exact words for as long as one desires: the student has them 'always in front of his eyes' and he can 'relive the lecture'. Evidently the recording methods normally used by students provided them only with 'paraphrases or similar words'. John emphasizes the need for 'word for word' recording, if not for learning. One senses also the fleetingness of human words in class and that John felt the students' pain of being unable to keep up with their teacher.

Though Burnett wrote his article to counter Carruthers's assertion about the power of memory in the schools, his work can also be seen as proof that there was no one approach to study common to everyone. Despite John's extravagant claims about his note-taking method, very few of the rules for it are extant. Notice, too, John's assertion that complete notes and careful rereading actually lead to a good memory of the material. The goal is to the get the material into one's head, by whatever method happens to work. John says that the continuous rereading of his complete lecture notes will give the student 'a ready and perfect memory of all things', allowing the student to become like his master. The student then will achieve success in the academic world. Remembering what one learned in class was not just a matter of personal enrichment; professional advancement depended on being able to draw upon the master's words.

[57] Translation from Burnett, 'Give him the White Cow', p. 4.

If note-taking, particularly in the early years[58] of the schools, did not necessarily provide a reliable aid to memory for students and masters, one might expect that they would have turned to the *Rhetorica ad Herennium*'s or Cicero's memory method, which was certainly known in the twelfth century. In fact, there was a kind of consensus in the scholarly world that Cicero's mnemonic method was too impractical to be of any real use. Numerous comments from rhetoricians and writers attest to this attitude. In mid-century, John of Salisbury wished for a practical memory method like the one that Seneca was supposed to have known but never seems to have written down. John claims not to have found Cicero's rules to be of much use.[59] At the end of the century, Geoffroi de Vinsauf agreed with John about the value of Cicero's memory rules: 'Cicero relies on unusual images as a technique for training the memory; but he is teaching himself, and let the subtle teacher, as it were in solitude, address his subtlety to himself alone.'[60] Unlike John of Salisbury, Geoffroi appears to have had a memory method that he preferred, which was to divide a text into pieces and then memorize each section separately, without overburdening his memory. His emphasis on sobriety and diligence may explain his disdain for Cicero's more elaborate method. Thomas of Chobham († *c.* 1233–36), a product of the schools in the late twelfth and early thirteenth century, also rejected Cicero's memory system in his *Summa*

[58] Obviously, many examples of students' notes in the form of *reportationes* exist from the thirteenth century and later. See for example, Thomas Williams, 'Transmission and Translation', in *Cambridge Companion to Medieval Philosophy*, ed. by Arthur Stephen McGrade (Cambridge: Cambridge University Press, 2003), pp. 328–43.

[59] *Ioannis Saresberiensis episcopi carnotensis Metalogicon Libri III*, ed. by Clement Charles Julian Webb (Oxford: Clarendon Press, 1929), I.20: 'Seneca se artem comparande memorie traditurum facillime pollicetur; ut utinam innotuisset michi, sed quod eam tradiderit, omnino non recolo. Tullius in Rhetoricis operam dedisse uisus est; sed similibus mei non multum prodest.' Fredborg thinks it is not surprising that John had trouble with the mnemonic rules in the *Ad Herennium* given the work's treatment by his teacher, Thierry of Chartres. See Karin Margareta Fredborg, 'Twelfth-Century Ciceronian Rhetoric: Its Doctrinal Development and Influences', in *Rhetoric Revalued: Papers from the International Society for the History of Rhetoric*, ed. by Brian Vickers, Medieval and Renaissance Texts and Studies, 19 (Binghamton, NY: Center for Medieval and Renaissance Studies, 1982), pp. 88–89.

[60] Geoffroi de Vinsauf, *Poetria nova*, in *Les Arts poétiques du XII*e *et du XIII*e, ed. by Edmond Faral, Bibliothèque de l'école des hautes études, 238 (Paris: Champion, 1924; repr. 1958), V.2018–19: 'sed se docet et sibi soli/ Subtilis subtile suum quasi solus adoret'; trans. by Mary F. Nims, *Poetria nova* (Toronto: Pontifical Institute of Mediaeval Studies, 1967), p. 89. See Carruthers's discussion in *Book of Memory*, p. 146.

*de arte praedicandi.*[61] In his introduction to the five parts of rhetoric, Thomas declared:

> [B]ut after the preacher has 'invented' and well adorned the matters to be said, memory is necessary for him, in order that he may retain the things which he invented and arranged and adorned. And although Tully handed down his art for this purpose, nevertheless memory works better from practise and diligence.[62]

Like Geoffroi, Thomas seems to have found Cicero's method too involved to be of much practical use. As Gillian Evans has commented, there was no scholar in the twelfth century with enough interest in the mnemonic system contained in the *Ad Herennium* to promote it.[63]

If twelfth-century scholars recognized their dependence on a good memory, but rejected Cicero's rules, were they using any other method? The answer is yes. There were in fact numerous memory methods available to twelfth-century scholars. As we have seen, Geoffroi de Vinsauf described a method of dividing up texts into small sections that seemed to suffice for his needs, and medieval monks seem to have had mnemonic practices that ministered to theirs.[64] Almost certainly, scholars in the universities continued to employ these methods. However, there was another method that is rarely emphasized by modern historians. For the writer or scholar trained in rhetoric and logic, there was no need to master the intricacies of Cicero's images, because he already had a way of remembering texts: noting arguments and topics. According to Karin Fredborg, 'it was [...] the ubiquitous eleventh- and twelfth-century drill in analysing a text into arguments and topics for arguments which served as a system of mnemonics'.[65] She gives as example Wibald, Abbot of Stavelot and Corvey's, comment in 1149: 'I have the habit, having read a book which holds any kind of difficult subject matter, to lay aside the book and by memory unfold the topics and arguments, the premisses in

[61] Thomas of Chobham, *Summa de arte praedicandi*, ed. by Franco Morenzoni, CCCM, 82 (Turnhout: Brepols, 1988). Thomas was a secular priest who composed, in addition to his preaching *summa*, a *summa* on penance and one on the virtues and vices (ibid., pp. ix–xix).

[62] *Summa de arte*, II.2, p. 268: 'Postquam autem predicator inuenerit et bene ornauerit ea que dicenda sunt, necessaria est ei memoria, ut bene retineat ea que inuenit et disposuit et ornauit. Et licet Tullius ad hoc artem suam tradiderit, melius tamen ex usu et diligentia memoria operatur.'

[63] Gillian R. Evans, 'Two Aspects of *Memoria* in Eleventh and Twelfth Century Writings', *Classica et mediaevalia*, 32 (1971–80), 263–78 (p. 278).

[64] See Carruthers, *Craft of Thought*. Carruthers connects Geoffroi's mnemonic schemes to earlier, monastic practice ('Late Antique Rhetoric', pp. 240–42, 250).

[65] Fredborg, 'Twelfth-Century Ciceronian Rhetoric', pp. 88–89.

the discussion and the traps of the conclusions.'[66] John of Salisbury's account of his time at Paris learning logic under Alberic and Robert de Melun seems to confirm Fredborg's view of the ubiquity of the topics:

> Drilled by them [Alberic and Robert] for all of two years, I became so accustomed to allotting places, and to rules, and to the other elementary rudiments with which the minds of boys are instructed and in which the aforesaid doctors were most capable and expeditious, that it seemed to me that I knew all of these things as well as my own nails and fingers.[67]

Why would the rhetorical and logical training of the twelfth century provide such a solid basis for memory that scholars and preachers will still be relying on it by the end of the Middle Ages?[68] The goal of both classical rhetoric and dialectic was to produce some kind of argument: either an argument about a judicial case, as in Latin rhetorical theory, or an argument about a dialectical proposition, as in dialectic.[69] A modern student can see the most basic aspect of the issue: as many modern college professors tell their students, simply grasping and retaining the main points of an author's argument is a good way to learn and store for future recall the contents of a book or article. Twelfth-century students were taught to analyse a text into its topics for argument.[70] Clearly this method worked for Wibald. But the topics could be even more useful mnemonically than this picture initially conveys.

[66] Fredborg, 'Twelfth-Century Ciceronian Rhetoric', pp. 88–89. Wibald of Corvey, 'Epistola 147', in *Epistolae*, PL, CLXXXIX, cols 1087–1508 (col. 1251D): 'et in hoc me exercere soleo, ut post lectum aliquod cuiuspiam nodosae quaestionis volumen, locos et argumenta et disputandi vias et conclusionum laqueos, amoto libro, memoriter replicem'.

[67] *Metalogicon*, ed. by Webb, 79. 22–29: 'Apud hos, toto exercitatus biennio, sic locis assignandis assueui et regulis et aliis rudimentorum elementis, quibus pueriles animi imbuuntur, et in quibus prefati doctores potentissimi erant et expeditissimi, ut hec omnia michi uiderer nosse tanquam ungues digitosque meos. Hoc enim plane didiceram, ut iuuenili leuitate pluris facerem scientiam meam quam esset. Videbar michi sciolus, eo quod in iis que audieram promptus eram.' Of course, as Keats-Rohan points out, John, at the time of his writing, no longer approved of this kind of logical training ('John of Salisbury', pp. 13–14). Translation from Lynn Thorndike, *University Records and Life in the Middle Ages* (New York: Columbia University Press, 1949), no. 4: 'The Education of John of Salisbury'.

[68] See Chapter 3, below.

[69] See Eleonore Stump, *Boethius's 'De topicis differentiis'* (Ithaca: Cornell University Press, 1978), pp. 160–65, for a lucid description of a classical disputation.

[70] Fredborg, 'Twelfth-Century Ciceronian Rhetoric', p. 90.

In classical theory, when one needed to come up with or 'invent' an argument, either before a case was argued in court or in the thick of a disputation, then one drew on the appropriate topics. Rhetorical and dialectical topics were both defined in antiquity as the 'seats of argument',[71] but they were not perceived to function in exactly the same way. We can get an idea of what ancient and twelfth-century scholars might have understood as rhetorical topics by looking at Cicero's *De inventione*.[72]

For Cicero, the topics (or *loci*) were the seats of argument, and an argument was 'what creates conviction in a doubtful matter', such as a judicial case.[73] Topics had a spatial sense; they were places where arguments 'resided', and one filled them up with the arguments necessary for each enquiry. One could also see them as a list of the sort of statements that could be made about a subject.[74] For a judicial case Cicero's topics were a list of attributes about the person involved in the case and his actions. The rhetor needed to ascertain information about the person, such as his name, nature, and manner of life. He also needed to cover the attributes of the act, which were divided into four parts: topics coherent with the act itself, topics involved in the performance of the act, topics dealing with adjuncts of the act, and topics dealing with consequences that follow from the act.[75] Once the rhetor had covered all of the above points, he had 'invented' much of the material of his argument. Other Latin rhetoricians who followed Cicero had somewhat different lists of topics, but the theoretical process was fairly similar.[76] These examples certainly do not exhaust the number of topics available to a rhetor, as they pertain only to the person and act involved in a judicial case.[77]

[71] Quintilian says that loci are 'the seats of argument in which they hide [and] from which they must be sought' (*Inst. orat.*, V.20, § 20).

[72] Although Cicero compiled two sets of topics, one in the *De inventione* and one in the *Topica*, in the Middle Ages the ones from *De inventione* were used as the topics of rhetorical invention. Marc Cogan, 'Rodolphus Agricola and the Semantic Revolutions of the History of Invention', *Rhetorica*, 2 (1984), 163–94 (pp. 168–69). For what follows, I have relied on Cogan, as well as Stump, *Boethius's 'De topicis differentiis'*; Michael C. Leff, 'Boethius' *De differentiis topicis*, Book IV', in *Medieval Eloquence*, ed. by Murphy, pp. 3–24, and Leff, 'The Topics of Argumentative Invention in Latin Rhetorical Theory from Cicero to Boethius', *Rhetorica*, 1 (1983), 23–44.

[73] Cogan, 'Rodolphus Agricola', p. 171.

[74] Cogan, 'Rodolphus Agricola', pp. 171–72.

[75] Leff, 'Topics of Argumentative Invention', pp. 27–28.

[76] Leff, 'Topics of Argumentative Invention', p. 37. See pp. 43–44 for a list of attributes of the person and act in several Latin authors.

[77] See Ernst Robert Curtius, *European Literature and the Latin Middle Ages*, trans. by William R. Trask (New York: Bollingen, 1953), p. 70.

There were also topics for dialectical argument. In Aristotle's original conception, dialectic was about a discussion, or disputation, between a questioner and an answerer. They started from a provocative question, such as 'Is the world eternal or not?' The questioner established a proposition to which he tried to compel the answerer to agree by asking him questions.[78] The answerer had to try to block the questioner's proposition. In order to fulfil their parts in the disputation, each side had to have a fund of arguments at his disposal and to be able to marshal them when appropriate. The topics aided in finding these arguments, and the authority that dominated medieval discussion of logical topics was Boethius's *De topicis differentiis*. Like other ancient authorities, Boethius defined a topic as a seat of argument, of which there were two types: topical principal (*propositio maxima*) and a topical difference (*maximae propositionis differentia*). Topical principals were self-evident propositions or the best-known premises for arguments. Examples of these would be 'What inheres in the parts must inhere in the whole' or 'Those things whose efficient causes are natural are themselves more certain than itself'.[79] Since there were so many topic principals, Boethius grouped them according to their differences; hence topical differences, which became topics themselves.[80] Boethius's topics were not empty spaces, like Cicero's, but were instead the foundations of arguments used in disputation; because they were well-established premises, they acted as guarantors of the argument's soundness or validity.[81] Twelfth-century scholars were likely familiar with both kinds of topics, though the rhetorical ones may have been the most useful ones for most of the people discussed above.

How could such topics serve a mnemonic function? In antiquity the relationship between mnemonic loci and argumentative loci may have been very close. Aristotle, in the *Topics*, certainly associates the two:

> For just as in a person with a trained memory, a memory of things themselves is immediately caused by the mere mention of their places (*topoi*), so these habits too will make a man readier in reasoning, because he has his premises classified before his mind's eye, each under its number.[82]

[78] Stump, *Boethius's 'De topicis differentiis'*, pp. 18, 160–61; Leff, 'Boethius' *De differentiis topicis*', pp. 3–4.

[79] Cogan, 'Rodolphus Agricola', p. 176.

[80] Leff, 'Boethius' *De differentiis topicis*', p. 7.

[81] Cogan, 'Rodolphus Agricola', p. 177; Stump, *Boethius's 'De topicis differentiis'*, p. 181.

[82] Yates, *Art of Memory*, p. 31; Evans, 'Two Aspects of *Memoria*', pp. 266–67.

Both Yates and Evans speculate that dialectical topics may have their origin in mnemonics. In her work on Boethius's *De topicis differentiis* Eleonore Stump agrees with this position: 'A certain sort of Topic that plays a role in the ancient methods for memorization antedates and is probably the source for the kinds of Topics used in discovering arguments.'[83] In the same way that one could use a mnemonic place over and over again to store things, one could use dialectical and rhetorical topics over again to create new arguments. By the twelfth century, however, the relative positions of the topics/loci may have been reversed, with dialectical and rhetorical topics acting as mnemonic prompts. Topics originally designed to provide an 'idea' and copiousness for material could also help one order and recall the same material later.[84] It may well have remained the memory method of choice for those who found image-based methods, particularly that of the *Ad Herennium*, too arcane. Hugh of St Victor's use of the seven circumstances, discussed below, will provide a compelling example of how fundamental the topics could be to pedagogical theory and practice in the twelfth century.

In the world of education, the twelfth century was a time of transition, as methods that had served students and masters for centuries persisted into the new world of the schools. However, both monks and scholars found themselves under pressure to perform in this faster-paced world, as one needed both to recall and to find information more quickly than in the past. No where can these issues be illustrated more clearly than in the works of Hugh of St Victor.

## *Memory on the Cusp of Change: Hugh of St Victor's Mnemonic Recommendations*

As an Augustinian canon who taught in the schools in Paris, Hugh of St Victor had his feet in both the world of monasticism and the world of the schools.[85] He

[83] Stump, *Boethius's 'De topicis differentiis'*, p. 16.

[84] See Carruthers on topical invention, *Craft of Thought*, chap. 1.

[85] As Thomas Head observes in 'Monastic and Scholastic Theology: A Change of Paradigm?', in *Paradigms in Medieval Thought Applications in Medieval Disciplines: A Symposium*, ed. by Nancy Van Deusen and Alvin E. Ford (Lewiston, NY: Edwin Mellen, 1990), pp.127–42 (p. 131). For Hugh of St Victor and his school, see also Ferruolo, *Origins of the University*, pp. 29–40; Robert W. Southern, *Scholastic Humanism and the Unification of Europe*, II: *The Heroic Age* (Oxford: Blackwell, 2001), chap. 5. For the differences between monks and canons in the twelfth century, see Caroline Walker Bynum, *Docere verbo et exemplo: An Aspect of Twelfth-Century Spirituality*, Harvard Theological Studies, 21 (Missoula, MT: Scholars, 1979).

had his own, rather idiosyncratic, approach to theology and scriptural studies, an approach that did not survive the twelfth century,[86] but in his most basic educational aims, he relied on ancient methods and his ideas were certainly picked up by future educators. In his *Didascalicon* and in his *De tribus maximis circumstanciis gestorum*, Hugh outlined a programme of educational goals that describe how memory methods may have been taught in the twelfth century. His methods demonstrate that the logical and rhetorical teachings about *divisio* served basic mnemonic purposes in Hugh's time. They also provide an indicator of how memory methods could aid in the transition from the world of oral teaching to one of written reference works. Finally, his works illustrate one aspect of the twelfth-century dependence on topics, in the guise of the circumstances.

## Memory, Division, and the Construction of Reference Works[87]

In their articles on medieval manuscripts, Mary and Richard Rouse have noted that thirteenth-century scholars had a more aggressive and utilitarian attitude toward the page than that of previous generations. Rather than merely reading and ordering the knowledge of the past, these scholars searched written works in order to answer new questions.[88] Developments in page layout such as running headlines, and the many new research tools that appeared in the late twelfth and thirteenth centuries, such as concordances, encyclopedias,[89] and exempla collec-

[86] Beryl Smalley, *The Study of the Bible in the Middle Ages*, 3rd edn (Oxford: Blackwell, 1983), pp. 105–06.

[87] Parts of this section of the chapter previously appeared in Kimberly A. Rivers, 'Memory, Division, and the Organization of Knowledge in the Middle Ages', in *Pre-modern Encyclopaedic Texts: Proceedings of the Second COMERS Congress, Groningen, 1–4 July 1996*, ed. by Peter Binkley (Leiden: Brill, 1997), pp. 147–58.

[88] Mary A. Rouse and Richard H. Rouse, 'The Development of Research Tools in the Thirteenth Century', in *Authentic Witnesses: Approaches to Medieval Texts and Manuscripts* (Notre Dame: University of Notre Dame Press, 1991), pp. 221–55 (pp. 221–22, 239).

[89] By encyclopedias I understand medieval works commonly called encyclopedias by modern scholars: works that attempt to collect and order as comprehensive a view of knowledge as possible. See Michael W. Twomey, 'Medieval Encyclopedias', in *Medieval Christian Literary Imagery: A Guide to Interpretation*, ed. by Robert Earl Kaske, Arthur Groos, and Michael W. Twomey (Toronto: University of Toronto Press, 1988), pp. 182–215 (p. 182), and Denis Hue, 'Structures et rhétoriques dans quelques textes encyclopédiques du moyen âge', in *L'Encyclopédisme: Actes du Colloque de Caen 12–16 janvier 1987*, ed. by Annie Becq (Paris: Éditions aux amateurs de livres, 1991), pp. 311–18 (pp. 311–12).

tions, are witnesses to this transformed attitude. Concomitant with a change in approach to the page may have come a change in approach to memory. The Rouses speculate that after the twelfth century memory may have made an inadequate finding device for retrieving information, as scholars attempted tasks for which memory was unsuited.[90] Memory was still relevant to medieval writers, but now it was aided by the new tools. In fact, it has been suggested by Carruthers and others that memory techniques influenced the organization of those tools.[91]

It is this connection between memory and the use of reference works that Hugh of St Victor's memory precepts, laid out in the early twelfth century before the fresh attitudes toward the page took effect, elucidate so well. Though Hugh is not much concerned with the quick retrieval of information, he does care about ordering material and sharing it with others. In this respect, he saw a role for the transferral of mnemonic techniques to the page. In particular, his use of mnemonic terms like division, collection, and *compendia* suggests that some written compilations were products of mnemonic techniques. Hugh's ideas about memory and the organization of information can be seen as a first step toward the thirteenth-century attitude toward the page. Hugh's mnemonic methods have recently received a good deal of attention.[92] Without wishing to duplicate that work, I would like to refine the interpretation of Hugh's memory system and to discuss how his ideas could affect the organization of information in a practical way.

Throughout his works, Hugh of St Victor holds memory in high esteem as an indispensable learning tool. He implies that modern students are not as proficient as the ancients in retaining what they have learned and thus provides some aids to help his students catch up. Hugh describes a variety of memory methods, but the one most quoted in educational contexts and the one that most elucidates the structure of reference works is a simplified method described in the *Didascalicon*.[93]

[90] Mary A. and Richard H. Rouse, '*Statim invenire*: Schools, Preachers, and New Attitudes to the Page', in *Renaissance and Renewal in the Twelfth Century*, ed. by Robert L. Benson and Giles Constable (Cambridge, MA: Harvard University Press, 1982), pp. 201–25 (pp. 202–03); also in Mary A. Rouse and Richard H. Rouse, '*Statim invenire*: Schools, Preachers, and New Attitudes to the Page', in their *Authentic Witnesses*, pp. 191–219.

[91] Carruthers, *Book of Memory*, pp. 101–02; Illich, *In the Vineyard of the Text*, p. 45; Hue, 'Structures et rhétoriques', pp. 311–12.

[92] Carruthers, *Book of Memory*, pp. 80–85, 162–65, 231–39; Carruthers, 'Poet as Master Builder', pp. 881–904. Illich, *In the Vineyard of the Text*, pp. 29–50; Grover A. Zinn, Jr, 'Hugh of Saint Victor and the Art of Memory', *Viator*, 5 (1974), 211–34.

[93] Hugh of St Victor, *Didascalicon: De studio legendi*, ed. by Charles Henry Buttimer (Washington, DC: Catholic University of America Press, 1939), III.3; English translation, *The*

A related, but not identical, method is found in the preface to the *Chronicon* (*De tribus maximis circumstantiis gestorum*).[94]

The mnemonic advice in the *Didascalicon* depends on two notions: collection (*collectio*) and division (*divisio*). Hugh connects the two terms in his chapter on memory:

> Concerning memory I do not think one should fail to say here that just as aptitude investigates and discovers through analysis [*divisio*], so memory retains through gathering [*collectio*]. The things which we have analyzed in the course of learning [*quae discendo divisimus*] and which we must commit to memory, we ought, therefore, to gather.[95]

'To gather or collect' is 'to reduce to a brief and compendious outline [*summa*] things which have been written or discussed at some length. The ancients called such an outline an "epilogue", that is, a short restatement, by headings, of things already said.'[96] Ancient orators did include an epilogue or *conclusio* at the end of their speeches. One type of conclusion, called the *enumeratio*, was intended to refresh the memory of the audience. The late antique rhetorician Victorinus used the term *collect*, saying that an orator may enumerate by 'touching briefly on and collecting those things which you said before'.[97] The advice, however, pertains to oratory, not to education. Hugh intends by the term something like a summary or an abstract: 'every exposition has some principle upon which the entire truth of the matter and the force of its thought rests, and to this principle everything else is traced back. To look for and consider this principle is to "gather".'[98] The end result of gathering or collecting is a 'compendious summa'.

The analysis or division that Hugh refers to is his method of expounding a text:

> Every analysis [*divisio*] begins from things which are finite, or defined, and proceeds in the direction of things which are infinite, or undefined. Now every finite or defined matter

*Didascalicon of Hugh of St. Victor*, trans. by Jerome Taylor (New York: Columbia University Press, 1961), p. 87. Green, 'Hugo of St. Victor'.

[94] A more complex mnemonic system is described in Hugh's ark and is analysed in Carruthers, *Book of Memory*, and in Kimberly A. Rivers, in 'Memory and the Mendicant in the Later Middle Ages' (unpublished doctoral thesis, University of Toronto, 1995), chap. 2.

[95] *Didas.*, III.11; trans. by Taylor, p. 93.

[96] *Didas.*, III.11; trans. by Taylor, p. 93.

[97] Victorinus, *Explanat. in reth.*, in *Rhetores Latini minores*, ed. by Halm, II.52.256. Cf. Cicero, *De inventione, De optimo genere oratorum*, trans. by Harry Mortimer Hubbell, Loeb Classical Library (Cambridge, MA: Harvard University Press, 1960), I.52.98.

[98] *Didas.*, III.11; trans. by Taylor, p. 93.

> is better known and able to be grasped by our knowledge; teaching, moreover, begins with those things which are better known and, by acquainting us with those, works its way to matters which lie hidden. Furthermore, we investigate with our reason (the proper function of which is to analyze) when, by analysis and investigation of the natures of individual things, we descend from universals to particulars.[99]

To talk of expounding as a process of 'dividing', of moving from better known things to the less well known, and of 'descending from universals to particulars' is at first puzzling. What does Hugh mean here? Because the concept of division is crucial to Hugh's mnemonic system, it is worth exploring it in some detail.[100]

Like the topics, *divisio* has both a rhetorical and a logical background. In ancient rhetoric, division was used to provide order to a speech and to aid memory. According to Quintilian, division is the best way of remembering what we have planned to say:

> For correct division will be an absolute safeguard against error in the order of our speech, since there are certain points not merely in the distribution of the various questions in our speech, but also in their development [...] which naturally come first, second, and third [...] while the connexion will be so perfect that nothing can be omitted or inserted without the fact of the omission or insertion being obvious.[101]

The arrangement of one's ideas contributes to order and consequently preserves the memory of what one wishes to retain. This confidence in division, however, does not delineate its functions. Quintilian defines it as 'the division of a group of things into its component parts', while the related concept of *partitio* is 'the separation of an individual whole into its elements'.[102] Partition is thus a subset of division and is the term Quintilian uses most frequently to refer to the enumeration of points or *propositiones* that an orator intends to cover in his proof. It delivers signposts to the speaker and to the audience of the material to follow and is obviously useful to memory. This function is likely what Quintilian means by division in its general sense, but it does not fully explain Hugh's conception of division.

However, there is also a logical background to division which seems to fit Hugh's meaning more closely.[103] Here *divisio* represents the starting point in the

[99] *Didas.*, III.9; trans. by Taylor, p. 92. See also *Didas.*, III.7, III.8, VI.12.

[100] Although Carruthers does discuss Hugh's use of *divisio*, she does not discuss the logical background of the term which makes it intelligible (*Book of Memory*, pp. 80–107).

[101] Quintilian, *Inst. orat.*, XI.2, § 37, trans. by Butler.

[102] *Inst. orat.*, VII.1, § 1.

[103] *Divisio* is mentioned in a number of logical texts that were available to Hugh in the early twelfth century, including Porphyry's *Isagoge*, Boethius's *De divisione*, and his commentaries on

reasoning process, followed by *definitio* and *collectio*. Division consists of separating genera into species in order to provide the basis for the definitions and propositions of logical argument.[104] *Collectio* concludes the reasoning process by arranging the propositions drawn from division and definition into a syllogism or proof.

Hugh has clearly adapted this logical vocabulary to talk about division. His explanation of divisions does not differ much from the explanations of the ancient authorities on the topic: Boethius and Porphyry. According to them, division must descend from universals to particulars, and must divide finite, not infinite things.[105] Division must necessarily move in a hierarchical fashion, from general concepts (*genera*) to specific ones (*species*); when drawn out schematically, division looks like one of those trees so beloved by medieval preachers. Hugh himself indicates how division must work in instruction in the early books of *Didascalicon*, where he divides the arts and sciences into their component parts, moving from universal concepts to particular subjects, 'thus dividing up philosophy from the peak down to the lowest members'.[106]

However, if Hugh's conception of division is clearly related to ancient logic, his notion of *collectio* is not, being drawn instead from the rhetorical models mentioned above. For him, *collectio* is not a matter of sorting out propositions for a proof but is instead a matter of making abstracts of important material. Thus, one might summarize the *Didascalicon*'s advice so: the diligent student or teacher

*Isagoge* and Cicero's *Topics*. Porphyry, *Categoriarum supplementa: Porphyrii Isagoge translatio Boethii et anonymi fragmentum vulgo vocatum 'Liber sex principiorum'*, ed. by L. Minio-Paluello and Bernard Geoffrey Dod, Aristoteles Latinus, 1, 6–7 (Bruges: de Brouwer, 1966), 6.13; Boethius, *De divisione*, PL, LXIV, cols 875–92; Boethius, *In topica Ciceronis commentaria*, PL, LXIV, col. 1045. For the availability of ancient logical texts in the early Middle Ages, see Sten Ebbesen, 'Ancient Scholastic Logic as the Source of Medieval Logic', in *Cambridge History of Later Medieval Philosophy: From the Rediscovery of Aristotle to the Disintegration of Scholasticism 1100–1600*, ed. by Norman Kretzman, Anthony Kenny, and Jan Pinborg (Cambridge: Cambridge University Press, 1982), pp. 101–27.

[104] Until the thirteenth century, Boethius's *De divisionibus* provided the standard teaching on divisions; see Ebbesen, 'Ancient Scholastic Logic', p. 122.

[105] Porphyry's *Isagoge* says that one descends from general to specifics by dividing and that one ascends back to generals by collecting (6. 13). Boethius, *De divisione*, PL, LXIV, cols 877, 882D.

[106] *Didas.*, trans. by Taylor, p. 44; 'ut autem sciri possit quid legendum sit aut quid praecipue legendum sit, in prima parte primam numerat originem omnium artium deinde descriptionem et partitionum earum, id est quo modo unaquaeque contineat aliam, vel contineatur ab alia, secans philosophiam a summo usque ad ultima membra': *Didas.*, *Praefatio*, p. 2.

will 'analyse' or 'divide' the text in order to discern universal and particular ideas and to indicate their order and relationship. He will then summarize (or 'collect') the main points of these discoveries and store them in memory. Exactly how the memory retains the collections is not entirely clear. However, a thirteenth-century text does provide a model for how this type of mnemonic division might function. In his *Rhetorica novissima* Boncompagno da Signa (*c.* 1165/75–*c.* 1240) articulates a potpourri of mnemonic precepts.[107] Though he does not use the term *divisio*, Boncompagno does offer some mnemonic advice based on the related idea of *ordo*. He provides the seating arrangement from the Fourth Lateran Council as an example of this principle. According to him, Pope Innocent III

> had, through knowledge of the greater people, memory of their inferiors under a certain 'generality'. By beginning with himself, as though from the most general *genus*, he descended, preserving by degree the dignities and offices of each, to individuals as though to subalternated species.[108]

Other dignitaries, such as emperors and kings, may imitate this method, which relies on order and hierarchy. Boncompagno outlines a similar scheme in his plan for the perfect schoolhouse. In it, the teacher occupies the highest seat (because of his greater authority and so that he can keep an eye on the door), while the students are arranged according to rank. On no account is the seating order to be changed, nor should any student dare to take another's spot.[109]

The key to Boncompagno's *ordo memorandi* is hierarchy, whether social, ecclesiastical, or logical. One begins with the highest part of a genus, as it were, and descends by dividing to individual members, or species. For those wishing to master the names of the inhabitants of the animal kingdom, Boncompagno advises finding the ruler of the appropriate realm, i.e., the lion is the king of the beasts, the eagle is the queen of the birds, the whale (*cetus*) is the emperor of the

[107] Boncompagnus, *Rhetorica novissima*, ed. by Augusto Gaudenzi, in *Scripta anecdota antiquissimorum glossatorum*, 3 vols (Bologna: [n. pub.], 1888–1903), II (1892), 251–97. See Terence Tunberg, 'What is Boncompagno's "Newest Rhetoric"?', *Traditio*, 42 (1986), 299–334 (p. 300 nn. 4–6), and Ronald G. Witt, 'Boncompagno and the Defense of Rhetoric', *Journal of Medieval and Renaissance Studies*, 16 (1986), 1–31, for details of his rhetorical innovations and for bibliography. For Boncompagno's biography, see 'Boncompagno', *Dizionario biografico degli italiani*, 72 vols to date (Rome: Istituto della Enciclopedia italiana, 1960–), XI, 720–25.

[108] *Rhet. novis.*, VIII.279: 'Sumat igitur ab Innocentio papa exemplum qui nuper generale concilium celebravit, in quo per maiorum personarum notitiam, memoriam inferior sub quadam generalitate habuit, incipiens a se ipso tanquam a genere generalissimo et faciens descensum, conservatis gradatim quorumlibet dignitatibus et officiis, ad singulos tanquam ad species subalternas.'

[109] *Rhet. novis.*, VIII.279.

fish, etc. One then moves down from the ruler to individuals, putting the worthier animals ahead of the lesser.[110] The system thus provides a classifying scheme that supplies each name with its proper slot.

This plan is clearly similar to division in the *Didascalicon* and might even be Boncompagno's attempt to put it into practice. A basic logical skill turns out to be a basic mnemonic and organizational skill as well; if one begins from the highest point of a genus (or whatever one's subject), one can arrive at the most particular point and hold it in memory by making logical divisions. Given that logical training was so pervasive in the schools, it is not surprising that divisions turn up everywhere and that mnemonic advice is rarer than one might expect. Evidently, one learned more than logical skills when one learned to divide.

Of course, it is hard to know how much information those divisions could hold: Hugh recommends summaries, and Boncompagno seems content to remember names and relationships by this method. Hugh may intend to provide a more comprehensive method in *De tribus maximis circumstantiis gestorum*.[111] In this little treatise, Hugh advocates three 'circumstances' as the key to memory: number, place, and time.[112] For our purpose, number is the most important of the three, for under it Hugh describes a memory method in language very similar to that above. Since Carruthers has already analysed the work, only a brief summary is necessary.

Hugh advises his young readers to contemplate in their minds a line of natural numbers extended lengthwise, starting with one (i.e., the integers from one to infinity).[113] The student should practise finding any desired number quickly

[110] *Rhet. novis.*, VIII.280: 'Ergo in cellule memorialis repositorio ad besties, aves, pisces et reptilia secundum genera singulorum per tuam industriam facies regularem descensum, digniora naturaliter premittendo.'

[111] Green, 'Hugo of St. Victor: *De tribus maximis*', pp. 484–93. See Carruthers, *Book of Memory*, pp. 93, 261–66.

[112] The significance of the circumstances is discussed below.

[113] Green, 'Hugo of St. Victor: *De tribus maximis*', p. 489: 'Disce contemplari in animo tuo lineam naturalis numeri ab uno in quamlibet longam porrectionem quasi oculos cordis tui extensam.' Carruthers translates 'linea naturalis numeri' as 'grid', but surely the phrase is 'a line of natural numbers'. *Naturalis numerus* was a mathematical term for the integers from one to infinity. See Boethius, *De institutione arithmetica libri duo, De institutione musica libri quinque*, ed. by Godofredus Friedlein (Leipzig: Teubner, 1867), 47.28, one of the major mathematical works until the twelfth century, where the term is defined. My guess is that Hugh's 'grid' would look a great deal like the canon-like tables that made up the *Chronicon*, the work to which the *De tribus* was attached as preface.

along this line until his searching routine becomes routine. Once mastered, the technique can be used to memorize many things: Hugh gives, as example, the Psalms. First, one places the initial words of each Psalm, such as 'Beatus vir', in order along the number line, from 1 to 150. When one can proffer the numbered place of any Psalm in any order, one should apply the same method to the verses of the Psalms:

> By dividing and distinguishing at first the book according to the Psalms, then the Psalms through the verses, I reduce the wordiness to a brief *compendium*. And, indeed, this method can easily be used with the Psalms or with other books possessing fixed divisions. But where there is a continuous flow of text, it is necessary for this to be done by art, as it pleases the reader, where it seems most appropriate. First the whole series is divided into some fixed parts, and these again into others, and those into yet others, until the entire text is brought under control.[114]

Brevity is the key to the entire process, and Hugh cautions that each set of divisions must contain a small number of items.

This explanation of *divisio* is more explicit than that in the *Didascalicon*. 'Dividing' literally means partitioning a text into increasingly smaller sections in order to create a 'brief compendium'. The division is a physical one but does not consist so much of breaking up the text every seven words or so[115] as of making hierarchical distinctions. For instance, in his example Hugh describes a hierarchical division of the Psalms. First he learns the beginning of each Psalm, then the beginning of each verse, then the rest of the verse. This division preserves the cohesion of the text, since each section is nested inside the preceding one.

The recommendation to divide up one's text for mnemonic purposes is related to, but not necessarily identical with, the logical division that we have already investigated. In the emphasis on hierarchical descent, the two methods are clearly related. However, in *De tribus maximis* Hugh does not divide his text by any logical distinction. Instead, he follows the verse divisions already present in the

[114] Green, 'Hugo of St. Victor: *De tribus maximis*', p. 490: 'Cognitis autem psalmis, idem facio in singulis psalmis de initiis versuum quod feci in toto psalterio de initiis psalmorum, totamque deinceps seriem in singulis versibus facile corde retineo postquam, dividendo et distinguendo imprimis librum per psalmos deinde psalmum per versus, tantam prolixitatem ad tantum compendium et brevitatem redigi. Et hoc quidem in psalmis sive in aliis libris certas distinctiones habentibus facile videri potest. Ubi autem continua series est lectionis, id ipsum artificio fieri oportet, ut scilicet secundum lectoris placitum, ubi competentius videbitur, primum tota series in certas aliquas partes dividatur, et illae rursum in alias, illae iterum in alias, donec tota prolixitas ita restringatur'; my translation.

[115] As Carruthers seems to see it (*Book of Memory*, pp. 80–107).

Psalms. If a text is not supplied with divisions, Hugh advises his students to create their own, a necessary skill in the twelfth century, when most manuscripts had few chapter divisions.[116]

To summarize the relationship of memory and division in Hugh's memory methods: the difference between division in *Didascalicon* and in *De tribus maximis* is that one divides ideas and the other divides a text. Taylor rightly translates *modus legendi*, the title of the chapter that explains division in *Didascalicon*, as 'the method of expounding'. His translation reflects one of the three types of reading that Hugh outlines in *Didascalicon*: reading to someone else, i.e., teaching.[117] Division is a method that Hugh himself employs as he teaches his students what to read. This kind of division aids memory by ordering the material and by indicating what a student should remember. In contrast, the kind of division elaborated in *De tribus maximis* is more clearly a memory method, providing a way of retaining a great deal of material.

The goal of collection in *Didascalicon* and of division in *De tribus maximis* is a *summa* or *compendium*; these terms may help explain the movement toward encyclopedism and other reference works in the late twelfth and thirteenth centuries when education was becoming professionalized. Certainly the terms *brevis summa* and *compendium* recur constantly in Hugh's educational and theological works, either as goals to be aimed at or as descriptions of his own work. In fact, he describes a *compendium* as the objective of teaching:

> When, therefore, we treat of any art — and especially in teaching it, when everything must be reduced to outline [*compendium*] and presented for easy understanding — we should be content to set forth the matter in hand as briefly and clearly as possible, lest by excessively piling up extraneous considerations we distract the student more than we instruct him. We must not say everything we can, lest we say with less effect such things as need saying.[118]

For Hugh, *compendia* reduce necessary knowledge to a memorable and intelligible form. The key to them is that the teacher or learner has selected and organized the most important information to learn and to remember. From these selections, all the other material may be derived.

[116] See Carruthers's discussion of chapter divisions, *Book of Memory*, pp. 94–96.

[117] *Didas.*, III.7. *Lectio* 'consists of forming our minds upon rules and precepts taken from books' and may occur in three ways: by teaching (reading to someone else), by learning (being read to by someone else), or by examining the text oneself (reading to oneself). *Didas.*, trans. by Taylor, p. 91.

[118] *Didas.*, III.5; trans. by Taylor, p. 90.

It is clear that Hugh regards many of his educational and theological works as *compendia*, the fruits of division and collection. For instance, in the preface to *De sacramentis*, his major work of theology, he refers to his new work as the foundation of allegorical interpretation:

> For I have compressed this brief *summa*, as it were, of all doctrine into one continuous work, that the mind may have something definite to which it may affix and conform its attention, lest it be carried away by various volumes of writings and a diversity of readings without order or direction.[119]

A previously composed historical work is a *compendiosum volumen* while *De sacramentis* is a *brevis summa*, the same words designating mnemonic practices in *De tribus maximis* and *Didascalicon*. Their use indicates what Hugh may mean by a *brevis summa* — in *De sacramentis*, a running outline of the mysteries of faith, comprehensive in scope but concise in elaboration.[120] When Hugh's words are understood in a mnemonic context, it is clear that he is not making modest disclaimers about *De sacramentis*, but rather that he sees his theological explanation as a short introduction to Christian doctrine, theological notes that were likely once held in Hugh's memory.[121]

For this reason, one should consider carefully what an author may mean when he classes his work as a *collectio*, a *compendium*, or a *brevis summa* (words often used to introduce encyclopedic works). Texts introduced with these words may be the product of mnemonic division and gathering now spread out on the page. Glorieux has noted that the term *summa* had many connotations in the Middle Ages; in some cases it could mean a compilation or even an encyclopedia. He also observes that one of its major senses is *compendium*, a brief summary of the

[119] Hugh of St Victor, *On the Sacraments of the Christian Faith (De Sacramentis)*, trans. by Roy J. Deferrari (Cambridge, MA: Medieval Academy of America, 1951), p. 3. Hugh of St Victor, *De sacramentis*, PL, CLXXVI, col. 183.

[120] Examples of Hugh's emphasis on the memorization of factual knowledge combined with *summa* language can also be found in his teachings on the arts. See Roger Baron, 'Hugonis de Sancto Victore Epitome Dindimi in philosophiam', *Traditio*, 11 (1955), 91–148 (p. 105); Jean Leclercq, 'Le "De grammatica" de Hugues de Saint-Victor', *Archives d'histoire doctrinale et littéraire du moyen âge*, 14 (1943–45), 263–322 (pp. 271, 273, 288). Both works can also be found in *Hugonis de Sancto Victore, Opera propaedeutica: Practica geometriae, De grammatica, Epitome Dindimi in philosophiam*, ed. by Roger Baron (Notre Dame: University of Notre Dame Press, 1966).

[121] Southern has recently pointed to Hugh's *De sacramentis* as 'the first original medieval *Summa theologica*' (*Heroic Age*, p. 57).

principles of a particular subject.[122] It is surely this sense of the word *summa* that Hugh intends. One could thus see Hugh's *compendia* as an early step toward encyclopedism, a step with a clearly mnemonic aspect.

Hugh's notion of a *compendium* indicates that there is a mnemonic context for the arrangement of material in compilations. One achieves a *compendium* or short *summa* when one divides or collects the material to be learned or when one divides up a text by his number line method. In either case, one has reduced a great deal of material to a manageable and organized form. His adoption of the same terms to describe his own work indicates both that his written works have a mnemonic aspect and that he sees a need to share his organizational skills by putting them on paper. Organization and brevity are the keys to his method. This desire to make mental organization accessible to others may have been a motivating factor for later medieval compilers and should be explored. One thing is certain: divisions soon made their appearance on the thirteenth-century page. The process of dividing and collecting seems to describe the job of a medieval compiler, as well as that of most teachers and preachers in the High Middle Ages, and may explain that curious passion for divisions so often remarked on by modern scholars. Scholars should not see medieval writers' passion for divisions as a kind of quirk but rather as an integral part of teaching, learning, and writing in the Middle Ages.

The resulting reference works became increasingly useful for scholars and preachers as they studied for their classes, prepared lectures and disputations, and composed their sermons. The fruit of someone else's memory spilled onto the page, as it were, could be incredibly useful for someone who had not read the original works for himself, and thus could not remember them. In this way, the changing scholarly world of the twelfth century adapted pedagogical methods from the past to suit their new needs.

## Memory and History in Hugh of St Victor's Scriptural Programme

Another aspect of Hugh of St Victor's pedagogy that elucidates twelfth-century mnemonic practice is his use of the topics in historical studies. Since Beryl Smalley published *The Study of the Bible in the Middle Ages*, scholars have stressed the importance of the literal or historical level of scriptural studies to Hugh of

[122] *Dictionnaire de théologie catholique: Contenant l'exposé des doctrines de la théologie catholique, leurs preuves et leur histoire*, ed. by Alfred Vacant, 15 vols (Paris: Letouzey et Ané, 1899–1950 ), XIV, pt II, 2341–43, s.v. 'Sommes théologiques'.

St Victor and his students. Smalley placed the Victorine school, especially Hugh and Andrew, at the beginning of a medieval continuum that raised the dignity of the literal sense of Scripture.[123] Her views have been reinforced by the work of Richard Southern and Grover Zinn, who have examined the role of historical development in Hugh's theological works, especially *De sacramentis*.[124] What has been given less attention, however, is the extraordinary degree to which Hugh equates memory work with the historical level of Scripture. For Hugh, history comprises the foundation of exegesis, and the details of the historical events described in the Bible have to be committed to memory in order for that foundation to stand. Memory also secures the bases of allegorical interpretation and even meditation. While historical understanding is not the end toward which scriptural interpretation is directed, it does provide the structure that allows one's mind to reach the heights of contemplation. This is why in *De tribus maximis circumstantiis*, *Didascalicon*, and the ark treatises, Hugh lays out a plan of exegetical study that advances from the memorization of historical facts and Christian doctrine to allegorical interpretation and meditation.

Hugh himself connects these areas by requiring the memorization of facts and doctrine before proceeding to more sophisticated approaches to scriptural texts and by using the rhetorical circumstances as an organizing tool in much of his writing, especially his works aimed at teaching elementary skills and concepts. His use of the circumstances as a heuristic binds together much of his teachings about history, memory, and the goals of a Christian education.[125]

The foundation of Hugh's thinking about history and memory is laid out in *De tribus maximis*, which served as the prologue to the *Chronicon*, a schoolboy's

[123] Smalley, *Study of the Bible*, p. 89.

[124] Richard W. Southern, 'Aspects of the European Tradition of Historical Writing: 2. Hugh of St Victor and the Idea of Historical Development', *Transactions of the Royal Historical Society*, ser. 5, 21 (1971), 159–79; Grover A. Zinn, Jr, '*Historia fundamentum est* and the Role of History in the Contemplative Life According to Hugh of St Victor', in *Contemporary Reflections on the Medieval Christian Tradition: Essays in Honor of Ray C. Petry*, ed. by George H. Shriver (Durham, NC: Duke University Press, 1974), pp. 135–58. Bert Roest, 'Reading the Book of History: Intellectual Contexts and Educational Functions of Franciscan Historiography 1226–ca. 1350' (unpublished doctoral thesis, University of Groningen, 1996), pp. 153–54, also comments on the importance of historical studies to Hugh of St Victor.

[125] Marie-Dominique Chenu remarks on Hugh's partiality to the historical sense of Scripture without discussing memory in *La Théologie au douzième siècle*, 3rd edn (Paris: Vrin, 1976), pp. 200–02, as does Smalley, *Study of the Bible*, pp. 83–106. Henri De Lubac, however, found Hugh's attitude entirely traditional, *Exégèse médiévale: Les Quatre sens de l'Écriture*, 4 vols (Paris: Aubier, 1959–64) II, pt I, 287–359.

history text written around 1130. As we have already seen, Hugh described an elementary mnemonic technique in this text, and it is the topic to which Hugh devotes the most space in his tract. However, the title remains instructive: *De tribus maximis circumstantiis gestorum, id est personis locis temporibus.* (On the three most important circumstances of deeds, i.e., persons, places, and times). The full import of the title only becomes clear in the second part of the treatise, where Hugh discusses the methods of explicating Scripture. The senses of Scripture are, as one would expect, the historical, the allegorical, and the tropological. Hugh puts the latter two aside in order to concentrate on history, because history is the foundation of all learning. Once it is mastered, all later learning can be understood and retained more easily. Mastery, for Hugh, means memorization: the deeds of the past should be committed to memory.

The difficulty of such an approach, as every first-year history student has already discovered, is that the events of the past are nearly infinite. How can the student create a foundation of historical learning that one's memory can actually retain? Hugh's recommendation is 'to collect from them all a certain kind of brief summary [*brevis summa*], like the foundation of the foundation, that is the first foundation, which the mind is easily able to comprehend and retain in memory'.[126] One may construct such a 'brief summary', or 'first foundation' of deeds, by consulting the three things on which the knowledge of deeds chiefly depends: the persons by whom the deeds were done, the places in which they were done, and the times when they were done.[127]

Using the number method already described, Hugh advises his young pupils to place important persons with their times along the numbered, longitudinal line 'in the ark of our heart' and to stretch out the places along the lateral line.[128] Hugh

[126] Hugh, *De tribus maximis*, p. 491: 'oportet nos ex omnibus brevem quandam summam colligere quasi fundamentum fundamenti, hoc est primum fundamentum, quam facile possit animus comprehendere et memoria retinere'.

[127] Green, 'Hugo of St. Victor: *De tribus maximis*', p. 489: 'Tria igitur sunt in quibus praecipue cognitio pendet rerum gestarum, id est, personae a quibus res gestae, le loca in quibus gestae sunt, et tempora quando gestae sunt.'

[128] Hugh's advice here neatly ties together his number-line method with his more sophisticated advice about meditating in the two ark treatises, discussed below. Note also how the language here reinforces the idea that Hugh's method depends on lines, not a grid. Green, 'Hugo of St. Victor: *De tribus maximis*', p. 491: 'Siquidem in archa cordis tempus et numerus longitudinem metiuntur, aream in latitudinem expandit locus, ut deinde cetera disponantur locis suis. Primum igitur personas cum temporibus suis ordine disponemus, in longitudinem lineam ab exordio porrigentes. Deinde loca etiam designabimus quantum capacitas adbreviationis patietur sufficinter ex universitate collecta.'

then gives an injunction to his students to use his memory method on the 'things which will be described below':

> Now, therefore, you have enough to do to imprint on your memory those things which will be described below, according to the mode and form of learning demonstrated to you above, in such a way that you are able to recognize by experience the truth of my words, when you will see how useful it is not only to weigh out one's zeal and effort for the hearing of Scriptures and their discussion, but also for their memory.[129]

He follows the injunction with an example: a quick narration of the six days of Creation and their works. Then he begins the list of the lines of generation starting with Adam, concluding that 'the other things follow below, arranged according to Hebrew Scripture'.[130] The *Chronicon* that follows this mnemonic advice contains pages of columns devoted to names, dates, and geographical place names, arranged for easy memorization. Green reproduces the first page of the chronological tables that follow Hugh's preface. It catalogues the six days of Creation and the lines of generation of the first age.[131] The example and the tables provide the students with their mnemonic assignment; they indeed 'have enough to do!'

The clear implication of Hugh's arrangement of mnemonic method, discussion of the historical level of interpretation, and then pages of historical information is that the foundation of the historical level of Scripture, 'the foundation of the foundation', is memorization. It is introductory work that schoolboys must master. Hugh's recommendation for remembering historical information might at first seem like sensible, if tedious, advice for young students. But his insistence on persons, places, and times as a filtering device for learning is not a temporary preoccupation: it appears whenever he recommends basic information

[129] Green, 'Hugo of St. Victor: *De tribus maximis*', p. 491: 'Nunc ergo satage ut ea quae subter describentur ita memoriae tuae imprimas, secundum modum et formam discendi superius tibi demonstratum, ut experimento dictorum meorum veritatem agnoscere possis, cum videris quantum valeat, non auditui scriptuarum sive loquacitati solummodo studium et operam impendere, sed memoriae.'

[130] Green, 'Hugo of St. Victor: *De tribus maximis*', p. 492: 'Et cetera sicut subter sequuntur secundum Hebraicam veritatem disposita.'

[131] Descriptions of the contents of the *Chronicon* can be found in Damien van den Eynde, *Essai sur la succession et la date des écrits de Hugues de St-Victor* (Rome: Apud Pontificium Atheneaum Antonianum, 1960), pp. 90–92, and Roger Baron, 'La Chronique de Hugues de Saint-Victor', *Studia Gratiana*, 12 (1967), 167–80. Some of the lists of rulers in the *Chronicon* are in Monumenta Germaniae Historica, Scriptores, 24 (Hannover: Hahn, 1879), 88–97.

to be learned and it ties together much of his teachings about memory and history. This near obsession requires some explanation.

First, why has he chosen these three rubrics? Hugh's choice depends on a subset of the rhetorical topics discussed above. As mentioned above, Cicero divided his topics in *De inventione* into person and act, a division he found in Hellenistic sources, such as Hermagoras of Temnos (150 BC). In his search to find the subject matter of rhetoric, Hermagoras distinguished the *thesis*, an abstract issue without specific circumstances, from the *hypothesis*, a concrete issue surrounded by circumstances (*peristaseis*), which could be explored by the questions who? (*quis*), what? (*quid*), when? (*quando*), where? (*ubi*), why? (*cur*), how? (*quem ad modum*), and with what resources? (*quibus adminiculis*).[132] Cicero included these circumstances among his list of topics, but he by no means stopped at seven topics in his attributes of person and act.[133] It was in the late antique period that rhetoricians began to use the seven circumstances to define the events surrounding an individual case, and their works, along with Boethius's *De topicis differentiis*, were transmitted to the Middle Ages.[134] The circumstances were most often used in the twelfth and thirteenth centuries in prologues for literary works and in medieval penitential and theological works as a way of organizing the questions or details of a given topic. As they were well known to an educated audience — there was a metrical verse to hold them in memory[135] — the circumstances provided a useful mnemonic and organizing tool. In *De scripturis et scriptoribus sacris praenotatiunculae*, Hugh gives a fuller list of circumstances as an aid to exegesis: *res, persona, numerus, locus, tempus, gestum*.[136] His version

[132] Leff, 'Topics of Argumentative Invention', p. 28. Johannes Gründel, *Die Lehre von den Umständen der menschlichen Handlung im Mittelalter*, Beiträge zur Geschichte der Philosophie und Theologie des Mittelalters, 39.5 (Münster: Aschendorf, 1963), pp. 15–16. See also Rita Copeland, *Rhetoric, Hermeneutics, and Translation in the Middle Ages: Academic Traditions and Vernacular Texts*, Cambridge Studies in Medieval Literature (Cambridge: Cambridge University Press, 1991), 67–68.

[133] Gründel notes that one will search Cicero's work in vain for a neat version of the seven circumstances (*Die Lehre von den Umständen*, p. 21).

[134] Gründel, *Die Lehre von den Umständen*, pp. 13–14, 24–37.

[135] Gründel notes that the hexameter 'quis, quid, ubi, quibus auxiliis, cur, quomodo, quando' appears in both theological and rhetorical works of the twelfth century (*Die Lehre von den Umständen*, p. 38 n. 5).

[136] Hugh of St Victor, *De scripturis et scriptoribus sacris praenotatiunculae*, in *Opera omnia*, PL, CLXXV, cols 9–28 (col. 21): 'res autem quaelibet tam multiplex potest esse in significatione aliarum rerum, quot in se proprietates visibiles aut invisibiles habet communes aliis rebus. Hae

represents a variation on the standard list of seven circumstances, but he always calls them *circumstantiae*.[137]

Second, it should be noticed that the circumstances appear not once, but twice in *De tribus maximis*. Though it seems clear that the title itself refers to the second half of the treatise, a variant of the circumstances is used in the first half as well. When Hugh begins to explain his number line method, he declares that one may retain all of what one learns by discerning things through number, place, and time. His mnemonic method is then arranged around these three distinctions: number indicates the number line mnemonic, place refers to the book that one learned from and the physical environment in which one studied, and time when the thing happened that one studies and also when one learned the material. One could argue that for Hugh, the variants of the circumstances function as a kind of mnemotechnic prior to his more obvious number line method. The circumstances order the material to be learned, and they help one select the most important principles and ideas from among the many things that could be learned in history. The number line mnemonic then aids one to memorize the information selected. In a similar way, the circumstances order Hugh's explication of the mnemonic method.

Since the circumstances were originally used to define the peculiarities of individual cases in ancient rhetoric, they were particularly appropriate for selecting the memorable aspects of historical events. In recommending these topics, Hugh showed, as Richard Southern has noted, a sensitivity for historical understanding.[138] The choice is not a random one but depends, as the title indicates, on a selection of the three circumstances most relevant for historical events. Many modern history teachers require their students to remember important people

autem res primae per voces significatae, et res secundas significantes, sex **circumstantiis** discretae considerantur: quae sunt hae, videlicet res, persona, numerus, locus, tempus, gestum. In his enim significatio rerum primarum ad secundas consideratur' (boldface per original). Like Hugh's *De modo di<s>cendi et meditandi* (PL, CLXXVI, cols 875–80), *De scripturis et scriptoribus sacris praenotatiunculae* is largely a compilation or revision of ideas found in the prologue to *De sacramentis* and *Didascalicon* (large excerpts of Books IV, V, and VI are found in *De scripturis*). Curiously, the section on the six circumstances is not found in these other works, though the use of the terms is consistent with some of Hugh's other writings, including *De tribus maximis* (Green, 'Hugo of St. Victor: *De tribus maximis*', pp. 484–93).

[137] Gründel, *Die Lehre von den Umständen*, pp. 33–34. The circumstances listed by the fourth-century Fortunatianus is not far from Hugh's list (*persona, res, causa, tempus, locus, modus, materia*), p. 26, as is Alcuin's (*persona, factum, tempus, locum, modum, occasio, facultas*), p. 33.

[138] Southern, 'Aspects of the European Tradition', pp. 165–66, 172–74.

and events by referring to the five *W*s: who, what, where, when, and why. For this reason, one might expect to find Hugh employing the circumstances most often in the context of the historical level of Scripture and in the context of memory injunctions, as indeed one does.

For instance, a very similar recommendation of the circumstances for learning historical information occurs in Book VI of the *Didascalicon*, where Hugh treats the order and method of reading the Bible, including the three levels of sense:

> First you learn history and diligently commit to memory the truth of the deeds that have been learned, reviewing from beginning to end what has been done, when it has been done, where it has been done, and by whom it has been done. For these are the four things which are especially to be sought for in history — the person [*persona*], the business done [*negotium*], the time [*tempus*], and the place [*locus*].[139]

This is essentially the same advice that he related in *De tribus maximis*, with the addition of *negotium*. As though expecting opposition (probably from his students), Hugh explains patiently the need to learn 'small things' like the recounting of God's deeds in the past, before rushing on to the more intellectually exciting field of allegory. When history is considered as the narration of events, Hugh recommends the historical books for study: Genesis, Exodus, Joshua, Judges, Kings, Chronicles, the four Gospels, and the Acts of the Apostles.[140]

Given his emphasis on the circumstances and memory in the works which discuss the importance of exegetical training, one might wonder whether a similar preoccupation appears in Hugh's biblical commentaries. Although he has not left many behind, the introductions to his commentaries demonstrate a leaning toward the literal sense of Scripture and the use of the circumstances.[141] Richard Hunt and A. J. Minnis have demonstrated the importance of the introductions to scriptural commentaries in the development of medieval literary theory.[142] They have noted in Hugh's scriptural prologues the use of a version of the rhetorical circumstances. Minnis notes a change in the eleventh century away

[139] *Didas.*, VI.3; trans. by Taylor, pp. 135–36.

[140] *Didas.*, VI.3.

[141] Smalley, *Study of the Bible*, p. 89.

[142] Richard William Hunt, 'The Introduction to the 'Artes' in the Twelfth Century', in *Studia mediaevalia in honorem admodum Reverendi Patris Raymundi Josephi Martin, Ordinis Praedicatorum s. theologiae magistri LXXum natalem diem agentis* (Bruges: De Tempel, 1948), pp. 85–112; Alistair Minnis, *Medieval Theory of Authorship: Scholastic Literary Attitudes in the Late Middle Ages*, 2nd edn (Aldershot: Wildewood House, 1988).

from the circumstances toward a 'Type C' prologue, so that Hugh's use of the circumstances constitutes a rare approach in the twelfth century.

Hugh's application of the circumstances to scriptural exegesis takes advantage of their mnemonic utility. For this reason, his prologues are not the usual type of the medieval *accessus ad auctores*. The *accessus* identified by Hunt and Minnis explain questions of authority and literary theory. For instance, the standard academic prologue of the twelfth century discussed the title of the book, the author's name and intention, the subject matter, method of procedure, etc.[143] Many of Hugh's prologues, however, differ from this model. He tends to employ three or more of the circumstances to establish the basic elements of the literal foundation, which must be in place before the rest of the exposition can continue. Within the literal level of Scripture, he emphasizes the historical events of the narration.

The best example of this procedure is found in Chapter 1 of Hugh's commentary on Leviticus:[144]

> Five points are treated [in the book of Leviticus], that is the sacrifices which are offered to God, and the persons by whom they are offered, and the times when they are offered, and the places where they are offered, and the causes for which they are offered. It therefore is necessary for us to examine something of each one, as the plan of the introduction demands.[145]

In the next several chapters, Hugh scrutinizes each point. The significance of Hugh's prologue is that he is clearly laying out for exposition the kind of information he told the reader to memorize in *De tribus maximis*. Because of the overlap between the points discussed in his biblical commentary and the points raised in *De tribus maximis*, it is reasonable to see the prologue to Leviticus as an injunction to memory. Hugh does not provide such an introduction to every book in his relatively slight corpus of exegesis, but he does use it more than once.[146] Thus, it appears that for Hugh, the historical level of Scripture forms the foundation of all exegetical learning. One must memorize the basic facts before

[143] Minnis, *Medieval Theory of Authorship*, pp. 19–24.

[144] *In Levit.*, PL, CLXXV, col. 74. Smalley noted that Hugh's prologue to Leviticus does not correspond to the usual *accessus* (*Study of the Bible*, p. 99).

[145] *In Levit.*, PL, CLXXV, col. 74: 'Quinque namque sunt: id est sacrificia quae Deo offeruntur, et personae a quibus offeruntur, et tempora quando offeruntur, et loca ubi offeruntur, et causae pro quibus offeruntur: quae in hoc libro distincte tractantur. Nos ergo de singulis, quantum ratio introductionis expostulat, aliquid praelibare oportet.'

[146] See Hugh of St Victor, *In librum Judicum*, PL, CLXXV, cols 87, 115.

proceeding to more sophisticated approaches, and the circumstances provide a guideline for what should be memorized.

What should also be noted about Hugh's attitude toward exegesis is that he is nearly as insistent about the need for the memorization of factual knowledge for allegorical interpretation as for the historical. In the *Didascalicon* he tries to restrain his students' zeal to get at the mysteries of allegory, lest they rashly presume incorrect meanings in the text. He urges them to lay a second foundation of knowledge over the first, this one relating to allegory: for while there may be ambiguities and contradictions in the literal level, there can be no opposition in the spiritual sense.[147] Allegory is the superstructure of scriptural exegesis resting on the foundation of historical studies. In turn, the superstructure of allegory is built from several courses (*ordines*) of stone, such as the Trinity, Creation, the origin of sin and punishment, the Incarnation, and the Resurrection. Each of these courses has a secure base on which to rest, which serve as 'the principles of the mysteries'. Such principles are obtained from learned teachers, and they should act as a gauge against which the student can measure each new idea about the faith. Only through this careful approach will students be able to avoid changing their views every time they read a new book.[148]

Once again, Hugh insists on the memorization of the basic tenets before one is turned loose on the text alone.[149] Significantly, the eight 'courses' of allegory named in the *Didascalicon* form the core of Hugh's *De sacramentis*, a work designed to provide students with basic doctrine and a work that Hugh identified as the next level of instruction after history.[150] In the prologue to *De sacramentis*, Hugh says,

> Since, therefore, I previously composed a compendium on the initial instruction in Holy Scripture, which consists in their historical reading, I have prepared the present work for those who are to be introduced to the second stage of instruction, which is in allegory. By this work they may firmly establish their minds on that foundation, so to speak, of the knowledge of faith, so that such other things as may be added to the structure by reading or hearing may remain unshaken.[151]

[147] *Didas.*, VI.4.

[148] *Didas.*, VI.4; trans. by Taylor, pp. 142–44.

[149] This insistence probably stems from Hugh's designation of the history and allegory as pertaining to knowledge, while the tropological level of exegesis pertains to morals. *Didas.*, V.6.

[150] See *Didas.*, trans. by Taylor, p. 223 n. 15, for a bibliography of scholars noting this relationship.

[151] Translation from Deferrari, *On the Sacraments of the Christian Faith*, p. 3. Hugh of St Victor, *De sacramentis*, PL, CLXXVI, col. 183: 'Cum igitur de prima eruditione sacri eloquii quae

As Green points out, the 'compendium' about history must be *De tribus maximis*, while the second stage of instruction, allegory, provides the foundation of doctrine.[152]

Just as the circumstances were an integral part of Hugh's idea of the historical level of Scripture, the circumstances also turn up in Hugh's rules for interpreting allegory. Roger Baron noted in *Science et Sagesse* that there were what he called six symbolic elements in Hugh's theory of allegory: '*res, persona, numerus, locus, tempus*, and *actus*'.[153] In *De scripturis et scriptoribus sacris praenotatiunculae*, Hugh defines allegory as 'when some invisible deed or fact is signified through a visible one'.[154] Never content to leave a reader unprepared to face the mysteries of Scripture, Hugh provides instructions for uncovering the hidden fruit of Scripture, that is, allegory. His thinking depends on Augustine's distinction between words and things. In most areas of knowledge, readers look only for the signification of the words in their books. Sacred Scripture is different and indeed superior to these other writings, because the signification of the things in it is more important than the signification of the words. Once one has got past the meaning of the things signified by words, one must consider the meaning of the things themselves, and the circumstances provide the framework through which to interpret them. For instance, Hugh understands the *res* of the circumstances to mean a material substance, such as stones, wood, or plants. Every material thing in Scripture can signify either an exterior form or an interior nature. Thus, snow by its interior nature signifies coldness, the extinction of the heat of desire, while by its exterior nature, whiteness, it designates the purity (*munditia*) of works.[155]

Here, the circumstances provide a mental checklist against which to determine the meanings of words in Scripture. They serve as guidelines for an approach in

in historica constat lectione, compendiosum volumen prius dictassem, hoc nunc ad secundum eruditionem (quae in allegorica est) introducendis preparavi; in quo, si fundamento quodam cognitionis fidei animum stabiliant, ut caetera quae vel legendo vel audiendo superaedificare potuerint, inconcussa permaneant. Hanc enim quasi brevem quamdam summam omnium in unam seriem compegi, ut animus aliquid certum haberet, cui intentionem affigere et conformare valeret, ne per varia Scripturarum volumina et lectionum divortia sine ordine et directione raperetur.'

[152] Chenu also notes the relationship of these two treatises as the first or second *eruditiones* of scriptural knowledge (*La théologie au douzième siècle*, p. 203).

[153] Roger Baron, *Science et sagesse chez Hugues de Saint-Victor* (Paris: de Brouwer, 1963), p. 122.

[154] *De scripturis et scriptoribus sacris praenotatiunculae*, PL, CLXXV, col. 12B.

[155] *De script.*, PL, CLXXV, col. 21B–C.

the difficult world of allegorical interpretation and restrain students from unsubstantiated interpretations of Scripture. In all of these instances Hugh relies on the circumstances to organize basic information and to provide an approach to difficult tasks. The circumstances act as a ready-made filter, screening out information extraneous to the task at hand, and rendering memorization easier.

Further confirmation of the essential role of memory and history in scriptural studies can be seen in a letter composed around 1170 by an unknown writer, probably a Victorine. He advises a young friend on 'the method and order of reading Scripture', following closely the programme laid out in the *Didascalicon*.[156] Like Hugh, he first sets out the names and order of the books of the Old and New Testaments for the student to learn. After mastering this information, he moves on to the threefold exegesis of Scripture. He begins, of course, with the historical level, by scrutinizing all the historical books three or four times. From this reading 'a *summa* must be collected and retained in memory': incidents worthy of such attention are the creation, construction of the ark, the promise made to Abraham, the names and number of the patriarchs, their wives, concubines, and sons, and the like.[157] The author refers to the same *circumstantiae* as memory headings; for instance, in the Gospels 'the number of sermons and miracles must be noted, and what, where, when and in the presence of whom a matter was done and said by the Lord'.[158] The list occupies almost a whole column of text.

Once the historical studies are completed, the student should move on to doctrinal and moral training. He must learn about the sacraments of the Church, 'which are found fully in the books of Master Hugh', and he must know the nature of the cardinal virtues and their opposing vices.[159] Only after all of this instruction may the student advance to exposition of Scripture. The letter reinforces the priority of memory, history, and factual knowledge in the Victorine school.

Hugh's use of mnemonic devices, including the circumstances, in education does not end with scriptural studies or exegesis, but, in fact, extends to all Chris-

[156] *Thesaurus novus anecdotorum. Tomus primus: Complectens regum ac principum aliorumque virorum illustrium epistolas et diplomata*, ed. by Edmundus Martene and Ursinus Durand (Paris: Delaulne [and others], 1717); cited in Smalley, *Study of the Bible*, pp. 88–89.

[157] *Thesaurus novus anecdotorum*, pp. 488–89.

[158] *Thesaurus novus anecdotorum*, p. 489C: 'in quibus [libri novi testamenti] diligenter & numerus sermonum & miraculorum notetur, & quid, ubi, & quando, & coram quibus à Domino factum dictumve sit'.

[159] *Thesaurus novus anecdotorum*, p. 489.

tian knowledge. In the ark treatises, Hugh discovers a way to arrange Christian knowledge through a visual design.[160] Hugh describes and moralizes the 'literal' ark's attributes in *De arca Noe morali* and explains how to build it in *De arca Noe mystica*.[161] In *De arca Noe morali*, Hugh describes the need for each person to construct an interior dwelling place for both God and oneself to inhabit. Many types of dwellings are possible, but Hugh settles on the ark as his metaphor. The treatise then describes four kinds of arks, two exterior and two interior: the literal ark that Noah built, the Church built up by Christ, the ark of Wisdom built by meditation on the law, and the ark of Grace. Hugh is most interested in the ark of Wisdom, devoting most of his time to it, but all are implied in the term *ark*.

The ark of Wisdom, as Carruthers notes, is crafted from meditation. One builds and lives in the ark simultaneously: the process is accomplished by casting one's thoughts back over what one has already learned and by forming it into a new whole. The planks of the ark are composed from the factual knowledge Hugh advised his students to memorize in *De tribus maximis* and *Didascalicon*. For instance, we measure out the length of the ark by leading our thoughts from the beginning of the world to the end, giving us the longitude of three hundred cubits. We fix the width by thinking about the Church and the height by becoming adept at Scripture, which is contained in thirty volumes (hence thirty cubits for the height).[162] Thus, in the pictorialized ark the longitude contains the lines of succession from Adam to the Incarnation, then the apostles and the popes up to Honorius II, with space for those to come. The north side of the column situated in the centre of the ark represents the Book of Life, to which ladders lead with the names of the volumes of Scripture inscribed on them.[163]

The priority of memorization and the circumstances can be seen in Book IV of the Moral Ark when Hugh describes the order and disposition of thoughts necessary for construction. To succeed, we must arrive at a right ordering of our thoughts, based on the order of things. And the things on which our minds should

[160] See Roger Bacon, *Opus tertium*, in *Opera quaedam hactenus inedita*, ed. by John Sherren Brewer, Rolls Series, 15 (London: Longman, 1859), chap. 58, p. 226, for his assertion of the usefulness of having images like Noah's ark and Solomon's temple before one's eyes in order to understand the literal sense of Scripture. For more on the visual aspects of Hugh's arks, see Patrice Sicard, *Diagrammes médiévaux et exégèse visuelle: Le Libellus de formatione arche de Hugues de Saint Victor*, Bibliotheca victoriana, 4 (Turnhout: Brepols, 1993).

[161] Hugh of St Victor, *De arca Noe morali*, PL, CLXXVI, cols 649–80; *De arca Noe mystica*, PL, CLXXVI, cols 681–704.

[162] Hugh of St Victor, *Arc. mor.*, PL, CLXXVI, cols 635–36.

[163] Hugh of St Victor, *Arc. myst.*, PL, CLXXVI, cols 685–88; 684, 693–94.

focus are the things of creation and of restoration (the things that pertain to salvation).[164] From the many works of restoration, one must pick out the most important deeds and persons with their places and times and then order them in the ark relative to one another according to their place, time, and worthiness. The latter circumstance will determine the person or event's dwelling place in one of the three levels or mansions of the ark and thus its altitude. In one sense both time and place run together along the longitudinal line of the ark, because the lines of succession enumerated their descent along the East/West axis. Thus, according to Hugh, the beginning of the world began in the East, with subsequent human actions moving their focus successively to the West, that is, from Eden to Assyria and Chalcedon to Greece to Rome.[165]

From this discussion it is clear that Hugh is relying on his use of the circumstances in their mnemonic context to describe the materials of the ark's construction. The kinds of things that Hugh has recommended his students to memorize in his elementary instruction books are now to be incorporated into the ark. The ark builders are not asked to learn this material now, but rather 'to cast their thoughts back' over such details, building their ark in meditation from things they already know. This is what meditation is for Hugh. One could say that for Hugh, history provides the 'hooks' for meditative thinking.

The significance of the ark is twofold. In the first place, through it Hugh finds a method of including all Christian belief into a unified visual whole. As he puts it:

> This ark is similar to a storeroom stuffed with a variety of delights. You will seek nothing in it that you shall not find, and when you find one thing, many things will seem laid open to you. There all the works of our restoration from the beginning of the world to the end are contained fully, and the universal status of the Church is figured. There the history of events is woven, there the mysteries of the sacraments are discovered, there the steps of emotions, thoughts, meditations, contemplations, good works, virtues, and rewards are arranged. There is shown what we ought to believe, to do, to hope for.[166]

[164] Hugh of St Victor, *Arc. mor.*, PL, CLXXVI, cols 663–77.

[165] Hugh of St Victor, *Arc. mor.*, PL, CLXXVI, col. 677.

[166] Hugh of St Victor, *Arc. mor.*, PL, CLXXVI, col. 680B: 'Haec arca similis est apothecae omnium deliciarum varietate refertae. Nihil in ea quaesieris quod non invenias, et eum inveneris unum, multa tibi patefacta videbis. Ibi universa opera restaurationis nostrae a principio mundi usque ad finem plenissime continentur, et status universalis Ecclesiae figuratur. Ibi historia rerum gestarum textitur, ibi mysteria sacramentorum inveniuntur, ibi dispositi sunt gradus affectuum, cogitationum, meditationum, contemplationum, bonorum operum, virtutum et praemiorum. Ibi quid credere, quid agere, quid sperare debeamus ostenditur.'

Hugh has produced for the early twelfth century a systemization of Christian belief that includes both doctrine and the steps of contemplation. In this endeavor he is similar to the other twelfth-century authors, such as Gratian and Peter Lombard, who imposed an order and unity upon their material. Hugh's synthesis is different in that there are no apparent contradictions for him to reconcile: the task is merely to gather all the knowledge into one place. Then, too, the product is a 'visual' one, even if we modern scholars could never hope to keep it before our mind's eye. Assuming that Hugh's visual conceit is a genuine one, he has afforded his students and confrères with a storehouse for any item of information they could desire.

In the second place, though the marshalling of information is certainly important to Hugh, it is not the sole goal of the ark. Indeed, he would be dismayed at anyone who got trapped at that level, for the ark's final purpose is to provide a dwelling place for God and for oneself. The ark is not merely a visual construct but a lived experience leading one through the five steps of contemplation. Thus it is not enough merely to know, but also to do. Only when one has passed from knowledge of virtue, to reach virtue's possession through its practice, will the architect have both built and lived in the ark.

The complexity and intricacy of Hugh's visual and pedagogical programme may even have implications for the systemization of theology in the twelfth century. Marcia Colish recently drew attention to the inadequacy of our understanding of twelfth-century theology by noting the tendency of modern scholars to underrate the efforts of theologians well known to contemporaries.[167] As an example of an overlooked theologian, she mentions Peter Lombard, whose masterwork, the *Sentences*, has often been considered 'a mere rehash of patristic theology, a *florilegium* with no originality'. However, if this is so, why was this 'rehash' the most popular theological textbook in the fledgling universities? Colish attributes the success of Lombard's *Sentences* to its coverage, use of technical terminology, resolution of conflicts within the Christian tradition, demonstration of Lombard's own theological positions, and, perhaps above all, to its organization. Among the authors whose theological *summae* she examines as contenders for the queen of textbooks is Hugh of St Victor, whose *De sacramentis* she describes as 'redundant and disorganized'.[168]

[167] Marcia Colish, 'Systematic Theology and Theological Renewal in the Twelfth Century', *Journal of Medieval and Renaissance Studies*, 18 (1988), 135–56. See also her 'Another Look at the School of Laon', *Archives d'histoire doctrinale et littéraire du moyen âge*, 53 (1986), 7–22.

[168] Colish, 'Systematic Theology', p. 144.

While there is undoubtably some truth to this accusation, especially when one compares *De sacramentis* to the *Sentences*, it is possible that Hugh's work is not as unorganized as it at first appears. Like many of Hugh's works, *De sacramentis* deals with God's *opera creationis* and *opera restaurationis*. Accordingly, it is divided into two parts: the first deals with events from the beginning of the World until the Incarnation, while the second considers the Incarnation to the end of the age. Unsurprisingly, Hugh begins the part dedicated to the works of creation with an account of Creation, which he follows by a discussion of our knowledge of God and God's will, and the creation of angels and of humans. Next comes an analysis of the Fall and the Reparation, and then of sacraments, defined in a broad sense as 'all the modes by which God manifests Himself to man and redeems man'.[169] The consideration of the Reparation allows Hugh to introduce the means of achieving it, including faith, and the natural and written laws. The second part continues this theme by focusing on the Incarnation and the unity of the Church with Christ. Thus, all the books of the second part deal with things of the Church, encompassing ecclesiastical orders, sacred clothing, the sacraments, the virtues and vices, penitence, and the like.

All of these themes and the order of treatment are perfectly consistent with their handling in *Didascalicon*, *De tribus maximis*, and the ark treatises; that is, if one were trained as a Victorine, the order of *De sacramentis* makes perfect sense. However, if one were not a Victorine, or if one wanted a resolution of conflicts within the tradition, which Hugh certainly does not provide, then Lombard's *Sentences* would indeed make a better introduction to the problems of theology than *De sacramentis*.

That Hugh was able to compress the Christian doctrine of the early twelfth century into one mental image tells us some important things about Hugh and his society. Though aware of the great number of books in the world (he often cautions his readers to make choices),[170] Hugh is confident enough of his own and his fellow canons' abilities to attempt his project. He has mastered the learning of the past. His emphasis on the memorization of factual knowledge is symptomatic of a conservative approach to learning. Hugh's attitude toward learning indicates why the twelfth century made the advances it did and perhaps even why his school's philosophy of history and learning did not become the norm: having mastered the learning of the past, the scholars of the twelfth and thirteenth centuries were ready for the new learning.

[169] Colish, 'Systematic Theology', p. 143.

[170] For instance, in *Didas.*, III.13, he cautions his students to read what is useful, if they cannot read everything.

The twelfth century was a time of transition in pedagogical methods. Scholars made use of ancient memory methods as they studied for their exams, prepared their lectures and disputations, and composed their sermons. They also had new reference works that better suited the new conditions of the schools. Using the fruits of someone else's memory spilled out onto the page, as it were, they could access works that they could not remember because they had never read the original works themselves. But by the thirteenth century, developments in thinking about the place of rhetoric in the hierarchy of the *trivium*, about ethics, and about cognitive psychology would cause the Dominicans, and perhaps the Franciscans, to rethink their opinion of mnemonic practice, as we shall see in Chapter 2.

Chapter 2

# The Influence of the Mendicant Orders on Mnemonic Theory

By the mid-thirteenth century, several changes within the schools and within European society coalesced to produce a re-evaluation of the usefulness of memory aids and of the *Ad Herennium* in particular.[1] This change in attitude came about for a numbers of reasons, including the study of Book IV of Boethius's *De topicis differentiis* in the schools, which encouraged a re-examination of the respective roles of logic and rhetoric; the foundation of the mendicant orders and the concomitant revival of preaching oratory on a widespread basis; and the recovery of Aristotle's works, which gave new status to the role of images in cognition and memory.[2] Armed with a new understanding of the place of rhetoric within the hierarchy of knowledge and possessed of an enhanced view of the need for images in cognition, Dominicans such as Albertus Magnus and Thomas Aquinas no longer disparaged the *Ad Herennium*'s memory system as twelfth-century authors had, and could even be said to have promoted it for rhetorical and ethical purposes.

The Franciscans, however, took a somewhat different approach. Exposed to the same influences described above as the Dominicans, they adhered more strongly to the monastic memory practices of the Cistercians and the Victorines (though the Dominicans certainly knew the memory theories of Hugh of St Victor). Guibert de Tournai studied at the same university (Paris) as Albertus Magnus and Thomas, but under Franciscan masters. He took a more ambiguous attitude toward the *Ad Herennium*'s rules for memory, describing a unique

[1] See also Carruthers, *Book of Memory*, pp. 153–55.

[2] Parts of this chapter previously appeared in Rivers, 'Memory and Medieval Preaching'.

Franciscan understanding of memory that still shared a number of assumptions with his Dominican contemporaries, chiefly the notion that mnemonics should be discussed in the context of cognitive theory. This chapter will look first at the pedagogical changes of the thirteenth century that influenced Dominican attitudes toward mnemonic aids. It will then turn to the Franciscan approach to memory as seen in the *De modo addiscendi* of Guibert de Tournai. Chapter 3 will examine Franciscan dependence on monastic models of memory through the works of David von Augsburg.

## *Logic versus Rhetoric*

In the thirteenth century, a shift in the schools' curriculum affected scholars' understanding of dialectic and rhetoric, which, while hardly flattering to the overall status of rhetoric within the *trivium*, did identify some basic differences between the procedures of each discipline.[3] Masters in the schools wrote commentaries and lectured on rhetorical textbooks just as they did for other subjects. Karin Fredborg has shown that while twelfth-century commentators chose Cicero as their authority, thirteenth-century commentators preferred the fourth book of Boethius's *De topicis differentiis*.[4] Following the interests of Boethius himself, thirteenth-century writers struggled to work out the relationship between rhetoric and dialectic and the appropriate settings for each discipline. Boethius ranked dialectic as a higher discipline because its subject matter was based on universal ideas, whereas rhetoric's subject was grounded in particular circumstances. For Boethius, the subject of dialectic was the thesis, 'a question proposed from debate that makes no reference to particular circumstance', whereas rhetoric deals with the hypothesis, 'a question that is framed by circumstances'. A way to think of the difference between the two types of questions lies in the presence of circumstances: 'Should a man marry?' versus 'Should Cato marry?'[5] Because Aristotelian epistemology ranked universal ideas above particular ones, the Boethian scheme carried the day in the thirteenth century.

[3] Karin Margareta Fredborg, 'The Scholastic Teaching of Rhetoric in the Middle Ages', *Cahiers de L'Institut du moyen âge grec et latin*, 55 (1987), 85–105.

[4] Fredborg, 'Scholastic Teaching of Rhetoric', pp. 88–89. By the end of the thirteenth century, rhetoricians had moved on to Aristotle's *Rhetoric*. See Chapter 1, above, for further discussion of Boethius's *De topicis differentiis*.

[5] Leff, 'Boethius' *De differentiis topicis*', p. 9.

The working out of the relationship between dialectic and rhetoric affected thirteenth-century attitudes toward memory. For instance, some writers noticed a difference in the kinds of demands made on the speaker's memory in a logical disputation and in a formal speech. A commentary on Boethius's *Topics*, written by an anonymous English master in Paris, possibly in the 1240s, compares the parts of logic and rhetoric and claims that artificial memory is necessary only for the rhetor:

> The disputant [*dialecticus*] does not need the art of memory; rather natural memory suffices for him; for he makes short speeches. But the rhetor does require the art of memory, for he makes continuous and long speeches, and for this reason natural memory alone will not suffice for him, but it is necessary that he have artificial memory.[6]

In his *Notule Priorum analyticorum Aristotelis*, Robert Kilwardby explains that rhetoricians require the aid of *dispositio* and *memoria*, when logicians do not, because the multitude of signs and arguments required in rhetorical speech can cause confusion and forgetfulness.[7] This reasoning implies that participants in the regular disputations of the schools had very little need for a formal art of memory, because they simply did not have to talk so long and so copiously as rhetors. There also seems to have been less anxiety about losing track of the order of one's discourse. The kinds of memory methods that logicians already knew, which did not seem to warrant the term 'artificial memory', sufficed for their purposes.[8] Kilwardby expands on the comparison of memorial requirements for rhetoricians and disputants in his *De ortu scientiarum*, where he notes that the rhetor has to keep track of a multitude of arguments by himself and by his opponent. He thus needs an art of arranging (*dispositio*) to collect and order them and an art of memory to hold on to them and produce them quickly when necessary.[9] The

[6] Patrick Osmund Lewry, 'Rhetoric at Paris and Oxford in the Mid-Thirteenth Century', *Rhetorica*, 1 (1983), 45–63 (pp. 46–48 n. 12): 'dialecticus non indiget arte memorandi, set sufficit ei memoria naturalis; vtitur enim (continua et longa *expunx. MS*) breui oracione. Set rethor indiget arte memorandi; vtitur enim continua (f. 78$^{va}$) et longa oracione: et ideo non sufficit ei memoria naturalis, set oportet quod habeat memoriam artificialem.'

[7] Lewry, 'Rhetoric at Paris and Oxford', pp. 46–48 n. 12: '<in> rhetorica affirmatur multitudo signorum et emptimematum continue ad probandum intentum, et proper talem multitudinem uel confusionem, ne aliqua tradantur obliuioni, necesse est in rhetorica tam disposicio quam memoria'.

[8] See the discussion of logical topics in Chapter 1, above. Also useful is Carruthers's distinction between elementary mnemonics and arts of memory (*Book of Memory*, chap. 4).

[9] Robert Kilwardby, *De ortu scientiarum*, ed. by Albert G. Judy, Auctores britannici medii aevi, 4 (London: British Academy; Toronto: Pontifical Institute of Mediaeval Studies, 1976), chap. 61, no. 620, pp. 211–12.

logician has no need of either of these crucial parts of rhetoric, because he does not have to speak for as long a time and because he does not have to wait as long to make his response to his opponent's argument.[10] This juxtaposition of the demands of dialectic with those of rhetoric was nothing new. As long ago as the sixth century, Cassiodorus, in his *Institutiones*, had contrasted the 'brevity' of dialectical argument with the copious nature of rhetoric with a telling metaphor taken from the Roman scholar Varro (116–27 BC): 'Dialectic and rhetoric are like the clenched fist and open palm in a man's hand, <the former encloses the proofs of argumentation briefly, the latter, in full flow of words, traverses through the fields of eloquence;> the former narrows its words, the latter expands them.'[11] However, this renewed comparison occurred in the thirteenth century, not the twelfth, perhaps because the study of each subject was now sophisticated enough to warrant such a comparison and perhaps also because Western Europe now had speakers, not just writers, who needed to draw on what had been some relatively unused aspects of rhetoric. Both dialectic and rhetoric were being put into practice in the thirteenth century in a way they had not been since antiquity. In the new universities, disputation was now a regular part of the curriculum, likely providing writers a chance to assess its requirements in a more practical way.[12] Likewise the demands of rhetoric were felt more acutely than in the recent past.

[10] We could add that the preacher Francesc Eiximenis, whose ideas are discussed in Chapter 3, below, also thought that one needed a memory method when one had a 'multitude of memorable things to retain', as in a sermon (*Ars praed.*, VII.3.2, p. 325).

[11] Cassiodorus, *Institutions of Divine and Secular Learning and On the Soul*, trans. by James W. Halporn, Translated Texts for Historians, 42 (Liverpool: Liverpool University Press, 2004), p. 189; 'Dialectica et rhetorica est quod in manu hominis pugnus astrictus et palma distensa, <illa brevi oratione argumenta concludens, ista facundiae campos copioso sermone discurrens,> illa verba contrahens, ista distendens': Cassiodorus, *Institutiones*, ed. by Roger Aubrey Baskerville Mynors (Oxford: Clarendon Press, 1937), II.3.

[12] For more on disputation in the medieval university, see *Les Questions disputées et les questions quodlibétiques dans les facultés de théologie, de droit et de médecine*, ed. by Bernardo C. Bazàn and others, Typologie des sources du moyen âge occidental, 44–45 (Turnhout: Brepols, 1985). Jim Ginther argues that disputations provided a way for medieval masters and students to enhance their memory of the text of the Bible: 'As most theologians committed the Bible to memory, engaging in disputation provided an ideal pedagogical venue for the memory to be enhanced, for the disputation was an event in which the student and master equally engaged and exploited the biblical *lemma* and its multi-valent *sententia*' (James R. Ginther, 'There is a Text in this Classroom: The Bible and Theology in the Medieval University', in *Essays in Medieval Philosophy and Theology in Memory of Walter H. Principe, CSB: Fortresses and Launching Pads*, ed. by James R. Ginther and Carl N. Still (Aldershot: Ashgate, 2005), pp. 43–73 (p. 49)).

The people most likely to need to speak 'copiously' in the thirteenth century were preachers, and the new sermon structure of the late twelfth and early thirteenth century may have exacerbated their anxiety of speaking copiously.[13] Robert of Basevorn declared that the 'ancient' sermon form (the homily) was 'good for those who have deficient or feeble memories, because it is easier for a man to recall the narrative of some large portion of the gospel, than a complex argument or a fine subdistinction of a division'.[14] The anonymous author of the *Ars concionandi* agreed that preaching on a whole passage of the Gospels aided the memory of the preacher, as did the Franciscan Francesc Eiximenis. The difficulty of remembering the complex thematic sermon may also explain an exemplum in Étienne de Bourbon's *Tractatus de diversis materiis*. He relates the ordeal of St Francis, who, asked to preach before a body of rich prelates, completely forgot the well-ordered sermon with which he had been supplied by a learned friend for the occasion. The implication is that the prelates expected the upstart preacher either to compose an inadequate sermon or to forget the one prepared, and hoped to mortify him.[15] Composing and remembering a sermon was an arduous enough task to function as a kind of ordeal for the would-be preacher in this story.

That composing and memorizing a sermon was an off-putting task is supported by the comments of William de Montibus (*c.* 1140–1213) in his second sermon collection. His handbook (mentioned in Chapter 4), written just before the flourishing of prescriptive manuals, reminds us that instead of struggling over their own creations, medieval preachers could memorize someone else's. This, in fact, was the purpose of William's sermon collection. He composed his sermons for those 'who are learned and capable of memorizing written sermons, but who are too lazy or negligent to undertake the task'.[16] William also hopes that his

[13] The development of the new sermon form is discussed at length below, in Chapter 4.

[14] 'Primus modus esset bonus eis qui sunt labilis memoriae vel debilis, quia facilius potest occurrere homini processus alicujus magni evangelii quam subtilis argumenti, vel parva divisio unius membri. Secundus modus est modo magis usitatus, quia curiosior': Robert of Basevorn, *Forma praedicandi*, in *Artes praedicandi: Contribution à l'histoire de la rhétorique au moyen âge*, ed. by. Thomas Marie Charland (Ottawa: Institut d'études médiévales, 1936), pp. 231–323 (pp. 246–47). Cited in H. Leith Spencer, *English Preaching in the Late Middle Ages* (Oxford: Clarendon Press, 1993), p. 239 (Spencer's translation). A similar point is made in the *Ars concionandi*, in St Bonaventura, *Opera omnia*, 10 vols (Ad Claras Aquas [Quaracchi]: Ex Typographia Collegii S. Bonaventurae, 1882–1902), IX, 8–21 (p. 11), and in Francesc Eiximenis's *Ars praed.*, III.7.3, p. 331 (see Chapter 3, below).

[15] Forny, 'Giacomo da Vitry', pp. 55–56.

[16] Joseph Goering, *William de Montibus (c.1140–1213): The Schools and the Literature of Pastoral Care*, Studies and Texts, 108 (Toronto: Pontifical Institute of Mediaeval Studies, 1992), p. 516.

efforts will serve as a model for his readers to compose their own sermons. He clearly expects most preachers to memorize their sermons, but he does not explain how they should go about it.

Of course, these examples do not prove that every preacher delivered an entire sermon from memory. For instance, the friars may have sometimes relied on written scripts to deliver their sermons. Portable *vademecum* books containing outlines of model sermons may have been used by friars in sermon presentation.[17] Such outlines also circulated as separate quires and were used by some preachers. Roger Bacon claimed that bishops, not having learned much about theology or preaching in school and finding that they now had to preach, 'borrow and beg the quires of boys' (mutuantur et mendicant quaternos puerorum).[18] Although this passage is evidence that quires were used for preaching preparation, it does not prove that they were used in the pulpit. In his examination of late medieval English sermons, G. R. Owst assumed that a small manuscript containing 'skeletons' of sermons (British Library, MS Additional 21253) was 'clearly meant to be expanded by the preacher, as he stands, book in hand, to deliver his address'.[19] On the other hand, Helen Spencer has pointed out that the iconography of medieval preachers depicts them without books. She acknowledges, however, that iconography is self-perpetuating and may cease to reflect common experience.[20] On the whole, however, these stories indicate that the pressure to construct and remember an appropriate sermon had likely increased by the early thirteenth century, when both the mendicant orders and the university system began to flourish. The recognition of the increased demands placed on memory by sermon delivery likely contributed to the sense that rhetoric needed an artificial memory

[17] For examples of *vademecum* books, see David L. d'Avray, 'Portable *Vademecum* Books Containing Franciscan and Dominican Texts', in *Manuscripts at Oxford: An Exhibition in Memory of Richard William Hunt (1908–1979)*, ed. by Albinia Catherine de la Mare and B. C. Barker-Benfield (Oxford: Bodleian Library, 1980), pp. 60–64. See also d'Avray, *Preaching of the Friars*, pp. 56–61.

[18] Cited and translated in David L. d'Avray, *Medieval Marriage Sermons: Mass Communication in a Culture Without Print* (Oxford: Oxford University Press, 2001), p. 19; 'Et quia praelati, ut in pluribus, non sunt multum instructi in theologia, nec in praedicatione dum sunt in studio, ideo postquam sunt praelati, cum eis incumbit opus praedicandi, mutuantur et mendicant quaternos puerorum': Roger Bacon, *Opus tertium*, ed. by Brewer, p. 309.

[19] Gerald Robert Owst, *Preaching in Medieval England: An Introduction to Sermon Manuscripts of the Period, c.1350–1450* (Cambridge: Cambridge University Press, 1926), pp. 235–36.

[20] Spencer, *English Preaching*, p. 75.

system more than dialectic did. In turn, this new pressure explains in part why the Dominicans and Franciscans utilized artificial memory when twelfth-century scholars did not.

## *Cognitive Psychology*

An additional influence in the new, more favourable consideration of the *Ad Herennium* was the rediscovery and assessment of Aristotle's works on the soul and the interior senses and of the Arab commentaries on these works. Views about the importance of imagery for mnemonics were supported by most medieval theories of cognition and of imagination, which considered the image the representative of human sensation. Aristotle's dictum that the intellect cannot think without an image was an understatement of the true situation: humans could not hear, see, or remember without an image either.[21] There were many theories of sensation and intellection in the Middle Ages, but all had to account for the problem of how the particularity of sensory information could be utilized by an intellect that dealt only with universals.[22]

The variation in the theories arose from Aristotle's vagueness in delineating the mediators between sensation and intellection, known as the internal senses.[23] Aristotle made references to the notion of a 'common sense', to *phantasia* (imagination), and to memory, which he said belongs to the part of the soul to which *phantasia* belongs.[24] However, he was not particularly clear in distinguishing their functions. Arabic and medieval Latin commentators were obliged

[21] *De anima*, in *The Basic Works of Aristotle*, ed. by Richard McKeon (New York: Random House, 1941), II.7–8.

[22] See Coleman, *Ancient and Medieval Memories*; Nicholas H. Steneck, 'The Problem of the Internal Senses in the Fourteenth Century' (unpubished doctoral dissertation, University of Wisconsin, 1970); Richard Sorabji, *Aristotle on Memory* (Providence: Brown University Press, 1972); Murray Wright Bundy, *The Theory of Imagination in Classical and Medieval Thought* (Urbana: University of Illinois Press, 1927); Henry A. Wolfson, 'The Internal Senses', *Harvard Theological Review*, 28 (1935), 69–133; Deborah L. Black, 'Estimation (*Wahm*) in Avicenna: The Logical and Psychological Dimensions', *Dialogue*, 32 (1993), 219–58. Also useful as a condensed explanation is Alastair J. Minnis, 'Medieval Imagination and Memory', in *The Cambridge History of Literary Criticism*, II: *The Middle Ages*, ed. by Alastair J. Minnis and Ian Johnson (Cambridge: Cambridge University Press, 2005), pp. 239–74.

[23] Black, 'Estimation (*Wahm*) in Avicenna', p. 219.

[24] Aristotle, *De memoria et reminiscentia*, in *Basic Works of Aristotle*, ed. by McKeon, 450[a].

to construct a more elaborate schema to explain the function of memory and the internal senses (often grouped together as the imagination) and their connections to intelligence.

Despite the variation in theories, it is possible to give a general picture of the internal senses, so that one can understand the relationship between memory, images, and intellection. Because Janet Coleman has discussed these theories exhaustively, my overview will be quite short. Most medieval philosophers in the thirteenth century thought that the soul had three parts: the vegetative, sensitive, and intellectual or rational. Only the latter two divisions were considered to play a role in cognition. The sensitive soul directed locomotion and apprehension, while the rational soul governed intellection and drew upon the powers of the sensitive soul. Both the external senses (hearing, sight, etc.) and the internal senses were considered part of the sensitive, rather than the rational soul. The external senses began the process of sensation by sensing their proper objects. This sensory experience was transmitted to the interior senses through 'species' or 'phantasms'. The interior senses occupied three cells in the brain, the first two of which were divided into two parts: in the first cell were located the common sense and imagination, in the second cell were the phantasy and estimation, and in the third memory. Each power either apprehended the species sent to it or stored some part of them away. First, the common sense received the species from the external senses and discerned the proper actions of the senses and the five common sensibles (i.e. size, shape, motion, rest, and number). It also prepared the image sent to the other internal senses.

Next, imagination received the species that were multiplied (i.e., transmitted) from the common sense and stored them away. They could be remultiplied to the other internal powers as needed. The estimative power then perceived the non-sensed species, which Avicenna called 'intentions'. The classic example of an intention is the sheep's instinctive flight from a wolf. Even if it has never seen a wolf before, it senses the hostile *intentio* of the animal. The phantasy (sometimes called the cogitative sense) produced new images from the species received from common sense and the estimative power, and was the power which imagines. This process was thought to be occasionally aided by reason in humans, but not in animals. Finally, memory stored the species and intentions received from all the other powers for future reference. Unlike the other treasure-house of the internal senses, the imagination, memory stored intentions and could refer to the past. It could also reminisce with the aid of the intellect.[25] The images stored in

[25] The above depiction is based on Steneck, 'Problem of the Internal Senses', pp. 10–15.

imagination and memory were then available for use by the intellect in rational thought.

The entire process of sensation to intellection was thus one of abstraction, of removing accidents, matter, and, eventually particularity, to derive an abstract concept or 'universal'. It is important to note that no part of the above description would have gone unchallenged by some medieval philosopher, as different schools of thought emphasized one power over the others. This was particularly true for the two most influential thinkers in the internal sense tradition, Avicenna and Averroes. Avicenna emphasized the estimation, considering it the highest power of the internal senses.[26] Averroes, however, rejected the idea of estimation as a special power, claiming that it had been invented by Avicenna (he was right). Averroes varied in delineating three or four faculties of the imagination, but, in both of his treatments, memory represents the most spiritual and abstracted of the internal senses.

Medieval Latin authors responded variously to these schemes, some preferring Avicenna and others following Averroes more closely. What is important for our purposes is that some version of the internal sense tradition was accepted by most writers trained in the university. Thus, when we see words like *phantasm* or *similitude* discussed in other contexts, we often can recognize the presence of a technical term.

The thirteenth-century desire to wrestle with Aristotle's human psychology was crucial to thinking about mnemonics, because the first positive discussions of the *Ad Herennium*'s rules for memory occur in the context of cognitive psychology. Albertus Magnus, Thomas Aquinas, and Guibert de Tournai all strived to reconcile the *Ad Herennium*'s notion of artificial memory with Aristotle's *De memoria et reminiscentia*. The two Dominican thinkers came to a fairly positive understanding of the *Ad Herennium*'s rules because they fit into the Aristotelian views of epistemology and ethics.

Both Albertus Magnus and Thomas introduce the topic of artificial memory in two contexts: in their commentaries on Aristotle's *De memoria* and in their discussion of prudence. In each of these settings, it is clear that artificial memory is not their main concern, but rather something to be fitted into the larger framework of psychological memory or prudence, as Janet Coleman has noted.[27] Yates

[26] Black, 'Estimation (*Wahm*) in Avicenna', p. 258.

[27] See Coleman, *Ancient and Medieval Memories*, pp. 416–19, 455 (n. 157), for her comments. She emphasizes that Albertus is less interested in the art of memory per se than in the use of memory for exemplary purposes as the habit of prudence.

was perhaps too ready to associate the medieval transformation of the art of memory with the ethical demands she saw in Albertus Magnus's and Thomas's writings. The context of the comments on artificial memory in the *De memoria* commentaries and in Albertus's *De bono* is clearly one of reconciling Cicero with Aristotle. Sabine Heimann-Seelbach has also recently expressed similar uneasiness with Yates's interpretation of Albertus's and Thomas's views on memory. She questions Yates's contention that Albertus's and Thomas's discussions of memory constituted a 'moral triumph' of memory arts in the Middle Ages. Indeed, she thinks that Albertus clearly subordinated Cicero's rules to Aristotle's authority and that he remained suspicious of the *Ad Herennium's* art except in certain contexts.[28] I would argue that their discussions demonstrate that they both knew quite a lot about Cicero's memory method and that their attitudes toward it were in fact favorable, especially for Albertus, if the art was used in the correct contexts. Obviously, Aristotle represented a higher authority than Cicero for both philosophers, but both saw a role for the art's rules that earlier scholars had denied.

Albertus has more to say about the art of memory than Thomas, especially in *De bono*, where he distinguishes the parts of prudence. He begins with Cicero's partition of prudence into three parts: *memoria*, *intelligentia*, and *providentia*.[29] He divides his treatment of memory into two main sections: 'what is memory' and 'concerning the art of memory'. In these two articles, he has several questions to resolve: how can memory be a part of prudence when they belong to different parts of the soul, whether memory or reminiscence should be equated with the art of memory, and what the relationship of the art's places and images are to the accepted psychological functions of memory.

He deals first with memory's definitions and how it might be a part of prudence. There are several objections to this idea. First, memory, which recollects things in the past, is a part of the soul, not a habit, and every part of prudence is a habit; therefore, memory is not a part of prudence. Second, memory belongs to the sensitive soul, while prudence is part of the rational; therefore, memory cannot be a part of prudence. Third, memory recollects past things, while prudence directs present and future actions: thus, memory cannot be of much use to prudence. Finally, Albertus points out that the recollection of past things either proceeds from a determined starting point, which is reminiscence, not memory,

[28] Heimann-Seelbach, *Ars und scientia*, pp. 373–87.

[29] See Yates, *Art of Memory*, p. 62.

or it proceeds according to sensible forms, which is not a part of the rational soul and thus not part of prudence. He begins to resolve these contradictions by suggesting that experience and a knowledge of the past might contribute to the recognition of good and evil, a necessary skill for prudence. Albertus thus concludes that memory is a part of prudence when considered as reminiscence:

> For because prudence selects those things which aid it from those which impede it in its work, it must proceed by enquiring and so it is necessary that it set off from a determined starting point [*principium*] and through probable middle terms arrive at a workable proposition. And for this reason, when it proceeds from past things, it uses memory as a part of reminiscence.[30]

He also decides that memory defined by Cicero is indeed a moral habit; since such a habit does not reminisce, but rather remembers, it is proper to refer to a habit of memory, rather than a habit of reminiscence.[31]

Having concluded that memory as reminiscence is a part of prudence, Albertus turns to a long discussion of the art of remembering. Here he decides that Cicero posits memory for reminiscence, so that, when memory is mentioned, we should understand reminiscence. He also tries to make sense of Cicero's rules for the art of memory, which the rhetorician had said could be strengthened by induction and precepts.[32] Albertus declares that remembering is the subject of this art, which is generated both by induction and by precept. Induction occurs from the images, and precepts begin, like reminiscence, from a starting point. It is therefore necessary that in the soul there be that from which reminiscence proceeds and that toward which it proceeds. That from which it proceeds is the starting point, that is, Cicero's precepts, and that toward which it proceeds, are the images, which are like letters in the soul.[33] Albertus seems to identify Cicero's precepts only with the

[30] Albertus Magnus, *De bono*, in *Opera omnia*, XXVIII, ed. by H. Kühle and others (Münster: Aschendorff, 1951), tr. IV, De prudentia, q. 2, art. 1, solution: 'Dicimus, quod memoria est pars prudentiae, secundum quod memoria cadit in rationem reminiscentiae. Cum enim prudentia eligat ea quibus adiuvatur, ab eis a quibus impeditur in opere, oportet ipsam procedere inquirendo et sic necesse est eam progredi a principio determinato et per media probabilia devenire in propositum operabile; et ideo cum proceditur ex preteritis, utitur memoria, secundum quod est pars reminiscentiae.' For the clearest presentation of Albertus's views on reminiscence, see his *Liber de apprehensione*, IV.7, in *Opera omnia*, V, ed. by Auguste Borgnet and others, 38 vols (Paris: Vrin, 1890–99).

[31] See Coleman's exposition of Albertus's desire to make memory a habit-serving prudence, *Ancient and Medieval Memories*, pp. 416–17.

[32] Albertus Magnus, *De bono*, tr. IV. q. ii. art. 2 obj. 3.

[33] Albertus Magnus, *De bono*, tr. IV. q. ii. art. 2 answer to obj. 4.

rules for places, perhaps because the notion of a starting point does accord more with places than images.

Although at first doubtful about the wisdom of employing metaphorical images to represent things (why not use the objects themselves?), Albertus comes to sanction Cicero's image-making. He concedes that wondrous images excite memory more than the objects themselves (*propria*) and are thus appropriate for the art of memory.

Albertus's reconciliation of Aristotle and Cicero conflates the art of memory with reminiscence, especially in the use of mnemonic places. Images are what reminiscence seeks after starting from a predetermined point or place. His comments deal more with loci than images, but he seems to approve of them. In his commentary on *De memoria*, however, he does touch on image-making, advising those wishing to reminisce to retire to solitary places, so that the images of sensible things will not be disturbed.[34]

Though Thomas is less verbose than Albertus Magnus on the topic of artificial memory, he is extremely clear in delineating the relationship of mnemonics to the psychological functions of memory. Like Albertus, he identifies the art of remembering with reminiscence or recollection in his *De memoria* commentary:

> Now, because it is necessary that a person recollecting take some starting point from which he begins the process of recollection, people sometimes seem to recollect from places in which are any matters said, or done, or thought. They use that place as a starting point for recollecting, because arrival at that place is a kind of starting point for all those matters which are set in motion in that place. Hence Cicero teaches in his *Rhetoric* (*Ad Herennium* 3.17.30) that in order to remember easily, it is necessary to imagine certain ordered places in which the phantasms of those things which we wish to remember are arranged in a particular order.[35]

Thomas thus more clearly identifies mnemonic places with reminiscence's starting points than Albertus does. He also condenses much of Aristotle's teaching on

[34] See the discussion of Albertus's comments on *De memoria* at the end of this chapter.

[35] Thomas Aquinas, *Commentary* on Aristotle, *On Memory and Recollection*, trans. by John Burchill, in *Medieval Craft of Memory*, ed. by Carruthers and Ziolkowski, pp. 153–88 (p. 179); 'Quia enim oportet reminiscentem aliquid principium accipere, unde incipiat procedere ad reminiscendum, inde est quod aliquando homines videntur reminisci a locis, in quibus aliqua sunt dicta vel facta vel cogitata, utentes loco quasi quodam principio ad reminiscendum: quia accessus ad locum est principium quoddam eorum omnium quae in loco aguntur. Unde et Tullius in sua Rhetorica docet, quod ad facile memorandum oportet imaginari quaedam loca ordinata, quibus phantasmata eorum quae memorari volumus quodam ordine distribuantur': Thomas Aquinas, *In Aristotelis libros de sensu et sensato, De memoria et reminiscentia commentarium*, ed. by P. F. Raymundi M. Spiazzi (Rome: Marietti, 1949), I, lect. IV.377.

the need for order and a starting point when recollecting into four rules of his own:

> Therefore, to remember or recollect well, we can learn four useful lessons from the foregoing [Lectio V in *De memoria*]. First one must be careful to reduce to some order what one wishes to retain; then one must apply the mind profoundly and intently to those things; next one must frequently meditate on them in order; finally one must begin to recollect from a starting point.[36]

One could also say that Aquinas's rules are less a distillation of Cicero than a reinterpretation as viewed through Aristotle. As we have just seen, all of his rules are consistent with Aristotelian thinking.

Aquinas also introduces the importance of images into a discussion of the part of the soul to which memory belongs:

> He [Aristotle] says that the part of the soul to which memory belongs is clear from what has been said, because it belongs in that part to which imagination belongs, and because the things which are essential objects of memory are those of which we have phantasms, that is sense objects, while intelligible matters, which are not perceived by man without his imagination, are incidental objects of memory. For this reason we cannot remember well those things which we regard as rarified and spiritual; those objects that are corporeal and perceived by the senses are better objects of memory. It is necessary, if we wish to facilitate remembering abstract ideas, to bind them to particular images, as Cicero teaches in his *Rhetoric* (see *Ad Herennium* 3.20.33–37).[37]

Aquinas's point is that anything that one can sense is memorable, because it is naturally preserved in memory by a phantasm or image. Anything that is intelligible, that is, ideas or notions, are not as easily preserved in memory, because they are not preserved naturally by the interior senses with an image. For this reason, he recommends making one's own images for such things that one wants to remember along the lines of Cicero's rules. In keeping with the context of the discussion, Aquinas's reasons for recommending Cicero's rules are epistemological.

[36] Thomas Aquinas, *Commentary*, trans. by Burchill, p. 177; Aquinas, *De memoria et reminiscentia*, ed. by Spiazzi, I, lect. V.371.

[37] Thomas Aquinas, *Commentary*, trans. by Burchill, pp. 164–65; Aquinas, *De memoria et reminiscentia*, ed. by Spiazzi, I, lect. II.326: 'Et dicit manifestum esse ex praemissis ad quam partem animae pertineat memoria, quia ad eam, ad quam pertinet phantasia; et quod illa sunt per se memorabilia, quorum est phantasia, scilicet sensibilia; per accidens autem memorabilia sunt intelligibilia, quae sine phantasia non apprehenduntur ab homine. Et inde est quod ea quae habent subtilem et spiritualem considerationem, minus possumus memorari. Magis autem sunt memorabilia quae sunt grossa et sensibilia. Et oportet, si aliquis intelligibiles rationes volumus memorari facilius, quod eas alligemus quasi quibusdam aliis phantasmatibus, ut docet Tullius in sua *Rhetorica*.'

Thus, because Cicero's system seems to adhere so closely to Aristotle's depiction of human psychology, both Albertus and Aquinas recommend it. Both recognize that Cicero's system of loci accords well with Aristotle's emphasis on the need for order in recollection. Both also present a reasonably positive view of the use of images in cognition and memory. One cannot think without an image: memory and imagination store away images and their intentions, which can then be utilized by the intellect. Natural memory may be good on its own, or it may be strengthened by artificial memory, as elaborated by Cicero. Because Albertus and Aquinas made this connection, it seems likely that other mendicants, especially those who had progressed reasonably high in the mendicant scholastic system, would have seen a similar resemblance between memory images and phantasms. Almost any image had the potential to help one remember. Because Albertus Magnus and Thomas Aquinas were such influential teachers and scholars within the Dominican order, we can assume that their views were shared by more than two people.

## *Ethics*

The other part of the *Ad Herennium*'s revival arose from an interest in ethics, though not perhaps to the extent that Yates emphasized. Albertus Magnus recommended Cicero's art of memory as the best one in certain contexts:

> We say that the *ars memorandi* which Tullius teaches is the best and particularly for the things to be remembered pertaining to life and judgment (*ad vitam et iudicium*), and such memories (i.e. artificial memories) pertain particularly to the moral man and to the speaker (*ad ethicum et rhetorem*) because since the act of human life (*actus humanae vitae*) consists in particulars it is necessary that it should be in the soul through corporeal images; it will not stay in memory save in such images.[38]

Cicero's rules serve the moral man because moral decisions must be made about particular actions, not universal rules. Because human experience is saved through memory and the images of past events, a system that enhances such memories through image-making will fit the requirements for a moral life. For similar reasons, Cicero's rules seem to Albertus to be appropriate for a rhetor. As we have already seen, Book IV of Boethius's *De topicis differentiis* defined one of the major differences between logic and rhetoric as relative universality: rhetorical argu-

[38] Trans. by Yates, *Art of Memory*, p. 67; Albertus Magnus, *De bono*, tr. IV. De prudentia. q. 2. solutio.

mentation was more tied to particular circumstances than dialectic was.[39] It is the particularity of ethics and rhetoric that make them suitable subjects for Cicero's mnemonic system, at least according to Albertus Magnus.

In this recommendation, he was followed by fellow Dominican Thomas Aquinas, as has been amply demonstrated.[40] In his consideration of whether or not memory is a part of prudence, Aquinas agrees that it is and that it applies universal knowledge to particulars, which come from the senses.[41] He adds that just as one's natural aptitude of prudence can be improved by practise, so, too, can memory, according to Cicero. He then proceeds to give four examples of how memory can be improved:

1) Tie the things that one wishes to remember to unusual similitudes.
2) Place the things that one wishes to remember in order.
3) Regard these things with solicitude and cleave to them with affection, for the more something is impressed in the soul, the less likely it is to slip away.
4) Meditate frequently on what one wishes to remember.[42]

His advice, though similar to what he advocated in his *De memoria* commentary, is a little different; here he emphasizes the need for images and for impressing them upon the soul, whereas the advice in *De memoria* neglects imagery altogether in favour of rules about order and the need to find a starting place for reminiscence. This version might be considered the briefest possible overview of the *Ad Herennium*'s rules, or even a simplified mnemonic independent of the rhetorical handbook's system, given that he does not say much about the manual's elaborate rules for creating places. However, the tenor of his advice is clearly different from the attitude of the twelfth-century writers we examined in Chapter 1. They stuck to dividing up their texts and rejected elaborate imagery and Cicero's rules, while Aquinas here explicitly recommends images and does not criticize Cicero for being over-subtle. Thus, it seems that the logical, rhetorical,

[39] Leff, 'Boethius' *De differentiis topicis*', pp. 9–13.

[40] Yates, *Art of Memory*, pp. 70–78.

[41] Thomas Aquinas, *Summa theologiae*, 2ª 2ªᵉ, in *Opera omnia*, III, ed. by E. Fretté and P. Maré (Paris: Vives, 1872), q. XLIX, art. 1.

[42] Thomas Aquinas, *Summa theologiae*, 2ª 2ªᵉ, q. XLIX, art. 1. Aquinas varies this formula in his commentary on *De memoria et reminiscentia*, where he replaces the precept to form images with an injunction always to begin remembering from a starting point (I, lect. V.371).

and cognitive studies of the time coalesced to make Cicero's mnemonic rules more attractive, as least to thirteenth-century Dominicans, than they had been to twelfth-century scholars.

## *The Influence of Hugh of St Victor on Dominican Education*

The *Ad Herennium* was not the only mnemonic source for the Dominicans. Because one argument of this book is that the Franciscans were more dependent on Victorine ideas about memory than were the Dominicans, it is worth noting that some of Hugh of St Victor's ideas about the role of memory in education did influence the Dominicans, at least in their views of early education. His influence should not be surprising, since the *Didascalicon* was recommended by Humbert de Romans as a good introductory text for Dominican novices planning a life devoted to study.[43] In particular, both Guillaume de Tournai and Vincent de Beauvais relied on the method of reading and memorization and the psychological analysis underlying that method laid out in Book III of Hugh of St Victor's *Didascalicon*.

According to the *Didascalicon*, the qualities of natural endowment, practise, and discipline enable the student to learn. Natural endowment, the ability to grasp easily and to retain what one hears, is particularly important in the learning process. It is composed of aptitude (*ingenium*) and memory, both of which are described as 'powers of the mind' (*vis animae*).[44] For Hugh these are innate capabilities which may be sharpened, but not transformed, by the standard exercises of medieval education, reading and meditation.[45] Both Guillaume and Vincent retain this analysis but differ in their recommendations for practise and in the amount of psychological and physiological description they provide as explanation.

[43] M. Michèle Mulchahey, *'First the Bow is Bent in Study': Dominican Education Before 1350*, Studies and Texts, 132 (Toronto: Pontifical Institute of Mediaeval Studies, 1998), pp. 92, 109–10.

[44] *Didascalicon* describes only *ingenium* in these terms, but *De modo di<s>cendi* (PL, CLXXVI, cols 875–80), a compilation of extracts concerning memory and learning from several of Hugh's works, adds a psychological description of memory: 'Memoria est rerum et verborum et sententiarum ac sensum formissima animae vel mentis perceptio [...]. Memoria per exercitium retinendi et assidue meditandi maxime juvatur et viget' (col. 877). Some manuscripts of *Didascalicon* also contain a similar explanatory phrase about memory's functions: 'Memoria est vis animae recentiva eorum quae sensibus supposita fuerunt vel etiam imaginibus' (*Didas.*, III.7).

[45] *Didas.*, III.7.

Although Guillaume de Tournai's *De instructione puerorum* does not list any memory precepts, it does discuss memory in the *Didascalicon*'s terms. *De instructione* is a simple tract on the education of young boys, written at the request of his brethren between 1249 and 1264.[46] In her formidable work on Dominican education, Michèle Mulchahey sees the tract as a teacher's manual for Dominican friars who instructed young boys in the preparatory schools that acted as feeder schools for the order.[47] Designed to teach children the path to salvation, it covers three broad areas of instruction: faith, morals, and knowledge. The knowledge section is based partly on *Didascalicon*. In it, Guillaume looks at the kinds of learning in which children should be instructed, how it should be acquired, and what its utility is. Hugh's *Didascalicon* provides the method of attaining knowledge. Guillaume quotes Hugh's dictum that 'the method of learning is in reading, its consummation in meditation'.[48] Three things are necessary for study: nature, practise, and discipline. Nature is rooted in aptitude and memory, both of which need to be polished, as all study and discipline cohere in them. Aptitude discovers wisdom; memory guards it.[49] Thus, although Guillaume omits Hugh's memory advice, he does indicate memory's psychological place in education.

Similarly, Vincent de Beauvais's *De eruditione filiorum nobilium* adopts Hugh's psychological valuation of memory, and, in addition, elaborates Hugh's precepts for memory. Written between 1245 and 1249, *De eruditione* was dedicated to Queen Margaret and is aimed at the sons of nobles.[50] It is longer and more comprehensive than Guillaume's work, but, like most of Vincent's literary endeavours, is largely a compilation of authorities on specific topics. His educational experts are Quintilian, Pseudo-Boethius, and Hugh of St Victor, the latter two affecting Vincent's views on memory. Like Guillaume, Vincent regards natural endowment, practise, and discipline as necessary qualities for learning and sees aptitude and memory as the component parts of natural endowment.[51] However, he separates

[46] *The De instructione puerorum of William of Tournai, O.P.*, ed. by James A. Corbett (Notre Dame: Medieval Institute, University of Notre Dame, 1955), p. 6.

[47] Mulchahey, *'First the Bow is Bent in Study'*, p. 87.

[48] *De instructione*, ed. by Corbett, p. 37.

[49] *De instructione*, ed. by Corbett, pp. 38–39.

[50] Vincent de Beauvais, *De eruditione filiorum nobilium*, ed. by Arpad Steiner (Cambridge, MA: Medieval Academy of America, 1938), pp. xv–xvi.

[51] *De eruditione*, V.21, XIV.52–53. Vincent includes Hugh's psychological analysis of memory and *ingenium* and their relationship to reading and meditation in a chapter entitled 'De proficiencium lectione', but he does so in a very cursory fashion. He lists the rules for order,

Hugh's memory precepts from this discussion, including them in a chapter division borrowed from Pseudo-Boethius's *De disciplina scholarium*.[52] According to this early thirteenth-century tract, a student must be attentive in listening, docile in understanding, and benevolent in retaining.[53] Under the third heading, Vincent includes much of Hugh's advice from the *Didascalicon*.

He begins with Hugh's injunction to his students to rejoice not because they had read many books, but because they had been able to retain them. To achieve retention through benevolence, three things are required. The first is that the student listen freely and diligently, that is, he must first listen to learn. He must also pay attention to what is said, not who says it. The second requirement is that the student collect briefly in memory the things he has heard: 'briefly', because it is not easy to recall all the words read aloud, much less all the words of a book. For this reason, the student should retain a *summa* of the *intencio* and the *materia*. Vincent quotes Hugh's directions on 'collecting' from the *Didascalicon* to explain how to make a *summa*, but he adds a further note of his own:

> For this reason in many tractates and books, epilogues, that is brief recapitulations of the words, are often found after extensive expositions of ideas, by which all the ideas are able to be commended to memory in summary fashion.[54]

Vincent provides a thirteenth-century 'gloss' on Hugh's notion of mnemonic 'collection'. For Vincent, collecting requires a summary of the *intencio* and *materia* of one's reading. Both expressions are technical terms commonly used in the medieval *accessus ad auctores*. *Intencio* refers to the author's reason for writing and is the kernel of the text; Gundissalinus claimed that whoever neglected a book's *intencio* ate only the shell and left the kernel intact.[55] The *materia libri* is the subject matter of the text or the materials from which it is

method, and part of those for memory, which occupy four chapters in the *Didascalicon*, in only one long paragraph.

[52] For more information about this anonymous treatise see Steiner's introduction to *De eruditione* and Beryl Smalley, *English Friars and Antiquity in the Early Fourteenth Century* (Oxford: Blackwell, 1960), p. 56.

[53] *De eruditione*, VIII.30.

[54] *De eruditione*, X.38: 'Ideo inquam breuiter, quia non de facile omnia uerba, que dicuntur, in leccione possent recolligi, ne dum uerba tocius libri. Ideoque summam intencionis et materie discenti conuenit memoriter retinere. Propter hoc eciam in multis tractatibus et libris frequenter post diffusas sententiarum exposiciones fieri solent epylogi, id est, breues dictorum recapitulaciones, quibus summatim possint omnia memorie commendari.'

[55] Cited in Minnis, *Medieval Theory of Authorship*, p. 20.

composed.[56] Therefore, if he remembers anything about his lesson, the student should strive to retain the author's purpose and his subject matter. This information illuminates Hugh's notion of a *summa*, as does Vincent's assertion of the mnemonic function of the epilogues found in any books.

Vincent's other recommendations for memory practise include repetition of the lesson and continuous study without interruption. The student may practise either by recollecting or ruminating to himself or by reading the things that he has learned to others.

Vincent adds some final comments on memory in his chapter on study and meditation. He begins with Hugh's definition of meditation: '[M]editation is sustained thought along planned lines [which] prudently investigates the cause and the source, the manner and the utility of each thing.'[57] The other authorities with which Vincent illustrates meditation equate it with rumination or recollection. Hence Ambrose in his sermon on Psalm 118:

> Let us not pass over perfunctorily that which we read [...] but also, when the codex is absent, let us recall to memory those things which we read and, like clean animals [...] let us bring forth from the treasury of our memory a spiritual fodder for ruminating.[58]

For Vincent, in meditation a man can be wise even without books and sometimes advance more.[59] Meditation in these terms is first a recollection of things already memorized (for the book is absent), and then 'a studious investigation', presumably of the questions arising from the recollected material. It is part of a continuum of learning, beginning with reading and including writing and disputing.[60]

Thus, Vincent bases his view of memory in education on Hugh's *Didascalicon*, though not in a systematic fashion. He gives memory an important psychological function but lists the rules for improving it in chapters on benevolence and meditation. He provides limited recommendations for improving it, citing neither

[56] Minnis, *Medieval Theory of Authorship*, p. 20.

[57] *De eruditione*, XVII.62; *Didas.*, trans. by Taylor, p. 92.

[58] *De eruditione*, XVII.62: 'non perfunctorie transeamus, que legimus [...] sed eciam, cum abest codex manibus, ea, que legimus, in memoriam reuocemus et tanquam animalia [...] munda [...] de noster memorie thesauro ruminandum nobis pabulum spirituale promamus'. Ambrose, *In Psalmum David CXVIII Expositio*, PL, XV, col. 1289C, Sermo VII.25.

[59] *De eruditione*, XVII.62: 'Igitur in meditacione potest homo sapiens eciam sine libris et aliquando melius proficere.'

[60] *De eruditione*, XIV.52.

*De tribus maximis* nor the *Ad Herennium*, nor for that matter, the division of a text into smaller parts favoured by twelfth-century scholars. Both the works by Guillaume de Tournai and Vincent de Beauvais prove that the Dominicans were aware of and influenced by Hugh of St Victor's pedagogical thought, but not decisively so. They seem to have considered his rules most relevant for early education rather than for more advanced study.

Moreover, Vincent's treatment of memory is as interesting for what it does not include as for what it does. We know from the *Speculum maius* that Vincent was familiar with almost all the roles that memory could play in the thirteenth century: in *Speculum naturale* he discusses memory as an internal sense, and in *Speculum doctrinale* he includes memory both as a part of rhetoric and as a part of prudence.[61] In none of these places does he discuss memory precepts, despite the fact that his fellow Dominicans Albertus Magnus and Thomas did link artificial memory to rhetoric and to prudence. His chapter on 'Study and Meditation' in *Speculum doctrinale* avoids all mention of memory, even of Hugh's rules, despite the chapter's obvious resemblance to its namesake in *De eruditione*.[62] Vincent's segregation of memory's various aspects differs markedly from Guibert de Tournai's consolidation of the same material in *De modo addiscendi*. In Guibert's *De modo*, we will find a distinctive, Franciscan approach to memory and learning.

## *The Franciscan View of Memory*

In the thirteenth century, the Franciscans were exposed to the same intellectual trends as the Dominicans. Like the Dominicans, they studied logic and rhetoric and the new psychological works. Also like the Dominicans, they opened up *studia generalia* at the sites of the new universities, as well as other local *studia* aimed at the training of its members.[63] Such *studia* enabled the Franciscans to participate in the great intellectual questions of the day. Because of these common factors, one would expect the orders to arrive at similar attitudes about the utility

[61] Vincent de Beauvais, *Speculum naturale*, XXVII.11–15, in *Speculum quadruplex sive, Speculum maius*, 4 vols (Graz: Akademische Druck-u. Verlagsanstalt, 1964–65), I, 1925–27; *Speculum doctrinale*, IV.21, ibid., II, 313.

[62] Vincent de Beauvais, *Speculum doctrinale*, chap. 45 (II, 5). The lack of memory precepts in *Speculum doctrinale* is especially striking since so much of the material in Books II, V, VI, and VIII duplicate the contents of *De eruditione*. See Steiner, 'Introduction', *De eruditione*, p. xv.

[63] For a detailed discussion of Franciscan mendicant schools, see the works by Bert Roest listed below and the sources cited in Chapter 7, below.

of ancient and medieval memory practices, and indeed, there was some overlap. However, there is enough evidence of Franciscan ideas about memory to conclude that they also had their own distinctive ways of thinking about memory training, ways that depended especially on the Cistercians and the Victorines. We will look first at Guibert de Tournai's views on memory to gain an insight into Franciscan ideas and practice. Guibert's work, the *De modo addiscendi*, reveals a number of peculiarly Franciscan themes: incorporation of memory into a theory of epistemology dependent on illumination from God; discussion of a wider array of memory experts than just Cicero, including Hugh of St Victor; and a particular respect for the memory of St Francis. In the next chapter, we will examine the influence of monastic practices on Franciscan ideas about memory through the works of David von Augsburg. In Chapter 4, we will also see how the Franciscan Francesc Eiximenis put his order's ideas about memory into practice as a preacher.

Much less has been written about Franciscan views about memory than about Dominican views. On the whole, scholars have tended to assume that because both orders were devoted to preaching, they both had the same reasons for promoting the *Ad Herennium*'s rules in the thirteenth century. It does certainly appear to be the case that the Franciscans grappled with Cicero's rules in the thirteenth century for the reasons discussed above. However, the Franciscan attitude toward Cicero is more ambiguous than the Dominican view. They acknowledge more authorities about memory than Albertus and Thomas do in their writings, and they have a greater commitment to Augustinian views about memory that needed to be reconciled with Aristotle and Cicero. In the mid-thirteenth century, Guibert de Tournai included an outline of several mnemonic methods, Cicero's among them, in his treatise on education, *De modo addiscendi*. His discussion of artificial memory turns up in the same context as those of Thomas and Albertus: a consideration of the newly translated Greek and Arab texts on memory and cognitive science. His inclusion of so many other mnemonic methods also reflects the varied ways that medieval people had used to remember material.

## Guibert de Tournai's *De modo addiscendi*

Guibert's reputation has fallen into that curious crack into which popular authors sometimes slip: he was well known and respected in his lifetime but has been largely ignored by modern-day scholars. This neglect is the more puzzling since Guibert was on intimate enough terms with Louis IX of France to compose the *Eruditio regum et principum* at the king's request and to write *De virginitate* for his sister, Isabella. Guibert was born probably a little after 1200 in Tournai of a noble family, and his continuing ties to the area can be seen in his writing *De modo addiscendi* for the benefit of the Count of Flanders's son, Jean de Dampierre.[64] He travelled to Paris at a young age, studying arts and theology. While at Paris, he joined the Franciscan order and eventually held the Franciscan chair in theology at Paris from *c.* 1257–60, probably immediately after St Bonaventura.[65] Indeed his association with such famous Franciscan scholars as Bonaventura and Jean de La Rochelle and the similarity of much of his thought to theirs renders his theological opus, the *Rudimentum doctrinae*, a fabulous repository of Franciscan theology in the thirteenth century.[66] In addition to his academic career, Guibert was also an influential preacher, whose *ad status* collection was widely copied and was printed in the fifteenth century and after.[67] Since Guibert was so well known in the thirteenth century, it seems unlikely that his thought was isolated from general trends in Franciscan thinking at the time.

Despite Guibert's undeniable influence in the thirteenth century, relatively little analysis has been made of much of his work.[68] Fortunately, there are critical

[64] Baudouin d'Amsterdam, 'Guibert De Tournai', in *Dictionnaire de spiritualité ascétique et mystique, doctrine et histoire*, ed. by Marcel Viller, Ferdinand Cavallera, and J. de Guibert, 17 vols (Paris: Beauchesne, 1932–95), VI, 1140. Palémon Glorieux also thought that Guibert accompanied St Louis on his first crusade in 1248: *Répertoire des maîtres en théologie de Paris au XIIIe siècle*, 2 vols (Paris: Vrin, 1933–34), II, 56. See also Léon Baudry, 'Wibert de Tournai', *Revue d'histoire franciscaine*, 5 (1928), 23–61.

[65] Glorieux, *Répertoire des maîtres en théologie*, II, 56. A few scholars have speculated that Guibert served two terms as a master in theology at Paris, once before he joined the Franciscan order and once after. See Baudry, 'Wibert de Tournai', pp. 26–27; Bonifacio, 'Introduction', *De modo addiscendi*, p. 12.

[66] D'Amsterdam, 'Guibert de Tournai', p. 1146.

[67] For works on Guibert's preaching career, see Jean Longère, *La prédication médiévale* (Paris: Institut d'études augustiniennes, 1983), pp. 101–02; David L. d'Avray, 'Sermons to the Upper Bourgeoisie by a Thirteenth-Century Franciscan', *Studies in Church History*, 16 (1979), 187–99; d'Avray, *Medieval Marriage Sermons*, pp. 274–316; Jenny Swanson, 'Childhood and Childrearing in *Ad status* Sermons by Later Thirteenth-Century Friars', *Journal of Medieval History*, 16 (1990), 309–31. A list of his sermon collections can be found in Johann Baptist Schneyer, *Repertorium der lateinischen Sermones des Mittelalters für die Zeit von 1150–1350*, Beiträge zur Geschichte der Philosophie und Theologie des Mittelalters, 43, 11 vols (Münster: Aschendorff, 1969), II, 282–318.

[68] For bibliography to 1974 see Benjamin Troeyer, *Bio-bibliographica Franciscana Neerlandica ante saeculum XVI*, I: *Pars Biographica, auctores editionum qui scripserunt ante saeculum XVI* (Nieuwkoop: de Graaf, 1974), pp. 15–48. See also Servus Gieben, 'Il *Rudimentum doctrinae* di

editions of *Eruditio regum et principum* and *De modo addiscendi*, and it is to the latter effort that we now turn.[69] Guibert probably wrote the *De modo* between 1264 and 1268 as the third tractate of his *Rudimentum doctrinae*, sometimes called the *Erudimentum doctrinae*, a theological, encyclopedic work resembling in some respects the *Summa theologica* attributed to Alexander of Hales.[70] The *Rudimentum*'s four parts correspond to the four causes of theology; Tractate I, on the end of study, constitutes the final cause; Tractate II, on qualities necessary to be a master, is the efficient cause; Tractate III (*De modo*), on the master's method, is the formal cause; while Tractate IV, on the sciences to be taught, is the material cause.[71] Although the *De modo* occupies an integral spot in the larger *Rudimentum*, it also stands as a coherent work on its own and circulated as such in at least one manuscript.[72] Certainly its style has clearly been adapted for a different audience than that of the *Rudimentum*. While the first two tracts proceed in *quaestio* format, the third does not, preferring a more expository style that tends to be as inclusive as possible — essentially an encyclopedic format.

Though the *De modo* is ostensibly directed to Michel de Lille for the education of his student Jean de Dampierre, the son of the Flemish count, it has more ambitious pretensions than the education of a young noble. For that, a compilation like Vincent de Beauvais's *De eruditione filiorum nobilium* would have sufficed,

Gilberto di Tournai con l'edizione del suo *Registrum* o tavola della materia', in *Bonaventuriana*, ed. by Francisco de Asis Chavero Blanco and Jacques Guy Bougerol (Rome: Edizioni Antonianum, 1988), pp. 621–80. More recently, Bert Roest has examined some of Guibert's views on Franciscan education. See Roest, '*Scientia* and *sapientia* in Gilbert of Tournai's *(E)rudimentum doctrinae*', in *Le Vocabulaire des écoles des Mendiants au moyen âge: Actes du colloque, Porto, Portugal, 11–12 octobre 1996*, ed. by Maria Cândida Pacheco, Études sur le vocabulaire intellectuel du moyen âge, 9 (Turnhout: Brepols, 1999), pp. 164–79, and Roest, *A History of Franciscan Education (c. 1210–1517)* (Leiden: Brill, 2000).

[69] A. de Poorter, 'Un traité de pédagogie médiévale: Le *De modo addiscendi* de Guibert de Tournai, O.F.M.', *Revue néo-scolastique*, 24 (1922), 195–228.

[70] Étienne Gilson, *History of Christian Philosophy in the Middle Ages* (New York: Random House, 1955), p. 327. Roest has noted that the ambiguity of the title highlights two important aspects of education: the work deals with both the basics of education (*rudimentum*) and with the act of teaching (*erudimentum*) ('*Scientia* and *sapientia*', p. 168.)

[71] There is some question as to whether the fourth tractate was ever completed. It certainly is not present in any of the five extant manuscripts; see Bonifacio, 'Introduction', p. 14; Baudry, 'Wibert de Tournai', p. 29. For further analysis of the educational import of Guibert's work, see Roest, '*Scientia* and *sapientia*', and Roest, *History of Franciscan Education*, pp. 264–71.

[72] One of the five manuscripts which contain all or part of the *Rudimentum* presents the *De modo* as a self-standing work; see Bonifacio, 'Introduction', pp. 53–54.

though both Guibert and Vincent seemingly regard theology as the crown of a good education, suitable even for certain portions of the laity.[73] However, Guibert's is a much more elaborate work than Vincent's. His method of learning deals with both the teacher and the student, but far more of the work is aimed at students, whom he separates into three grades: those in the state of beginners (*status inchoationis*), those in the state of progression (*status progressionis*), and those in a state of perfection (*status perfectionis*), that is, cloistered monks.[74] Overall, Guibert's vision of education seems more appropriate for the training of a Franciscan than for a noble, which is probably the best way to view it. As Bert Roest has observed, though one cannot see the *Rudimentum* as a whole as a straightforward blueprint of Franciscan educational practices, 'The doctrine that it upholds is a specific Franciscan brand of the *doctrina christiana*, cast in an encyclopedic form, to make it accessible for a diversified audience of teachers and pupils.'[75] The overall goal of the education laid out by Guibert is to obtain wisdom, which depends on the eternal wisdom of God and thus on illumination (*influentia lucis increatae*).[76] This illumination helps to make the soul deiform and a house of God.[77]

To teach the beginning students, Guibert lays out four main areas of discussion related to learning: the factors that precede learning (*antecedentia)*, those that accompany it (*comitantia*), the consequences of learning (*consequentia*), and things which impede learning (*extranea*).[78] One might loosely translate the first three topics as the things that instill discipline in the student, the faculties of the soul

[73] Vincent de Beauvais's *De eruditione* was written between 1245 and 1249 (probably 1246–47) and bears such a remarkable similarity to Guibert's pedagogical work in some places that the question of dependence has arisen. See Bonifacio, 'Introduction', pp. 49–53, and de Poorter, 'Un traité de pédagogie médiévale', p. 201. Bonifacio concedes that Guibert may have relied on Vincent, since the latter finished his treatise first and had access to the same royal circle as Guibert. Bonifacio also notes, however, that the two may have simply used similar florilegia and that Guibert's version is more systematic and sustained than Vincent's (p. 53). De Poorter thought it was nearly impossible to judge dependence.

[74] *De modo*, p. 105 (all translations from *De modo* are mine unless otherwise noted). Note that these are the same stages used by David von Augsburg in his works. The ultimate source of the three stages comes from Gregory the Great. Roest, 'Franciscan Educational Perspectives', p. 171.

[75] Roest, '*Scientia* and *sapientia*', p. 177.

[76] Roest, *History of Franciscan Education*, p. 264.

[77] Roest, 'Reading the Book of History', p. 193.

[78] *De modo*, p. 105.

that aid learning, and the moral attributes that should be consequences of learning, such as humility and studiousness.[79]

## Guibert's Ideas about Memory

Guibert's description of memory occurs in his discussion of the faculties of the soul that accompany learning, which include *sensus*, *ingenium*, *memoria*, and *ratio* (sense, aptitude, memory, and reason). Sense apprehends objects, aptitude searches out undiscovered things, memory stores away the judgements and offers them back up for determination, and reason judges the things found.[80] For each faculty, Guibert explains its functions and how it may be trained. Naturally, memory is of the greatest interest here, though we will touch on the other aspects. He devotes four chapters to memory, investigating memory's quiddity, its quality, its power, and its *formabilitas*. In the first two chapters he establishes what memory is, how it fits into a kind of 'divine chain of memory', what it can and cannot do, and where the sensible memory is situated in the brain. In the third chapter he marvels at the power of memory, fitting its capacity, spirituality, and utility firmly into an Augustinian format, while the fourth chapter contains a round-up of mnemonic precepts.

Like his Dominican counterparts, Guibert sees the need to reconcile Cicero with other authorities; where he differs is in his initial choice of authorities and his stance toward them. Guibert begins the chapter on quiddity by defining memory, not according to Aristotle, but according to Cicero, John of Damascus, and Augustine. From Cicero he takes the well-known definition of memory as a part of prudence. From John of Damascus he finds the definition: '[M]emory is a phantasy [*phantasia*] left from something sensed according to a visible action, or a "heaping up" [*coacervatio*] of sense and intelligence.' Without actually naming Augustine, Guibert borrows from him, likening memory to an 'enormous hall containing innumerabiles treasures of diverse corporeal things and images brought in through the senses'.[81]

Because he avoids the *quaestio* format in the *De modo*, Guibert does not so much reconcile his authorities as gather them together in an organized manner.

[79] Roest, '*Scientia* and *sapientia*', pp. 171–72.

[80] *De modo*, p. 135: 'Sensus enim apprehendit obiecta, ingenium exquirit incognita, ratio iudicat inventa, memoria recondit iudicata et offert adhuc diiudicanda.'

[81] *De modo*, p. 194.

He subsumes all the types of memory he intends to discuss under a hierarchy dependent on a few crucial distinctions. According to Augustine, memory is divided into a sensible part and an intelligible part. Sensible memory grasps sensible things and from it opinion arises; intelligible memory grasps things through the intellect and from it understanding arises.[82] Of these, the intelligible may be divided into that which is not part of the image of God in us and that which is, while, according to Cicero the sensible memory can be separated into the natural and the artificial.[83] Guibert also posits a divine memory that imposes its form on everything; the more any memories conform to this divine memory, the better and purer they are. Beneath this highest memory comes all created memory. Given these distinctions, it then follows that the highest type of memory is the divine, which informs all others. Next comes the created intelligible memory that is part of the image of God. It is present in both angels and in humans, but the angelic kind is more noble. So in turn is the human intelligible memory that is a part of the image of God nobler than the part which is not a part. All of human intelligible memory is nobler than the sensible memory, and the natural sensible memory nobler than the artificial. Finally, both of these are superior to animal memory.[84]

Guibert's hierarchy allows him to reconcile Augustine's ideas about memory with the Aristotelian and Arabic ideas coming into fashion at Paris. By dividing memory into an intelligible part and a sensible part and a part which is part of the image of God and a part which is not, Guibert can differentiate between the highest functions of memory, which reflect Augustinian views, and the more mundane, such as preserving sensory impressions, described by Aristotle and the Arabic writers. One important aspect of this distinction is memory's relationship to time. Divine memory is eternal and thus beyond the limits of time, while the created memory that is a part of the image of God and in angels is not eternal, but does participate in eternity (*aeternitatis particeps*) through contemplation and beatitude. It is thus beyond the vicissitude of time in a way that memory in humans is not. Memory in humans is subject to time, but in varying degrees. Human intelligible memory that is part of the image of God is a *vis intelligibilis* that has the ability to abstract intelligibles from differences in time but is still able to keep before itself some knowledge of the unity of God, that is, it has some

[82] *De modo*, pp. 194–95.

[83] *De modo*, p. 195.

[84] *De modo*, p. 195.

relationship to a world beyond time.[85] The human intelligible memory that is not a part of the image of God is more mundane, being a *vis conservativa* that preserves intelligible species with an acknowledgement of the passage of time.[86] When one moves on to sensible memory, then one encounters the world of Aristotle, in which memory is the repository of things sensed in the past. If intelligible memory is a *vis*, then sensible memory is a *virtus*. Cicero's distinction between natural and artificial memory allows Guibert to include both the emerging ideas about the internal senses (*memoria sensibilis* is the power or faculty situated in the back chamber of the brain) and artificial memory in the discussion. This valient attempt to summarize all of memory's functions might be Guibert's most original contribution to memory and to the internal sense tradition. Certainly, neither Albertus nor Thomas mention such a hierarchy. As we will see below, Guibert, like many of his fellow Franciscans at Paris, was committed to an Augustinian view of memory and knowledge that depended on light illumination. Because he had also studied the new books of Aristotle and his Arab commentators, he seems to have been unwilling to ignore their views completely.

## Franciscan Memory

It is in the third chapter on memory's power and utility that Guibert's commitment to an Augustinian, and perhaps uniquely Franciscan, view of memory becomes evident. Here he explicates the power of memory — its capacity, spirituality, dignity, and utility — rather than memory's operations. His wonderment at the capacity and spirituality of memory is firmly Augustinian: in six printed pages of text he quotes Augustine ten times, relying especially on Book X of the *Confessions*, *De Trinitate*, and *Contra Julianum*.[87] He selects quotations from the *Confessions* that emphasize the unlimited power of memory: 'its end is nowhere, such is the power of memory'.[88] He also follows Augustine in admiring

[85] 'Memoria vero intelligibilis in hominibus prout est pars imaginis est vis intelligibilis abstrahens ab omni differentia temporis secundum superiorem portionem eius conversa in Deum, tenens apud se praesentiam notitiae primae unitatis in habitu aliquo innato, ut patet in libro Augustini *De Trinitate*': *De modo*, p. 196; cf. Augustine of Hippo, *De Trinitate libri XV*, ed. by William J. Mountain, CCSL, 50–50A (Turnhout: Brepols, 1968), IX, 6, and XI, passim.

[86] 'Memoria vero intelligibilis quae non est pars imaginis est vis conservativa specierum intelligibilium secundum differentias temporis diversas de rebus prius acceptis': *De modo*, p. 196.

[87] *De modo*, pp. 208–13.

[88] *De modo*, p. 209: 'et finis nusquam est, tanta vis est memorie'.

the spirituality of memory, meaning memory's ability to transcend its corporeal dimension:

> You have frequently seen the image of your face in the mirror, nor did the dimensions of the image exceed the size of the mirror: for your image shone larger in a large mirror, smaller in a small mirror — never did it exceed the mirror. But the image of the city of Tournai appeared to you in your memory just as it appeared to your eyes when it was viewed in its nature and quality. Therefore, since the image of the aforesaid city was impressed on your memory, and its image is not able to exceed the size of the thing on which it is imprinted, it is necessary to say that your memory is larger than the aforesaid city. If therefore your memory is able to look at the whole world and everything it contains, its image will appear to you as the same size which it has in reality. But no corporeal thing is able to exist in which an image of the whole world could be painted without diminution of its size. Therefore the memory of man is greater than the world, not in its corporeal size but in its spiritual nature.[89]

Guibert's idea is not quite an original one, as Ælred of Rievaulx makes a similar point about the memory's ability to encompass London and Westminster Abbey.[90]

The dignity of the spirituality of memory comes from the possibility of the similitude of God being found there, an idea based on Augustine's contention that God lives in the mind when we remember him. Guibert builds on this idea and on the thinking of Isaac de l'Etiole's *Epistola de anima* (see below) to argue that the soul must transcend itself to see the image of God:

> Therefore a soul purged of the senses and phantasms of sensible things and made mirror-like ascends to itself [*ad se*] and is elevated above itself and proves the worthiness of its memory. And just as in the purest mirror, the similitude of divine wisdom and the image

[89] *De modo*, p. 209: 'Vidisti enim frequenter imaginem vultus tui in speculo, nec tamen speculi mensuram excessit imaginis magnitudo: nam in maiori speculo maior et in minori minor imago tua fulgebat: numquam tamen speculum excedebat. Imago autem civitatis Tornacensis tanta apparet tibi in memoria tua quanta apparebat oculis tuis cum videbatur in natura et qualitate sua. Ergo cum imago dictae civitatis sit impressa memoriae tuae et imago eius rei magnitudinem cui imprimitur non possit excedere, memoriam tuam necesse est fateri maiorem praedicta civitate. Si ergo totum mundum et quidquid in eo est posset aspicere memoria tua appareret tibi eius imago in eadem magnitudine in qua est in veritate. Sed res corporea esse non potest in qua totius mundi imago posset depingi sine magnitudinis suae diminuatione. Est ergo memoria hominis maior mundo non mole corporea sed spirituali natura.'

[90] In fact some of the wording of Guibert's comment is nearly identical to that of Ælred's *De anima*, II.5–8, in *Opera omnia*, ed. by Anselm Hoste and Charles H. Talbot, CCCM, 1 (Turnhout: Brepols, 1971). As we will see below, Guibert was probably quite familiar with a number of Cistercian authors. He quotes from Ælred's *Speculum caritatis* in the *De modo* (p. 183). For more on Ælred's passage, see also Evans, 'Two Aspects of *Memoria*', p. 265, and Coleman, *Ancient and Medieval Memories*, pp. 212–23.

> of the first unity will shine in it. For the more that I come toward the knowledge of God, the more I approach him through similitude.[91]

Guibert adds that it is the rational mind (which he seems sometimes to conflate with memory) that is able to rise toward divine knowledge.[92] Guibert's ideas about the cleansing of memory and its ability to rise toward a knowledge of God parallel his ideas about the intellect and its need for cleansing and illumination from God in order to achieve true knowledge.

## Sense and Illumination in Guibert's Thought

A number of thirteenth-century authors, including Robert Grosseteste, Bonaventura, and Henry of Gent, explained human cognition through a combination of Pseudo-Dionysian thought and Augustinian illumination theory.[93] Guibert was also highly influenced by the English Cistercian Isaac de l'Etoile's *Epistola de anima*, written around 1162. Isaac was probably the abbot of the abbey of Notre-Dame des Châteliers on the island of Ré, a short distance from the French port of La Rochelle. He was a student in the schools before 1130, and his work reflects the interests of Chartrians like Guillaume de Conches and Thierry de Chartres, and the school of St Victor.[94] Much of what Guibert says about sense and memory is drawn directly from this twelfth-century mystical work.[95]

[91] *De modo*, p. 210: 'Igitur anima purgata et specularis effecta a sensibus et phantasmatibus rerum sensibilium ascendat ad se et elevetur supra se et dignitatem experietur memoriae suae, et sicut in speculo purissimo relucebit in ea similitudo divinae sapientiae et imago unitatis primae. Nam tanto magis ad cognitionem Dei accedo quanto magis et per similitudinem appropinquo.'

[92] A similar idea is expressed in what seems to be a previously written work by Guibert, *De doctrina Dei*, which he quotes from earlier in the treatise: 'Praecipuum enim speculum ad videndum Deum mens est rationalis, cum sit ymago Dei expressa' (*De modo*, p. 120 n. 1, and de Poorter, 'Un traité de pédagogie médiévale', p. 217). The quotations listed in Bonifacio's edition and in de Poorter's article are from the *Rudimentum* in Paris, BnF, cod. lat. 15,451.

[93] See Joseph Owens, 'Faith, Ideas, Illumination, and Experience', in *Cambridge History of Later Medieval Philosophy*, ed. by Kretzmann, Kenny, and Pinborg, pp. 440–59; Colish, *Medieval Foundations*, pp. 291–306.

[94] Coleman, *Ancient and Medieval Memories*, p. 215. For the text of the *Epistola de anima*, see PL, CXCIV, cols 1875–90, and *Three Treatises on Man: A Cistercian Anthropology*, ed. by Bernard McGinn, Cistercian Fathers Series, 24 (Kalamazoo: Cistercian, 1977), pp. 153–78.

[95] Throughout *De modo*, Guibert claims to quote from 'Isaac's *De spiritu et anima*', seemingly a conflation of Isaac de l'Etoile's *Epistola de anima* and the *De spiritu et anima*, by an anonymous Cistercian. Bonifacio assumes Guibert's references are to the latter work, but eight of the nine

Isaac describes a fivefold ascent of *rationabilitas* (essence of the soul) to God, each of which has its proper object: *sensus* investigates bodies, *imaginatio* knows the similitudes of bodies, *ratio* perceives the incorporeal forms of corporeal things, *intellectus* the forms of incorporeal things, and *intelligentia* information about God.[96] There is a tension in this schema between matter and spirit. Sense knowledge and imagination function on the corporeal level, but they are not able to transcend it: they cannot reach the part of the soul that perceives incorporeal reality:

> Sense knowledge and imagination thrive on the level of the natural states of the existence of corporeal things, but without reason they are insufficient. They do not rise to the rational level, but remaining below, from a distance as it were point out the incorporeal form to reason as it rises. Certainly they are able to bring reason itself to this point, but they cannot accompany it up to the incorporeal forms of corporeal things.[97]

Reason operates on a middle ground between the corporeal and incorporeal worlds. It abstracts from a body the forms of corporeal things, which, because they are founded in a body, are 'scarcely incorporeal'.[98] *Intellectus* and *intelligentia* deal with the truly incorporeal. *Intelligentia*, the power of the soul closest to God, is aided by theophanies descending into it. Isaac also employs a light analogy, that God, in whom there is light, illuminates the soul's understanding to acknowledge truth.[99]

Guibert reproduces this entire schema in one chapter devoted to the senses. Taking his attitude toward them from the notion that *disciplina* begins with the apprehension of the senses and reaches completion with their purification, Guibert views the senses in a somewhat more positive light than Isaac. Learning

quotations can be found more fully in Isaac's *Epistola*. This unusual plurality of potential sources is explained by the fact that *De spiritu* is a late twelfth-century compilation of several mystical works, including Isaac's *Epistola*. Thus, a number of Guibert's quotations are found in both works, but *De spiritu* does not contain the entire quotation. For more information on Isaac de l'Etoile and *De spiritu*, see Bernard McGinn, 'Introduction', in *Three Treatises on Man*, ed. by McGinn, pp. 1–100.

[96] Coleman, *Ancient and Medieval Memories*, p. 216; Isaac de l'Etoile, *Epistola de anima*, PL, CXCIV, cols 1884–88.

[97] Isaac de l'Etoile, *Epistola de anima*, PL, CXCIV, col. 1884: 'Circa naturales ergo rerum corporearum status sensus et imaginatio vigent, sed absque ratione non satis valent; ad rationem vero non ascendunt, sed infra remanentes, eum ascendenti rationi quasi a longe ostendunt. Deducere nimirum rationem ipsam aliquatenus possunt, sed usque ad rerum corporearum incorporeas formas comitari eum non possunt.' Translation from *Three Treatises on Man*, ed. by McGinn, pp. 169–70.

[98] Isaac de l'Etoile, *Epistola de anima*, PL, CXCIV, col. 1884.

[99] Isaac de l'Etoile, *Epistola de anima*, PL, CXCIV, cols 1888–89.

has its foundation in communication, which occurs through *voces* and *signa*. Though imperfect transmitters of thought, *voces* are recognized by Guibert to be perceived by the senses. Once this initial perception has happened, there is a progression of powers reaching from the senses to the understanding, based on Isaac's analysis. Guibert immediately juxtaposes this progression of the senses to an Aristotelian one, the progression from sensory impressions to knowledge. Only creatures who have the capacity for sense, memory, hearing, imagination, and reason may learn from experience and achieve knowledge:

> For a thing is first sensed, then it is commended to memory, and experience is gained through the multiplication of sense and memory. From many experiences arises a universal, which is the beginning of art and science.[100]

Learning (*disciplina*) reaches completion through the purification of the senses by an infusion of light from God.[101] Guibert's proof for light infusion comes from Isaac's *Epistola de anima*, where it had been used to explicate how understanding (*intelligentia*) is aided by superior light to know truth. His ideas about light infusion are explained more fully elsewhere in the *De modo*. He explains that the rational soul is positioned on the horizon of two worlds, the sensible and the intelligible, the world below and the world above. The sensible or lower world is a world of darkness as far as our intellect is concerned, which can see nothing of sensible things in as much as they are sensible, but the intellect is illumined by them toward knowing intelligible things. This knowledge occurs through the mediation of sense, imagination, and memory, because they pass along the species of sensible things to the intellect.[102] According to Guibert,

> The senses stand outside in sensible forms and the intellect reads them inside, just as its name shows, because *intellectus* is said to mean *intus legens* (reading inside), and it ascends up to the intelligible world and the eternal light, which is God, which projects itself to the soul and touches it from on high.[103]

[100] *De modo*, p. 141: 'Res enim prius sentitur, deinde memoriae commendatur et ex sensus et memoriae multiplicatione experimentum habetur, et ex multis experimentis fit unum universale quod est principium artis et scientiae.' This conception of science is drawn from the opening paragraphs of Aristotle's *Metaphysics*: *Metaphysica libri I–IV.4; translatio Iacobi sive 'vetustissima' cum scholiis et translatio composita sive 'vetus'*, ed. by Gudrun Vuillemin-Diem (Leiden: Brill, 1970), 980a21–982a1. For a similar, thirteenth-century presentation of the same idea, see Robert Kilwardby, *De ortu scientiarum*, ed. by Judy, pp. 8–14.

[101] *De modo*, pp. 144–45.

[102] *De modo*, p. 121.

[103] *De modo*, p. 121: 'Sensus enim stant foris in sensibilis formis et intellectus intus legit, sicut nomen eius ostendit, unde intellectus dicitur quasi intus legens, et ascendit usque ad

If the soul were free and healthy, it would easily be able to raise itself up to the region of light and enter it in the way that now it can enter the region of darkness.

It is Guibert's contention that the soul cannot think *pure* unless it returns to itself and directs its attention above itself.[104] Reaching this highest knowledge, which he calls revelation, usually cannot happen for humans because of sin. For humans to approach the first light, either the divine light which is above them through nature or the angelic light which is sent for illuminating them through the grace of God, their souls have to be abstracted from exterior things and from their bodies. The soul could then look at itself and because it is the image of God, it could read what is written or received or infused within itself, and it would be free to raise himself and understand if corruption did not block it. Corruption impedes the process of revelation because the dregs of sin, the tying of the soul to our bodies, and the corporeal things which intrude too much into the soul prevent the mind from being abstracted, just as an inscription on a wax tablet prohibits another inscription from being made or the filling of a vessel with one liquid prevents it from receiving another one.[105] The grace of God and the cleansing of the rational mind allow for the illumination of revelation, which happens when souls are *in spiritu* rather than *in corpore*. To be *in spiritu* means to be apart from the region of darkness and free from the cares and thoughts coming into our souls from that region. To be *in corpore* means to be submerged in the body, whose walls block the rays of illumination. Guibert says those walls have to be leapt over, which happens at death, or windows can be made, which happens when the soul is *in spiritu*. In the end, the highest knowledge available to humans occurs through the revelation received by divine illumination.

Guibert also applies the idea of illumination to memory in a discussion of memory's utility. Here he declares that certain people have used memory in place of books ('quidam memoria usi sunt pro codicibus') 'just as we read about both St Antony the Anchorite or concerning the Order of the Friars Minor'. Guibert claims that the fewer things (i.e., books or parchment) that memory needs, the better and more like God it is ('Nam quanto memoria paucioribus indiget, tanto

mundum intelligibilem et lucem aeternam, quae Deus est, quae super eminet animae et tangit eam a vertice.'

[104] *De modo*, p. 118: 'Nec potest anima quidquam pure intelligere nisi prius redeat ad se et convertat se super se prout dicit Augustinus in libro *De ordine* et *De quantitate animae*.' See also *De modo*, p. 119.

[105] *De modo*, p. 122.

melior et deiformier est').[106] He compares the perfection of memory with the perfection of the intelligence, which is only complete and perfect when it can see all things with one glance of the eye, as it were. This only happens when the mind has been taken up above the world in the divine light, as happened to St Benedict of Nursia. Guibert refers to the story from Gregory the Great's *Dialogues*, in which Benedict was praying in the middle of the night when he suddenly saw an enormous ray of light shining down from the heavens. Then the whole world was gathered up before his eyes in one ray of light, and he saw the soul of Germanus, Bishop of Capua, carried up to heaven in a ball of fire.[107] Guibert quotes Gregory's comment on the incident: 'Why should it surprise us, then, that he could see the whole world gathered up before him after this inner light had lifted him so far above the world.'[108] Guibert says that this light which shone in front of Benedict's 'outer' eyes was the inner light in the mind, which showed to his soul when he had been taken up on high, how narrow (*angusta*) all things below him were. 'So I say concerning memory that it is not able to be perfect unless it is illuminated by an incorporeal light.'[109] He then quotes Augustine in *De Trinitate*, 'by the light of incorporeal truth is fixed in memory what was not found fixed there before'.[110] According to Guibert, memory is especially godlike when it performs with wondrous speed and without whirling thoughts.[111] However, Guibert is uncertain whether such memory is possible in this life, although it will be common in the next one, where forgetfulness will be unknown.

So for Guibert some people can use 'memory in place of books'.[112] Guibert's notion is not only the kind of distinction that Carruthers makes between a book and a text carried in memory (that sense is implicit here), but is also based on Franciscan ideas of illumination that we have already seen.[113] For Guibert such

[106] *De modo*, p. 213.

[107] Gregory the Great, *Dialogorum libri IV De vita et miraculis patrum italicorum*, II. 35, PL, LXXVII, cols 149–430 (col. 200B).

[108] Translation from Gregory the Great, 'Dialogues', in *Readings in Medieval History*, ed. by Patrick J. Geary, 3rd edn (Peterborough, ON: Broadview, 2003), pp. 199–220 (p. 233).

[109] *De modo*, p. 213: 'Ita dico de memoria quod non potest esse perfecta nisi illuminetur luce incorporea.'

[110] Augustine, *De Trinitate*, XII.14, ed. by Mountain.

[111] Elsewhere Guibert says that the more things conform to divine memory, the better and purer they are: *De modo*, p. 195.

[112] This idea falls under one of Guibert's four useful aspects of memory, *De modo*, pp. 211–13.

[113] Carruthers, *Book of Memory*, pp. 8–13.

memory is impossible without the aid of illumination from God, as his examples of people receiving such memory or divine illumination show: St Antony the Anchorite, St Francis of Assisi, and St Benedict.

There is another Franciscan element to this discussion. When Guibert says that some people have used memory for books, 'just as we read about both St Antony the Anchorite or concerning the Order of the Friars Minor', he is most likely referring to a tradition in the Franciscan order about St Francis's memory. According to St Francis's biographer, Tommaso da Celano, although Francis did not receive a scholarly education, he was irradiated by flashes of eternal light concerning Scripture. In addition,

> He sometimes read the Sacred Books,
> and whatever he once put in his mind,
> he *wrote* it indelibly *in his heart.*
> His memory took the place of books [*Memoriam pro libris habebat*],
> Because, if he heard something once,
> it was not wasted,
> as his heart would mull it over with constant devotion.
> He said that this was the fruitful way to read and learn,
> rather than to wander through a thousand treatises.[114]

Although Guibert mentions the Order of the Friars Minor rather than St Francis specifically, this passage seems to fit his meaning quite clearly. Tommaso claims Francis received flashes of eternal light to illuminate his understanding of Scripture and that he had memory in place of books. Tommaso's account of St Francis's life implies a familiarity with St Athanasius's *Life of Saint Antony*. Athanasius had had much the same thing to say about this saint, 'For he paid such close attention to what was read that nothing from Scripture did he fail to take in, rather he grasped everything, and in him the memory took the place of books.'[115]

[114] Translation from *The Francis Trilogy of Thomas of Celano: The Life of Saint Francis, The Remembrance of the Desire of a Soul, The Treatise on the Miracles of Saint Francis*, ed. by Regis J. Armstrong, J. A. Wayne Hellman, and William J. Short (Hyde Park: New City Press, 1998), p. 232. Thommaso da Celano, *Vita secunda S. Francisci*, Analecta franciscana, 10.1 (Florence: Quaracchi, 1927), chap. 67. See also Carruthers, *Book of Memory*, p. 174, where this passage is briefly discussed. Bonaventura also includes the same story in his life of Francis: Bonaventura, *Legenda maior S. Francisci*, Analecta franciscana, 10.1 (Florence: Quaracchi, 1941), chap. 11, p. 605.

[115] Translation from Robert C. Gregg, *The Life of Antony*, III, in *Athanasius: The Life of Antony and The Letter to Marcellinus* (New York: Paulist, 1980), pp. 31–32, cited in *Francis Trilogy*, p. 232 note a; PL, LXXIII, col. 128.

Tommaso links Francis with the early saint, thereby increasing his prestige. But the story is no mere topos, for Tommaso several times makes reference to Francis's memorial powers. Perhaps the most telling is what he says in the first *Life of Saint Francis* after he relates the saint's response to the call to the apostolic life found in Matthew's Gospel: 'For he was no a deaf hearer of the gospel; rather he committed everything he heard to his excellent memory and was careful to carry it out to the letter.'[116] It is significant that Tommaso praises Francis's memory at one of the most important moments of his life and seems to attribute to his memory Francis's fulfilment of scriptural teachings. At least for Guibert, Francis's life, along with that of St Benedict and of St Antony, demonstrated the role of illumination in real life. Francis's memory had also clearly become legendary among the Franciscans, for Guibert's reference to the order is as brief as could be. Given the importance of the life of St Francis to the development of the order, it is likely that stories about Francis's memory would not have needed explanation for a Franciscan.[117]

Guibert's explanation of memory used in place of books occurs in a discussion of memory's utility. Another utility of memory is that it aids us in reminiscing. Guibert thinks that humans should be sure to recall the benefits that they have received both from other people and from God. He calls men ungrateful and evil who do not remember the benefits they have received and are ungrateful — these are similar to lynxes. Even worse are those who do not follow Caesar's lead and forget nothing except injuries: they remember only injuries, making them similar to camels.[118] One other utility of memory for Guibert that should be mentioned briefly for now is that the memory of benefits aids us in loving God.[119] In this context, he quotes at length from Seneca's *De beneficiis*, where Seneca chastises some philosophers who complain that the gods have not sufficiently endowed

[116] Translation from *Francis Trilogy*, p. 42; Thommmaso da Celano, *Vita prima S. Francisci*, Analecta franciscana, 10.1 (Florence: Quaracchi, 1926), chap. 9.

[117] J. A. Wayne Hellman, 'Francis of Assisi: Saint, Founder, Prophet', in *Francis of Assisi: History, Hagiography, and Hermeneutics in the Early Documents*, ed. by Jay M. Hammond (Hyde Park: New City Press, 2004), pp. 15–38 (pp. 24–29). It must be pointed out, though, that the Dominicans also used the same topos to describe the memorial powers of some of their saints. See Lina Bolzoni, 'The "Triumph of Death Cycle" Frescoes in the Pisan Camposanto and Dominican Preaching', in her *The Web of Images: Vernacular Preaching from its Origins to St Bernardino da Siena* (Aldershot: Ashgate, 2004), pp. 11–40 (p. 34).

[118] *De modo*, pp. 211–12.

[119] *De modo*, p. 212.

humans with the same attributes that they have given to various animals.[120] The idea that memory should remind us of past benefits, especially of those from God, is a standard one in the High Middle Ages, although little discussed by scholars, and one which played nicely into the new theology of penitence and confession that the mendicant orders were promoting. Vincent de Beauvais strikes the same note near the end of *De eruditione* in a chapter entitled 'Quod vir preterita debet recolere et presencia attendere'.[121] Vincent recommends that a mature man will remember past miseries, faults, and benefits: miseries, that he might remember his origins and remain humble; faults, that he might be penitent; and benefits, that he might not be ungrateful to God.[122] In the early fourteenth century, John Ridevall's chapter on memory in the *Fulgentius metaforalis* also brings up the same issues.[123] We will return to the implications of this theme in the next chapter.

Once he has explained how memory works and marvelled at its immense capacity, Guibert is ready to explain the more mundane, but essential, task of improving it.

## Guibert's Mnemonic Precepts

Guibert's handling of memory's *formabilitas*, its capacity to be molded, like his other chapters on memory, is less the advocacy of a single mnemonic system than an ordering of many different kinds of mnemonic advice. If Guibert outlines no complete mnemonic system, he is at least notable for his astonishing familiarity with the mnemonic literature. He is one of the few medieval writers to quote the fifth-century rhetorician, Martianus Capella, on mnemonics,[124] and he utilizes at least selections from Cicero's *De oratore*, perhaps obtained from a *florilegium*, as

[120] *De modo*, p. 212. Cf. *L. Annaei Senecae De beneficiis et De clementia*, ed. by Martinus Clarentius Gertz (Berolini: Weidmannos, 1876), II.29, p. 34.

[121] *De eruditione*, p. 159.

[122] *De eruditione*, pp. 159–65.

[123] *Fulgentius Metaforalis: Ein Beitrag zur Geschichte der antiken Mythologie im Mittelalter*, ed. by Hans Liebeschütz, Studien der Bibliothek Warburg, 4 (Leipzig: Teubner, 1926), pp. 89–93.

[124] Guibert is the only medieval writer I have seen to quote Martianus Capella in conjunction with the *Ad Herennium*'s advice on memory. The only other authors that I know to quote Martianus on memory are Ulrich of Bamberg and Bene of Florence, both experts on the *ars dictaminis*. Terence Tunberg includes a transcription of Bene's brief section on memory in 'What is Boncompagno's "Newest Rhetoric"?', pp. 333–34. For Ulrich, see Hajdú, *Das mnemotechnische Schriften*, pp. 59–60, and Murphy, *Rhetoric in the Middle Ages*, p. 127.

well as from the *Ad Herennium*.[125] He also knows Hugh of St Victor's chapters on memory in the *Didascalicon*. He arranges precepts from all of these authors under four ordering principles: time, practice, place, and method (*tempus*, *actus*, *locus* and *modus*). Each of these in turn has three rules of its own. Since Guibert's rules for memory have not received scholarly attention, it is worth examining them with some care before considering the impact of thirteenth-century influences on them.[126]

Guibert's first heading is the time for molding memory, for which he lists three main rules: that it be quiet, that it be nocturnal, and that digestion be completed.[127] Guibert quotes Martianus Capella in advising one to memorize by night rather than by day, because it is generally quieter at night and one is less likely to be distracted. Again, according to Martianus, one can memorize either the *res* or *verba*, but memorizing *verba* should not be attempted unless one has a great deal of time and a naturally good memory.[128] Guibert adds his own advice on the topic, warning against memory work right after dinner, because the vapours released after eating disturb the sense organs, especially those of vision and hearing, which are necessary for learning. Memory is weakened then, because the *phantasmata* are indistinguishable from one another. Instead it flourishes after sleep (perhaps after a little nap) when digestion is completed and the soul can apply all its powers toward the job at hand.

Place also evokes three precepts: it must be dark, familiar, and marked with signs and images. First, those wishing to reminisce seek solitary, dimly lit spots, fleeing both other people and light, since images of sensible things are scattered in a bright, public place, and their movement is confused. However, in a dark place, they are united and moved in order. That is why Cicero advises one to see out dark and solitary places. Thus, when we see those who wish to remember

[125] Incomplete copies of the *De oratore* seem to have circulated, but a complete copy became available only after 1422. Reynolds, *Scribes and Scholars*, p. 123.

[126] Pierre Riché is one of the few writers to allude to Guibert's memory precepts: 'Le Rôle de la mémoire dans l'enseignement médiévale', in *Jeux de mémoire: Aspects de la mnémotechnie médiévale*, ed. by Bruno Roy and Paul Zumthor (Paris: Vrin, 1985), pp. 133–46.

[127] *De modo*, p. 214.

[128] Yates, *Art of Memory*, p. 51. Guibert repeats substantially the same advice in the conclusion of his chapter on mnemonics with the words of Encheriades (who may be the rhetorician Fortunatianus) on the usefulness of having the very best writers to hand in one's memory. He recommends word-for-word memorizing if time permits, but if not, that one should assure oneself of knowledge of the matter (*res*) of the speech. Faulty verbatim memorization is dangerous, for the forgetting of one word can lead to hesitation or a complete cessation. He, like Martianus, also prefers to memorize at night, meditating his lesson with a quiet murmur in the silence.

something, we notice that they close their eyes or frequently look at the ground.[129] Although it is true that the author of the *Ad Herennium* advised memorizing one's loci in a deserted place, because it was harder to fix the images in one's mind in a crowd of people, he did not recommend dark places.[130] In fact, it was Albertus Magnus who gave this advice, in words nearly identical to Guibert's.[131] As we shall see below, it is almost certain that Guibert knew Albertus's commentary in Aristotle's *De memoria et reminiscentia*, in which he refers to Cicero's mnemonic advice.

Next, a place can be familiar because memory is sometimes excited by places in which we saw or heard those things which we are trying to remember and which we know to have been done or said there. This is an ancient piece of advice, one so well known that Guibert would not have needed a direct source for it. Quintilian recognized long ago that Simonides' use of mental places arose from common experience: 'For when we return to a place after considerable absence, we not merely recognise the place itself, but remember things that we did there, and recall the persons whom we met and even our unuttered thoughts which passed through our minds when we were there before.'[132] Certainly it was an idea well known in the Franciscan order. One of Guibert's predecessors as lector to the Franciscans in Paris, Jean de La Rochelle, described reminiscence in his *Summa de anima* as

> a searching by means of similar things, for forms deleted from memory through forgetfulness, just as, having forgotten someone whom we saw, we return to the place and time and activity [*ad locum et tempus et actus*] through which we recall the person in such a place, at such and such a time, doing such things.[133]

[129] *De modo*, p. 215.

[130] *Ad Her.*, III.19.

[131] Guibert: 'Volentes enim reminisci trahunt se ad locum solitarium et obscurum, publicum fugientes et lucidum, quia in publico loco et lucido sparguntur imagines sensibilium et confunduntur motus earum, in obscuro vero adunantur et ordinate moventur. Unde Tullius in Secunda Rhetorica ubi traduntur memoriae praecepta dicit quod quaeramus loca obscura, parum lucis habentia' (*De modo*, pp. 214–15). Albertus Magnus: 'Et hujus causa bene volentes reminisci trahunt se a publico lucido, et vadunt ad obscurum privatum: quia in publico lucido loco sparguntur imagines sensibilium, et confunduntur motus eorum. In obscuro autem adunantur et ordinate moventur. Hinc est quod Tullius, in arte memorandi quam ponit in secunda Rhetorica, praecipit ut imaginemur et quaeremus loca obscura parum lucis habentia' (Albertus Magnus, *De memoria et reminiscentia*, II.1, in *Opera omnia*, ed. by Borgnet and others, IX, 108. See Yates's comments on this passage in *Art of Memory*, p. 68.

[132] *Inst. orat.*, XII.2, § 17.

[133] See Jean de La Rochelle, *Tractatus de divisione multiplici potentiarum animae*, ed. by P. Michaud-Quantin (Paris: Vrin, 1964), II.10, p. 77: 'reminiscentia vero est requisitio formarum

Since Guibert includes a long excerpt of Jean's *Summa,* including this very quotation, to explain reminiscence in his chapter on memory's quality, we can be sure he had seen this exact wording before.[134]

Guibert's first two kinds of 'places' refer to one's physical location when storing away or recalling a piece of information and should be contrasted with the last kind of place, a mental one, in which images of things to be remembered are set. Cicero tells us:

> Therefore in the same way that those who know letters are able to write what was said and to recite what they wrote, so those who learn mnemonics are able to set what they learned in places and from them to deliver the memory. For the places are similar to wax or to papyrus, the images to letters, the disposition and arrangement of the images are like writing and the delivery is like reading. Therefore, if we wish to memorize many things, it is necessary that we prepare for ourselves a large number of places, so that we are able to set many images in many places.[135]

Guibert obtains this advice from the *Ad Herennium*, but he also quotes the same comparison of images and places to wax and letters from Martianus Capella and Cicero's *De oratore*.[136] Although Guibert follows his comparison of the places to wax tablets with a long quotation from Cicero's *De oratore* about how Simonides discovered the principals of his art of memory, he does not actually explain how to form the kind of memory places to which these authors are referring.

a memoria deletarum per obliuionem per similia, sicut obliti alicuius persone, quam vidimus, recurrimus ad locum, ad tempus, ad actus, per que recordamur persone, quam vidimus tali loco, tali tempore, talia facientem'. Bonifacio does not include John as a source in his table of fontes at the end of the edition.

[134] *De modo*, p. 202: 'inquisitio formarum a memoria deletarum per oblivionem per consimilia, sicut obliti alicuius persona quam vidimus recurrimus ad locum et tempus et actus per quae recordamur personae, quam vidimus tali loco, tali tempore, talia facientem'. Cf. Jean de La Rochelle, *Tractatus*, II.10 (see n. 133, above). Hugh makes a similar comment in *De tribus* (Green, 'Hugo of St. Victor: *De tribus maximis*', p. 490), as does Quintilian, *Inst. orat.*, X.2, § 17. Coleman (*Ancient and Medieval Memories*, p. 392 n. 10) calls John's definition of reminiscence a synthesis of Aristotelian *reminiscentia* and Ciceronian place theory. It is probably more correct to see John's mnemonics as a combination of Aristotle and a long-established use of the topics, especially the seven circumstances. As we saw above, time and place were two of the circumstances that Hugh used to remember the facts of history in his number-line method and in his ark. John's and Guibert's use of these terms indicate a pronounced mnemonic function for the circumstances.

[135] *De modo*, p. 215.

[136] *Ad Her.*, III.17, p. 278; Capella, *De nuptiis*, V.538, ed. by Willis; Cicero, *De oratore*, I.86, ed. by Wilkins.

According to Guibert, the third memory precept, *actus* or practise, is exceedingly important, for, unless memory is used, it will wither away, no matter how much help it gains from art. Guibert cites three ways to exercise one's memory: reading, writing, and meditating. He has little to say about how reading aids mnemonic practice, other than to quote Martianus Capella that an item for memorization should first be read aloud, and not with a loud voice but rather with the murmur of meditation.[137] In an earlier chapter on how the *ingenium* can be sharpened, Guibert also discussed reading, recommending there some useful tips for memory work, such as limiting one's reading list to a few works that can actually be mastered, rather than trying to read everything, and sticking to shorter works, because, 'since the memory of man is weak, it rejoices in brevity'.[138]

Practice may also be obtained by writing, so long as one writes briefly and moderately. Too much writing fatigues the body, destroys the *ingenium*, and confuses memory. If there is any mnemonic point that seems to reflect Guibert's personal habit, it is the usefulness of writing as an aid to memory. In justification of this point, he quotes Augustine's criticism that some men neglect to write things down because they presume too much on their memory. Guibert seems to have a fairly elastic sense of what writing (*scribere*) means. His only concrete advice here again comes from Martianus Capella: one should first write out what one wishes to memorize and then divide longer selections for memorization into smaller parts, adding *notae* or 'signs' to individual things that one especially wants to retain.[139] Hugh of Saint Victor also gave this advice in *De tribus maximis.*

However, in an earlier chapter on how the *ingenium* can be sharpened by moderate amounts of writing, Guibert includes a cluster of ideas that can elucidate his meaning here. For him, writing can mean correcting exemplars, excerpting notable things that one has read, reducing concepts to the pen, and imprinting memorable things on one's mind![140] Chastising those who so love the beauty of their books that they hesitate to spoil them with corrections, Guibert lists the many reasons why books might need correcting.[141] By excerpting things one has read, Guibert may mean taking notes on one's reading, possibly in the manner of a *florilegium*. The language he uses to describe this process is quite close to what Hugh of St Victor says about collecting: 'Therefore, because time is brief, and we

[137] *De modo*, p. 217.

[138] *De modo*, p. 162.

[139] *De modo*, pp. 217–18.

[140] *De modo*, p. 173.

[141] *De modo*, pp. 174–76.

are occupied with many matters and memory is weak and there are many books [...] it is necessary to collect the better things from many and to serve brevity.'[142] Guibert also seems to think that writing down one's thoughts serves to fix them and keep them from wandering off: 'For the mind [*animus*] is frail [*fluxus*] and transient [*labilis*] and therefore the running about and wandering of one's thoughts ought to be restrained by the chains of writing.'[143] At the end of his sections on writing, Guibert returns to a point he had only mentioned before, that one should imprint memorable things on one's mind. He says that he is passing over the topic now but will cover it more fully in a later chapter on memory. For the present this advice will suffice: that memory is aided by letters.[144] Though he says nothing else about memory in this chapter, Guibert's ultimate point may well be that writing and memorizing are intimate processes and each feeds off the other. One writes from one's well-stocked memory, and one can help stock the memory by writing things down.

There is one kind of writing, however, of which Guibert disapproves as a memory aid. He hastens to warn his students away from those arts called *notariae* or *notoriae*: 'notarial' from the notes or signs which are used in them, or 'notorious' for the knowledge which they give to memory, based on superstition and error. There are two kinds of these notorious arts, major and minor, and both are prohibited. Guibert says that he once made a study of these arts, and discovered 'superficially' devout prayers that he thinks were added so that the arts would look more credible. He also discovered many words which seem to be neither Greek, Hebrew, or Latin and which he could not understand. In one of these arts, observation is made of the stars, as though they could impart ability through their power. In the other art, wondrous signs and drawings are inspected in order to generate the sciences and the arts in memory.[145]

Like most accounts of the mysterious *ars notoria*, Guibert's description is not completely clear, perhaps because the rules for this type of 'memory' are obscure to him. His observations are quite similar to those made in the *Summa theologica/ Summa Alexandri*, where the *ars notoria* is condemned as a superstition because of the mysterious words, observation of the stars, and drawings and lines designed

[142] *De modo*, p. 176.

[143] *De modo*, p. 179. He also says that '[f]or just as the mind wanders when thinking, so it does in reading, and just as reading is beneficial when it is reduced to certitude, so thinking is beneficial when it is recollected in writing'.

[144] *De modo*, p. 187.

[145] *De modo*, p. 218.

to engender knowledge of the arts and sciences.[146] There was obviously a high medieval tradition of condemning the *ars notoria* on theological grounds, and Guibert takes pains to criticize it on technical grounds as well.[147] He quotes the *Ad Herennium* to the effect that using prepared lists of images is bad mnemonic practice, since what works for one person may not aid another.[148]

For Guibert, the last and best type of memory practice is meditation, because it fixes the intention of the mind on a subject. *Meditatio*, according to Hugh of St Victor, is 'sustained thought investigating the manner, the source, and the definition of any thing: manner, what it is; source, why it is; definition, how it is'.[149] Or, following Richard of St Victor's definition, it is 'studious intention of the mind diligently insisting on the investigation of something'. There are three kinds of meditaiton: meditation on creatures, which arises from admiration; on Scripture, which comes from reading; and on mores, from circumspection. Guibert says little more on meditation here, because, as he notes, he has already discussed it above and will say more about it later.[150] We will come back to his ideas about meditation below.

The fourth memory principle that Guibert considers is the method (*modus*) of fashioning memory, and there are three: the collective, divisive, and suppositive of examples. The collective method is one mentioned frequently by Guibert and again comes from Hugh of St Victor:

[146] The work ordinarily attributed to Alexander of Hales is now thought to have been compiled by a number of Franciscan theologians: Alexander of Hales, *Summa theologica* (Florence: Quaracchi, 1930), III.8.1 (775ab), 'De orationibus et figuris artis notorie'.

[147] For other condemnations of the *ars notoria*, see Frank Klaassen, 'English Manuscripts of Magic, 1300–1500: A Preliminary Survey', in *Conjuring Spirits: Texts and Traditions of Medieval Ritual Magic*, ed. by Claire Fanger (University Park: Pennsylvania State University Press, 1998), pp. 14–15. For background on the *ars notoria*, which has been little studied, see Lynn Thorndike, *History of Magic and Experimental Science*, 8 vols (New York: MacMillan, 1923–58), II (1929), 279–89; Yates, *Art of Memory*, pp. 39–43, 204–05; and the articles in Fanger's *Conjuring Spirits*.

[148] *De modo*, p. 218.

[149] *De modo*, p. 218. I have adapted Taylor's translation of *meditatio* from the *Didascalicon* (p. 92) for the sake of consistency.

[150] In saying that he has already discussed meditation, Guibert is probably referring to a discussion in Tractate II, *De causa efficiente doctrinae*, of the *Rudimentum*, in which he discusses how a prelate ought to teach. See Gieben, 'Il *Rudimentum doctrinae*', p. 660 (III.1). Guibert discusses meditation again in *De modo*, pp. 266, 274–75.

> Just as aptitude [*ingenium*] investigates and discovers through analysis [*divisio*], so memory retains through gathering. The things which we have analysed [*dividere*] in the course of learning and which we must commit to memory we ought, therefore, to gather. Now 'gathering' is reducing to a brief and compendious outline things which have been written or discussed at some length.[151]

Collecting would appear to lead inevitably toward *florilegia*, and one often finds advice on the necessity of collecting in the face of mountains of books, brevity of time, and dullness of memory.[152] Division requires that longer things for memorization be broken up into parts, just as Martianus advised above. An unknown Encheriades declares composition and division to be the best aids to memory. Because Guibert's language of method offers us some ideas about how *collectio* and *divisio* were understood in the thirteenth century, we will give extended discussion to them below.

The last method is the *exemplorum suppositivus*, which proceeds through similitudes. Cicero prescribes forming similitudes of things one wishes to remember. Guibert says that

> if we wish to remember a judicial opponent, we should imagine something with huge horns in judgement coming at us in the dark. For the horns prompt us to recall our adversary, and the memory of milk is recalled through whiteness, and so on concerning other things, as is obvious in the art of memory.[153]

Cicero identifies two kinds of these similitudes, one for things and one for words. When one reduces an entire fact under a 'simple image, or similitude, or exemplum', one creates a similitude for things. These images ought to be as striking as possible, and here Guibert quotes the passage from the *Ad Herennium* describing *imagines agentes*. Guibert prefers not to discuss images for words, since words are infinite in number. Nor does he much approve of a book entitled *Liber de notis Senecae*, again because he dislikes prepared images.[154]

[151] Because Guibert has quoted Hugh's *Didascalicon* nearly exactly, I have used Taylor's translation, p. 93.

[152] Vincent de Beauvais lists two pages of classical and medieval allusions to the problem, *De eruditione*, XVIII.66–67.

[153] *De modo*, p. 220: 'ut si voluerimus recordari eius qui adversatur nobis in iudicio, imaginemur aliquem in obscuro magnis cornibus in iudicio [*sic*] contra nos venientem: cornua enim ducunt memoriam in reminiscentiam adversarii; et memoria lactis reducitur per album; et ita de aliis, ut patet in arte memoriae'.

[154] Perhaps this is the work on memory prepared by Seneca that John of Salisbury wished that he could read? See Chapter 1, p. 40, above.

Guibert's advice about forming similitudes offers a rare example of a synthesis of the *Ad Herennium*'s advice and Aristotle's scientific thinking about memory in his *De memoria et reminiscentia*. In this he is not alone, for Albertus Magnus made very similar comments in his commentary on *De memoria*. Albertus's version is very similar but not identical. In a discussion of reminiscence, he comments:

> For example, if we wish to recall the person who opposes us in a court case, we should imagine some ram in the dark with great horns and great testicles coming against us; for the horns prompt us to recall our opponent and the testicles prompt us to recall the arrangement of those testifying.[155]

Without a knowledge of the *Ad Herennium*, it is not clear why a horned ram attacking us in the dark should aid our memory; because these two examples provide illustrations of memory images, it is worth trying to tease the meaning out of them.

We should first examine Albertus's similitude, which is significant both for its resemblance and its dissimilarity to the exemplar given in the *Ad Herennium*. The rhetorical manual's one example of a memory image for *res* runs as follows:

> For example, the prosecutor has said that the defendant killed a man by poison, has charged the motive for the crime an inheritance, and declared that there are many witnesses and accessories to this act. If in order to facilitate our defense we wish to remember this first point, we shall in our first background [*locus*] form an image of the whole matter. We shall picture the man in question as lying ill in bed, if we know his person. If we do not know him, we shall yet take some one to be our invalid, but not a man of the lowest class, so that he may come to mind at once. And we shall place the defendant at the bedside, holding in his right hand a cup, and in his left tablets, and on the fourth finger a ram's testicles.[156]

Albertus's own commentary on this passage, which he quotes in *De bono*, is

> in the cup is the memory of the poison, which he [the defendant] administered, and in the tablets is the memory of the inheritance, on which he wrote, and in the doctor is the figure of the accusor and in the testicles the figure of the witnesses <and> accomplices and in the ram the prosecution of the defendant in court.[157]

[155] Albertus, *De memoria et reminiscentia*, II.1, ed. by Borgnet, p. 108: 'sicut si volumus recordari ejus quod adversatur nobis in judicio, imaginemur aliquem arietem in obscuro magnis cornibus et magnis testiculis contra nos venientem. Cornua enim ducunt in recordationem adversarii, et testiculi ducunt in dispositionem testium.' Translation from Albertus Magnus, *Commentary* on Aristotle, *On Memory and Recollection*, trans. by Jan M. Ziolkowski, in *Medieval Craft of Memory*, ed. by Carruthers and Ziolkowski, pp. 118–52 (p. 138).

[156] *Ad Her.*, III.20, pp. 33–34 (Caplan's translation).

[157] Albertus Magnus, *De bono*, tr. IV. De prudentia. q. 2. art. 2 (16): 'ut scilicet in poculo sit memoria veneni, quod propinavit et in tabulis memoria haereditatis sit, quas subscripsit, et in

Here Albertus appears to have a good understanding of how the *Ad Herennium*'s memory image was supposed to function. Because Albertus seems to understand the *Ad Herennium*'s similitude perfectly in *De bono*, Yates found Albertus's image-making in *De memoria* odd, attributing the ram 'careening loose in the darkness' to too much nocturnal memory work.[158] Interestingly, Albertus probably wrote his commentary on *De memoria* after he wrote *De bono*.[159] Why then the change in the later commentary? One possibility may be that Albertus was trying to simplify the example to suit readers of his commentary on *De memoria*. He merely wanted to demonstrate Aristotle's reminiscence through Cicero's advice.

Guibert's version of the memory image may offer us additional information. He has added the association of whiteness to milk as an example of image-making. Though this association is not part of the original court case, a reading of Thomas Aquinas's commentary on *De memoria* can make Guibert's connection intelligible. In *De memoria* Aristotle tells us that

> it is necessary [in remembering] for there to be a beginning point; for this reason some people sometimes are seen to recall from places. The reason for this is that they move quickly from one thing to another, as from milk to white, from white to air and from it to dampness.[160]

medico figura sit accusatoris et in testiculis figura testium <et>? consciorum et in ariete defensio contra reum in iudicio'. Albertus here takes the *medicum* to mean 'doctor', while the original text has *medico* 'on the fourth finger.'

[158] Yates, *Art of Memory*, pp. 68–69.

[159] Carruthers assumes that he wrote the commentary on *De memoria* first, gaining a better comprehension of the example given in *Ad Herennium* by the time he wrote about artificial memory in *De Bono* (*Book of Memory*, p. 143). Unfortunately for this sensible explanation, Albertus probably wrote *De Bono* first. According to James Weisheipl, all parts of Albertus's *Summa Parisiensis*, which includes *De Bono* (Part IV), were finished by the time Albertus started writing Book II of the *Sentences* in 1246. Weisheipl places the date of the commentary on the *Parva naturalia* (and thus, *De memoria et reminiscentia*) after the *De anima*, written between June 1254 and June 1257, and before *De vegetabilibus*, composed before 1260–61. This would give us a rough chronology of *De bono* by 1246, *De memoria* between June 1257 and December 1261, and Guibert's *De modo* 1264–68 (James Weisheipl, 'The Life and Works of St. Albert the Great', in *Albertus Magnus and the Sciences: Commemorative Essays 1980*, ed. by James Weisheipl (Toronto: Pontifical Institute of Mediaeval Studies, 1980), pp. 13–53 (pp. 22, 569–72)).

[160] Aristotle, *De memoria et reminiscentia*, chap. 2, 452, in Thomas Aquinas, *De memoria et reminiscentia*, ed. by Spiazzi, I, lect. VI.372: 'Oportet autem acceptum esse principum. Propter quod a locis viduntur reminisci aliquando. Causa autem est, quia velociter ab alio in aliud veniunt: ut a lacte in album, ab albo autem in aërem et ab hoc in humidum.'

Thomas's response to this is, 'For instance, if we think or speak of milk, we easily pass to white on account of the whiteness of milk; and from white to air on account of the clarity of the transparent medium of light which causes whiteness; and from air to moisture, because air is moist.'[161] According to Thomas, people's minds pass easily from one idea to another through the principles of likeness, contrariety, or closeness. Guibert must have had the same Aristotelian principles in mind when he drew on Albertus's exemplum to make his point. Thus, his conclusion, 'for the horns prompt us to recall our adversary, and the memory of milk is recalled through whiteness, and so on concerning other things, as is obvious in the art of memory' is an example of two kinds of mnemonic association: the horns for the adversary and whiteness for milk. Read this way, his image makes more sense. Because of the closeness of the texts, it seems likely that Guibert had been exposed to Albertus's writings or teachings. Their careers overlapped at Paris (Albertus Magnus was at Paris from 1245 to 1248, while Guibert was a master of arts in Paris in 1240, when he decided to join the Franciscans there). He quite likely had access either to Albertus's writings themselves or had heard him or a fellow Dominican speak on this point. Given Albertus's influence on the Dominican study of natural philosophy, Guibert might have picked up Albertus's ideas from a Dominican other than Albertus himself.[162] The verbal echoes of these accounts could also testify to a tradition of medieval memory interpretation developing in the schools.

Guibert's and Albertus's dissection of the *Ad Herennium*'s memory image demonstrates how medieval authors confronted ancient mnemonic texts. They attempted to reconcile Cicero with Aristotle, sometimes in an obscure fashion. Thus, their nocturnal ram is probably not an indication of too much memory work or an interest in the occult, as Yates surmised, but rather represents a simplified memory image used to illustrate Aristotelian principles.

Now that we have looked at all of Guibert's instructions for forming memory, we can ask what mnemonic system Guibert practised. If one reviews his precepts, one will see that most are not incompatible with one another. He declares that one needs four things to improve one's memory: time, practise, place, and method. Time refers mainly to when one should memorize, practise to the need to test out the precepts that one has so diligently learned, whether by reading, writing, or meditating. Guibert equivocates on the term *locus*, meaning sometimes the

[161] Thomas Aquinas, *De memoria et reminiscentia*, ed. by Spiazzi, I, lect. VI.378: 'sicut si cogitemus vel loquamur de lacte, de facili pervenimus in album propter lactis albedinem'; Thomas Aquinas, *Commentary*, trans. by Burchill, p. 179.

[162] See Mulchahey, *'First the Bow'*, pp. 254–67.

place where one goes to memorize or where one first saw or heard something and sometimes the places of the *Ad Herennium*. Finally, method may refer to what one actually does, either keeping mental or written notes as in 'gathering' and 'dividing' what one reads, or memorizing images for what one wishes to remember. Since only two of the many kinds of recommendations actually come from the *Ad Herennium*, my conclusion is that, if he used a system at all, it was something close to Hugh's or to Martianus's recommendations, and having come upon the place and images system, tried to work it in. It is entirely possible that one might use the rules for images to construct more elaborate *notae* along the lines of Martianus's plan. However, though Guibert probably drew heavily on these earlier ideas, he put them in a thirteenth-century context, as his language of method shows.

## *Method and Division in the Thirteenth Century*

Method (*modus*) was a thirteenth-century concern. As Alastair J. Minnis has demonstrated, thirteenth-century theologians investigated the grounds for true knowledge or science as related in Aristotle's *Metaphysica*. They were particularly interested in the degree to which theology could be called a science. Some theologians, such as Alexander of Hales, Robert Kilwardby, and Richard Fishacre, distinguished between human science, whose end is knowledge, and divine science, whose end is wisdom.[163] Each kind of science was thought to possess its own methods. According to Hales and Kilwardby, human science depends on reason and thus employs the definitive, divisive, and collective methods. Divine science has need of more rhetorical methods, such as the preceptive, exemplifying, and revelatory. The methods for human reason are drawn from Aristotle's rules for syllogisms, but can be applied to science. Thus, the definitive method delimits the subject matter of a science, division names the parts of a science, and collection or *ratiocinatio* is necessary for the knowledge of complex things, that is, propositions.[164] One other method, the *modus exemplorum suppositivus*, is not strictly necessary for human science, but can be useful for beginners.

[163] Minnis, *Medieval Theory of Authorship*, p. 119.

[164] Robert Kilwardby, *De natura theologiae*, ed. by Fridericus Stegmüller (Münster: Aschendorff monasterii, 1935), quest. 3.28: 'Et ideo istae scientiae quae humana ratione perquirunt verum, necesse habent definire, dividere et colligere [...]. Divisio, ut per eam cognoscatur subiectum scientiae [...]. Definitio autem est necesse propter partes et species subiecti, ut diviso genere subiecto per proprias differentias seu partes, ipsae partes aut species per priora se definitive cognoscantur. Collectio vero sive ratiocinatio est necessaria propter cognitionem complexorum.'

This is the terminology that Guibert uses to discuss memory precepts, applying the methods of human science to order the rules for memory. Evidently syllogistic language has become so commonplace that it will describe any subject: Guibert uses the same terms when he discusses preaching in the second part of the *Rudimentum*.[165] However, the authorities that he employs to illustrate definition, collection, and division are not logical works but Hugh of St Victor and Martianus Capella. For Guibert, collection is equivalent to Hugh's epilogue or a 'brief recapitulation' of a reading. Division is the separation of the material to be learned into parts. Guibert stresses that division provides order:

> As Martianus says, the divisive method is so that, if the longer things which need to be memorised are divided by parts, they stick in the memory more easily. Encheriades asks, 'What especially aids memory? Composition and division. For order strongly serves memory, just as we can see from Simonides' party'. Nevertheless, notice that we ought not always to seek things in the order in which they were seen, but to distribute them in appropriate places. Every division begins from finite things and progresses to infinite ones: every finite thing is better known and more easily understood by knowledge.[166]

Following the rhetoricians Fortunatianus and Martianus, Guibert thinks that division provides a retrievable order for the text.

One further way to understand the variable meanings of division in the thirteenth century is to look at the *forma tractandi* and the *forma tractatus* of the *accessus ad auctores* or introductions to texts in the High Middle Ages. These two related methods of describing the authorial role developed in the thirteenth century.[167] The *forma tractandi* refers to the form of writing; for Scripture it indicates the method of a particular book and is based on the discussion of knowledge indicated above. Thus, the exemplifying mode might be used in the Apocrypha and the prophetic mode in Isaiah. The divisive mode in this sense could be used in composing a text to give the parts of the subject of a science, to divide genera into species, arts into component parts, etc. An example might be Kilwardby's *De ortu scientiarum*, which proceeds by separating the sciences and

[165] See Bonifacio's table of the *Rudimentum*'s contents, *De modo*, p. 26.

[166] *De modo*, p. 220: 'Modus autem divisivus est "ut, sicut dicit Martianus, si longiora fuerint quae sunt ediscenda divisa per partes facilius inhaerescant." Unde Encheriades: "Quid maxime memoriam adiuvat? Divisio et compositio. Nam memoriam vehementer servat ordo sicut accepimus ex Simonidis convivio." Tamen hoc attende quod non semper eo ordine quo aspecta sunt debemus repetere, sed opportunis locis disponere. Omnis divisio incipit a finitis et ad infinita progreditur: omne autem finitum magis est notum et magis scientia comprehensum.'

[167] Minnis, *Medieval Theory of Authorship*, p. 118.

their parts one from another. This kind of division is similar to that discussed in Hugh's *Didascalicon*.

A second kind of division, a physical one of the text, can be seen in the *forma tractatus*. It refers to how an author orders his material and is also called *divisio textus*.[168] This kind of division does not arbitrarily parcel up the text but rather divides according to the ideas contained in the narrative. It reflects a general interest in the thirteenth century in ordering material in a logical way. This second sense of division may be a descendent of the mnemonic division described in Hugh's *De tribus maximis*. In fact, Guibert's own work is an ideal example of how rubrics could be used to divide and recombine well-known material into something new. Whatever principles of mnemonics Guibert recommended, his practice was likely something close to this kind of division.

These are some of the ways that the thirteenth-century authors adapted Hugh's advice. Because of the changing literary needs of the thirteenth century caused by the new preaching industry and the expansion of the universities, thirteenth-century pedagogues could be relentlessly practical in the ways they put ideas like Hugh's into effect. A good example of this practicality are Robert Kilwardby's *Tabulae super originalia*. They consist of a threefold system of patristic aids: an *Intencio*, a *Tabula*, and a *Concordancia*. In the *Intencio*, also called *Conclusiones* or *Capitula*, Kilwardby summarizes the contents of selected patristic writings for students. He divides each book into small sections and analyzes the contents. Thus laid out the teachings of the works can be grasped and remembered at a glance. One manuscript pointed out this twofold utility:

> But in front of these volumes of blessed Augustine are placed *conclusiones* of certain books by blessed Augustine, compiled in the order of chapters by brother Robert Kilwardby, of the Order of Preachers, Archbishop of Canterbury and finally Cardinal of Porto. Which *conclusiones* are especially useful for him who wishes to know the teachings of St Augustine and to retain it in memory.[169]

These conclusions are likely a version of Hugh's collection method: they grasp the heart of a chapter (as in Vincent de Beauvais's *intencio*) and lead the student into

[168] Minnis, *Medieval Theory of Authorship*, p. 145.

[169] Cambridge, Gonville and Caius College, MS 108, fol. 2$^r$, cited in Daniel A. Callus, *The 'Tabulae super originalia patrum' of Robert Kilwardby, O.P.* (Bruges: De Tempel, 1948), p. 255: 'Sed ante ista volumina beati Augustini premittuntur conclusiones quorundam librorum beati Augustini secundum capitula eorundem compilate, sicut estimo, per fratrem Robertum de Killwardeby ordinis Predicatorum, archiepiscopum Cantuariensem ac tandem Cardinalem Portuensem, que sunt nimis utiles volenti scire doctrinam sancti Augustini et eam memoriter retinere.'

the whole of Augustine's thought. Hugh probably would not have provided his students with such a tool, preferring them to create their own collection as they read Augustine's works. By the thirteenth century, students and preachers were in a bigger hurry to get information.

## *The Influence of Hugh of St Victor on the Franciscans*

Guibert's treatment of memory in *De modo addiscendi* represents some changed attitudes toward memory and learning since the time of Hugh of St Victor. It has become more important to explain how memory functions, and the sources are available to attempt such an explanation. Guibert also seems to know more mnemonic sources than Hugh did and to try to merge them together. Because of this conflation, Guibert's description of memory precepts is less coherent than Hugh's.

However, in some ways he has much in common with Hugh. Both Guibert and Hugh include memory as part of an educational programme. Both also attempt to order the knowledge available to himself. The influx of the new learning rendered Guibert's task much more difficult than Hugh's. Guibert does not arrange his material pictorially, as Hugh does in the ark, but instead chooses well-known medieval rubrics to act as mnemonic 'hooks' for the ensuing material: the *Rudimentum*'s four causes, subdivided into *De modo*'s formal cause, then master and pupil, etc. These are memorable subheadings, dependent on the all-important concepts of order and division. This, then, is an example of how mnemonic precepts were used to order material on the page as well as in the memory. Guibert's scheme was one that required a certain educational background to appreciate, that is, familiarity with Hugh of St Victor, Pseudo-Dionysius, and Aristotle. It would not be immediately accessible to anyone lacking that background. In Chapter 4, we will see how these concepts were applied to preaching.

In drawing so extensively on the mnemonic ideas of Hugh of St Victor, Guibert was completely in step with other Franciscan writers. In *Reading the Book of History*, Bert Roest has shown the importance of Franciscan historiography to Franciscan self-identity and to Franciscan education. Though the Franciscans put a great deal of emphasis on preaching to the laity, they were still a religious order with concern for the religious lives of their members. Roest thinks the Franciscans inherited a monastic legacy of *lectio* and *meditatio*.[170] The point of their spiritual

[170] Roest, 'Reading the Book of History', p. 134.

exercises in Franciscan terms was to acquire *christoformitas*, a concept that we have already encountered in Guibert's work.[171] To help prepare its members both for their preaching ministry and for their religious formation, the Franciscans, like the Dominicans, developed a series of provincial schools.[172] Within these schools, theology naturally played an important part, and within their theological programme, biblical exegesis was paramount. Roest thinks that the Franciscans saw history as a primary tool for exegetical studies, and that Franciscan theologians looked back to twelfth-century scholars, especially to the Victorines, as models.[173] Since we have already seen how integral mnemonic learning was to Hugh's sense of history as the foundation of biblical studies, it should not come as a surprise to see the same emphasis in Franciscan historical writing and exegesis.

Although this topic could be explored in greater depth, I want to point to just one example here: the *Satirica ystoria* of Paolino da Venezia (*c.* 1274–1344).[174] The *Satirica* was a kind of universal history, consisting of 238 chapters devoted to pre-Christian history, the history of the Gospels and the apostles, and the subsequent history of Roman emperors in the West down to Henry VII of Luxembourg.[175] What is most pertinent to our interests here is the supplementary material to the main text. Paolino placed sixteen thematic and alphabetical registers (*tabulae*) in the manuscript preceding the chronicle, which include lists of Gospel readings for the lectionary, lists of saints, hermits, Church fathers, and classical philosophers, as well as heretics and heresies.[176] They all refer to the corresponding chapters and paragraphs in the main text. The inclusion of this material seems to accord well with Hugh of St Victor's advice to learn the 'circumstances' of history, especially of people. Two other learning supplements that reflect Hugh's influence are a *linea regularis* and a *mappa mundi*.[177] The *linea* functions as a kind of time table, with all the rulers 'depicted' with distinctive features. There are also parallel *lineae* listing contemporary events. These *lineae*

[171] Roest, 'Reading the Book of History', p. 138.

[172] Roest, 'Reading the Book of History', pp. 130–31. We will return to the topic of the Franciscan schools in Chapter 8, below.

[173] Roest, 'Reading the Book of History', p. 153.

[174] Roest, 'Reading the Book of History', chap. 7.

[175] Roest, 'Reading the Book of History', pp. 259–62.

[176] Vatican City, Biblioteca Apostolica Vaticana, MS fondo vaticano latino 1960, fols 28$^{r}$–47$^{r}$, cited in Roest, 'Reading the Book of History', pp. 254–55.

[177] Roest, 'Reading the Book of History', pp. 255–56.

are clearly an offshoot of Hugh's mnemonic advice in the preface to the *Chronicon*, as we saw in Chapter 1. They act as timelines to aid the reader while reading and memorizing the text and are an example of a once invisible mnemonic function used to organize material on the page. Roest also sees Paolino's work as a summa for meditation for the Franciscans. It could act as a promptbook for memory and for new compositions.[178]

[178] Roest, 'Reading the Book of History', p. 274.

Chapter 3

# FRANCISCAN MEMORY AND MEDITATION

Though Guibert de Tournai's *De modo addiscendi* specifically addresses the topic of artificial memory techniques, it was not the only conduit of training in *memoria* for the Franciscans. An older, monastic view was transmitted to the order through the writings of David von Augsburg, among others. One of the most influential Franciscan works on monastic exercises was his *De exterioris et interioris hominis compositione secundum triplicem statum incipientium, proficientium et perfectorum*. Although often referred to under the composite title above, the book more regularly circulated as three works: the *Formula de compositione hominis exterioris ad novitios*; the *Formula de interioris hominis reformatione ad proficientes*; and *De septem processibus religiosorum* or *De profectu religiosorum*.[1] Master of novices at Regensburg starting around 1240, David von Augsburg (*c.* 1200–1272) wrote the works as three separate books for the novices at Regensburg and for those of the Strasbourg province of the Franciscan order.[2] His works reflect the growing importance of the noviciate in

[1] Roest, *History of Franciscan Education*, p. 244. I have used the Latin edition available in Bonaventura, *Opera omnia: Sixti V., pontificis maximi jussu diligentissime emendata*, ed. by Adolpho Carolo Peltier, 15 vols (Paris: Vives, 1864–71), XII, 292–442. In this edition, the sections of David von Augsburg's works are titled differently: the *Formula de compositione hominis exterioris ad novitios* is entitled *De institutione novitiorum*, pp. 292–312. This work in turn is divided into two parts: 'Pars prima seu de compositione hominis exterioris' and 'Pars secunda seu viginti passus de virtutibus bonorum religiosorum'. The *Formula de interioris hominis reformatione ad proficientes* is called *De profectu religiosorum*, bk I, pp. 326–61, and *De septem processibus religiosorum* is *De profectu religiosorum*, bk II, pp. 362–442. For translations into English, I have relied on David von Augsburg, *Spiritual Life and Progress*, trans. by Dominic Devas, 2 vols (London: Burns, Oates, and Washbourne, 1937), except where a more literal translation helps to illustrate my arguments.

[2] Roest, *History of Franciscan Education*, p. 244. For biographical and bibliographical information about David von Augsburg, see John Moorman, *A History of the Franciscan Order from*

the Franciscan order. They also demonstrate the kind of religious programme that the friars were expected to follow, a programme that incorporated earlier Benedictine, Cistercian, and Victorine practices.[3] Though I will concentrate on David's work in this chapter, I argue that because of the widespread diffusion of his work both within the Franciscan order initially and then across Europe in the later Middle Ages, his ideas offer insight into the practices of the order as a whole.

## *Disciplining Memory*

In the *De exterioris et interioris hominis compositione*, the disciplining and refashioning of memory forms a crucial part of the religious life. While the first book on the exterior man occasionally recommends some disciplining of memory, not surprisingly, it is in the two books on the interior man and on progress in the spiritual life that David von Augsburg treats memory most fully. Drawing upon a Cistercian anthropology (one that had been heavily influenced by St Augustine), he identifies three powers, or faculties, of the soul: understanding (*ratio*), memory (*memoria*), and will (*voluntas*).[4] Because of sin, the image of God in the soul along with these three powers has been distorted. The way to God involves restoring the image, and it can only be done by reforming the three faculties.[5] Sin has had the effect of blinding the reason, weakening the will, and setting the memory wandering along an endless number of useless paths.[6] Injuries to all of these areas block spiritual progress, but here we will concentrate only on memory. David says memory should be able to touch the eternity of God, because once one has

*its Origins to the Year 1517* (Oxford: Clarendon Press, 1968), p. 263 n. 275; André Rayez, 'David d'Augsbourg', in *Dictionnaire de spiritualité*, ed. by Viller, Cavallera, and de Guibert, III, 42–44; Kurt Ruh, 'David von Augsburg', *Die deutsche Literatur des Mittelalters: Verfasserlexikon*, ed. by Kurt Ruh and others, 2nd edn (Berlin: de Gruyter, 1977–), II, 47–58. For a full and recent discussion of the evidence for the biographical details of David's life, see Cornelius Bohl, *Geistlicher Raum: Räumliche Sprachbilder als Träger spiritueller Erfahrung, dargestellt am Werk De compositione des David von Augsburg*, Franziskanische Forschungen, 42 (Werl: Coelde, 2000).

[3] Roest, *History of Franciscan Education*, pp. 243–44.

[4] Ruh, 'David von Augsburg', p. 50. David von Augsburg, *De profectu religiosorum*, I.4, pp. 335–36; David von Augsburg, *Spiritual Life and Progress*, trans. by Devas, I, 81.

[5] Roest, *History of Franciscan Education*, p. 246, also stresses the importance of this theme in David von Augsburg's thought.

[6] David von Augsburg, *De profectu religiosorum*, I.4, p. 336: 'Sed per peccatum ratio caeca facta est, voluntas curva et foeda, memoria instabilis et vaga'; David von Augsburg, *Spiritual Life and Progress*, trans. by Devas, I, 84.

learned to keep God in mind at all times, one is no longer separated from God.[7] Unfortunately, such utter concentration is beyond the capacity of most people's memories in an unreformed state.

Memory's problem is thus that it cannot control itself. Rather than fixing itself upon God, it wanders from topic to topic, seduced by one distraction after another. The solution to memory's instability is order and discipline, and David outlines how such discipline might be attained:

> The beginning of the renovation of the memory is to strive to recall it from its habitual wandering to the thought of God by means of prayer, reading, recollection and reflection, however shallow still. Progress is seen by the success attained in freeing meditation and prayer from importunate distractions. [...] Its perfection lies in being so caught up with and absorbed in God as to be forgetful of self and all created things, and, without any stir of fugitive thoughts and imaginings, to rest sweetly in God alone.[8]

As one sees throughout his discussion of religious life, there are three stages to the overhaul of memory: one for beginners, one for those becoming proficient, and one for those nearing perfection. These stages are the same ones identified by Guibert de Tournai. Beginners train memory to think about God through the spiritual exercises of prayer, reading, and the like. Proficients see their progress in increased concentration on God while meditating and praying; and those reaching perfection can focus so completely on God as to be entirely forgetful of self. One might see the ultimate goal of memory as the kind of 'flow' desired by athletes, in which they perform perfectly without any conscious thought. According to J. Heerinckx, all of these concepts likely had their origin in Guillaume de Saint-Thierry's *Golden Epistle*.[9] David took the idea of the three stages of religious from William, as well as the need to have God always in memory.

Having identified the problems of the three faculties in Book II, David returns to the topic in the third work, *De septem processibus religiosorum* or *De profectu religiosorum*. Progress for a religious soul has seven stages, though not every soul has to pass through each one of them: 'Fervour, Austerity and Consolation — these are the first three — Temptation, Self-mastery, Holiness, Wisdom; these are

[7] David von Augsburg, *De profectu religiosorum*, I.7, p. 337; David von Augsburg, *Spiritual Life and Progress*, trans. by Devas, I, 81.

[8] David von Augsburg, *De profectu religiosorum*, I.7, p. 337; David von Augsburg, *Spiritual Life and Progress*, trans. by Devas, I, 86.

[9] P. Jacques Heerinckx, 'Influence de l'Epistola ad Fratres de Monte Dei sur la composition de l'homme extérieur et intérieur de David d'Augsbourg', *Études franciscaines*, 45 (1933), 330–47 (pp. 334 and 339).

the remaining four.'[10] The soul can find the third stage, consolation, through 'the supernatural adornment of the natural powers of the mind'.[11] The powers of the mind or soul, in which there is the image of the highest Trinity, are again the understanding, will, and memory (*ratio*, *voluntas*, and *memoria*), which have no good in them until they have been adorned and filled by God. God illuminates the understanding toward the knowledge of the True; he inflames the will toward the love of God; and he helps memory to be quieted toward adhering to and enjoying the good. None of these powers can be perfected without the adornment of the others.[12] David says that memory's adornment consists in 'an abundance of holy thoughts, a flow of useful meditations, a firm (*stabilis*) memory of God, and the shutting out of wandering thoughts, and the tranquil clinging to God, and the repression of bodily imaginings, and the complete forgetfulness of all worldly matters, and to be *one Spirit* with God'.[13] David here adds slightly to his earlier explanation of improving memory's role in spiritual development. As before, he identifies the need to stop memory's tendency to wander from thought to thought. What is needed is a *stabilis* or firm memory of God, along with useful meditations, and the shutting out of 'corporeal' imaginings and worldly matters in order to become one with God.

How does one accomplish this task? In the same way that he scatters his identification of memory's problem throughout his texts, David also offers numerous solutions throughout his works. One solution is the spiritual exercise, 'De suspensione mentis in Deum'.[14] By this exercise, he means keeping the mind constantly raised up to or focused on God, which one does 'by praying, thinking, remembering, meditating, reading, directing one's attention, and by contemplating good things'.[15] That this exercise is about memory can be seen in Augsburg's

[10] David von Augsburg, *Spiritual Life and Progress*, trans. by Devas, II, 3. Cf. David von Augsburg, *De profectu religiosorum*, II.1.

[11] David von Augsburg, *De profectu religiosorum*, II.1, p. 363; David von Augsburg, *Spiritual Life and Progress*, trans. by Devas, II, 5.

[12] David von Augsburg, *De profectu religiosorum*, II.1, p. 363; David von Augsburg, *Spiritual Life and Progress*, trans. by Devas, II, 4–5.

[13] David von Augsburg, *De profectu religiosorum*, II.1, p. 363; my translation (though Dominic Devas's translation is expressed more felicitously than mine, a somewhat more literal translation is helpful for my argument).

[14] David von Augsburg, *De profectu religiosorum*, II.20, p. 380; David von Augsburg, *Spiritual Life and Progress*, trans. by Devas, II, 43–52. It is one of seven important spiritual exercises.

[15] David von Augsburg, *De profectu religiosorum*, II.20, p. 380.

comment that '[t]he summit of heavenly bliss is found in the uninterrupted vision of God; and, for us on earth, the nearest approach to such beatitude is found in being unceasingly mindful of God'.[16] The memory of God should occupy the religious not only in leisure but also when occupied with other matters.

Another solution involves interior discipline and the 'memory of the benefits of God'. In the first book on the exterior man, David stresses the need for discipline in the various contexts of the novice's life. Discipline in serving the Mass requires a reminder that the Mass is the daily descent of God upon the altar: 'Here he has left to us a memorial of all His love, a summary of all His benefits.'[17] He reveals what those benefits are in his next sentence: 'The Incarnation, the redemption, the resurrection, our own justification and glorification, all are gathered here as it were in open vision before us.'[18] He also recommends dwelling on one of those benefits as part of discipline in the dormitory. Whenever the novice wakes in the night, he should 'bring to mind at once the gracious memory of Christ and His Passion'.[19] The trope, the 'memory of the benefits of God', is clearly influenced by Cistercian authors, as we shall see. His recommendation to bring the Passion to mind when waking at night also recalls the emphasis on the Passion in *De domo interiori* as a way to drive away depraved thoughts, as outlined below.

Another recommendation for interior discipline occurs in the final chapters of the third book. Here David becomes a little more specific about how recollection can progress. Much of his advice occurs in his chapter on prayer. As any one who has ever participated in a church service knows, it is very easy to let one's mind wander during prayers, whether one is hearing set prayers or praying in one's own words. For David the key to this problem is to fix one's attention on the

[16] David von Augsburg, *De profectu religiosorum*, II.20, p. 380; David von Augsburg, *Spiritual Life and Progress*, trans. by Devas, II, 53.

[17] David von Augsburg, *De institutione novitiorum*, I.11, p. 296; David von Augsburg, *Spiritual Life and Progress*, trans. by Devas, I, 13.

[18] David von Augsburg, *De institutione novitiorum*, I.11, p. 296: 'Et ideo hoc est memoriale totius dilectionis suae, et quasi compendium quoddam omnium beneficiorum suorum, quos nobis reliquit: incarnationis, redemptionis, glorificationis et justificationis figuram in hoc inclusit, sicut patet his, qui considerant hujius sacramenti institutionem, celebrationem, et fructus participationem'; David von Augsburg, *Spiritual Life and Progress*, trans. by Devas, I, 13.

[19] David von Augsburg, *De institutione novitiorum*, I.9, p. 295: 'Quoties autem evigilaveris, statim occurrat tibi memoria Dei et ejus passionis, cum gratiarum actione, quia ipse vigiliat super nos, quando dormimus, ut ipse custodiat nos'; David von Augsburg, *Spiritual Life and Progress*, trans. by Devas, I, 10–11.

business at hand. First, the religious should pay attention to be sure that he is saying the right prayer in the right place. Then he should pay attention to the literal meaning of the words. Focusing on the actual words, rather than merely mouthing them, helps to keep the mind from wandering.[20] David does not think this fixing of attention is easy, but it is part of the control of imagination necessary for success in religious life. He also lists the control of imagination as the first step going up the ladder of prayer.[21]

Finally, one other way that David suggests for refashioning his memory pertains to the inculcation of virtue and the rooting out of vice, matters which fall under the provenance of the will. It must be remembered that for David, reforming one's memory is only part of the problem, along with reforming one's understanding and will. But the process was begun in the first book about improving the exterior man, where much time was spent on the vices and their remedies, the virtues. One can hardly concentrate on God when one's attention is still taken up with sinful and worldly matters. He returns to these issues in the last book by talking about temptation, self-mastery, and the virtues. For David memory provides the weapons for self-mastery, another step in spiritual progress. Returning again to his theme of memory's tendency toward idle thoughts, he warns about the need to drive them away the moment they appear:

> Not only should we drive away immediately carnal and shameful thoughts, but also idle [*vanas*], and bitter [*amaras*], and gluttonous [*gulosas*] ones, and we ought not to paint in imagination the likeness [*simulacra*] of similar vices in the temple of our hearts. Theaters and taverns [*tabernae*] are accustomed to be adorned with paintings of worldly and theatrical stories, but temples are decorated with sacred histories and mystical pictures. By the quality of the picture, the quality of the house and of the lord residing there is discerned. Sometimes pride paints for itself prelacies and lordships, the obsequies of servants, and other pompous things. Vain glory paints for itself any kind of ornate thing and the means by which it can acquire the praise of men. And sometimes it paints moral purity and miracles, prophecies and great devotions, and edifying sermons, and many similar things, from which public admiration arises, and hidden praise and reverence may be displayed. So envy moves fraud and detraction, anger brawls and contention, wars and outcries. [...] Therefore he who does not wish to drive away the good guest [*hospitem*] Christ from the lodging of his heart, must not receive his enemies, namely the vices, with himself.[22]

[20] David von Augsburg, *De profectu religiosorum*, II.57, pp. 411–12; David von Augsburg, *Spiritual Life and Progress*, trans. by Devas, II, 131–32.

[21] David von Augsburg, *Spiritual Life and Progress*, trans. by Devas, II, 71.

[22] David von Augsburg, *De profectu religiosorum*, II.15, p. 378; my translation.

Here David begins to get to the heart of how memory gains control of itself. The soul of a monk or friar is like a dwelling decorated with the images of what it thinks about or remembers. It is covered either with the stories of worldly life, pictures of fights and brawls and scenes of public admiration, or it can be painted with scenes from Scripture and religious images. As David says, 'curiosity paints some beautiful and curious things; greed, full tables and various kinds of food and drink; lechery, also, paints fantastically the things which are congruent to itself'. The reader should not take this passage purely as metaphor. Rather David really means that the religious should expunge from his memory images of vice and replace them with images of a more fitting nature. 'Here are the idols which God showed painted on the walls of the temple to Ezechiel, which he also called "abominations". He should wipe these things with care from the temple of our heart, lest we become abominable to God, just as they are.'[23] Memory works both to extirpate vice and to construct a better focus for itself: the cultivation of virtue. Like his earlier recommendations about the Passion, David implies that thinking about the virtues helps memory to concentrate. Virtuous thought also helps to make the monk more virtuous, which he must become before he can advance toward God. As we shall see and as Mary Carruthers has demonstrated, the religious literature of the High and late Middle Ages is shot through with calls for 'painting' in one's heart what one wants to dwell on, to remember.

## *Cistercian Influences*

Many of these ideas about memory, meditation, and the human soul were not original to David von Augsburg but rather derive from previous monastic practice. David was especially influenced by Cistercian thinkers.[24] Their influence is most obvious in his emphasis upon the need to reform the triad of understanding, memory, and will. The three linked powers of the human soul gained their influence first from Augustine's use of them as an analogy of the Trinity in *On the Trinity*.[25] However, our author is probably not drawing directly from Augustine

[23] David von Augsburg, *De profectu religiosorum*, II.15, p. 378; my translation.

[24] Roest, *History of Franciscan Education*, p. 249, notes the continuity between Franciscan and high medieval monastic spirituality.

[25] Walter H. Principe, *Introduction to Patristic and Medieval Theology* (Toronto: Pontifical Institute of Mediaeval Studies, 1987), pp. 87–88. Augustine, *The Trinity*, trans. by Stephen McKenna, Fathers of the Church, 18 (Washington, DC: Catholic University of America Press, 1963), Book X. See Heerinckx, 'Influence de l'Epistola ad Fratres', p. 341.

himself but from a Cistercian tradition of human psychology, most likely from Guillaume de Saint-Thierry.[26] As Bernard McGinn has demonstrated, a number of Cistercian authors wrote about the human soul as part of their 'anthropological and spiritual program designed to provide a theoretical basis for man's return to God'.[27] P. Michaud-Quantain notes that it was inconceivable for Cistercian authors to teach about spirituality without discussing the soul. For them, psychology functioned as an introduction to the spiritual life and a way to raise oneself toward God.[28] These Cistercians thought that humans had been made in the image and likeness of God, but because of sin they had fallen and gotten lost in a region of dissimilarity (*regio dissimilitudinis*).[29] Their texts explained the results of sin and how the image of God could be restored. One such result was that the powers of the soul, including memory, did not function according to their capacity.

One way that some Cistercian authors addressed the soul's problems was through treatises that analysed *conscientia*. Such treatises were less about the nature of the soul itself than a programme to gain self-knowledge through reflection on conscience.[30] The self-knowledge would then reveal the sinfulness of the monk's past life and indicate the need for an 'ascetic programme' to get out of sin. An example of these texts is *De domo interiori* or *On the Interior House*, a work erroneously attributed to St Bernard, in which the discussion of memory was especially noteworthy.[31] It outlines a plan of meditation and contemplation that helps the human soul ascend to God, and like some other twelfth-century tracts, such as Hugh of St Victor's *De arca Noe*, describes meditation as the construction

[26] Athanasius Matanic thinks that the basic stance toward the interior and exterior man came to the Franciscan school from the Cistercians and Victorines, 'La "hominis compositio" tra la scuola vittorina e la prima scuola francescana', in *L'Antropologia dei maestri spirituali: Simposio organizzato dall'Istituto di spiritualità dell'Università gregoriana, Roma, 28 aprile–1 maggio 1989*, ed. by Charles André Bernard, Pontificia Università Gregoriana, Istituto di spiritualità (Cinisello Balsamo: Edizioni Paoline, 1991), pp. 163–77 (p. 163).

[27] *Three Treatises on Man*, pp. 20–21, 81–82. See also Coleman, *Ancient and Medieval Memories*, pp. 194–227.

[28] Pierre Michaud-Quantin, 'La Classification des puissances de l'âme au XII^e^ siècle', *Revue du moyen âge latin*, 5 (1949), 15–34 (p. 20).

[29] *Three Treatises on Man*, pp. 77–79.

[30] *Three Treatises on Man*, p. 81.

[31] PL, CLXXXIV, cols 507–52. See also Philippe Delhaye, 'Domo (De interiori)', in *Dictionnaire de spiritualité*, ed. by Viller, Cavallera, and de Guibert, III, 1548–51.

of an interior dwelling place for their soul and for God.[32] The author advises his presumably monastic readers that the interior house rests on seven pillars and in order to erect them, one should try to put the three powers of the soul — reason (sometimes also called the understanding), the will, and memory — in order. The right ordering of these powers comprises three of the pillars: the first column is a good will, the second is the memory of the benefits of God, and the seventh is an illumined reason or understanding. Only the first two pillars need interest us here. The author says that a good will is a gift from God and is important because all good comes from a good will. He leaves room for merit by saying that God does not grant a good will to one who is unwilling. Here we see the idea that a good will is needed to start off the process of meditation and in some senses precedes the demands of memory.

The second pillar is the memory of the benefits of God, which we should remember 'so that we may be set aflame with his love'. According to the anonymous author, the kind of benefits that one should keep in mind are mainly actions: the way that God warns sinners who have become forgetful of God; the ways that he guards the perseverant Christian; the ways he forgives sins and frees us from dangers. 'For this reason, just as there is no moment in which we do not use or enjoy the piety and mercy of God, so there ought to be no moment in which we do not have him present in our memory.'[33] To this writer, the human relationship with God is that of an inferior receiving favours or *beneficia* from a superior, perhaps not unlike that of a knight receiving land or favours from his lord.[34] The major favour conferred on humanity is salvation from sin. The proper

[32] For a discussion of the use of architectural motifs in twelfth-century contemplation, see Christiania Whitehead, 'Making a Cloister of the Soul in Medieval Religious Treatises', *Medium aevum*, 67 (1998), 1–29. Here Whitehead argues that before the twelfth century, commentaries allegorizing the House of God as a temple of tabernacle saw them as 'vessels for the ineffable presence of God'. With Hugh of Fouilloy's *De claustro animae*, which instead allegorized the cloister, one sees a shift in metaphors from the building as a metaphor for God to the building as a metaphor for 'the contemplative condition of the soul' (p. 5). These Cistercian treatises seem to straddle the conceptual shift identified by Whitehead, as the *De domo interiori* sees the allegorized house as a dwelling place for both God and the soul, but also clearly outlines a contemplative journey for the soul. Whitehead expands on some of her conclusions about architectural motifs in *Castles of the Mind: A Study of Medieval Architectural Allegory*, Religion and Culture in the Middle Ages (Cardiff: University of Wales Press, 2003).

[33] *De domo interiori*, PL, CLXXXIV, cols 511D.

[34] A parallel example would be Robert Scribner's likening of the Virgin Mary's intercessory role before Christ to that of noblewomen in feudal society: Robert W. Scribner, 'Elements of

response to the great good granted by God is not just gratitude but love: we should love him with our whole hearts. Since people are known to become forgetful of past favours, monks should cultivate the memory of God's gifts. This is why 'there ought to be no moment in which we do not have him in our memory'. His point here is similar to David von Augsburg's injunction to keep the mind raised up to God.

For this author, good will or intention begins with meditation, bolstered by the love flowing from the memory of God's benefits. Without that love, no rational understanding of Christianity will suffice for salvation or for contemplation. Love spurs Christians, or in this case monks, on to higher and more difficult feats. Later in the text, the author advises the soul to remake itself in the image of God and explains his injunction by drawing on Augustine's analogy of the three powers of the soul to the Trinity:

> From these three more excellent powers, we are commanded to love God, so that we love him with our whole heart, our whole soul, our whole mind, that is, with the whole intellect, the whole will, and the whole memory. [...] But knowing God is not enough if his will is not accomplished by our loving him in return. And even knowledge and love are not enough, unless memory also comes into play so that God may always be present to the person who knows and loves him. Just as there cannot be a moment in which a person does not use or enjoy God's goodness and mercy, so too there should not be a moment in which God is not present in memory.[35]

The author recognizes that keeping God in memory at all times is not an easy task. To make the ascent toward God, the mind must enter into itself and then focus its attention on things that are above it. The great obstacle blocking the mind's ascent is the wandering of one's thoughts and the dwelling on exterior, rather than interior, matters.[36] In the same way, memories of one's past, especially of one's past sinful actions, can distract the mind from its proper focus. For these problems, too, memory holds the answer. The author suggests that the remedy against depraved (*pravas*) thoughts is the memory of the Passion of Christ and of the Last Judgement. He advises that the monk should look (*intuere*) at how Judas handed Christ over to the Jews and how vilely he was handled (*pertractatur*), reviled and cuffed about, judged, and condemned, plundered and whipped,

Popular Belief', in *Handbook of European History, 1400–1600: Late Middle Ages, Renaissance and Reformation*, I: *Structures and Assertions*, ed. by Thomas A. Brady Jr, Heiko Oberman, and James D. Tracy (Leiden: Brill, 1994), pp. 231–62 (p. 242).

[35] *De domo interiori*, PL, CLXXXIV, col. 547.

[36] *De domo interiori*, PL, CLXXXIV, cols 513–14.

and at the end hung on the Cross between two thieves.[37] These memories should suffice to drive away illicit thoughts, as should the recollection of what will happen at the Last Judgement. The anonymous author's description of the Passion is couched in a quick series of passive verbs, suggesting that the memory of the Passion should become (and perhaps already was) a well-practised exercise. He reminds his readers that if they wish to drive away evil thoughts, think of these things often. 'For where your thoughts are, there will be your emotions, and where your heart is, there is your desire.'[38]

The author of *De domo interiori*'s concern about the inability of memory to control wandering thoughts would seem to support some of Mary Carruthers's observations about monastic memory in *The Craft of Thought*.[39] In her analysis of Johannes Cassianus's *Conferences*, Carruthers notes Cassianus's warning against wandering thoughts, expressed by him as *curiositas*. He describes how the mind can find it difficult to concentrate on only one scriptural passage: 'Ever on the move, forever wandering, it [the mind] is tossed along through all of the body of Scripture, unable to settle on anything, unable to reject anything or hold on to anything, powerless to arrive at any full and judicious study.'[40] For Cassianus, three things can help to stabilize a wandering mind: 'vigils, meditation, and prayer. Constant attention to them and a firm concentration upon them will give stability to the soul.' Carruthers interprets the monastic solution to the problem of the wandering mind to be the creation of a 'way' or 'route' through one's thoughts. Medieval monks created patterns, especially mental images, as maps for the mind to keep it from wandering off the chosen route. To her, the frequent injunctions in monastic texts to climb ladders can be seen as an example of following the 'way'.[41]

[37] *De domo interiori*, PL, CLXXXIV, cols 530–31: 'Intuere quomodo a Juda Judaeis traditur, et quam viliter pertractatur, blasphematur et colaphizatur, judicatur et condemnatur, exspoliatur et flagellatur; ad ultimum vero contumeliis et opprobriis affectus inter duos latrones suspenditur: clavis cruci affixus, sputis derisus, spinis coronatus, lancea perforatus. Ex omnibus partibus sanguis emanat, et inclinato capite emittit spiritum.'

[38] *De domo interiori*, PL, CLXXXIV, col. 532: 'Si vis omnes malas cogitationes a corde tuo expellere, haec saepe cogita. Ibi namque est cogitatio tua, ubi est affectio tua; ibi cor tuum, ubi est desiderium.'

[39] Carruthers, *Craft of Thought*, pp. 82–84.

[40] Carruthers, *Craft of Thought*, p. 83.

[41] Carruthers, *Craft of Thought*, pp. 80–81.

The author of *De domo interiori*'s recommendation to visualize the Passion as a way to focus the mind does create a mental picture of the Passion and it does assume a certain order for the meditation. The scenes of the Passion are listed in the order they are described in the Gospels, and, as I noted before, their description implies the habit of frequent practise. Meditation on the Passion keeps the mind from wandering from its chosen path. The choice of the Passion as a frequent source of meditation, aside from its obvious importance to Christianity, arises from its centrality in the trope of the *memoria beneficiorum Dei*, or the 'memory of the benefits of God'.

The phrase 'the memory of the benefits of God' is found in many works outside of *De domo interiori*. In fact, one can almost regard it as a standard trope of sermon and contemplative literature from at least the twelfth century through the later Middle Ages. It comes up often in the context of sermons on Psalms 77 and 105, both of which focus on God's aid for Israel. Most authors see the role of such memory to be to kindle devotion towards God or to make the believer grateful to God. Thomas of Chobham, a twelfth-century English cleric, expressed the sentiment most succinctly in his *Summa de arte praedicandi*: '[T]here is nothing that so moves the human soul toward loving God than to call back to memory all the benefits that God did for us.'[42] Vincent de Beauvais, in his *Speculum morale* declared the memory of the benefits of God to be 'praiseworthy, indeed necessary, for returning thanks'.[43] Few authors explain exactly what they mean by 'the benefits of God' — the author of *De interiori domo* is more explicit than most — but the Cistercian Ælred of Rievaulx in one of his sermons claims that Christ, aware of the corruption of human memory through forgetfulness, provided humans with a way to be always mindful of his benefits by having them recited to us through Scripture and represented to us through spiritual practices like the Eucharist.[44] His understanding of the Eucharist's role in preserving the memory of God's *beneficia* is nearly identical to David von Augsburg's and suggests a connection.

[42] *Summa de arte*, IV, l. 1413.

[43] Vincent de Beauvais, *Speculum morale*, in *Speculum quadruplex sive, Speculum maius*, Liber I, pars III, dist. XXXVIII (III, 295).

[44] Ælred of Rievaulx, *Sermones I–XLVI*, ed. by Gaetano Raciti, CCCM, 2A (Turnhout: Brepols, 1988), Sermo 9, l. 8: 'Sed quia nobis expediebat semper memores exsistere beneficiorum eius quae nobis per praesentiam suam corporalem exhibuit, <et> quia sciuit memoriam nostram esse corruptam per obliuionem, intellectum per errorem, studium per cupiditatem, pie prouidit nobis ut ipsa sua beneficia non solum recitarentur nobis per Scripturas, sed etiam nobis repraesentarentur per quasdam spirituales actiones.'

Though many authors refer to the trope of the memory of the benefits of God, Cistercian authors often tie together the memory that kindles love for God with the memory of our own sins that produces compunction or affliction of the heart (*compunctio cordis*). According to the Cistercian monk Hermannus de Runa, writing in the twelfth century,

> [D]evotion excites reason, illumines the will, chases away forgetfulness [...]. Devotion is therefore the death of vice, the life of virtue, the strength of fighters, the palm of victory. [...] It must indeed be known that just as compunction arises from the memory [*recordatio*] of our sins or the desire for eternal joy, so also does devotion proceed from the memory of divine benefits.[45]

Bernard de Clairvaux counted the compunction arising from the memory of sin and the devotion from the memory of benefits as two of the three spiritual unguents for Christ's body.[46] One might conclude that for monastic authors, especially Cistercians, one role of memory is to stir up strong emotions, either sadness or love, without which further progress in meditation is impossible. As we saw in Chapter 1, Carruthers's *The Craft of Thought* illustrates how strong emotions like fear or extreme sadness began the process of prayer and meditation.[47] The memory of the benefits of God, then, had the effect of focusing one's thoughts to keep them form wandering and, by arousing love or compunction, enabling the soul to begin meditation.

If the Cistercians worked out much of these ideas, they were certainly taken up by other authors. Riccardo Quinto comments that Stephen Langton, in his moral commentary on the Book of Leviticus, saw the memory of past sins and the memory of the benefits one acquired through Christ's passion as aids in penitence and confession.[48] Quinto notes that Langton stayed at the Cistercian abbey of

[45] Hermannus de Runa, *Sermones Festivales*, ed. by Edmundus Mikkers, CCCM, 64 (Turnhout: Brepols, 1986), Sermo 82, l. 121: 'Sciendum sane, quod sicut compunctio surgit ex recordatione peccatorum uel desiderio aeternorum, ita et deuotio procedit ex diuinorum memoria beneficiorum, siue quae unusquisque in seipso assidue experitur, siue quae cunctis simul credentibus per sacramenta dominicae incarnationis impensa reminiscitur.'

[46] St Bernard, *Sententiae*, sententia 169, in *Opera*, ed. by Jean Leclercq and H. M. Rochais, 8 vols (Rome: Editiones Cistercienses, 1957–77), VI, pt II, 56: 'Unguenta tria sunt: compunctio de memoria peccatorum, quae infundit pedes Iesu; devotio ex recordatione beneficiorum, qua perungitur caput Iesu; pietas ex consideratione miserorum, quae ad ungendum corpus Iesu a mulieribus praeparatur.'

[47] Carruthers, *Craft of Thought*, pp. 95–103.

[48] Riccardo Quinto, 'Peter the Chanter and the "Miscellanea del Codice del Tesoro" (Etymology as a Way for Constructing a Sermon)', in *Constructing the Medieval Sermon*, ed. by Andersson, pp. 33–81 (p. 65).

Pontigny with its excellent library, suggesting one way that Langton could have absorbed such Cistercian ideas. The point of his article is to suggest that secular masters at Paris like Stephen Langton and Petrus Cantor were conduits of earlier monastic thinking (as well as of their own important theological ideas) to the early Franciscans who studied at the University of Paris. He argues that it is less likely that the early friars had rich libraries at their disposal in which to absorb older ideas; rather, they learned from the theological tools that the secular masters had compiled, such as Petrus Cantor's *Distinctiones Abel* and *Verbum abbreviatum*.[49] This is an important argument that certainly helps to explain the prevalence of Cistercian and Victorine themes in the works of the early friars.

David von Augsburg was not the only Franciscan to see the value of the memory of the benefits of God. Included with the works by Bonaventura in the Peltier edition is a little work called *De exercitiis spiritualibus* that outlines the role of the memory in meditation in terms very similar to those we have been discussing.[50] The author, who may or may not be Bonaventura, begins his short tract with a warning to the reader that although all things found in divine Scripture speak and instruct about God, not all of them are useful for meditation. Instead one should take up for meditation only those things that either incite one more fully with fear or cause you to burn with love. He recommends certain general themes that he feels are more likely to accomplish this goal, namely, 'the memory of one's sins, [...] the memory of death, [...] the memory of the Last Judgement, [...] the memory of pains of Hell, [...] the memory of celestial glory, [...] and the memory of the benefits of God, and especially of the benefit of the Incarnation'.[51] It would be hard to find a clearer statement that the author sees memory as the foundation of meditation. Wishing to provide the reader material at hand for meditation, the author provides some general thoughts for each of the above-mentioned topics. He advises the reader, therefore, to 'be a clean animal [*animal mundum*], chewing and turning over these things and things similar to them in your heart, so that you are able to remove empty things from your memory'.[52] The implication is that, much as in David von Augsburg's works, the reader should replace the vain things that have filled his memory with the memory of the topics that the author has laid out.

[49] Quinto, 'Peter the Chanter', pp. 69–70.

[50] Bonaventura, *De exercitiis spiritualibus*, in *Opera omnia*, ed. by Peltier, XII, 171–79.

[51] Bonaventura, *De exercitiis spiritualibus*, ed. by Peltier, XII, 171.

[52] Bonaventura, *De exercitiis spiritualibus*, ed. by Peltier, XII, p. 171: 'Esto igitur animal mundum, ruminans et revolvens ea, et ipsis similia, in corde tuo, ita inutilia et vana possis e memoria removere.'

In the chapter on the *beneficia Dei*, the author gives the reader 'a plan [*modum*] of meditating on the benefits of God and of reforming your memory'. Again, much as we saw in David , memory is in need of reformation, and it can be repaired by focusing its attention on different things. In this chapter, the author says that one can vary and expand one's meditations by meditating first on the benefactor and then by meditating on the benefits that God has given to the reader.[53] Considering the greatness and goodness of God, his infinite powers, infinite wisdom, and great solicitude for one should have the effect of kindling love and gratitude in the meditator. For the benefits themselves, one should first think of the many evils that God no longer counts against you and then the actual gifts that he has given you. Recognizing that no one can easily count up all of these gifts, the author gives a *modum cogitandi*, a way of proceeding through the material, saying 'think how he gave to you gifts of nature, gifts of grace, and then the gift of surpassing excellence [*superexcellentia*], the Incarnation'.[54] He says that one should 'run through' each one of them, because in any one of them there are many useful things. He sees the Incarnation as the most important benefit given to humans, one that explains all of God's interactions with the human race. 'For why else would he have done all of these things [speak to the prophets, lead the Hebrews out of Egypt and into the promised land, etc.] except to illuminate your understanding through figures and through the prophets toward the knowledge of the Truth and to draw your emotions [*affectus*] toward the love of the Good?'[55] He ends the small tractate with one chapter on the Lord's Supper and on the Passion. Both of these fall under the rubric of the greatest *beneficium Dei*, the Incarnation, and both require extensive meditation. It is obvious how important the topic of meditation on the Passion became in medieval practice.

Enough has been said to demonstrate the importance of the idea of the memory of the benefits of God to both Cistercian and Franciscan thought. Far from being a 'throw-away line', the phrase came to represent a trope in contemplative and homiletic literature and to indicate an author's stance toward memory. David von Augsburg's writings were doubtlessly only one way that the trope entered into Franciscan thought.

[53] Bonaventura, *De exercitiis spiritualibus*, ed. by Peltier, XII, 175.

[54] Bonaventura, *De exercitiis spiritualibus*, ed. by Peltier, XII, 175: 'Attamen, ut his habeas modum cogitandi, cogita quomodo dedit tibi dona naturae, dona gratiae, dona superexcellentiae.'

[55] Bonaventura, *De exercitiis spiritualibus*, ed. by Peltier, XII, 176: 'Ut quis autem haec omnia fecit, nisi ut per figuras et per prophetas intellectum tuum in cognitione veri illuminaret, et affectum tuum detraheret ad amorem boni.'

## *Long-term Influence of Monastic and Franciscan Spiritual Exercises*

It would be impossible to enumerate all of the influence that monastic spiritual exercises had on the later Middle Ages. However, I do think that it is worth emphasizing two aspects of these exercises: their influence on the prominence of the virtues and vices in medieval preaching, especially but not exclusively by the mendicant orders, and on the noticeable flourishing of artificial memory tracts by the beginning of the fifteenth century. In the first instance, I want to suggest that the recommendation to drive away pictures of vices and to implant more virtuous ones in the soul helped to drive the promotion of the virtues and vices in Franciscan and other medieval preaching in the thirteenth and fourteenth centuries. In this chapter, I want only to expand on the importance of visualizations of virtues and vices in monastic spirituality. Later chapters in the book will demonstrate their importance in medieval preaching. In the second instance, I would argue that the increased desire to practise meditation across certain sections of medieval society and the substantial demands that the meditative methods they used made upon memory help to explain in part the flourishing of mnemonic tracts in fifteenth-century Europe. However, this is a topic for another book.

## **The Virtues and Vices**

In advising mental painting of the virtues, David von Augsburg was in no way unique. As Carruthers has demonstrated, the religious literature of the High and late Middle Ages is shot through with calls for 'painting' in one's heart. Her analysis emphasizes the compositional aspects of the pictures, which serve both to aid in creating new compositions and to anchor the organization of the resulting texts.[56] Carruthers mentions the Benedictine Pierre de Celles's *On Conscience*, in which he paints a mental picture of a king at a banquet table with Conscience as a guest.[57] Pierre also paints Charity. As another example, in *De arca Noe mystica*, Hugh of St Victor places images of the virtues on the ladders leading from one level of the ark to the next. For instance, at the foot of one of these ladders, Hugh imagines a young nude woman emerging from a cave to be greeted by an inciter

[56] Carruthers, *Craft of Thought*, p. 208: 'This is not the only picture in Peter's book. There are several smaller pictures, which serve to structure his materials into paragraph-sized divisions.'

[57] Carruthers, *Craft of Thought*, pp. 205–09.

of vice emitting fire from his mouth and nose in order to portray concupiscence.[58] A little higher on the same ladder another nude maiden is beaten to portray patience, while on a second ladder a woman distributes alms to signify mercy.

But why the need for mental images of virtues and vices? As we have noted above, calls for interior reformation by monastic authors required a change in one's exterior and interior lives. As Morton Bloomfield, Siegfried Wenzel, and Richard Newhauser have shown in their work on the concept of the seven deadly sins, the need for monks to withdraw from the world in order to combat sin and vice is present almost from the beginnings of Christian monasticism.[59] Newhauser identifies the monk Evagrius Ponticus as the originator of the tradition of the eight chief vices.[60] The goal of Evagrius's ascetic programme was the knowledge of divinity, but the monk could reach it only after the passions had been brought under control. The chief categories of sinfulness, which became the capital vices, were evil thoughts utilized by demons to stir up the passions and to keep the monks from achieving a state of peace (or *apatheia*).[61] As long as a monk was under the sway of these passions, he could not concentrate on meditating, his true job. This is why Evagrius's initial stage of monastic discipline was set up as a way to purify the part of the soul where the passions resided. Johannes Cassianus († *c.* 435) brought to Marseille from Egypt and Syria the idea of eight cardinal (i.e., chief) sins. His *Institutes* has a chapter devoted to each of them: *gula*, *luxuria*, *avaritia*, *ira*, *tristia*, *acedia*, *vana gloria*, *superbia*.[62] Because no progress can be made in the interior life when one's soul is full of vice, the vices have to be extirpated and virtues implanted in their place. Later medieval writers accepted this basic idea of the role of the vices and virtues in the interior life. Hugh of St Victor's *De sacramentis* contains a telling image of the effect of the vices on the rational soul:

[58] Hugh of St Victor, *De arca Noe mystica*, PL, CLXXVI, col. 696.

[59] Morton W. Bloomfield, *The Seven Deadly Sins: An Introduction to the History of a Religious Concept; With Special Reference to Medieval English Literature* (East Lansing: Michigan State College Press, 1952), pp. 69–83; Siegfried Wenzel, 'The Seven Deadly Sins: Some Problems of Research', *Speculum*, 43 (1968), 9–22 (p. 4). See also Siegfried Wenzel, *The Sin of Sloth: Acedia in Medieval Thought and Literature* (Chapel Hill: University of North Carolina Press, 1967). Richard Newhauser, *The Treatise on Vices and Virtues in Latin and the Vernacular*, Typologie des sources du moyen âge occidental, 68 (Turnhout: Brepols, 1993), p. 99.

[60] Newhauser, *Treatise on Vices and Virtues*, p. 103.

[61] Newhauser, *Treatise on Vices and Virtues*, pp. 100–01.

[62] Bloomfield, *Seven Deadly Sins*, p. 69; Newhauser, *Treatise on Vices and Virtues*, p. 108.

> The rational soul in its health is a strong and sound vessel without any corruption. When the vices enter into it, they spoil [*vitiant*] and corrupt it in this way: through pride it becomes blown up, through envy it dries out, through wrath it cracks, through *acedia* it breaks, through greed it is scattered about, through gluttony it is stained, and through lust it is trodden under foot, and reduced to clay.[63]

This focus on vice and virtue became more or less standard in contemplative works of the Middle Ages. Much of David 's writings on spiritual progress is occupied with these two topics. For instance, his second book on the interior man dwells at length on the seven capital sins and their remedies. His most lengthy reflection on the virtues comes in the third book on spiritual progress, presumably a sign that virtue is associated with progress toward the contemplative life.

The mental images of virtue and vice stem from the need to refocus the mind. It is in this connection between virtue and memory that the recent work of Brian Stock on Augustine and medieval meditation becomes most helpful. The programme for spiritual progress outlined in David von Augsburg's works and the kinds of mental images of virtues and vices noted above support Brian Stock's insight that medieval contemplative practices, especially after the eleventh century, formed a programme of self-improvement involving the reshaping of ethical values.[64] He sees Augustine of Hippo as the first to embark upon a plan for spiritual self-reform based upon reading and action arising from reading. Later medieval writers followed his example by moving from reading and meditation on the Bible, or *lectio divina*, to reading and meditation on other genres within the Christian tradition, such as saints' lives, contemplative works, and the like, an activity he labels *lectio spiritualis*.[65] Stock thinks that by the late Middle Ages this meditation became increasingly less text based and more image based, that is, one could meditate on ideas and images gleaned from a text no longer present.[66]

Stock also sees memory as critical to the programme of self-improvement that Augustine outlined for himself. For him, Augustine linked memory and narrative by ethics in Book X of the *Confessions*, where Augustine advanced the idea that one no longer reads for aesthetic reasons but rather for an ascetic programme. 'Moral precepts are read (or heard): they are then transformed from thought to practice as they are recalled. The specific recollections are the points of departure

[63] Cited in Wenzel, *Sin of Sloth*, p. 40.

[64] Brian Stock, *After Augustine: The Meditative Reader and the Text* (Philadelphia: University of Pennsylvania Press, 2001), pp. 1, 16–17.

[65] Stock, *After Augustine*, pp. 101–14.

[66] Stock, *After Augustine*, p. 104.

for a meditative ascent. As this proceeds, the study of scripture gradually becomes a form of life (*forma vivendi*).'[67] Memory then forms a crucial part of self-mastery.[68] Whether or not later writers drew explicitly on the *Confessions* for their ideas of self-reform, it is clear that some medieval writers, including David von Augsburg, saw an integral role for memory.

Reforming one's habits is not that easy. As Newhauser noted for Evagrius's ideas about evil thoughts and as Brian Stock has noted for Augustine's plan of spiritual reform, vices like gluttony are about the mind, not the stomach, so that one has to reform the mind, not the stomach. The monk needs a different kind of food. Clearly, some of that 'food' could come from oral teaching by other monks.[69] Implicit in Augustine's thought and in Stock's analysis, however, is the sense that this different kind of food will often come from texts. Since one cannot keep the texts always in front of one's eyes, they have to be memorized.[70]

It seems clear that later monastic writers agreed with Augustine's emphasis on reading as a way to find better interior guides. For instance, in *The School of the Cloister*, Pierre de Celles praises the role of reading in cloistered life:

> Constant and attentive reading devoutly done purifies our innards of the bones of dead men and the corpses of thoughts which should be cut out. Even if the fruit of understanding and knowledge does not result from reading, reading is nevertheless always useful in that our minds are occupied and exempted from the vain and useless thoughts which weigh them down and stubbornly intrude themselves.[71]

For Pierre, reading becomes a way of cutting out old ways of thought and of fixing one's attention and keeping it from the vice of distraction. In *Affliction and Reading*, Pierre lists among reading's many merits the fact that 'it constantly tells of the clash of virtues and vices, so that this clash is never passed over in silence'.[72] David von Augsburg more than once calls attention to the role of reading in spiritual progress, claiming that reading, especially of Scripture, 'gives the material and, as

[67] Brian Stock, *Augustine the Reader: Meditation, Self-Knowledge, and the Ethics of Interpretation* (Cambridge, MA: Belknap Press of Harvard University Press, 1996), p. 14.

[68] Stock, *After Augustine*, p. 30.

[69] Newhauser remarks on the oral aspects of monastic teaching, *Treatise on Vices and Virtues*, p. 108.

[70] Stock, *Augustine the Reader*, p. 229.

[71] Pierre de Celles, 'The School of the Cloister', in *Peter of Celle, Selected Works*, trans. by Hugh Feiss, Cistercian Studies, 100 (Kalamazoo: Cistercian, 1987), pp. 63–130 (p. 103).

[72] Pierre de Celles, 'Affliction and Reading', in *Peter of Celle, Selected Works*, trans. by Feiss, pp. 131–41 (p. 135).

it were, the seed of good thinking'.[73] He also sees it as furnishing the basis of meditation and prayer:

> As for reading, it should be of such sort as may react profitably upon our prayers. It should help us to know God better and love Him; it should help us to order our lives aright, to bear trials well, to instil into us a contempt of the world and a longing for heaven, to teach us how to distinguish between vice and virtue, to master temptation, and in other ways to promote a spiritual life. Prayer should frequently mingle with our reading — as indeed with all of out other duties — so that the mind may be often raised up towards God.[74]

Reading is thus one of the ways that the spiritual person can discover how to behave.

The need for mental pictures comes from the need to remember the fruit of all of this reading. While I would not dispute Carruthers's observation about the utility of mental pictures in creating and remembering compositions, I think that it is worth remembering that the purpose of both Pierre's and Hugh's treatises, like that of the author of *De domo interiori*, is to construct a dwelling place for the soul and for Christ. The dwelling should be ornamented with worthy objects of remembrance and mental focus, especially the virtues. Pierre introduces his banquet table with the injunction to 'fix in your mind something which will both goad the mind to the piety of devotion and be a visible example to enkindle the soul to invisible contemplation'.[75] Whether or not David von Augsburg read these particular texts, the practices of the Cistercians and the Victorines were certainly a source for Franciscan spirituality as a whole.

However, we do know that David's plan of spiritual exercises was read by many Franciscans, as well as by other people with spiritual leanings in the Middle Ages.[76] Herein may lie a partial explanation for the need to depict virtues and vices in later Franciscan preaching: the better to discern vice and cultivate virtue in one's soul through meditation. In his works on Franciscan education, Roest has noted the importance of individual mental prayer for all Franciscans, as has I. Brady.[77]

[73] David von Augsburg, *De institutione novitiorum*, II.4, p. 306; David von Augsburg, *Spiritual Life and Progress*, trans. by Devas, II, 1.

[74] Translation adapted from David von Augsburg, *Spiritual Life and Progress*, trans. by Devas, II, 128; David von Augsburg, *De profectu religiosorum*, II.58, p. 412.

[75] Pierre de Celles, 'Affliction and Reading', p. 152.

[76] Bohl, *Geistlicher Raum*, p. 49. Bohl notes that David's work was the most widespread spiritual handbook before *The Imitation of Christ*.

[77] Roest, *History of Franciscan Education*, p. 252; I. Brady, 'The History of Mental Prayer in the Order of Friars Minor', *Franciscan Studies*, 11 (1951), 317–45.

Brady comments, 'Prayer was considered by Saint Francis so much a part of the Franciscan vocation that he saw no need for formal legislation.'[78] It would not be surprising if meditative practices of visualizing the Passion and the virtues and vices eventually spilled out into Franciscan sermons. The audience for Franciscan sermons had neither the ability nor the time to spend on meditative reading. As we will see in later chapters, sermons instructed the laity in the knowledge of virtue and vice and provided them with a way to remember what they heard. Monastic practices may have continued to influence the transmission of the ideas about the virtues and vices as mendicant preachers who practised their own spiritual meditation transferred some of their practices into their sermons.

This idea would require an addition to the current picture of the transmission of the virtues and vices to medieval Europe, which stresses the role of the schoolmen of the twelfth and thirteenth century, as they applied abstract speculation to the familiar categories.[79] By the thirteenth century, the concept of the virtues and vices became popular within the wider culture. Bloomfield thinks that the requirement for the laity to confess their sins once a year after 1215, the establishment of the friars, and similar developments, such as the decree by Archbishop John Pecham in England in 1281 that priests should instruct people in the seven *capitalia peccata* 'stimulated the composition of a large number of works of instruction designed to help individual priests to carry out their duties. The moral tractates of the later Middle Ages are closely related to these works of instruction, and most of them list the chief sins.'[80] Exempla collections for preachers, about which we will have much to say later, were especially important in popularizing knowledge of the sins. According to Bloomfield, 'These different types of instructional material, then, are largely responsible for the transference of our concept from the theologians to the clerics and the people and for the movement from the Latin to the vernaculars.'[81] Without in any way wishing to challenge the general outline of this picture of the transmission of the vices from fourth-century Egypt to the medieval West, I would like to suggest that monasticism continued to play a larger role in the transmission of knowledge of the vices and virtues than is usually considered.

[78] Brady, 'Mental Prayer', p. 319. Francis thought one could not make progress in the service of God without prayer.

[79] Newhauser, *Treatise on Vices and Virtues*, p. 122.

[80] Bloomfield, *Seven Deadly Sins*, pp. 91–92.

[81] Bloomfield, *Seven Deadly Sins*, p. 92.

To conclude, David von Augsburg adopts the Cistercian view of human psychology and stresses the need for the understanding, will, and memory to be refashioned. Memory needs to be cleansed of the recall of past sins and must learn to devote its attention to God. One way to achieve this goal is by focusing memory's attention on the benefits of God, particularly the great gift of the Passion. Another way to focus memory's attention is to strip away evil and depraved thoughts by painting one's soul with images of the virtues instead. This idea that the weakened state of memory requires active attempts at reformation comes up in art of memory treatises in the late Middle Ages as an explanation of why one should learn such mnemonic techniques. It probably also explains why some preachers insist on great elaboration of details in sermon imagery. If the memory of a monk or mendicant has been damaged, imagine the problems of the laity.

# Part II. Constructing the Preacher's Memory

Chapter 4

# Mnemonic Advice for Preachers

As we have seen in the last three chapters, memory techniques inherited from long monastic practice were supplemented in the twelfth and thirteenth centuries by practices developed in the schools.[1] In addition, the mnemonic method advised by the *Rhetorica ad Herennium*, long out of favour among scholars, was revived as a mnemonic option by the mendicant orders in the mid-thirteenth century. Chief among their reasons for choosing the architectural mnemonic was its usefulness for oratory, newly important in the preaching revival of the time. Surprisingly, however, the most abundant sources available for understanding the preaching of the friars, sermons and *ars praedicandi* treatises, rarely address the topic of memory explicitly. The silence of the preaching tracts contrasts noticeably with the handbooks of the other forms of medieval rhetoric like the *ars dictaminis* and the *ars poetriae*.[2] Their authors comment relatively frequently about memory and Cicero's rules, even if, as we have seen, they did not find his advice particularly useful.

This lack of direct information about the role of memory in preaching makes the *Ars praedicandi* of Francesc Eiximenis extremely important. This short treatise

[1] A version of this chapter was previously published as Kimberly A. Rivers, 'Memory and Medieval Preaching: Mnemonic Advice in the *Ars praedicandi* of Francesc Eiximenis (c. 1327–1409)', *Viator*, 30 (1999), 253–84.

[2] For examples of the comments of other medieval rhetoricians, see Carruthers, *Book of Memory*, pp. 85–88. See also Rivers, 'Memory and the Mendicants', chap. 1, for an overview of comments about memory in the *ars dictaminis* and the *ars poetriae*. The most accessible introductions to these fields may be found in Douglas Kelly, *The Arts of Poetry and of Prose*, Typologie des sources du moyen âge cccidental, 59 (Turnhout: Brepols, 1991), and Martin Camargo, *Ars dictaminis, Ars dictandi*, Typologie des sources du moyen âge occidental, 60 (Turnhout: Brepols, 1991).

by a fourteenth-century Franciscan is the only *ars praedicandi* that I have found to give specific advice to preachers for remembering their sermons.[3] His directives explain how some medieval preachers remembered their sermons and illustrate what medieval audiences were meant to take away from a sermon by revealing what he thought makes a sermon memorable. He exhibits a constant concern to aid the memory of both the preacher and the listener. Though one might argue that this is a negligible concern, it is actually quite important. Classical mnemonic treatises advocated schemes that would aid the speaker's memory and pass unnoticed by the audience; the authors of preaching treatises advised techniques that would help their listeners recall the salient points of the sermon later. As Francesc's treatise reveals, medieval mnemonic methods aided both speaker and listener and taught the people the learning of the schools almost imperceptibly. Procedures that medieval preachers recognized as mnemonic devices, but did not explicitly name so, have not been readily identified by modern researchers. Many of the methods that preachers used to structure and recall their sermons depend on the theological, rhetorical, and logical teaching of the schools, and these same mechanisms served as a way of teaching the laity the things that the medieval church determined that they needed to know for salvation.

To demonstrate these ideas, we will begin by examining the explicit advice given about memory in the *artes praedicandi* written before Francesc's, before turning to a detailed analysis of Francesc's treatise. Then we will compare some of his practices to that of other medieval preachers.

In making this survey of *ars praedicandi* treatises, I am assuming that they do have something valuable to convey about the practice of medieval preaching. In *The Preaching of the Friars*, David d'Avray argued against the influence of the *ars praedicandi* as a tool for educating medieval preachers in favour of model sermon collections.[4] D'Avray was quite right to point out the importance of model sermon collections in the array of handbooks to aid preachers in the composition of sermons. However, a study of the *ars praedicandi* is indispensable for the study of medieval mnemonics. Since many memory aids were derived from ancient rhetoric, and since the *ars praedicandi* was one offshoot of rhetoric in the Middle Ages, these handbooks cannot be ignored. In addition, whether or not every

[3] The mnemonic aspects of Francesc's treatise have been little discussed by modern scholars. The only extended discussion that I know of is Xavier Renedo, 'Una imatge de la memòria entre les *Moralitates* de Robert Holcot i el *Dotzè* de Francesc Eiximenis', *Annals de l'Institut d'estudis Gironins*, 31 (1990–91), 53–61 (pp. 53–56).

[4] See d'Avray, *Preaching of the Friars*, p. 78.

preacher reached for an *ars praedicandi* treatise at the moment of beginning of a new sermon, there is no reason to think that the advice contained in these manuals was divorced from the world of medieval preaching. Indeed, Yuichi Akae's recent article comparing Robert of Basevorn's *Forma praedicandi* and the sermons of John Waldeby, OESA, found a high degree of congruence between the methods exhibited in the two homiletic works. In fact, his study 'succeeds in rehabilitating the *ars praedicandi* for understanding contemporary techniques of sermon composition, techniques that are sometimes difficult to recognize without this analytical tool'.[5] Though one can never know whether a particular preaching handbook actually influenced another preacher, it is fair to assume that the views contained in the manual reflect the opinions and practices of the writer and very likely of other preachers at the time.

## *Memory Techniques in 'Ars praedicandi' Treatises*

In twelfth- and thirteenth-century Europe interest in preaching and pastoral concerns increased dramatically,[6] as can be seen by the contemporary references to preaching 'revivals', by the outpouring of handbooks and manuals devoted to pastoral care from the schools, and by the number of sermon manuscripts extant from that time.[7] In response to what David d'Avray calls 'an almost feverish market for preaching', a new approach to composing sermons was developed. Before the mid-twelfth century, most sermons followed a homiletic style in which a long biblical text of the day was explicated carefully. In the new sermon style,

[5] Roger Andersson, 'Introduction', in *Constructing the Medieval Sermon*, ed. by Andersson, pp. 1–7 (p. 2), commenting on Yuichi Akae, 'Between *Artes praedicandi* and Actual Sermons: Robert of Basevorn's *Forma praedicandi* and the Sermons of John Waldeby, OESA', ibid., pp. 9–31.

[6] Scholarly interest in medieval preaching has increased dramatically in the past few decades. For some of the most useful recent work and useful bibliographies, see Marianne G. Briscoe and Barbara H. Jage, *Artes praedicandi and Artes orandi*, Typologie des sources du moyen âge occidental, 61 (Turnhout: Brepols, 1992); and Beverly Mayne Kienzle, *The Sermon*, Typologie des sources du moyen âge occidental, 81–83 (Turnhout: Brepols, 2000). See also Carolyn Muessig, 'Sermon, Preacher and Society in the Middle Ages', *Journal of Medieval History*, 28 (2002), 73–91, for an overview of recent developments in the field.

[7] See d'Avray, *Preaching of the Friars*; Goering, *William de Montibus*; Harry Caplan, *Mediaeval 'Artes praedicandi': A Hand-List*, Cornell Studies in Classical Philology, 24 (Ithaca: Cornell University Press, 1934); and Harry Caplan, *Mediaeval 'Artes praedicandi': A Supplementary Hand-list*, Cornell Studies in Classical Philology, 25 (Ithaca: Cornell University Press, 1936).

more emphasis was placed on moral persuasion reinforced by numerous, authoritative citations than on explication of the scriptural text.[8] This change in focus is evidenced by what celebrated preachers and authors of preaching tracts identified as the goals of the new sermon style (the *sermo modernus*): the need to preach right action and prohibit vice. For instance, Alain de Lille, in his *Summa de arte praedicandi*, defined preaching as 'the manifest and public instruction of morals and of the faith'.[9] Another preacher saw his duty as 'the public announcement of the word of God, enjoining morality and prohibiting wrong actions'.[10] The graduates from the recently developed schools in Europe, and later the members of the mendicant orders, were eager to use and promote the innovative preaching style, and the rules for writing it were contained in the *artes praedicandi*. Alain de Lille's *Summa de arte praedicandi*, written near the end of the twelfth century, is often seen as a harbinger of the new sermon method.

Though the *ars praedicandi*, like the *ars dictaminis* and the *ars poetriae*, was clearly influenced by classical rhetorical rules, it can sometimes be hard to see that influence in the handbooks written to advise readers how to compose the *sermo modernus*. Rather than following the classical division of rhetoric (*inventio*, *dispositio*, *elocucio*, *memoria*, and *actio*), the *artes praedicandi* generally arrange their material according to some discussion of the goals of preaching, the demeanour of a preacher, and the structure of the new style, consisting of five parts: the theme (a statement of the day's scriptural quotation); an opening prayer for divine aid; a protheme or second scriptural quotation; the division or statement of the parts of the theme; the *dilatatio* or development of the members of the division; and sometimes a conclusion.[11]

Most *ars praedicandi* authors include this outline and offer rules to construct such a sermon, but not all authors cover the various components of the sermon

[8] Briscoe and Jage, *Artes praedicandi*, pp. 27–28.

[9] Étienne Gilson, 'Michel Menot et la technique du sermon médiéval', *Revue d'histoire franciscaine*, 2 (1925), 301–50 (p. 304): 'Praedicatio est manifesta et publica instructio morum et fidei, informatione hominum deserviens, ex rationum semita et auctoritatum fonte proveniens' (PL, CCX, col. 111C).

[10] Jean Leclercq, 'Le Magistère du prédicateur au XIII^e siècle', *Archives d'histoire doctrinale et littéraire du moyen âge*, 15 (1946), 105–47 (p. 111): 'Praedicatio vero est verbi Dei publica annuntiatio jubens honesta, prohibens illicita.' Francis of Assisi told his followers to announce the vices and virtues as well as the penalties and glory to come.

[11] Briscoe and Jage, *Artes praedicandi*, pp. 54–62; see also Murphy, *Rhetoric in the Middle Ages*, p. 299.

equally. Some of the most fully developed handbooks, such as those by John of Wales, Thomas Waleys, and Ranulf Higden, treat nearly every aspect in depth. Others, especially in the later fourteenth and fifteenth centuries, take a shorter and more practical approach, and it is among these that Francesc Eiximenis's *ars* falls.[12] Within these handbooks it is relatively rare to find a chapter entitled 'memory' or 'delivery', as in the types of medieval rhetoric, such as the *ars dictaminis* or the *ars poetriae*, which followed the old rhetorical rules more closely. For this reason, discussions of mnemonic techniques among preaching experts are quite a rare occurrence. Thomas of Chobham's manual is one of the few that does discuss the five parts of rhetoric and thus has a 'memory' section.

Classical discussions of mnemonic techniques, such as those found in Cicero's *De oratore*, Quintilian's *Institutio oratoria*, and the *Rhetorica ad Herennium*, always focused on ways to improve the orator's memory so that he could remember either the gist of his ideas or the exact words he had composed. Though the methods advocated by these authors differed somewhat, most of their advice would have remained unknown to the audience. The places and images that Cicero and the author of the *Ad Herennium* described lived only in the head of the speaker and were not aimed at listeners. Only Quintilian's emphasis on right order, or *compositio* and *divisio*, would have been immediately useful for the audience's comprehension, but this was not his primary concern.

When one examines the rather small body of comments about memory in the *artes praedicandi*, it is immediately clear that their authors most often connect problems of recall to the laity, not to the preacher. This concern seems to weigh particularly heavily on Thomas of Chobham and Thomas Waleys, who focus most of their mnemonic advice on ways to aid the memory of their listeners.

The *Summa de arte praedicandi* of Thomas of Chobham († *c.* 1233–36) is the earliest to discuss mnemonics. Unlike many later preaching experts, Thomas spends far less time directing his readers in the art of arranging sermon material than he does in explaining who should preach, what the purpose of a sermon is, and what the content of a good sermon should be. Only the last part of his *ars* covers the practicalities of sermon construction, and here Thomas carefully connects the five parts of classical rhetoric to the art of composing sermons according to the *sermo modernus*.[13] Consequently, he actually has a memory section in the last part of his work. However, Thomas's *ars memorandi* aids the listener's

[12] Briscoe and Jage, *Artes praedicandi*, pp. 42–43.

[13] Thomas of Chobham, *Summa de arte*, pp. 268–303.

memory, rather than the preacher's. In fact, though Thomas evidently admires Cicero (he is referred to throughout the *Summa* as *philosophus*),[14] he consciously rejects the classical art of memory commonly attributed to him in the Middle Ages. In his introduction to the five parts of rhetoric, Thomas declares

> But after the preacher has invented and well adorned the matters to be said, memory is necessary for him, in order that he may retain the things which he invented and arranged and adorned. And although Tully handed down his art for this purpose, nevertheless memory works better from practise and diligence.[15]

Thomas admits that a memory art might be useful to a preacher, but, like the twelfth-century scholars examined in Chapter 1, he does not recommend Cicero's art. Despite this concession to memory's role in preaching oratory, he omits any discussion of the preacher's need to remember his sermon in the chapter on memory. Instead, Thomas declares that an art of memory is useful to preachers 'so that their listeners may firmly remember what they hear'. Since listeners will not be able to retain a 'wandering and disordered' sermon whose parts do not cohere, he stresses the importance of a well-constructed sermon:

> A sermon ought to be ordered so that after the head has been heard, that is the theme of the sermon, the listener immediately understands from the head the members which the preacher joins to it; and from these members he ought to preserve and anticipate the sermon. And so he will hold in memory what he is about to hear, and when the sermon is finished, he will remember how to retain the aforesaid because he understands them so to cohere to one another that they are not able to be separated.[16]

[14] See for instance Thomas of Chobham, *Summa de arte*, p. 262, where Thomas cites Cicero's *De inventione*, referring to its author as 'philosophus'. See also p. 369, ll. 309–10 for another example.

[15] Thomas of Chobham, *Summa de arte*, p. 268: 'Postquam autem predicator inuenerit et bene ornauerit ea que dicenda sunt, necessaria est ei memoria, ut bene retineat ea que inuenit et disposuit et ornauit. Et licet Tullius ad hoc artem suam tradiderit, melius tamen ex usu et diligentia memoria operatur.'

[16] Thomas of Chobham, *Summa de arte*, pp. 296–97: 'A simili ita debet ordinari predicatio, quod audito capite, id est themate predicationis, statim ex ipso capite intelligat auditor que membra predicator ei adiungat, et de quibus membris debeat seruare sermonem et expectare. Et ita memoriter tenebit quod auditurus est, et finito sermone memoriter tenebit quomodo possit predicta retinere cum intelligat ita sibi coherere ut separari non possint.' This advice is exactly that which the minor rhetoricians Fortunatianus and Julius Victor recommended for an orator: Thomas seems to have obtained it from Cicero. Morenzoni lists Cicero, *De oratore*, II.80, l. 325, and *De inventione*, I.19, as likely sources. For the views of the minor rhetoricians on memory, see C. Chirius Fortunatianus, *Artis rhetoricae libri III*, and C. Iulius Victor, *Ars rhetorica*, both in *Rhetores Latini minores*, ed. by Halm (cited in the 'Introduction', above); *Artif. eloq.*, and Carruthers, *Book of Memory*, pp. 85–87.

For Thomas, it is not Cicero's places and images that help a listener to recall a sermon, but rather a logically ordered sermon. Thomas's point is that there is little point in preaching a sermon that no one will remember afterwards. Evidently he felt that would-be preachers might resist his call to clarity and get carried away by the attractions of a complicated theme; he adds that the less 'copious' theme ought not to be condemned in favour of a more copious one, if the less complicated one is effectively followed. Besides incoherence, the preacher should avoid verbosity and inattention to time constraints, since both harm 'the art of remembering'. To address these inevitable problems, the preacher should have on hand elements that are either extremely useful or obviously pleasing, so that one's listeners are glad to delay their departure; if not, he should defer his sermon to a more opportune time.[17]

Thomas's remarks about a well-ordered sermon depend in part on the division of the theme. It is the careful marking out of topics and their order of consideration that causes the head and members of a speech to cohere closely. Thomas is hardly unusual in discussing the importance of divisions in medieval preaching, but he does provide a kind of medieval synthesis of ancient teachings about division in his own chapter on the topic. He finds two kinds of division in preaching. The first is when the whole sermon is divided into several parts, much as an author divides his work into chapters or books, and occurs when a preacher divides his theme into parts.[18] The second kind of division is of one word rather than a whole *negotium*. According to 'secular literature', there are seven types, which we will not detail here. Significantly, Thomas takes these seven variations from Boethius's *De divisione*, thereby integrating logic and rhetoric into the new preaching medium. Of Boethius's list, Thomas thinks the most commonly used is the division of a word (*vox*) into its various significations, as when all the ways that 'lion' or 'rock' may be interpreted in Scripture are shown.[19] Thomas also advises preachers to avoid too many divisions, lest their listeners be unable to retain in memory so many divisions and not understand what they hear.[20]

[17] Thomas of Chobham, *Summa de arte*, p. 297.

[18] Thomas of Chobham, *Summa de arte*, p. 284: 'Fiunt autem in predicationibus diuisiones dupliciter. Quandoque enim diuiditur tota predicatio in simul accepta in plures partes, sicut aliquis auctor diuidit opus suum per plura capitula uel per plures libros.'

[19] Thomas of Chobham, *Summa de arte*, p. 285.

[20] Thomas of Chobham, *Summa de arte*, p. 286: 'Iterum, uitiosum est facere diuisiones in predicatione multorum membrorum, quia ita possunt fieri auditores minus capaces, et potest obtundi animus eorum ut non intelligant quod dicitur.'

Finally, Thomas identifies a mnemonic purpose for the epilogue or conclusion of a sermon. He calls an epilogue a 'brief recapitulation' of the more salient points of the sermon, which the preacher judges to be most likely to move the hearts of his listeners.[21] Thomas sees two reasons to end his sermon with an epilogue: first, that he may repeat the most important reasons supporting his main point, and second, 'that he may better imprint on the memory those things which were preached'. Otherwise, the audience departs from a vain and empty exercise.[22] Thomas thinks that the 'simple' and 'less skilled' are most likely to benefit from repetition and to retain what they had heard before.[23]

Thomas's suggestions for memory work are relentlessly practical and draw on the simple ideas of *compositio* and *divisio* that Quintilian and his successors recommended. But one could call him medieval in his concern for his listeners' ability to retain the sermon, which seems to outweigh his solicitude for the preacher's memory. Presumably, following these rules will assist the preacher to remember his sermon as well.

Writing over one hundred years later, Thomas Waleys († 1349) confirms much of Thomas of Chobham's advice.[24] In his extensive manual on the art of writing sermons, *De modo componendi sermones*, Thomas considers the audience's memory by counselling preachers to be brief. Even the most exquisitely worded sermons that exceed 'the capacity and satiety of their listeners' ears' are wasted, because the superfluity provokes their memories to nausea, and 'they vomit those useful things they heard before', because their memories cannot absorb and digest the edifying material.[25] What Thomas means by brevity differs somewhat from what a modern reader might expect. When used by a medieval preacher, the term *brevitas* can simply mean shortness in length, as in delivering a short sermon.

[21] See Chapter 1 for Hugh of St Victor's views on epilogues and Chapter 2 for Vincent of Beauvais's.

[22] Thomas of Chobham, *Summa de arte*, p. 303: 'Potest etiam alia de causa facere epilogum, scilicet ut melius inprimat memorie ea que predicta sunt. Aliter enim recederent auditores uacui et inanes, nisi memoriter tenerent que audierunt.'

[23] Thomas of Chobham, *Summa de arte*, p. 267.

[24] Smalley, *EFA*, pp. 75–108. For biographical detail, see also Smalley, 'Thomas Waleys, O.P.', *AFP*, 24 (1954), 50–107.

[25] Thomas Waleys, *De modo componendi sermones*, in *Artes praedicandi*, ed. by Charland, pp. 325–403 (p. 339): 'quia et pulchri sermones qui ultra mensuram et satietatem auditorum eorum auribus inseruntur perduntur, quia eis non prosunt, et quandoque provocantur ex tali superfluitate ad nauseam, quia evomunt ea quae prius utiliter audierunt, quia excedunt a memoriis eorum eo quod eorum memoria non sufficit ad tot retinenda et bene digerenda'.

However, one should not assume that that is all the word means. Bernardino da Siena, by all accounts an immensely popular preacher and one exceedingly solicitous of his listeners' memories, is said to have preached regularly for three or four hours at a time.[26]

Among rhetoricians, *brevitas* usually referred less to the length of one's discourse than to its conciseness. The enemy of brevity was *prolixitas*, 'wordiness', and was something to be avoided in both written, but especially in spoken, discourse.[27] Curtius notes that in the Middle Ages, *brevitas* was often linked to a *fastidium* formula, i.e., that too much of a good thing promotes nausea.[28] In fact, Thomas employs the word in this very context, comparing memory to an overburdened stomach. Curtius also draws attention to an opposition in twelfth- and thirteenth-century poetical arts between *dilatatio*, amplifying or extending one's material, and *abbreviatio*, compressing it for the sake of brevity.[29] The preaching treatises regularly address the topic of *dilatatio* (likely because the great fear of a novice speaker is not having enough to say), while skipping over abbreviation. The call for brevity in Thomas's manual may be a way of including abbreviation, though he gives no rules for how to achieve it.

What Curtius does not mention is how often the terms brevity and prolixity turn up as opposing ideas within the context of memory work. Thomas Waleys fears that if his listeners' satiety for words is exceeded, they will retain nothing of what they have heard. A similar assumption about memory (in this case, the preacher's memory) being oppressed by prolixity can be seen in the pastoral work of William de Montibus (*c.* 1140–1213). He composed his second sermon collection for preachers unable to make the effort of writing their own. For those who fear 'difficult or wordy' sermons, William provides a more attractive alternative:

> Desiring by the goad of artificial brevity to motivate you to the task of preaching, I have composed short and easy sermons, so that this simple collection of them might rouse your delicate spirit, which can be deterred from the labour of memorization by the length or difficulty of other sermons, to that same work.[30]

[26] Iris Origo, *The World of San Bernardino* (New York: Harcourt, Brace, and World, 1962), p. 31.

[27] Curtius, *European Literature*, pp. 487–94, on the judicial origins of *brevitas* as a *virtus narrationis*.

[28] Curtius, *European Literature*, p. 487.

[29] Curtius, *European Literature*, p. 490.

[30] Goering, *William de Montibus*, p. 516 (trans. by Goering); Latin p. 545: 'Quia ergo tibi amice huiusmodi negligentiam inesse perpendi, cupiens te quodam artificiose breuitatis stimulo

Here brevity seems to mean a number of things: shortness in length, simplicity of thought, and lack of labour (since the preachers did not have to write the sermon themselves). For William, brevity is certainly an aid to memory.[31] As Geoffroi de Vinsauf notes, 'the glory of a brief work consists in this: it says nothing either more or less than is fitting'.[32]

Hugh of St Victor provides one more example of what brevity could mean in the context of memory work: order. As we saw in Chapter 1, Hugh of St Victor devised a number-line method for remembering texts like the Psalms, a method which Hugh claimed attacked prolixity. According to Hugh, 'By dividing and distinguishing at first the book according to the Psalms, then the Psalms through the verses, I reduce the wordiness to a brief compendium [*tantam prolixitatem ad tantum compendium et brevitatem redigi*].'[33] The Psalms have not been made any shorter by mnemonic division, but they have, in Hugh's eyes, been made 'briefer', that is more orderly, with only a few words attached to each division of the text.

Besides counselling brevity, Thomas claims that a proper division of the theme will both support the audience's memory and aid the preacher in developing his sermon. Thomas says:

> But given that there be only one division of the theme, it will be useful for both the preacher and the listener. For not on account of curiosity alone, as some believe, do modern preachers divide the theme, which formerly preachers did not do. Rather, it is useful for the preacher, because the division of the theme into diverse members offers the opportunity of expansion in the prosecution of the rest of his sermon. But the division

ad opus predicationis excitare, sermones breues et leues composui, ut animum tuum delicatum quem in aliis sermonibus aut difficultas aut prolixitas a labore recordationis deterrere potuit, horum facile compendium ad eundem laborem prouocaret. Hiis sermonibus si uti consueueris tam magnum pariet tibi consuetudo profectum, ut quandoque iuxta horum exemplar alios eque bonos et forte meliores proprio possis ingenio formare, quibus sonorus incedas et precepta sapientie predices ne legis censura moriaris set cum elucidantibus sapientiam uita perfrui merearis eterna.'

[31] Note Carruthers's discussion of brevity as an aid to memory, *Book of Memory*, pp. 83–85.

[32] Geoffroi de Vinsauf, *Poetria nova*, trans. by Nims, p. 42.

[33] Hugh of St Victor, *De tribus maximis* (Green, 'Hugo of St. Victor: *De tribus maximis*', p. 490): 'Cognitis autem psalmis, idem facio in singulis psalmis de initiis versuum quod feci in toto psalterio de initiis psalmorum, totamque deinceps seriem in singulis versibus facile corde retineo postquam, dividendo et distinguendo imprimis librum per psalmos deinde psalmum per versus, tantam prolixitatem ad tantum compendium et brevitatem redigi. Et hoc quidem in psalmis sive in aliis libris certas distinctiones habentibus facile videri potest. Ubi autem continua series est lectionis, id ipsum artificio fieri oportet, ut scilicet secundum lectoris placitum, ubi competentius videbitur, primum tota series in certas aliquas partes dividatur, et illae rursum in alias, illae iterum in alias, donec tota prolixitas ita restringatur'; my translation.

> is especially useful to the listener, because, when the preacher divides the theme and afterwards follows the members of the division in an orderly and distinct fashion, both the matter of the sermon and the form and method of preaching are easily grasped and retained. This will not be the case if the preacher proceeds obscurely and in a disorderly and confusing manner.[34]

The division of the theme provides the blueprint for both the preacher and the listeners to remember the sermon to come. It also furnishes the preacher with the form of material to be preached. After the theme, the division is the most fundamental part of the sermon, and possibly the most important mnemonically. Though Thomas provides an especially clear mnemonic function for the theme and its division, he was far from the only preaching authority of the time to value them. As Siegfried Wenzel has written, their importance can be seen in the definition of preaching given by the thirteenth-century Franciscan, John of Wales: 'Preaching is the clear and devout expounding of the announced *thema* by means of dividing and confirming it with fitting authorities after God's help has been invoked, for the purpose of enlightening the mind in the faith and kindling the heart in love.'[35] For John, preaching was about announcing the theme and dividing it. The anonymous Franciscan author of the *Ars concionandi*, writing in the thirteenth century, recommended dividing the theme of the sermon explicitly when preaching to the people, though he declared that this was not necessary in sermons for the clergy.[36]

Although Thomas seems most solicitous of his listeners' retention of sermon material, Thomas does consider the preacher's memory. Perhaps in an effort to avoid a purely theoretical approach to composition, his *De modo* lists practical qualities that a good preacher ought to possess. For instance, he warns new

[34] *De modo comp.*, p. 370: 'Dato vero quod tantum una fiat divisio thematis, adhuc illa divisio erit bene utilis [ut ilis Charland], tam praedicatori quam etiam auditori. Non enim propter solam curiositatem, sicut aliqui credunt, invenerunt moderni quod thema dividant, quod non consueverunt antiqui. Immo, est utilis praedicatori, quia divisio thematis in diversa membra praebat occasionem dilatationis in prosecutione ulteriori sermonis. Auditori vero est multum utilis, quia, quando praedicator dividit thema et postmodum membra divisionis ordinate et distinctim prosequitur, faciliter capitur et tenetur tam materia sermonis quam etiam forma et modus praedicandi; quod non erit si praedicator indistincte ac sine ordine et forma confuse procedat.' See Carruthers, *Book of Memory*, p. 103, for her comments on this passage.

[35] 'Predicacio est, invocato Dei auxilio, propo[s]iti thematis dividendo et concordando congrue clara et devota exposicio, ad intellectus catholicam illustracionem et affectus caritativam inflammacionem': cited in Siegfried Wenzel, 'The Arts of Preaching', in *Cambridge History of Literary Criticism*, ed. by Minnis and Johnson, pp. 84–96 (pp. 86–87).

[36] Cited in Spencer, *English Preaching*, p. 243.

preachers to be moderate in their gestures while speaking, as he has seen some who have become so carried away that they seem to be fighting a duel with someone else, to the extent that they would have fallen if others had not caught them![37] So it is not surprising that Thomas would have something to say about a practical issue like the preacher's memory. Here he has two rules to impart.

First, a preacher should not tie his discourse to certain exact words when preparing to speak. Words slip easily from memory and a slight action may disturb one's memory. Indeed even the dropping of one syllable may cause the loss of the whole word, resulting in the preacher's confusion.[38] Thomas claims that the forgetting of words and subsequent bewilderment occur when the whole sermon is produced in a rhymed, or in an affected, style, or when there are too many authorities.[39] To avoid this danger, the preacher should remember the full sense of his authorities (the *sententia*), whether or not he recites them verbatim.[40] Should he decide that some words in a quotation merit a complete narration, then he should direct his attention to memorizing and repeating them and take less care over other words.[41] Thomas is of the opinion that many authoritative texts are too obscure and difficult anyway for recitation and that the audience would benefit from a pithy paraphrase.

Thomas distinguishes between direct quotation and paraphrase, much as the *Ad Herennium* separates memory for words from memory for things. Thomas, however, does not tell the preacher how to memorize the sense or *sententiae* of

[37] *De modo comp.*, p. 332: 'Vidi enim aliquos qui quoad alia in sermonibus [optime] se habebant, tamen ita motibus corporis se jactabant quod videbantur cum aliquo duellum inisse, seu potius insanisse, in tantum quos seipsos cum pulpito in quo stabant nisi alii succurissent praecipitassent.'

[38] *De modo comp.*, pp. 335–36: 'Octavum documentum est ut videlicet ad certa et limitata verba non se nimis allegat. Verba enim de facili memoria excidunt, et ex levi actione sic turbatur dicentis memoria quod verba prius concepta non occurrunt. Immo, saepe cadens syllaba, cadit a toto. Tunc praedicator confunditur, quia se verbis plus quam sententiae alligavit.'

[39] *De modo comp.*, p. 336: 'Et accidit frequenter talis verborum oblivio et sequitur praedicta confusio, quando fit totus sermo in rhythmis vel stylo nimis polito et divisionibus auctoritatum superfluis.'

[40] *De modo comp.*, p. 336: 'Unde, ne praedicatori tale periculum accidat, provideat semper sibi quod, quidquid contingat de verbis auctoritatum hujusmodi, sententiam auctoritatum plene et distincte retineat.'

[41] *De modo comp.*, p. 336: 'Et si qua sunt verba in auctoritatibus illis quae sunt merito singulariter ponderanda, illa singulariter conetur memoriter retinere et dicere, de aliis minus curans.' See also Carruthers, *Book of Memory*, pp. 89–90.

these passages; he only tells him to recite the gist of the matter, rather than the exact words. He seems to fear the mishandling of 'authorities' most, perhaps because such texts, especially those by the Fathers, would be couched in unusual vocabulary and in someone else's words. Presumably, many preachers could have discoursed effortlessly on standard topics like the virtues and vices.[42]

Thomas's second counsel to the preacher about memory seems grounded in experience. He warns a novice preacher to overcome his apprehension when about to preach, because 'nervousness greatly disturbs one's memory and induces forgetfulness'.[43] He recommends practising one's sermon privately to gain confidence.

The emphasis on brevity, division of the theme, and practise as aids to memory constitute the bulk of mnemonic advice in most of the *artes praedicandi*. Though such counsel was undoubtably beneficial to novice preachers, it was hardly a thorough grounding in the mnemonic advice that should have been available to preachers in the twelfth and thirteenth centuries. Other than Thomas of Chobham's dismissal of Cicero's rules, there is virtually no reference to the *Ad Herennium*'s memory section.

## *The 'Ars praedicandi' of Francesc Eiximenis*

However, one of the few such treatises that does contain specific mnemonic information, Francesc Eiximenis's *Ars praedicandi*,[44] has a chapter on memory techniques that may explain why memory advice is mentioned so infrequently. Francesc's mnemonic precepts are relentlessly practical and rely partly on medieval adaptations of ancient mnemonic techniques and partly on ordering

[42] Francesc Eiximenis, at least, thought that most preachers could come up with one thing to say on single points: 'Et modus tamen predicta scilicet diuidendi euangeli uel notandi ibi aliqua puncta seriose et per ordinem, est modus ualde expeditus ad predicandum subito et ex improuiso. Raro enim est quod quilibet eciam modicum sciens, non habeat aliquid ad dicendum super uno puncto solo et quin sibi occurrat aliquid predicabile' (*Ars praed.*, p. 331.)

[43] *De modo comp.*, pp. 340–41: 'Pusillanimitas valde turbat memoriam et oblivionem inducit.'

[44] P. Martí de Barcelona, '*Ars praedicandi*', in *Hometage a Antoni Rubió i Lluch: Miscellània d'estudis literaris històrics i lingüístics*, 3 vols (Barcelona: [n. pub.], 1936), II, 300–40. The same edition is available in P. Martí de Barcelona, 'L'*Ars praedicandi* de Francisco Eixemensis', *Analecta sacra tarraconensia*, 12 (1936), 301–40. For a translation of the parts of the text covering mnemonic advice, see Francesc Eiximenis, *On Two Kinds of Order*, trans. by. Rivers, pp. 189–204.

conventions developed in the schools and available in many works well diffused by the late fourteenth century. The seven gifts of the Holy Spirit, the seven virtues and vices, the four causes and the like are explicitly mentioned by Francesc as ordering devices for generating and remembering preaching material. From his advice, it appears that late medieval preachers may have absorbed mnemonic training when they received their theological and logical instruction. It also implies that the laity learned these same kinds of things when they heard sermons.

Because Francesc is a figure unfamiliar to many English speakers, a brief biography of his life is in order.[45] He was born in the Catalan city of Girona, where he may have been educated and where he likely joined the Franciscan order.[46] A document in the Episcopal Archives in Barcelona records that he was ordained subdeacon or deacon at the church of Santa Maria de Sants in Barcelona in 1351, while in 1357 he attended a chapter meeting at the Franciscan house in Girona.[47] From perhaps 1357 to 1374 he studied philosophy and theology in schools all over Europe, including Paris, Oxford, and Rome; with the support of the royal family of Aragon, Francesc obtained a degree in theology in 1374 from the University of Toulouse.[48] He then returned to Barcelona as lector to the Franciscans and probably began his *Lo Crestià* (The Christian) at the request of Pere III, King of Aragon. After finishing volume one, he moved to Valencia, where he spent most of his remaining career and wrote his major Catalan works. He also had official duties, preaching at the funeral of Pere III, serving as royal confessor, and organizing a crusade to clear the African coast of Berbers. In 1408 the Aragonese pope Benedict XIII invited Francesc to attend the Council of

[45] For bibliography about Eiximenis to 1980, see David J. Viera, *Bibliografia anotada de la vida i obra de Francesc Eiximenis (1340?–1409?)* (Barcelona: Fundació Salvador Vives Casajuana, 1980). For biographical details in English, see my introduction to Francesc Eiximenis, *On Two Kinds of Order*, pp. 189–92, as well as Francesc Eiximenis, *Psalterium alias Laudatorium Papae Benedicto XIII dedicatum*, ed. by Curt J. Wittlin (Toronto: Pontifical Institute of Mediaeval Studies, 1988), and David J. Viera, *Medieval Catalan Literature: Prose and Drama*, Twayne's World Authors Series, 802 (Boston: Twayne, 1988).

[46] Viera, *Medieval Catalan*, p. 63; Isaac Vazquez, 'Francesc Eximenis', in *Dictionnaire d'histoire et de géographie ecclésiastiques*, ed. by Alfred Baudrillart, Albert Vogt, and Urbain Rouziès (Paris: Letouzey et Ané, 1912–), XVI, 252–53.

[47] Viera, *Medieval Catalan*, p. 63.

[48] Viera, *Medieval Catalan*, p. 63; Jill Rosemary Webster, 'A Critical Edition of *El Regiment De Princeps* by Francesc Eiximenis' (unpublished doctoral thesis, University of Toronto, 1969), pp. 2–3. Wittlin, in his edition of *Psalterium*, p. 3, puts the beginning of Eiximenis's study tour at 1357 at the earliest.

Perpignan, where he was named Patriarch of Jerusalem and Bishop of Elne. He died in Perpignan in 1409.[49]

During his time at Valencia, Francesc composed several works, all concerned in some manner with lay devotional life. His most famous works are *The Christian* (1378–91), an encyclopedic work planned for thirteen books (only four of which were completed) that deals with the Christian life, temptation, the seven deadly sins, and public life;[50] *Llibre dels àngels* (The Book of Angels, 1392), *Llibre de les dones* (The Book of Women, 1396), and *Vida da JesuCrist* (The Life of Christ, 1397–98). He showed his concern for lay understanding of religious doctrines by writing these works in the vernacular. In *The Christian* he declares that he is proceeding 'in a simple and unrefined way, so that although this book can be of profit to learned and well-trained individuals, I intend, rather, to speak to simple lay persons who are not trained in this subject matter'.[51] He is also careful to translate or paraphrase most Latin quotations in the *Christian* into Catalan.[52] Thus, Francesc demonstrates a concern for lay devotion in his vernacular works that also appears in his preaching treatise, which he wrote in Latin, the *Ars praedicandi populo*.[53]

Written most likely in the early part of Francesc's career, his *ars praedicandi* survives in three manuscripts.[54] Originally, the treatise was meant to introduce

[49] Viera, *Medieval Catalan*, pp. 63–64; Webster, 'Critical Edition', p. 3; *Psalterium*, ed. by Wittlin, pp. 9–11; Vasquez, 'Francesc Eximenis', p. 253.

[50] Webster, 'Critical Edition', pp. 8–28. Parts of the *Crestià* have been edited. For selections from the text, see *Lo Crestià: Selecció*, ed. by Albert Hauf (Barcelona: Edicions 62, 1983). Parts of the twelfth book of *Lo Crestià* have been edited in *Dotzè llibre del Crestià*, ed. by Curt J. Wittlin (Girona: Col'legi Universitari de Girona, Diputació de Girona, 1986).

[51] Viera, *Medieval Catalan*, pp. 63–64.

[52] Over half of the authors cited are quoted first in Latin and then translated or paraphrased into Catalan. The rest are quoted only in Catalan, though the translations from the Latin are rather free: Jorge J. E. Gracia, 'Francesc Eiximenis' Sources', in *Catalan Studies: Volume in Memory of Josephine de Boer*, ed. by Joseph Gulsoy and Josep M. Sola-Solé (Barcelona: Hispam, 1977), pp. 173–87 (p. 179).

[53] Briscoe and Jage, *Artes praedicandi*, pp. 45–48.

[54] The manuscripts are Cracow, Biblioteka Jagiellońska, MS 471. Aaa. I. 8 (*c.* 1444), fols 466$^{r}$–487$^{r}$; Budapest, Egyetemi Könyvtár (University Library), Bibliotheca Regiae Scientiarum, MS 73, no. 1 (xv), fols 109$^{r}$–144$^{v}$; and Biblioteca Apostolica Vaticana, MS fondo ottoboni 396 (xv), fols 29$^{v}$–44$^{r}$. According to Wittlin in his edition of *Psalterium*, p. 5, the preaching manual is listed in an inventory in Mallorca in 1499: see Jocelyn N. Hillgarth, 'Una biblioteca cisterciense medieval: La Real (Mallorca)', *Analecta sacra tarraconensia*, 32 (1960), 89–191 (p. 168).

three volumes of sermons, which have unfortunately been lost.[55] Because of Francesc's wide-ranging education and travels and because of his influence with the Crown of Aragon and the Pope, we need not fear that his *Ars praedicandi populo* represents the views of a preacher isolated from general European currents.[56] In fact, it falls into a genre of highly practical preaching manuals written in the later fourteenth century and is consistent in style and content with developments elsewhere in Europe.[57] Moreover, we know from his own writings that he seemed particularly well acquainted with English authors.[58] He may even have been familiar with Thomas Waleys's much-studied *Ars praedicandi*.[59]

Like his other religious works, Eiximenis's preaching manual exhibits concern for the religious life of the laity by insisting on the responsibility of the preacher to his audience and on the importance of his vocation as a preacher. The treatise is arranged, like many other medieval treatises, around the four causes of preaching: the final cause is the reason for preaching, the efficient cause is the demeanour

[55] See Josep Perarnau Espelt, 'Un fragment del Liber sermonum de Francesc Eiximenis', *Arxiu de textos catalans antics*, 10 (1991), 284–92.

[56] In fact, as William Courtenay shows in a recent article, scholars from the Iberian Peninsula were hardly isolated from intellectual trends in the rest of Europe. A number, like Francesc, studied theology in schools north of the Pyrenees. Even more significantly, a large number of manuscripts of texts written by European scholars survive in Spanish manuscript collections. See William J. Courtenay, 'Spanish and Portuguese Scholars at the University of Paris in the Fourteenth and Fifteenth Centuries: The Exchange of Ideas and Texts', in *Medieval Iberia: Changing Societies and Cultures in Contact and Transition*, ed. by Ivy A. Corfis and Ray Harris-Northall (Woodbridge: Tamesis, 2007), pp. 110–19.

[57] Briscoe and Jage, *Artes praedicandi*, pp. 42–43.

[58] Webster, 'A Critical Edition', p. 2 n. 9, lists works in which Eiximenis mentions his travels. Webster says he constantly refers to English theological treatises and to books he could not have obtained in Catalonia, such as Bede, John of Salisbury, Alexander Neckham, and William of Ockham. Wittlin, in *Psalterium*, p. 3, emphasizes the influence of John of Salisbury's political ideas on Francesc, which he probably absorbed through John of Wales's *Breviloquium* and *Communiloquium*.

[59] Albert G. Hauf, 'El "Ars praedicandi" de Fr. Alfonso d'Alprao, O.F.M.: Aportación al estudio de la teoría de la predicación en la Península Ibérica', *AFH*, 72 (1974), 233–329 (p. 240 n. 1), notes that there are several points of overlap in the preaching treatises of Thomas Waleys and Eiximenis. For instance, in Francesc's treatise, the material covering 'the form of preaching' and the seven conditions of a preacher (pp. 8–20) resembles Thomas Waleys's chapter on various 'examples' concerning the quality of a preacher. Several of the examples are nearly identical to Waleys's. Hauf attributes this overlap to coincidence, but if Eiximenis was so well travelled, he might have had access to Waleys's preaching treatise.

of the preacher, the formal cause is the method of preaching, and the material cause is the substance to be preached.[60] To Francesc, the most important final cause of preaching is the praise and glory of God. In every sermon, the preacher should attend most carefully to the task of explaining to the people God's attributes of goodness, wisdom, justice, sweetness, and truth. Such preaching should inform and inflame the people toward the praise of God. Approached properly, such sermons should also result in the salvation of both the people and the preacher.[61] Francesc particularly castigates those speakers who ignore the proper ends of preaching and instead focus on their own reputation. These preachers can be distinguished by their sermons, which are clearly not intended to stoke the fires of popular devotion. Instead, some preachers

> in contempt of the word of God and to the enticement of their listeners, turn themselves toward elaborate, rhymed and rhetorically ornate words, to which they add for their greater ostentation sayings from the *quadrivium*, such as arithmetic, geometry, astrology, and music, although often they know nothing of which they speak.[62]

In order that preachers might avoid these faults, Francesc devotes the second section (the efficient cause) of his treatise to recommendations of appropriate demeanour. Preachers should strive for chastity and poverty, and they should set a good moral example for the people. Francesc indicates that he thinks mendicant preachers might be more likely to accomplish this goal than secular ones.

The last seven chapters of the treatise turn to the form of preaching. It is in this section that Francesc imparts his most practical advice for the composition of sermons. He divides the section into seven 'conditions' of a sermon: preaching of the Divine Word should be done 'very briefly, very fervently, leisurely, devoutly, with a moral purpose [*moraliter*], prudently, and in an ordered manner [*ordinate*]'.[63] Most of these 'conditions' are justified by the effect that they will have on listeners and on their powers of recollection. For example, like other *ars praedicandi* writers, Francesc recommends brief sermons because the briefer the

[60] *Ars praed.*, Prologue, p. 304.

[61] *Ars praed.*, I, pp. 304–05.

[62] *Ars praed.*, I, p. 306: 'Et ad hoc in contemptum uerbi Dei et in scandalum audiencium conuertunt se ad uerba picta, rimata et rhetorice ornata, quibus coniungunt pro sui maiore ostentacione dicta quadriuii ut arismetice, geometrie, astrologie et musice, licet sepius illa ignorent que dicunt.'

[63] *Ars praed.*, III.1, p. 308: 'Forma autem ordinate praedicacionis quod est principale tercium hic discuciendum, hoc exigit seruare, uidelicet, ut predicacio uerbi diuini fiat breuissime, feruentissime, spaciose, deuote, moraliter, prudenter, ordinate.'

sermon, the more likely it is that the sermon will profit the listeners and that they will take away the sermon with them, a point very similar to Thomas Waleys's.[64] In fact, brevity seems so important to Francesc that he thinks it will serve all of the other 'conditions' of preaching, because 'he who speaks briefly is able to preach more securely, more quickly, in a more leisurely manner, and more devoutly, and can speak more acutely concerning morality'.[65] Like Hugh of St Victor, Francesc connects the ability to speak briefly with an ability to reduce material to order: '[T]he preacher who loves brevity must place his words in some certain order lest because of a weakness in order he may ramble [*discurrendum sine ordine*], often repeat the same thing, or, on account of forgetfulness, become bogged down in prolixity.'[66] Similarly, the preacher should speak in a fervent fashion so that his words will be more likely to imprint themselves in his listeners' minds.[67]

Francesc's memory advice appears as the seventh 'condition' of the method of preaching. According to Francesc, an apostolic messenger or excellent preacher should preach in an ordered manner (*ordinate*), not in disorder, not obscurely, lest he confuse himself and hinder his listeners.[68] The topic of order is so important to Francesc that he provides three chapters on its benefits: the first describes how order can aid understanding, the second how it aids memory, the third how it supports study and language. In fact, these three chapters serve the ancient rhetorical principles of *inventio*, *memoria*, and *dispositio*, as the first chapter actually shows how order can be used to generate or 'invent' preaching material, the second how order can help one to remember the material generated, and the third how order can be used to arrange the entire sermon. The first two chapters are densely packed with memory precepts and demonstrate nicely how theological and logical concepts could both support the preacher's memory and instruct the laity.

We will deal with the third section first, because its contents are very like those of the *artes* that we have already examined. Once the preacher has invented his material and stored it away, then he must arrange it. Francesc says that this third

[64] *Ars praed.*, III.1, p. 309.

[65] *Ars praed.*, III.1, p. 309.

[66] *Ars praed.*, III.1, p. 309: 'Propter quod oportet quod predicator breuitatis amore ponat uerba sua in aliquo certo ordine ne propter deffectum ordinis habeat discurrendum sine ordine, sepe eadem repetere, uel propter obliuionem prolixius immorari.'

[67] *Ars praed.*, III.2, p. 310.

[68] *Ars praed.*, III.7.1, p. 321: 'Septimo, nuncius apostolicus siue tuba Christi et predicator excellens debet ordinate loqui, non confuse, nec inuolute, ne confundat se et suos impediat auditores.'

chapter will aid study (*studium*) and language by producing an ordered sermon, because this kind of order teaches the preacher how to compose a sermon and the words to be said in a certain order. The preacher, observing this order attentively, 'as if reading a book, remembers while he preaches, and by remembering produces eloquently and clearly what he has to say. And so the preacher avoids all verbal obscurity and perturbation of mind.'[69] Clearly, Francesc has a good deal of confidence in his sermon method! He describes a number of ways one might arrange one's sermons, praising the use of divisions, because they help the preacher to remember. He, like many a late medieval preacher, notes that formerly doctors did not use divisions, as they were so imbued with the Holy Spirit that they translated into 'lofty' (*supernalia*) words without any order when they explicated the scriptural text in homiletic style. Francesc also describes the 'modern' style of preaching, which involves an introduction, an introduction of the theme, and a *distinctio* and *prosecutio* with its expansion. This is the method that he describes most fully. It has several advantages: a preacher using it finds copious preaching material, develops a habitual style that will aid his memory, and achieves the eloquence arising from a properly timed sermon.[70] All of this advice is consistent with earlier preaching tracts, and it is not as unusual as the advice in the first two chapters on order.

These first two chapters on order have in common the idea that preachers should rely on things they already know to compose, remember, and arrange a sermon. In the first chapter, devoted to inventing preaching material, Francesc assumes that most preachers already have some familiarity with basic theological and logical concepts, and launches directly into a series of rules for finding material. The four Aristotelian causes (final, efficient, formal, and material) provide a good example of Francesc's methodology.[71] According to Francesc, if a preacher needs to compose a sermon about charity, he might use the causes to invent his material. First, he should ask 'what is charity's final cause?' 'its efficient cause?', and so on. He could answer that charity's final end is to love God and neighbour, its efficient cause is God and a good life, and so on. If a preacher follows this advice, he will then have both something to say and an order in which

[69] *Ars praed.*, III.7.3, p. 331: 'Et hec species docet componere sermonem et uerba predicanda in aliquo certo ordine ad quem intellectum aduertens seriose, quasi legens in libro, dum predicat memoret et memorando proferat diserte et distincte quod habet dicere, et sic excludatur a predicante omnis inuolucio uerbalis et turbacio mentis.'

[70] *Ars praed.*, III.7.3, p. 332.

[71] *Ars praed.*, III.7.1. p. 321. See also p. 329.

to proceed. Medieval preachers and writers found the four causes a useful form of division; Francesc bases his own preaching manual on it, as did Robert of Basevorn. Guibert de Tournai organized the four parts of his *Rudimentum doctrinae* on the same principle. In addition, thirteenth-century scriptural exegetes often discussed questions of authorship in their academic prologues in these terms. As Aristotle's works on metaphysics and physics became textbooks accepted in the university curriculum, the four causes became standard ways to analyse material.[72] Understanding the causation of something helped scholastics to understand the event or thing itself; by Francesc's time, the fourfold scheme was being imparted to the laity in sermons. Thus, the four causes represented an order with which most school-trained preachers would be familiar and something Francesc thought listeners needed to learn.

Another suggestion for generating copious material for a sermon is to prove a proposition through an accustomed order of authorities. For example, if a preacher wants to base his sermon on the proposition that parents should be honoured, he should first find a proof text from the Bible to establish his first argument. The second authority should be supplied from *originalia* of the saints, the third from natural reason or common experience, the fourth from exempla of perceptible things, and the fifth may come from histories.[73] Canon law texts, philosophical examples, poetry, and fables should be avoided as proof texts in sermons to the people. Francesc here relies on a fairly common order of precedence for authoritative texts. His advice shows preachers how to remember the order of their citations, that is, texts from the Bible precede texts from saints' lives or natural histories, and warns them away from material inappropriate for the laity's ears.

Another particularly interesting suggestion is to construct a diagram comprised of several standard ordering schemes. A preacher places his theme or whatever he wishes to preach about in the centre of a circle. Around the ring of this circle he should arrange (*ordinare*) the Ten Commandments, the articles of faith, the gifts of the Holy Spirit, the eight Beatitudes, the five corporeal senses, the seven works of mercy, the seven virtues, and the seven vices.[74] If the preacher compares each of these items to his theme, he should be able to find something to preach about.

[72] Minnis, *Medieval Theory of Authorship*, pp. 28–29.

[73] *Ars praed.*, III.7.1, p. 322.

[74] *Ars praed.*, III.7.1, p. 323.

The material that Francesc includes in his diagram would have been reasonably well known to medieval preachers by the end of the fourteenth century. Since the Fourth Lateran Council in 1215, pastoral care had been recognized as a major concern of the Church. The schools of the twelfth century had begun to define the elements of pastoral instruction, a process which continued throughout the thirteenth century in the schools and universities.[75] An example of what would constitute the syllabus of pastoral care can be seen in the following mnemonic verse:

> Hec sunt precipua sermonibus insinuanda,
> Bis sex articuli fidei septemque petenda,
> Virtutes, uitia, presertim crimina septem,
> Septem sacra, duo Domini mandata decemque [precepta]
> Legis, iustorum merces penesque malorum,
> In quibus erratur, quid uitandum, quid agendum.[76]

The poem's phrases summarize the chapter titles of Richard of Wetheringsett's *Summa qui bene presunt*. Francesc uses similar material as ordering schemes. As in his advice about proof texts, the orders that Francesc recommends his preachers to follow are exactly the things the laity are supposed to learn from preaching.

Francesc tells us that the Aristotelian categories can be used in the same way:

> Under this rule is included the whole categorical order, so that if you should seek out the proposed matter or theme under the order of the categories concerning your proposition — what it is, how much, what sort, whose, where, when, etc. — much material would occur to you. Also under this rule falls the whole order of logical places, by the ordering of which many mental prompts will occur to you immediately if you look for material for your theme. And any order disposing our intellect toward finding mental prompts about a theme usefully falls under this rule.[77]

[75] Goering, *William de Montibus*, pp. 58–99.

[76] Goering, *William de Montibus*, p. 90 and n. 92; 'These things especially ought to be placed in sermons | The twelve articles of faith and the seven petitions | The virtues, the vices, especially the seven deadly sins | The seven sacraments, the two injunctions of the Lord and the Ten Commandments | Of law, the reward of the just and the pangs of the damned | Matters of error, what should be avoided, what performed'; my translation. Goering thinks that the verse's author, Richard of Wetheringsett, was one of the first writers to set out these particular prescriptions for teaching that became so ubiquitous (pp. 82–93).

[77] *Ars praed.*, III.7.1, p. 323; Francesc Eiximenis, *On Two Kinds of Order*, trans. by Rivers, p. 196.

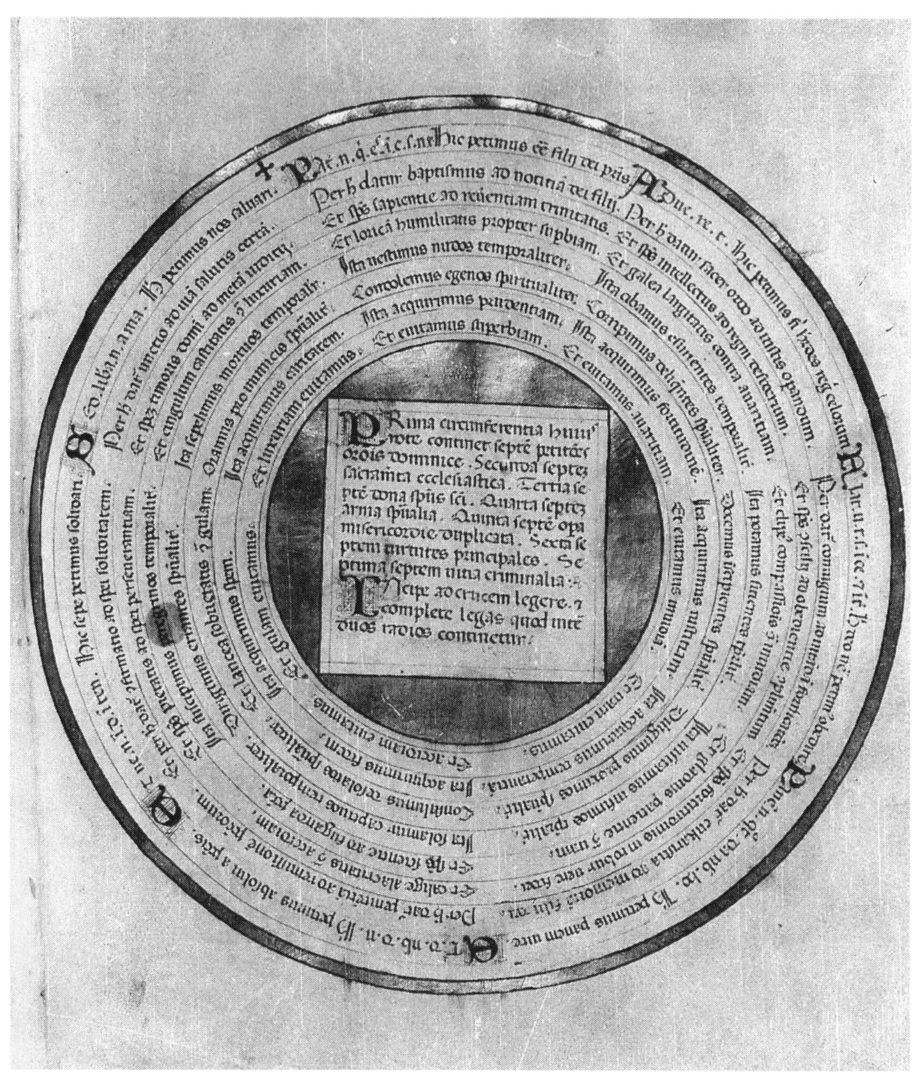


Fig. 1. 'Rota of the Sevens', present location of manuscript unknown, fol. 6r. Fifteenth century. Photograph courtesy of the Warburg Institute.

By this advice Francesc wishes the novice preacher to understand that the essence of finding preaching material is to turn to some sort of established order, whether it is one of the theological schemes, the categories, or logical loci. To preachers trained in logic, which must have been most medieval preachers, the categories and the logical places would have been deeply ingrained in their mental equipment. Preaching will seem a much less daunting task if the sermon can be based on such well-known material.

Constructing diagrams like circles to invent preaching material was also not unusual in the late Middle Ages. An example of a very similar circle can be seen in Figure 1. Beginning from the outermost ring and moving inwards, the circle contains the seven petitions of the Lord's Prayer, the sacraments, the gifts of the Holy Spirit, the metaphorical weapons of the Christian, the works of mercy, the virtues, and the vices. As Michael Evans has explained, the text in the central square of the diagram explains that to read the circle, one should begin at the cross (near the top on the outer ring) and move towards the centre of each radius. So the first section reads:

> Our Father which art in heaven, hallowed be Thy name. Here we ask to be sons of God the Father/ through this baptism is given for knowledge of the Son of God/ and the Spirit of Wisdom for reverence of the Trinity/ and the breastplate of Humility against Pride/ thus we clothe the naked physically/ we suffer with the needy spiritually/ thus we acquire Prudence/ and we drive our Pride.[78]

Though one could make many uses of the circle (Evans suggests that it could be used as an object of contemplation),[79] an obvious one would be to use the mix of lists in each sector to create sermons, just as Francesc advised. If one could also mentally rotate the various circles, one could create a plethora of outlines for sermons. As will be discussed in Chapter 8, Francesc's circle is a nice example of how images could be used to generate preaching material and how texts could inspire images.

While Francesc's advice in this chapter aims mainly to solve the problem of deciding the content of a sermon, it also provides a way to remember the final composition. In his chapter on the use of order in remembering a sermon,

[78] Michael Evans, 'The Geometry of the Mind', *Architectural Association Quarterly*, 12 (1980), 32–55 (p. 54) (Evans's translation).

[79] Evans, 'The Geometry of the Mind', p. 42. See also his comments on the use of circle diagrams generally in the Middle Ages, as well as John Block Friedman, 'Les images mnémotechniques dans les manuscrits de l'époque gothique', in *Jeux de mémoire*, ed. by Roy and Zumthor, pp. 169–83.

Francesc says that a preacher can memorize his material by utilizing some of the orders for generating preaching content.[80]

After describing how to invent the content of a sermon through order, Francesc provides additional aids to remember that material in the second chapter on order. His advice consists of an amalgam of medieval rules about memory. His description of a number-line method bears some resemblance to the one set out by Hugh of St Victor in his preface to the *Chronicon*, as does his recommendation to place mnemonic cues in the book in which one studies.[81] His method is also similar to that of the *Rhetorica ad Herennium* and perhaps seemed a simpler and more practical method to his contemporaries. Certainly he knows the work and quotes its supposed author, Cicero, at least three times.[82] The wording of his advice, however, is couched in the vocabulary and teachings of the schools. His ideas do not seem to be affected by the works of another Iberian author, Ramon Llull, as least as far as I can discover.

Francesc begins, as so many mnemonic experts of the late Middle Ages begin, by noting that one has memory either of names and words (*nomina* or *vocabula*) or of signified things (*res significatae*). Words are more difficult to remember because one must imagine some similitude or figure for each word. When one needs to remember things, however, then only one similitude or figure can represent a whole story. For example, a crucifix signifies the entire passion story or an image of a king with a lance indicates a triumph in war.[83] However, Francesc makes it clear that associating images with words or stories does not provide an entirely reliable retrieval system unless the images are stored in a clear order.[84]

[80] *Ars praed.*, III.7.2, p. 329: 'Et universaliter hoc habeas pro regula generali, quod ubicumque intellectus non potest inuenire ordinem, ibi habeas fundamentum memorandi, quia ordo rerum tibi notus est magister memorie tue. Et quia infinitis modis intellectus potest sibi fingere ordines, ideo infinitis modis potest tibi occurrere materia memorandi, quod eciam supra, precedenti capitulo, diximus de ordine inuenire potest multum iuuare memoriam racione ordinis connexi, sicut est ordo causarum principalium et ordo predicamentorum, et sic de aliis ordinibus supradictis.'

[81] Green, 'Hugo of St. Victor: *De tribus maximis*', pp. 484–93.

[82] Francesc Eiximenis, *On Two Kinds of Order*, trans. by Rivers, p. 191.

[83] *Ars praed.*, III.7.2, p. 325.

[84] *Ars praed.*, III.7.2, p. 325. 'Concerning each kind of remembering, Aristotle posits a similar example in his book, *On Memory and Reminiscence*, namely, that every memorable thing results from a past action, that is, it often comes before a sense, as before the eyes or the ears or the touch, or according to what was once sensed by one or several senses. It should, however, be noted that past sensation is useful to memory only if through that sensation is perceived some order in the

Having indicated that order and images are the keys to remembering, Francesc describes two methods of remembering words (*nomina* or *vocabula*), five for remembering things (*res significatae*), and three for remembering phrases. To remember names, one should arrange them on a long road under some similitude in an ordered way. To retain the names of the apostles, for example, one should think of a familiar road at the start of which is located a large stone: the stone will represent Peter. Next, one should think of some farm situated near the same stone in which two people are kissing; they represent Paul or peace. One may then place a large lamb (*agnus*) near the farm, which will stand for Andrew (in Latin both words start with *a*).[85] In this way, one is able to remember the other apostles and any other incomplex names to be remembered.[86]

One can also adapt this method of memorizing incomplex names to include the numbers (*nomina numeralia*), so that if someone mentions many names, and then asks in what place a certain name was said, one will be prepared to answer. Francesc's advice is to form for oneself an extremely familiar set of places and to locate, in the imagined places, a series of numbers, beginning from one to whatever final number one wishes.[87] When one recalls the images of the names set in each place, one will also automatically remember the number. Francesc admits that including numbers is more difficult, but worth the effort. As an example, Francesc mentions someone who recalled numbers or *res* through an ordered series of things whose names indicated a certain number. This friend would imagine a straight line from the heavens to the earth, and on the first part of the line he placed the firmament, which stood for one; on the second place he placed the luminous bodies, the sun and the moon, which represented two. For the number three, he used three elements, fire, air, and water; for four, the four corners of the globe; and for five, a hand. In this way, the places, by their very being, also revealed their numbered order.[88]

Francesc's system clearly preserves some ancient mnemonic principles, but they have been adapted to a medieval context. This change is most evident in his terminology: Cicero's expressions have been translated into the nomenclature of

thing sensed, for it is difficult to retain a multitude of memorable things'; Francesc Eiximenis, *On Two Kinds of Order*, trans. by Rivers, p. 198.

[85] *Ars praed.*, III.7.2, pp. 325–26.

[86] *Ars praed.*, III.7.2, p. 326: 'et sic procedas de aliis apostolis et de quibuscumque uoleris incomplexis nominibus recordari'. The edition reads 'in complexis nominibus'.

[87] *Ars praed.*, III.7.2, p. 326.

[88] *Ars praed.*, III.7.2, p. 326.

medieval logic, that is, the *Ad Herennium*'s *verba* and *res* have become *nomina* and *res significatae*. A *nomen* may be either a 'name' or a 'noun', though Francesc also calls it a 'word' (*vocabulum*).[89] Hence, Francesc has modified the concept of memory for words, as most of his rules for *verba* are for memorizing names, or at least strings of single words, not whole sentences. This is clear both from the apostle example and from his use of the phrase *incomplexum nomen*, or 'term'. Aristotle's *Categories* defines incomplex names as 'those without complexity, such as "man", "ox", "runs", "conquers". Complex names are 'those which are said with complexity, as "man runs," "man conquers," i.e. propositions'.[90] Incomplex names are, by necessity, single words. Evidently logical terms came more naturally to Francesc, and perhaps to his audience, than Cicero's vocabulary.

In addition, the idea of memorizing places and images seems close to the advice given in the *Ad Herennium*. However, Francesc's example of a line stretching from heaven to earth is not dissimilar to the number-line method described in Hugh of St Victor's *De tribus maximis circumstantiis gestorum*,[91] in which Hugh advises his young readers to contemplate in their minds a line of natural numbers extended lengthwise, starting with one.[92] Francesc's method may have originated from either of these sources or perhaps have been a practical amalgamation of both.

The phrase *res significatae per nomina* is used in a way that is closer to the classical usage, designating the things signified by the names, rather than the names, or words, themselves. A *res* signified by a name may be not just a 'thing', but a whole story or perhaps a section of a sermon. For example, the crucifix does not signify simply Christ on the Cross but the whole story (*tota series*) of the

[89] See Joseph Patrick Michael Mullally, *The Summulae logicales of Peter of Spain*, Publications in Mediaeval Studies, 8 (Notre Dame: University of Notre Dame Press, 1945), p. 2; Charlton Thomas Lewis and Charles Short, *A Latin Dictionary*, 2nd edn (Oxford: Oxford University Press, 1975), p. 1213.

[90] Aristotle, *Categoriae vel Praedicamenta, 'Translatio Boethii'*, ed. by Lorenzo Minio-Paluello, Aristoteles latinus, 1, 1–5 (Bruges: de Brouwer, 1961), 1a15: 'Eorum quae dicuntur alia quidem secundum complexionem dicuntur, alia vero sine complexione. Et ea quae secundum complexionem dicuntur sunt ut homo currit, homo vincit; ea vero quae sine complexione, ut homo, bos, currit, vincit.'

[91] Green, 'Hugo of St. Victor: *De tribus maximis*', pp. 484–93. Francesc says that 'ipse imaginabatur lineam rectam a firmamentum usque ad terram' (*Ars praed.*, III.7.2, p. 326).

[92] Green, 'Hugo of St. Victor: *De tribus maximis*', p. 489: 'Disce contemplari in animo tuo lineam naturalis numeri ab uno in quamlibet longam porrectionem quasi oculos cordis tui extensam.'

events of the Passion.[93] Such a simple mental notation could very well be a sufficient reminder for a preacher, who presumably would know the events of the Passion story in some detail.

Having explained the method for remembering incomplex names, Francesc turns to *res significatae per nomina*. He offers one basic principle: '[A]lways order the things to be remembered in some order corresponding to the things to be remembered.'[94] There are many ways to find an order and Francesc offers eight: 1) in major roads and paths known to us; 2) in anything that is straight or situated in an orderly way; 3) in large and ornate homes; 4) in the human body and its ordered members; 5) in the book in which one studies; 6) in a mixture of all these possibilities; 7) in the joining of syllables to form words and names; 8) when the end of one phrase cues the beginning of the next.

Five options demonstrate ways to remember things, while three are really ways to remember strings of words. In the first example, we imagine a direct road from Rome to Santiago de Compostella, along which we think of six other cities — Florence, Genoa, Avignon, Barcelona, Saragossa, and Toledo — chosen for their fame, familiarity, and distinctiveness from one another.[95] Then, supposing that we have eight matters to remember, we match each item to the city which most closely corresponds to it. Thus, we will place in Rome the material concerning clerics, because it is the city of clerics. In the Florence of our imagination we will place money, because it is a city famous for money.[96] For Avignon, Francesc makes a pun on the word *pons* (bridge), saying that there he places the material concerning a great *pons*, 'because there is the most famous *pons* in Christendom', that is, probably both the famous Pont St Bénézet and the 'pontiff' or pope, who in the mid-fourteenth century resided in Avignon.[97]

[93] This view is consistent with the *Ad Herennium*, which declares, 'Often we encompass the record of an entire matter by one notation, a single image' (trans. by Caplan); 'Rei totius memoriam saepe una nota et imagine simplici comprehendimus' (*Ad Her.*, III.20.33).

[94] *Ars praed.*, III.7.2. pp. 326–27: 'Memorare autem res significatas per nomina potest quis faciliter accipiendo hoc pro fundamento ut semper ordinet memoranda in aliquo ordine rerum concordancium cum rebus memorandis'; Francesc Eiximenis, *On Two Kinds of Order*, trans. by Rivers, p. 199.

[95] *Ars praed.*, III.7.2. p. 327: the cities are 'Roma, Florencia, Ianua, Auinio, Barchinona, Cessaraugusta, Toletum et Sanctus Iacobus'.

[96] *Ars praed.*, III.7.2, p. 327.

[97] *Ars praed.*, III.7.2, p. 327: 'Quarto, ponam in Auenione materiam magni pontis, quia de facto ibi est pons famosior qui sit in christianitate'. The Pont St Bénézet was built between 1177

As in the exercise for recalling the apostles' names, we match the item to be remembered with an appropriate place. Francesc seems not to advocate an accustomed order of places to be used every time we store away information, but rather recommends that we match the places to the objects of memory. One assumes that Francesc suggests this particular example of order only for topics that can produce associations with the cities. The same principle applies when we use the human body as a series of ordered places. We can begin from the feet and move up to the head or vice versa. In this manner the body may become a model of society:

> For the feet can signify peasants or the foundation of a house; just as the feet support the whole body and the peasants support the republic by their labor, so also their feet labor the most in the body. And the shins and the legs signify the burgesses, who are immediately above the peasants; the stomach represents those who receive the money of the republic, just as the stomach contains and receives everything. The arms symbolize the knights, because the knights labor by warring with their arms.[98]

Continuing the analogy up to the head, which designates the king of the state, Francesc again conflates the place and the image: the head is both the last place and the king. The lines between mnemonic strategy, idea, and physical representation are blurred, so that Francesc's method becomes much less rigid than the *Ad Herennium*'s with its strict definitions of images and places. As a way of summing up his precepts on remembering *res*, Francesc tells us that, if we have to memorize something quickly, we may combine elements from all of these possibilities. As a general rule, an order of things known to us is the director of our memory.[99] Because there is an infinite number of ways that our intellect can discover order, it follows that an infinite number of ordering schemes for re-

and 1185, long before Francesc's lifetime; Yves Renouard, *The Avignon Papacy: The Popes in Exile, 1305–1403*, trans. by Denis Bethell (New York: Barnes and Noble, 1970), p. 35. The French nursery tune 'Sur le pont d'Avignon' reflects the importance of the bridge in the popular imagination.

[98] *Ars praed.*, III.7.2, p. 328: 'pedes enim possunt significare tibi rusticos uel fundamenta domus, sicut ipsi pedes sustinent totum hominem et rustici rem publicem in labore suo sicut eciam pedes eorum plus laborant in corpore humano; et tibie et crura burgenses qui sunt immediate super rusticos; uenter, recipientes peccunias rei publice, sicut uenter omnia continet et recipit; brachia, milites, quia milites laborant brachiis bellando'; Francesc Eiximenis, *On Two Kinds of Order*, trans. by Rivers, p. 201. Francesc's image of the human body representing the parts of the community closely follows a similar image in John of Salisbury's *Policraticus*, V.2. I am indebted to Mary Rouse for this reference.

[99] *Ars praed.*, III.7.2, p. 329: 'Et universaliter hoc habeas pro regula generali, quod ubicumque intellectus non potest inuenire ordinem, ibi habeas fundamentum memorandi, quia ordo rerum tibi notus est magister memorie tue.'

membering exists. He adds that the rules for remembering verbal material ('ad recordandum materias uerbales') can be handled like *res*, 'so that if you wish to remember the titles of the *Decretals* or the *Corpus iuris civilis* or any material contained therein', you may do so by applying the titles in an orderly way to places. Francesc has no other rules for recalling verbatim memorization of longer texts (as opposed to names).

Francesc's final rules rely on wordplay. For instance, if I wish to remember several names, I may grasp them all by taking one syllable from each in order to form another word. This method is still used today. American students of the French language are sometimes taught to remember the verbs of departing and returning that require *être* as the auxiliary for the past tense by the name 'Mrs Vandertramp'. Each letter stands for the first letter of a verb; thus, *M* is for *monter*, *r* is for *retourner*, and so on. Another approach advocated by Francesc is to cue the first word of a phrase through the last word of the preceding one. That is, if I had to speak on the subjects the heavens, fire, and water, I might arrange my introduction just so:

> First the heavens must be discussed and it is obvious that it is made of fiery matter, while fire must be investigated secondly, because it is situated near air. And I will talk about air thirdly because it is vaporous.[100]

Such advice recognizes the practical difficulties of preaching and would probably be easily utilized by someone more sceptical of the other practices.

One other method is to learn by the order in the book where one studied the subject one wants to remember. According to Francesc, the ancients, like many moderns, would impress in their minds notable signs, such as a paragraph or ink marks, in the book near the line of text they wished to remember. When they preached, they could recount their sermon as though reading from a book by referring to these signs. Francesc is so impressed by this method that he wants the scribes who copy the sermons that follow his treatise in the manuscript to reproduce the exact arrangement of lines, because Francesc arranged them in the way best suited to aid fallible memories.[101] (Unfortunately, the sermons are absent

[100] *Ars praed.*, III.7.2, p. 330: 'primo loquendum est de celo et ostendendum quod est materie ignite; ignis secundo est discuciendum quia situatur prope aërem; de aëre tercio est dicendum qui uaperosus est'.

[101] *Ars praed.*, III.7.2, p. 330. Francesc's *ars praedicandi* originally served as the prologue to three volumes of sermons which have unfortunately been lost; see P. Martí de Barcelona, 'Ars praedicandi', p. 3. The autograph might have demonstrated what scribal practices he thought most likely to aid memory. See also Espelt, 'Un fragment'.

from the three surviving manuscripts of the *Ars*). The ancients to whom Francesc refers may be very ancient indeed, as this is substantially the same mnemonic advocated by Quintilian, Martianus Capella, and, much later, Hugh of St Victor. His mnemonic advice in this chapter favours utility over adherence to any one 'art of memory'. It also shows less concern for content likely to serve the laity than the advice dispensed in the previous chapter. Some of the methods here would aid mental recall of a sermon without necessarily affecting the content and structure of a sermon.

One other noteworthy point about Francesc's mnemonic rules is a rather puzzling aside about Cicero's memory method:

> Note that Tully and many others, wishing to aid memory artificially, discovered that on the aforesaid places images of memorable things ought to be made and commended to these places. Nevertheless, because he has a long tract concerning the difficulty and magnitude of remembering because of the images of things so located in them (places), for this reason the moderns of this time do not approve that method, but, considering more effective and easier that method which we just set forth, they direct themselves to it, passing over the ancient method. For this reason, I took care to speak only about this new mode.[102]

According to Francesc, modern preachers and mnemonic experts considered Cicero's method too cumbersome to use. Instead they preferred the method which Francesc himself had just set out. Now, this is a somewhat puzzling statement, since he has explained several different mnemonic strategies. This statement could be interpreted in one of two ways. First, as the *Ad Herennium* only remarks on the difficulty of memory for words, not memory for things, what Francesc may mean is that modern preachers do not often employ Cicero's rules to remember long, written material, reserving it for incomplex names and for things. A reason for preferring this interpretation is that Francesc inserts the comment about Tully immediately after mentioning that the titles of the *Decretals* or the *Corpus iuris civilis* can be memorized using places. The context is one of remembering what he calls 'verbal material' rather than *res*.

It is clear that he has not fully rejected the use of places and images in memorizing, but rather that he, and likely other preachers (the *moderni*), have

[102] *Ars praed.*, III.7.2, p. 329: 'Nota quod Tulius et multi alii, uolentes iuuare artificialiter memoriam, inuenerunt super locis predictis deberi fingi imagines memorabilium et commendare eas locis. Tamen quia hic habet longum tractatum de difficultate atque magnitudine in recordacione quia imaginum sic rerum collocatarum in eis, ideo modum istum non approbant moderni huius temporis sed, magis expeditum et facilem estimantes illum quem statim diximus et premissimus, ad istum se conuertunt, antiquo pretermisso. Ideo de isto premisso nouo modo solum curaui hic loqui.'

merely simplified the method. Francesc quotes from Cicero's mnemonic art approvingly. The key to this method is to discover some association of a place with the memorable point and to discover a new order or series of places for each set of things one wants to remember. Francesc does not tell us to reuse the places nor does he make the usual comparison of the places to wax and the images to letters. Rather, he advocates a more limited arrangement. This point can be seen in a number of places in his text. For instance, he says that 'when one has to memorize things quickly and no order appears that lends itself to arranging our proposition in a memorable way, then mix the orders together'.[103] Presumably one would not have to find a new order every time one had new material if one used the ancient memory method: one would either reuse old places or simply place the new things to be remembered in the first free places that one had prepared already. He also says that the fundamental rule for remembering things signified by words is 'always order the things to be remembered in some order corresponding to the things to be remembered'.[104] In the memory arts of the fifteenth century, one plays association games with the things to be remembered and the image. In Francesc's system, the association is made between the thing to be remembered and the place.

A second way this statement could be interpreted, as Mary Carruthers has recently done, is to see it as a wholesale rejection of Cicero's mnemonic system and view it instead as an advocation of the kind of monastic practices outlined in Chapter 1.[105] It seems clear that Francesc does not slavishly follow Cicero's method and instead advocates a mix of methods that draw on simpler systems, including that of the monks. However, I would still argue that he does not completely reject Cicero, as can be seen in his quotations from the *Ad Herennium*, his use of loci, and in his transformation of the old classical vocabulary into a scholastic nomenclature.

## *The Use of Francesc's Methods by Other Medieval Authors*

What does Francesc's mnemonic advice tell us about how medieval preachers remembered their sermons? Is there any evidence that other medieval speakers utilized the same kinds of methods? What does it reveal about what the laity

[103] *Ars praed.*, III.7.2, pp. 328–29; Francesc Eiximenis, *On Two Kinds of Order*, trans. by Rivers, p. 202.

[104] *Ars praed.*, III.7.2, pp. 326–27; Francesc Eiximenis, *On Two Kinds of Order*, trans. by Rivers, p. 199.

[105] Carruthers, 'Late Antique Rhetoric', p. 251.

were expected to remember? Francesc's memory advice implies that mnemonic techniques were known in the later fourteenth century and were combined with medieval concepts to remember homiletic material. The emphasis was less on sticking to an 'art' than on utilizing any method suitable for one's particular mnemonic situation. Francesc's practicality suggests one reason why medieval mnemonic advice is so hard to find: there was no one, definitive mnemonic scheme. Preachers used any method that would work, especially methods that served more than one function.

Francesc's mnemonic advice also stresses the importance of order in remembering sermon material. The entire discussion of memory occurs in the context of speaking in order (*ordinate*), and he says that the key to remembering is 'to find an order of things known to you'. The orders that he provides as examples are either concepts learned in the schools or basic images like streets and the parts of the body. This advice is similar to his recommendations for inventing preaching material, and here may be another reason why medieval discussions of preaching mnemonics are so infrequent.

Other preaching experts utilize 'ordering' methods like Francesc's, but they rarely identify their practices as mnemonically useful. To illustrate how other preachers relied on ordering mechanisms, even though they seldom make this relevance explicit, we may divide Francesc's ordering examples into those that rely on common orders, those that depend on the theological or logical teaching of the schools, and those that rely on imagery.

An example of common orders is given by Étienne Gilson in a well-known article about the *ars praedicandi*. Gilson describes the concordance of texts in one of Michel Menot's († 1518) sermons, an example he considered 'un cas manifestement pathologique'.[106] Menot ties together a string of biblical quotations by relying on the notes of the scale: Ut. Re. Mi. Fa. Sol. La. He warns his listeners about the souls of the damned, who sing a song with six miserable notes in it. The souls chant biblical texts, each corresponding in its first letter to a note. So one soul sings the first note, saying 'Utinam consumptus essem, ne oculus me rideret' (Job 10. 18). Then he adds the second note, singing 'Repleta est malis anima mea' (Ps 87. 4). The other souls join in with texts to fill out the rest of the scale.[107] In its reliance on a well-known order and on wordplay, Menot's sermon method corresponds perfectly to Francesc's mnemonic advice. In general, one

[106] Gilson, 'Michel Menot', p. 337.

[107] Gilson, 'Michel Menot', pp. 337–38. *Sermons choisis de Michel Menot (1508–1518)*, ed. by Joseph Nève, Bibliothèque du XV^e siècle, 25 (Paris: Champion, 1924), pp. 246–47.

might take it as a rule that the odder the sermon construction, the more likely it is that the author is using a mnemonic device, either for himself or for his audience.

Carruthers notes that Robert of Basevorn also recommends that preachers divide their themes by musical notes. He divides his example theme, 'Ego vox clamantis in deserto, parate viam Domini', by the same six notes as Menot and then attaches the texts of the subdivision to correspond by their first letters to each note:

> 1) UT filii lucis ambulate; 2) REvertere, revertere, Sulamitis, revertere, revertere ut intueamur te; 3) MIsere animae tuae placens Deo; 4) FAcite dignos fructus poenitentiae; 5) SOLve vincula colli tui, captiva filia Syon; 6) LAvamini, mundi estote.[108]

Many of Robert's other suggestions for dividing a theme fit Francesc's requirements for finding an order. For example, he subdivides a sermon on the Passion according to the vowels, an obviously well-known order:

> Subdividitur tunc sic: Quinque sunt vocales, scilicet *A E I O U*, quae omnem vocem faciunt. Sic quinque vulnera Christi omnem sonum, sive doloris sive gaudii faciunt. Vide *in manibus A* et *E*: [Jer. 31. 3] 'Attraxi te miserans' et: [Is. 49. 16] 'Ecce in manibus meis descripsi te'; *I in latere*: talem enim figuram imprimit vulnus lanceae, hoc est 'ostium arcae' quod 'in latere', etc. in Gen. [6. 16] et in Joan. [20. 27]: 'Infer digitum tuum huc et mitte in latus meum, et noli esse incredulus, etc:, *O* et *U in pedibus*: [Ps 8. 6] 'Omnia subjecit Deus sub pedibus ejus'. Ideo ut consequaris dicas facto: [Job 23. 11] 'Uestigia ejus secutus est pes meus'.[109]

As Carruthers remarks, the five subdivisions are marked by two sets of five, both the five wounds in the Crucifixion and the five vowels. The biblical texts are tied to the subdivisions by references to the wounds within the quotations and by the first word of each citation, which begins with the requisite vowel.

George Ferzoco has examined a sermon for the feast of the canonization of St Bridget (or Birgitta) of Sweden that shows an example of the rhetorical device *notatio per litteras* to construct and undoubtably also to recall a sermon. The sermon has the theme 'Benedictus Dominus, qui creauit celum et terram' and was probably written by the Vadstena monk Acho (or Ako) Iohannis. He expands on the qualities of Birgitta's character that correspond to the letters of her name: '"b" for *benedicta*, "i" for *illuminata*, "r" for *roborata*', and so on.[110] In his study of the

[108] Robert of Basevorn, *Forma praedicandi*, in *Artes praedicandi*, ed. by Charland, p. 312; cited in Carruthers, *Book of Memory*, p. 105.

[109] Robert of Basevorn, *Forma praedicandi*, pp. 311–12; cited in Carruthers, *Book of Memory*, p. 105.

[110] George Ferzoco, 'Preaching, Canonization and New Cults of Saints in the Later Middle Ages', in *Prédication et liturgie au moyen âge*, ed. by Nicole Bériou and Franco Morenzoni

*ars poetriae*, Edmond Faral observes that ancient writers placed *notatio per litteras*, or the use of etymology, among the topics of invention.[111] Medieval writers followed the same practice and give many examples in their manuals of using the first letters and syllables of phrases to spell out a given word or name.

Other authors, such as Robert of Basevorn, mention the use of theological concepts as ordering devices, such as St Bernard's seven mercies of God, the eight beatitudes, the nine orders of angels, and the Ten Commandments.[112] Unlike Francesc, Robert never identifies the mnemonic function of these arrangements of the text. Kirsten Berg's study of mnemonic schemes in the Old Norwegian Homily Book gives several examples of theological concepts used as structuring devices, including the four evangelists, the virtues of the dove, and the hierarchy of angels.[113] Again, these are not identified in the sermon text as memory aids.

Nor does the Franciscan author of the *Ars concionandi* refer to mnemonic utility when he recommends dividing one's theme by the Aristotelian categories. As an example, he chooses the text 'Evangelizo vobis gaudium magnum, quod erit omni populo, quia natus est vobis hodie Salvator, qui est Christus dominus, in civitate David' (Luke 2. 10). Using the categories as a guide, he then asks a series of questions about the text, such as 'Quis evangelizat? Quid? De quo? Cui?' Each question is answered by a reference to the text, providing a way both to divide the theme and to expand on it, if desired. Gilson notes that Bonaventure had recourse to the same technique, while Michel Menot employed the rhetorical circumstances in a similar fashion.[114]

In all of these examples, I have stressed the importance of order over imagery, because as important as imagery is (and the rest of the book will be devoted to it), order is the key to homiletic mnemonics. One could almost claim that the structure of the sermon is its message.[115] Certainly, many sermons could reasonably be

(Turnhout: Brepols, 2008), pp. 297–312 (p. 305). He has transcribed the text of the sermon in the appendix. He also lists other examples of wordplay in sermons on p. 305 n. 44.

[111] *Les Arts poétiques*, p. 65.

[112] Robert of Basevorn, *Forma praedicandi*, p. 312; Carruthers, *Book of Memory*, p. 107. For an enlightening comparison between Robert of Basevorn's *ars praedicandi* and John of Waldeby's sermons, see Akae, 'Between *Artes praedicandi* and Actual Sermons', pp. 9–31.

[113] Berg, 'On the Use of Mnemonic Schemes', pp. 222–27.

[114] Gilson, 'Michel Menot', p. 327.

[115] Jussi Hanska comes to a similar conclusion in his article '*Uidens Iesus ciuitatem fleuit super illam*: The *Lachrymae Christi* Topos in Thirteenth-Century Sermon Literature', in *Constructing the Medieval Sermon*, ed. by Andersson, pp. 237–51 (p. 251): 'For a medieval preacher, constructing the structure of a sermon was essentially about making decisions on the content at the same time.'

reduced to the skeletal form found in the *vademecum* books. The structure also holds much of the 'material' that the laity might be expected to learn from the sermon, such as the seven virtues and vices, the seven gifts of the Holy Spirit, and the like, and it was up to the oratorical skill of the speaker to provide the fervour that would move their souls in the right direction.

It can be difficult to prove that the laity absorbed these structural messages, but there are some hints in discussions of preaching that this was the case. Certainly preachers complained that some audiences, particularly 'fashionable' or sophisticated ones, ignored the message of the sermon in favour of its structure. A thirteenth-century preacher, speaking before the canons of St Victor in Paris, remarked that

> There are many, who, when they come to sermon [*sic*], [...] do not care what the preacher says; but only how he says it. And if the sermon be well 'rhymed', if the theme be well 'divided', if the brother discourses well, if he pursues his argument well, if he 'harmonizes' well, they say: 'How well that brother preached!' 'What a fine sermon he made!' That is all they look for in the sermon, nor do they attend to what he says.[116]

In fifteenth-century England, Thomas Gascoigne complained about listeners who disdained sermons without form: 'They say, "This sermon has no shape." The man spoke, and he didn't know what he was talking about. He had no idea of what he was saying and he couldn't organize his ideas.'[117] Gascoigne (who wanted to revive the ancient sermon form over the modern one) thought that his audience was ignoring the content of the sermon in favour of its structure. His difficulty was that his predecessors had been too successful in training their listeners to learn the structure of sermons. While he chided them for favouring the branches of the tree over the fruit, in fact for many laity, the branches *were* the fruit of the tree.

Such an argument does not mean that listeners could learn nothing else from medieval sermons. Medieval writers occasionally express their astonishment over the knowledge that laypeople had been able to gain from listening to sermons. One sees this especially in the context of heretics, whose diligence in learning was brought up as a contrast to the more idle habits of orthodox laypeople. For example, G. G. Coulton noted Étienne de Bourbon's astonishment at the learning of some heretics:

[116] Cited in Owst, *Preaching in Medieval England*, p. 312.

[117] Thomas Gascoigne, *Loci et libro veritatum*, ed. by J. E. T. Rogers (Oxford: Oxford University Press, 1881), p. 179, cited in Spencer, *English Preaching*, p. 241.

> They know the Apostle's Creed excellently in the vulgar tongue. They learn by heart the Gospels of the New Testament in the vulgar tongue, and repeat them aloud to each other. [...] I have seen a young cowherd who had dwelt but one year in the house of a Waldensian heretic, yet had attended so diligently and repeated so carefully all that he heard, as to have learned by heart within that year forty Sunday gospels, not counting those for feast-days [...] and other extracts from sermons and prayers. [...] This I say on account of their diligence in evil and the negligence of the Catholics in good.[118]

Though this example hardly proves the effectiveness of Catholic preaching, it does indicate the hunger some laity had for religious teaching and their ability to learn it without an ability to read. D'Avray has compared the communications reach of medieval sermons to the modern newspaper, noting that the constant repetition of ideas, in his case, about marriage in marriage sermons, must have influenced the minds of some people:

> We cannot tell what any single reader makes of ideas on, say, a common European currency constantly reiterated in tabloid newspapers. If we think in terms of aggregate and of reasonable probabilities, we can be reasonably sure that a rather large number of people understand these topoi and that a subset of this subset are convinced by them.[119]

In any case, proving that the laity absorbed the messages aimed at them is the subject of another study.

Because I intend to deal with this topic in the next few chapters, I have not given much attention to mnemonic imagery in sermons, except to note that Francesc's example of the body signifying the parts of society is a good example of the kinds of moralization of images that one often finds recommended or practised in homiletic material.

## *Conclusions*

To conclude, Francesc of Eiximenis's *Ars praedicandi populo* is revealing of attitudes about memory among twelfth- to fourteenth-century writers and preachers. His inclusion of mnemonic principles in his preaching tract reveals the practices of medieval preachers at which other sources only hint. Francesc's mnemonic advice accords with the basic principles of organization laid out by earlier writers of *ars praedicandi*: aim for brevity, construct a logically ordered text by using divisions, and stick to concepts rather than exact words when memorizing. Unlike

[118] Cited in *From St. Francis to Dante*, ed. by G. G. Coulton, 2nd edn, Sources of Medieval History (Philadelphia: University of Pennsylvania Press, 1972), p. 302.

[119] D'Avray, *Medieval Marriage Sermons*, p. 30.

them, he includes a great deal of specific mnemonic advice; unlike the twelfth-century rhetoricians, such as Geoffroi de Vinsauf, he advocates a method similar to the *Ad Herennium*'s, which they had rejected. He builds on this mnemonic method, but he adapts the ancient text to the practical demands of mendicant preaching. His generally positive attitude toward Cicero's rules reflects the changes that the thirteenth century had made to the world of rhetoric and memory: the rise of the mendicant preachers, the influx of Aristotle's works on memory and cognition, and the study of Boethius's *De topicis differentiis* created an atmosphere more welcoming of the *Ad Herennium*'s mnemonic system than the twelfth-century schools had been.

However, Francesc did not adopt the ancient work's rules without change. He adds to these rules the need to find an order to generate, to remember, and to arrange one's material. Many of the 'orders' that he recommends reflect the theological and logical teachings of the schools, for example, the seven circumstances, the seven gifts of the Holy Spirit, and the like. These orders functioned like rhetorical topics and would doubtless have been very useful to many preachers. While Francesc is so practical in outlook that one might worry that his recommendations are idiosyncratic, the similarity between Francesc's heuristic devices and those of other writers should relieve such a fear. The task of imposing order on information created a kind of community of systems that one could both expect other educated people to know and which one could personalize for better effect. It is this ubiquity that may explain why medieval mnemonic advice is relatively hard to find unless one knows what to look for.

Finally, the tone of Francesc's entire *ars praedicandi*, as well as the advice of Thomas of Chobham and Thomas Waleys, indicates that aids for the laity's memories were as important as aids for the preacher's memory. The same ordering schemes that preachers knew from their training were deemed the kinds of religious teaching that the laity should learn. Knowledge of the virtues and vices was supposed to help Christians shun vice and become virtuous. These were not the only expected 'outcomes' (as modern educational jargon puts it), but they were important ones. In the end, medieval mnemonic schemes served the goals of the Church as well as the mental recall of the preacher.

Chapter 5

# Theoretical Justifications for the Use of Images in Preaching

When discussing the precepts for remembering and for preaching, most of the medieval writers that we have encountered so far stressed the priority of order over imagery. However, their emphasis on order did not exclude imagery. On the contrary, most mnemonic experts thought that images, that is, things seen, imprinted themselves in human memory much more effectively than things merely heard. In this opinion, the mnemonic theorists were supported by psychological theories, which presupposed a basic role for images in human cognition. The particular challenge for preachers was how to incorporate recommendations about the memorial function of images into a medium that depended almost exclusively on the spoken word. The problem was less acute for their own memories, since preachers trained in mnemonics could form mental images of the things they wished to remember. But how were they to convey this talent to their audiences? The next few chapters will explore the ways in which preachers, especially mendicant preachers, sought to render their sermons memorable through verbal imagery. This chapter will focus on their reasons for wanting to do so.

We will begin by examining the ways in which theologians and preachers justified the use of imagery — both pictorial and verbal — in the church and in sermons. Because we are most concerned with preaching, this discussion will concentrate on preaching imagery, that is, exempla. Finally, we will finish by scrutinizing a late medieval debate about appropriate kinds of exempla and preaching techniques that may indicate that acceptance of mnemonic techniques was not universal.

## *Theories about Images and the Laity in the Church*

The traditional thinking in the West about the role of images for the laity in the Church as expressed in artwork had its roots in Pope Gregory the Great's (590–604) assessment of images:[1]

> Pictures are used in churches so that those who are ignorant of letters may at least read by seeing on the walls what they cannot read in books (*codicibus*).
>
> What writing (*scriptura*) does for the literate, a picture does for the illiterate looking at it, because the ignorant see in it what they ought to do; those who do not know letters read in it. Thus, especially for the pagans (*gentibus*), a picture takes the place of reading. [...] Therefore, you ought not to have broken that which was placed in the church in order not to be adored but solely in order to instruct the minds of the ignorant.[2]

Gregory's contention that pictures were an ideal way to educate the laity was reiterated endlessly throughout the Middle Ages as a defence of religious art. In our period Guilelmus Durandus declared in his *Rationale divinorum officiorum*:

> It is seen that a painting moves the feeling more than what is written. In a painting some action is placed before the eyes, but in literature that action is recalled to the memory as it were by the hearing, which touches the feelings less. And so it is that in church we do not show as much reverence to books as we do to images and pictures.[3]

St Bonaventura seemed essentially to agree with this opinion when he listed the reasons for religious art:

[1] For general arguments and bibliography see Lawrence G. Duggan, 'Was Art Really the "book of the illiterate"?', *Word and Image*, 5 (1989), 227–51; Michael Camille, 'Seeing and Reading: Some Visual Implications of Medieval Literacy and Illiteracy', *Art History*, 8 (1985), 26–49; Margaret Aston, *Lollards and Reformers: Images and Literacy in Late Medieval Religion* (London: Hambledon, 1984); William R. Jones, 'Art and Christian Piety: Iconoclasm in Medieval Europe', in *The Image and the Word: Confrontations in Judaism, Christianity and Islam*, ed. by Joseph Gutmann (Missoula, MT: Scholars Press for the American Academy of Religion, 1977), pp. 75–105; G. G. Coulton, *Art and the Reformation* (Cambridge: Cambridge University Press, 1953).

[2] *S. Gregorii Magni registrum epistularum libri VIII–XIV*, ed. by Dag Ludvig Norberg, CCSL, 140A (Turnhout: Brepols, 1982), IX.209, p. 768, and XI.10, pp. 873–76, cited in Duggan, 'Was Art Really the "book of the illiterate"?', p. 227.

[3] Guilelmus Durandus, *Rationale divinorum officiorum I–IV*, ed. by Anselme Davril and Timothy M. Thibodeau, CCCM, 140 (Turnhout: Brepols, 1995), bk I, chap. 3, par. 4, ll. 63–67, p. 24: 'Pictura namque plus uidetur mouere animum quam scriptura. Per picturam quidem res gesta ante oculos ponitur quasi in presenti generi uideatur [...] sed per scripturam res gesta quasi per auditum, qui minus animum mouet, ad memoriam reuocatur. Hinc etiam est quod in ecclesia non tantam reuerentiam exhibemus libris quantam ymaginibus et picturis.'

> (1) They [images] were made for the simplicity of the ignorant, so that the uneducated who are unable to read Scripture can, through statues and paintings of this kind, read about the sacraments of our faith in, as it were, more open scriptures.
>
> (2) They were introduced because of the sluggishness of the affections, so that men who are not aroused to devotion when they hear with the ear about those things which Christ has done for us will at the least be inspired when they see the same things in figures present, as it were, to their bodily eyes. For our emotion is aroused more by what is seen than by what is heard.
>
> (3) They were introduced on account of the transitory nature of memory, because those things which are only heard fall into oblivion more easily than those things which are seen. For frequently is verified that common saying: the word enters through one ear and exits through the other.[4]

For Bonaventura religious art is effective because the ignorant can in some way 'read' it, unlike the Bible; because images more effectively rouse the emotions than words do; and because things seen are more likely to be remembered than things that have only been heard. He was followed in this estimation by several writers, including Thomas Aquinas and Johannes Balbus (*Catholicon*).[5] However, artwork was not the only kind of image influencing medieval thought.[6] Mental images were at least as important in the spiritual lives of both clergy and laity in the Middle Ages.

[4] Cited in Duggan, 'Was Art Really the "book of the illiterate"?', p. 232; Comm. III. dist. IX. art. 1, q. 2, concl., in St Bonaventura, *Opera omnia*, III, 203: 'Propter simplicium ruditatem inventae sunt, ut simplices, qui non possunt scipturas legere, in huiusmodi sculpturis et picturis tanquam in scripturis apertius possint sacramenta nostrae fidei legere. Propter affectus tarditatem similiter introductae sunt, videlicet ut homines, qui non excitantur ad devotionem in his quae pro nobis Christus gessit, dum illa aure percipiunt, saltem excitentur, dum eadem in figuris et picturis tanquam praesentia oculis corporeis cernunt. Plus enim excitatur affectus noster per ea quae videt, quam per ea quae audit [...]. Propter memoriae labilitatem, quia ea quae audiuntur solum, facilius traduntur oblivioni, quam ea quae videntur. Frequenter enim verificatur in multis illud quod consuevit dici: verbum intrat per unam aurem et exit per aliam'; trans. by Charles Garside, Jr, *Zwingli and the Arts* (New Haven: Yale University Press, 1966), p. 91.

[5] Duggan, 'Was Art Really the "book of the illiterate"?', p. 232; see also Michael Baxandall, *Painting and Experience in Fifteenth-Century Italy: A Primer in the Social History of Pictorial Style*, 2nd edn (Oxford: Oxford University Press, 1988), pp. 40–45.

[6] For a discussion of the connections between wall paintings and sermons in medieval England, see Miriam Gill, 'Preaching and Image: Sermons and Wall Paintings in Later Medieval England', in *Preacher, Sermon and Audience in the Middle Ages*, ed. by Carolyn Muessig (Leiden: Brill, 2002), pp. 155–80, as well as the other essays on preaching and art in the volume.

## *Cognitive Psychology, Images, and the Will*

One kind of mental image that was the topic of much discussion in the Middle Ages was the kind of image used in cognition. Since we have already discussed cognitive psychology (see Chapter 2), there is no need to say anything more about it here other than to note that Aristotle's theories about the role of images in cognition served to buttress traditional ideas about the role of images in educating the laity. Scholars like Albertus Magnus and Thomas Aquinas present a reasonably positive view of the use of images in cognition and memory. One cannot think without a (mental) image: memory and imagination store away images and their intentions, which can then be utilized by the intellect. Natural memory may be good on its own, or it may be strengthened by artificial memory. Memory techniques could be particularly effective in saving memories of 'incorporeal things', that is, concepts and ideas. For Thomas Aquinas in particular, there was a natural link between memory images and phantasms. Almost any image had the potential to help one remember if utilized properly.

As we saw in Chapter 2, Aristotle's views about the soul and its powers co-existed in the High Middle Ages with an older view that still had many adherents at this time, St Augustine's division of the soul's three powers into memory, intellect, and will. One of the implications of medieval thinking about Augustine's powers of the soul and indeed about Aristotle's theories is that there is a connection between the movement of the will and the images stored in memory.[7] One can see intimations of this connection in Gianfrancesco Pico della Mirandola reconsideration of the internal senses, *On the Imagination*, written around 1501.[8] Towards the end of his analysis, he observes that

> the affections are known from the phantasies which a man especially produces, and on which he dwells, when he is moved by nothing from without. If, therefore, we find ourselves moved by good phantasies of the sort that give birth to good affections, it remains for us to follow these affections, and to assist them with reason and intellect, and even with external effort. If we find ourselves moved by evil phantasies, another remedy offers itself: that in our position on that lofty watch-tower of the intellect we continually

[7] Minnis makes the same point about Aristotle's thinking about images in 'Medieval Imagination and Memory', p. 241. He notes that for Aristotle, the imagination was important in moral conduct, because it can produce images related to past, present, or even future things. Minnis says this has enormous implications for ethics: 'Thus mental pictures help in moving the will to initiate courses of action. These ideas underlie many medieval manifestations of ethical poetics and "affective piety", as we will see.'

[8] Gianfrancesco Pico della Mirandola, *On the Imagination*, trans. by Harry Caplan (Westport, CT: Greenwood, 1957).

> observe phantasy, and anticipate its reckless attacks. As Epictetus teaches, we must from the beginning strive to prevent the imagination from corrupting us.[9]

The kinds of phantasies produced in the imagination have the ability to move our affections and thus to bring about good or bad actions. Pico says we should follow the affections that rise from good phantasies and set the intellect to guard against the evil ones. This line of reasoning suggests that one might have some control over the images or phantasies in the imagination. The kinds of images with which one fills one's memory, such as images of the Passion or of the virtues and vices or of the events of the Last Judgement, should work to move the will to act in a moral fashion.

In fact, Pico says almost exactly that in his chapter on how to prepare oneself against the darkness of the imagination which arise from 'the wounds of evil spirits'.[10] He thinks that the intellect must be strengthened by the light of Faith in this battle. In addition, he identifies two levels of imagination, the brutish and the human, the first being the kind of imagination common to both animals and humans, the second present only in humans. The light of Faith can minister to either type of imagination. It has particular aids for the brutish, which he thinks is the type of imagination that children mostly live by:

> For example, it [the light of Faith] places before the youth, who live for the most part in that imagination which we have called the brutish [...] the punishments and fires of Hell, the rewards and delights of Paradise; and all these in a way which is most agreeable to the imaginative power, so that they are easily comprehended and with no difficulty retained. It presents, on the one hand, the lakes of fire and brimstone, tortures, demons, and the like; on the other hand, the golden ramparts of the Heavenly Jerusalem, girt with precious stones, celestial banquets, the marriage of the Lamb, the societies of the blessed, choruses of angels chanting harmonious tunes, and whatever scenes of this kind there are, scattered through Holy Writ. As a result, children are delighted by the one, and saddened and terrified by the other. And by both [...] they are warned, and at the same time led away from evil images.[11]

Pico thus thinks that the 'light of Faith' speaks to the less sophisticated imagination, as it were, of children through particularly effective images that help young people to shun voluptuous images and lead to right action. Even adults will continue to find such images morally effective, though they should eventually move on to a deeper understanding of the Sacred Scriptures.[12]

[9] Pico della Mirandola, *On the Imagination*, trans. by Caplan, p. 85.

[10] Pico della Mirandola, *On the Imagination*, trans. by Caplan, p. 85.

[11] Pico della Mirandola, *On the Imagination*, trans. by Caplan, p. 89.

[12] Pico della Mirandola, *On the Imagination*, trans. by Caplan, pp. 90–93.

Lest one think that this sixteenth-century example is a little late to be a good indicator of medieval thinking, one can look to a similar connection between images and action in the *Colloquio spirituale*, written in Italian in the late fourteenth century by the Dominican Simone da Cascina and analysed by Lina Bolzoni in *The Web of Images*.[13] Simone's text is a dialogue with four speakers that seeks to explain to a nun named Caterina the way to grasp the hidden meanings of the Mass. Much of the text hinges on how to interpret and create images, and Bolzoni sees the same connection between images in memory and their effect on the will. 'Simone's text [...] is concerned with modelling the vast spaces of the soul, filling all the "places" with emotionally effective images that will persist in the memory, speak to the intellect through the play of allegorical meaning and facilitate the uphill journey to God.' Simone says to Caterina, 'Above all, my child, make your penitence perfect so that, removing obstacles and removing yourself from evil, you may direct your path to a good end, *adorning your inner self with virtuous images*.'[14] Here internal images clearly lead the will toward moral choices. The interaction between memory, will, and intellect is even clearer when Simone says, 'Church doctrine, when it takes hold of the will, will guide the faculties of thought and imagination solely towards spiritual things, allowing one to think of or imagine only celestial things; it will fill the memory with holy and virtuous imaginings.'[15] One sees in the text the concomitant idea that vicious images, ideas, and emotions need to be purged from the memory, will, and intellect.[16]

Given these ideas, it would be hard to conceive that medieval preachers would not utilize mental imagery and even artwork in their sermons, especially given the oft-repeated dictum that images were peculiarly appropriate for the laity. The incorporation of mental images into sermons involved careful descriptions by the preachers and an equal imaginative effort by their listeners. Certainly imagining scenes from the life of Christ or from the lives of the saints was something some preachers expected people to be able to do. One anonymous English preacher declared in a sermon that 'we ought to see Job sitting in the dung-heap, and John the Baptist clad in camels' hair fasting in the desert, and Peter on the gallows of

[13] Lina Bolzoni, 'Allegories and Memory Images: The *Colloquio spirituale* and the "Tower of Knowledge Cycle"', in her *Web of Images*, pp. 41–81. See also Lina Bolzoni, 'Il *Colloquio spirituale* di Simone da Cascina: Note su allegoria e immagini della memoria', *Rivista di letteratura italiana*, 3 (1985), 9–65.

[14] Bolzoni, 'Allegories and Memory Images', p. 47.

[15] Bolzoni, 'Allegories and Memory Images', p. 47.

[16] Bolzoni, 'Allegories and Memory Images', p. 53.

the cross, [...] and James falling upon the sword of Herod'.[17] The fifteenth-century Franciscan, Johannes von Werden, cautioned his listeners that they should always carry the Passion of Christ in memory.[18] One way for preachers to incorporate this kind of mental imagery into their sermons was through exempla, which we will examine now. Another way was through the encouragement of meditative practice, which we will examine in Chapter 8.

## *The Cognitive and Memorial Functions of Exempla*

The same arguments used to support the retention of imagery in the churches for the laity were espoused to explain the importance of the imagery most often used in preaching, exempla.[19] Gregory the Great was equally profuse in his praises for exempla as he was for imagery. His pastoral works are strewn with references to the value of exempla: 'Toward the love of God and neighbour, exempla excite the hearts of listeners more than words'; 'there are some whom exempla inflame more to the love of the celestial homeland than *praedicamenta*'.[20] Gregory's point is that exempla have an emotional appeal that other preaching conventions lack and they seem also to transcend words. This appeal is conceded by the later mendicant experts in exempla and added to other benefits.

Perhaps the best articulation of the usefulness of exempla in preaching was laid out by the Dominican Étienne de Bourbon in the prologue to his famous exempla collection, the *Tractatus de diversis materiis predicabilis* in the mid-thirteenth century:

[17] London, BL, MS Additional 21,253, fol. 15, cited and translated in Gerald Robert Owst, *Literature and Pulpit in Medieval England: A Neglected Chapter in the History of English Letters and of the English People*, 2nd edn (Oxford: Blackwell, 1966), p. 136.

[18] Johannes von Werden, *Dormi secure de tempore* (Nuremberg: Anton Koberger, 1498), Sermo 57.

[19] For background on exempla see Jean Thiébaut Welter, *L'Exemplum dans la littérature religieuse et didactique du moyen âge* (Paris: Guitard, 1927); Claude Bremond and Jacques Le Goff, *L' 'Exemplum'*, Typologie des sources du moyen âge occidental, 40 (Turnhout: Brepols, 1982); H. Petré, R. Cantel and R. Ricard, '*Exemplum*', in *Dictionnaire de spiritualité*, ed. by Viller, Cavallera, and de Guibert, IV, 2; Frederic C. Tubach, '*Exempla* in the Decline', *Traditio*, 18 (1962), 407–17.

[20] 'Ad amorem Dei et proximi plerumque corda audientium plus exempla quam verba excitant' (PL, LXXVI, col. 1300); 'Sunt nonnulli, quos ad amorem patriae coelestis plus exempla quam praedicamenta succendunt' (PL, LXXVII, col. 153). See Welter, *L'Exemplum*, pp. 14–15, for a list of similar citations in Gregory's works.

> Exempla are especially valuable for furnishing, bestowing, and imprinting these things [the things necessary for human salvation] on human hearts. And they instruct the ignorance of simple people, and they heap up and imprint more easily, longer, and tenaciously in memory. (As St Gregory proves in his *Book of Dialogues*, deeds teach more than words and exempla more than *predicamenta*.)[21]

Exempla imprint themselves more firmly in people's hearts and minds than mere words and are also especially efficacious for simple folk. In this view of exempla, Étienne considered himself to be following the example of Christ,

> who first taught by deeds rather than by words and rendered the subtlety of preaching and of doctrine coarse, as it were, corporeal and visible, surrounding and vesting it with diverse similitudes, parables, miracles, and exempla, in order that his teaching might be more quickly grasped, more easily understood, more strongly retained in memory, and more efficaciously fulfilled in practice.[22]

Étienne even saw Christ himself as a kind of physical manifestation of the invisible, incorporeal, eternal wisdom: Christ is an exemplum or similitude of the eternal God. To strengthen this conception of exemplum, he draws on Pseudo-Dionysius: 'Wise philosophers embody their words by clothing them in similitudes and exempla. For a corporeal word passes more easily from sense to imagination and from imagination to memory.'[23] This idea substantially agrees with Aquinas's point that 'it is necessary, if we wish to facilitate remembering abstract ideas, to bind them to particular images, as Cicero teaches in his *Rhetoric* (see *Ad Herennium* 3.20.33–37)'.[24]

[21] *Stephani De Borbone Tractatus de diversis materiis praedicabilibus: Prologus, Prima Pars De dono timoris*, ed. by Jacques Berlioz and Jean-Luc Eichenlaub, CCCM, 124 (Turnhout: Brepols, 2002), pp. 3–4: 'quia autem ad hec suggerenda et ingerenda et imprimenda in humanis cordibus, maxime ualent exempla, que maxime erudiunt simplicium hominum ruditatem, et faciliorem et longiorem ingerunt et imprimunt in memoria tenacitatem (magis, ut probat beatus Gregorius in Dyalogorum libro, docent facta quam uerba et magis mouent exempla quam predicamenta)'.

[22] *Stephani De Borbone Tractatus*, ed. by Berlioz and Eichenlaub, p. 4: 'ideo summa Dei sapientia, Christus Ihesus primo docuit factis quam uerbis, et subtilitatem predicacionis et doctrine grossam quasi corpoream et uisibilem reddidit, muniens et uestiens eam diuersis similitudinibus, parabolis, miraculis et exemplis, ut eius doctrina citius caperetur, facilius cognosceretur, fortius in memoria retineretur et efficacius opere adimpleretur'.

[23] *Stephani De Borbone Tractatus*, ed. by Berlioz and Eichenlaub, p. 4: 'Sapientes philosophi incorporant sermones suos uestiendo eos similitudinibus et exemplis. Sermo enim corporeus facilius transit de sensu ad ymaginationem et de ymaginatione ad memoriam.'

[24] Thomas Aquinas, *Commentary*, trans. by Burchill, pp. 164–65; Aquinas, *De memoria et reminiscentia*, ed. by Spiazzi, I, lect. II. 326.

Other compilers of exempla collections evidently considered Étienne's estimation of exempla to be accurate, for many either echoed his points or copied them completely. Humbert de Romans, in his *De dono timoris* (which owed much to Étienne's *Tractatus*) rephrased Étienne's premise and added a few ideas of his own:

> Since exempla move more than words, according to Gregory, and are more easily seized by the intellect and fixed more deeply in memory and are also heard more freely by many and attract many to sermons by a certain delight, it is expedient for men dedicated to the preaching office to have many exempla of this kind available, which they may use now in common sermons, now in *collationes* for persons fearing God, now in easy *collocuciones* for every kind of person and for the edification and salvation of all.[25]

Humbert seems to feel even more strongly than Étienne that exempla are particularly suited to human cognitive capacity, not just to those of the simple people, although a preacher may match his exemplum to his audience. However, he qualifies this statement in his rules for using exempla, where he cautions preachers against using exempla when preaching to wise men unless the stories are 'laudable and worthy of religion'. Instead, they should be reserved for those of less intelligence, for whom exempla are as mother's milk.[26] While Humbert probably means that learned men require fewer illustrative stories to augment their understanding, he may also be hinting to inexperienced preachers that a learned audience is likely to be critical of inappropriate exempla. Certainly, Humbert included exempla in his own explanations to preachers about the importance of the preaching office.[27]

Carlo Delcorno has remarked that such recommendations of exempla say less about the definition of an exemplum than about its function.[28] Étienne's prologue

[25] Cited in Welter, *L'Exemplum*, p. 72; 'Quoniam plus exempla quam verba movent secundum Gregorium et facilius intellectu capiuntur et alcius memoria infiguntur necnon et libencius a multis audientur suique delectacione quadam pluros attrahunt ad sermones, expedit viros predicacionis officio deditos in hujusmodi habundare exemplis, quibus utantur modo in sermonibus communibus, modo in collacionibus ad personas Deum timentes, modo in facilibus collucucionibus sc. ad omne genus hominum et ad edificacionem omnium et salutem.'

[26] Welter, *L'Exemplum*, pp. 72–73 n. 13: 'Non enim viris alte sapiencie sunt hujusmodi exempla facile proponenda, nisi multum sint laudabilia religionisque digna, sed aliis minoris intelligencie quibus magis competunt sicut lac parvulis.'

[27] Humbert de Romans, *Treatise on the Formation of Preachers*, in *Early Dominicans: Selected Writings*, ed. by Simon Tugwell, Classics of Western Spirituality, 33 (New York: Paulist, 1982), p. 235.

[28] Carlo Delcorno, *Exemplum e letteratura: Tra medioevo e rinascimento* (Bologna: Il Mulino, 1989), p. 9.

merely distinguishes exempla from similitudes, parables, and miracles without defining any of them. It is thus worth considering what an exemplum is in order to understand why the friars considered them such a vital part of preaching.

Most *artes praedicandi* include exempla among the proofs of a sermon, along with *auctoritates* and *rationes*, a formula that Étienne follows in his prologue.[29] *Auctoritates* formed the heart of much medieval discourse, being the ubiquitous call to a higher authority than the preacher could claim for himself, while *rationes* were simple doctrinal arguments.[30] Defining an exemplum is more difficult. Most scholars would agree that our 'example' is not quite the right idea.[31] A good place to start is with a provisional definition advanced by Claude Bremond and Jacques Le Goff in their volume on the exemplum for the series Typologie des sources: 'un récit bref donné comme véridique et destiné à être inséré dans un discours (en général un sermon) pour convaincre un auditoire par une leçon salutaire'.[32] They stress the brevity, verisimilitude, and didactic nature of the exemplum and give some notion of how it was distinguished from other ornaments of the sermon in the Middle Ages. It was not a *fabula*, at least as the latter was defined by Remigius of Auxerre — 'a fictive narration of something, which is neither true nor seems to be true, but which is posited in arguments, because, although it never happened, nevertheless, if it had happened, it would have happened in this way'[33] — because a crucial feature of the exemplum is its verisimilitude. It was also generally differentiated from the *similitudo* in that the latter was a comparison while an exemplum was a story.[34] This distinction was not always maintained; in the quotations below, both Thomas of Chobham and Thomas Waleys refer to

[29] Bremond and Le Goff, *L'Exemplum'*, p. 28; *Artes praedicandi*, ed. by Charland, p. 195; *Anecdotes historiques, légendes et apologues tirés du recueil inédit d'Étienne de Bourbon, dominicain du XIII^e^ siècle*, ed. by A. Lecoy de la Marche (Paris: Librairie Renouard, 1877), pp. 3–4.

[30] *Artes praedicandi*, ed. by Charland, p. 195.

[31] Bremond and Le Goff, *L'Exemplum'*, pp. 27–28.

[32] Bremond and Le Goff, *L'Exemplum'*, pp. 37–38: 'a short story presented as true and meant to be inserted in a discourse (in general, a sermon) in order to persuade a listener by a salutary lesson'.

[33] Bremond and Le Goff, *L'Exemplum'*, p. 32: 'fabula est ficta rei narratio, quae nec vera est nec veri similis, sed ponitur in argumentis, quia licet numquam factus est, tamen si fuisset, ita utique fuisset'.

[34] Bremond and Le Goff, *L'Exemplum'*, pp. 30–31, 156–57. According to Isidore of Sevilla, 'inter exemplum et similitudinem hoc interest quod exemplum historia est, similitudo re adprobatur'.

the functions of exempla as *similitudines*. Neither was an exemplum exactly a miracle.

Above all, Bremond and Le Goff emphasize that the final goal of preaching in general and of the exemplum is eternal salvation. In this sense, it is 'un gadget eschatologique'. Bremond and Le Goff are surely correct to see the greater goal of preaching as salvation. They note as one of the differences between the ancient and medieval kinds of exempla the medieval preacher's desire to transform the life of the listener. Ancient orators were content merely to change their audience's opinions.[35]

However, their definition passes over some of the short-term goals of preaching, in which a certain kind of behaviour, belief, or memory of a sermon's contents is desired in order to achieve the long-term goal of salvation. It is quite clear that preaching was sometimes meant to stimulate a specific response, such as penitence, and a specific action, such as confession.[36] The appeal to emotion laid out by the medieval authors above also indicates a desired response from listeners. Moreover, the same authors' emphasis on memory indicates that the sermon's contents were not meant to be ephemeral but to provide some kind of lasting life in the hearts and minds of the listeners.

For this reason, Bremond and Le Goff's definition requires some modification to include the memorial function of exempla. They were not unaware of the importance of memory and in fact note that the development of the 'new rhetoric' for preachers and theories of memory appeared at about the same time as the full-fledged exemplum. They ask what place the exemplum might have in memory's proceedings. Both Jacques Berlioz and Carlo Delcorno have begun to explore that question. Berlioz defines exempla as 'ces courts récits que les prédicateurs inséraient dans leurs sermons pour faire passer auprès de l'auditoire, et offre à sa mémoire, une vérité religieuse utile à son salut'.[37] His definition has the merit of leaving open the possibility of short-term goals of preaching, such as affectivity and memory. In fact, he lays great stress on memory, seeing the exemplum as 'a signifying object whose structure is isomorphic to the conducting of a situation

[35] Bremond and Le Goff, *L'Exemplum'*, p. 45.

[36] See Jacques Berlioz, '"Quand dire c'est faire dire": Exempla et confession chez Étienne de Bourbon († v. 1261)', in *Faire croire: Modalité de la réception des messages religieux du XII^e^ au XIV^e^ siècle; Table Ronde organisée par l'École française de Rome, en collaboration avec l'Institut d'histoire médiévale de l'Université de Padoue (Rome, 22–23 juin 1979)* (Rome: École française de Rome, 1981), pp. 299–335.

[37] Berlioz, '"Quand dire c'est faire dire"', p. 299.

which ought to be that of the hearer (conversion by example), to which the hearer can return at an opportune moment'.[38] The exemplum's metaphoric character also aids this process, as it is an image aimed at the imagination to reach memory. Delcorno concurs with Berlioz's emphasis on the exemplum's memorable nature and thinks that in the context of Dominican preaching the exemplum 'assumes the function of the *imago agens*, which impresses itself in the memory of the hearer and sometimes summarizes the internal message of the sermon'.[39] In other words, every exemplum can be seen as a mnemonic image. Calling every exemplum an *imago agens* puts too much emphasis on the *Ad Herennium*'s memory system; however, exempla clearly were meant to lodge in a listener's memory. Some, as we shall see, were specifically designed to stay there.

We have already seen an insistence in exempla and sermon collection prologues that exempla imprint themselves in listeners' memories. Another reason that exempla seemed to stick in people's minds was their 'corporeal nature' and their familiarity. In his prologue to *Sermones vulgares*, Jacques de Vitry († 1240) declared:

> For the edification of the uncultivated and the instruction of the boorish, corporeal and palpable things and such things as they know through experience must frequently be put forward, for they are moved more by exterior exempla than by authorities or by profound statements.[40]

According to John Bromyard,

> More often through exempla are posited teachings about the habits of people than about animals or other unknown things since human mores are better known and more believable for persuasion to the people to whom one must speak or preach.[41]

Thomas of Chobham justified the use of similitudes on the basis of the weakness of the human intellect, declaring similitudes to be a better method of persuasion than the naked truth:

[38] Berlioz, '"Quand dire c'est faire dire"', p. 305.

[39] Delcorno, *Exemplum*, p. 10.

[40] Cited in Welter, *L'Exemplum*, p. 68: 'Ad edificacionem rudium et agrestium erudicionem, quibus quasi corporalia et palpabilia et talia que per experienciam novunt frequencius sunt proponenda, magis enim moventur exterioribus exemplis quam auctoritatibus vel profundis sententiis.'

[41] Welter, *L'Exemplum*, p. 71: 'Sepius tamen per exempla ponuntur accepta de moribus hominum quam de animalibus vel de aliis rebus ignotis utpote hominibus quibus loquendum et predicandum est magis nota et credibiliora persuasionis.'

> So that if a man wishes to say to another that perverse society ought to be avoided since often a person will pick up bad conduct and evil habits from such society, he will more effectively persuade him by quoting from *Ecclestiaticus* 'who touches pitch will be soiled by it', than if he would simply say, 'He who frequents evil society will learn evil habits from it'. [...] For the human intellect is naturally weak in seeing the truth for itself. And for this reason, it desires the help of similitudes through which it can see the truth more openly.[42]

Like Étienne, he concludes that since the Lord himself and all the apostles used similitudes to explain the truth, so should preachers.

Thomas Waleys recommends similitudes for a similar reason:

> It is agreed that speech through similitudes [*similitudines*], if well adapted, delight more and are more strongly imprinted in memory than a simple word or *ratio*, because the cognition of our intellect naturally, while we are here *in via*, is through conversion to *phantasmata*, which are similitudes of things — which, if they are well adapted, delight very much. And, for this reason, speech through similitudes of things, as though causing in us cognition of our nature and conforming more to our natural understanding, delights much. Hence it is that Scripture often uses symbolic speech, which occurs through similitudes of other things.[43]

Thomas here ties the use of *similitudines* to the contemporary understanding of cognitive psychology, hence the reference to *phantasmata*. While Thomas does not here elaborate on the connections between memory and images, he clearly means one to think that images stick in our memories because they are aesthetically pleasing and because they suit our cognitive capabilities.

From this discussion, we can see that many medieval preachers appreciated the aid of exempla in their sermons because such stories were accessible to the laity, appealed to the emotions and to previous experience, were appropriate for

[42] *Summa de arte*, p. 282: 'Vt si uelit homo dicere alii quod praua societas uitanda est quia sepe colligit homo sordes et malitias ex praua societate, efficacius persuadebit ei dicens hoc modo ut in Ecclesiastico: *qui tangit picem iniquinabitur ab ea*, quam si diceret simpliciter: qui propinquus est prauo socio prauos mores addiscet ab eo [...]. Intellectus enim humanus naturaliter inbecillis est per se ad uidendum uerum. Et ideo desiderat adiutorium similitudinum per quas expressius ueritatem possit uidere.'

[43] *De modo comp.*, pp. 396–97: 'Constat etiam quod locutio per similitudinem, si bene aptetur, magis delectat naturaliter et fortius imprimitur memoriae quam dictum simplex vel ratio, quia naturaliter cognitio nostri intellectus, dum sumus hic in via, est per conversionem ad phantasmata, quae sunt rerum similitudines; quae, si bene aptentur, magis delectant. Et ideo, locutio per similitudines rerum, tanquam causans in nobis cognitionem naturae nostrae et modo nostro intelligendi naturali magis conformem, plus delectat. Hinc est quod Sacra Scriptura multum utitur locutionibus symbolicis, quae fiunt [de rebus] per similitudines aliarum rerum.'

the human intellect, and stuck in people's minds: exempla were persuasive and memorable.

## *Criticisms of Mendicant Preaching*

Given this nearly universal approbation of exempla and their oft-expressed helpfulness to memory, it is odd that one rarely finds a recommendation of exempla in a specifically mnemonic context. Only Guibert de Tournai makes the connection when he declares that one of his 'methods' of forming the memory is the 'method which supplies exempla' and which proceeds through similitudes. He links these similitudes to those recommended by Cicero as a way of imagining the things we wish to remember.[44] It is not clear whether he is referring to preaching exempla or to 'examples' as we would understand them, but this is the closest connection yet found. However, we may be able to get at this question in a back-handed manner by looking at some criticisms of preaching by mendicants, the most frequent employers of exempla.

In his *Ars faciendi sermones*, written in the first half of the fourteenth century, the Franciscan Géraud du Pescher, criticized certain kinds of preachers:[45]

> But we must not pass over the fact that some preachers, pursuing their fantasies, build cities and castles with towers and doors and other things in imagination, and they arm knights with shield, helmet, lance, sword, and breast plate. They moralize these images in themselves and prove nothing through Scripture; they devise their own similitudes, as if Scripture needed to be strengthened by human similitudes. Such preachers detract from Scripture and they destroy and confound theology.[46]

Géraud is clearly unhappy with the way that some preachers use imagery in their preaching. A large part of the criticism seems to depend on preachers relying too much on their own imaginations and disregarding the sole authority of Scripture.

[44] *De modo*, p. 220.

[45] 'L'"Ars faciendi sermones" de Géraud du Pescher', ed. by F. M. Delorme, *Antonianum*, 19 (1944), 169–98. Géraud (or Giroldus de Piscariis) was a Franciscan on good terms with Pope John XXII, who made him the first master of theology at the University of Toulouse (p. 170). See also C.-V. Langlois, 'Géraud du Pescher', *Histoire littéraire de la France*, 36 (1927), 614–17.

[46] Géraud du Pescher, 'L'"Ars faciendi sermones"', ed. by Delorme, p. 186: 'Istud autem non est pretermictendum quod aliqui sue fantasie insistentes predicantes, civitates et castella edificant cum turribus et portis et aliis fingentes, et armant milites cum scuto, galea, lancea, ense quoque et lorica, et hec per seipsos moraliçando et nihil per sacram Scripturam probando, faciendo similitudines suas adinventas ac si sacra Scriptura curatur similitudinibus aprobatis. Tales enim divine Scripture derogant et sacram doctrinam destruunt et confundunt.'

His criticism seems to echo that of many hostile, or at least concerned, observers of mendicant preaching in the later Middle Ages. This censure was particularly vehement in England, where an anti-fraternal tradition sprang up in vernacular literature and in certain more 'radical' religious groups, such as the Lollards.[47] Though the hostile consideration touched on many aspects of the mendicant lifestyle, from the friars' cultivation of the rich and famous to their alleged theft of children, much of it was directed towards mendicant preaching. Wyclif, for instance, chided the friars for not expounding the Gospel and the standard preaching topics in a brief and pithy manner, as St Francis of Assisi had instructed them, and for instead dwelling on long fables or even constructing their own novelties.[48] In 1401 'Jacke Upland' also upbraided the friars for their preaching:

> What cause hast thou that thou wilt not preach the gospel,
> as God saith that thou sholdst,
> sith it is the best lore,
> and also our beleeve?[49]

In his reply, 'Friar Daw' interpreted this point as a slur on the content of mendicant preaching:

> Aȝens that that thou saist, that we prechen
> but fallace
> and fables,
> and leue the gospel
> that moste vs al saue.[50]

It was not just outsiders who criticized methods of preaching. The English Carmelite John Baconthorpe (early fourteenth century) singled out the use of

[47] Carolly Erickson, 'The Fourteenth-Century Franciscans and their Critics', *Franciscan Studies*, 35 (1975), 107–35; Arnold Williams, 'Chaucer and the Friars', *Speculum*, 28 (1953), 499–513; David Knowles, *The Religious Orders in England*, II: *The End of the Middle Ages* (Cambridge: Cambridge University Press, 1955).

[48] *The English Works of Wyclif Hitherto Unprinted*, ed. by Frederic David Matthew, 2nd rev. edn, EETS, o.s., 74 (London: Kegan Paul, Trench, Trübner, 1902; repr. Millwood, NY: Kraus, 1973), p. 50: 'And ȝit þei tellen not schortly ne plenerly þe gospel, & vices & vertues, & peynes and ioie, but maken longe talis of fablis, or cronyclis, or comenden here owen nouelries.'

[49] *Political Poems and Songs Relating to English History*, ed. by Thomas Wright, Rolls Series, 14, 2 vols (London: Longman, Green, Longman, and Roberts, 1861), II, 23.

[50] *Political Poems and Songs*, II, 55.

fables as a problem in both teaching and preaching. In the introduction to his postill on St Matthew, he lays out his plan of exposition, claiming that 'the fables of the poets must not be introduced, nor indeed should they be moralized in preaching. [...] One reason is that fables signify in themselves falsehood, just as a parable in itself is an *exemplum* significative of truth. But something false ought to be destroyed, not brought into teaching.'[51] Baconthorpe is very clearly protesting against the contemporary practice of introducing moralized fables into both scriptural commentaries and sermons, a practice made famous by the classicizing friars whom we shall examine in the next chapter.[52]

Besides the concerns about the use of fables in sermons, there were also complaints across Europe about the style of modern preaching. That notorious critic of the later thirteenth-century, the Franciscan Roger Bacon, disliked the use of elaborate divisions and rhymes in sermons:

> The vulgar [...] turn themselves to the highest and limitless curiosities, namely through Porphyrian divisions, and through agreement of words and clauses, and through rhymes, in which there is only a wordy vanity, lacking every kind of rhetorical argument and power of persuading.[53]

Pierre de Baume's (fl. 1320s) concerns reflected Bacon's:

> In the old days sermons were such as to profit the people. But now they have rhymes and curious comparisons, and philosophical subtleties are mixed with them; so many sermons do no good; they only please the hearers as oratory.[54]

Religious authorities were conscious of these problems and counselled their followers not to fall prey to them. Humbert de Romans, Minister General of the Dominicans to 1263, in his *De eruditione praedicatorum* includes in a chapter

[51] Beryl Smalley, 'John Baconthorpe's Postill on St Matthew', in *Studies in Medieval Thought and Learning from Abelard to Wycliff*, ed. by Beryl Smalley (London: Hambledon, 1981), pp. 289–343 (pp. 306–07): 'Non tamen sunt fabule poetarum admittende, immo nec moraliter exponende in predicatione [...]. Alia ratio est quia fabula per se significat falsum, sicut parabola per se exemplum est veritatis significativum; sed falsum ubique est destruendum, non introducendum.'

[52] Smalley, 'John Baconthorpe's Postill', pp. 310–11. It is clear that his protest involves not just scriptural commentary but also preaching. Later in his postill, he says, 'Nota quod per fabulas non est predicandum.'

[53] Bacon, *Opus tert.*, ed. by Brewer, I, 304: 'vulgus (sc. praedicatorum) [...] convertit se ad summam et infinitam curiositatem, scilicet per divisiones Porphyrianus, et per consonantias ineptas verborum, et clausularum, et per concordantias vocales, in quibus est sola vanitas verbosa, omni carens ornatu rhetorico et virtute persuadendi'.

[54] Cited in Smalley, *EFA*, p. 43.

'Against Preachers Who Speak about Vain Things in the Manner of Secular Teachings' a warning to preachers against the use of worthless stories (*nugae*) and fables in their sermons.[55] Archbishop John Pecham of England clarified the proper content of sermons to the people in the canons propagated by the Lambeth Council of 1281, when he said,

> [E]very priest bearing rule over the people [should expound] plainly in their vulgar tongue without any fantastical imagination or invention of any manner subtlety or curiosity either by himself or by some other, four times in the year, that is to wit every quarter of the year once, and that in one solemn feast or more the 14 Articles of the Faith, the 10 Commandments, the Two Precepts of the Gospel [...] the Seven works of mercy, the Seven Deadly Sins with their branches, the Seven principal Virtues and the Seven Sacraments of Grace.[56]

But were the friars really as careless of their preaching vocation as these criticisms imply? After all, in the early thirteenth century, the mendicants were most heralded for the excellence of their preaching. The Dominicans, in particular, put all the considerable resources of their order to the training and promotion of preachers and were careful about allowing their members to preach.[57] Was all this effort abandoned by the fourteenth century? Might not there be a genuine disagreement about the procedures of correct preaching?

The rest of Géraud's censure may offer a pointer towards the essence of the argument: 'But if they wish to discourse about cities or arms or those things which they speak about, let them argue through Scripture or explain this figure concerning the city which John in Revelations saw, which had twelve doors and many other things; this, at least, ought to be preached.'[58] With a closer look at his comment, one discovers that the Franciscan does not disapprove of using imagery per se in sermons. What he does dislike is the preachers' inclusion of their own imagery instead of scriptural imagery. In fact, he implies that Scripture is conveyed

[55] Welter, *L'Exemplum*, pp. 70–71.

[56] Cited in Spencer, *English Preaching*, p. 203.

[57] William A. Hinnebusch, *The Early English Friars Preachers*, Dissertationes historicae, 14 (Rome: Institutum historicum ff. praedicatorum Romae ad S. Sabinae, 1951), pp. 280–86.

[58] Géraud du Pescher, 'L'"Ars faciendi sermones"', ed. by Delorme, p. 186: 'Si autem vellent distinguere de civitate vel de armis et ista que dicunt probarent per Scripturam vel exponerent istam figuram de civitate quam vidit Johannes in Apoc., que habebat xii portas vel multa alia, illud esset utique adprobandum.' Carlo Delcorno notes the importance of Géraud's comments and compares them to San Bernardino of Siena's approach to preaching: '"Ars praedicandi" e "Ars memorativa" nell'esperienza di San Bernadino da Siena', *Bullettino della deputazione abruzzese di storia patria*, 70 (1980), 77–162 (pp. 110–11).

largely through such means. As it is, the moralization of castles and knights' equipage seems to have little to do with the Bible or theology. An English commentator, who decried preachers indulging 'in vanis fabulis et turpiloquiis scurilitatibus ociosis et luxuriosis verbis', had a similar vision of good preaching:

> And techeth vs goode vertues euene
> That bryngen vs to þe blisse of heuene
> Of such þyng men shulde her matere take
> That writen rymes and hem can make
> As of oure lady and of hire sone
> And of seyntis þat wiþ hem wone
> Of holywrit þe exemplis loke
> And holy myraclis writen in boke.[59]

For him, rhymes and songs in sermons should be taken not from the poets but from the lives of Mary, Christ, and the saints, and from the Bible generally.

But clearly, not everyone would agree with Géraud's and the English writer's assessments of proper preaching. In his *Chronicon* the Franciscan Salimbene de Adam wrote approvingly of the preaching abilities of the friar Hugh Pocapaglia of Reggio:

> He was a master of grammar in the world, a great jester and a great orator, and a solemn and outstanding preacher of the order of the Friars Minor, who silenced the scandal-mongers of the order and abashed them with his sermons and examples. [...] He was filled with proverbs, stories [*fabulae*] and examples, and these resounded perfectly in his mouth, as he employed all of them to moral purposes. And he had an eloquent and agreeable tongue and was willingly listened to by the populace.[60]

Hugh's use of fables and examples elicited no criticism from Salimbene, because he put them to a moral purpose and because he was effective in gaining the attention of his audience.

[59] Homer G. Pfander, 'The Popular Sermon of the Medieval Friar in England' (unpublished doctoral dissertation, New York University, 1937), pp. 21–22.

[60] *Cronica Fratris Salimbene de Adam Ordinis Minorum*, ed. by O. Holder-Egger, Monumenta Germaniae Historica, Scriptores, 32 (Hannover: Hahn, 1905–13): 'fuit magister in grammatica in seculo et magnus truphator et magnus prolocutor et in ordine fratrum Minorum sollemnis et optimus predicator, et qui mordaces ordinis confutabat et confundebat predicationibus et exemplis [...] Hic erat totus plenus proverbiis, fabulis et exemplis, et optime sonabant in ore suo, quia hec omnia reducebat ad mores, et habebat linguam disertam et gratiosam, et libenter audiebatur a populo'; cited and translated in Roest, 'Reading the Book of History', p. 217.

John Bromyard discussed the issue in the prologue to his *Summa praedicantium*, stating that 'in the case of herbs, no one seeks to find out in what land, or in the charge of what gardener, or by what culture they grew, provided that they possess healing power'.[61] The same applies to exempla: 'For, from the moralizations of Gentile fables a form of instruction is sometimes derived; and it is right, also, to be taught by the enemy, and to enrich the Hebrews with the spoils of the Egyptians.'

Similarly, Simon Alcock, in his fifteenth-century *ars dilatandi*, was still endorsing the very procedure that Géraud despised. He recommends using a physical place like a castle, a ship, a shield, a temple, a door, and the like, as a basis for expanding one's theme, because one can moralize both the spatial properties and its physical characteristics.[62] The idea of moralizing the properties of a figure was a perfectly proper tenet of the *ars praedicandi*: Thomas of Chobham included a section in his chapter on narration on how to discover properties and expand on them in sermons. The chief point of contention seemed to be of subject matter. Thomas lists six persons for whom he is willing to discover properties: God with his angels, the devil with his demons, the Church Militant, the Church Triumphant, the soul generally considered, and the synagogue of the devil.[63] These are all scriptural themes, while Simon's 'places', like the shield, swords, and lances that Géraud disdains, are not. This, then, is a dispute about method, and probably about a mnemonic method.

Géraud's comment points to a debate both inside and outside the mendicant community about how the truths of the faith could best be conveyed to the laity. The criticisms levelled against the friars' preaching indicate that what some preachers thought proper *materia praedicabilis* might be considered by other observers to be foolish 'fancies and fables'. Undoubtably, there must have been preachers who included lively stories purely for their entertainment value or to rouse a lethargic audience.[64] But there were others, like Simon Alcock, who thought moralized shields, mythological stories, and the like to be carefully planned tools based on sound pedagogical and psychological theory. Many of these fancies were designed to help sermon audiences to remember.

[61] Cited in Owst, *Literature and Pulpit*, p. 180.

[62] 'Simon Alcock on Expanding the Sermon', ed. by Mary Fuentes Boynton, *Harvard Theological Review*, 34 (1941), 201–16 (p. 214).

[63] *Summa de arte*, p. 279.

[64] Jacques de Vitry claimed to have used such methods to wake up a sleepy listener: 'Ille qui in loco illo dormitat secreta mea vel concilium meum non revelabit' (Welter, *L'Exemplum*, pp. 68–69).

This debate about proper preaching matter certainly cannot be conceived in purely mnemonic terms. Throughout the Middle Ages, there was a tension between those who wanted to 'despoil the Egyptians' by including classical and pagan culture in the Christian world and those who thought it too dangerous.[65] For those who were interested in classical books, such as Smalley's classicizing friars, the world of homiletics must have seemed an ideal way to combine their interests with their vocation. Then, too, an element of pure entertainment value must have crept into the medieval audience's enjoyment of such stories.

But the arguments that we examined in the first part of the chapter indicate that medieval preachers took exempla seriously. We should probably not dismiss these stories as frivolities as quickly as Géraud did. In fact, his description does offer us some rules for distinguishing specifically mnemonic exempla from ordinary ones. While I agree with Delcorno that any exemplum could potentially be considered a memory image, some exempla were clearly designed to function as such. Here are some criteria for distinguishing them:

1) An exemplum clearly defined as an image, even if it at first does not seem easily depicted. Examples can be seen in Géraud's shield, helmet, castle and in Hugh of St Victor's ark.

2) Elaborate moralizations. As a general rule, one might say that the more elaborate and fantastic an exemplum, the more likely that it is designed as a mnemonic image.

3) Structuring function. Does the image or exemplum furnish the main outline of the sermon or a goodly part of the sermon? Some even store the themes of several weeks worth of sermons.

4) The presence of verses or sayings as parts of the picture, particularly if they either form the basis of the moralization or sum up the gist of the story.

These 'rules' are really just suggestions for sorting through the many exempla left to us. A final observation that I will bring forward, and which will be demonstrated in the next chapter, is that the mnemonic exempla of northern Europe tend to be of the type that Géraud particularly deplored — fantastic or mythogra-

[65] See Gerald L. Ellspermann, *The Attitude of the Early Christian Latin Writers Toward Pagan Literature and Learning*, Catholic University of America Patristic Studies, 82 (Washington, DC: Catholic University of America Press, 1949); James J. O'Donnell, 'Augustine's Classical Readings', *Recherches augustiniennes*, 15 (1980), 144–75; Henri Irénée Marrou, *Saint Augustin et la fin de la culture antique* (Paris: de Boccard, 1938).

phic — while those in the South, especially Italy, tend to be based more on Scripture. This distinction accords with Smalley's findings; when she compared the English classicizing friars to the Italian pre-humanists, she found very few points of overlap.[66] She attributed this fact to differences in culture, suggesting that Italian preachers and audiences possessed a stronger classical tradition and an increased sophistication in exempla. I have no further insights as to the reasons for this disjunction, except to suggest that perhaps the Italian preachers had read Géraud. In any case, we will turn in the next chapter to an examination of mnemonic exempla, chosen on the basis of their congruence to the above rules.

## *Conclusions*

Medieval preaching experts considered exempla to be cognitive aids for the laity. They were supported in this opinion by psychological theory and centuries of approval for ecclesiastical imagery. These ideas made it possible for preachers to conflate the theory of exempla with that describing mnemonic imagery. Not all preachers approved of this move, however, considering the results frivolous and deleterious of Scripture. These complaints do not seem to have hindered the preaching experts considered in the next chapter. We will see how some mendicants created a new kind of exemplum specifically designed to aid their own memories and then adapted it for their listeners.

[66] Smalley, *EFA*, pp. 272–79.

Chapter 6

# THE MNEMONIC EXEMPLA OF THE CLASSICIZING FRIARS

Given the strong preference for exempla expressed by medieval preachers and the evidence for mnemonic methods that we have already examined, it should not surprise anyone to find examples of mnemonic exempla in medieval homiletic works. Although, admittedly, it can be difficult to identify the detritus, as it were, of mnemonic methods in written texts and visual images, the effort is not a vain one.[1] Occasionally, a feature of a sermon, an exempla collection, and the like, will seem so odd that a mnemonic function may provide the best explanation of its presence in a text. In the chapters that follow, I do not want to provide a deterministic model for all exempla. Medieval preachers were quite capable of combining mnemonic goals with literary and doctrinal ones. However, a systematic examination of the way some exempla functioned mnemonically provides a useful insight into late medieval preaching and spirituality.

With this caveat out of the way, I would like to concentrate in this chapter on certain exempla so odd that they have drawn comment from puzzled scholars for years. In the fourteenth and fifteenth centuries, some northern European preachers participated in a kind of craze for composing in rhyme verbal *picturae* or *imagines* as personifications of virtues, vices, and ancient gods.[2] Though a number of scholars had commented on what seemed to them eccentricities, the *picturae* received their first serious scholarly treatment in Beryl Smalley's *English*

[1] Here I have to disagree with Peter Parshall's point, in his article, 'The Art of Memory and the Passion', *Art Bulletin*, 81 (1999), 456–72, that it is impossible to discover remains of mnemonic methods.

[2] Smalley, *EFA*, pp. 115–18, 165–82.

*Friars and Antiquity in the Early Fourteenth Century*. In two chapters on the friars John Ridevall and Robert Holcot, Smalley pointed out their curious exegetical technique of verbal 'pictures'. She was puzzled by it because the pictures seemed difficult to represent visually and because their sources were obscure. She concluded that they were a curious kind of preaching aid with some visual appeal. Later Frances Yates, in a chapter of *The Art of Memory* devoted to the interrelationship between memory and the formation of imagery, suggested that the friars' pictures were images in the medieval art of memory, a suggestion recently seconded by Mary Carruthers.[3]

While scholars have postulated that such 'pictures' served a mnemonic function, no one has demonstrated how they functioned in texts and how they may be elucidated by the references to mnemonic techniques in the *artes praedicandi* already examined and by later *ars memorativa* tracts.[4] In addition, no one has appreciated how widespread the phenomenon actually was in the late Middle Ages. Nor have scholars noticed that there are several types of mnemonic pictures, from rhymed verses that I speculate may have been intended mainly to aid preachers' memories to non-rhymed, to more visually appealing verbal images, possibly designed to aid the laity's memories. The latter type indicates the friars' commitment to the inculcation of the precepts of the faith in their audience and explains the direction that many of the devotional practices of the laity took in the fifteenth century.

## *Background of the Classicizing Friars*

The picture tradition was popularized in the works of John Ridevall, Robert Holcot, and the author of the *Fasciculus morum*. These writers belonged to the circle of English scholars whom Smalley first designated as 'the classicizing friars'. For her, the word *classicizing* pointed to 'a fondness for classical literature, history and myth without suggesting that the group played any special part in the rise of humanism'.[5] To be included in her group, a scholar's classical interest had to manifest itself in homiletical endeavours, such as scriptural commentaries, ser-

[3] Yates, *Art of Memory*, pp. 96–99; Carruthers, *Book of Memory*, pp. 230–31.

[4] I made a first step in this direction in Kimberly A. Rivers, 'Pictures, Preaching and Memory in Robert Holcot's Commentary on the Twelve Prophets' (unpublished MSL thesis, Toronto, Pontifical Institute of Mediaeval Studies, 1993).

[5] Smalley, *EFA*, p. 1.

mons, and preaching aids. She identified a diverse group of writers, all mendicants, who were active in England between about 1320 and 1350. They included the Franciscans John Ridevall and John Lathbury, both Oxford theologians, as well as the Oxford Dominicans Thomas Waleys, Robert Holcot, William D'Eyncourt and the Cambridge Dominicans Thomas Hopeman and Thomas Ringstead.[6] Recent research by Siegfried Wenzel has revealed that the anonymous Franciscan author of the *Fasciculus morum,* a handbook of stories and doctrinal material for preachers, should be included in the classicizing circle. More will be said about this work later in the chapter.[7]

In addition to the first group, Smalley pointed to another group of mostly English scholars, also mendicants, whom she called the classicizers' forerunners. For her, thirteenth- and early fourteenth-century writers such as the Dominicans Vincent de Beauvais, Simon Hinton, and Nicholas Trevet, and the Franciscans Thomas Docking, Roger Bacon, Walter Wimborne, and John of Wales all displayed significant classical interests. She excluded these authors from the group of classicizing friars either because they did not exercise their classical interests in biblical commentaries or because their attitude to antiquity was 'encyclopedic'.[8] Smalley saw the thirteenth-century encyclopedists as forerunners, but not classicizers, because in their works, classical studies were not distinct from other kinds of learning: 'Ancient history and myth went shares with natural science and all other known branches of learning in their claims on [their] attention.'[9] One other writer with similar interests whom Smalley did not include is Jacopo da Cessole, OP. Like the English classicizing friars, he promoted classical authors in exempla with a moralizing, and probably even mnemonic, intent.[10] More will said about him in Chapter 9.

Though one might quibble with some of Smalley's exclusions from the classicizing group (for instance, I might push harder for John Bromyard's and Trevet's inclusion), it is fair to see the classicizers as exhibiting a more intense interest in incorporating classical sources into their writings than the encyclopedists.

[6] Smalley, *EFA*, p. 1.

[7] D'Avray notes another friar's interest in antiquity in 'Another Friar and Antiquity', in *Modern Questions about Medieval Sermons: Essays on Marriage, Death, History and Sanctity*, ed. by Nicole Bériou and David L. d'Avray (Spoleto: Centro italiano di studi sull'alto medioevo, 1994), pp. 247–57.

[8] Smalley, *EFA*, pp. 45–65.

[9] Smalley, *EFA*, p. 47.

[10] I owe this insight to Roger Andersson and the anonymous reader of the book manuscript.

Without ignoring stories drawn from natural history or saints' lives, writers like Waleys, Ridevall, Holcot, and Ringstead pushed exempla from classical works and mythological accounts onto their readers. And there was something about their writings to which readers, preachers, and likely audiences responded. Holcot's Commentary on *Wisdom* and his *Moralitates*, John Lathbury on *Lamentations*, and Thomas Ringstead on *Proverbs* were 'best-sellers' of their day.[11] This was also not a group that only Smalley recognized as having common interests. As she herself noticed, later compilers of medieval books tended to group the classicizers' works together as constituting 'a classicizing type of pastoral literature', a kind of *figmenta anglicana*.[12]

## *The 'Pictures'*

As we shall see further in Chapter 7, one aspect of the friars' style which had almost irresistible appeal on the Continent in the later fourteenth and fifteenth centuries was the *picturae* technique. Smalley supposed that John Ridevall pioneered the trick of composing verbal pictures in rhyming jingles in his *Lectura in Apocalypsim* and the *Fulgentius metaforalis* and passed it along to Robert Holcot. Holcot rhymed his pictures in his *Commentary on the Twelve Prophets* but then enhanced the *picturae* in his *Moralitates* by making them more visually appealing and by removing their rhymes.[13] There are also a few pictures in his sermon collection and in his Wisdom commentary.[14] However, Siegfried Wenzel's work on the *Fasciculus morum*, a preacher's handbook written in England at the very beginning of the fourteenth century, suggests that its anonymous Franciscan author[15] may have been the first to make consistent use of the *picturae*

[11] Minnis, *Medieval Theory of Authorship*, p. 165.

[12] See Chapter 8, below, for more on this topic.

[13] Smalley, *EFA*, p. 2.

[14] There are two pictures of Justice and one of the Roman gods in Holcot's sermon collection: Cambridge, Peterhouse, MS 210, Sermones 92h, 105b, and 69g; in his commentary on Wisdom are pictures of Drunkenness (Bacchus), Minerva, Mercury, Fortune, and the Three Graces (Smalley, *EFA*, p. 171 nn. 1–5).

[15] For the arguments about the authorship of *Fasciculus morum*, see Siegfried Wenzel, *Verses in Sermons: Fasciculus Morum and its Middle English Poems* (Cambridge, MA: Medieval Academy of America, 1978), pp. 35–41; Alan J. Fletcher, 'The Authorship of the *Fasciculus morum*: A Review of the Evidence of MS Barlow 24', *Notes & Queries*, n.s., 30 (1983), 205–07, and Susan Powell, 'Connections between the *Fasciculus morum* and Bodleian MS Barlow 24', *Notes &*

for preaching purposes.[16] His creations resemble the un-rhymed pictures in Holcot's *Moralitates* rather than Ridevall's type.[17]

Besides these three authors, who for now may be regarded as the popularizers of the *picturae*, other members of the classicizing circle occasionally included a picture or two in their sermons, preaching aids, and biblical commentaries. For instance, the Dominican Thomas Hopeman (fl. 1340–56) has pictures of Holy Scripture and of Venus in his commentary on Hebrews, while Thomas Ringstead,

*Queries*, n.s., 29 (1982), 10–14. See also Annette Kehnel, 'The Narrative Tradition of the Medieval Franciscan Friars on the British Isles', *Franciscan Studies*, 63 (2005), 461–530.

[16] Although Wenzel on the whole is inclined to connect the *Fasciculus morum* more to late thirteenth-century works like John of Wales's *Breviloquium* than to fourteenth-century authors like Holcot, he does acknowledge that the pictures in the *Fasciculus morum* relate it to the classicizing friars (Wenzel, *Verses in Sermons*, pp. 26–29, 59). See also *Fasciculus morum: A Fourteenth-Century Preacher's Handbook*, ed. by Siegfried Wenzel (University Park: Pennsylvania State University Press, 1989). Nigel F. Palmer comes to a similar conclusion in '"Antiquitus depingebatur": The Roman Pictures of Death and Misfortune in the *Ackermann aus Böhmen* and *Tkadlecek*, and in the Writings of the English Classicizing Friars', *Deutsche Vierteljahrsschrift für Literaturwissenschaft und Geistesgeschichte*, 57 (1983), 171–239 (p. 180). As Wenzel points out in 'The Classics in Late-Medieval Preaching', in *Medieval Antiquity*, ed. by Andries Welkenhuysen, Herman Braet, and Werner Verbeke (Leuven: Leuven University Press, 1995), pp. 127–43 (p. 130 n. 23), the use of the formulae *picturae* and *depingebatur* was not initiated in the *Fasciculus morum*. Both are quite commonly found in mythological literature from Fulgentius through the end of the Middle Ages. See Smalley, *EFA*, pp. 112–18, 165–83, and Jean Seznec, *The Survival of the Pagan Gods: The Mythological Tradition and its Place in Renaissance Humanism and Art*, trans. by Barbara F. Sessions, Bollingen Series, 38 (New York: Pantheon, 1953). This point will be discussed at length in Chapter 7. Mental pictures also turn up in meditational literature throughout the Middle Ages. For a long discussion of monastic pictures and their relation to ekphrasis, see Carruthers, *Craft of Thought*, chap. 3.

[17] Some of the exempla in the appendix of Oesterley's edition of the *Gesta Romanorum* (*Gesta Romanorum*, ed. by Hermann Oesterley (Berlin: Weidmännische Buchhandlung, 1872; repr. 1963)) also appear to overlap considerably with those found in Holcot's *Moralitates*. However, Palmer points out that Oesterley did not make it clear enough that many of texts printed in his appendix are not really extracted from manuscripts of the *Gesta Romanorum*; some of the exempla used by Oesterley include material derived from *Moralitates*; see Palmer, '"Antiquitus depingebatur"', p. 182 n. 33. The provenance of the 'original' *Gesta Romanorum* is uncertain, but the earliest dated manuscript (Innsbruck, Universitätsbibliothek, MS 310, Franciscan, S. German, 1342) has Middle English verses and words, showing use of English preaching materials on the Continent. For more on the origins of the *Gesta Romanorum* and its relation to the works of the English friars, see also Nigel F. Palmer, 'Das "Exempelwerk" der englischen Bettelmönche: Ein Gegenstück zu den "Gesta Romanorum"', in *Exempel und Exempelsammlungen*, ed. by Walter Haug and Burghart Wachinger, Fortuna vitrea, 2 (Tübingen: Niemeyer, 1991), pp. 137–72.

also a Dominican and a contemporary of Hopeman, incorporates what Smalley calls a 'debunking' picture of Peace into his commentary on Proverbs.[18] In his *Summa praedicantium*, John Bromyard includes a *pictura* of Gratitude modelled along the lines of Holcot's True Friendship and a picture of the Wheel of Fortune.[19] Of these examples, the pictures of John Ridevall and Robert Holcot were by far the most popular.

## *Background of Ridevall and Holcot*

Before turning to the main discussion, it is useful to consider briefly Ridevall's and Holcot's careers and writings. John Ridevall, OFM, and Robert Holcot, OP, were contemporaries at Oxford in the 1330s. What little information that we possess about Ridevall is connected with his life as a Franciscan theologian at Oxford.[20] In 1331 he incepted in theology at Oxford Greyfriars and became the fifty-fourth lector there. In October 1340, he attended a council of the order at Basel.[21] He wrote several works which place him in Smalley's circle of classicizing friars: the *Fulgentius metaforalis*, a moralized commentary on the fifth-century writer Fulgentius's *Mitologiarum libri tres*;[22] a *Lectura* on the

[18] Smalley, *EFA*, pp. 211, 216.

[19] See Wenzel, *Verses in Sermons*, p. 58 n. 201. Wenzel points out that Bromyard's picture was presumably written before Holcot's, as the part of the *Summa* that contains the picture was written before 1330, before the possible date of Holcot's *Moralitates* (between 1334 and 1342; Palmer, '"Antiquitus depingebatur"', p. 182). See Leonard Boyle, 'The Date of the *Summa praedicantium* of John of Bromyard', *Speculum*, 48 (1973), 533–37, and Smalley, *EFA*, p. 146.

[20] For information about Ridevall, see Alfred Brotherston Emden, *A Biographical Register of the University of Oxford to A.D. 1500*, 3 vols (Oxford: Clarendon Press, 1957–59), III, 1576; *DNB*, XVI, 1164; Smalley, *EFA*, pp. 109–32; Judson B. Allen, 'Commentary as Criticism: The Text, Influence and Literary Theory of the "Fulgentius Metafored" of John Ridevall', in *Acta Conventus Neo-Latini Amstelodamensis: Proceedings of the Second International Congress of Neo-Latin Studies*, Amsterdam, 19–24 August 1973, ed. by P. Tuynman, G. C. Kuiper, and Eckhard Kessler (Munich: Fink, 1979), pp. 25–47, and Jane Chance, *Medieval Mythography*, II: *From the School of Chartres to the Court at Avignon, 1177–1350* (Gainesville: University of Florida Press, 2000), pp. 281–304.

[21] Smalley, *EFA*, p. 109.

[22] Jane Chance, *Medieval Mythography*, I: *From Roman North Africa to the School of Chartres, A.D. 433–1177* (Gainesville: University of Florida Press, 1994), p. 97; for the Latin edition, see Fabius Planciades Fulgentius, *Opera*, ed. by Rudolph Helm (Leipzig: Teubner, 1898; repr. 1970), and for the English translation, see *Fulgentius the Mythographer*, trans. by Leslie George Whitbread (Columbus: Ohio State University Press, 1971).

Apocalypse, which survives in excerpts; and commentaries on Augustine's *De civitate Dei*, Books I–III, VI–VII,[23] and on Walter Map's *Dissuasio Valerium ad Rufinum de uxore non ducenda*.[24] His works clearly influenced Holcot, who cites Ridevall several times as a source for his pictures.[25]

Holcot's life is less of a mystery than Ridevall's.[26] In fact, Holcot (*c.* 1290–1349) was a very popular author in the late Middle Ages and a respected theologian and logician; Katherine Tachau has pointed out that the extant manuscripts of Holcot's Commentary on the *Sentences* outnumber those of William of Ockham by more than a dozen.[27] Holcot was probably born in Northampton, in the village of Holcot that lies in the region; he may also have joined the Dominican order there.[28] He was at Oxford from about 1326 to about 1334.[29] The study of his scholastic career aids in determining the date of his published works.

[23] See Helmut Boese, 'John Ridevalle und seine Expositio zu Austins Gottesstaat', in *Xenia medii Aevi historiam illustrantia oblata Thomae Kaepelli O.P.*, ed. by Raymond Creytens and Pius Künzle (Rome: Storia e letteratura, 1978), pp. 371–78.

[24] See Smalley, *EFA*, pp. 109–32, for a detailed analysis of the importance of Ridevall's commentaries on Augustine and Walter Map.

[25] Holcot quotes Ridevall as an authority for pictures of Hope, Sweetness, Grace, and Truth, and borrows Ridevall's pictures of Idolatry and Faith without citation.

[26] Secondary sources for details of Holcot's life include Smalley's studies of Holcot, 'Robert Holcot', *AFP*, 26 (1956), 5–97, and *EFA*, pp. 133–202; *BRO*, II, 946–47; 'Robert of Holcot', *DNB*, IX, 1007–09; Kimberly Georgedes, 'Robert Holcot', in *A Companion to Philosophy in the Middle Ages*, ed. by Jorge J. E. Gracia and Timothy B. Noone, Blackwell Companions to Philosophy, 24 (Malden, MA: Blackwell, 2003), pp. 609–10. William J. Courtenay, *Adam Wodeham: An Introduction to his Life and Writings* (Leiden: Brill, 1978), pp. 95–106; and Courtenay, *Schools and Scholars in Fourteenth-Century England* (Princeton: Princeton University Press, 1987), pp. 64–65; *Seeing the Future Clearly: Questions on Future Contingents by Robert Holcot*, ed. by Katherine H. Tachau and Paul A. Streveler, Studies and Texts, 119 (Toronto: Pontifical Institute of Mediaeval Studies, 1995). For works on Holcot written before 1983, see Hester Goodenough Gelber, *Exploring the Boundaries of Reason: Three Questions on the Nature of God by Robert Holcot, OP*, Studies and Texts, 62 (Toronto: Pontifical Institute of Mediaeval Studies, 1983).

[27] Tachau, 'Introduction', *Seeing the Future Clearly*, ed. by Tachau and Streveler, pp. 1–56 (p. 3).

[28] Joseph C. Wey, 'The *Sermo finalis* of Robert Holcot', *Mediaeval Studies*, 11 (1949), 219–24 (p. 219); Smalley, *EFA*, p. 135.

[29] *BRO*, II, 946.

Like all students of theology at Oxford in the fourteenth century, Holcot had to spend several years listening to lectures on the Bible and on Peter Lombard's *Sentences*. After a year or two spent participating in debates, the theological candidate lectured first on the *Sentences* and then on the Bible.[30] These years usually produced major commentaries which were sometimes revised for publication. The chronology of Holcot's Oxford years hinges on the date of his two-year reading of the *Sentences* and on the lectures of Holcot's fellow students. The traditional dating, based on Joseph Wey's edition of Holcot's *Sermo finalis*, puts the end of Holcot's reading of the *Sentences* in 1332. Wey fixed on this date because of references to student unrest which may have preceded the Stamford migration of 1333.[31] However, several revisions have been made recently to that schema. The most recent moves Holcot's reading to 1331–33, based on an almost indisputable dating of Richard FitzRalph's inception as Master of Theology.[32]

If Holcot lectured on the *Sentences* in 1331–33, then his regency in theology must have been in 1333–35.[33] He likely wrote his *Commentary on the Twelve Prophets* (about which more will be said below), his quodlibetal questions, and *Sex articuli* during this period.[34] Two sermon collections have also been attributed

[30] Tachau, 'Introduction', pp. 3–5. For more on Oxford theological studies in the fourteenth century, see Courtenay, *Schools and Scholars*, pp. 41–43, 58–84; William J. Courtenay, 'The Lost Matthew Commentary of Robert Holcot, OP', *AFP*, 50 (1980), 103–12; Beryl Smalley, 'Problems of Exegesis in the Fourteenth Century', *Antike und Orient im Mittelalter: Miscellanea Mediaevalia*, 1 (1962), 266–74.

[31] Wey, '*Sermo finalis*', p. 219; *Victoria History of the County of Oxford*, III: *University of Oxford*, ed. by Herbert Edward Salter and Mary Doreen Lobel (London: University of London, Institute of Historical Research, and Oxford University Press, 1954), p. 8.

[32] Both Holcot's and Adam Wodeham's reading of the *Sentences* must take FitzRalph's inception into account. Katherine Walsh, in her *Richard FitzRalph in Oxford, Avignon and Armagh: A Fourteenth-Century Scholar and Primate* (Oxford: Oxford University Press, 1981), pp. 43–45, puts his inception between May and September 1331. For a full rehearsal of all the revisions of the dates for Holcot's *Sentences* commentary, see Katherine H. Tachau, *Vision and Certitude in the Age of Ockham: Optics, Epistemology, and the Foundations of Semantics, 1250–1345*, Studien und Texte zur Geistesgeschichte des Mittelalters, 22 (Leiden: Brill, 1988), p. 244 n. 3; Courtenay, *Adam Wodeham*, pp. 95–106; and Tachau, 'Introduction', pp. 1–27.

[33] Before becoming a regent master, Holcot still needed to lecture on the Bible as a bachelor, which at Oxford in the fourteenth century would have taken place during one term or even over the long vacation. See Courtenay, *Schools and Scholars*, p. 43.

[34] Smalley, *EFA*, pp. 138–39; Courtenay, *Schools and Scholars*, p. 45 n. 53. Georgedes, 'Robert Holcot', p. 609.

to him, though these have not been systematically studied.[35] His other biblical and moral writings — his commentaries on Wisdom and Ecclesiasticus, the *Moralitates* and possibly the *Convertimini*[36] — must have been written after his Oxford career. Smalley constructed a rough chronology of these works: the Wisdom commentary, written after he left Oxford, perhaps during a second regency at Cambridge, after 1334 and before 1342, maybe 1334–36; the *Convertimini* and *Moralitates*, after the Wisdom and before the Ecclesiasticus commentary (done at Northampton, 1343–49, at the end of Holcot's life), putting them somewhere between 1334 and 1343.[37]

After he finished his regency at Oxford, Holcot seems to have moved into Richard de Bury's *familia*. According to William de Chambre's *Continuatio historiae Dunelmensis*, Holcot, along with other well-known scholars of the early fourteenth century, was associated with Bury's household sometime between 1334 and 1345.[38] Though Bury was made Bishop of Durham in 1333, he seems to have considered London the centre of his operations. In 1334 Bury became Lord Treasurer of England, and from September 1334 until June 1335, he was Lord High Chancellor and guardian of the Privy Seal.[39] Thus, it is likely that the learned members of his retinue, including Holcot, spent much time at his residence in London, especially from the mid-1330s.

This suggestion would also account for a peculiar feature of the manuscripts of Holcot's *Sentences* commentary. William Courtenay points out that all the manuscripts derive from a later version which mentions London so often as an

[35] Smalley examined one sermon collection attributed to Holcot in Cambridge, Peterhouse, MS 210 (*EFA*, p. 137 n. 1). Schneyer identified another *de tempore and de sanctis optimos* collection with sixteen manuscripts, *Repertorium der lateinischen Sermones*, 43.5, pp. 192–95.

[36] The authorship of the *Convertimini* is open to some doubt. Only one of the eight extant manuscripts (London, BL, MS Sloane 1616) mentions Holcot as the author, and it adds the faintly damning qualification 'ut quidam dicunt'. Herbert, Smalley, and Welter attributed the work to Holcot, while Wenzel cites the book as anonymous. See John Alexander Herbert, *Catalogue of Romances in the Department of Manuscripts in the British Museum*, III (London: Trustees of the British Museum, 1910; repr. 1962), pp. 116–17; Welter, *L'Exemplum*, p. 362; Smalley, *EFA*, p. 147; and Wenzel, *Verses in Sermons*, p. 118.

[37] Smalley, *EFA*, pp. 147–48.

[38] Courtenay, *Schools and Scholars*, p. 134. See also Noël Denholm Young, 'Richard de Bury (1287–1345)', *Transactions of the Royal Historical Society*, ser. 4, 20 (1937), 135–63, and Janet Coleman, 'English Culture in the Fourteenth Century', in *Chaucer and the Italian Trecento*, ed. by Piero Boitani (Cambridge: Cambridge University Press, 1983), pp. 33–63.

[39] Courtenay, *Schools and Scholars*, p. 137.

example that it may have been revised there.[40] Perhaps Holcot corrected it while in Bury's service after 1335. In any event, his association with Bury puts the possibility of a second regency at Cambridge in doubt.

## *Rhymed Pictures in the 'Fulgentius metaforalis'*

Ridevall composed two works arranged around his pictures: the *Lectura* on the Apocalypse and the *Fulgentius metaforalis*. Extracts from the first survive in a single Venetian manuscript, while the second is found in several manuscripts scattered throughout Eastern Europe.[41] The subsequent circulation of the *Fulgentius* is curious and complex, and even now far from certain. In 1926, Hans Liebeschütz prepared a critical edition of the mythographic commentary. However, he based his edition on Venice, Biblioteca Nazionale Marciana, codex latinus I. 139, which contains only half of the material commonly associated with the work in the nine surviving manuscripts.[42] Liebeschütz considered the long recension an 'enlarged' version. Judson Allen pointed out that there is no evidence to place the Venice manuscript closer to the exemplar than the longer version.[43] Both recensions follow the proper order for a commentary on the original *Mythology* by Fulgentius, reflecting the order of its chapters. The Liebeschütz edition contains chapters on Idolatry, Saturn, Jupiter, Juno, Neptune, and Pluto, while the other version adds chapters on Apollo, Pheton, Mercury, Dane, Ganymede, Perseus, Alceste, Paris, Minerva, Juno, and Venus. Jane Chance, however, has marshalled some good arguments against Allen's contention. She points out that the texts of both the long and the short versions of the *Fulgentius* were not stable.[44] In addition, the gods included in Liebeschütz's edition form a certain coherence of their own, with Saturn interpreted as Prudence, Jupiter as Benevolence, Juno as Memory, Nepture as Intelligence, and Pluto as Providence. Jupiter,

[40] Courtenay, *Schools and Scholars*, p. 106.

[41] For a list of manuscripts, see *Fulg. meta.*, 'Introduction', pp. 47–53; Allen, 'Commentary as Criticism', pp. 25–38.

[42] As Allen points out, Biblioteca Nazionale Marciana, cod. lat. I. 139 also contains the Apocalypse fragments, which may have influenced the editor's decision: 'Commentary as Criticism', pp. 25–26; idem, *The Friar as Critic: Literary Attitudes in the Later Middle Ages* (Nashville: Vanderbilt University Press, 1971), pp. 51–52.

[43] Allen, 'Commentary as Criticism', p. 26.

[44] Chance, *Medieval Mythography*, II, 294 n. 85.

Juno, Neptune, and Pluto are Saturn's children, while Memory, Intelligence, and Providence can be seen as the three parts of Prudence.[45] Regardless of whether or not Ridevall composed both parts of the entire work, it was certainly known as an entirety to a large medieval audience and deserves a full edition.[46]

The first type of verbal picture (or Type I), as developed by Ridevall, can be exemplified by his picture of Neptune/*Intelligencia*, taken, as he says, from the 'ancient poetic picture':

| | |
|---|---|
| Cornutus, opibus exutus,<br>Arpiis adiutus, statura levatus<br>Et mole gravatus, canicie dealbatus,<br>Sale coronatus, tridente sceptrizatus,<br>Stigi maritatus.[47] | Horned, despoiled of riches,<br>aided by the Harpies, lofty in stature<br>and weighty in size, white-haired,<br>crowned with salt, sceptred with a trident,<br>married to the Styx. |

Such pictures possess several notable characteristics: they are usually personifications of a virtue, vice, or ancient god; they are expressed as Latin jingles; are not easily presented visually; and are attributed to an ancient source. To see how Ridevall and Holcot meant them to function in context, it is necessary to analyse a section from each author's commentary, and then to investigate three considerations that arise from this analysis: biblical *distinctiones*, preachers' rhymes, and specific aspects of mnemonic techniques.

Ridevall's use of the pictures is far more consistent and precise than Holcot's. Each chapter in both the edited and unedited halves of the *Fulgentius metaforalis* is devoted to one god and its moralization, expressed in a picture. These pictures depend on the goal of the work. In the introductory chapter on Idolatry, Ridevall claims that it was the intention of the original Fulgentius 'under the veil of fables devised by the poets, to describe various kinds of vices and the virtues opposed to them, in order that the knowledge of the honour of the virtues and the baseness of the vices might lead his listeners to the exercise of virtue and the hatred of vice'.[48]

[45] Chance, *Medieval Mythography*, II, 296. Chance, *Medieval Mythography*, II, 282 interprets the personifications of the gods as 'faculties' of the soul, without defining what she understands as a 'faculty'.

[46] Professor Nigel F. Palmer has announced his intention to prepare a new and complete edition of *Fulgentius metaforalis*. Palmer, '"Antiquitus depingebatur"', p. 175 n. 11.

[47] *Fulg. meta.*, p. 93.

[48] *Fulg. meta.*, p. 65: 'Institucio venerabilis viri Fulgencii in sua mithologia est sub tegmine fabularum a poetis fictarum describere diversa genera viciorum et virtutum eis oppositarum, ut cognita virtutum honestate et viciorum deformitate inducat auditores ad virtutum exercitacionem et viciorum detestacionem.'

For Ridevall, unless such poetic tales are introduced for moral reasons, theologians ought to avoid them as vain and silly or run the risk of falling into idolatry. Following Maimonides, he recognizes idolatry as the sin most displeasing to God and defines it, like Fulgentius, as 'inordinate' or 'un-ordered' love.[49] From this discussion, one can conclude that Ridevall intends more by his pictures than mere 'frivolity'. As we saw in the last chapter, this was a charge often levelled against the friars, sometimes unfairly.

Ridevall illustrates his definition of Idolatry by referring to Augustine's *De civitate Dei* and Fulgentius's story of the first idol. Augustine compares two kinds of love to two kinds of cities: love of self creates an earthly city which leads to contempt of God; love of God creates a celestial city which leads to contempt of self.[50] The creation of the first idol provides an illustration of the first kind of love, disordered love. A certain rich Egyptian named Cirophanes loved his son so much that when the youth died, he fell into inordinate grief. To relieve his despair, he made an image of the boy, which he called an *ydolum*, that is, 'an image of sadness'.[51] Thus, disordered love produced inordinate grief, which in turn resulted in Idolatry.

Ridevall grounds his discussion firmly in antiquity: his sources are frequently ancient ones, and he relies on Fulgentius as much as possible. Fulgentius wants to show how the four principal human passions — love, sadness, hope, and fear — lead humans into sin when they are not governed by right reason. There follows a discussion as to which people first practised idolatry, the Egyptians as Fulgentius posits, or the Babylonians as Petrus Comestor, the Master of the Histories, asserts. Ridevall concedes that Fulgentius writes not history but rather 'a fabulous and apologetic discourse ordered to the description of virtues and vices'.[52] If one might doubt Fulgentius's purpose in writing, one could not assert that Ridevall had any other design than to showcase the virtues and vices.

After this discussion, Ridevall introduces the 'ancient' picture of Idolatry, which he claims accords well with Fulgentius's treatment in the order of his mythology:

[49] *Fulg. meta.*, p. 65.

[50] Augustine, *De civitate Dei, libri XI–XXII*, ed. by Bernhard Dombart and Alfans Kalb, CCSL, 48 (Turnhout: Brepols, 1955), XIV.28.

[51] *Fulg. meta.*, p. 66: 'quam ymaginem vocavit ydolum [...]. Ydolum quasi species vel forma doloris; dolor autem vocabulum est Latinum.'

[52] *Fulg. meta.*, p. 70: 'Dicendum quod auctor iste Fulgencius non intendit texere historiam, sed pocius mithologiam, sermonem scilicet fabulosum et apologicum ordinatum ad descripcionem virtutum et viciorum.'

| | |
|---|---|
| Mulier notata, oculi orbata, | A woman of ill-repute, deprived of sight |
| Aure mutilata, cornu ventilata, | and hearing, announced by a horn, |
| Vultu deformata et morbo vexata.[53] | Misshapen of face, and tormented by disease. |

According to Ridevall, Idolatry is a woman of ill fame and deprived of sight and hearing. She is *ventilata cornu*, because she has been convicted of *lèse-majesté*. She is sad because the origin of idolatry was unmitigated grief. Finally, she is painted *morbo vexata* because excessive love makes one ill.

In this chapter Ridevall's picture serves to consolidate the preaching material outlined throughout. Several of the attributes refer back to the story of Cirophanes and thus reinforce the memory of the origin of idolatry. The picture is adduced casually, with no indication of its curiosity. Like all of Ridevall's and Holcot's pictures, the image is a person adorned with several attributes, some of them more easily depicted than others. Idolatry is the first image described and serves to introduce Ridevall's method. In the following chapters, he places the picture nearer the beginning of the chapter in order to structure the entire discourse. In the unedited part of the *Fulgentius*, the picture is always positioned at the beginning of the chapter.

Sometimes Ridevall's pictures are more complex, reinforcing their mnemonic function. His chapter on Pluto as Providence includes multiple pictures. Pluto is

| | |
|---|---|
| Ligno coronatus, opibus ditatus | Crowned with wood, rich, |
| Inferis prelatus, Cerbero delatus | Lord of the Underworld, carried away by Cerberus, |
| Etati ligatus, Furiis armatus | Tied to the state of marriage, armed with the Furies |
| Et Fatis vellatus.[54] | And protected by the Fates. |

Ridevall expands four of the seven attributes into their own pictures. *Ligatus Etati*, 'tied to the state of marriage', refers to Pluto's wife Proserpine, who merits her own short picture: *A Cibele nata, litteris arata, | Cithara letata et lucis prelata*.[55] Cerberus, the Furies, and the Fates also figure in separate pictures, though the Fates are represented only by a poetic tag: *Onerate, ocupate et obstinate*. But as Liebeschütz remarks in a note, the addition of extra pictures allows the author or preacher to include extra material in an organized fashion.[56] Even if a preacher

[53] *Fulg. meta.*, p. 70. Holcot uses this same image in his *Commentary on the Twelve Prophets* (Smalley, *EFA*, pp. 173–74).

[54] *Fulg. meta.*, p. 100.

[55] *Fulg. meta.*, p. 107: 'Born from Cibele, ploughed with letters, gladdened by the lute, and Lady of the light'.

[56] *Fulg. meta.*, p. 103 n. 4.

never included Pluto or his band of courtiers in a sermon, he could hardly fail to note such a useful device for including digressions into the main discourse.

## *Rhymed Pictures in 'The Commentary on the Twelve Prophets'*

Holcot employed his first picture method, the rhymed pictures, in his *Commentary on the Twelve Prophets*. The commentary survives in four manuscripts, all of them representing one recension of rather rough lecture notes. Smalley put the *terminus a quo* at 1332 (which should be corrected to 1333), because Holcot mentions his *Sentences* commentary. There are also references to seemingly contemporary events that may indicate Edward II's deposition in 1327. It would make sense for this reason to put the commentary during Holcot's regency *c.* 1333–35, as masters of theology were expected to lecture on one book of the Old Testament and one of the New concurrently.[57] Thus, the Twelve Prophets commentary likely represents his earliest biblical work, with the possible exception of fragments from a commentary on Matthew.[58]

Because the work is obviously still close to its original form as a series of lectures, it is less polished than Holcot's better-known commentary on Wisdom. However, the literary infelicity is more than compensated for by the opportunity to watch Holcot employing his exegetical techniques firsthand. The commentary is divided into twelve books corresponding to the twelve minor prophets. Its two most striking features are Holcot's delight in classical stories and allusions and the picture technique. Because the commentary has not been edited, I have concentrated on only one section, the Book of Nahum. I chose Nahum because it contains more pictures than the other books and was a manageable length to edit.

Holcot's methodology resembles Ridevall's, though he is more idiosyncratic. In Book VII of his *Commentary on the Twelve Prophets* (on Nahum), Holcot seeks classical stories wherever they may be found. He quotes from the following classical and medieval authors: Aristotle, Augustine, Aulus Gellius, Bernard de Clairvaux, Isidore of Sevilla, Jerome, Justin, Remigius of Auxerre, Petrus Comestor, Servius, the three Vatican Mythographers (anonymous writers whose works on the gods were found in a manuscript in the Vatican Library),[59] and

[57] Smalley, *EFA*, pp. 138–41; William J. Courtenay, 'The Bible in the Fourteenth Century: Some Observations', *Church History*, 54 (1985), 176–87.

[58] Smalley, *EFA*, pp. 142–43; Courtenay, 'Lost Matthew Commentary', pp. 103–12.

[59] Among Holcot's and Ridevall's favourite sources were the second and third 'Vatican Mythographers'. See *Scriptores rerum mythicarum latini tres Romae nuper reperti I–II*, ed. by

Vegetius, as well as the Bible and the *Glossa ordinaria*. Many of these classical sources Holcot must have known at secondhand, from *florilegia* like Thomas of Ireland's *Manipulus florum* and Vincent de Beauvais's *Speculum maius*. Still we know from asides in his lectures that Holcot took special pride in tracking down certain elusive volumes, such as thirty-six of Seneca's letters, beyond the traditional eighty-eight.[60]

Leaving aside the question of why Holcot used so many classical authors, let us consider how he uses them in the Nahum commentary. Most he adduces in support of sections he has identified in the text through division and through his pictures. Both are an integral part of his methodology, as can be seen in the first chapter. He cites the opening lines of the text, *Onus Ninive*, and interprets Nahum as meaning *germinans eis* or *consolatio*. He next divides the chapter into five parts, citing the scriptural text which marks the division: '[I]n the first part of the first chapter he [Nahum] posits the vengeance and fury of the Lord. In the second part, he posits his patience and strength, *Dominus patiens, et caetera*.'[61]

After partitioning the chapter, he returns to its beginning to discuss the theme of the vengeance of the Lord. He cites the scriptural text *ulciscens Dominus in hostes suos* and advises his audience not to be too quick to take vengeance on its enemies, quoting Seneca twice, St Bernard, the Code of Justinian, and Scripture to explain why.[62]

Then Holcot draws on a picture to explain the division at *Dominus patiens*. Patience is

| | |
|---|---|
| homo sedens ditatus, vilibus cibatus, | A rich man sitting, fed with vile foods, |
| vultu laetatus, omnibus inclinatus, | Joyful of face, turned towards all, |
| purpura vestitus, hostibus munitus, | Clothed in purple, protected from enemies, |

Georg Heinrich Bode, 2 vols (Cellis: Schulze, 1834; repr. Hildesheim: Olms, 1968); *Mythographi Vaticani I et II*, ed. by Peter Kulscár, CCSL, 91C (Turnhout: Brepols, 1987); *Le Premier mythographe du Vatican*, ed. by Nevio Zorzetti and Jacques Berlioz (Paris: Les Belles Lettres, 1995); E. Rathbone, 'Master Alberic of London, "Mythographus Tertius Vaticanus"', *Medieval and Renaissance Studies*, 1 (1941), 35–38; K. O. Elliot and J. P. Elder, 'A Critical Edition of the Vatican Mythographers', *Transactions of the American Philological Association*, 78 (1947), 189–207; Richard M. Krill, '"Vatican Mythographers": Their Place in Ancient Mythography', *Manuscripta*, 23 (1979), 173–77; Seznec, *Survival of the Pagan Gods*.

60 Smalley, *EFA*, p. 153.

61 Nahum, ll. 8–9. All references to Holcot's Commentary on the Book of Nahum, part of his larger commentary on the Twelve Prophets, are to my edition of Holcot's Nahum commentary, contained in Rivers, 'Pictures, Preaching and Memory'.

62 Nahum, ll. 24–56.

| | |
|---|---|
| cum manu arida et alia extenta, | With one hand shrivelled and the other extended, |
| sine pedibus, sine lingua et auribus.[63] | Without feet, without tongue and ears. |

Each of the ten attributes of Patience then forms one of the ten remaining divisions of the text. In each division, Holcot unpacks the meaning of the attribute. A patient man is 'sitting rich and quiet' because he possesses himself and God, therefore he is rich. The patient man's quiet nature is implied through a string of biblical quotations: 'An angry man provokes quarrels, he who is patient quiets excitement.'[64]

Sometimes Holcot summons other authorities to reinforce his initial moralizations of the attribute. Augustine and Seneca support Holcot's assertion that patience should be joyful. Sometimes, too, Holcot clearly has an exempla collection in front of him or has followed a train of associations in memory. For instance, in an aside on Patience's clothing, he moves from a story found in Aulus Gellius's *Attic Nights*, about a bearded man clothed in a pallium who thus considered himself a philosopher, to three more tales connected only by the mention of beards or the four signs of the ancient philosopher.[65]

Holcot employs the same method in the rest of Book VII. He includes one picture of Impatience in Chapter 1 and one of Lechery in Chapter 3, which absorbs most of the exegesis in that chapter. Impatience is

| | |
|---|---|
| homo pauper splendide cibatus, | A poor man fed splendidly, |
| maestitia respersus, omnibus adversus, | Sprinkled with the tears of grief, opposed to all, |
| vestibus nudatus, aculeis vallatus, | Divested of clothing, defended by barbs, |
| cum manibus leprosis et pedibus vulpinis, | With leprous hands and the feet of a fox, |
| cum lingua serpentina et auribus leoninis.[66] | With a serpentine tongue and the ears of a lion. |

The picture of Impatience clearly derives from that of Patience. Many of the attributes are antithetical to Patience's virtues: Patience is rich, Impatience is poor. Patience is fed with vile foods, is joyful of face, and inclined toward all, while Impatience is fed ostentatiously, besmeared with grief, and against everyone. The other attributes are clearly interrelated as well, each set involving hands, feet, and

[63] Nahum, ll. 59–63. Holcot attributes this picture to 'Boralensis'. I, like Smalley, have been unable to determine who Boralensis might be. Holcot quotes him as a source for a picture two other times in the Twelve Prophets, of a King on Osee 3. 4–5 and of Devotion on Zachariah 10. 2 (Smalley, *EFA*, pp. 173, 177).

[64] Nahum, ll. 64–68.

[65] Nahum, ll. 144–70.

[66] Nahum, ll. 272–77.

ears. Holcot himself signals the two pictures' close relationship, for he ends his description of Impatience with the comment 'the exposition of this picture is obvious from the aforesaid description of Patience, therefore I will pass on'.[67] Whatever the ultimate source of Patience may have been, the author of Impatience was almost certainly Holcot himself.

The most interesting of the three pictures is that of *Luxuria*, or Lechery, for here it is possible to discover Holcot's sources and to observe how he weaves them together to form a *pictura*. Holcot says that Lechery, according to some, was depicted as

| | |
|---|---|
| mulier plena sorde, sine corde, | A woman full of uncleanliness, without a heart, |
| excaecata, spoliata, | Blind, despoiled, |
| ignita, columbis custodita, | Aflame, guarded by doves, |
| cum damno de mari nata, | Born with damage from the sea, |
| Vulcano maritata, | married to Vulcan, |
| concha marina onerata, rosis adornata.[68] | Burdened with a sea shell, adorned with roses. |

Holcot's depiction of Lechery slides into a description of Venus, an affinity which is born out by the sources he quotes. Attributes six through ten are all standard characteristics of Venus drawn from the accepted medieval authorities on classical mythology, such as Servius, Fulgentius, and the three Vatican Mythographers. Lechery is 'kept by doves' because, according to Servius, Venus is, and Holcot relates the fable of how Venus acquired this characteristic.[69] For the same reason, Lechery is 'born from the sea', 'married to Vulcan', 'carries a sea shell', and is 'adorned with roses'. Most of these depictions must have been familiar to anyone at all acquainted with classical mythology. What is new here is that Holcot has drawn them together with five scriptural attributes as a rhymed picture. In this moralization, as in others in the Twelve Prophets, we can see Holcot combining his two over-riding interests of classicism and his pictures.[70]

[67] Nahum, ll. 276–77.

[68] Nahum, ll. 486–89.

[69] Nahum, ll. 580–86. Although Holcot claims Servius as his source for nearly all of these attributes, I have found few of them in Servius. Sometimes Fulgentius or one of the three Vatican Mythographers, particularly the third, seems a closer match. See the *Apparatus fontium*, ll. 579–621, for Holcot's sources for this picture.

[70] Other pictures with classical sources or motifs are those of Cupid, Charity, Bacchus, Hope, Peace, Mercy, Grace; Smalley, *EFA*, pp. 172–78. Because Smalley has transcribed all the pictures in the Twelve Prophets commentary from Oxford, Bodleian Library, MS SC 2648 (Bodl. 722), in *EFA*, I will generally cite her and not the manuscripts themselves when I refer to pictures outside Nahum.

If the pictures in the Nahum commentary are compared to the pictures in the other eleven books, we see that none of them is wholly original. Many of the attributes, even whole phrases, can be interchanged. Boy, Hope, and Poverty, as well as Patience, are *vultu laetatus*; both Grace and Impatience are *Veste nudatus*, and Poverty as well as Patience is *sedens quietatus*. As Smalley pointed out, once Holcot had mastered his technique, there was no end to the pictures he could create.

Despite the allure of his pictures, Holcot did not always structure his chapters around them. In Chapter 2 of the Nahum commentary he alters his plan. As in Chapter 1, he divides the text into parts. He then expounds the phrase *clypeus fortium* (shield of the strong) by discussing the kinds of shields found in Scripture. He discovers four — *clypeus aeneus*, *clypeus aureus*, *clypeus sermocinalis*, and *clypeus igneus* — each possessing three angles. The bronze shield is the shield of faithful constancy, with three angles because one should display constancy by believing in one's heart, confessing with one's mouth, and persevering in deed.[71] Once he has explained the four *clypei*, he then expounds four *scuta* (oblong shields). Another option is similar to the picture method. At the chapter's close Holcot comments on the text *miles captivus est* with the following jingle:

| | |
|---|---|
| notatur quod bonus miles debet esse | It is noted that a good knight ought to be an |
| Alexander in donariis, | Alexander in gifts, |
| monachus in ecclesiis, | A monk in churches, |
| virgo in eloquio et consiliis, | A maiden in eloquence and counsels, |
| leo in campis et proeliis.[72] | A lion in the fields and battles. |

Each of these phrases is then expounded in much the same manner as the pictures and the shields.

Neither Ridevall's nor Holcot's techniques of exposition is quite what we would expect. What is the point of these pictures, the shields, and the jingles? What have Alexander the Great and Venus to do with Old Testament prophecy, or Neptune and Pluto with the virtues and vices? Other scholars have asked these same questions. Smalley was particularly intrigued by the pictures. She considered them to be a literary, rather than visual phenomenon, because they seemed so difficult to paint. Smalley eventually concluded that whatever the pictures' origin, they were meant as preaching aids, since '[a]n image which could be grasped easily,

[71] Nahum, ll. 311–15: 'clypeus aeneus est clypeus fidelis constantiae. Primo Reg. 17: "Clypeus tegebat umeros eius." Iste clypeus habet tres angulos, quia constantiam debet homo ostendere in corde credendo, ore confitendo, et opere perservando.'

[72] Nahum, ll. 424–27.

complex enough to intrigue without confusing, projected back into antiquity and supplied with inscriptions to intrigue still further, this made first-class preaching material'.[73]

I think that Smalley is certainly correct in seeing these pictures as preachers' aids. What I think needs to be explained is exactly how they functioned. To answer that question, three related topics need to be addressed: the medieval tradition of biblical distinctions, preachers' rhymes, and specific references to mnemonic techniques and to preaching in *ars praedicandi* and *ars memorativa* treatises.

## *Biblical Distinctions and Preachers' Rhymes*

Ridevall's and Holcot's pictures capitalize on practical, medieval responses to the exigencies of preaching. This can be seen most clearly in the resemblance of the picture to a *distinctio* and in the use of preachers' rhymes. In Holcot's Zachariah commentary, Pride is

| | |
|---|---|
| rex coronatus, ut aquila exaltatus, | A king crowned, exalted like an eagle, |
| vestibus laceratus, capite infirmatus, | Whose clothes are torn and whose head is injured; |
| cum dentibus aprinis et pedibus taurinis, | With the teeth of a boar and the feet of a bull; |
| colore denigratus, familia stipatus, | Coloured black, surrounded by family, |
| magnam habens prolem et impugnans solem, | Possessing great offspring and assailing the sun, |
| vermibus infestatus, in fetibus collocatus, | Infested with worms, established in unclean places, |
| tenebrescens et intumescens.[74] | Growing dark and swelling up. |

If one reads the Rouses's work on *distinctiones*, one is immediately struck by how close these pictures are to a catalogue of attributes, such as one might find in a *distinctio*. The Rouses follow P. Moore's definition of a distinction, which 'distinguishes — thus the name — the four senses or levels of meaning (literal, allegorical, anagogic, tropologic) of a term found in the scriptures; and for each meaning it furnishes a scriptural illustration'. They modify the definition only by noting that a distinction may list levels of meaning other than the four senses, and that the illustrations may not necessarily be scriptural.[75]

[73] Smalley, *EFA*, p. 182.

[74] Smalley, *EFA*, p. 178.

[75] Mary A. and Richard H. Rouse, 'Biblical *Distinctiones* in the Thirteenth Century', *Archives d'histoire doctrinale et littéraire du moyen âge*, 41 (1974), 27–37 (pp. 27–28).

Distinctions, though based on patristic practice, flowered in the twelfth century. They began by simply providing an intelligent understanding of a biblical term. By the end of the twelfth and in the thirteenth century, compilers culled more citations from patristic and profane sources and incorporated exempla. This practice allowed preachers and teachers to graft secular and moral teaching onto the scriptural ones. Stephen Langton, for instance, drew on natural history and bestiaries: 'the raven is black, he feeds on carrion, he cries "cras cras"; hence he signifies the wicked, blackened with sin, who feed on vanity, who procrastinate'.[76] Collections of distinctions became increasingly popular in the thirteenth century; those complied by Maurice de Provins, Nicolas de Biard, and Nicolaus Gorran were frequently copied in the thirteenth and fourteenth centuries.[77]

During the thirteenth century, such distinctions began to be used to construct divisions of sermons. For instance, in a sermon preached in 1230, the Dominican John of St Giles, builds the second half of his sermon on a distinction of the word *lumen*: 'Est autem lumen gratiae, lumen rationis et item intentionis et item fidei.'[78] These phrases form the topic headings of the four subdivisions of the latter part of the sermon. Holcot's use of the 'shields' in Chapter 2 of the Nahum commentary is analogous, as is, of course, the way he divides his commentary in Chapters 1 and 3 around the ten attributes of his pictures.

Distinctions could also be presented in verse form, especially for divisions in sermons, which brings us to the topic of preachers' rhymes. According to d'Avray, 'The use of rhymed divisions is normal in this period; from the mid-thirteenth century it would be harder to find exceptions than examples.'[79] The Rouses demonstrate that Bonaventura used them to divide his sermons: 'a sermon on the

[76] Smalley, *Study of the Bible*, p. 247, from Langton's gloss on Genesis 8. 6 (n. 3).

[77] Louis-Jacques Bataillon, 'L'agir humain d'après les distinctions bibliques du XIIIe siècle', in Bataillon, *La Prédication au XIIIe siècle en France et Italie*, ed. by David d'Avray and Nicole Bériou (Aldershot: Variorum, 1993), pp. 776–90. Bataillon suggests that the large number of manuscripts stems from their official authorization by the University of Paris. All appear on the taxation list for 1304, though in 1275 only Maurice de Provins's is mentioned. The Rouses, however, point out that no set reading list was provided by the university to the stationers, in 'The Book Trade at the University of Paris, ca. 1250–ca. 1350', in their *Authentic Witnesses*, pp. 259–338 (p. 305).

[78] Mary A. and Richard H. Rouse, *Preachers, Florilegia and Sermons: Studies on the 'Manipulus florum' of Thomas of Ireland*, Studies and Texts, 47 (Toronto: Pontifical Institute of Mediaeval Studies, 1979), pp. 75–76.

[79] David L. d'Avray, 'The Wordlists in the "Ars faciendi sermones" of Geraldus de Piscario', *Franciscan Studies*, 16 (1978), 184–93 (p. 186 n. 8).

octave of Epiphany has as its divisions, "dulcedo benignae allocutionis, amaritudo magnae tribulationis, sollicitudo discretae inquisitionis"'.[80] Many *artes praedicandi* recommended the practice and even gave elaborate instructions for the procedure. For instance, Thomas de Tuderto explained to preachers how to form proper rhymes in Latin:

> The fourth rule that a sermon writer ought to use, as far as he is able, is that in words from which rhymes are composed, the vowels [*vocales*] be similar. This rule especially ought to be applied to the last and penultimate vowels; whence these two words, *deficiens* and *concinans*, are not easily associated, because they do not agree in the beginning, the end, or the middle. For the last vowel of the first word is *e*, while the last vowel of the second word is *a*. But these two words, *sufficiens* and *subveniens*, are well joined, because they agree in the beginning, and in the middle, and in the end. For the penultimate and the final vowels of both words are the same, as was noted.[81]

Thomas Waleys also discusses the use of jingles in his treatise on composing sermons.[82] Waleys considers whether or not preachers should employ metres and rhymes in their sermons. Observing that many preachers certainly do use them, he concedes that the practice is licit as long as it is not overdone. Once the licence has been granted to use rhyme, Waleys immediately advises his readers on the best ways to incorporate them into their work.[83] A preacher should have many written lists of words that end in a similar way to which he can refer at will. In this way, he can avoid the disaster of discovering the perfect idea for a sermon, only to

[80] Rouse and Rouse, *Preachers*, pp. 76–77.

[81] D'Avray, 'Wordlists', p. 186 n. 8. D'Avray has transcribed the passage from Munich, Bayerische Staatsbibliothek, clm 19608 and the textual emendations in the Latin are his: 'Quarta regula quod sermocionator (*cod.* sermaciotor) debet conari pro posse quod in dictionibus (dictionibus] dictienibus *ante corr.*) ex quibus rigmi componuntur vocales sunt similes; que regula maxime debet intelligi de ultima et penultima vocalibus, unde non bene sociarentur ille due dictiones: *deficiens* et *continans*, eo quod nec in principio nec in fine nec in medio conveniunt, quia ultima vocalis prime dictionis est *e*, ultima vero secunde dictionis est *a*, sed ille due dictiones *sufficiens* et *subveniens* bene sociarentur, quia in principio et in medio et in fine conveniunt, quoniam penultime (*cod* pul[e] *sive* pnl[e]) et ultime vocales utriusque dictionis sunt similes ut notum est.'

[82] Smalley, *EFA*, pp. 78, 101. Waleys wrote *De modo componendi sermones* around 1342, after he was released from a stint in the papal prisons for his opinions on the Beatific Vision. Waleys was sometimes eccentric in his opinions, but his preaching advice seems sensible and likely reflected contemporary custom.

[83] *De modo comp.*, p. 374: 'Qua licentia concessa, dico quod volentibus rhythmis uti et multos sermones componere valde expedit multas summas verborum colligere quae simili modo terminentur, et eas habere in scriptis semper in promptu, ut ad eas possint recurrere quando volunt.'

discard it when he cannot find an appropriate word to rhyme.[84] Waleys probably did not repudiate rhyming divisions of his own sermons, because he employs one himself as an example of a proper division in a prior chapter entitled 'On Dividing the Theme and the Utility of its Division':

> V.g. accepi forsan thema istud, de Adventu Domini: *Hora est jam nos de somno surgere.* Postquam autem ipsum introduxi, dico sic: Apostolus in hiis verba tria facit, *quia excitat, suscitat, et incitat. Excitat negligentes ut considerent, suscitat dormientes ut vigilent, incitat torpescentes ut [se] praeparent.*[85]

> (For example, I took this theme about the Advent of Christ: 'Now is the hour for us to arise from sleep'. After I introduced it, I say the following: 'The Apostle does three actions in the quotation, because he excites, he revives, he incites. He excites the negligent to take thought; he revives the somnolent to keep watch; he incites the indolent to prepare themselves.')

It appears that rhyming distinctions in Holcot's and Ridevall's time appear to constitute an integral part of sermon division.

Although Waleys does not provide examples of his word lists, the Franciscan Géraud du Pescher, does.[86] In the seventh chapter of his *Ars faciendi sermones*, Géraud lists a seemingly incomprehensible conglomeration of words. D'Avray insightfully untangled them. Taking several examples from the section joining adjectives and substantives, he arranged the words in columns:

| **(A)** | **-1** | **-2** | **-3** |
|---|---|---|---|
| Inexpressibilis | malorum punitio | miseria | calamitas |
| Optabilis | Dei dilectio | divina gratia | proximi caritas |
| Odibilis | culpe transgressio | superbia | iniquitas[87] |

A preacher could match the adjectives in column A with the substantives in column 1 to create a rhymed division: for example, 'Inexpressibilis punitio', 'Optabilis dilectio', 'Odibilis transgressio'. The same principle works for each column; the same adjectives combined with the words in column 3 would yield 'Inexpressibilis calamitas', 'Optabilis caritas', 'Odibilis iniquitas'. As d'Avray

[84] *De modo comp.*, p. 374: 'et tamen, propter defectum unius vocabuli quod non occurrit memoriae ipsius volentis auctoritatem dividere, quia scilicet non occurrit vocabulum quod in rhythmo concordare possit cum alio vel aliis, oportet eum dimittere sententiam bonam quae occurrit'.

[85] *De modo comp.*, p. 369; my emphasis.

[86] Also known as Geraldus de Piscarius. This is the same author discussed in Chapter 5.

[87] D'Avray, 'Wordlists', p. 189. I have removed the formatting of his table in order to increase legibility.

noted, the words are not aligned exactly in columns in the manuscript, nor do all the examples fall into such neat divisions, but this must be the way the lists were designed to function.

A comparison to Ridevall's jingles will quickly reveal that he worked on a much more superficial level. Nearly all of the phrases of his jingles, in both the edited and unedited portions of the *Fulgentius metaforalis*, depend on the past participle of verbs of the first conjugation.[88] Pheton is

| | |
|---|---|
| Sole generatus, curis inflammatus | Engendered by the Sun, inflamed by trouble, |
| Situ sublimatus, in curru locatus, | High in position, seated in a chariot, |
| Literis aratus, loris ocupatus, | Ploughed with letters, busy with the reins, |
| Mole incuratus, timore turbatus, | Oblivious to his burden, disturbed by fear, |
| Honore priuatus, morti condempnatus, | Deprived of honour, condemned to death, |
| Versibus ornatus et fletu rigatus.[89] | Decorated with verses and dampened with weeping. |

while Juno is

| | |
|---|---|
| Vertice velata, iride sertata, | Veiled from the crown of her head, wreathed in the rainbow, |
| Unguentis afflata, sceptro decorata | Wafted with perfume, adorned with a sceptre |
| Et auro ligata, Iovi maritata, | and bound with gold, married to Jove, |
| Herculi irata, avibus vallata, | Angry with Hercules, surrounded by birds, |
| Humore rigata et luce lustrata.[90] | Dampened with rain, and illuminated with light. |

Holcot also depends on the same participle but does sometimes vary his rhymes. Suavitas, for example, is an image

| | |
|---|---|
| Sexus virilis, infacilis, | Of the virile sex, not lazy, |
| Cor madens cruore, oculis [*sic*] amore; | Heart dripping blood, eyes [dripping] love, |
| Os spirat dulcorem, manus fundunt rorem.[91] | Mouth breathing sweetness, the hands shed dew. |

[88] This similarity in style may be one indication that the unedited half of the *Fulgentius* is indeed by Ridevall, as Holcot and the other picture writers either vary their rhymes or leave the rhymes out altogether. Of course, the practice could have been imitated by an admirer.

[89] London, BL, MS Royal 7.C.I, fol. 338$^{rb}$. Liebeschütz transcribes this picture from Vatican City, Biblioteca Apostolica Vaticana, MS Palatinus latinus 1066, which gives a slightly different version: Sole generatus, curru inflammatus | Situ sublimatus, in curru locatus | Litteris aratus, loris occupatus | Mole minoratus, timore turbatus | Morti condempnatus, versibus ornatus | Fletibus rigatus (*Fulg. meta.*, p. 176).

[90] *Fulg. meta.*, p. 88.

[91] Smalley, *EFA*, p. 176.

There is a good deal of repetition in these attributes; several personifications are *vallata/us* or *maritata/us*, which may indicate that Holcot and Ridevall could have profited from aids such as Géraud's word list to compose their rhymes.

But for whom were the rhymes intended, the preacher or the audience? Waleys brings up that point in *De modo componendi*. Even though he decides that preachers may use rhymes in their preaching to clergy, he is adamantly opposed to their use in preaching to the people in the vernacular:

> For I do not consider it vicious that they [the preachers] use them [*talibus coloribus*] in preaching to the clergy, so long as they do not dwell on them or use such rhymes too often. But a preacher, when he is about to preach to the people in the vernacular, should not make such rhymes for them.[92]

Some preachers excuse their use of rhymes by claiming that their listeners require it. Clerics are accustomed to eating the rich food of the table of Scripture; thus, those who would minister to them need to prepare their delicacies in a 'curious and subtle' manner. For this reason, Waleys concedes that modern preachers should be allowed their rhymes in sermons to clerics, in order that they might remove the distaste of their listeners, as long as they do not use them excessively.[93]

From Waleys's comments, it seems likely that these Latin jingles cannot have been intended for a non-clerical audience. In the first place, it seems that it was an accepted custom to insert jingles in sermons to the clergy. The excuse that clerics require more subtle fare is a topos here. In the second place, Waleys's advice on collecting rhyming words in writing indicates that the composition of jingles was likely not impromptu. But in order to preach the Latin jingles to a non-clerical audience, the friars would have had to translate the jingles into the vernacular. It is unlikely that they could arrive at suitable rhymes on the spot. A consensus has been reached by those who have researched the friars' preaching habits that the friars delivered their sermons in the vernacular, but wrote them down in Latin.[94] Undoubtably, some sermons were originally composed in the vernacular, whether written down or not, but model sermon and skeleton sermon collections were generally preserved in Latin. This habit was one reason why mendicant sermons travelled so well: they were not area-specific. Of course, the friars included ver-

[92] *De modo comp.*, p. 373: 'Non enim reputo vitiosum quod eis utantur praedicando clero, dummodo eis non immorentur nimio vel tales colores frequentent. Absit autem a praedicatore ut, praedicaturus populo in vulgari, tales rhythmos eis faciat.'

[93] *De modo comp.*, p. 374.

[94] D'Avray, *Preaching of the Friars*, pp. 90–95; Owst, *Preaching in Medieval England*, pp. 222–30.

nacular verses in some of their sermons, and several scholars have studied macaronic English sermons that switch back and forth from English to Latin in mid-sentence. No doubt Waleys would have been less adamant in his denunciation if the practice of rhyming the vernacular were not widespread. But the question is whether or not these particular Latin jingles were delivered to lay audiences, and on the whole, it seems unlikely.[95]

Thus, I think Holcot's and Ridevall's pictures were designed for a clerical audience, not a lay one. Because of the difficulty of transferring the multiple rhymes to another language on the spot (though perhaps not an impossibility), it is likely that these jingles were meant as both memory aids for the preachers, and perhaps attention-grabbers for a clerical audience. The pictures may never have been stated out loud. We will shortly examine Holcot's manner of overcoming this difficulty.

## *Mnemonic Aspects*

Holcot's and Ridevall's pictures may also be elucidated by remarks in *ars praedicandi* and *ars memorativa* treatises specifically addressing the mnemonic needs of preachers. These sources resolve difficulties about the mnemonic points of verses and the need for loci in the pictures.

Like Thomas de Tuderto and Thomas Waleys, Francesc Eiximenis reviews the topic of rhyming verses in his *Ars praedicandi*. Unlike them, however, he is critical of their inclusion in sermons, unless they aid the memory. Those who fill their sermons with rhymes are more like triflers (*trufatores*) and actors (*histriones*) than preachers of God's words.[96] It is not necessary to use rhymes in the division of the theme, 'except to aid one's memory or some other pious intent'.

Some *ars memorativa* treatises are more explicit about how to use verses as a memory aid. A French codex of the fifteenth century contains three memory treatises written in the same hand.[97] The only French *ars*, called *Notables enseignemens pour avoir memoire et souvance des choses veries*, contains recommendations for using verses. One can make verses by choosing a notable word from each part

[95] For examples of the inclusion of English verses in Latin sermons, see Wenzel, *Verses in Sermons*.

[96] *Ars praed.*, III.7.3, p. 337.

[97] Jean Phillipe Antoine, 'Ancora sulle Virtù: La "nuova iconografia" e le immagini di memoria', *Prospettiva*, 30 (1982), 13–29 (p. 23).

of the lesson or book one wants to remember, putting it in meterd form, ordering its parts, and remembering the whole. The scribe adds that he in fact has done this many times and always found it beneficial. In order to aid the reader in fulfilling this recommendation, four verses covering the principal teachings of the tract are listed at the end of the text.[98]

Holcot and Ridevall are clearly following this kind of advice. Each attribute in their pictures picks one word from a large body of information about the relevant virtue or vice. The picture and verse provide an order to follow in their composition and would be memorable. A final example of using this method of mnemonic verses can be found in Simon Alcock's fifteenth-century *De divisione thematis*. He supplies forty-four methods of dividing a theme through one mnemonic poem:

> Ad, quare, per, propter; notat, in, similiat que gerundi,
> Ad quos, ne, de quot; locus, impedit, atque processus.
> Accidit, adverbium; circumstat, que relative,
> Participans, variis, ablative, genitive,
> Ostendit, movet, ut; historia, cum quia, contra.
> Pertinet, effectus; conclusio, quaestio, stat que,
> Comparet, adveniunt; argutio, littera, signa,
> Adquirit, causa; postil, diffinit, et inter.[99]

Taking as his theme *Te salvum fecit*. Alcock demonstrates how each element of the verse can divide the theme:

> An example of dividing the theme through the first word of the first verse, that is, the word or preposition *ad* may be had by taking *Te salvum fecit* for the theme. From this theme, proceed with the aforementioned word by so dividing: *'Te salvum fecit' ad tui ab inferno liberationem* through the power of the sacraments, *ad viciorum evacuationem* through the observance of the laws, *ad future beatitudinis fruitionem* in attendance on the saints.[100]

By creating a verse to hold together the disparate methods of dividing a theme, Alcock creates his own order. The rhythm of the verse holds the methods

[98] Antoine, 'Ancora sulle Virtù', p. 25.

[99] Boynton, 'Simon Alcock', p. 206.

[100] Boynton, 'Simon Alcock', p. 206: 'Exemplum dividendi thema per primam dictionem primi versus scilicet hanc dictionem sive prepositionem *ad* sic patet capiendo pro themate, *te salvum fecit*. A quo themate per predictam dictionem sic dividendo procede: *Te salvum fecit* ad tui ab inferno liberationem per virtutem sacramentorum, ad viciorum evacuationem per observantiam preceptorum, ad future beatitudinis fruitionem in contubernio beatorum.'

in his mind. Then the methods that he provides order the sermon. This method thus functions very similarly to Ridevall's and Holcot's pictures. The mnemonic aspects of the verses will distinguish these pictures from the verses in the Type II pictures (explained below).

The other mnemonic aspect of the pictures' composition is their visual presentation. Many scholars have remarked on the curiously unimaginable quality of the pictures. The large number of attributes in most of the 'images' produces a jumble seemingly impossible to reproduce visually. This problem is exacerbated by the characteristic of some attributes: how does one paint *ore dulcorata* or *numero sacrata*?[101]

Part of this difficulty may be resolved by looking at the pictures as mnemonic images. Yates rightly pointed out that mental images might require less coherence of composition than a wall painting or manuscript illumination. In fact, as we have seen, a good indicator that either a verbal 'picture' or even a manuscript illumination is intended as a mnemonic aid is the presence of unusual objects or extreme intricacy.[102] Hugh of St Victor's ark is an exemplary type of memory image. Its intricate design is so difficult to visualize in its entirety that Hugh provides a physical illustration of the ark before he teaches anything else. One assumes that mentally one could keep any single aspect of the ark before one's eyes.[103] Still, even a preacher with the most vivid imagination would require a method of keeping the attributes straight. This problem may be overcome by examining the notion of mnemonic 'loci' with respect to the pictures, and there are three ways to do this.

The first is to follow Carruthers and Bolzoni in looking for 'a place' in which to put the pictures. Both scholars have suggested that the Bible could serve as a repository of mnemonic places for preachers and writers of mystical texts.[104] They note that Holcot, for instance, often introduces a new picture in his *Commentary*

[101] Smalley, *EFA*, pp. 176–77; Oxford, Bodleian Library, MS SC 2648 (Bodl. 722), fol. 107v.

[102] Antoine, 'Ancora sulle Virtù', discusses the characteristics of memory figures in several fourteenth- and fifteenth-century illuminated manuscripts. He sees the arrangement of human figures engaged in some unusual activity with an odd object to be a sign that the figures are to be used mnemonically. His ideas accord with the manuscript figures identified by Ludvig Volkmann in several *ars memorativa* tracts, '*Ars memorativa*', *Jahrbuch der Kunsthistorischen Sammlungen in Wien*, Neue Folge, 30 (1929), 111–200. These have large figures surrounded by unusual objects; however, they are often more static than Antoine's images.

[103] Hugh of St Victor, *De arca Noe morali*, PL, CLXXVI, col. 622B.

[104] Bolzoni, 'Il "Colloquio spirituale"', pp. 23–24; Carruthers, *Book of Memory*, p. 231.

*on the Twelve Prophets* with the words 'pono picturam super illam litteram' (I place a picture on this letter). They infer from this statement that Holcot sees the chapter and verses of the Bible as places onto which pictures representing his interpretation may be 'placed'. This is an important idea, but it must also be recognized that Holcot uses the formula *super illam litteram* throughout his commentary as a way of introducing any new point. For instance, he expounds on the phrase 'ulciscens Dominus in hostes suos' in Chapter 1 of Nahum with this sentence: 'Super illam litteram, "ulciscens Dominus in hostes suos", dicitur quod Dominus ulciscitur quando homines nolunt paenitere, hoc est, inferet eis poenam.'[105] In addition, it should be noted that Holcot does not use the word *pono* at all in his commentary on Nahum. His wording may indeed imply that he sees the text as having physical places to which to attach interpretations or it may just be a convenient way for him to raise a new point.

However, a second, more promising, kind of place may be found in Holcot's and Ridevall's pictures. Francesc Eiximenis provides this alternative kind of place in the mnemonic section of his *ars praedicandi*. As we saw in Chapter 4, Francesc lists several methods of providing mnemonic order: one of these is to use the human body as an ordering device. We can begin from the feet and move up to the head or vice versa. In this manner the body may become a model of society:

> For the feet can signify peasants or the foundation of a house; just as the feet support the whole body and the peasants support the republic by their labor, so also their feet labor the most in the body. And the shins and the legs signify the burgesses, who are immediately above the peasants; the stomach represents those who receive the money of the republic, just as the stomach contains and receives everything. The arms symbolize the knights, because the knights labor by warring with their arms.[106]

If we compare our pictures to Francesc's recommendations, we will immediately notice that each of them features a human figure as the starting point and that many of their attributes centre on a body part: Impatience has 'leprous hands', 'foxy feet', 'a serpentine tongue', and 'leonine ears'; Boy is 'of moderate stature', 'prepared to walk', 'with his hands extended', and 'his mouth prepared for

[105] Nahum, ll. 24–26.

[106] *Ars praed.*, III.7.2, p. 328: 'pedes enim possunt significare tibi rusticos uel fundamenta domus, sicut ipsi pedes sustinent totum hominem et rustici rem publicem in labore suo sicut eciam pedes eorum plus laborant in corpore humano; et tibie et crura burgenses qui sunt immediate super rusticos; uenter, recipientes peccunias rei publice, sicut uenter omnia continet et recipit; brachia, milites, quia milites laborant brachiis bellando'; Francesc Eiximenis, *On Two Kinds of Order*, trans. by Rivers, p. 201.

kissing'.[107] These attributes also possess an implicit order, the order that the verse follows in listing them. One can see this order more clearly when one follows the exposition of the pictures in the commentaries. Each attribute in Holcot's Patience is recalled to the reader by the formula *primo patientia pingitur, secundo pingitur*, etc. Sometimes he alters the phrase to *prima conditio, secunda conditio*. Unlike Francesc, neither Holcot nor Ridevall moves always from head to foot or vice versa.[108]

If we examine a manuscript copied one hundred years later, we find both confirmation of the above analysis and a sense of the evolution of medieval mnemonic practice. Ludvig Volkmann's 1929 monograph on illustrated *artes memorativae* describes a fifteenth-century codex (Vienna, Nationalbibliothek, cod. 5393) which contains an illustrated memory treatise. The eleven pen-and-ink drawings form the nucleus of the tract and evidently predate the three pages of text included with them.[109] Each of the eleven drawings features a large human figure with outstretched arms, surrounded by a numbered series of smaller objects. See Figure 2, of Christ surrounded by scenes relating to his life, as an example. Not all of the smaller pictures have numbers next to them, but those that do are consistent in their order; number one is the head, two the right hand, three the space under the right hand, four the space above the head, five the neck or the breast, six the trunk of the body, seven the knees, eight the feet, nine the left hand, and ten the space under the left hand.[110] The large pictures are varied, including a young woman, a knight, a Christ-figure, a nun, and a friar. The eleventh drawing is a mnemonic device to recall the preceding ones. The large figure reproduces the young woman in picture one, with small reproductions of the other illustrations placed in the usual numbered loci around her body, though not in the same order in which they were originally presented.[111] A note in the text advises the reader as to the pictures' purpose:

[107] Smalley, *EFA*, pp. 174–75.

[108] Antoine also mentions the practice of using body parts as mnemonic loci. He adds that human figures can add to the number of places already established. Thus, this interpretation is not incompatible with Carruthers's and Bolzoni's. Antoine, 'Ancora sulle Virtù', p. 19.

[109] Volkmann, '*Ars memorativa*', p. 124. See also Susanne Rischpler, 'Die Ordnung der Gedächtnisfiguren: Der bebilderte Mnemotechnik-Traktat im Cod. 5393 der Österreichischen Nationalbibliothek', *Codices Manuscripti: Zeitschrift für Handschriftenkunde*, 25 (2004), 73–87.

[110] Volkmann, '*Ars memorativa*', pp. 129–30.

[111] Volkmann, '*Ars memorativa*', pp. 127–28.

Fig. 2. Memory image of Christ surrounded by scenes relating to his life, Vienna, Österreichische Nationalbibliothek, cod. 5393, fol. 335r. Reproduced with permission.

> These images are placed here as examples, not that one ought to use them oneself; for if he did, he would greatly err. Rather he should study to rely on the living thing and matter, which the image here represents.[112]

The student should not adopt these pictures for immediate use, but rather look at them as models for making his own memory pictures. (This advice accords with the *Ad Herennium*'s prohibition of ready-made *imagines agentes*, though authors were bound to be disappointed by actual practice). Other notes written around the picture give further recommendations for their use. One explains the limit of ten places in each image, beyond which one should not go lest the memory be confused.[113]

This fifteenth-century manuscript indicates one direction in which Holcot's and Ridevall's pictures were headed. It has illustrated the 'imagines' and replaced the mnemonic jingles with a prescribed order of body parts. The attributes are more easily depicted, but because we do not know what the figures were used to remember, we cannot judge their efficacy.

There is also a third way of linking these images to the idea of 'place', that is, to a description of a physical place. Simon Alcock recommends using a physical place like a castle, a ship, a temple, a door, and the like, as a basis for expanding one's theme, because one can moralize both the spatial properties and its physical characteristics. He takes a shield as an example. One can note its spatial features, that is, its triangular shape, the pictures painted on it, its upper and lower parts. One can also moralize its natural qualities, commenting on a golden shield's heaviness and durability.[114] Alcock's suggestion sounds very like Holcot's use of *clypei* and *scuta*; each made from a different metal and representing some different virtue. Sometimes the shields can be very elaborate: the *Fasciculus morum*'s shield of patience is 'purple, with a silver lion rampant in the middle, wearing a red rose, that is in *goules,* on its chest'.[115] These shields could probably be used either as mnemonic devices or as ordinary exempla. Their function in Holcot's commentary is certainly very like the pictures.

Ridevall's pictures in *Fulgentius metaforalis* and Holcot's pictures in the *Commentary on the Twelve Prophets* combine the established practices of *distinctiones*

[112] Volkmann, '*Ars memorativa*', p. 128: 'Iste imagines sunt posite pro exemplificatione/ non quid sibi quisque debeat incorporare, quia valde erraret/sed unus studeat unamquamque applicare rem vivam et materiam, quam imago hic representat.'

[113] Volkmann, '*Ars memorativa*', pp. 129–30.

[114] Boynton, 'Simon Alcock', p. 210.

[115] *Fasc. mor.*, pp. 722–23: 'purpureum, cum leone argenteo *rampaunte* in medio, ac in pectore unam rosam de minio, idest *gowles*, gestante'; trans. by Wenzel. Other elaborate shields in the *Fasciculus* are on pp. 103, 235–37, 569.

and preachers' jingles with mnemonic techniques to produce a useful mnemonic device for preachers. The combination of a visual image and a list of attributes couched in rhyming language resulted in the framework for a lecture or sermon. Ridevall and Holcot may have utilized this system in their commentaries for two reasons. First, they may have simply presented their lessons orally, using this system to remember their lectures. A more detailed investigation into classroom techniques might shed light on this possibility. Second, they may have been teaching the technique to their students. It is possible that, if used in sermons, the pictures and rhymes were never meant to leave the preachers' mental world; they would learn the image and jingle and then present a sermon on say, patience, relying on what they had memorized.

## *Non-rhymed Pictures in the 'Fasciculus morum' and the 'Moralitates'*

By the time Holcot composed his *Moralitates*, his method had changed. His format for the later work is quite different from that of *The Commentary on the Twelve Prophets.* Instead of expounding Scripture and producing his lively fables to explain it, he begins here with either a story or an *imago* or *pictura*, which he then proceeds to moralize. His interest in classical motifs is even more pronounced. The most significant aspect of the *Moralitates* for our purposes is Holcot's creation of his pictures in a new manner. They are far simpler than before and the jingles have disappeared, to be replaced by verse inscriptions. I call this type of picture 'Type II'. These verses scan, but seldom rhyme. A typical example is his picture of the god of piety and clemency:

> Deus autem pietatis clementia depingetur ad similitudinem hominis, qui tenebat in manu sua cor scissum in duas partes. Et in circitu cordis scribebatur literis aureis sic:
>
> Pietas & misericordia tota die expectant,
> quando peccator à suo peccato recedere curet.
>
> In vna parte cordis scriptum erat literis aureis sic:
>
> Nisi esset peccatum, non esset misericordia.
> Si venia petatur, citò habetur.
>
> In altera parte cordis scribebatur:
>
> Ibi est misericordia, vbi est peccatum:
> Ibi nulla est misericordia, vbi nullum est peccatum.[116]

[116] *M. Roberti Holkoth Liber moralizationum historarium, In librum Sapientiae regis Salomonis praelectiones ccxii* (Basel: [n. pub.], 1586), pp. 709–48 (pp. 710–11). The *Moralitates* is printed as an appendix to Holcot's Wisdom Commentary in this edition.

(The god of piety and clemency shall be depicted in the image of a man, who holds in his hand a heart cut in two parts. And around the heart is written in gold letters the following:

> Piety and mercy wait the entire day
> for when a sinner should care to depart from his sin.

In one part of the heart is written in gold letters:

> If there were no sin, there would be no mercy.
> If indulgence is sought, it is quickly possessed.

In the other part of the heart is written:

> There is mercy where there is sin:
> there is no mercy where there is no sin.)

The rhyming verse and long lists of attributes have been abandoned, to be replaced by a simpler image. Holcot prefers inscriptions now, and these are of a kind which would, I think, more easily bear translation into a vernacular language. In short, I think Holcot's pictures in the *Moralitates* are still memory images, but now they are also accessible to a lay audience. And this change represents Holcot's deliberate effort to improve an existing technique.

But like the Type I pictures, this second type was also likely borrowed from a Franciscan, this time the anonymous author of the *Fasciculus morum*. Wenzel's work on the preaching manual, which he conjectures was written early in the fourteenth century, reveals pictures nearly identical to some of Holcot's in the *Moralitates*.[117]

The relative chronology of these two works is a little puzzling, since, of his two different picture methods, Holcot employs what some scholars have called the more effective in the later text, when both methods were at least theoretically available to him from the start. Wenzel places the *terminus ad quem* for the *Fasciculus* near the end of the fourteenth century, because the earliest manuscripts can be dated palaeographically from this period. He puts the *terminus a quo* about a century earlier, probably during the reign of Edward I (1272–1307), because of internal references.[118] The author of the *Fasciculus* is still unknown, although Robert Selk, OFM, is the most likely candidate; the author is almost certainly Franciscan.[119] This dating would give us the following relative chronology for our

[117] Wenzel, *Verses in Sermons*, p. 118.

[118] Wenzel, *Verses in Sermons*, pp. 26–28.

[119] Wenzel, *Verses in Sermons*, p. 39.

picture books: *Fasciculus morum* (following Wenzel's conjecture of the beginning of the fourteenth century), Ridevall's *Fulgentius metaforalis* (*ante* 1331–32), his *Lectura in Apocalypsim* (1331–32?), Holcot's *Commentary on the Twelve Prophets* (1333–35) and the *Moralitates* (1334–43).

The pictures in the *Fasciculus morum* and *Moralitates* are striking for a number of reasons. First, they are far simpler in composition and thus easier to depict visually. For example, in the *Fasciculus morum*, the Fickleness of the World is depicted:

> Unde fertur poetice quod antiquitus mundus sic depingebatur, scilicet in specie muliebri sedens cum tribus capitibus coronatis et inscriptis. Nam in fronte primi capitis scribebatur hoc verbum: 'Promisi'. Set in eius corona sic: 'Celum fecit fabulam'. In fronte secundi capitis scribebatur hoc verbum: 'Derisi', set in eius corona: 'Mare fecit statuam'. In fronte vero tercii capitis scriptum erat hoc verbum: 'Dimisi', set in eius corona sic: 'Terra legit literam.[120]

> (The poets tell us that in old times the world was depicted in the form of a woman, sitting, with three crowned heads that bore inscriptions. On the first forehead was written, 'I have promised', but on its crown, 'Heaven has made a fable'. On the second forehead was written, 'I have laughed at', but on its crown, 'The sea has made a statue'. And on the third forehead was written, 'I have abandoned', but on its crown, 'The earth has read out a letter'.)

In fact, Fritz Saxl found some illustrations in a fifteenth-century manuscript of the Bibliotheca Casanatense in Rome that he traced back to Holcot's *Moralitates*.[121] Some of the illustrations are also drawn from Ridevall's *Fulgentius*, the *De prudentia* image collection, and the *Gesta Romanorum*. Saxl notes that no English illustrated copy of these manuscripts has survived, but an illustrated version of the *Fulgentius* did circulate in Germany in the early fifteenth century.[122] The pictures in the Casanatensis manuscript are derived from the same source as the illustrated *Fulgentius*. Saxl also describes a Wellcome manuscript with some similar illustrations.[123] It contains the Holcot and the *De prudentia* illustrations, but not the ones from the *Fulgentius*. Despite these discoveries, no copies of these works seem to have been illustrated until the fifteenth century, and even then drawings were rare.

[120] *Fasc. mor.*, p. 328; trans. p. 329.

[121] Fritz Saxl, 'A Spiritual Encyclopaedia of the Late Middle Ages', *Journal of the Warburg and Courtauld Institutes*, 5 (1942), 82–134 (p. 102). He also describes this manuscript in 'Aller Tugenden und Laster Abbildung', in *Festschrift für Julius Schlosser zum 60. Geburtstage*, ed. by Arpad Weixlgärtner and Leo Planiscig (Zurich: Amalthea, 1927), pp. 104–21.

[122] Saxl, 'A Spiritual Encyclopaedia', p. 102.

[123] Saxl, 'A Spiritual Encyclopaedia', pp. 110–17.

The second striking characteristic of these pictures is the change in verse style. Gone are the rhymed preachers' jingles and in their place appear elaborate inscriptions, which Holcot calls verses or 'sentences'. His picture of Penitence offers a particularly good example of his method:

> Poenitentia depingebatur ad modum vnius hominis nudati per totum corpus, qui tenebat in manu sua quoddam flagellum quinque folia ferens, in quo scribebatur quinque versus vel sententiae. Scriptura primi folii talis erat: Peccaui, cessare volo, quod peccaui, grauiter doleo. Scriptura secundi folii haec erat: Poenitentia libenter me affligo, quia contra Deum iniustè egi. Scriptura tertii folii talis erat: Totam meam spem pono in coelum, ubi Deus propitius est & pro misericordia lachrymabiliter precor Deum. Scriptura quartii folii talis erat: Exercere volo opera misericordiae, vt mihi aperiatur porta veniae. Scriptura quinti folii talis erat: In vita bona perseuerabo propter gaudium coeli, etc.[124]

> (Penitence is painted as a completely nude man, who holds in his hand a scourge with five leaves, on which is written five verses or thoughts. The writing on the first leaf was thus: 'I sinned, I wish to cease: the sin that I did, I greatly regret'. The writing on the second leaf was: 'With penitence I freely strike myself, because I acted unjustly against God'. The writing on the third leaf was: 'I place my whole hope in heaven, where God is well-disposed, and I beseech God mournfully for mercy'. The writing on the fourth leaf was: 'I wish to perform the works of mercy, in order that the gate of kindness is opened for me'. The writing on the fifth leaf was: 'I will persevere in a good life because of the joy of heaven'.)

The change in method is particularly evident in Penitence. Instead of an illustration composed in verses, each phrase of which refers to an attribute to be memorized, Holcot now provides a picture which incorporates written inscriptions into the illustration. The verses now express complete thoughts and are obviously meant to be memorable. The rest of the image provides a framework for the inscription, a place in which to put it.

In addition, because these verses are usually not rhymed but rather depend on metre, and because they are simpler than the Type I pictures' verses, they could more easily be translated into the vernacular. That this indeed happened can be seen in the *Fasciculus morum*, in which verses of several exempla, including some of the pictures, appear in both Latin and Middle English versions. Here is a image of Prayer from the handbook:

> Fertur autem quod antiquis temporibus a commentatore Iuvenali Oracio depingebatur ad modum hominis pulcherrimi habentis corpus igneum et capud in celum erectum, super unam lanceam rectam et altissimam, cum quatuor angelis illam supportantibus et rotul<u>m in manibus singulis tenentibus codicem condiciones Oracionis continentem. In quorum primo rotulo scribebatur:

[124] Holcot, *Liber moralizationum historiarum*, p. 718.

Terris, igne, mari, ventis peto dominari.
Anglice sic: Fyre, watur, wynd and lond
Y wylne to haue in my honde.

In secundo: Vir, pete, sum presto; si plangas, cercior esto.
Anglice sic: Byd faste and Y come sone;
Yf þow sorow, þe tyt þy bone.

In tercio: Si petor, accedo: sin autem, inde recedo.
Anglice sic: Whyle þou bydde, redy Y am;
When þou leuyst, Y go þe fram.

Et in quarto: Adiuvo ferventer, non desero, pugno libenter.
Anglice sic: <Smertly> I helpe <and noght> forsake.
Gladly Y fyȝt þe maystry to take.[125]

(In ancient times, Prayer is said to have been depicted, by the commentator Juvenal, as a most beautiful man with a body of fire, his head lifted to heaven, leaning on a straight and tall lance, and supported by four angels who held scrolls in their hands which expressed the qualities of prayer.

On the first was written: Lands and fire, sea and winds I strive to rule.

In English:

Fire, water, wind, and land
Firmly I wish to have in hand.

On the second: Pray, I am at your will; if you weep, you may be more sure.

In English:

Fast you pray, and I come soon,
If you are sorry, you get your boon.

On the third: If I am asked, I come, but leave as soon as you stop.

In English:

As long as you pray, ready I'll be,
But when you stop I go from thee.

And on the fourth: With fervor I help, I do not forsake, and gladly I fight.

In English:

I eagerly help and not forsake,
And gladly fight the crown to take.)[126]

[125] *Fasc. mor.*, p. 522; trans. pp. 521, 523.

[126] *Fasc. mor.*, pp. 522–23.

Although both the Latin and the English verses have rhymed elements in this picture, the verses are short enough to be translated relatively effortlessly. The composition of the picture in prose style with easily translated verse inscriptions meant that a preacher could include a picture in his sermon and use it as a mnemonic device both for himself and for his audience. As the other pictures had several mnemonic aspects to recommend them to a sermonizing audience, so too did the Type II picture have much to recommend it to a lay audience.

The first is the character of the verse transcriptions themselves. Wenzel has noted several important functions of verses in sermons, some of which are relevant here. The verses may summarize some material that needs to be memorized, so that the verse carries most of the mnemonic burden. They may summarize a story or an exemplum or give the moral. Wenzel calls this type 'message verses', and it is the type most commonly found in popular preaching. Often the stories would lose their point without the verses. Finally, verses may be used for structural purposes, as in the pictures examined here.[127]

Another aspect of the pictures which would recommend them to a lay audience is the character of the images. As mentioned before, they are far easier to depict than the rhymed pictures in Ridevall's works. For this reason, they could likely be grasped much more easily by a listening audience and more easily serve a mnemonic function for them, as well as the preacher. An example of a mnemonic text that sheds light on the Type II pictures can be found in the fifteenth-century *ars memorativa* tract with the *incipit Memoria fecunda Deus Pater eternus*, 'With fruitful memory, God the eternal father', edited by Roger Pack in 1979.[128] For his edition he used the text contained in Vienna, Nationalbibliothek, MS Vind. 4444, which was copied in Bologna in July 1425.[129] The treatise lists verbal

[127] Wenzel, *Verses in Sermons*, pp. 66–75.

[128] Roger A. Pack, 'An *Ars memorativa* from the Late Middle Ages', *Archives d'histoire doctrinale et littéraire du moyen âge*, 46 (1979), 221–75. This manuscript has been discussed a number of times by scholars interested in various aspects of the *ars memorativa*. See Roger A. Pack, 'A Life of Saint Marina in an Ars Memorativa', *Classical Folia*, 31 (1977), 78–84; Berlioz, 'La Mémoire du prédicateur'; Jacques Berlioz, 'Comment se souvenir d'un *exemplum*: Marine déguisée en moine', in *Prêcher d'exemples: Récits de prédicateurs du moyen âge*, ed. by Jean-Claude Schmitt (Paris: Stade, 1985), pp. 173–78 (a shorter version of the 1982 article); Hajdú, *Das mnemotechnische Schrifttum*, pp. 101–03; Bolzoni, *Gallery of Memory*, trans. by Parzen, pp. 150, 213; Giuseppa Saccardo del Buffa, 'Dalla narrazione alla scena pittorica mediante la tecniche della memoria (Wien, Ö.N.B. 4444)', *Arte lombarda*, 105–07 (1993), 79–84; Heimann-Seelbach, *Ars und scientia*, pp. 28–34.

[129] When Roger Pack prepared his edition, he thought that only one copy of the manuscript existed. However, Sabine Heimann-Seelbach's work on fifteenth-century mnemonic

descriptions of the virtues and vices for the would-be mnemonist to remember. For example, Justice is a young woman holding a sword in her right hand and a book in her left; Faith wears on her head a crown with twelve stars (the articles of faith); Humility wears black clothing, bending her head and knee, and beats herself with a branch of hyssop, while Pride has three crowns and is dressed with style.[130] Each of these mental images draws on attributes of the virtue or vice and helps one to remember it. Pride and Faith in particular are nearly identical to images found in contemporary exempla collections.[131] The presence of these images in a mnemonic tract indicates that this author considered the virtues and vices to be worth remembering and that the kind of personifications that had been used in religious texts for at least the last century made good mnemonic images.

## *'Picturae' in other English Authors*

Given that the *picturae* and *imagines* (as the non-rhymed, Type II images are often called in the manuscripts) appear to be ideal vehicles for lay instruction, it makes sense to ask whether other preachers and writers of homiletic aids made use of them. As we shall see in the next few chapters, the classicizing *picturae* and *imagines* were wildly popular on the Continent in the fourteenth and fifteenth centuries. How did they fare in England? Siegfried Wenzel, who has probably spent more time with the sermon manuscripts of late medieval England than anyone else, asked the same question. He wondered whether Smalley's *picturae* were used in sermons after 1350, and if they were, to what extent.[132] He was particularly interested in whether they remained a fixture of mendicant preaching, since they had started out in a mendicant context. He found that one could certainly find the pictures in some mendicant authors, but that they did not make

treatises has turned up a total of sixteen manuscripts of the text, although they are not all identical. Some of them have a much longer introduction than the others: *Ars und scientia*, pp. 28–34, 472–76.

[130] Pack, 'An *Ars memorativa*', p. 243.

[131] Kimberly A. Rivers, 'The Fear of Divine Vengeance: Mnemonic Images as a Guide to Conscience in the Late Middle Ages', in *Fear and its Representations in the Middle Ages and Renaissance*, ed. by Anne Scott and Cynthia Kosso, Arizona Studies in the Middle Ages and Renaissance, 6 (Turnhout: Brepols, 2002), pp. 66–91 (p. 90).

[132] Siegfried Wenzel, *Latin Sermon Collections from Later Medieval England: Orthodox Preaching in the Age of Wyclif*, Cambridge Studies in Medieval Literature (Cambridge: Cambridge University Press, 2005), p. 293.

up a very large number of examples out of the total pool of mendicant sermon collections.[133] However, he also found just as many examples in monastic collections.[134] His conclusion was that '[t]o say the least, then, by the end of the fourteenth century and later, pseudo-classical lore and the moralized *picturae* had becomes part of the *koiné* of pulpit rhetoric and were no longer a distinguishing feature of mendicant preaching'.[135]

## *Mnemonic Pictures in the Religious Lives of the Laity*

The final question that we might consider is why medieval preachers would be so eager to have their listeners retain images of Humility, Death, Prayer, Penitence, and the like. The answer to this question lies in the issues that we explored in the last few chapters. As we have seen, medieval monks and friars (especially the Franciscans) developed a style of meditation that favoured mental images as a focus for inducing stability in a wandering memory. Images of virtues and vices were useful in this regard, and the inculcation of virtue and removal of vice were regarded as indispensable in repairing the wounds to the soul caused by original sin. Given this thinking, it should not be surprising that images of virtues and vices would find their way into medieval sermons and homiletical aids by the fourteenth century and that Franciscans appear to be the creators of the *picturae*. The fact that Holcot and Ridevall called their method of picture making 'painting' (*depingens*) is also suggestive, because, as we saw in Chapter 2, the same language was used by monks to describe their meditative techniques. We know that Ridevall was familiar with the idea of making memory more 'stable', because he employed this concept in his picture of Juno as the virtue of Memory.

[133] Wenzel, *Latin Sermon Collections*, p. 293. He lists Nicholas Philip, John Waldeby, the anonymous authors of P1 (Cambridge, Pembroke College, MS 199) and P2 (Cambridge, Pembroke College, MS 257), and D (Toulouse, Bibliothèque municipale, MS 342).

[134] O (= Oxford, Bodleian Library, MS Bodley 649), W (= Worcester, Cathedral Library, MS F. 10), RY (= London, BL, MS Harley 4894), and E (= Hereford, Cathedral Library, MS O.iii.5). Patrick Horner has prepared an edition of MS Bodley 649: Patrick J. Horner, *A Macaronic Sermon Collection from Late Medieval England: Oxford, MS Bodley 649* (Toronto: Pontifical Institute of Mediaeval Studies, 2006).

[135] Wenzel, *Latin Sermon Collections*, pp. 293–94. I would add that some exempla collections compiled in late medieval England also include moralized *picturae* and *imagines*. Some examples include London, BL, MSS Harley 2316, Harley 7322, and Royal 12.E.xxi.

According to Ridevall, Juno is

| | |
|---|---|
| Vertice velata, iride sertata, | Veiled from the crown of her head, wreathed in the rainbow, |
| Unguentis afflata, sceptro decorata | Wafted with perfume, adorned with a scepter |
| Et auro ligata, Iovi maritata, | and bound with gold, married to Jove, |
| Herculi irata, avibus vallata, | Angry with Hercules, surrounded by birds, |
| Humore rigata et luce lustrata.[136] | Dampened with rain, and illuminated with light. |

Ridevall moralizes each of Juno's attributes to accord with the virtue of memory. Nearly all of memory's attributes deal with the role of memory in the life of the sinner and his reconciliation with God. Ridevall says that memory is a woman, because memory is soft and fragile like a woman. She is veiled because of her shame at the memory of past sins. She is crowned with the rainbow as a sign of her reconciliation with God, which occurs because of the calling to mind of sins that the sinner has committed.[137] In like vein, the perfume with which Juno is wafted figures the spiritual consolation received by the sinner after reconciliation. Perhaps most interesting in light of our discussion in Chapter 3, Ridevall says that Juno is bound by golden chains which represent memory's stability or strength (*stabilitas*) and permanence. He quotes Remigius's commentary on Martianus Capella that all things which are seen or heard quickly vanish like clouds and slip away from the mind unless they are held by the chains of memory. He also ties this aspect to his theme of the memory of sin by noting that there is little value in remembering sins if one promptly forgets them.[138]

Ridevall's teachings about memory accord with views of the role of memory in contrition, the emotional state considered part of penitence and confession. One can hardly regret the sins one has committed if one cannot remember what they are. Memory is thus a necessary part of the sinner's reconciliation with God, and for this reason Ridevall celebrates its strength and durability even while acknowledging that it is prone to serious weaknesses. The memory of sins leads to tears of remorse and sadness of the heart, from which process the conscience is made fair. In the end, memory of past sins leads to a good conscience. It is hard not to draw the conclusion that the memory of all of the other virtues in Ridevall's

[136] *Fulg. meta.*, p. 88.

[137] *Fulg. meta.*, p. 88: 'Secundum enim ficcionem poeticam ipsa coronam portat de yride, de archu scilicet celesti in signum federis et reconsiliacionis cum deo, quam reconsiliacionem homo consequitur per peccati perpetrati rememoracionem.'

[138] *Fulg. meta.*, p. 90.

work would also aid in constructing a good conscience, which may be another reason for his inclusion of poetic pictures.

Holcot, too, was familiar with the idea of the memory of divine benefits and its role in human salvation. In a chapter of his Wisdom commentary on 8. 13, 'preterea habebo per hanc inmortalitatem et memoriam aeternam his qui post me futuri sunt relinquam'(Moreover, by the means of her I shall have immortality: and shall leave behind me an everlasting memory to them that come after me),[139] Holcot discusses the ideas of immortality and memory. Interestingly, he incorporates in this chapter one of his rare *picturae* in the Wisdom commentary as well as the idea of the memory of divine benefits. He declares that the ancient poets considered Minerva to be the goddess of wisdom and interprets her name as meaning *non mortalis*, that is 'immortalis'. According to Holcot,

> Ista dea pingebatur quasi virgo decora, triplicem habens vestem, et in pectore caput Gorgonis portabat depictum, sicut dicit Alexander Nequam in *Scintillario poetarum*, capitulo de Pallade. Dicitur etiam nata de Jovis vertice, et sine matre. Et dicitur Tritonia, Pallas, et Minerva, cui septenarius numerus consecratur, et est dea sapientie et omnium artium et bellorum.[140]

> (This goddess was depicted as a beautiful maiden, having three garments and wearing on her breast a picture of the head of the Gorgon, just as Alexander Nequam says in the *Anthology of the Poets*, in the chapter on Pallas. It is also said that she was born from the crown of Jove's head and without a mother. And she is called Tritonia, Pallas, and Minerva, to whom the number seven is consecrated. And she is the Goddess of Wisdom and of all the arts and of war.)

He then moralizes each of Minerva's attributes, usually in such as way as to elucidate her relationship to wisdom, rather than to immortality. After a little more consideration of immortality, he introduces the three kinds of memory found in Scripture: the memory of benefits or gifts, the memory of examples, and the memory of injuries. Holcot is most interested in the first kind of memory, as he devotes most of the rest of his lecture to it. He begins by declaring that we should have memory of divine benefits, quoting Isaiah 43. 25–26: 'Ego sum qui deleo iniquitates tuas propter me et peccatorum tuorum non recordabor. Reduc me in memoriam et iudicemur simul' (I am he that blot out thy iniquities for my own sake, and I will not remember thy sins. Put me in remembrance, and let us

[139] Wisdom 8. 13, *The Holy Bible: Douay Rheims Version, Revised by Bishop Richard Challoner* (Rockford, IL: Tan Books, 1989).

[140] Holcot, *Super libros sapientiae* (Haguenau: [n. pub.], 1494; repr. Frankfurt: Minerva, 1974), Lectio 112; my translation.

plead together).[141] He interprets *Reduc me in memoriam* according to the gloss as 'remember the good things that I did for you by creating, by redeeming, and by preparing beatitude'. Three things block this kind of memory, which are prosperity, curiosity, and desire (*voluptas*). Prosperity causes ungrateful people to forget the friends who helped them out during difficult times. It also explains the many people who keep God in their memories during times of affliction and persecution, but who hand God over to oblivion when they reach a more tranquil state. He quotes Seneca on the mutual benefits possible between friends. Finally, he concludes this section by deciding that if we owe benefits and gratitude to other men, how much more should we be grateful to God, and that 'just as there is no moment when we do not use or enjoy the goodness and mercy [of God], so there ought to be no moment when we do not have [him] present in our memory'. Though he attributes this thought to Hugh of St Victor's *De claustro anime*, it is, as we have seen, actually from *De domo interiori*.

Holcot's lecture is a reminder that the memory of the benefits of God was a very widespread concept by the end of the Middle Ages and likely one of the reasons why there was an increasing emphasis on remembering the Passion and other religious ideas. After all, the Redemption was one of the major benefits provided by God. Though he does not draw explicit connections between the *pictura* and the memory of the benefits of God, it is suggestive that Holcot includes both in a chapter on memory.

Thus, both Holcot and Ridevall are well aware of the larger implications of devotional memory, as well as the specific uses to which mnemonic aids could be put. In the next two chapters, we will examine the ways that their *picturae* were put to use in homiletic aids in other parts of Europe.

[141] Isaiah 43. 26: 'reduc me in memoriam et iudicemur simul'.

# Part III. The Spread of Mnemonic Exempla

Chapter 7

# France: Mythography and the Virtues and Vices

If the 'pictures' of Smalley's classicizing friars had remained an isolated, English phenomenon, their interest to historians would be that of a rather curious footnote to the study of the classics in the Middle Ages. Smalley herself emphasized that the classicizing tendency of her subjects was a short-lived development and was not something to be equated with Italian humanism.[1] Now nearly forty years after her work appeared, historians are in a position to modify some of her conclusions.

Smalley was right to note that few English writers followed the classicizing group in composing classicizing biblical commentaries.[2] The future of the classicizing movement lay on the Continent, not in England, and in the area of classicizing exempla rather than biblical commentaries. Jean de Hesdin, in Paris, seems to have been the main follower in biblical work. Smalley also was aware that works like Holcot's commentary on Wisdom and his *Moralitates* became the medieval equivalents of best-sellers.[3] Inspired in part by Holcot and Ridevall,

[1] Smalley, *EFA*, pp. 299–307.

[2] Smalley, *EFA*, pp. 299–301.

[3] If one examines the manuscripts of the *Moralitates* listed in Stegmüller's *Repertorium* of medieval biblical commentaries, those listed in the forward of Hans Liebeschütz's edition of the *Fulgentius metaforalis*, and those in Welter, *L'Exemplum*, one discovers over forty manuscripts of at least part of the text, only four of which are still in England. Friedrich Stegmüller, *Repertorium biblicum medii aevi*, 11 vols (Madrid: [n. pub.], 1949–80), V, 141; *Fulg. meta.*, pp. 49–53; Welter, *L'Exemplum*, p. 366 n. 63. Stegmüller, *Repertorium*, V, 141–49, no. 7416, lists twenty-three printed editions and over one hundred manuscripts of Holcot's commentary on Wisdom.

scholars in France like Pierre Bersuire and Jean de Hesdin created their own pictures for the use of preachers and university students. Their books, in turn, had considerable success on the Continent.

However, what she underestimated was the kind of craze for the classicizing friars' pictures and their classicizing homiletics that took off on the Continent during the fourteenth and fifteenth centuries. In addition to the original work done in France was the compilation of collections of pictures taken from Ridevall's, Holcot's, and some anonymous authors' books. These collections circulated all over Europe but were particularly popular in Germany and central Europe. They inspired the craze for *figmenta anglicana*, as Smalley puts it, that could compete with the *theologica anglicana* coming out of Oxford and Cambridge at the same time. The collections also provided exempla that preachers could insert into their sermons, thus reaching a wider audience than the original authors could ever have envisioned.

This chapter and the next will concentrate on the spread of the classicizing friars' pictures in France and Germany. In each case, we will discuss first how the English homiletic works were transmitted to that area, before turning to a study of the principal authors involved.

While there may have been many French preachers and scholars who eagerly snatched up copies of Holcot's and Ridevall's picture books, the two who made the most consistent use of them were the Benedictine Pierre Bersuire and the Hospitaller Jean de Hesdin. They are important to this study because they both describe how they found the materials for their pictures and why they wanted to use them. In each case, the writer describes a difficult search for the sources which would provide the pictures of the gods and/or the virtues (Hesdin seems to regard them as virtually the same thing) they needed. For Hesdin, the first book of Bersuire's *Ovidius moralizatus* proved a gold mine of material, while for Bersuire, Petrarch's poem *Africa* and Ridevall's *Fulgentius metaforalis* served the same function. In addition, they had in common access to books in Avignon and Paris and a desire to incorporate mythographic material into their works.

Both authors concentrated on the moral implications of the ancient gods, helping to create an indissoluble tie between the figures of ancient mythology and Christian virtues and vices; the literary and visual components of the 'pictures' of the gods and the virtues and vices also made them increasingly attractive as mnemonic images. The mnemonic pictures that resulted from this tie became indispensable for preaching and teaching purposes, while later, 'formal', mnemonic treatises incorporated mythological figures into their mnemonic systems.

## *Pierre Bersuire, OSB*

Pierre Bersuire is a well-known figure to scholars of medieval literature. Famous for the classical and mythological interests displayed in his commentary on Ovid's *Metamorphoses*, the *Ovidius moralizatus*, and in his translation of Livy, he has been the subject of numerous studies.[4] My main purpose here is to sketch out his relation to the development of the picture technique and to establish him as an important influence on Jean de Hesdin. I will give a brief outline of his life (somewhat different from the standard interpretation) in order to establish his opportunities for finding unusual sources.[5]

Bersuire's career took him to exactly the right places in France to further an interest in the classics. Bersuire was born around 1290 at Saint-Pierre-du-Chemin and came from a noble or recently ennobled family, but not a wealthy one. Virtually nothing is known about his formal education except for a notice in a papal bull of 1336, which states that Bersuire had laboured in the study of theology since his youth.[6] Evidently, Bersuire began his career as a Franciscan but was unhappy with his life with them. As a young Franciscan, he had abandoned his habit and wandered about for a time. He did return to his order and was received by his superiors, but transferred to the Benedictine order at an unknown date, very likely after he moved to Avignon. A petition from Bersuire to Pope Clement VI, sent in 1343, reveals that Bersuire was received into the Benedictines at the

[4] For more on Bersuire's life and works, see: Smalley, *EFA*, pp. 261–64; Joseph Engels, 'Berchoriana, I: Notice bibliographique sur Pierre Bersuire', *Vivarium*, 2 (1964), 62–124; F. Ghisalberti, 'L'Ovidius moralizatus di Pierre Bersuire', *Studi Romanzi*, 23 (1933), 5–136; Charles Samaran and Jacques Monfrin, 'Pierre Bersuire, Prieur de Saint-Éloi de Paris (1290?–1362)', *Histoire littéraire de la France*, 39 (1962), 259–450; Chance, *Medieval Mythography*, II; Betty Nye Quinn, 'Venus, Chaucer, and Pierre Bersuire', *Speculum*, 38 (1963), 479–80; William D. Reynolds, 'Sources, Nature, and Influence of the *Ovidius Moralizatus* of Pierre Bersuire', in *The Mythographic Art: Classical Fable and the Rise of the Vernacular in Early France and England*, ed. by Jane Chance (Gainesville: University of Florida Press, 1990), pp. 83–99; Ernest Wilkins, 'Descriptions of Pagan Divinities from Petrarch to Chaucer', *Speculum*, 32 (1957), 511–22; Seznec, *Survival of the Pagan Gods*, pp. 174–79; *Petrus Berchorius, Reductorium morale, liber XV: Ovidius moralizatus, cap. i: De formis figurisque deorum*, ed. by Joseph Engels and the Instituut voor Laat Latijn of Utrecht, Werkmateriaal, 3 (Utrecht: Rijksuniversiteit, Instituut voor Laat Latijn, 1966).

[5] For the details of Bersuire's life, I, like most scholars, have depended heavily on Samaran and Monfrin, 'Pierre Bersuire'. See also Kimberly A. Rivers, 'Another Look at the Career of Pierre Bersuire, O.S.B.', *Revue bénédictine*, 116 (2006), 92–100.

[6] Samaran and Monfrin, 'Pierre Bersuire', p. 260.

curia by a brother John, Abbot of San Salvador de la Torre in the diocese of Tuy in Spain.[7]

Bersuire made his way to the papal court at Avignon, probably in the early 1320s, where he obtained the patronage of Cardinal Pierre des Prés.[8] While in Avignon, Bersuire received a number of benefices, likely through the influence of his patron. It seems unlikely that Bersuire ever resided at any of these priories but instead remained in Avignon. While there, he also met Petrarch on a number of occasions, who encouraged him in his interest in classical studies. Bersuire's many years in Avignon were productive ones. It was here that he composed some of his best-known works, including the *Reductorium morale* and the *Repertorium morale*.

Bersuire was in Avignon during the reign of three popes (John XXII, Benedict XII, and Clement VI), and remained there probably until 1349, though there is a tradition that he moved to Paris in 1342.[9] Charles Samaran thinks the 1349 date the more likely, because in December of that year, Bersuire was granted the office of *chambrier* of Notre-Dame de Coulombs in the diocese of Chartres. If he was still in Avignon in 1349, he may well have desired to leave the city because of the ravages of the Black Death. In any case, the new benefice turned out to be less than beneficial for Bersuire. He quickly discovered that the head of the abbey, Gauthier, had arranged for his cousin to collect the revenues for Bersuire's new position. When Bersuire complained, Gauthier responded by accusing Bersuire of heresy. At the end of 1350 or the beginning of 1351, Bersuire was arrested by officials of the Bishop of Paris and thrown into the bishop's jail. In the process,

[7] In 1902, the Benedictine scholar Ursmer Berlière published a transcription of a petition sent from Pierre Bersuire to Pope Clement VI in August 1343 that gives some hitherto unknown details about Bersuire's life: Ursmer Berlière, 'Pierre Bersuire', *Revue bénédictine*, 19 (1902), 317–20. I have seen a reference to this article in only one place: Philip Edward Burnham, 'Cultural Life at Papal Avignon, 1309–1376' (unpublished doctoral thesis, Tufts University, 1972), p. 255. The article is not listed in Engels, 'Berchoriana, I', pp. 62–124, which may be why scholars have overlooked it. The petition clearly refers to the Pierre Bersuire in question, for it names Bersuire as prior of the Priory of la Trinité de Clisson in Nantes, a benefice which we know Clement had granted to Bersuire the year before (Clement VI's bull granting Bersuire the priory of Clisson is contained in Antoine Thomas, 'Extraits des Archives du Vatican pour servir à l'histoire littéraire', *Romania*, 11 (1882), 177–87 (pp. 186–87)). The letter also notes Bersuire's position as a member of the household of Cardinal Pierre des Prés. For a detailed recounting of the effect of this petition on our views of Bersuire's life, see Rivers, 'Another Look'.

[8] Samaran and Monfrin, 'Pierre Bersuire', p. 265.

[9] Samaran and Monfrin, 'Pierre Bersuire', p. 279; Smalley, *EFA*, p. 261.

many of his possessions were destroyed and he himself was tortured.[10] Official records say that Bersuire had been detained 'on account of presumptions against him, because he used forbidden sciences, evil and smacking of heresy'.[11] Because Bersuire had enrolled in the University of Paris as a student in theology, the university intervened in the dispute on Bersuire's behalf, resulting in a full-scale battle between the Bishop and the university. King John (Jean le Bon) had interested himself in the case. The King, hoping to pacify the two parties, asked that the matter be brought before him. The King came down on the side of the university, Bersuire was released, and his property was to be restored to him.[12]

After his release from prison, Bersuire spent the rest of his life in Paris. He was made Prior of Saint-Éloi in April 1354. King John asked him to translate Livy's histories from Latin into French. He also was able to resume his friendship with Petrarch. In 1361, Petrarch was sent to Paris by Galeazza Visconti as part of a congratulatory embassy to King John after his release by the English. While there, he saw much of Bersuire.[13] Bersuire must have been dead by the end of 1362 because a datable document speaks of him as already dead in January 1363.[14]

Bersuire's contributions to the picture tradition lie in his *Ovidius moralizatus*, a commentary on Ovid's *Metamorphoses* which comprised Book XV of a much larger project, the *Reductorium morale*. The *Reductorium* was a vast work of sixteen books: the first thirteen books moralized the natural phenomenon described in Bartholomaeus Anglicus's *Liber de proprietatibus*. Bersuire then added a fourteenth book on the wonders of the world, a fifteenth on Ovid's *Metamorphoses*, and a sixteenth containing a moralization of the Bible. The book on Ovid, known as the *Ovidius moralizatus*, circulated independently from the rest of the *Reductorium*. It survives in several versions, two prepared at Avignon in the 1340s,

[10] This episode is described in Samaran and Monfrin, 'Pierre Bersuire', pp. 280–85.

[11] 'Propter presumptiones contra ipsum, quia utebatur scientiis prohibitis et malis et sapientibus heresim': Charles Jourdain, *Index chronologicus chartarum pertinentium ad historiam Universitatis parisiensis: Ab ejus originibus ad finem decimi sexti saeculi* (Paris: Hachette, 1862; repr. Brussels: Culture et civilisation, 1966), p. 146. See also *Chartularium Universitatis Parisiensis*, ed. by Heinrich Denifle and Emile Chatelain, 4 vols (Paris: Delalain, 1889–97; repr. Brussels: Culture et civilisation, 1964), pp. 4–7.

[12] Samaran and Monfrin, 'Pierre Bersuire', pp. 284–85; Pearl Kibre, *Scholarly Privileges in the Middle Ages: The Rights, Privileges, and Immunities of Scholars and Universities at Bologna, Padua, Paris, and Oxford* (Cambridge, MA: Mediaeval Academy of America, 1962), p. 151.

[13] Ernest Hatch Wilkins, *Life of Petrarch* (Chicago: University of Chicago Press, 1963), pp. 173–77.

[14] Samaran and Monfrin, 'Pierre Bersuire', pp. 299–301.

and a third after 1350 when Bersuire was in Paris.[15] His Ovid commentary had three main parts: a prologue, an introductory chapter describing the pagan gods and goddesses and providing moralized interpretations of their descriptions, and fifteen books moralizing Ovid's fables.[16]

Bersuire placed his version of the *picturae* in the introductory chapter. He entitled the chapter 'De formis figurisque deorum' and went to some trouble to find the material for it.[17] He declared that he wanted to begin the work with the forms and figures of the gods, but that he could not find their images described or painted in an orderly way anywhere. Unsatisfied with other authors, he turned to Petrarch's poem *Africa*, in which the famous Italian poet described the gods in elegant metre without any sort of moralization.[18]

The key to Bersuire's dilemma must have been the need for an 'orderly' or 'systematic' (*ordinate*) series of images of the gods, for it was certainly not impossible to find descriptions of many of the classical gods in the early fourteenth century. He could have found exemplars in the *Mithologiae* of the fifth-century writer Fulgentius; in Rabanus Maurus's *De universo*; in the mythography of the Third Vatican Mythographer (often attributed to Alexander Nequam in the Middle Ages); or in Ridevall's *Fulgentius metaforalis*, among other authors. Bersuire evidently consulted the first three authors, but he did not encounter Ridevall's work, which he much admired, until he got to Paris, where he was exposed to books that he had not encountered in Avignon.[19] In fact Bersuire implies that it was something of a chore to use the other mythographers in order to find images of the gods. He says, 'I have also had to leaf through [*transcurrere*] the works of Fulgentius, Alexander, and Rabanus and thus assemble from various

[15] Reynolds, 'Sources, Nature, and Influence', pp. 86–87; Wilkins, 'Descriptions of Pagan Divinities', p. 513.

[16] Reynolds, 'Sources, Nature, and Influence', pp. 86–87; Wilkins, 'Descriptions of Pagan Divinities', p. 513.

[17] Reynolds, 'Sources, Nature, and Influence', p. 88.

[18] Smalley, *EFA*, p. 262; Wilkins, 'Descriptions of Pagan Divinities', p. 513. See *Petrus Berchorius, Reductorium morale, liber XV*, ed. by Engels and the Instituut voor Laat Latijn of Utrecht, p. 3: 'necessarie habui consulere venerabilem virum magistrum Franciscum de Pentraco [...] qui prefatas ymagines in quodam opere suo eleganti metro describit'.

[19] In Paris Bersuire was also introduced to the *Ovide moralisé* by Philip de Vitry; Smalley, *EFA*, pp. 262–63; Pierre Bersuire, '*The Moral Reduction*, Book XV: *Ovid Moralized*: Prologue and Extracts', in *Medieval Literary Theory and Criticism, c. 1100–c. 1375: The Commentary-Tradition*, ed. by Alastair J. Minnis and A. Brian Scott (Oxford: Clarendon Press, 1988), pp. 366–72 (p. 368).

sources the figures and the images which the ancient writers assigned to their fictional gods in conformity with the teachings of history or natural history.'[20] He adds, 'Having weighed up all of these sources, I have put together, as best I could, the image of each god, and having blended all of them together I have drawn up an allegorical or moral exposition, separated out the straw from the wheat and gathered the wheat in my barn.'[21]

It seems clear from his introduction that Bersuire regarded the first chapter of his moralized Ovid as the orderly presentation of the gods that he could not find elsewhere. Judging from the use made of it by later authors, he evidently filled a perceived gap in the scholarship of his time. The *De formis figurisque deorum* had an independent manuscript circulation of its own, apart from both the rest of Bersuire's *Ovidius moralizatus* and from the *Reductorium*. It was translated into French and attached to the *Ovide moralisé* as an introduction. Moreover, Bersuire's images of the gods formed the nucleus of the *Libellus de imaginibus deorum*, a distillation of Bersuire's pictures without the moralizations, which became an important source for artists wishing to depict the gods in the fifteenth century.[22]

What has not been adequately discussed is why Bersuire felt it so important to begin his commentary with an orderly series of descriptions of the gods and goddesses. I would suggest that Bersuire desired to provide images of the gods before embarking on his moralization of Ovid, because he thought the ancients had discussed their forms and because the images provided an excellent focus for multiple interpretations. Since Bersuire aimed his work at least in part at preachers, the images furnished first-class preaching material. As mentioned above, he says that he had to leaf through sources like Fulgentius trying to find what the ancients had said about the images of the gods. Bersuire also implies that he is free to interpret the meaning of the gods, because the ancients had done the same thing themselves when they interpreted natural processes as gods, i.e., Saturn as time and Jove as the ether, etc., and when they applied stories to the gods.[23] When he begins his interpretations with the first of the gods, Saturn, he finds it natural to begin with the depiction 'he was thought to have'. Again, he implies

[20] Translation from Bersuire, '*Moral Reduction*', p. 369.

[21] Translation from Bersuire, '*Moral Reduction*', p. 369.

[22] Reynolds, 'Sources, Nature, and Influence', p. 88; Seznec, *Survival of the Pagan Gods*, pp. 174–79.

[23] Ghisalberti, 'L'Ovidius moralizatus', p. 90.

this is a tradition inherited from the ancients, which, as we shall see below, was certainly the belief of fourteenth-century mythographers. Bersuire makes the same implication in his treatment of Mercury: 'Because Mercury, like the other planets, was believed by the gentiles to be a god, they wished to paint his image in this way.'[24]

Bersuire thus sees himself as following ancient precedent in providing multiple interpretations of the gods and in providing their depictions. What becomes clear as one reads Bersuire's first chapter is that the pictures themselves provide a uniquely efficient way of organizing multiple interpretations of each god. Bersuire declares in the opening chapter of the *Ovidius moralizatus* that he wants most of all to give the moral interpretation of Ovid's fables, following the precedent set by Scripture of using fables to point out some truth.[25] But, as William Reynolds has pointed out, the sheer number of moral interpretations set out by Bersuire is dazzling.[26] Reynolds assumes that the interpretations are designed to give preachers ample material for composing sermons, surely a correct assessment. I would add that the pictures provide a convenient way of organizing these multiple interpretations. A preacher had only to memorize the basic picture, and he then had a key to recalling a number of different ways of moralizing the figure and thus the nucleus of a number of different sermons or sermon parts. Because Bersuire's depictions provide clearer visual clues than many of the mnemonic pictures that we have examined thus far — his book became the basis for an artists' handbook on painting the gods — it is easy to see how useful the pictures would have been as a mnemonic device.

To see how the images might function, it helps to examine an example of Bersuire's method. According to him,

> Saturnus ergo depingebatur homo senex curvus tristis et pallidus, qui cum una manu falcem tenebat et in eadem drachonis portabat ymaginem qui dentibus caudam propriam commordebat, altera vero filium proprium ad os applicabat et eum dentibus propriis devorabat. Quattuor iuxta se habebat liberos s. Iovem, Iunonem, Neptunum et Plutonem. Quorum etiam Iupiter patris virilia amputavit. Mare etiam ante eum pictum erat in quo dicta virilia proiecta videbantur, de quibus Venus puella pulcherrima nascebatur. Iuxta ipsum autem Opes uxor sua in cuiusdam matrone similitudine picta erat, que opem ferens omnibus etaim panem pauperibus erogabat.[27]

[24] Ghisalberti, 'L'Ovidius moralizatus', p. 96.

[25] Bersuire, '*Moral Reduction*', p. 367.

[26] Reynolds, 'Sources, Nature, and Influence', p. 89.

[27] Ghisalberti, 'L'Ovidius moralizatus', pp. 90–91; my translation.

> (Saturn was depicted as an old man, bent over, sad, and pale, who held a sickle in one hand and in the same hand carried an image of a dragon, who bit its own tail with its teeth; but in the other hand he steered his own son toward his mouth and devoured him with his own teeth. He had next to him his four children, namely Jove, Juno, Neptune, and Pluto, one of whom, Jupiter, cut off his father's private parts. In front of him was pictured the sea, into which the private parts are shown to have been thrown, and from which Venus, that most beautiful maiden, was born. Next to him, however, was pictured Opes, his wife, in the guise of a matron, who, bearing aid, disbursed bread to all the poor.)

Unlike Ridevall's picture of Saturn, Bersuire's is unrhymed and written in a way to favour easy visualization. Bersuire's depiction of Saturn is a standard one, but it provides him much material for interpretation.[28] He says that the image can be exposited in many different modes, that is, literally, historically, naturally, and spiritually. For him, the literal interpretation is that Saturn, the first of the gods, was Saturn, the first of the planets. The interpretation through nature is that Saturn signifies time, because he had four children, who also signify the four elements. The historical interpretation is that Saturn was the King of Crete, to whom his brother Titan said that his son would expel him from his kingdom. What really seems to motivate Bersuire, however, are the spiritual interpretations. He does not confine himself to one, but supplies several, each explaining the major elements of the picture. So he says that Saturn could be seen as an evil superior or an old prelate with evil morals, or he could be seen as a tyrant, or he could be seen, as in the mythology of Fulgentius (and here he means Ridevall's *Fulgentius metaforalis*), as Prudence.[29]

The sheer variety of interpretations must have been a godsend to the classically minded preacher searching for material for a sermon. The image of Saturn is easily memorable and fits the criteria of memory images that they be violent and sensual.[30] The preacher needed only to hold the image in mind, decide on the central interpretation he would take, and then moralize the picture accordingly. Presumably, also, the images of the gods with their interpretations provided an introduction to anyone who remained unfamiliar with the classical gods before

[28] See Raymond Klibansky, Erwin Panofsky, and Fritz Saxl, *Saturn and Melancholy: Studies in the History of Natural Philosophy, Religion, and Art* (London: Nelson, 1964).

[29] Klibansky, Panofsky, and Saxl, *Saturn and Melancholy*, pp. 91–94.

[30] On the role of fear, violence, and sensuality in medieval mnemonics, see Carruthers, *Craft of Thought*, pp. 95–103, and Jody Enders, *The Medieval Theater of Cruelty: Rhetoric, Memory, Violence* (Ithaca: Cornell University Press, 1999); Jody Enders, 'Rhetoric, Coercion, and the Memory of Violence', in *Criticism and Dissent in the Middle Ages*, ed. by Rita Copeland (Cambridge: Cambridge University Press, 1996), pp. 24–55; Rivers, 'Fear of Divine Vengeance'.

embarking on a study of Ovid. Bersuire's little treatise must have served as an ideal introductory textbook to mythology and its interpretation. Certainly his treatise inspired the biblical commentaries of Jean de Hesdin.

## *Jean de Hesdin*

In the midst of his commentary on Paul's epistle to Titus, the French Hospitaller and biblical scholar Jean de Hesdin (fl. 1350–70) paused to ask what the ancients and the poets thought about the vice of Lechery. His source for their opinion was Brother Robert Holcot, who described Lechery as the image of Venus. According to Holcot, 'in antiquity Venus was painted with a bare body, anointed with myrrh, with a beautiful face, crowned with fig leaves, standing on a sea shell'.[31]

Modern readers might be surprised to see a nude Venus rising from the pages of a scriptural commentary, but to Hesdin and many of his contemporaries, her picture did not seem out of place. He discussed her image not to titillate but to instruct his readers, for to him she had at least three functions: she served as a 'visual' example of the kind of vice that clerics and prelates should avoid, as a memorial cue to those who would seek to avoid her, and as a icon of the medieval style of classical culture that was about to be overthrown by the new humanism pioneered by Hesdin's contemporary, Petrarch.

### Hesdin's Career and Writings

Because few people are familiar with Jean de Hesdin's life, we will begin with a brief resume of his career and writings. Jean de Hesdin is a figure remembered chiefly because of an epistolary dual he fought against Petrarch over the validity of the Avignon papacy in the later fourteenth century. Well known for his disdain of the papacy's residence in Avignon (which he called the 'Babylonian captivity'), Petrarch wrote to Pope Urban V both before and after the Pope's return of the papal court to Rome in 1367.[32] In his letters he made several uncomplimentary

[31] Oxford, Balliol College, MS 181, fol. 101$^{vb}$: 'Quantum ad primum sciendum quod frater Robertus Holcot, qui moralizauit figuras deorum, sub ymagine Veneris luxuriam descripsit. Depingebatur antiquitus Uenus nudata corpore, mirra delibuta, visu pulcra siue facie, foliis ficus coronata, sub pedibus concha marina.'

[32] Grover Furr, 'France vs. Italy: French Literary Nationalism in "Petrarch's Last Controversy" and a Humanist Dispute of ca. 1395', *Proceedings of the Patristic, Medieval and Renaissance*

observations about France, Avignon and its climate, and the quality of French scholarship. Naturally enough, the French resented Petrarch's insinuations and put up Ancel Choquart, a professor of canon law, to defend the honour of Avignon and the advantages of the protection of the French king just before Urban left for Rome.

After Choquart died in 1368/69, Jean de Hesdin joined the fray, becoming known as the *Gallus calumpniator* (the Gallic challenger). Because of his solid career at the University of Paris, Hesdin would have seemed a natural choice for the French side. Hesdin was a member of the Order of the Hospitallers of St John of Jerusalem and likely held the position of regent master of theology at the order's house in Paris for over twenty-five years.[33] By the late 1360s, he had written a number of biblical commentaries and sermons, most of them studded with references to classical culture. He was also Dean of the Faculty of Theology at Paris by 1364, a respected position at the university rarely held by a member of a religious order.[34] In addition, he had spent at least a few months in Avignon itself, on his way back from a mission to Hungary with his patron, Guy de Boulogne, later Bishop of Porto. Wishing to defend the reputation of France, he wrote to Petrarch, probably in 1369 or 1370. Among the disputed points was a differing idea of classical culture and the uses to which it should be put. While Petrarch valued the eloquence of the ancient writers and the sense of Italian

*Conference, Villanova University*, 4 (1979), 115–25; also available at <http://petrarch.petersadlon.com/submissions/Furr.pdf> [accessed 8 February 2010]. For more on Hesdin's involvement in the dispute, see also Beryl Smalley, 'Jean de Hesdin O. Hosp. S. Ioh.', *Recherches de théologie ancienne et médiévale*, 28 (1961), 283–330 (pp. 283–89); Pierre de Nolhac, *Pétrarque et l'humanisme*, 2 vols (Paris: Champion, 1907), II, 307–11; and Burnham, 'Cultural Life at Papal Avignon'. For Urban V's return of the papacy to Rome, see Guillaume Mollat, *The Popes at Avignon, 1305– 1378*, trans. by Janet Love (London: Nelson, 1963), pp. 154–60, and Renouard, *Avignon Papacy*, pp. 53–61.

[33] Smalley, 'Jean de Hesdin', p. 284, and Anthony Luttrell, 'Jean and Simon de Hesdin: Hospitallers, Theologians, Classicists', *Recherches de théologie ancienne et médiévale*, 31 (1964), 137–40. See also Rolf Sprandel, *Altersschicksal und Altersmoral: Die Geschichte der Einstellungen zum Altern nach der Pariser Bibelexegese des 12.–16. Jahrhunderts* (Stuttgart: Hiersemann, 1981).

[34] Smalley, 'Jean de Hesdin', p. 284. A roll of petitioners for papal provisions sent in June 1365 lists him as dean of theology: 'Primo fratri Johanni de Hesdinio, Ord. S. Johannis Jherusolimit. decano ad presens theologice facultatis Parisius, qui per xxv annos fuit quasi continue actu regens, excepto tempore quo in Avinione cum domino cardinale Boloniensi peregit lecturam supra Job, quam Parisius inceperat, et postea Parisius fecit lecturam supra epistolam Pauli ad Titum, cum pluribus sermonibus et aliis operibus, que per copiam habentur Parisius' (*Chartularium*, ed. by Denifle and Chatelain, III, 127, no. 1305; see also nos 1299, 1336, and 1429).

history that he drew from Rome's past, Hesdin and the French defenders subordinated verbal eloquence to Christian wisdom: to them the riches of the past should be put to a Christian use.[35]

The careful appropriation of classical culture was, in fact, the approach that Hesdin had taken in his own scholarship. During his career, he composed three or four biblical commentaries which are still extant: a commentary on Job, a commentary on Paul's epistle to Titus, another on the Gospel of Mark, and possibly one on the Song of Solomon, which has not been studied.[36] Smalley describes all of them as *lecturae*, products of his years in the classroom in Paris. In the commentaries on Job, Mark, and Titus, Hesdin makes liberal use of secular authorities, as well as the standard biblical and theological ones, but he incorporates the most classical sources and the picture technique into his work on Titus. I have for this reason concentrated my efforts on Titus, which Hesdin started in Paris in 1362 and finished in 1364 on the Feast of the Exaltation of the Holy Cross (14 September). It must have been a fairly popular title, as it survives in at least thirty manuscripts.[37] Its popularity almost certainly stems from its abundance of classical citations and of the picture technique, which we will address shortly. I have used a copy from Oxford's Balliol College, MS 181 (= *B*), copied in 1444 in two hands, either Dutch or German, supplemented by Paris, Bibliothèque Mazarine, MS 271 (= $P^{1}$).[38]

## *Use of Pictures in the Commentary on Titus*

In the *Commentary on Titus* the things worthy of remembrance are the virtues and the virtuous behaviour of people in the past, along with the vices and salutary reminders of the punishments visited upon past sinners. Rather than merely listing or discussing the virtues and vices, in *Titus* Hesdin often uses the distinctive technique of describing *picturae* of virtues or vices, a technique he does

[35] Furr, 'France vs. Italy', p. 120.

[36] As in so many areas related to medieval biblical commentaries, Beryl Smalley has already laid the groundwork for a study of Hesdin's writings and drawn attention to his pictures. Smalley, 'Jean de Hesdin', pp. 289–91, and Stegmüller, *Repertorium*, III, nos 4551–56, VII, no. 10707, and IX, nos 4551–56.

[37] See Stegmüller above. Smalley, 'Jean de Hesdin', p. 289, lists only nineteen manuscripts, but seems to have miscounted the number listed in Stegmüller.

[38] Roger Aubrey Baskerville Mynors, *Catalogue of the Manuscripts of Balliol College, Oxford* (Oxford: Clarendon Press, 1963), p. 184.

not use in his other biblical commentaries. As in the example of Lechery depicted as the goddess Venus mentioned before, most of his pictures are drawn from classical mythology. I have found eighteen of these pictures (see Table 1), which include Apollo moralized to represent Truth, Saturn as Pride, Mars as Anger, Bacchus as Drunkenness, and Pluto as Prudence.

**Table 1. *Picturae* in Jean de Hesdin's Titus Commentary.**[39]

| Folio | *Picturae* |
|---|---|
| $90^{vb}$ | Fides |
| $92^{va}$ | Veritas/Apollo |
| $93^{va}$ | Pietas |
| $102^{ra}$ | Luxuria/Venus |
| $103^{rb}$ | Superbia/Homo crudelis |
| $103^{vb}$ | Superbia/Saturnus |
| $104^{ra}$ | Iracundia/Mars |
| $105^{ra}$ | Ebrietas/Bachus |
| $108^{vb}$ | Iusticia |
| $115^{ra}$ | Mendacium/Mulier |
| $123^{rb}$ | Senectus |
| $125^{rb}$–$125^{va}$ | Prudencia/Pluto |
| $126^{va}$ | Amicicia |
| $132^{vb}$ | Castitas/Minerva |
| $135^{rb}$ | Vers/Iuuenis |
| $136^{va}$ | Integritas/Dyana |
| $153^{va}$ | Obediencia |
| $159^{ra}$ | Malicia |

Hesdin makes no claims for originality in his pictures and indeed is always careful to state a source for them, even if it is the wrong one. Living as he did in Paris and Avignon, Hesdin had the opportunity to encounter a number of the 'picture books', including Holcot's *Moralitates*, Fulgentius's *Mithologiae*, and probably Ridevall's *Fulgentius metaforalis*.[40] He also relied heavily on one other source, Pierre Bersuire's *De formis figurisque deorum*. Referring to Bersuire as the 'Prior of Saint-Éloi', Hesdin names him explicitly as a source for his pictures, even

[39] Folio references are to *B*.

[40] See the next chapter, on Germany, for a discussion of the picture books.

when Bersuire was not actually the author. On the whole, Hesdin prefers to draw on authors like Bersuire to provide his pictures, rather than to create his own. His attitude emerges clearly when he explains the difficulty of finding a ready-made model of Justice. He says he searched through the works of Fulgentius, Rabanus Maurus, Remigius of Auxerre, Robert Holcot, and the Prior of Saint-Éloi, who worked very hard in composing these images, but could not find what he wanted. Eventually he found an image of Justice painted as a maiden in Aulus Gellius's *Attic Nights*, but he added a few details of his own.[41]

As Smalley pointed out, Hesdin does seem to have ventured into the field of picture creation with his image of Old Age:

> Concerning which Remigius says that the ancients [...] created images for the virtues and vices, so that they also painted an image of Old Age. Moreover it was a bent figure, and Hope in the form of a maiden gave to it a rod to support its body. It had under its feet two ravens. With a sad expression on its face, it looked backwards. On one side were young men laughing at the image, while on the other side were important and mature men, who crowned it with various crowns.[42]

[41] *B*, fols 108$^{vb}$–109$^{ra}$: 'Et quia iustitia tantam excellenciam inter alias virtutes antiquitus obtinuit, ut nunquam aliquis ex istis quorum scripta vidi et studui, videlicet Fulgencius, Rabanus, Remigius, Robertus Holcoth, et prior sancti Eligii, qui circa istas imagines componendas multum insudauerunt, sub aliqua figura deorum aut astrorum iustiticiam descripserunt, nisi quod Fulgencius sub ymagine Paridis, filii Priami, iusticiam describere videtur in ii° Mithologiarum, verumtamen in legendo Agellium libro noctium atticarum li° xvi° c v quarto, iusticie ymaginem /fol. 109$^{ra}$/ descriptam ab antiquis, ut ipse dicit, in hunc modum adinueni.' See also Smalley, 'Jean de Hesdin', p. 315. It is actually surprising that Hesdin had such a hard time finding a picture of Justice, since Justice was one of the most common pictures in the genre and was generally depicted as either a blind girl or man (the female version is a little more common) and occasionally without hands. A selection of the *Iusticia* pictures can be found in the *Fasc. mor.*, p. 502; in MS Bodley 649, fol. 185$^{b}$; in BAV, MS Pal. lat. 1066, fol. 232$^{r}$; in Holcot's *Convertimini* (see Herbert, *Catalogue of Romances in British Museum*, III, 119); in Basel, Universitätsbibliothek, MS A.X. 118; the *De prudentia* collection contained in Paris, BnF, cod. lat. 590, fols 177$^{r}$–178$^{r}$; and the Oesterley edition of the *Gesta Romanorum*.

[42] *B*, fol. 123$^{rb}$: 'Super quod dicit Remigius quod antiqui ex hoc finxerunt diuerso [*Sprandel* diversa] in honore uel commemoracione amicorum et in tantam vesaniam euenerunt quod eciam ad [*Smalley, Sprandel add.* ad.] virtutes et vicia ymagines formuerunt, sic quod eciam senectutis ymaginem depinxerunt. Erat autem ymago curva, et spes in specie domicelle dabat sibi vnum baculum pro sustenacione corporis. Habebat autem sub pedibus duos coruos [*Sprandel* cornos]. Vultu tristi et euerso retro se respiciebat. Ex uno latere erant iuuenes et adolescentes illam ymaginem deridentes, ex alio latere graues et maturi homines, qui eam coronabant diuersis coronis.' For a transcription of Hesdin's entire moralization of Old Age, see Sprandel, *Altersschicksal und Altersmoral*, pp. 164–86.

In the middle of his moralization of Old Age, Hesdin admits that the things he had recited to his students above 'were not written in books in these same words, but in the same sense, and so I was able to collect them together in order to have a clearer understanding'.[43] Like Smalley, one can legitimately take this confession to mean that he made up the picture of Old Age and felt a little guilty about it![44] On the other hand, his acknowledgment shows that it was not difficult for him to adopt the picture method to his own purposes.

The question that should be asked is what purpose these pictures could possibly have served in a biblical commentary on Titus. Smalley suggested that they were a digression designed to amuse the students listening to Hesdin's lectures at the University of Paris.[45] Hesdin does say more than once that he has introduced a picture 'for the sake of hilarity'. It is also true that the theologians who incorporated the pictures into their commentaries and exempla collections were fascinated by classical culture and probably appreciated an outlet for their interest, but, as Siegfried Wenzel has pointed out, late medieval preachers had more serious intents for their rhetorical strategies.[46] In fact, the verbal images served at least two functions within the text: they served as a 'visual' example of the kind of vice that clerics and prelates should avoid or model of a virtue they should practise; and second, they aided the memories of Hesdin and his students through their well-defined structure.

In Hesdin's commentary, the pictures' initial function was to introduce a new virtue or vice into the discussion. Hesdin devoted much of his commentary to the virtues and vices, because he viewed Titus as a kind of 'Mirror for Princes' aimed at prelates and clerics.[47] This idea is borne out by his letter of dedication to Philip d'Alençon, the Archbishop of Rouen, which concludes with the following sentiment:

> And because I considered that in this brief epistle [i.e., to Titus] [there is] learning necessary and useful for the regulating of all prelates with respect to the life, doctrine, and instruction of all clerics, whatever their grade or status; for the governing of temporal

[43] *B*, fol. 124$^{rb}$, marked in the margin as 'Excusacio': 'Et sciant auditores quod ista, que ibi recitaui, non eodem modo nec sub hiisdem verbis scribuntur in libris, sed eodem sensu et sicud potui ad habendum clariorem intellectum in breuibus collegi.' See Sprandel, *Altersschicksal und Altersmoral*, p. 172.

[44] Smalley, 'Jean de Hesdin', p. 315.

[45] Smalley, 'Jean de Hesdin', pp. 300, 315.

[46] Wenzel, 'Classics in Late-Medieval Preaching', pp. 127, 143.

[47] Smalley, 'Jean de Hesdin', p. 305.

> domains with respect to themselves and their subjects; for the obedience and subjection of their subjects and servants; for the condition and bettering of all sexes and estates; and for the hatred and repulsion of heretics and infidels, I set out to labour over a worthy work concerning these things and to humbly present it to your bountiful paternity.[48]

And, in fact, in Paul's epistle to Titus, there is much discussion of the virtues necessary for and the vices repulsive to prelates and their subjects. Hesdin thus sees the epistle as a peculiarly appropriate place to discuss the virtues and vices. Since nearly all of Hesdin's pictures represent a virtue or vice (Youth and Old Age are the two exceptions), this is almost certainly the reason that he reserves the picture technique for Titus. Often, then, when Hesdin reaches a place in the epistle where Paul introduces a new virtue or vice, he begins his own discussion with a picture. For example, when Hesdin reaches the point in the text when Paul discusses the sin of anger (Titus, I.7), he says:

> As proof and declaration of this vice, just as has been our habit concerning the others, let us first examine the vice in itself and second, how it should be avoided by clerics and especially by prelates. Concerning the first point, it should be known that, just as Fulgentius, in the second book of the *Mythologies*, and Rabanus, in *The Natures of Things*, say, the ancients described the vice of anger in the form of Mars.[49]

The examination of the first point consists in the recitation and examination of how anger was painted by the ancients in the form of Mars. He considers a description of an ancient painting of the vice to be the method he has been following in this work, not an unusual digression. He makes the same point when he introduces the virtue of Piety: 'It remains to say something about piety, and, if we wish to allude for the sake of hilarity and erudition to what the ancients thought about piety, just as in the other virtues posited above, let us see also about piety.'[50]

Hesdin is even more explicit about his methodology and his interpretation of Titus as a kind of 'Mirror for Prelates' in his discussion of drunkenness. After he has treated the vices of Lechery, Pride, and Anger, considering the ways in which they are detestable in themselves and especially to prelates and ecclesiastics,

[48] *B*, fol. 86$^{ra-b}$; transcription from Smalley, 'Jean de Hesdin', pp. 323–24.

[49] *B*, fol. 104$^{ra}$: 'Ad evidentiam istius uicii et declaracionem, sicud moris est de aliis, videamus primo de vicio in se et secundo quomodo vitandum est clericis et maxime prelatis. Circa primum sciendum quod, sicud dicit Fulgencius, ii° Mithologiarum, et Rabanus, De naturis rerum, sub specie Martis et ymagine antiqui vicium ire describebant.'

[50] *B*, fol. 93$^{va}$: 'Restat aliquod dicendum de ipsa pietate, et si velimus, sicut in aliis virtutibus superius positis, alludere causa jocunditatis et erudicionis quid antiqui de pietate senciebant, videamus eciam de ista pietate.'

Hesdin turns to Drunkenness. He is careful to stress that he is following the very same order of vices as the apostle does in his epistle, and he, of course, begins his discussion with a picture, in this case, one of Bacchus drawn from Bersuire's *De formis figurisque deorum*.[51] Given Bersuire's known predilections for criticizing the immoral behaviour of prelates, it is not hard to see why Hesdin might have felt his pictures to be especially appropriate for inclusion in an exposition of Titus. Occasionally he quotes Bersuire's moralizations specifically. For instance, he states that 'the Prior of Saint-Éloi' explained the proud prelate under the figure of Saturn,[52] and the angry prelate under the figure of Mars.[53]

Besides presenting an introduction to the kinds of vices that prelates should avoid or of the virtues to be cultivated, Hesdin's pictures aided the memories of Hesdin and his students through their well-defined structure. His picture of Justice can serve as an example. When Hesdin reaches the text 'For a bishop, as God's steward [...] must be just' (Titus, I.8), he declares:

> And, as we have been accustomed to do in this lecture, treating the vices and virtues, three things must be done: first, to see for the sake of consolation how the ancients painted the image of justice, reducing it to morals for the sake of our instruction; second, what the philosophers, ancients, and doctors said and felt about its effects. [...] Third [...] how necessary it is to princes, judges, and prelates.[54]

He then describes the ancient picture of Justice that he found in Aulus Gellius's *Attic Nights* as a graceful, incorruptible virgin with a formidable glance, full of dignity, seated on a throne with a crown on her head and a sceptre in her hand.

[51] *B*, fol. 105$^{ra}$, Leccio xxii$^{a}$, Titus, I.7: 'Sequitur *non vinolentum*. Postquam visum fuit de uiciis luxurie, superbie, et iracundie, quomodo in se sunt detestabilia et maxime prelatis et viris ecclestiasticis, videndum est de vinolencia siue ebrietate; eo scilicet modo quo Apostolus in epistola ista ipsa vicia per ordinem nominat et prohibet, et eo ordine quo visum fuit de predictis viciis. Causa nostre solacionis et erudicionis videbuntur tria per ordinem circa ebritetatem siue vinolenciam, quia pro eodem accipitur in proposito. Primo quomodo antiqui de ipso senciebant ipsum figurando [...] tercio applicando ad propositum quomodo istud vicium est execrabile viris ecclestiasticis et maxime principibus et prelatis.'

[52] *B*, fol. 103$^{vb}$: 'Circa primum sciendum quod prior Sancti Eligii in libro suo, quem intitulauit de moralizacione deorum, exponit statum superbi prelati sub figura Saturni.'

[53] *B*, fol. 104$^{ra}$: 'Moraliter istud exponendo secundum priorem sanci Eligii et secundum Fulgencium, Mars representat speciem alicuius principis et prelati iracundi.'

[54] *B*, fol. 108$^{vb}$: 'Et ut consueuimus in ista lectura facere [*Smalley* sacra], tractando de viciis aut virtutibus, tria sunt facienda: primo videre causa consolacionis quomodo antiqui iusticie ymaginem depinxerunt, reducendo ad mores causa nostre instructionis; secundo quid de ea philosophi et antiqui et doctores dixerunt et senserunt et de eius effectibus [...]. Tercio ad propositum erit videndum quomodo necessaria sit principibus, iudicibus aut prelatis.'

He adds that Eustachius, in his commentary on Aristotle's *Ethics*, said that the philosophers taught that Justice had a golden face and scale in one hand.

He has thus outlined his usual procedure of examining a topic, first according to what the ancients or the poets thought (*poetice*), then according to what the philosophers and doctors thought, then according to a proposition. The picture almost always comes first and provides Hesdin with a method of discussing the tropological, or moral, aspect of the text.[55] The picture is always described as a series of attributes that can then be analysed: it thus also provides a structuring device for one section of the commentary. As we saw in the last chapter, many preachers and commentators employed pictures for exactly this purpose. The picture thus solved the rhetorical problem of copiousness of material by giving the preacher or commentator the outline of everything he had to say.

In its position as the first part of a threefold methodology, Hesdin's picture anchored the material about Justice in place in the reader's or listener's mind. In the *Craft of Thought* Mary Carruthers has drawn attention to verbal pictures placed at the beginning of works or at the start of important sections of works as *Bildeinsätze*.[56] These mental pictures acted as the foundation for what followed, a kind of map of the themes to come. She connects such verbal pictures to a long tradition of monastic rhetoric that depended on mental images as a form of invention.

Beginning a new topic with an image also served as a valuable way of imprinting the material in the minds of the speaker and of the readers or listeners of the material as a more specific mnemonic image. I would argue that Hesdin's images, like those of the classicizing friars, sprang from a tradition of medieval *memoria* that depended on the use of places and/or images to remember things. The structure of the pictures aided the memories of Hesdin and his students by providing a framework of the material. For instance, Hesdin borrowed from Holcot the picture of *Superbia* (Pride), which was depicted as a cruel man, with three crowns on his head and two lions under his feet. Each crown had a verse written on it, which could be moralized in order, as could the significance of the lions.[57] The crowns functioned as mnemonic placeholders for the verses in the

[55] For more on the tropological sense, see Smalley, *Study of the Bible*, p. 8; Henri de Lubac, *Medieval Exegesis*, trans. by Mark Sebanc, 4 vols (Grand Rapids: Eerdmans, 1998), I, 66–74; II, chap. 9.

[56] Carruthers, *Craft of Thought*, pp. 197–203.

[57] *B*, fol. 103$^{rb}$, Leccio xx$^{a}$, Titus, I.7, *Oportet episcopum sine timore esse et cetera*: 'Quantum ad primum sciendum quod frater Robertus Holcot in moralizatione sua de figura (*sic*) deorum

crown, while all the parts of the image acted as places for the more important moralizations that Hesdin wished to present.

Similarly, the picture of Faith, which Hesdin claims that he found in Fulgentius's *Mithologiae*, has an easily discernable structure: 'As Fulgentius says in the second book of the *Mythologies*, the ancients painted Faith with a darkened and veiled face, with bare shoulders and breast, crowned with a laurel, holding a sceptre in her hands and having two wolves beneath her feet.'[58] A speaker had merely to hold the picture in mind to have a guide to the presentation. As well as helping Hesdin remember his material, the attributes of the pictures likely gave the students listening to his lectures a ready method of remembering the material later for examination purposes, the composition of their own scriptural commentaries, or for their own sermons.

## *The Ancient Tradition of the Pictures of the God and Virtues and Vices*

Hesdin did not insert his pictures into his commentary merely because they constituted a fashionable teaching technique in the mid-fourteenth century. For him, as for Bersuire, there was an intimate connection between ancient teachings, the classical gods, and visual representations of virtue and vice. This complex interaction also came to make mythological images seem the ideal mnemonic device by the fifteenth and sixteenth centuries. We can begin to see the relationship between these many different elements of medieval culture in a passage from Hesdin. Commenting on the phrase 'of truth' in Titus, I.1, he declares:

> Therefore, it should be known that Servius, who was a commentator on Virgil, said on the *Georgics* that the ancients made the virtues gods so that when the poets, who were clerics and learned, spoke about the properties of some virtue or vice to the people, they would immediately construct and build an idol or statue, in which the meaning of the property of that virtue or vice was signified. And so such images were for the 'rude people'

narrat quod Rabanus, libro de naturis rerum, dicit quod Socrates depinxit superbiam ad modum hominis crudelis, coronati tribus coronis, et sub pedibus duo leones. In prima corona erat uersus scriptus: Effluo, descendo, quo quis priuatur habendo. In secunda corona erat uersus: Transmigrat, excedit, et cuiquam numquam obedit. In tercio corona erat scriptum: Turbo perturbor, affligo, sed undique ledor.'

[58] *B*, fol. $90^{vb}$, Titus, I.1: *secundum fidem electorum Dei*: 'Et ideo, ut dicit Fulgencius li. ii° Mithologiarum, antiqui fidem depingebant vultu obscuram et quasi velatam, circa spatulas et pectus nudam, lauro coronatam, ceptrum in manibus tenetem, sub pedibus duos vulpes habentem et in modo constantiam.'

> books; now in churches there are pictures, which are commonly called the books of country people (*rustici*).[59]

Hesdin here accepts the notion that the ancient poets, whom he, like other medieval scholars imagined as clerics like themselves, associated their gods with virtues and vices and created idols of them to teach the people. Unlike other authors, he connects that activity with the same function of images in his own time, following the well-worn idea that pictures could serve as books for the unlettered. He adds that, according to Fulgentius's *Mithologiae*, the Greeks connected the virtue of truth with Apollo, giving him license to do the same thing in his own commentary.[60]

In fact, among the English classicizing friars and their contemporaries there was a tradition that the ancients had composed pictures books of the gods and goddesses depicted as the virtues and vices. An anonymous author of a fourteenth-century English manuscript claimed that 'the ancient authors say that there was a book entitled "On the ancient pictures", which some say Antistenes explained and others Archimedes. In this book many such modes of painting images of the virtues and vices were described.'[61] Holcot also mentions that Servius claimed that the 'gentiles' had books with pictures of the virtues.[62]

Though no modern scholar has been able to a find a specific 'book of pictures' created in antiquity, the fourteenth-century classicizers had reasonable grounds for their assumption. They were well aware of the existence of books that contained pictures of the ancient gods moralized as virtues and vices, that is, books

[59] *B*, fol. 92[va] on Titus, I.1: *Et cognicionem veritatis que est iuxta pietatem*, cap. 1, leccio 7[a]; 'Primo inquiramus quid antiqui de veritate senciebant, secundo quid moderni. Est ergo primo sciendum quod Sergius, qui fuit commentator Virgilii, super Georgicam dicit quod antiqui faciebant uirtutes deos ita quod quando poeta, qui clerici et litterati erant, de aliqua virtute aut vicio populo proprietates dicebant, illi statim ydolum aut statuam construebant et fabricabant in quo signifacio proprietatis illius uirtutis aut vicii significabatur, et sic tales ymagines populo rudi erant pro libris: nunc in ecclesiis fiunt picture, que dicuntur communiter libri rusticorum.'

[60] *B*, fol. 92[va] on Titus I: 'Vnde Fulgencius, li.° ii° Mithologiarum, dicit quod sub significationibus ymaginum diuersorum deorum Greci antiquitus ponebant uirtutes et vicia quare ut ipse dicit illi ponebant veritatem sub figure Appollinis.'

[61] Anon. exempla collection, Worcester, Cathedral Library, MS F 154, fol. 38[r]: 'Notandum hic est, quod dicunt antiqui auctores vnum esse librum intitulatum "De picturis antiquis", quem exposuisse dicunt Antistenem philosophum et alii Archimenidem. In hoc libro describuntur tales modi depingendi ymagines virtutum et viciorum, sicut in proposita pictura Parisidis.'

[62] Smalley, *EFA*, p. 171 n. 3: 'In cuius signum Servius super primum librum Eneidarum refert quod apud gentiles, qui picturas virtutum habebant in libris, isto modo gratia pingebatur.'

devoted to mythography, such as Fulgentius's *Mithologiae*, the Vatican Mythographers, and the sections of encyclopedic works by Isidore of Seville and Rabanus Maurus that were devoted to pagan gods. As Jane Chance defines it, mythography is the 'moralization and allegorization of classical mythology'. It differs from mythology in that '[m]ythology is a unified system of myth, often in narrative form, whereas "mythography" is an explanation and rationalization of one or more myths, often in didactic form'.[63]

While the tradition of mythography seems to have started with the Greek Stoics' attempts to rationalize Homer, it was Fulgentius (Fabius Planciades Fulgentius), a Christian grammarian who probably flourished during the reign of the Vandal kings, between 439 and 533, who began the medieval, Christian tradition of mythography.[64] He seems to have been the first writer to make extensive use of the 'pingitur' formula, describing verbally how ancient gods and goddesses were represented. As we have seen from Hesdin's use of Fulgentius, he also moralized the gods to make them more acceptable to a Christian audience, a practice already begun by early Christians.[65] Later Christian authors, such as Isidore, Rabanus Maurus, and the Vatican Mythographers, who used Fulgentius as a source for their mythographic teachings, also adopted the 'pingitur' formula, at least in part, though they sometimes changed the wording slightly to 'fingitur' or 'describitur'.[66] Thus, these ancient writers were important for our authors because they both moralized the gods as virtues and vices and described them through the pingitur formula. The notion that the ancients had started the practice of associating the gods with the virtues explains why almost all of the pictures found in the many image collections of the fourteenth and fifteenth centuries have some association with the virtues and vices. The ancients had already worked out the relationships between the gods and the virtues or vices; all the moderns needed to do was follow them. When Hesdin or Holcot moralized a god as a virtue or vice, each thought

[63] Chance, *Medieval Mythography*, I, 1–2; Jane Chance, 'The Origins and Development of Medieval Mythography: From Homer to Dante', in *Mapping the Cosmos*, ed. by Jane Chance and Raymond O'Neil Wells (Houston: Rice University Press, 1985), pp. 36–37.

[64] Chance, *Medieval Mythography*, I, 97. For bibliography on him, see pp. 97–98 n. 8.

[65] Chance, *Medieval Mythography*, I, 1–29; J. D. Cooke, 'Euhemerism: A Medieval Interpretation of Classical Paganism', *Speculum*, 2 (1927), 396–410 (p. 397).

[66] For instance, see Rabanus Maurus, *De universo libri viginti duo*, XV.6, PL, CXI, col. 432: 'Cupidinem vocatum ferunt propter amorem. Est enim daemon fornicationis, qui ideo alatus pingitur: quia nihil amantibus levius, nihil mutabilius invenitur. Puer pingitur, quia stultus est, et irrationabilis amor.'

he was simply following classical precedent. Holcot even stated that the pagans considered there to be as many gods as there were virtues.[67]

As a number of scholars have noted, the 'pingitur' formula followed the ancient rhetorical technique of *ekphrasis*, that is literary descriptions of visual images.[68] Most scholars who have studied both the ancient and the fourteenth-century use of the 'pictures' have distinguished between the attitude toward visual representation in the two time periods. They see Fulgentius and Isidore as using 'pingitur' to speak of real works of art, while the fourteenth-century writers reserved the word for literary or verbal descriptions.[69] This view is well summarized in the words of Alistair Minnis: 'Ridevall, and Bersuire after him, were thinking of literary images rather than visual art, whether paintings or statues: each and every "picture" was the work of the poets (pingitur a poetis).'[70] Of course, all of the pictures were expressed in words rather than drawings, but Minnis's point is that writers like Bersuire and Ridevall saw the ancient pictures as created by wordsmiths rather than painters. Poets in antiquity had used fables, stories of the gods, as a way to cover up truth with a story.[71] Almost every important work of poetry in the fourteenth century repeats Horace's *dictum* that 'the poet's aim is to teach or please, or to combine that which delights with what is useful in life'.[72] Their fables had a didactic aim beyond the delights of the story itself. Hesdin, too, attributes his pictures to the poets and sometimes calls his method of discussing the figures of the gods a poetic one.[73]

[67] Holcot, *Liber moralizationum historiarum*, p. 710 (*Moral.* III).

[68] Seznec, *Survival of the Pagan Gods*, p. 106: Chance, *Medieval Mythography*, I, 141, emphasizes Isidore of Seville's descriptions of the gods as a rhetorical device.

[69] Meg Twycross, *The Medieval Anadyomene: A Study in Chaucer's Mythography*, Medium Aevum Monographs, n.s., 1 (Oxford: Blackwell, 1972), p. 18; Chance, *Medieval Mythography*, I, 530 n. 13.

[70] Alastair J. Minnis, *Chaucer and Pagan Antiquity* (Totowa, NJ: Rowman and Littlefield, 1982), p. 20.

[71] Jane Chance, 'The Medieval "Apology for Poetry": Fabulous Narrative and Stories of the Gods', in *Mythographic Art*, ed. by Chance, pp. 3–44 (pp. 5–8).

[72] Richard Hamilton Green, 'Classical Fable and English Poetry in the Fourteenth Century', in *Critical Approaches to Medieval Literature*, ed. by Dorothy Bethurum, Selected papers from the English Institute, 1958–59 (New York: Columbia University Press, 1960), pp. 110–33 (p. 119).

[73] For instance, in his picture of Prudiencia, Hesdin discusses his method of proceeding: 'Ideo sicud supratractatum est de aliis virtutibus et viciis, ita hoc est tractandum, et primo figuratur et magis poetice, secundo de prudencia in se, tercio de eius effectibus et concludemus ad propositum' (*B*, fol. 125$^{rb}$).

Without wishing to deny the literary importance of the fourteenth-century writers' understanding of the pictures, I would like to draw attention to the extent to which they saw these pictures in more visual terms. If one looks carefully at the fourteenth-century writers' manner of describing the pictures, it is clear that they sometimes do see the pictures as descriptions of real paintings or statues. One example can be seen in Hesdin's treatment of the image of *Mendacium*. He says that according to Robert Holcot and the Prior of Saint-Éloi, the ancients did not create an image of Untruth as a god or worthy of adoration, but rather *sculpted* it as a vice of detestation and confusion.[74] The word *sculpted* implies a much greater affinity to a work of art than to a literary work. Hesdin also described the source for this point as Holcot's *Moralizations of Idols*, which also rather suggests physical pieces rather than literary works. If we look again at the quotation cited above, we can see the same visual emphasis:

> When the poets, who were clerics and learned, spoke about the properties of some virtue or vice to the people, they would immediately construct and build an idol or statue, in which the meaning of the property of that virtue or vice was signified. And so such images were for the 'rude people' books; now in churches there are pictures, which are commonly called the books of country people [*rustici*].[75]

Hesdin says explicitly that the ancients made actual statues of their gods as virtues and vices and compares their practice to the teaching practices of his own day, the only picture writer to my knowledge to do so. Hesdin made it clear that he understood the value of imagery as a teaching tool and that he understood himself to be following classical precedent in describing the pictures. The further implication of Hesdin's attitude about the gods is that his verbal descriptions of the virtues and vices could teach people through their character as a kind of image.

[74] *B*, fol. 115$^{ra}$: 'Quantum ad primum est sciendum quod frater Robertus Holcot, in moralitatibus ydolorum quas composuit, mendacii ymaginem descripsit prout sibi imponit; prior sancti Elegii, non, ut dixit, quod antiqui hoc finxissent tamquam ymaginem aliquid diuinum habentem et causa adoracionis, sed magis eam sculpserunt vt vicium detestacionis et confusionis. Erat enim ymago ad modum mulieris, habitu meretricis variis distincto [*Smalley* distincta] coloribus, oculis orbata, vultu deformis et morbo languida.'

[75] *B*, fol. 92$^{va}$ on Titus I.1: *Et cognicionem veritatis que est iuxta pietatem*, cap. 1, leccio 7a: 'Primo inquiramus quid antiqui de veritate senciebant, secundo quid moderni. Est ergo primo sciendum quod Sergius, qui fuit commentator Virgilii, super Georgicam dicit quod antiqui faciebant uirtutes deos ita quod quando poeta, qui clerici et litterati erant, de aliqua virtute aut vicio populo proprietates dicebant, illi statim ydolum aut statuam construebant et fabricabant in quo significacio proprietatis illius uirtutis aut vicii significabatur, et sic tales ymagines populo rudi erant pro libris: nunc in ecclesiis fiunt picture, que dicuntur communiter libri rusticorum.'

When he immediately follows his observation with a 'picture' of Apollo as Truth, one cannot avoid the implication that his verbal images should serve the same function. We should thus consider that Hesdin's pictures may well have been used by himself or his students in sermons, putting them to use as didactic images for the laity. Certainly medieval preachers put enormous emphasis on moral behaviour as part of their pastoral mission, and more will be said about this topic in the next chapter. Though few peasants would ever have read Hesdin's *Commentary on Titus*, they could have come in contact with a picture of Venus through the sermons composed by readers of Hesdin's commentary. While I have not yet examined a sermon by Hesdin, I have seen such pictures used in sermons by other preachers in the fourteenth and fifteenth centuries.

## *Mythological Memory Images*

The literary and visual components of the 'pictures' of the gods and the virtues and vices also made them increasingly attractive as mnemonic images. There were a number of strands of medieval culture that reinforced the mnemonic aspect of mythographic figures. One such aspect was the delight that medieval authors took in mythography, which they also called fables, and in mythological pictures. It is clear in the examples cited from Bersuire and Hesdin that they regarded their pictures as the creation of ancient poets who deliberately hid moral pills, as it were, in the sugar-plum coating of stories about the gods. It was this very character of the delightfulness and unfamiliarity of fables that made them ideal mnemonic images. Albertus Magnus commented on the aptness of fable and poetic discourse for mnemonics in his *De bono*.[76] During the course of his careful examination of the *Ad Herennium*'s rules for memory, Albertus Magnus considered the usefulness of metaphorical language. He concluded that metaphorical, poetic, or unusual language 'moved' memory more than ordinary language. He noted that

> what is marvelous [*mirabile*] is more moving than what is ordinary, and so when images of this metaphorical sort are made out of marvels [*ex miris*] they affect memory more than commonplace literal matters. So indeed early philosophers translated their ideas in poetry, as the Philosopher says, because a fable, since it is composed out of marvels is more affecting.[77]

[76] Albertus Magnus, *De bono*, quest. 11, art. 2, p. 251.

[77] Translation from Carruthers, *Book of Memory*, Appendix B, p. 279. See also Rossi, *Logic and the Art of Memory*, pp. 10–11.

For him, the wonder excited by poetic creations could even lead to scientific knowledge, 'because what is wonderful [*mirum*] by its vigorous motion causes questioning, and thence gives rise to investigation and recollection'.[78] The *picturae* of mythological figures met the requirements of delight and wonder and were thus peculiarly suitable to function as mnemonic images. The fact that they were available in so many different collections in the fourteenth and fifteenth centuries must have heightened their appeal to would be mnemonists.[79]

The ancient gods were also known to medieval people in other guises than moralizations. A particularly important association existed from antiquity between the gods and the planets. These associations were also depicted pictorially and from antiquity one could find books outlining the relationships. It was in the twelfth century that medieval scholars began to study ancient astronomy in earnest, and it is from this time that one begins to see depictions in art of the gods and planets. A particularly important doctrine showing how the astronomical identification of the gods could have mnemonic consequences can be seen in the doctrine of *melothesia*: the ancient pagan notion that the twelve signs of the zodiac affected various parts of the body.[80] Each sign was thought to have particular influence over one body part; for instance, Aries governed the head, Taurus the neck, and Gemini the shoulders and arms. The *melothesia* idea had been carried from antiquity into Middle Ages, but pictorial representations are common only from the thirteenth and fourteenth centuries.[81] An example of such an illustration can be seen in Figure 3. Here the figure of a man is depicted with a tiny image of the appropriate zodiac sign on the twelve affected parts of the body. If one compares this figure to depictions of mnemonic figures in fifteenth- and sixteenth-century *artes memorativae* as in Figure 2, above, the similarity in principle becomes obvious. Each has one large figure with ten to twelve spots marked on its body that are meant to be followed in order. Each spot is then filled with a smaller image. The purpose of the entire image is to help one recall the

[78] Minnis, *Medieval Theory of Authorship*, pp. 139–40, notes that Ulrich of Strasbourg, in his *Liber de summo bono* (1262–72), quotes the same idea as Albert of the poet as philosopher, because the 'poet feigns a fable in such a way that he excites to wonder, and by wonder subsequently excites to inquiry; and this science takes shape, as the 'Philosopher' says in his Rhetoric'.

[79] See the next chapter for a detailed discussion of collections of *picturae*.

[80] *Survival of the Gods: Classical Mythology in Medieval Art; An Exhibition by the Department of Art, Brown University, Bell Gallery, List Art Center*, ed. by S. Bonde (Providence: Brown University, 1987), p. 176.

[81] *Survival of the Gods*, p. 176.

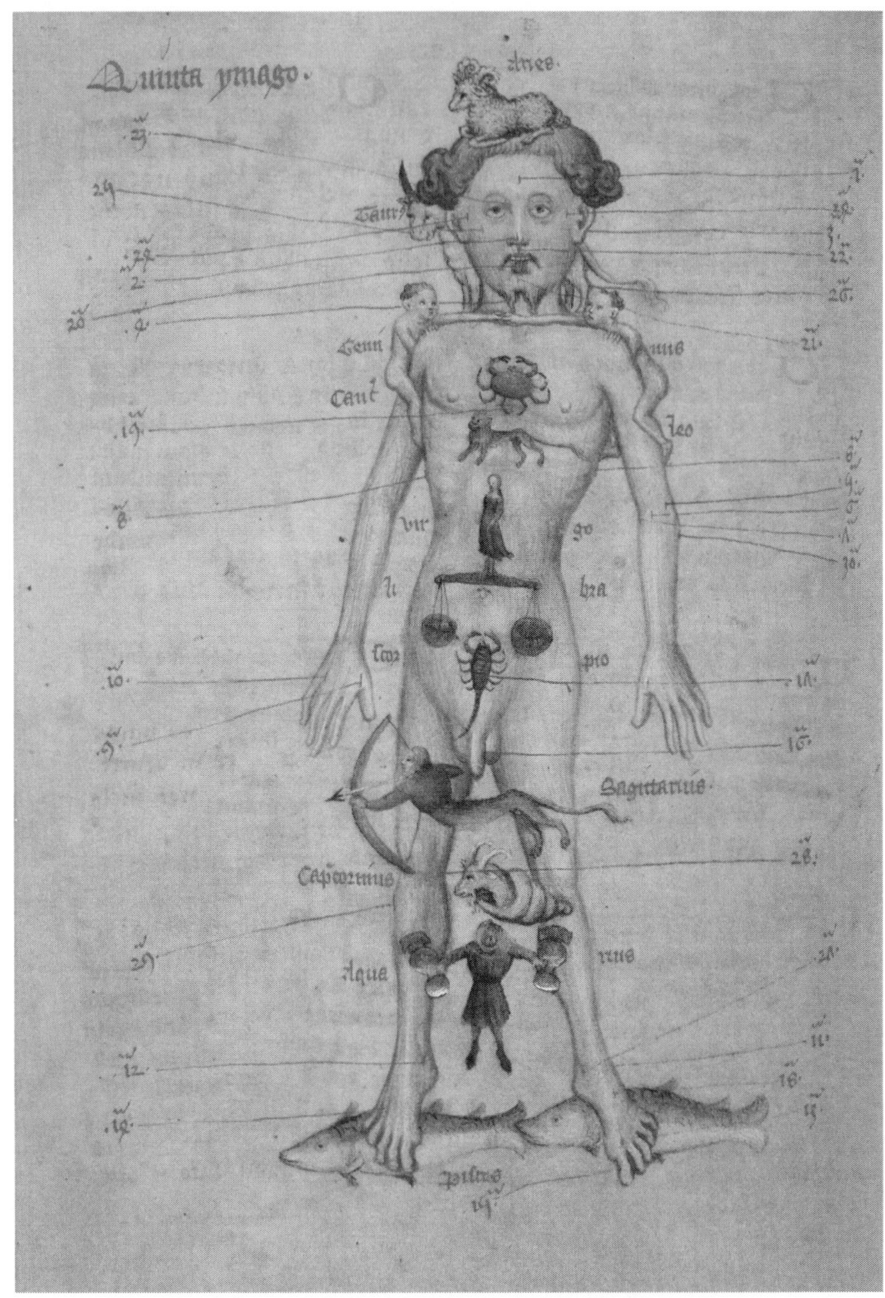


Fig. 3. 'Bloodletting-Zodiac Man', in John de Foxton, *Liber cosmographiae*, Cambridge, Trinity College, R.15.21, fol. 28v. Reproduced by permission of the Master and Fellows of Trinity College, Cambridge.

order and significance of the smaller figures, and the whole thing can either be depicted in a piece of visual art or recalled as a mental image. Surely the illustrations of *melothesia* were to meant to help out people who needed to remember the associations, probably physicians in particular.[82]

The mnemonic usefulness of images of the gods and goddesses can also be seen in the mnemonic treatises of the later Middle Ages themselves. Some of them specifically discuss how to recall the gods or goddesses or recommend their images to memorize something else. An early example occurs in Thomas Bradwardine's *De memoria artificiali*.[83] When he comes to explain the way to create memory images, his first example is the signs of the zodiac:

> Suppose that someone must memorize the twelve signs of the Zodiac, that is the Ram, the Bull, etc. So he might, if he wished to, make for himself in the front of the first location a very white ram standing up and rearing on his hind feet, with golden horns. And he might put a very red bull to the right of the ram, kicking the ram with his rear feet; standing erect, the ram with his right foot might kick the bull in his large and super-swollen testicles, causing a copious effusion of blood. And by means of the testicles one will recall that it is a bull, not a castrated ox or a cow.[84]

Bradwardine includes equally vivid depictions of the other signs, creating in the process perhaps the most visually detailed instructions for mnemonic images in the medieval tradition up to his time. His examples follow all the best advice for creating long-lasting memory images: they are vivid, violent, sensual, and colourful.

It is quite likely that Bradwardine gives instructions for the signs of the zodiac first, because they can be used to recall other things, either metaphorically, as signs of virtues, vices, or other characteristics, or as place-making images, as described in the last chapter. Mnemonic authors often began with examples that seem staid and obvious, but which turn out to have useful connotations outside of the

[82] At least one author was quite up front about the connections between the picture tradition and the doctrine of *melothesia*. This was John de Foxton, author of the *Liber cosmographiae*. For the text, see *John de Foxton's Liber cosmographiae (1408): An Edition and Codicological Study*, ed. by John Block Friedman, Brill's Studies in Intellectual History, 5 (Leiden: Brill, 1988). For secondary literature, see Chance, *Medieval Mythography*, II, 302–04; John Block Friedman, 'John de Foxton's Continuation of Ridewall's *Fulgentius metaforalis*', *Studies in Iconography*, 7–8 (1981–82), 65–79; John Friedman, 'John Siferwas and the Mythological Illustrations in the *Liber cosmographiae* of John de Foxton', *Speculum*, 58 (1983), 391–418.

[83] For an edition of the Latin text, see Mary J. Carruthers, 'Thomas Bradwardine, "De memoria artificiale adquirenda"', *Journal of Medieval Latin*, 2 (1992), 25–43.

[84] Thomas Bradwardine, *On Acquiring a Trained Memory*, trans. by Mary J. Carruthers, in *Medieval Craft of Memory*, ed. by Carruthers and Ziolkowski, pp. 205–14 (p. 209). Carruthers also provided a translation of the same text in *Book of Memory*, Appendix C, pp. 281–88.

mnemonic text. For instance, at first glance, it might seem odd that any educated person would need help in remembering the twelve signs of the zodiac. Even a modern person finds the standard imagery associated with them easily memorable. I would argue that Bradwardine begins with the zodiac precisely because they make excellent examples of active images and because they will be so useful to the would-be mnemonist in the rest of his career.[85]

Certainly later mnemonic authorities included advice either for memorizing mythological figures or for using them to remember some other item. For instance, in 1542 Lodovico Dolce, in his (unacknowledged) translation of Johannes Romberch's *Congestorium artificiosae memoriae* (1520), recommends how to remember the celestial bodies. His advice is to recall them through images based on their properties, such as using the figure of an evil old man of our acquaintance to remember Saturn, a Soldier to remember Mars, and a lustful girl to recall Venus.[86] He also recommends the authors who describe the nature of the gods and how the ancients painted (*dipingeuano*) them, singling out for attention Boccaccio's book on the nature of the gods, an attempt to distill the contents of the Latin picture books into Italian.

A little later, in 1553, Thomas Wilson, in his *Rhetorique*, found it quite natural to use Venus as an example of a memory image:

> And now to make this hard matter somewhat plain, I will use an example. My friend, whom I took ever to be an honest man, is accused of theft, of advoutry, of riot, of manslaughter, and of treason: if I would keep these words in my remembrance and rehearse them in order as they were spoken, I must appoint five places, the which I had need to have so perfectly in my memory as could be possible. As for example, I will make these in my chamber. A door, a window, a press, a bedstead, and a chimney. Now in the door I will set Cacus the thief, or some such notable varlet. In the window I will place Venus. In the press I will put Apitius, that famous glutton. In the bedstead I will set Richard the Third, king of England, or some like notable murderer. In the chimney I will place the blacksmith, or some other notable traitor.[87]

[85] For another example of mythological figures used as mnemonic devices, see Madeleine Jeay, 'La Mythologie comme clé de mémorisation: *La Glose des Échecs Amoureux*', in *Jeux de mémoire*, ed. by Roy and Zumthor, pp. 91–122.

[86] Lodovico Dolce, *Dialogo [...] nelquale si ragiona del modo di accrescere et conservar la memoria* (Venice: Heredi di Marchiò Sessa [Appresso Enea de Alaris], 1575), fol. 86$^{r}$: 'Ma, per tornare a i corpi celesti, di questi per le proprietà potremo raccordarci: come per Saturno imaginaoci alcun maluagio vecchio da noi conosciuto: per Marte vn Soldato: per il Sole vn'huomo illustre: per Venere vna fanciulla lusuriosa.'

[87] Thomas Wilson, *The Art of Rhetoric (1560)*, ed. with notes and commentary by Peter E. Medine (University Park: Pennsylvania State University Press, 1994), p. 238. Rossi, *Logic*

By his time, the association of Venus with the vice of Lechery was so complete that there was no need even to comment on why Venus would make a perfect image for 'advoutry'.

Other mnemonic experts in the sixteenth century advise using the zodiac and the constellations as 'places' on which to put images of the things they wish to recall. For example, Johannes Romberch, a German Dominican, in his *Congestorium artificiose memorie* (1533) thought that the signs of the zodiac would provide an easily recalled order of places, adding that one could extend the number of places available by including the images of the constellations, as described by Hyginus.[88] Cosmas Rossellius, in the *Thesaurus artificiose memorie* (Venice, 1579) gives similar advice. Both authors support their precepts with an ancient authority — Metrodorus of Scepsis.[89] According to Quintilian, Metrodorus (fl. first century BCE) was able to find 360 mnemonic loci in the signs of the zodiac.[90] L. A. Post described how Metrodorus might have designed his memory system:

> I suspect that Metrodorus was versed in astrology, for astrologers divided the zodiac not only into twelve signs, but also into thirty-six decans, each covering ten degrees; for each decan there was an associated decan figure. Metrodorus probably grouped ten artificial backgrounds under each decan figure. He would thus have a series of *loci* numbered from one to 360, which he could use in his operation.[91]

One way that Metrodorus could have found ten places for each decan was to use the parts of the body, as described above: ten was about the highest number of places that could fit on or around the human body. Metrodorus seems to have been well known in antiquity as a memory expert, but one does not hear about him in the Middle Ages.[92] By the time that Romberch wrote, the medieval tradition of memory was being merged with reinterpretations of the classical rhetorical rules, so it is impossible to know for sure whether Romberch's and Rossellius's recommendation of the zodiac represent a long tradition or a re-reading of Quintilian.[93]

*and the Art of Memory*, p. 66, saw Wilson's use of Venus as an anticipation of Bruno in use of mythological images.

[88] Johannes Romberch, a German Dominican, in his *Congestorium artificiose memorie* (Venice: Melchior Sessa, 1533), fol. 25r. See Yates, *Art of Memory*, p. 116.

[89] Yates, *Art of Memory*, p. 122.

[90] *Inst. orat.*, IX.2, § 22.

[91] L. A. Post, 'Ancient Memory Systems', *Classical Weekly*, 25 (1932), 105–10 (p. 109).

[92] For instance, Cicero testified to the fame of Metrodorus's powerful memory in *De oratore*, II.88, l. 360.

[93] Yates notes Giordano Bruno's use of the decans in *De Umbris idearum* (1582) and compares it to Metrodorus's system (*Art of Memory*, pp. 212–13, 217).

## *Conclusion*

By the beginning of the fourteenth century, scholars and preachers had created an indissoluble tie between the figures of ancient mythology and Christian virtues and vices; the mnemonic pictures that resulted from this tie became indispensable for preaching and teaching purposes. Why did the pictures burst forth in the fourteenth century? The use of pictures begins about two generations after the revival of the *Ad Herennium* and after the study of classical authors in general, from Aristotle to the mythographic writers, had become widespread among the educated elite.[94] The sense that it was now acceptable to study pagan culture may have allowed the Dominicans and then others to feel more comfortable using memory methods from the Roman past. The possibility is the more intriguing given Janet Coleman's recent observation that one reason why the *Ad Herennium*'s memory system may have gone out of fashion in the fourth century was its association with pagan culture and even sorcery.[95] The revival of interest in the classics, which started in the twelfth century and which reached new heights in the fourteenth century, probably fuelled interest in ancient memory methods.

[94] For instance, Jane Chance notes that Ovid's *Metamorphoses* became a school text in the twelfth century, with commentaries appearing only late in the century: 'The Medieval "Apology for Poetry"', pp. 3–44. See also Chance, 'Origins and Development', p. 47.

[95] Coleman, *Ancient and Medieval Memories*, pp. 118–19.

Chapter 8

# JOHANNES VON WERDEN'S *DORMI SECURE* AND THE CIRCULATION OF *PICTURAE* IN GERMANY AND CENTRAL EUROPE

The *picturae* pioneered by the English classicizing friars were even more popular in Germany and central Europe than they were in France. Separated from their original contexts, the *picturae* were compiled into new exempla collections by anonymous compilers. Once they were made available to preachers in this new form, they found their way into sermons across Europe. This chapter will examine the current scholarship about the picture collections and look at the use made of them in the sermon collection *Dormi secure*, probably compiled by the German friar, Johannes von Werden. The chapter will also outline the scholarly connections between England and Germany in the late fourteenth and fifteenth centuries that permitted the easy circulation of the *picturae*. I have chosen the *Dormi secure* because it was an extremely popular sermon collection in the late Middle Ages, and thus one which reached a good many preachers and likely many audiences as well.

## *The 'Dormi secure'*

Although the *Dormi secure* was wildly popular at the booksellers in the late Middle Ages, it has not been treated kindly by scholars. Many have viewed the model sermon collection as representative of two of the worst faults of late medieval preachers, laziness and irrelevance to Christian faith. Indeed, until recently, the *Dormi secure*'s full title itself was an object of opprobrium: 'Sunday sermons with expositions of the Gospels of the year sufficiently noteworthy and useful to all priests, pastors, and chaplains which are called *Sleep Securely* or *Sleep Without Care* because without great effort they can be easily digested and preached to the people.'[1] The idea that members of the clergy could get a good night's sleep, secure in the knowledge that their sermon had already been written (by someone else), symbolized to some historians the laziness of the clergy and the decadence of medieval preaching.[2] Gerald Owst, in his *Preaching in Medieval England*, thought the collection 'dreary' and a mass of dull and predictable material, occasionally enlivened by the preacher's feeble attempt to tell an amusing anecdote that the congregation had probably heard before anyway. Overall, Owst considered *Dormi secure* representative of 'the conventionalism and stagnation of mind' into which the pulpit had fallen by the fifteenth century.[3]

There have been some defenders of the *Dormi secure*. Anscar Zawart cautioned against misreading the title as an indictment of preachers, noting that at the very least the sermon had to be translated into the vernacular before it could be delivered.[4] Johann Schneyer and John Dahmus point out that the work was one of the most widely used and disseminated sermon collections of the late Middle Ages.[5] The change in appreciation of the *Dormi secure* is due in part to a better understanding of the nature of sermon collections, although much more work in this area is still needed. As the work of D. L. d'Avray on thirteenth-century model sermons has shown, writers of sermon collections drew together previously delivered sermons, as well as newly written ones, to provide a resource for other

[1] Translation from John W. Dahmus, '*Dormi secure*: The Lazy Preacher's Model of Holiness for his Flock', in *Models of Holiness in Medieval Sermons: Proceedings of the International Symposium (Kalamazoo, 4–7 May 1995)*, ed. by Beverly Mayne Kienzle, Textes et études du moyen âge, 5 (Louvain-la-Neuve: Fédération internationale des Instituts d'études médiévales, 1996), pp. 301–02. I have used the 1498 Anton Koberger, Nürnberg edition of the *Sermones dormi secure de tempore* for the study and have checked some of its readings against the Basel edition (printer of the Meffreth, 1489). I have also made limited use of Cologne, Historisches Archiv der Stadt Köln, HAStK 7002 119 (formerly Cod. GB fol. 119) through the microfilm resources of the Hill Monastic Manuscript Library at the University of St John in Collegeville, Minnesota (HMML 36041).

[2] Longère, *La Prédication médiévale*, p. 105.

[3] Owst, *Preaching in Medieval England*, pp. 237–38. In contrast, Siegfried Wenzel sees the period of *c.* 1350 to *c.* 1450 as 'the golden age of preaching in post-Conquest England before the Reformation' (Wenzel, *Late Sermon Collections*, p. xv). Granted, Wenzel is speaking of England rather than the Continent, but in general late medieval preaching has been undervalued.

[4] Anscar Zawart, 'The History of Franciscan Preaching and of Franciscan Preachers (1209–1927): A Bio-bibliographical Study', *Franciscan Educational Conference*, 9 (1927), 242–587 (p. 329): 'Perhaps any sermon-book of our day might with more justice be entitled "Dormi secure".'

[5] Johann Baptist Schneyer, 'Winke für die Sichtung und Zuordnung spätmittelalterlicher Lateinischer Predigtreihen', *Scriptorium*, 32 (1978), 231–48 (p. 239); Dahmus, 'Lazy Preacher', p. 301.

preachers.[6] Sermon collections were part of the same effort to raise the standard of preaching begun in the late twelfth century as *ars praedicandi* treatises, *distinctiones* and exempla collections, and biblical concordances. In d'Avray's opinion, sermon collections can be a much better indicator of actual preaching than these other aids that have received more scholarly attention.[7] Rather than indict the author of the *Dormi secure*, one should recognize his effort to fulfil the need for good preaching in German parishes in the early fifteenth century by providing an aid to preachers.

In fact I would argue that the author (probably Johannes von Werden) had a very clear idea of what preaching to the people should entail. Rather than being 'dreary', his sermons were clearly organized, boasted lengthy quotations of the day's pericope, and emphasized the demands of a moral Christian life. Any novice preacher would have found Johannes's sermons, perhaps especially his Sunday sermons, worth memorizing for delivery to his parish or else helpful models for his own efforts.[8] Johannes not only organized his compositions clearly, he also incorporated into them mnemonic exempla that served a variety of purposes: they structured the sermon for the preacher's easier recall; they captured his listeners' attention and helped them to recall what they had heard; they encapsulated salient features of the virtues and vices in a form the laity could remember; and

[6] For more on sermons in Latin, including model sermon collections, see Nicole Bériou, 'Les Sermons Latins après 1200', in *Sermon*, ed. by Kienzle, pp. 323–447, and Nicole Bériou, *L'Avènement des maîtres de la Parole: La Prédication à Paris au XIII^e^ siècle*, Collection des études augustiniennes, Série moyen âge et temps modernes, 31–32, 2 vols (Paris: Institut d'études augustiniennes, 1998).

[7] 'However it may be with the *artes praedicandi*, there can be no doubt about the influence of model sermon collections, which may probably be regarded as the most important single genre of preaching aid' (d'Avray, *Preaching of the Friars*, p. 78). In the late Middle Ages, the scope of sermon collections expanded to include not only sermons for Sundays, feast days and saints' days, the most common arrangements in the thirteenth century, but also for Lent and moral topics like the Ten Commandments, the Creed, the Our Father and the Sacraments (d'Avray, *Preaching of the Friars*, pp. 78–79); Johann Baptist Schneyer, *Geschichte der katholischen Predigt* (Freiburg: Seelsorge, 1969), p. 229. In his examination of sermon collections still in manuscript form, Wenzel avoids the term model sermon collections, which he sees as a much broader notion than d'Avray: 'It surely becomes reasonable to claim that any sermon that got written down could, and probably was intended to, function as a model to be used by other preachers' (Wenzel, *Latin Sermon Collections*, p. 3). Still, given the *Dormi secure*'s title, it seems reasonable to see this collection as a model sermon collection.

[8] There had long been a presumption in the early church that ordinary priests could memorize the sermons of other preachers. See D. W. Robertson, Jr, 'Frequency of Preaching in Thirteenth-Century England', *Speculum*, 24 (1949), 376–88 (p. 376).

almost certainly, they provided a focus for later meditation. His *De tempore* collection, in particular, is filled with the kinds of exempla pioneered by the English classicizing friars. Johannes also included mnemonic exempla of more devotional/scriptural imagery around which many medieval preachers built sermons.[9]

The impressive printing history of the *Dormi secure* suggests that Johannes's sermons must have reached a very wide audience of preachers and others who could read Latin, as well as the audiences to whom versions of his sermons were eventually delivered. Certainly it was well enough known in sixteenth-century Germany for Martin Luther to deride it as an example of the misguided scholarship of the 'monks': 'Instead of worthwhile books, the stupid, useless, and harmful books of the monks, such as *Catholicon*, *Florista*, *Grecista*, *Labyrinthus*, *Dormi secure*, and the like asses' dung were introduced by the devil.'[10] The *Dormi secure* is thus an indicator of the kind of preaching that late medieval preachers favoured and quite likely of the kind of sermons reaching the laity in fifteenth-century Germany.[11] To demonstrate these points, we will first discuss briefly the authorship of the work, Werden's relation to the English classicizing friars, and the ways that their influence travelled to Germany before turning to the mnemonic function of his exempla and that of the late medieval exempla in general.

## *Authorship of the 'Dormi secure'*

Although the *Dormi secure* was one of 'the widest and [...] most long-lastingly disseminated sermon collections of the late Middle Ages',[12] its author is hardly known. Most modern scholars attribute the sermon collection to Johannes von

[9] Schneyer, 'Winke für die Sichtung', p. 239, notes that Johannes evidently drew on many other medieval authors, such as Berthold of Wiesbaden, 'Meffreth', and Johannes Nider, to build up his collection, making it difficult to determine his independence. Rudolf Cruel, *Geschichte der deutschen Predigt im Mittelalter* (Detmold: Mener'sche Hofbuchhandlung, 1879), pp. 478–79, lists six unacknowledged sermons that Johannes borrowed from other collections.

[10] Martin Luther, 'To the Councilmen of All Cities in Germany that They Establish and Maintain Christian Schools', in *Selected Writings of Martin Luther, 1529–1546*, ed. by Theodore G. Tappert, 4 vols (Minneapolis: Fortress, 1967), II, 66.

[11] Anne Thayer reaches a similar conclusion about the *Dormi secure* in her *Penitence, Preaching and the Coming of the Reformation* (Aldershot: Ashgate, 2002), p. 4. See also her use of the sermon collection in 'Judge and Doctor: Images of the Confessor in Printed Model Sermon Collections, 1450–1520', in *Penitence in the Age of Reformations*, ed. by Katharine Jackson Lualdi and Anne T. Thayer (Aldershot: Ashgate, 2000), pp. 10–29.

[12] Schneyer, 'Winke für die Sichtung', p. 239.

Werden, thought to be a Franciscan originally from Werden in the Ruhr and a member of the order's convent in Cologne around 1400.[13] While the attribution of the *Dormi secure* to Johannes von Werden is not as 'secure' as its title, the author of the collection probably was German and may well have been the Franciscan that tradition claims for him.[14] Because Johannes von Werden was a determined borrower of other preachers' sermons, it is hard to draw firm conclusions from the evidence of the sermons themselves as to his identity.[15] Despite

[13] As in Zawart, 'History of Franciscan Preaching', pp. 328–29; Longère, *La Prédication médiévale*, p. 105; Franz Josef Worstbrock, 'Johannes von Werden', *Die deutsche Literatur des Mittelalters*, ed. by Ruh and others, IV, 811–13; Patricius Schlager, *Beiträge zur Geschichte der Kölnischen Franziskaner-Ordensprovinz im Mittelalter* (Cologne: Bachem, 1904), pp. 165–67. Other biographical notices include Cruel, *Geschichte der deutschen Predigt*, pp. 478–80; Clément Schmitt, 'Jean de Werden', in *Dictionnaire de spiritualité*, ed. by Viller, Cavallera, and de Guibert, VIII, 790–91; and 'Jean de Werden, Franciscain', *Histoire littéraire de la France*, 25 (1869), 74–84. The little information we have about Johannes von Werden's life depends on a biographical notice in Johannes Trithemius, *Catalogus illustrium virorum*, in *Opera historica*, ed. by Marquard Freher (1601; repr. Frankfurt a.M.: Minerva, 1966), p. 150, which names Johannes as the author of a *De tempore* and a *De sanctis* sermon collection collectively entitled *Dormi secure*, recognizes him as 'the most famous preacher of popular sermons of his time', and places him in Cologne around 1300 at the time of Emperor Wenceslas (see also the less informative biography in *De scriptoribus ecclesiasticis*, p. 336). As there was no Emperor Wenceslas in 1300, this date is suspect. In addition, the *Supplement to Wadding* undermines the date by noting that one of the authors cited in a sermon on the Immaculate Conception could not have written before 1330 (Giovanni Giacinto Sbaralea, *Supplementum et castigatio ad scriptores trium ordinum S. Francisci a Waddingo, aliisve descriptos*, 3 vols (Rome: Nardecchia, 1908–36), II, 140). However, there was both an Emperor Wenceslas and a Johannes von Werden living in Cologne around 1400, which makes the early fifteenth century a more likely date for the author.

[14] In the nineteenth century, many scholars considered the English Carmelite Richard Maidstone to be the author of the collection, while Wadding attributed it to Matheus Hus. See Owst, *Preaching in Medieval England*, pp. 237–38, who rejected the idea of Maidstone's authorship.

[15] For instance, the 1498 Nürnberg edition of the *Sermones dormi secure de tempore* includes a sermon by Jacobus de Voragine on the Passion. Still, it is worth considering some small pieces of evidence. A few of the sermons contain German words and phrases. For example, in a sermon on St Katherine, the author explains the meaning of *contubernium* with the German word *geselschafft*, implying that the German word would be more familiar to readers. The use of German is not in itself conclusive, but it suggests a familiarity with either a German audience or German texts (*Dormi secure de sanctis*, Sermon 66). In addition, a sermon on the Immaculate Conception of the Virgin Mary contains an exemplum about Bonaventure with German phrases (Johannes von Werden, *Sermones dormi secure de sanctis*, Sermon 5). Some scholars have also been reluctant to consider the author of the *Dormi secure* a Franciscan, mainly because the *De sanctis* section does not contain sermons dedicated to prominent Franciscan saints, such as St Francis

the divergent opinions, I assume that the author of the *Dormi secure* was a Franciscan, since this is still the view held by most scholars.

It is less important for my purposes to see Johannes as the author than to note the author's connections to a German-Franciscan milieu and the collection's widespread availability to German preachers in the fifteenth and sixteenth centuries. Roughly forty editions of the *Dormi secure* appeared by 1500 with almost ninety eventually in print. After Johannes Herolt's *Sermones de tempore et de sanctis*,[16] Johannes von Werden's work was probably the most popular sermon collection in Germany.[17] The question one might ask is, what made the collection so popular? I would argue that beyond the collection's catchy title and its intention of aiding parochial clergy, the sermons' use of mnemonic exempla attracted users. These exempla came ultimately from England and the classicizing friars.

## *Relation to the Classicizing Friars*

Johannes von Werden consistently incorporated exempla known variously as *picturae* and *imagines* in his sermons. A number of scholars have noted their presence in the *Dormi secure* without saying much about them.[18] Johannes em-

himself, St Anthony of Padua, or St Clare of Assisi, and because the sermon on the Immaculate Conception mentioned above places Bonaventure in Purgatory for denying the doctrine (Schmitt, 'Jean de Werden', pp. 790–91, and 'Jean de Werden, Franciscain', pp. 74–84). Though the author of this sermon criticizes Bonaventura, he does defend the Immaculate Conception, which was a favourite Franciscan doctrine. There are also several favourable references to Franciscans in his sermons. For instance, in an Ascension Day sermon (*De tempore*, Sermon 35), Johannes names only seven individuals, as opposed to types like martyrs and prophets, among the choir of angels (Saints Bernard, Anthony, Francis, Paul, Benedict, Katherine, and Barbara); one of these is St Francis and two others, Saints Bernard and Anthony, were much admired by the Franciscans. Overall, the sermons display a favourable attitude toward Francis; there is also a claim that the head of St Barbara was in the Franciscan choir in Colonia (Cologne), something a Franciscan from Cologne might be likely to know (*De sanctis*, Sermon 2).

[16] For more on Herolt's preaching, see Richard Newhauser, 'From Treatise to Sermon: Johannes Herolt on the *Novem peccata aliena*', in *De Ore Domini: Preacher and Word in the Middle Ages*, ed. by Thomas L. Amos, Eugene A. Green, and Beverly Mayne Kienzle (Kalamazoo: Medieval Institute Publications, 1989), pp. 185–209.

[17] Dahmus, 'Lazy Preacher', p. 301 n. 2; Worstbrock, 'Johannes von Werden', p. 812. Anne Thayer lists sixty-four editions of Johannes's work printed between 1450 and 1520 ('Sermon Collections in Print, 1450–1520', *Medieval Sermon Studies*, 36 (1995), 50–63 (pp. 60–62)).

[18] Dahmus, 'Lazy Preacher', p. 303; Schneyer, *Geschichte der katholischen Predigt*, p. 230. Zawart, 'History of Franciscan Preaching', p. 329, calls Johannes's sermons 'typically emblematic',

ployed them most often in the *De tempore* collection, and they constitute one of his most characteristic sermon techniques. In the 1498 Nürnberg edition of the *De tempore* series, I have counted eighteen classicizing *picturae* and exempla.

For example, in a sermon for the twenty-third Sunday after Pentecost, Johannes includes an *imago* of *Vanus Honor*, claiming that, according to Fulgentius,

> De hac imagine et superscriptione dicit Fulgentius quod romani faciebant imaginem vani honoris ad modum mulieris vage, scribentes super eam aureis letteris: 'Hec est imago vani honoris. Hanc inspice et semper eam fuge'. Hec imago habuit coronam in capite et sceptrum in manu sinistra, et pauonem in manu dextra, et oculis ceca et velata et sedebat super currum quem trabebant quatuor leones.[19]

> (The Romans made an image of Vain Honour in the form of a roving woman, writing over her head in golden letters 'This is the image of Vain Honour. Look at this woman and always flee her'. The woman wore a crown, carries a sceptre in her left hand and a peacock in her right, her eyes were blinded and veiled, and she was sitting atop a chariot drawn by four lions.)

Johannes invented neither the image of Vain Honour nor the method of creating verbal images. His visualization resembles John Ridevall's *pictura* of Juno in the *Fulgentius metaforalis*[20] and is very close to Robert Holcot's *pictura* of Riches and Honour:

> Narrat Fulgentius & Homerus in scintillario poetarum quod status diuitiarum depingebatur vt mulier vaga, habens coronam in capite, oculis velata, sceptrum regale tenens & pauonem in manu, variis vestimentis induta, sedens in curru, quem trahebant quatuor leones truculenti et immanissimi.

> (Fulgentius and Homer in the *Anthology of the Poets*, say that the state of Riches used to be painted as a roving woman, wearing a crown on her head, with veiled eyes, holding a royal sceptre and a peacock in her hand, sitting in a chariot, which four ferocious and extremely savage lions draw.)[21]

Interestingly, though the elements of Johannes's *imago* are so close to Ridevall's and Holcot's pictures, it is clear that Johannes has not copied his image directly from either one of them. The wording is not exactly the same, Johannes gives the

by which he seems to mean sermons that incorporate exempla drawn from natural history (see also pp. 365, 368).

[19] *Sermones dormi secure de tempore*, Sermo 64, twenty-third Sunday. Dahmus notes that the sermon is labelled the twenty-third Sunday after Pentecost, but is really the twenty-third after Trinity Sunday (Dahmus, 'Lazy Preacher', p. 303 n. 12).

[20] *Fulg. meta.*, p. 88. See Chapter 6 for the Latin text and a translation of the picture.

[21] Holcot, *Liber moral. hist.*, no. 40 (p. 742). The *Scintillarius poetarum* refers to Mythographus Tertius, probably Alberic of London. See Smalley, *EFA*, p. 171 n. 4.

image a different title, and he includes an inscription in his picture that the other two examples lack.[22]

## *The 'Picture' Collections*

If one asks how the author of the *Dormi secure*, writing in Germany nearly a century after Holcot and Ridevall, came to incorporate an exemplum so similar to theirs into his sermons, one discovers a fascinating and still largely unexplored world of mendicant travel and preaching. To understand this process, it is necessary to look first at the texts through which these exempla travelled, and then the mechanisms by which they made it to the Continent.

We will begin with the texts. The major work on manuscripts of the picture collections has been done by Judson Allen and Nigel Palmer.[23] They point out that of the major picture collections (discussed in Chapter 6), only Holcot's *Moralitates* circulated widely on the Continent.[24] The earlier picture books, the *Fasciculus morum* and the *Fulgentius metaforalis*, exerted an indirect influence on the circulation of the pictures through excerpts of their work in exempla collections compiled from the English authors and from other, unknown contributors to the genre. The contents of the complete *Fulgentius metaforalis*,[25] the *Morali-*

[22] Another picture of Riches and Fortune, which is similar, though again not identical, to Johannes von Werden's, can be found in the picture collection contained in Biblioteca Apostolica Vaticana (BAV), MS Pal. lat. 1066, fol. 237$^{rb}$: 'Fulgencius et Honorius [...] statum diviciarum et fortunam sic describunt: Mulier vaga, facie velata, corornam habens in capite, sceptrum tenens in manu et in altera manu pavonem' (cited in *Fulg. meta.*, p. 53). The manuscript, which is one of the few to illustrate the *picturae*, includes a drawing of this *pictura* on fol. 236$^{v}$. It can also be viewed in *Fulg. meta.*, Abb. 14.

[23] Allen, 'Commentary as Criticism', pp. 25–33; idem, *Friar as Critic*, pp. 51–52; Palmer, '"Antiquitus depingebatur"', pp. 171–239; Palmer, 'Das "Exempelwerk"', pp. 137–72.

[24] If one examines the manuscripts of the *Moralitates* listed in Stegmüller's *Repertorium* of medieval biblical commentaries, those listed in the forward of Hans Liebeschütz's edition of the *Fulgentius metaforalis*, and those in Welter, *L'Exemplum*, one discovers over forty manuscripts of at least part of the text, only four of which are still in England (Stegmüller, *Repertorium*, v, 141; *Fulg. meta.*, pp. 49–53; Welter, *L'Exemplum*, p. 366 n. 63). The *Fulgentius metaforalis* was, according to Palmer, extremely rare on the Continent; see '"Antiquitus depingebatur"', p. 227 and n. 177. He lists only two Continental manuscripts: Trier, Stadtbibliothek, MS 1975/642 4° (sxv$^{2}$), and Berlin, Staatsbibliothek, Stiftung Preussischer Kulturbesitz, MS theologicus latinus quarto 159.

[25] The critical edition prepared by Liebeschütz in 1926 was based on one manuscript, Venice, Bibliotheca Nazionale Marciana, codex latinus I. 139, which contains only half of the material commonly associated with the work in the other eight surviving manuscripts. Liebeschütz considered the long recension an 'enlarged' version. Cod. lat. I. 139 also contains the Apocalypse

*tates*, and some pictures from *Fasciculus morum* were distilled into three exempla collections that circulated sometimes as one collection and sometimes separately.[26] The three most common incipits for these collections are *Imagines Fulgentii*, *De prudentia depingebatur* (or occasionally as *De quattuor virtutibus*), and *Refert Fulgentius de ornatu orbis*. They had their greatest impact in central Europe, as their manuscript circulation attests.[27] Their anonymous authors condensed the material from the original works into a standard formula of picture followed by a short moralization. There are at least eighty manuscripts of Continental provenance of these collections, testifying to the popularity of the pictures. In addition to these collections devoted solely to pictures, other exempla collections also include pictures among other types of exempla.[28]

Palmer has also noted that the *Moralitates* and the *Imagines Fulgentii* often travelled together with two other classicizing exempla collections: the *Enigmata Aristotelis moralizata* and the *Declamationes Senece moralizate*.[29] They are found together so often that he has examined the four together as a kind of exempla collection of its own. He also compared this extended collection to the *Gesta Romanorum*, noting that it has not been definitely proven whether its origins should be sought in England or in southern Germany.[30] Given the overlap in

fragments, which may have influenced the editor's decision: Allen, 'Commentary as Criticism', pp. 25–33; idem, *Friar as Critic*, pp. 51–52. Liebeschütz's decision to edit only those six chapters makes some sense, since there is a unity to material based on the parts of Prudence, but both recensions follow the proper order for a commentary on the original *Mythology* by Fulgentius, reflecting the order of its chapters.

[26] Palmer, '"Antiquitus depingebatur"', p. 176, groups all three collections under the title *Imagines Fulgentii* and notes that it could have three parts: 1) an abridgment of Ridevall's *Fulgentius metaforalis*; 2) picture descriptions of the four cardinal virtues, known as *De prudentia*; 3) picture descriptions of various virtues and vices with the most common incipit being *Refert Fulgentius de ornatu orbis*. The whole collection has fifty-three chapters and is found only in BnF, cod. lat. 590, and Bordeaux, Bibliothèque municipale, MS 267. He speculates that the larger collection was compiled from shorter ones with an independent existence. This seems to me the most likely scenario, especially since the separate collections each have their own incipit and explicit in BnF, cod. lat. 590.

[27] See Liebeschütz, 'Introduction', *Fulg. meta.*, pp. 49–53, for a list of manuscripts consulted in his edition, including those for the picture collections. See also Allen's additions to this list, 'Commentary as Criticism', pp. 25–38, and Palmer, '"Antiquitus depingebatur"', pp. 175–78.

[28] Rivers, 'Memory and the Mendicants', chap. 5.

[29] Palmer, 'Das "Exempelwerk" der englischen Bettelmönche', pp. 139–54.

[30] Palmer, 'Das "Exempelwerk" der englischen Bettelmönche', p. 132. For new research on the origins of the *Gesta Romanorum*, see Brigitte Weiske, 'Die "Gesta Romanorum" und das

contents of antique exempla between the earliest manuscript of the *Gesta Romanorum* and Holcot's *Moralitates*, an answer to this question could shed light on the circulation of these exempla on the Continent.

It is impossible to decide with certainty from which of the many potential sources Johannes drew in the *Dormi secure*. He often attributes his images and exempla to either the *Gesta Romanorum* or occasionally to a *Gesta Graecorum*.[31] He once refers to a *liber de picturis* (book about pictures) as his source for a story about a rich and powerful king who had two cities, one safely defended atop a high mountain and another besieged by enemies in a valley.[32] As the same exemplum is found in Holcot's *Moralitates*, it is possible that a version of that text was his source. Certainly, Holcot is the most likely candidate. In the 1498 Nürnberg edition of Johannes von Werden's *De tempore* series, I have counted eighteen *picturae* and exempla of the type utilized by the classicizing friars, of which twelve can be found in some form in Holcot's *Moralitates*.

Among the classicizing-type exempla that could not have come from Holcot, at least two are common to many homiletic works that otherwise show no particular interest in *picturae* or classicizing themes. These two *picturae* are the Wheel of Fortune and Justice as a blind man with no hands. Justice was one of the most common pictures in the genre and was generally depicted as either a blind girl or man (the female version is a little more common) and occasionally without hands.[33] The Wheel of Fortune is an even more recurrent image, found in both picture collections and manuscript illuminations. As a picture, some variant of a

"Solsequium" Hugos von Trimberg', in *Exempel und Exempelsammlungen*, ed. by Haug and Wachinger, pp. 173–207.

[31] Smalley notes that a number of fourteenth-century exempla are ascribed to a 'Flaccianus in gestis grecorum', and assumes that the work's author was one of a number of successful 'forgers' of the time (*EFA*, p. 238).

[32] Sermo 20, Dominica Letare, in Palmer, '"Antiquitus depingebatur"', p. 227, mentions one copy of the *Imagines Fulgentii* that names it a *liber de picturis* in its explicit, the only example he has found: 'Explicit liber de picturis diuersis diuersorum doctorum' (Prague, Státní knihovna, MS XII.B.20). Although I have not seen this manuscript, the particular exemplum that Johannes says he took from the *liber de picturis* is not usually found in the *Imagines Fulgentii*.

[33] For the source of the picture of Justice, see Palmer, '"Antiquitus depingebatur"', p. 180. Versions of the *picturae* of Justice can be found in the *Fasc. mor.*, p. 502; in MS Bodley 649, fol. 185$^{b}$; in BAV, MS Pal. lat. 1066, fol. 232$^{r}$; in Holcot's *Convertimini* (see Herbert, *Catalogue of Romances*, p. 119); in Basel, Universitätsbibliothek, MS A.X. 118; the *De prudentia* collection contained in BnF, cod. lat. 590, fols 177$^{r}$–178$^{r}$; and the Oesterley edition of the *Gesta Romanorum*.

woman turning a wheel with four men sitting on it is present in the *Fasciculus morum*, Holcot's *Commentary on the Twelve Prophets*, the collection of exempla in London, British Library, MS Harley 7322, and the *Gesta Romanorum*.[34] The image was just as common in manuscript illumination; for example, an almost exact replica of Johannes's image can be found in an early fifteenth-century manuscript of *Histoire ancienne*.[35] Bromyard even refers to a wall painting of Worldly Fortune in his *Summa praedicantium*.[36] Holcot may thus have been Johannes von Werden's main source, with additional input either from manuscript illumination or from his perusal of other exempla collections. Johannes was probably not above creating his own mnemonic pictures; he certainly had a better pictorial sense than even Holcot, adding details to exempla that he had lifted from other collections and illuminations.

Of the other four classicizing-type exempla not found in Holcot, only one is a *pictura*.[37] The other two are narratives similar to the ones found in Holcot's *Moralitates* and in the *Gesta Romanorum*. It is possible that Johannes von Werden composed these stories himself or that he drew them from sermon collections incorporating pictures.[38]

[34] *Fasc. mor.*, IV. 4, p. 332; Holcot's *Commentary on the Twelve Prophets*, MS Bodley 722 (SC 2648), fol. 91[v] (Smalley, *EFA*, p. 175); BL, MS Harley 7322, fol. 79[a].

[35] London, BL, MS Stowe 54, fol. 197. See Millard Meiss, *French Painting in the Time of Jean de Berry: The Limbourgs and their Contemporaries*, 2 vols (New York: Braziller, 1974), II, pl. 84, and I, 7, 25, 62–65.

[36] Bromyard, *Summa praedicantium*, s.v. 'Mundus'. See also s.v. 'Invidia', cited in Owst, *Literature and Pulpit in Medieval England*, p. 239.

[37] *Sermones dormi secure de tempore*, Sermo 3, third Sunday in Advent: 'Amor Mundi Quid sum discerne, cum scieris fugo et desideria sperne. | Recedo, scilicet a Deo cum amor me trahit per vinculum superbie. | Sum charus dum vivo quia mundus diligit quod suum est sed post mortem valde amarus est. | Ludo illudit enim hominem et in tantum decipit quod discernere verum nescit. | Excedo mentum et hoc patet de Salmone cuius mentem excessit amor munde.'

[38] Though there is every reason to think that exempla collections were used (and some concrete examples of how will be shown below), sermon and sermon collections demonstrate pictures being put to use. This is the area where the least amount of work has been done and is one reason why Johannes von Werden's *Dormi secure* is so important. It proves that the pictures were not mere curiosities, but were picked up by preachers and transmitted to people all over Germany through manuscripts and then through the many printed editions of the collection. Although I will focus here on Johannes, it should be noted that he was not the only German preacher to incorporate pictures into his sermons.

## *Scholastic Connections between England and Germany*

The second question to consider is how these exempla texts made it to the Continent, particularly to France and Germany.[39] In his dependence on English preaching sources, Johannes von Werden was not alone. In fact, it should not be in the least surprising to find a German Franciscan from Cologne utilizing the homiletic works of an English writer like Holcot in the mid-fourteenth or early fifteenth centuries. By doing so, Johannes was participating in the circulation of English intellectual thought in Germany at his time. As William Courtenay has shown, English scholars in theology and philosophy at Oxford entered a period of high creativity starting around 1315 and peaking in the decade from 1330 to 1340.[40] Their innovations in logic, physics, and theology had a great impact on the Continent in the fourteenth century.[41] The influence of English thought was felt not just at the University of Paris, where it would be most expected, but all over Europe, not least in Germany and Eastern Europe. Travelling scholars, especially mendicant scholars, helped spread English scholastic thought. The spread of the *picturae* can be seen as a subset of this movement, because they were transported to the Continent in the same manner as other English works.

As Courtenay explains, English ideas and manuscripts were carried to the Continent by the travel of English scholars abroad and by Continental scholars who studied in England for a while before returning home. The main places to find English students abroad in the fourteenth century were at the papal curia at Avignon, and at the University of Bologna.[42] Ties between Paris and Oxford, which had been very strong in the thirteenth century, began to diminish even before the outbreak of the Hundred Years' War.[43] Nevertheless, English scholastic works did arrive in Paris through other avenues, primarily through Scottish and Italian scholars who had previously studied in England.[44] So Avignon, Paris, and Bologna were places where one could find English works, presumably through the influence of English scholars and travellers themselves.

[39] Palmer, '"Antiquitus depingebatur"', p. 171 n. 3, noted that the reception of the works of the English friars in central Europe and Bohemia still awaits investigation.

[40] Courtenay, *Schools and Scholars*, p. 153.

[41] Courtenay, *Schools and Scholars*, p. 163.

[42] Courtenay, *Schools and Scholars*, p. 157.

[43] Courtenay, *Schools and Scholars*, p. 154.

[44] Courtenay, *Schools and Scholars*, pp. 164–67. He also mentions the influence of English Cistercians studying at the Collège St Bernard at Paris.

A German scholar in the fourteenth or early fifteenth century was probably most likely to encounter new English books and ideas through an institution of higher learning, and a number of different institutional options were available to such a scholar at this time. Because Germany had no universities of its own before the mid-fourteenth century, German students wishing an education in theology had become accustomed either to studying at schools for secular or religious clergy established in Germany or German-speaking lands or to travelling to foreign universities.[45] Until the end of the fourteenth century, Germans often chose to study at Paris, where they were in the same nation as English students. Presumably, English students could have shared their knowledge of the new developments in English thought with the other students in their nation. However, since the number of English scholars at Paris began to drop from the second and third decades of the fourteenth century, Paris was likely not the primary source of English-German contacts.[46]

Those scholars who chose to stay in German-speaking lands often gravitated to cities where schools for both secular and religious clergy were present. Such cities became important scholarly centres; Cologne is a good example. The Dominican *studium generale* there was one of the most important *studia* in the order: both Albertus Magnus and Thomas Aquinas taught there, while Duns Scotus was associated with Cologne's Franciscan convent.[47] English works of logic, physics, and theology were flowing into Germany and Italy as early as 1337, and Cologne, along with Erfurt, was one of the first centres in Germany to receive such works.[48] Assuming that Johannes was a Franciscan at the Cologne convent, he may well have been able to consult English works there.

One of the most plausible ways that English manuscripts and ideas found their way to German scholars and to places like Cologne is through the travel of German students to and from Oxford University. During the fourteenth century, Oxford saw an increase in the number of foreign students, most of whom were members of mendicant orders. They were mendicant because each of the major mendicant orders — the Dominicans, Franciscans, Carmelites, and Augustine

[45] Courtenay outlines the opportunities in the German clerical schools in 'The Role of English Thought in the Transformation of University Education in the Late Middle Ages', in *Rebirth, Reform and Resilience: Universities in Transition 1300–1700*, ed. by James M. Kittelson and Pamela J. Transue (Columbus: Ohio State University Press, 1984), pp. 103–62 (p. 138).

[46] Courtenay, *Schools and Scholars*, p. 158.

[47] Rashdall, *Universities in the Middle Ages*, II, 254–55.

[48] Courtenay, *Schools and Scholars*, p. 163.

Hermits — maintained a system of provincial *studia* and *studia generalia* for the purpose of training their friars in the lectorate programme of theology. In all of these orders, each province had the right to send two to three students to study theology or law at the orders' *studia generalia* in Paris, Oxford, and Bologna, among others. Most of these students never went on to take doctorates at these universities. Instead they went back to their home provinces to act as lectors in provincial *studia*.[49] In addition, before they advanced to the highest levels of scholarship, mendicants often studied at a variety of less highly ranked *studia* within their home provinces in order to learn logic, natural philosophy, and the like.[50] This picture of mendicant schooling indicates that manuscripts and ideas were probably even more mobile than scholars have previously imagined.

During much of the fourteenth century, the largest group of foreigners at Oxford was Italian, mostly Franciscan. By 1370, the number of students from Germany and Eastern Europe had nearly caught up to the number of Italians. Again, most of these students were friars studying at their orders' *studia* connected to the university.[51] Starting in the 1360s, Bohemian students attended Oxford and encountered works of English scholastics like John Wyclif. In the last

[49] William J. Courtenay, 'Study Abroad: German Students at Bologna, Paris, and Oxford in the Fourteenth Century', in *University and Schooling in Medieval Society*, ed. by William J. Courtenay, Jürgen Miethke, and David B. Priest, Education and Society in the Middle Ages and Renaissance, 10 (Leiden: Brill, 2000), pp. 7–31 (pp. 15–17); William J. Courtenay, 'The Instructional Programme of the Mendicant Convents at Paris in the Early Fourteenth Century', in *The Medieval Church: Universities, Heresy, and Christian Life: Essays in Honour of Gordon Leff*, ed. by Peter Biller and Barrie Dobson, Studies in Church History, Subsidia 11 (Woodbridge: Boydell and Brewer, 1999), pp. 77–92. For an overview of the Dominican *studia*, see M. Michèle Mulchahey and Timothy B. Noone, 'Religious Orders', in *A Companion to Philosophy in the Middle Ages*, ed. by Jorge J. E. Garcia and Timothy B. Noone, Blackwell Companions to Philosophy, 24 (Malden, MA: Blackwell, 2003), pp. 45–54; Mulchahey, *'First the Bow is Bent in Study'*; Mulchahey, 'The Dominican *Studium*-System and the Universities of Europe in the Thirteenth Century: A Relationship Redefined', in *Manuels, programmes de cours et techniques d'enseignement dans les universités médiévales: Actes du Colloque international de Louvain-la-Neuve (9–11 septembre 1993)*, ed. by Jacqueline Hamesse (Louvain-la-Neuve: Institut d'études médiévales de l'Université Catholique de Louvain, 1994), pp. 277–324. For the Franciscan schools, see Mulchahey and Noone, 'Religious Orders', and Roest, *History of Franciscan Education*.

[50] See his description of the Franciscan *studia* in Germany; William J. Courtenay, 'The Franciscan studia in Southern Germany in the Fourteenth Century', in *Gesellschaftsgeschichte: Festschrift für Karl Bosl zum 80. Geburtstag*, ed. by Ferdinand Seibt, 2 vols (Munich: Oldenbourg, 1988), II, 81–90.

[51] Courtenay, *Schools and Scholars*, pp. 159–60.

two decades of the fourteenth century Oxford's foreign population was affected by ecclesiastical politics. Because of the Great Schism and the subsequent siding of nations with either the pope in Rome or Avignon, after 1382 neither German nor Italian students could attend Paris. Many Italian students who had been studying in Paris went home, while German authorities became much more rigorous about founding their own universities. Some of both groups went to Oxford, further increasing their numbers at the university.[52]

Mendicant *studia* thus provided an important communications link between England and the Continent. *Studia* within Germany were receptive of English ideas and could provide a place for German scholars to consult new texts. German and Italian friars also studied at Oxford and then took home ideas, and perhaps more importantly, manuscripts that they and their confrères could consult.

Courtenay's main objective in laying out this picture of foreign study at Oxford is to show how English innovations in logic, philosophy, and theology were translated to the Continent. But for our purposes it should be noted that another genre of literature, homiletic works, was carried to the Continent through the same process. As Smalley's work on the classicizing friars demonstrates, the early fourteenth century in England was an innovative period in the production of biblical commentaries and preaching aids.[53] The English friars made ancient literature and mythology a part of biblical studies and preaching, at least for a time. One of their number, Robert Holcot, was writing both biblical commentaries and the kind of theological works that Courtenay describes. Holcot was a well-known name in the late Middle Ages for his nominalist theological positions and for his *Wisdom* Commentary, a late medieval best-seller. The fame of his other writings may have recommended his *Moralitates*. It is certainly not surprising that mendicants, with their obvious interest in preaching and pastoral theology, should return from a study-tour in England with

[52] Courtenay, *Schools and Scholars*, pp. 160–61.

[53] As is shown in Smalley, *EFA*. With respect to biblical commentaries, both Smalley and Courtenay note a resurgence across Europe in the number of commentaries from 1310 (Courtenay thinks it began a bit earlier) to *c.* 1350 after a slump in their production in the last decades of the thirteenth century and the first decade of the fourteenth. The increasing interest in biblical studies at this time was most marked among mendicants, and not just at Paris and Oxford, but across Europe. Holcot's work on Wisdom was part of this new effort: Smalley, 'The Bible in the Medieval Schools', in *The Cambridge History of the Bible*, II: *The West from the Fathers to the Reformation*, ed. by Geoffrey William Hugo Lampe (Cambridge: Cambridge University Press, 1969), pp. 197–220 (p. 207); *EFA*, pp. 30–32; Courtenay, 'Bible in the Fourteenth Century', pp. 183–84. See also Smalley, 'Problems of Exegesis', pp. 266–74.

manuscripts of homiletic works along with the new works of English logic and theology, especially when they were written by the same person. Holcot's *Moralitates*, his Wisdom commentary, and his commentary on Ecclesiasticus circulated widely on the Continent, especially in Germany and Eastern Europe, in the fourteenth and fifteenth centuries;[54] Thomas Ringstead's commentary on Proverbs and John Bromyard's *Summa praedicantium* also maintained a respectable circulation in the same areas.[55] Some of these texts were very likely taken there by the same mendicants that Courtenay identifies.

## *The Career of Johannes Sintram, A German Franciscan*

This picture need not be a matter for speculation, since we can actually trace the career of a German friar from the fifteenth century who studied in both English and German schools and who copied English manuscripts for a German audience. Johannes Sintram († 1450), a Franciscan from Würzburg, transcribed the *Fasciculus morum* for himself and copied over thirty-five *Moralitates*-type (Type II) pictures into an exempla collection contained in London, British Library, MS Additional 44055.[56] Sintram was born in Würzburg around 1380, was the son of burgher parents, and entered the Franciscan order in his home city around 1400.[57]

[54] Stegmüller, *Repertorium*, V, 141–49, no. 7416, lists twenty-three printed editions and over one hundred manuscripts of Holcot's commentary on Wisdom; he also notes eleven manuscripts of Holcot's commentary on Ecclesiasticus (no. 7421). Eight remain in German-speaking countries and central Europe, one is in Italy, and two are in England.

[55] Smalley, *EFA*, p. 215; Stegmüller, *Repertorium*, V, 371–72, no. 8172, lists twenty-one surviving manuscripts of Ringstead's commentary on Proverbs. Ten of these manuscripts are in German, Dutch, or central European libraries, four are in Rome, and seven are in English libraries.

[56] A colophon notes the compiler: 'these things were written in Reutlingen by brother Johannes Sintram, lector there in the year of our Lord 1415'; *British Museum Catalogue of Additions to the Manuscripts 1931–35* (London: Trustees of the British Museum, 1967), pp. 286–87, fol. 117: 'Haec scripta sunt in Rutlinga [Reutlingen, in Würtenberg] per fratrem Iohannem Sintram lectorem ibidem sub Anno domini M°ccccxv°'.

[57] Nigel F. Palmer, 'Sintram, Johannes OFM', *Die deutsche Literatur des MA*, ed. by Ruh and others, VIII, 1284. Overviews of Sintram's career may also be found in the following articles: Dorothy K. Coveney, 'Johannes Sintram de Herbipoli', *Speculum*, 16 (1941), 336–39; Theodore C. Petersen, 'Johs. Sintram de Herbipoli in Two of his MSS', *Speculum*, 20 (1945), 73–83; P. Ludger Meier, 'Aufzeichnungen aus vernichteten Handschriften des Würzburger Minoritenklosters', *AFH*, 44 (1951), 191–209 (pp. 204–08); *BRO*, III, 1703. See also Rivers, 'Memory and the Mendicants', pp. 223–26. Finally, a very useful online guide to the literature on Sintram and

We can trace much of Sintram's subsequent activity through personal comments written in the remains of sixty-one manuscripts amassed, and probably copied, by Sintram himself.[58] His comments reveal that he led a truly peripatetic lifestyle, studying at several Franciscan convents within the province of the Upper Rhine of the Franciscan order, including Regensburg, Ulm, and Strasbourg, the *studium generale* of the province. He was then at Oxford in 1412. From 1415 until at least 1425 he served as lector in a number of convents in the order, both within and without his home province.[59] These convents include Reutlingen, Cologne, Schwäbisch Hall, Paris, Augsburg, Colmar, and Esslingen. He was guardian of the convent in Würzburg in 1437 and died there in 1450.[60] Before he died, he made a gift of sixty-one manuscripts to the library of the Würzburg convent.

Sintram's career indicates that he came into contact with English homiletic collections in England itself. Two manuscripts point to a stay in Oxford. The rear cover of New York, Morgan Library and Museum, MS 298 declares that 'this book is entitled *Fasciculus morum* and was written in England at Oxford by brother Johannes Sintram of Würzburg'. Two other notes within the same manuscript add that he was studying at Oxford and that the date of the copy was 1412.[61]

on other Franciscan authors is Maarten van der Heijden and Bert Roest, 'Franciscan Authors, 13th–18th Century: A Catalogue in Progress', <http://users.bart.nl/~roestb/franciscan/> [accessed 9 February 2010].

[58] According to a note (not in Sintram's hand) in London, BL, MS Additional 30,049, fol. 96v, Sintram donated sixty-one volumes to the Franciscan library in Würzburg in 1444: 'frater johannes Sintram librum istum posuit hic ad librariam herbippolensem et cum hoc sexaginta volumina hic in quatuor pulpeta convenienter posita quod factum est anno 1444 post festum sancti valentini' (Coveney, 'Johannes Sintram', p. 336 n. 4).

[59] The manuscript notes give us an overview of his scholastic career: in 1403–04, he studied at Regensburg (Meier 204); in 1405 at Ulm, in 1408 at Strasbourg, in 1412 at Oxford. After studying in England, Sintram served as lector at Reutlingen in 1415, at Halle in Swabia in 1416, at Colmar in 1421, at Esslingen in 1422, and then returned to Würzburg by 1425. He donated his library to the Würzburg convent in 1444 and remained there until his death in 1450. Emden summarizes the biographical information gleaned from the various manuscript notations, *BRO*, III, 1703.

[60] Palmer, 'Sintram', p. 1284.

[61] Coveney, 'Johannes Sintram', p. 337 n. 4: 'liber iste intytulatur fasciculus morum et est scriptus in anglia oxoniis per fratrem johannem Sinntram de herbippoli. Fol. 2r: librum istum scripsit frater johannes Sinttram dum erat studens oxoniis'. Petersen, 'Johs. Sintram', p. 73, notes that fol. 169v reads, 'librum ipsum scripsit frater Johannes Sinttram oxoniis, anno 1412' (not in Sintram's hand). He also observes that the title of Morgan Library and Museum, MS 298 is on the rear cover of the manuscript, not on 'the inside front cover', as Coveney cited.

An entry in Leeds, University Library, Brotherton Collection, MS 102 says that 'Johannes Sintram wrote this book';[62] another reference within the same manuscripts reveals that Sintram preached in Oxford in 1412.[63] From this information we know that Sintram studied in England in 1412 and that he not only read *Fasciculus morum*, the earliest known picture book, but actually made a copy of it for himself.[64]

In fact, when Sintram needed to compose a new sermon, one of the first books he reached for was the *Fasciculus morum*. The manuscript of his sermon outlines directs the reader to finish a sermon so: '[H]ere apply, if you wish, an example about mercy, *concerning the spiritual house*, namely *on the soul or conscience*. Look in the *fasciculus morum*.'[65] Sintram found the *Fasciculus* such a useful resource that he kept the book in his possession for at least the ten to fifteen years of his scholarly career that he spent at Reutlingen, Hall, Colmar, and Esslingen.[66] During this time, he added a second subject index to his copy of the work and numerous cross-references and annotations.[67] Indeed an exempla collection in BL, MS Add. 44055, written in 1415 in Reutlingen, has a cross-reference to Sintram's own copy of the *Fasciculus*.[68]

One could ask what Sintram found so compelling about this preacher's handbook. As we have seen, two of the *Fasciculus morum*'s distinctive features are verbal pictures of virtues and vices placed within an antique setting, and verses, in both Latin and Middle English, which occasionally appear as 'inscriptions' within the pictures. An example of one of the handbook's pictures with both Latin and

[62] Coveney, 'Johannes Sintram', p. 337: 'Librum istum scripsit Iohannes Sinttram de herbipoli'; see also Neil Ripley Ker, *Medieval Manuscripts in British Libraries*, 5 vols (Oxford: Clarendon Press, 1969–2002), III, 65.

[63] Ker, *Medieval Manuscripts*, III, 63–64: 1) 'Explicit Hugo venerabilis de vanitate mundi script' anno m° cccc xii° in anglia'; 5) 'Sermo ad clerum in concepcione virginis quem predicaui Oxoniis M° cccc° xii° Iohannes Sintram'.

[64] Notes contained in two sermons found in the manuscript of the *Fasciculus morum* (Morgan Library and Museum, MS 298) indicate that he was still revising the manuscript's contents in 1423 and 1426: Petersen, 'Johs. Sintram', p. 73.

[65] Petersen, 'Johs. Sintram', pp. 76–77. Folio 150r of the Brotherton manuscript advises the preacher to end a sermon on evil thoughts with material from the *Fasciculus morum*: 'Item materiam applica in fasciculo morum folio 2° ibi contra malas cogitaciones'; Ker, *Medieval Manuscripts*, III, 64.

[66] Petersen, 'Johs. Sintram', p. 75.

[67] Petersen, 'Johs. Sintram', p. 75; Wenzel, *Verses in Sermons*, p. 22.

[68] Wenzel, *Verses in Sermons*, p. 22 n. 49.

Middle English verses is 'Prayer'. 'In ancient times, Prayer is said to have been depicted, by the commentator Juvenal, as a most beautiful man with a body of fire, his head lifted to heaven, leaning on a straight and tall lance, and supported by four angels who held scrolls in their hands which expressed the qualities of prayer':

Terris, igne, mari, ventis peto dominari.

Anglice sic:

Fyre, watur, wynd and lond
Y wylne to haue in my honde.

In secundo:

Vir, pete, sum presto; si plangas, cercior esto.

Anglice sic:

Byd faste and Y come sone;
Yf þow sorow, þe tyt þy bone.[69]

(Lands and fire, sea and winds I strive to rule.

In English:

Fire, water, wind, and land
Firmly I wish to have in hand.

On the second:

Pray, I am at your will: if you weep, you may be more sure.

In English:

Fast you pray, and I come soon,
If you are sorry, you get your boon.)

It is clear that Sintram was entranced by both picture and verse. Sintram's encounter with the *Fasciculus*'s pictures may have stimulated his interest in the genre, for the first collection of exempla that he copied out in BL, MS Add. 44055 boasts over thirty. He could have found only four of these in the Franciscan preaching manual, and thus needed other sources; one of these was likely Holcot's *Moralitates*, for there is an overlap of ten pictures as well as several other

[69] *Fasc. mor.*, V.20, pp. 520–23. 'Fertur autem quod antiquis temporibus a commentatore Iuvenali Oracio depingebatur ad modum hominis pulcherrimi habentis corpus igneum et capud in celum erectum, super unam lanceam rectam et altissimam, cum quatuor angelis illam supportantibus et rotul<u>m in manibus singulis tenentibus codicem condiciones Oracionis continentem'; trans. by Wenzel, pp. 521, 523.

non-picture exempla with the Basel edition.[70] Interestingly, on the back cover of MS Add. 44055 is a vellum label which reads: 'Narraciones miracula et exempla multa et ymagines fulgencii et diversa documenta cum tabula decretalium et cetera videlicet'.[71] Although there is very little overlap between the pictures in Sintram's collection and those found in most of the incarnations of the *Imagines Fulgentii*, it could be that the fluidity of the *Imagines* collection (which both Palmer and Allen have noted) caused contemporary observers to consider all picture collections *Imagines Fulgentii*.[72]

Versifying in both Latin and German also appealed to Sintram, as can be seen in the things he chose to copy down. Theodore Petersen points out that fifteen pages of the Morgan manuscript have German translations of Latin verses in the text. A method of combining his two loves was bound to be a hit: MS Add. 44055 has a number of *picturae* with German translations of the Latin verses in the exempla. For instance, Sintram's collection includes a picture of Humility found also in Holcot's *Moralitates*. Humility is figured as a man with downcast head. Each hand and foot is supported by a wing, as is his breast. On each wing is written a Latin verse, for which Sintram appends a German translation. He also includes German translations of Latin verses in *Fasciculus morum*.[73] His sense of the mnemonic possibilities of verse can also be seen in the inclusion of verses for the *tituli* of Pope Gregory IX's five books of the Decretals contained in MS Add. 44055.[74]

Johannes Sintram thus fits the profile of a German friar and scribe who studied at a number of Franciscan *studia* both within and outside his home province of Upper Swabia. Like most friars, his education included arts subjects, such as

[70] Other sources Sintram may have used are the *Conuertimini*, possibly also by Holcot (see Smalley, *EFA*, p. 147 and Herbert, *Catalogue of Romances*, pp. 116–36) and the *Gesta Romanorum*. See *British Museum Catalogue of Additions to the Manuscripts*, pp. 279–83.

[71] The *British Museum Catalogue of Additions to the Manuscripts*, p. 287, records the title as 'Narraciones [...] ymagines fulgences' (Stories [...] glittering images). It seems very likely that someone copied down *Fulgentii* incorrectly.

[72] When contemporary observers did not attribute picture collections to Fulgentius, they often considered them *Moralitates* by Holcot. Liebeschütz's list of manuscripts reveals that many picture books were called Holcot's *Moralitates* that were not actually written by him.

[73] Wenzel, *Verses in Sermons*, p. 22; Petersen, 'Johs. Sintram', p. 81, transcribes two of Sintram's translations of the *Fasciculus*'s verses, which may be compared to Wenzel's edition, pp. 314, 316.

[74] *British Museum Catalogue of Additions to the Manuscripts*, p. 286.

dialectic and philosophy, as well as theology.[75] He encountered English homiletic works in England itself and probably in Germany. While in England he became particularly entranced with the works of the classicizing friars and copied the *Fasciculus morum* for his own use. When he returned to Germany, he continued to take an interest in mnemonic pictures, copying a number of them into one exempla collection. That in Germany he could compile an exempla collection filled with English *picturae* implies either that he still had access to books with such pictures in them or that he copied the pictures down from memory. Sintram also regularly translated verses into the vernacular, presumably to aid preachers and listeners. His fascination with the pictures and with English preaching materials and his constant travels demonstrate how the English pictures could make their way to Germany. What remains to be examined is what his Franciscan confrères did with such exempla once they read collections like his. Johannes von Werden's *Dormi secure* provides a fine example of how the classicizing *picturae* were used in sermons once they had escaped from the confines of exempla collections. Although I will focus here on Johannes, it should be noted that he was not the only German preacher to incorporate pictures into his sermons. More can be found in collections by Johannes Herolt, Geiler von Kaiserberg, Konrad Grütsch, 'Meffreth', and the collection known as *Parati sermones*.[76] My main interest here is to show how Johannes von Werden used the exempla in his sermons.

[75] Meier, 'Aufzeichnungen aus vernichteten Handschriften', pp. 204–08, lists the manuscripts donated by Sintram to the Würzburg convent. Naturally many of these contain sermons, the homiletic works we have already discussed, and other works of theology, but a number contain dialectic and philosophical treatises as well. For example, Würzburg, Bibliothek des Minoritenklosters, cod. I. 51, which has a note saying that the Sintram used it, contains works on both the old and the new logic, as well as *Questiones de generatione et corruptione* and *Questiones de caelo et mundo*, p. 207. In addition, London, University College Library, Cod. 4 contains a work on dialectic, as well as a commentary and 'exercise' on the *Summulae logicorum* of Petrus Hispanus, and logical works by Petrus Zech, 'De Pulka', of the University of Vienna, which were written by Sintram at Ulm and dated 1405. See Meier, 'Aufzeichnungen aus vernichteten Handschriften', p. 205.

[76] Schneyer, *Geschichte der katholischen Predigt*, p. 230. For other examples of pictures used in German preaching see a very useful article that I received too late to incorporate into the book: Nigel F. Palmer, 'Bacchus und Venus: Mythographische Bilder in der Welt des späten Mittelalters; Mit einem Textanhang', in *Literatur und Wandmalerei*, II: *Konventionalität und Konversation*, ed. by Eckart Conrad Lutz, Johanna Thali, and René Wetzel (Tübingen: Niemeyer, 2005), pp. 189–235.

## *Johannes von Werden's Preaching Method*

Though Owst found the sermons in *Dormi secure* dreary, the charge that these sermons contributed to lazy and uninspired preaching is unfair. Rather, the author of these sermons was extremely solicitous to ensure that the listeners of his sermons remembered the gist of the moral teachings they heard. Each sermon in the *De tempore* collection follows a regular plan of a quotation of the day's theme, a pro-theme, a lengthy reading of the pericope, a division of the theme into parts (usually four), a development of the theme's parts, and an extremely brief conclusion. While Johannes's compositions are no more detailed expositions of the biblical reading than most other late medieval sermons, his lengthy scriptural quotations did mean that listeners potentially could hear the Word translated into the vernacular. This is a tricky matter, because we can never be sure whether or not these sermons were actually preached, and if they were, how close was the relationship between the live version and the extent text. Still, it seems fair to conclude that in his consistent use of long quotations Johannes was anxious for his listeners to hear the scriptural text.[77]

What was it in his sermons that Johannes von Werden was so concerned that his listeners remember and understand? As a good Franciscan, Johannes often reminded his listeners of the need for penitence and confession.[78] Equally frequent themes of his sermons were the need for Christians to lead a moral life and the need to understand the basic ceremonies and functions of the church. An emphasis on moral behaviour was hardly unique to Johannes's pastoral mission. In his *Summa de arte praedicandi* the English cleric Thomas of Chobham addressed the topic of what ought to be preached to Christians. In his view

> It is well known that preaching ought to be about faith and good works or morals and about their opposites, namely it should be about the virtues and vices. For a preacher ought not to preach anything except the things that make a person better. For we can teach knowledge but not preach. But if any matters are touched on in a sermon besides the virtues and vices, this is teaching [*lectio*] and not preaching. For this reason, a preacher ought to reflect carefully lest he confuse these things, that he not teach as if lecturing when he ought to be preaching or that he not be merely preaching when he ought to be lecturing [*quando legendum est*].[79]

[77] In his comparison of Johannes von Werden's sermons with those by Johannes Herolt († 1468) and Johannes Nider († 1438), Dahmus noted that considerably more of Werden's sermons were devoted to the reading of the pericope than the sermons of the other friars ('Lazy Preacher', p. 315).

[78] Moorman, *History of the Franciscan Order*, pp. 272–77.

[79] *Summa de arte*, p. 143: 'Secundum ordinem prenotatum, restat uidere de quibus sit predicandum. Et constat quod de fide et bonis operibus uel moribus et eorum contrariis, scilicet de

Thomas, writing in the early thirteenth century, was a student of Petrus Cantor. Petrus and his circle of students in Paris at the end of the twelfth century desired to reform the morals of the clergy and laity throughout Christendom.[80] Their teaching had a great effect on reform-minded church leaders like Innocent III. Though Thomas was not a contemporary of Johannes von Werden or even a Franciscan, Johannes and most Franciscans could not have followed Thomas's advice any more closely than if they had written the passage themselves. Their job was less to teach doctrine than how to avoid vice and cultivate virtue. Johannes's themes are penitence and confession, virtue and vice, and the role of the church in these activities.

## *Mnemonic Exempla*

Often, Johannes von Werden's method of cultivating knowledge of virtue and vice, penitence and confession is the inclusion in his sermons of exempla that are specifically mnemonic. The pictures found in Johannes's sermons and in the works of the classicizing friars are probably examples of the kind of simplified mnemonic practice described by Francesc Eiximenis (see Chapter 4). The images are not only memorable as a whole but also provide 'places' within themselves for short speeches or inscriptions. In order to analyse Johannes's exempla, I have divided them into two groups: the 'classicizing' (Type II) and the 'devotional/scriptural'. The classicizing exempla are *Amor mundi*, *Vanus honor*, *Mutatio mundi* (the Wheel of Fortune), *Vera penitentia* as a knight, *Superbia* as a devil with three crowns, *Dilectio* as a youth clothed in green, *Peccatum mortale*, *Iusticia* as a blind man with no hands, *Humilitas*, *Honor mundi*, and *Pentitencia* as a nude man with a scourge.[81] The devotional/scriptural pictures are the fingers of the hand

uirtutibus et uitiis. Non enim debet predicator aliqua predicare nisi ea unde homo melior fiat. Docere enim possumus scientiam, sed non predicare. Si autem de aliis agatur in sermone quam de uirtutibus et uitiis, lectio est, non predicatio. Vnde debet predicator considerare ne ista confundat, scilicet ne legat quasi lectionem quando predicandum est, uel ne tantum predicet quando legendum est. Melius tamen est miscere predicationem lectioni quam lectionem predicationi.'

80 Franco Morenzoni, *Des Écoles aux paroisses: Thomas de Chobham et la promotion de la prédication au début du XIIIe siècle*, Collection des études augustiniennes, Série moyen âge et temps modernes, 30 (Paris: Institut d'études augustiniennes, 1995), p. 67. See also Baldwin, *Masters, Princes and Merchants*, and Smalley, *Study of the Bible*, chap. 5.

81 I have also found seven other 'classicizing-type' exempla that do not include pictures: a king with two sons, one lives in a valley (*Moral.* 2); a woman runs off with tyrant, receives four rings

moralized as parts of five virtues, the image of a sinner, St Macharius imagining the virtues crucifying Christ, choirs of angels, and the heavenly Jerusalem.

By labelling one group of exempla 'classicizing', I do not mean to imply that they have no Christian content, only that these exempla have an antique setting that the other group lacks. Johannes moralizes the classical pictures as virtues and vices and nearly all of them can be found in the exempla collections of classicizing friars like Holcot. The devotional/scriptural examples pertain to the virtues and vices, to the formation of conscience, and to scriptural imagery. All but the St Macharius example are of a type found in many medieval sermons, even when the wording is not exactly the same.

To see how Johannes von Werden incorporated mnemonic exempla into his sermons, I would like first to examine one instance of each type and then explore larger questions about mnemonic exempla in late medieval preaching. We can begin with a sermon written for the fourth Sunday after Easter on the theme 'And when he is come, he will convince the world of sin, and of justice, and of judgement' (John 16. 8).[82] His protheme picks up the phrase 'convince the world of sin', declaring that anyone who wants to accuse another ought to consider four things: whether he whom he plans to blame ought to be blamed; whether he whom he wishes to accuse ought not to be contradicted; whether the timing is appropriate; whether he whom he plans to blame might be made worse by criticism. His elaboration of these considerations leads him back to a rereading of the gospel pericope and finally to the theme, 'And when he is come, he will convince the world of sin'. Johannes explains that by 'the world' is understood 'human being' (*homo*), for just as the greater world is composed of the four elements, so is a human, who is called a small world (*mundus minor*). The flesh and bones of the human body are from the earth, its blood comes from water, its breath is from air, and the body's natural warmth comes from fire. Christ will accuse humans on four matters which are touched on in the Gospel: one, for not believing in God; two, for committing sins; three, for not seeking justice; and four, for not fearing judgement.

As befits a medieval preacher, Johannes fleshes out each division of the theme. The second division concerns us here, as the author uses a Roman picture of

from her prince (*Moral.* 24); a king with two sons, one good, one evil; a king with a merciful son; dolphins and north wind (*Moral.* 36); a Greek story, Christ as fighter/king's daughter elopes (*Moral.* 7); a large mountain, fountain in India (*Moral.* 20).

[82] 'Conuenerit ille arguet et mundum', *Dormi secure de tempore*, Sermo 32, on the third Sunday after the octave of Easter.

Mortal Sin to structure and explain his contention that Christ will censure those who commit the sin of denying God. He reminds his listeners that God dealt severely with Cain when he killed his brother, and with Adam, when he ate the apple. How much more severely, then, will he deal with those who abandon and deny God, their creator, which a sinner does through mortal sin. Here he adduces a picture as proof of the heinous nature of sin. The Romans painted Sin in a horribly arranged picture of a man:

> Sicut legimus de Romanis quod depingebant peccatum mortale ad imaginem hominis que erat valde horribilis disposita. Circa quam stabant quatuor imagines. Vna imago supra caput et erat hec imago dei, ad quam ait: 'Deum meum negavi: heu mihi quod natus sum'. Ad dexteram stetit imago pulcerrimi hominis ad quam ait, 'Dignitatem humane conditionis non cognoui. Ve mihi quod natus sum'. Ad imaginem sinistram et hec erat imago diaboli, ad quam ait: 'homagium diabolo feci. Heu mihi quod natus sum'. Infra infernus aperiens os suum et expectans ad devorandum ad modum draconis.[83]

> (Around which were standing four other images. One image stood above his head, and this was the image of God, to which he (the image of Mortal Sin) said: 'I have denied my God. Alas that I was born'. To the right stood the image of a very beautiful man, to which he said: 'I did not know the dignity of the human condition. Woe is me that I was born'. To the image on his left, which was the image of the devil, he said: 'I paid homage to the devil. Woe is me that I was born'. Below was hell opening its mouth and waiting to devour in the mode of a dragon.)

Johannes declares that the picture of the Romans certainly pertains to his teaching, for 'when a sinner in mortal sin denies God above, he trembles'.

Several points should be made about Johannes von Werden's use of this mnemonic image. First of all, it, like his other classical images, is borrowed from another source, likely Holcot's *Moralitates*. Holcot's picture is not identical to Johannes's:

> Varro depinxit peccatum ad similitudinem Deae, cuius ponebantur tres imagines. Prima fuit imago Dei; secunda fuit imago Diaboli; tertia fuit imago hominis. Et ista imago vnicuique imagini vnam literam siue chartam porrigebat. Et tenor chartae primae Deo exhibitae, iste erat: Deum cum suis angelis finaliter amisi, vae quod natus fui. Secunda charta directa Diabolo sic erat: Diabolo et eius angelis imaginem feci, quando per consensum in peccatum cecidi. Charta scripta homini talis erat. Verecundia et confusio est finis peccati, declinans in peccato finaliter confundetur, et cetera.

> (Varro painted Sin in the likeness [*similitudo*] of a goddess, around whom were placed three images. The first was the image of God, the second was the image of the Devil, the third was the image of a man. And this image of the goddess offered to each image a letter

[83] Johannes von Werden, *Dormi secure de tempore*, Sermo 32.

> or document. And the tenor of the first document given to God was this: 'I lost God with his angels to the very end; woe is me that I was born'. The second document directed to the Devil was so: 'I made the image[84] to the Devil and his angels, when I murdered through consent to sin'. The document written for the man was such: 'shameful and confusing is the end of sin, turning aside into sin he is at last confounded'.)[85]

Rather than attributing the picture vaguely to the 'Romans', as Johannes does, Holcot attributes it to Varro. In addition, Holcot's main figure is a woman rather than a man, and she hands letters with sayings written on them to the surrounding images, whereas Johannes's image of Sin speaks for himself. On the whole, Johannes's picture simplifies the message conveyed in Holcot's and makes it more accessible to a sermon audience. Johannes's addition of the dragon's mouth of hell to Holcot's initial scene also clarifies the picture's point. The dragon as mouth of hell is a very common element in judgement and Harrowing of Hell scenes in manuscript illuminations, so Johannes is hardly exhibiting artistic daring in adding the extra detail. Still, the dragon shows a dependence on contemporary art that is often lacking in mnemonic pictures.[86]

A second point is that both pictures serve the same basic mnemonic function of structuring the discussion of one division of a sermon (or, in Holcot's case, of the moralization that follows the picture). By recalling the elements of the picture and the speech of the sinner, Johannes von Werden has everything he needs to make up part of the sermon. All he needs to do is explain what each element means, remembering to treat the image of God first and that of the dragon last. The picture is thus a very useful tool for the preacher and likely one reason for the popularity of 'picture collections'.

But this image is also mnemonically useful to the listener (or to the reader) of a sermon. A listener hearing about Christ judging sinners for denying God could recall the image of a man surrounded by the figure of God, a beautiful man, the devil, and the open mouth of a dragon, waiting to devour the sinner. The listener of this version of the picture might recall the scene by projecting himself/herself into it as speaker of the forlorn lines. Notably, Johannes's image of sin speaks to

[84] The Basel edition of Holcot's *Moralitates* reads 'Diabolo & eius angelis imaginem feci' in the picture, but 'facit homagium Diabolo' in the moralization of the picture. The second reading obviously makes more sense, especially in light of Johannes's version of the picture.

[85] Holcot, *Liber moral. hist.*, pp. 734–35.

[86] Smalley comments on how hard many of Ridevall's and Holcot's pictures are to depict visually, *EFA*, pp. 112–13, 166; Saxl, 'Spiritual Encyclopaedia', p. 102, and Saxl, 'Aller Tugenden', pp. 104–21. Palmer, '"Antiquitus depingebatur"', p. 192, notes that some *picturae* of Death are easier to visualize than others, and that a few show signs of influence from contemporary art.

the images of God, Christ, and the Devil. In other versions, including Holcot's, the goddess, whom one author calls 'the Goddess of the nether regions' (*dea infernalium*), hands the surrounding images signs with inscriptions longer than Johannes's speeches on them.[87] Both methods carry a mnemonic punch, but Johannes's has a more dramatic quality in which a hearer could participate.[88] Jody Enders has seen all mnemonics as a kind of mental theater; Johannes's gives us a more specific example of theatrical possibilities.[89]

Finally, Johannes's picture of Mortal Sin is frightening. Indeed, I would argue that Johannes's picture of Mortal Sin is more likely to convey the dread of hell and judgement than Holcot's. Johannes says that sinners tremble, as well they might if looking at a picture containing both the devil and a dragon.[90] As modern commentators on medieval mnemonics like Carruthers and Enders have noted, mnemonic images could be violent or frightening, a point many people overlook.[91]

[87] Other examples of Mortal Sin can be found in *Imagines Fulgentii* in BnF, cod. lat. 590, fol. 101ᵛ; BL, MS Harley 2316, fol. 25ᵃ. Wenzel, *Verses in Sermons*, p. 75 n. 80, lists a picture of Sin in Cambridge, University Library, MS Kk.IV.24, fol. 187ʳ. In the Harley manuscript, the picture is described very briefly but a long verse in Middle English has been added. In the Paris manuscript, the image is closer to Holcot's than to Johannes's, though again it is not exactly the same: 'Capitulum 10: Peccatum mortale aput antiquos depingebatur stabat vna regina tremens continue et vocabatur dea infernalium. In cuius circuitu ponebantur tres ymagines, scilicet ymago Dei, ymago dyaboli, et ymago hominis. Et quelibet ymago tenebat vnam cedulam quas ymaginibus predictis porrigebat. Vnam scilicet Dei: "Saluatorem meum perdidi et omnes angelos eius. Ve, ve, ve quid natus sum". In carta ad dyabolum porrecta, sic continebatur: "dyabolo et angelis eius ymaginem feci, quando in peccatum per consensum cecidi". Carta directa homini talis erat: "Omnia mala hominis, omnis tribulatio, finis meus. Hoc solum cupio, vt si quis diligit me hic innotescat."'

[88] Palmer, '"Antiquitus depingebatur"', p. 188, describes the same process of change in the *picturae* of Death that he examined. Michael of Hungary's *pictura* takes the English verses presented as inscriptions in other versions of the picture and places them in the mouth of Death. For a list of the *picturae* of Death used by Palmer, see ibid., pp. 185–86.

[89] Enders, *Medieval Theater of Cruelty*.

[90] The idea of the trembling sinner may have accompanied the idea of the picture of Sin without always making it into the picture of Sin itself. Johannes says that the sinner trembles, but he does not include the tremor as an element of his picture. The picture of Mortal Sin in the *Imagines fulgencii* collection in BnF, cod. lat. 590, fol. 101ᵛ, which is quite similar to Holcot's version, says that the picture actually trembles: 'Peccatum mortale aput antiquos depingebatur: stabat vna regina tremens continue et vocabatur dea infernalium. In cuius circuitu ponebantur tres imagines, scilicet ymago dei, ymago dyaboli, et ymago hominis. Et quelibet ymago tenebat vnam cedulam quas ymaginibus predictas porrigebat.'

[91] Enders, 'Rhetoric, Coercion', pp. 25–27; Carruthers, *Craft of Thought*, p. 101.

Like Frances Yates before us, it is easy to see how stately pictures of regal maidens might be mnemonic images of virtues and even vices, and certainly these images did function memorially. Mnemonic images of Sin and Death were perhaps easier to disfigure than the virtues. Many of the *picturae* of Death studied by Palmer incorporate unusual or frightening elements: one is of a tyrant holding two swords in his mouth; another is of a monster with a diseased face; still another is of a maiden smeared with blood.[92] Such strikingly ugly images could be as mnemonic as more beautiful imagery, and these might be more likely to frighten Christians into a virtuous life and a clean conscience.

The second type of mnemonic exemplum in Johannes's repertoire is the devotional/scriptural variety. These exempla have no ancient overtones and can be drawn from Scripture, saints' lives, or pastoral works. An example that draws on a long history of practical mnemonics occurs in a sermon written for the octave of Easter.[93] Its theme is 'Put in thy finger hither and see my hands' (John 20. 27). Johannes's division of the theme plays on the kinds of hands one ought to see, and he identifies four: the directing hand, the writing hand, the striking hand, and the giving hand. He compares the directing hand to the signpost marking the way at a crossroads; in the same way a virtuous man should be directed by his own hand: 'for just as the hand of a man has a thumb and four fingers, so the virtuous man ought to have a hand which he looks at in order to direct him to the right path'. He then assigns a virtue to each digit of his hand: the thumb is justice, the index finger is prudence, the middle finger is fortitude, the ring finger (*annularis*) is love, and the 'ear finger' (*auricularis*) is obedience. Each joint of a finger stands for a part of its virtue. For instance, the three joints of one's index finger represent the three parts of prudence: prudence thinks about the past; it arranges present circumstances, and it foresees future contingencies.[94] In the same way, the three joints of the ring finger (which signifies love because it has a vein which touches the heart)[95] correspond to the three appropriate recipients of love: God, one's neighbour, and one's soul.

By moralizing the hand, Johannes provides a physical place for his listeners to deposit his teaching about five virtues. Nothing that he says advances beyond the

[92] Palmer, '"Antiquitus depingebatur"', pp. 190–91.

[93] Johannes von Werden, *Dormi secure de tempore*, Sermo 29.

[94] Johannes von Werden, *Dormi secure de tempore*, Sermo 29: 'Nam prudentia cogitat de preteritis, ordinat de presentibus, et providet de futuris.'

[95] The fourth finger was also called the *medicus* for the same reason: John Murdoch, *Antiquity and the Middle Ages*, Album of Science (New York: Scribner, 1984), p. 80.

most basic knowledge, but he is helping his listeners to learn and retain the names of the virtues and their parts. His audience might quite literally apply the sermon's method to their own lives by following the spiritual path set forth by their hands. The hand here thus clearly functions as a mnemonic device: the fingers and their joints provide 'places' onto which the virtues are mapped. The hand is a locational image, an image which contains places. As we saw above, using parts of the body was not an unusual mnemonic strategy in the Middle Ages.[96]

The hand itself often served as a common mnemonic device.[97] The appeal of the hand in mnemonics was probably due to the ease of visualizing the places. If one flexes one's fingers only slightly at the joints, it is easy to see 'places' marked out on each fingers. Perhaps the best-known example of the hand's mnemonic possibilities is the 'Guidonian hand', which taught the content of medieval music by illustrating the sequence of twenty notes in the scale as well as other information useful to musical theory.[98] The hand was also used to jog the memory in religious contexts. Thomas of Chobham, in his *Summa confessorum*, relies on the hand's clear places to help parish priests new to the job of hearing the frequent confessions of their parishioners remember the rules for consanguinity after the changes that the Fourth Lateran Council brought in 1215, Christians were not allowed to marry within four degrees of kinship.[99] One of Johannes Sintram's manuscripts (Leeds, Brotherton 102) includes a drawing of a hand that has texts

[96] John Bromyard also moralized parts of the hands and fingers in his *Summa praedicantium*; see Owst, *Preaching in Medieval England*, p. 304.

[97] For an encyclopedic overview of the hand as a guide for memory and knowledge in the early modern period, see Claire Richter Sherman, *Writing on Hands: Memory and Knowledge in Early Modern Europe* (Carlisle, PA: Trout Gallery, Dickinson College; Washington, DC: Folger Shakespeare Library; Seattle: University of Washington Press, 2000).

[98] See Murdoch, *Antiquity and the Middle Ages*, p. 81, and Carol Berger, 'The Hand and the Art of Memory', *Musica disciplina*, 35 (1981), 87–120.

[99] Thomas of Chobham, *Summa confessorum*, ed. by F. Broomfield, Analecta mediaevalia namurcensia, 25 (Louvain: Nauwelaerts, 1968). Broomfield, p. xlix, discusses whether Thomas could have known about the new provisions of Lateran IV when he wrote his *Summa* (finished and in circulation *c.* 1216). See also James A. Brundage, *Medieval Canon Law* (London: Longman, 1995), p. 75. 'De consanguinity': 'Et est vulgaris regula talis. Quotiens queritur consanguinitas inter aliquas personas semper recurrendum est ad stipitem aliquem unde descendunt ille persone, et ille stipes scilicet pater vel mater ponendus est in medio palme, et proles primo procedentes ab illo stipite, vel duo fratres vel due sorores vel frater et soror ponende sunt in duabus iuncturis primis duorum digitorum quorum unus dicitur medicus, alter medius' (Thomas of Chobham, *Summa confessorum*, ed. by Broomfield, p. 162). I owe this reference to Professor Joseph Goering of the University of Toronto.

beginning with the word *Meditare* written on the thumb, each finger, and two places on the palm.[100] Undoubtedly Sintram saw the hand as a focus for meditation on the texts associated with each finger.

Because we do not know whether all or any of Johannes's sermons were actually delivered, we should also consider the possibility that the mnemonic image of the hand may have been aimed at least as much at the parish clergy for whom the *Dormi secure* was designed as at the laity. Cuing the parts of virtues, which are, after all, parts of the sermon, to the digits of the hand would have been quite useful to a preacher. And since Johannes von Werden's sermons are shorter than those by his near contemporaries, Johannes Herolt and Johannes Nider, they may have been designed as outlines on which the preacher could expand. Mnemonic images, along with divisions and other recollective strategies, aided the preacher to keep the outline in mind and to aid related ideas *ex tempore* or by design.

## *Preaching and Meditation*

Besides aiding preachers and listeners in recalling the major points of a sermon, the kinds of imagery that we have been discussing whole may have served some psychological functions. In *Chaucer and the Imagery of Narrative*, V. A. Kolve examined the 'imagery of narrative', focusing not on metaphor or simile but on 'those larger images created by the narrative action itself, which it invites us to imagine and hold in mind as we experience the poem, and which later serve as memorial centers around which we are able to reconstruct the story and think appropriately about its meaning'.[101] Kolve explored the relationship between imagery and the audience of Chaucer's poems, noting the reliance placed upon the visual sense and mental imagery in the faculty psychology (i.e., the interior senses discussed in Chapter 2) of the time. Kolve also conceded that the problem of remembering a literary experience was 'a great deal less urgent for man's soul than the need to hold the great truths of the Church (historical and doctrinal) in mind, ready to be summoned for guidance, clarification, meditation, sorrow, or joy'.[102] Given this acknowledgment, it is surprising how little attention has been given to

[100] Ker, *Medieval Manuscripts*, III, 64 (no. 4). Illustrated examples of the hand as a focus for meditation can be found in Sherman, *Writing on Hands*, pp. 65, 153–55.

[101] V. A. Kolve, *Chaucer and the Imagery of Narrative: The First Five Canterbury Tales* (Stanford: Stanford University Press, 1984), p. 2.

[102] Kolve, *Chaucer and the Imagery of Narrative*, p. 48.

the ways in which imagery in sermons provided a source for later reflection and meditation for those who heard them.

In particular such images could provide a springboard for meditation. One of the best examples from Johannes von Werden's sermons combines the emphasis on virtues and vices found in his classicizing pictures with the appeal of a saint's life and accounts of the Passion. The image appears in a sermon written for the third Sunday after Easter. Its theme is 'Jesus stood in the midst of them and [...] he shewed them his hands and feet' (Luke 24. 36–40).[103] The division of the theme declares that Christ showed his disciples four parts of his body for four reasons; he showed them his hands, so that he would provoke them and us to fight; he showed them his side in order to incite them and us to love; his feet in order to call them and us to serve; and his whole body, in order to invite us to suffer with him.

His picture concerns the elaboration of the fourth point of the division. In order to explain how Christ called his disciples to suffer with him, he tells a story about St Macharius:

> De isto ostensione sui corporis legitur de quodam sancto videlicet machario qui deum multis annis exorauit dicens, 'O domine quomodo pro me et quilibet peccatore tot mala pati in tuo sanctissimo corpore potuisti cum non ex operibus iusticie que fecimus nos meruimus?' Cui apparauit dominus dicens, 'Misericordia me spinis coronauit./ caritas latus meum perforauit,/ patientia me flagellauit,/ benignitas clauum in dexteram manum fixit,/ clauum in sinistram manum mansuetudo./ Pietas clauum in dextrum pedem fixit,/ humilitas clauum in sinistrum pedem fixit,/ bonitas me ligauit,/ sed iusticia in his locum non habet.' Unde ait apostolus ad Tytum, 'Non ex operibus iusticie que fecimus nos sed secundum misericordiam saluos nos fecit. Et ideo ex quo audiuit talia de Christo quod iste virtutes cum cogeret ad sustinendum talia pro homine depinxit Christum in cruce pedentem et supra crucem imaginem pulcerrime virginis supra quam scripsit misericordiam aureis litteris et huic coronam spineam impressit. Item in latere dextro pulcram puellam latus eius aperientem et iuxta eam scripsit 'charitas.' Item ad dextrum brachium puellam pulchram que clauum in dextram manum incussit cum malleo ferreo et iuxta illam scripsit patientiam. Item iuxta sinistram manum puellam que clauum infixit, et iuxta illam scripsit 'benignitas.' Item iuxta dextrum pedem puellam, et iuxta illam scripsit 'pietas.' Iuxta sinistram scripsit 'mansuetudo' et puellam depinxit. Item ex alia parte stetit puella depicta et funem in manu tenuit et captiuauit. Et hanc imaginem sanctus ille omni die honorauit iuxta reuelatiuone saluatoris.[104]

[103] Johannes von Werden, *Dormi secure de tempore*, Sermo 28: 'Feria tecia [*sic*] post pasca': 'stetit iesus in medio discipulorum suorum et ostendet illis manus, etc'.

[104] Johannes von Werden, *Dormi secure de tempore*, Sermo 28.

(St Macharius prevailed upon the Lord for many years, saying 'O Lord, how were you able to suffer so many evils in your blessed body for me and every sinner when we do not deserve it from the works we do?' The Lord appeared to him and said, 'Mercy crowned me with thorns, Charity pierced my side, Patience flagellated me, Kindness [*benignitas*] fixed a nail in my right hand, Meekness a nail in my left hand. Piety put a nail in my right foot, Humility put a nail in my left foot. Goodness bound me, but Justice does not have a place in these things'. For this reason, the Apostle said to Titus, 'Not by the works of justice, which we have done, but according to his mercy he saved us' [Titus 3.5]. And because Macharius heard from Christ that these virtues forced him to endure such things for human beings, he painted Christ hanging on the Cross; and above the Cross he painted an image of a very beautiful maiden, above whom he wrote 'Mercy' in golden letters, and she impressed a crown of thorns on him. Then on the right side [he painted] a beautiful maiden opening his side and next to her he wrote 'Charity'. Then next to the right arm [he painted] a beautiful girl who struck a nail into the right hand with an iron hammer and next to her he wrote 'Patience'. Then next to the left hand a girl who fixed a nail, and next to her he wrote 'Kindness'. Then next to the right foot [he painted] a girl, and next to her he wrote 'Piety'. Next to the left foot he wrote 'Meekness', and he painted a maiden. Then on the other side stood a woman he had painted, and she held a rope in her hand and bound Christ. And the saint venerated the image every day according to the revelation of the Saviour.)

The story of St Macharius's encounter with Christ and his subsequent painting constitute the entire discussion of Johannes's fourth division of the theme. Immediately after relating the exemplum, he concludes the sermon.

Johannes's description of Christ's crucifixion by the virtues offers a fascinating example of the interplay between texts and images in the Middle Ages and of their use in meditation and devotion. Like his other exempla, this one is borrowed, but perhaps not from a preaching text. Instead, the literary picture was influenced by one of a number of images painted between the thirteenth and fifteenth centuries in Germany and Switzerland.[105] For example, Figure 4 shows a painting from a fifteenth-century German manuscript now held in the Biblioteca Casanatense in

[105] Saxl, 'Spiritual Encyclopaedia', pp. 105–06; Hanns Swarzenski, *Die lateinischen illuminierten Handschriften des XIII. Jahrhunderts in den Ländern an Rhein, Main und Donau, Denkmäler deutscher Kunst: Die Deutsche Buchmalerei des XIII. Jahrhunderts* (Berlin: [Deutscher Verein für Kunstwissenschaft], 1936), p. 19 n. 1, and pp. 95–96; Saxl, 'Aller Tugenden und Laster Abbildung', p. 107; Adolf Katzenellenbogen, *Allegories of the Virtues and Vices in Medieval Art from Early Christian Times to the Thirteenth Century*, Medieval Academy Reprints for Teaching, 24 (Toronto: University of Toronto Press, 1989), pp. 38–39; Wilhelm Molsdorf, *Christliche Symbolik der mittelalterlichen Kunst* (Leipzig: Akademische Druck- u. Verlagsanstalt, 1926), pp. 201–02; Heike Kraft, 'Die Bildallegorie der Kreuzigung Christi durch die Tugenden' (unpublished doctoral thesis, Freie Universität, Berlin, 1976).

Fig. 4. 'Christ Crucified by the Virtues and Vices', Rome, Biblioteca Casanatense, Cod. Cas. 1404, fol. 28$^{v}$. German, fifteenth century. Photograph courtesy of the Warburg Institute.

Rome. Here Patience, Humility, Charity, Faith, Hope, Justice, and Mercy surround the Cross, while Adam, the Church, and the Synagogue stand at its foot.[106]

Hanns Swarzenski demonstrated that this iconographical tradition took its source from the sermons of Bernard de Clairvaux. In an Easter sermon, Bernard enumerated the virtues that Christ exhibited on the Cross: he was humble when reviled by the Jews, patient when wounded by the nails; charity and obedience were perfected in him. Bernard added that the four ends of the Cross were adorned with the 'gems' of these virtues.[107] Fritz Saxl noted that the thirteenth-century paintings tend to depict only four virtues: Charity piercing Christ's side with a lance and three other virtues nailing his hands and feet to the Cross. The artists of the later versions chose virtues to accord with their own purposes. Something similar has occurred in Johannes's story. He did not rely on Bernard to formulate his exemplum but rather on a combination of literary and pictorial sources. The evidence for this view comes from a fourteenth-century painting on the Fronleichnamsaltar (Corpus Christi Altar) in Doberan, Germany. The altar there has an image of Christ and the virtues; it once had a lengthy inscription with exactly the same verse that Christ recites to St Macharius in Johannes's exemplum.[108] However, the Doberan painting does not contain the same virtues that are named in the verse. Interestingly, Johannes's exemplum does contain the virtues described in the verse. The implication is that Johannes von Werden (or whoever he may have borrowed the exemplum from) knew the verse and had seen a painting of Christ crucified by the virtues. His literary image is based directly on the verse and only indirectly on an actual painting. It may well be that the verse, with its complicated imagery, appealed more to Johannes than the paintings he

[106] Rome, Biblioteca Casanatense, MS 1404, fol. 28v. The manuscript has been dated to the second quarter of the fifteenth century and is thus contemporary with the *Dormi secure*. Cited in Saxl, 'Spiritual Encyclopaedia', p. 105; see also Parshall, 'Art of Memory', pp. 462–63.

[107] An early example of the theme is the manuscript illumination that precedes Bernard's Easter sermon in a collection of his sermons (Düsseldorf, Landesbibliothek, MS HS B. 31, fol. 122v). Swarzenski, *Die lateinischen illuminierten Handschriften*, pp. 95–96; Bernardus Claraevallensis Abbas, "In Coena Domini," in *Sermones De Tempore*, PL, CLXXXIII, col. 275. Cf. *Fasciculus morum*'s quotation of this very section from St Bernard (*Fasc. mor.*, pp. 228–29).

[108] 'Misericordia me spinis coronavit | Charitas latus meum perforauit. Patientia me flagellauit | Benignitas clavum in dextram manum fixit, | Mansuetudo clavum in sinistram manum. | Pietas clavum in dextrum pedem fixit, | Humilitas clavum in sinistram. | Bonitas me ligavit. | Sed iustitia in his locum non habet'; cited in Friedrich Schlie, *Die Kunst- und Geschichts-Denkmäler des Grossherzogthums Mecklenburg-Schwerin*, 4 vols (Schwerin i.M: Bärensprung [u.a.], 1899), III, 607–08, and Heinrich Jerchel, 'Die Bayerische Buchmalerei des 14. Jahrhunderts', *Münchner Jahrbuch der bildenden Kunst*, Neue Folge, 10 (1933), 74–78 (pp. 74, 77–78).

had seen or that it was easier to remember which virtues to include and where to place them in the image by following the verse than by visualizing the picture alone.

The literary description of the painting has been adapted to the context of preaching and memorial meditation. Johannes has emphasized the mnemonic elements of the original image. The beautiful mnemonic maidens have returned to participate in an example of supreme suffering. In fact, they are the agents of Christ's suffering, with Mercy crowning him with thorns, Patience flagellating him, and the other virtues nailing him to the Cross. In addition, the standard mnemonic signals of the word *depingebatur* and the writing in gold letters are present. Anyone could remember St Macharius's painting from the preacher to the most humble parishioner. The Latin verse helped the preacher to recall the scene (probably more than a vernacular translation would have aided the listeners). The image, which several art historians have seen as striking and dramatic, could last in both the preacher's and the listeners' memories.[109] Indeed, the painting in the Casanatense manuscript is part of what Saxl calls 'a spiritual encyclopaedia' that contains images of many items from Holcot's *Moralitates*, Ridevall's *Fulgentius metaforalis*, and the anonymous *De prudentia* collections (also sometimes attributed to an unspecified chancellor of Paris).[110] Both Saxl and Peter Parshall point to the value of such a collection for preachers preparing their sermons. According to Parshall, 'The manuscript is a model of how to invent pictures out of abstract ideas and, conversely, how to stimulate the construction of a new and private text on the basis of a picture.'[111] But why should the parishioner remember it?

Johannes's images of the various virtues do not so much explain what the virtues are as give examples of them in action. In other words, it was Christ's patience, mercy, and charity that kept him on the Cross. The ultimate goal of the many medieval treatises and sermons on the virtues and vices was to tear out vice by the roots from the human soul and to plant in its place new virtues. Preachers wanted their sermons to result in a change of life. Imagining Christ on the Cross and the infliction of suffering by nails, rope, and thorn was probably also meant to whip up an affective response from the audience both at the time of the sermon's delivery and later, when the listener recalled the sermon in private. An

[109] Katzenellenbogen called the thirteenth-century miniature, in Cologne, Stadtarchiv, MS W, fol. 255, 'a scene of intense dramatic quality' (*Allegories of the Virtues and Vices*, p. 38).

[110] Saxl, 'Spiritual Encyclopaedia', pp. 99–102. See also Saxl, 'Aller Tugenden', pp. 109–12.

[111] Parshall, 'Art of Memory', p. 463.

emotional response to sermons, art work, and religious treatises was increasingly considered a desired outcome in the later Middle Ages.[112]

The rousing of emotion required an appeal to ordinary people's imagination, even its training. Michael Baxandall has remarked that if a painter was a 'professional visualizer of the holy stories', one should remember that 'each of his pious public was liable to be an amateur in the same line, practiced in spiritual exercises that demanded a high level of visualization of, at least, the central episodes of the lives of Christ and Mary'.[113] He notes that preaching prepared the ground for emotional and visual identification with scriptural scenes.

It also taught the laity the fundamentals of meditation on a religious image. In a well-known article, Jeffrey Hamburger traced the evolution of the idea of imageless devotion for monks to one in which the use of images was permitted. One of his examples of the change towards meditation on images was the image of Christ crucified by the virtues.[114] By the fifteenth century, that image had made its way into the sermon literature as an appropriate vehicle for the laity's education in meditation. Not all preachers were confident of people's abilities in this skill. A common argument used to justify the place of images in Christian worship was their affective power. John Mirk went so far as to question most people's imaginative powers without the help of images: 'I say boldly that ther ben mony thousand of pepull that couth not ymagen in her hert how Crist was don on the rood, but as thai lerne hit be syȝt of ymages and payntours.'[115] And yet, imagining scenes from the life of Christ or the saints was something that preachers expected people to be able to do. One anonymous English preacher declared in a sermon that 'we ought to see Job sitting in the dung-heap, and John the Baptist clad in camels' hair fasting in the desert, and Peter on the gallows of the cross, [...] and James falling upon the sword of Herod'.[116] Visualization was especially important for scenes from the life of Christ. Johannes emphasizes this theme in a sermon on how the Passion is symbolized in the Mass.[117] Johannes thinks the representation

[112] Parshall explains the role of emotion in formulating mnemonic images by looking at a premodern understanding of the psychology of affect ('Art of Memory', p. 456).

[113] Baxandall, *Painting and Experience*, p. 45.

[114] Jeffrey Hamburger, 'The Visual and the Visionary: The Image in Late-Medieval Monastic Devotions', *Viator*, 20 (1989), 161–82 (pp. 170–71).

[115] Cited in Owst, *Literature and Pulpit*, p. 146; *Mirk's Festial*, ed. by Theodor Erbe, EETS, e.s., 96 (London: Paul, Trench, and Trübner, 1905; repr. Millwood, NY: Kraus, 1975), p. 171.

[116] BL, MS Add. 21,253, fol. 15; cited and trans. in Owst, *Literature and Pulpit*, p. 136.

[117] Johannes von Werden, *Dormi secure de tempore*, Sermo 68.

of aspects of Christ's crucifixion ought to move a good man to compassion when he is at Mass and that his soul ought to stand as though it were standing on the Mount at Calvary and watching all the things that happened there. Johannes thus invites ordinary parishioners to recall the events of the Passion at every Mass and to participate vicariously, remembering that their sins are the reason that Christ was put to death.

In giving these careful references to the Passion, Johannes clearly belongs to the medieval practice of reflecting and meditating on the scenes from the life of Christ. It is well known to scholars of the late Middle Ages that the Passion became an increasingly important subject for religious art and religious devotion.[118] Meditational works like the *Meditationes vitae Christi* and devotional themes like the *Arma Christi* flourished in the hothouse atmosphere of late medieval piety. Relatively rarely have the inputs of preaching and mnemonics been analysed as incitements to these late medieval developments, but they both played a role.[119]

When Johannes depicts his image of Christ fixed to the Cross by virtue and when he tells his readers that they should always carry the memory of the Passion with them,[120] he is thus drawing his audience's attention to a well-worked medieval theme. Certainly, the Franciscans contributed much to this theme with their insistence on the humanity of Christ and his suffering.[121] Sermon literature contributed to meditation on the Passion in the Middle Ages by teaching the people rudimentary techniques of visualization and memorization that enhanced their ability to meditate privately.[122] The kinds of images used by Johannes that

[118] David Freedberg, *The Power of Images: Studies in the History and Theory of Response* (Chicago: University of Chicago Press, 1989), pp. 168–78; James H. Marrow, *Passion Iconography in Northern European Art of the Late Middle Ages and Early Renaissance: A Study in the Transformation of Sacred Metaphor into Descriptive Narrative*, Ars Neerlandica, 1 (Kortrijk: Van Ghemmert, 1979); Richard Kieckhefer, 'Major Currents in Late Medieval Devotion', in *Christian Spirituality*, II: *High Middle Ages and Reformation*, ed. by Jill Raitt, World Spirituality: An Encyclopedic History of the Religious Quest, 17 (New York: Crossroad, 1987), pp. 75–108 (pp. 83–89). See also the essays in *The Broken Body: Passion Devotion in Late Medieval Culture*, ed. by Alasdair A. MacDonald, Bernhard Ridderbos, and R. M. Schlusemann (Groningen: Forsten, 1998).

[119] An exception is the article by Parshall, 'Art of Memory'.

[120] Johannes von Werden, *Dormi secure de tempore*, Sermo 57.

[121] Moorman, *History of the Franciscan Order*, p. 256; John V. Fleming, *An Introduction to the Franciscan Literature of the Middle Ages* (Chicago: Franciscan Herald, 1977).

[122] Preaching handbooks like the *Fasciculus morum* taught preachers themselves much of the lore they needed to know about the Passion. See pt III.10, 'On Christ's Passion', pp. 201–15.

I have labelled devotional/scriptural could certainly have been an aid to lay meditation; the classicizing images may or may not have provided as fruitful a ground for meditation.

Chapter 9

# Memory Precepts in Italian Preaching

The northern European friars that we have examined thus far were not the only preachers who dreamed up elaborate methods for remembering sermons and teaching the laity. In Italy, we also find references in sermons and exempla collections to the usefulness of mnemonic precepts in preaching. Indeed, the sources are so rich that they merit an independent study of their own, which cannot be undertaken here. Fortunately, Lina Bolzoni has done a great deal of work on Italian preachers, and her work can be used to illustrate the kind of mnemonic preaching found in late medieval Italy.

Future work on Italian preaching should take into account Heimann-Seelbach's thesis that the *ars memorativa* tradition was not dependent on medieval practice but rather began independently in the fifteenth century, likely as a result of Greek influences.[1] Because the earliest exemplars of the fifteenth-century *ars memorativa* treatises are Italian, we must be careful about making two common assumptions about the sources: 1) that the kind of mnemonic precepts on preaching found in the memory treatises necessarily reflect medieval practice; and 2) that the kind of mnemonic examples found in fifteenth-century Italian sermons were subject to the same influences as were fourteenth-century varieties. Indeed, it is likely that a preacher like Bernardino da Siena was aware of the mnemonic advice available in the fifteenth century and may well have utilized some of the new treatises' precepts in his sermons. Certainly the *ars memorativa* tradition was stronger in early fifteenth-century Italy than elsewhere in Europe. Indeed, Bernardino's sermons often offer methods closer to the *Ad Herennium*'s precepts than the ones found in the classicizing friars' works. We will examine the use to which two Italian friars put their mnemonic methods, one in his exempla collection, the other in his

[1] Heimann-Seelbach, *Ars und Scientia*, pp. 477–88, 506.

sermons. These examples will both reinforce the picture of the importance of mnemonics in mendicant preaching sketched above and demonstrate alternative methods of instilling religious precepts in the laity's memory.

## *Giovanni da San Gimignano*

The most careful medieval adapter of mnemonic rules to the needs of preachers and the laity was undoubtably Giovanni da San Gimignano. Born between 1260 and 1270, by 1299 he was lector at the Dominican convent at Arezzo. In 1305 he was assigned to the capital of Rieti to act as lector to the Roman convent of Santa Maria sopra Minerva. From 1310 to 1313, he was prior at Siena. He also helped found the convent at San Gimignano, where he remained until his death in 1333.[2] Almost all of his literary works are dedicated to preaching, the most famous of which, the *Summa de exemplis et rerum similitudinibus*, contains mnemonic advice.[3] Giovanni's *Summa* is particularly interesting because of the ways in which he adapts explicit mnemonic precepts, rules for order, and cognitive theory about imagery to the office of preaching. Most scholars interested in these issues have concentrated on the chapter in which he lists several rules for improving one's memory.[4] However, even the construction of the *Summa* proclaims Giovanni's interest in maximizing the learning potential and recall of all who would come into contact with its contents, from preachers to their audience.

Giovanni makes this desire abundantly clear in his Prologue. In explaining his reason for compiling the *Summa*, he discusses the role of exemplars in the human arts. In the performance of all of them, there are two kinds of examples, an internal one (*forma artis*) available to those skilled in the arts, and an external one

[2] Cesare Vasoli, 'Arte della memoria e predicazione', *Lettere italiane*, 38 (1986), 478–99 (pp. 483–84). See also Antoine Dondaine, 'La vie et les oeuvres de Jean de San Gimignano', *AFP*, 9 (1939), 128–83; Tommaso Kaeppeli, *Scriptores ordinis praedicatorum medii aevii*, 3 vols (Rome: Santa Sabina, 1970–80), II, 539–43; and Massimo Oldoni, 'Giovanni da San Gimignano', in *L'enciclopedismo medievale*, ed. by Michelangelo Picone, Memoria del tempo, 1 (Ravenna: Longo, 1994), pp. 213–28.

[3] Unfortunately no modern edition of this work exists. I have here used Giovanni da San Gimignano, *Summa de exemplis et rerum similitudinibus locupletissima Verbi Dei Concionatoribus cunctisque litararum studiosis maximo usui futura* (Lyon: Simphorianum Beraud et Stehanum Michaelem, 1585). Mulchahey, *'First the Bow Is Bent in Study'*, emphasizes the great popularity within the Dominican order of all of Giovanni's homiletic works, pp. 429–30.

[4] Yates, *Art of Memory*, pp. 85–86; Vasoli, 'Arte della memoria', pp. 483–88.

(*factum artificium*) for those learning the art.[5] Just as there is a twofold exemplar for the arts, so is there a twofold exemplar in human morals and deeds: the first is the internal example of Christ attained through faith, and the second is the 'created nature of things' outside the soul. From this second type of exemplar, one may draw an abundance of useful exempla pertaining to our morals:

> This abundance [...] especially of external things, which are known to us, and also concerning the wondrous works which nature continually produces or human diligence discovers, not only makes them pleasing to curious listeners [...] but also fruitful and acceptable to the vulgar and the simple, so that through examples of sensible things, they disclose spiritual and subtle things.[6]

Giovanni thinks that the multitude of external things, such as the wonders of the natural world, provide examples of more spiritual matters appropriate to simple folk. Therefore 'for the convenience of those preaching' and 'desiring to serve the progress of the simple listeners', Giovanni compiled this book of examples. However, the book is not an indiscriminate mass of stories, but rather a collection of examples carefully ordered and selected according to two principles.[7]

The first principle is adapted to the necessities of human cognition. According to Aristotle, Giovanni argues, knowledge involves sense, imagination, and reason. Starting with exterior things, there is first movement in the sense, then movement in the phantasy or imagination, and finally from the phantasy and the agent intellect, the possible intellect completes the act of understanding. Thus, Aristotle is right to say that there is no understanding without phantasms (images).[8] Arranging his material according to the best scientific research available to him, Giovanni posits his examples according to the order of human cognition, that is, first he adduces exempla about sensible things, then about imaginable things, and then about rational things. He further distinguishes the sensible things into the simple and the composite, the animate and the inanimate, the vegetative

[5] *Summa de exemplis*, fol.1r.

[6] *Summa de exemplis*, fol. 1r: 'Quae copia [...] praecipuè de rebus extrinsecis, quae nobis sunt in aperto, & etiam de mirandis operibus, quae continuè natura producit, vel adinuenit humana industria, non eos tantum apud curiosos auditores faciet gratiosos [...] sed etiam apud vulgus & simplices fructuosos & acceptos constituet, dum per exempla ad sensum spiritualia & subtilia declarabunt.'

[7] Giovanni declares in the Prologue that he has deliberately excluded stories from the Bible, from saints' lives, and from the lives of the gentiles, because other books have covered the material sufficiently (*Summa de exemplis*, fol. 1r).

[8] *Summa de exemplis*, fol. 1v.

and the sensitive, and water, land, and air animals to arrive at the ten books of the *Summa*:[9]

**Table 2. Exempla in Giovanni da San Gimignano's *Summa de exemplis et rerum similitudinibus*.**

| Sensibles | Imaginibles | Rationals |
|---|---|---|
| I) elements and celestial bodies (simple bodies)<br>II) minerals and stones<br>III) vegetables<br>IV) birds and fish<br>V) terrestrial animals<br>VI) humans | VII) dreams and visions | VIII) laws<br>IX) the arts<br>X) human deeds and morals |

Giovanni's first principle of selection serves two purposes. One, it presumably marks a learning curve. Items in the first two books should be easier to understand and would be more appropriate for inclusion in sermons for simple people than items in the books concerned with 'rational' exempla. Two, his ordering principle provides readers with a kind of index to the book's contents. If a preacher desires a story about animals, he knows to look in Book V, while information about plants can be found in Book III.

But this is not the end of Giovanni's organizational plan. His second ordering principle depends upon a distinction between *materiae* and exempla, *materiae* being the spiritual and subtle matters to which the exempla are compared. He arranges the *materiae* alphabetically in each book.[10] He concludes the Prologue with a final note about his method:

> In each of these ten books, I do not particularly intend to follow the order of the exempla but only to locate or place those matters [*materiae*] to which the exempla are adapted in alphabetical order. For example, in the first book, where exempla about simple bodies are found, I do not follow the order of the simple bodies [...] but they are mixed together, according to the various topics (which I put in alphabetical order) to which they are compared.[11]

[9] *Summa de exemplis*, fols $1^v$–$2^r$.

[10] *Summa de exemplis*, fol. $1^r$: 'Intendo autem in opere isto, sequi praecipuè rerum ordinem, de quibus adducentur exempla, nihilominus tamen materias, quibus aptabuntur exempla, reducam vt melius potero in singulis rerum generibus in ordine alphabeti.'

[11] *Summa de exemplis*, fol. $2^r$: 'In singulis autem predictis decem libellis, non intendo particulariter sequi ordinem exemplorum, sed solum illas materias, quibus adaptantur exempla locare seu ponere sub ordine alphabeti, verbi gratia, In primo libro, vbi ponuntur exempla de corporibus

In other words, the exempla in each book are arranged under the matters to which Giovanni thinks they may be compared, not under the exempla themselves. Giovanni also notes that the *materia* may be found in more than one book, arranged alphabetically in each one. As an example of his method, we might take the *materia* 'Grace'. In Book I, Giovanni compares Grace to the exemplum 'primum mobile', in the second to the exemplum 'sapphire', and in the third to the exemplum 'frumentum'.

This second ordering principle, though at first confusing, is actually particularly useful for preachers. If a preacher were working up a sermon on the *materia* 'Blessed Mary' for a crowd of peasants on Monday and maybe another for some merchants on Friday, he might choose to look in the first book under *m* for the first audience, where Mary is compared to the moon, or in the second book where she is compared to chalcedony and to the emerald. For the merchants, he might prefer a later book, where she appears as the active life. It is essential to the *Summa*'s purpose that the same matters recur from book to book, so that the 'spiritual' matters have appropriate exempla for each cognitive level.

Giovanni clearly understands the role of images in memory and learning and has arranged his material according to that understanding. But his specific treatment of memory in Book VI (on humans) reveals yet another dimension to his work. In this chapter Giovanni discovers three ways to compare memory (the spiritual matter) to the stomach (the exemplum): by reason of reception, by reason of purgation, and by reason of conception. He likens memory's retentive function to the stomach's role as receptacle of the body's food. Just as a stomach is rounded, elongated, and encompassing on account of the food inside it, so the memory is best disposed when it is enlarged through capacity and lengthened through long duration. To achieve these results, one needs methods of improving one's memory. He then relates Thomas Aquinas's four rules for extending memory (naming Aristotle, the Philosopher, rather than Aquinas as their author):

> For according to the Philosopher, there are four things which help people to remember. The first is that one place the things which one wishes to remember in some order. The second is that one cling to these things with affection. The third is that one reduce those things to some unusual similitudes, and the fourth is that one repeat them through frequent meditation.[12]

simplicibus, non sequar in eis ordinem ipsorum simplicium corporum [...] sed mixtim ponentur omnia, nunc de vno, nunc de alio, secundum quod rebus diuersis, quas ponam sub alphabeti ordine, variè adaptantur.'

[12] *Summa de exemplis*, fol. 159$^{v}$: 'Sunt enim quatuor secundum Philosophum quae iuvant hominem ad bene memorandum. Primum est, vt illa quorum benè vult recordari, aliquo ordine

It is not surprising that Giovanni, a Dominican, might know Thomas Aquinas's memory rules. What is unexpected is the use to which he puts them, for the most obvious one is the arrangement of his *Summa*. Even his language in his description of his method accords with this interpretation: he placed (*loco* and *pono*) the *materia* in alphabetical order, and he reduced the *materia* to similitudes.

He also notes a role for memory in penance and confession when he compares memory to the purgation of the stomach. Purgation from sin is born in memory because the dolor of contrition by which the soul is purged arises from the memory of sin.[13] This is not an unusual point; many medieval theologians emphasized the role of memory in penance and confession. John Ridevall, in his picture of Juno as Memory, links several of her attributes to the memory of sin and tears of contrition.[14] Their attitudes imply that confession is impossible without the contrition that arises from one's remembrance of sins. A systematic approach to recalling those sins also relies on rules for memory, a theme that deserves further study.[15]

Thus, Giovanni's recommendation of mnemonic rules rests upon a scientific understanding of the function of images in learning and on Thomas Aquinas's memory rules. The virtual identification that he makes between exempla and memory images means that imagery may be used in sermons as an aid to memory and learning. Aquinas's memory rules also influence the organization of the *Summa* itself, so that the entire work may be seen as a trained memory laid out on parchment. Massimo Oldoni emphasizes that the contents of this work are oriented toward homiletic ends; he calls it 'un vocabolario dell'anima'.[16]

As a final comparison of Giovanni's mnemonic method to the English friars, it should be noted that the *Summa* contains at least one *pictura* similar in style to those seen above. In Book VI, which is devoted to similitudes of the human body, Giovanni includes a chapter that shows why angels used to be painted in antiquity through corporeal members:[17]

disponat. secundum est, vt circa ea affectum adhibeat, tertium est, vt ea ad aliquas similitudines non omnino consuetas reducat, quartum est, vt illa per frequentem meditationem repetat.'

[13] *Summa de exemplis*, fol. 159v.

[14] *Fulg. meta.*, pp. 87–93.

[15] Bolzoni also remarks on the need for a study of memory's role in confession in 'Il "Colloquio spirituale"', p. 21.

[16] Oldoni, 'Giovanni da San Gimignano', pp. 226–27. Oldoni also recognizes the mnemonic structure of the *Summa*.

[17] *Summa de exemplis*, fol. 145r: 'Angelos quamplurimis rationibus corporeis membris iure solere antiquitus depingi, ostentatur.'

> Although they are incorporeal, nevertheless, one reads that angels appear in the figure of the human body, and so they are also painted. Also, various members of the body are attributed to them in divine Scripture through a certain similitude, in which their various invisible actions are expressed. Indeed, angels are painted first with long hair and curly locks, in order that through them they signify the angels' mental affections and ordered thoughts.[18]

Giovanni then explains the significance of every other body part as it pertains to angels. Like the mnemonic advice for using body parts as mnemonic places seen in Francesc Eiximenis's work, he proceeds in an orderly fashion, from head to toe. The references to painting and to antiquity suggest that Giovanni may have known the classical images of the English friars and was trying to adapt them to his similitudes.

## *Memory and Italian Dominicans in the Fourteenth Century*

Since the work of Frances Yates, scholars interested in memory techniques have seen an especially strong link between the Dominican order and the revival of the art of memory. As discussed in the introduction, Heimann-Seelbach has challenged the whole notion that the ancient art of memory was practised at all in the Middle Ages. I would argue that the *Ad Herennium*'s rules were known and sometimes used, though certainly not to the exclusion of other memory methods. Regardless of what form of memory aid was most practised in the medieval period, this book has shown that such aids were certainly used by preachers.

An important area for future research is the relationship between Dominican preachers living in Italy and interest in memory techniques. Lina Bolzoni has suggested that there is real evidence that the art of memory was known at the Pisan convent of St Catherine's from the late thirteenth and fourteenth centuries both in the old form and in the reinvention by Thomas Aquinas and Albertus Magnus. She thinks that the writings of Pisan Dominicans such as Bartolomeo da San Concordio (1262–1347) contributed to this new version of art of memory.[19]

[18] *Summa de exemplis*, fol. 145$^{r}$: 'Angeli licent sint incorporei, tamen in figura humani corporis apparere leguntur, & sic etiam depinguntur. Vnde & varia membra corporis etiam in diuina scriptura per quandam similitudinem eis attribuuntur, in quibus variae actiones eorum inuisibiles exprimuntur. Depinguntur siquidem angeli primo cum longa coma, & reflexis capitis: vt per haec eorum mentales affectiones, & ordinatae cogitationes significant.'

[19] Lina Bolzoni, 'Trees and Other Schemas: Some Examples of their Use', in her *Web of Images*, pp. 83–117 (pp. 83–84).

Bartolomeo's most famous work was *Gli ammaestramenti degli antichi*, a text meant to be used and remembered by both preachers and the laity. Like Yates, Bolzoni notes that the work contains many rules for remembering and assumes that they are meant to help readers remember the text as a whole. Both scholars note that in the fifteenth century Bartolomeo's work was accompanied in the manuscripts by the *Trattato della memoria artificiale*, the vernacular translation of the memory section of the *Rhetorica ad Herennium*.[20] Against this view, Heimann-Seelbach argues that the inclusion of the Italian translation of the *Rhetorica ad Herennium*'s memory rules in some fifteenth-century manuscripts explains nothing about Bartolomeo's goals for the text. She rejects the idea that the memory rules advocate the ancient art of memory, as well as the notion that they were intended to help the reader memorize the text as a 'memory book'.[21]

Heimann-Seelbach's point about the fifteenth-century manuscript circulation is a fair one, but she underplays the importance of Aquinas's memorial principles for the Dominican order.[22] Bolzoni's many articles on Italian Dominican preaching suggest an important role for memory within the order, regardless of the type of mnemonic scheme the friars employed. She thinks such teachings may help explain the many comments in Convent Chronicles about the fantastic memories of members of the Dominican community. For instance, a certain Filippo Borsa (whose last name means 'bag') was held to have lived up to his name by memorizing the Bible, making him 'an extremely capacious bag full of the Holy Scriptures'.[23] In fact, the Pisan Dominicans seem to have a regard for memory that was very similar to that recorded by Guibert de Tournai for the Franciscan order, who said that the order used 'memory for books'.[24] The Dominicans may even have drawn on the same model of St Antony that the Franciscans used. In his vernacular translation of the *Vitae Patrum* (Lives of the Desert Fathers) Domenico Cavalca (*c.* 1270–1342) said that St Antony Abbot 'learnt the Holy Scriptures so assiduously that he never forgot them. He kept all the Holy Commandments in his heart; instead of books he had a memory that was almost a cupboard of Holy Scriptures.'[25]

[20] Bolzoni, 'Trees and Other Schemas', p. 84; Yates, *Art of Memory*, p. 88.

[21] Heimann-Seelbach, *Ars und Scientia*, pp. 403–16.

[22] See Heimann-Seelbach, *Ars und Scientia*, pp. 377–78, for her analysis of Aquinas's rules.

[23] Bolzoni, 'Trees and Other Schemas', p. 84.

[24] See above, Chapter 2.

[25] Cited in Bolzoni, 'Trees and Other Schemas', p. 84. See also, Bolzoni, '"Triumph of Death Cycle"', p. 15.

Another example that argues in favour of the importance of mnemonic training within the Dominican order is the *Libellus super ludo schacorum* of Jacopo da Cessole, OP. In 1973, Raymond DiLorenzo wrote an article arguing that Jacopo used mnemonic techniques to arrange his collection of exempla and *sententiae*.[26] He saw Jacopo's work as a 'thoroughly structured regimen of the prince' that employed the chess game both as a symbol of society and as an aid to the memory of its readers.[27] He noted that Jacopo gave a verbal description of the chess pieces in terms that corresponded well to the rules for mnemonic imagery. For instance, the pawn who stands in the square in front of the king's *miles* or knight is described as 'a man who has a mallet in his right hand, a mattock in his left hand, and a mason's trowel in his cincture'.[28] The figure's attributes are then moralized to explain their functions. Even the chess board functions as a repository of mnemonic places, as Jacopo explains why each pawn stands in front of the particular higher status piece behind it.[29] DiLorenzo comments, as I have done throughout the book, that a once private memory method now affects what the author says and becomes a means of communication to his audience.[30]

Though not a lot is known about the background of Jacopo da Cessole other than that he was a Dominican, current scholarship links him to the Dominican house in Genoa in the early fourteenth century.[31] Jacobus de Voragine and Johannes Balbus were two other well-known Dominicans from the same house. Jacopo da Cessole's work was a very popular text in the late Middle Ages, with over two hundred extant manuscripts and printed editions. Its classical content and mnemonic images would have made for ideal preaching material and seem to fit in well with the interests of other fourteenth-century Italian Dominicans, as well as the English classicizing friars.[32]

[26] Raymond D. DiLorenzo, 'The Collection Form and the Art of Memory in the "Libellus Super Ludo Schachorum" of Jacobus de Cessolis', *Mediaeval Studies*, 35 (1973), 205–21.

[27] DiLorenzo, 'Collection Form', pp. 211, 213.

[28] DiLorenzo, 'Collection Form', p. 217: 'Nam factus fuit ipse faber in forma humana, habens in manu dextra malleum, dolabrum in leva, et scementarii trullam ad corrigiam'; trans. p. 219.

[29] DiLorenzo, 'Collection Form', p. 217.

[30] DiLorenzo, 'Collection Form', p. 207.

[31] DiLorenzo, 'Collection Form', pp. 205–06.

[32] Gösta Hedegård, 'Jacobus de Cessolis' Sources: The Case of Valerius Maximus', in *Chess and Allegory in the Middle Ages*, ed. by Olle Ferm and Volker Honemann (Stockholm: Sällskapet Runica et Mediaevalia, 2005), pp. 98–159, notes that Jacopo drew most of his sources from either Vincent de Beauvais or John of Wales. Both of these sources put him firmly in the orbit of Dominican and mendicant thinking.

Only more research on Dominican attitudes toward memory can decide which schemes they most used. Such research will require moving beyond what Thomas Aquinas and Albertus Magnus have to say to the works of other, less well known Dominican authors. The work of Bolzoni suggests that they, like the Franciscans, made use of various schemes, from the ancient art of memory, to Aquinas's rules, to Augustine's emphasis on memory, will, and intellect.

For our last author, we will return to the Franciscan order to study a fifteenth-century author who self-consciously made use of the art of memory in his sermons.

## *St Bernardino da Siena*

The main characteristic that we have seen in all our medieval mnemonic practicians is a determined practicality and inventiveness in adapting the rules of memory to their purposes. Carruthers is thus right to distinguish between memory 'arts' and elementary memory systems in that the latter's creations are fluid and subject to adaptation, while an art has fixed rules that are not subject to wholesale change. Bernardino da Siena offers a particularly good example of how a preacher could experiment with varying techniques of structure and imagery to captivate an audience.

Unlike our other preachers, St Bernardino's career has been extremely well documented, so that we have a record of how he preached as well as the contents of his sermons. By all accounts, he was an extremely effective and mesmerizing speaker who could preach for hours without losing his audience. His practice was to celebrate Mass at sunrise and then preach for two or three hours before releasing his audience for the day's work.[33] Because of the copious information available, St Bernardino has been well studied, especially from a mnemonic standpoint.[34] I will rely on these studies to demonstrate the possibilities of mnemonic techniques in the hands of an expert.

[33] Origo, *World of San Bernardino*, pp. 31–32.

[34] Carlo Delcorno and Lina Bolzoni have provided numerous articles on the Sienese preacher. See Bolzoni, 'Oratoria e prediche', *Letteratura italiana*, 3 (1984), 1041–74; Bolzoni, 'Teatralità e tecniche della memoria', pp. 271–87; Bolzoni, 'Predicazione e arte della memoria: Un quaresimale di Bernardino da Siena e l'immagine del Serafino', in *Musagetes: Festschrift für Wolfram Prinz zu seinem 60. Geburtstag am 5. Februar 1989*, ed. by Ronald G. Kecks (Berlin: Mann, 1991), pp. 179–95; Delcorno, 'L'ars praedicandi di Bernardino da Siena', pp. 441–75; Delcorno, '"Ars praedicandi"', pp. 77–162. See now also Lina Bolzoni, 'St Bernardino da Siena', in her *Web of Images*, pp. 117–95.

St Bernardino's preaching style appears at a time of renewal of preaching in the Church, after the Schism and the formation of the observant Franciscans.[35] He contributed to this revival by a shrewd recognition of the value of theatrical and imaginative techniques in ministering to urban populations. Carlo Delcorno has shown that this recognition took place over several years as the preacher's style moved from a close reliance on the traditional *sermo modernus* to one more liberal in several of its most basic techniques.[36] St Bernardino himself placed the beginning of his adaptation of the old model around 1412, but his boldest experiments began around 1424/25. He became much less dependent on the liturgical readings, choosing his theme more with an eye to the catechetical content than to its relation to the daily pericope. His plan, especially in the Florentine Lenten Cycle of 1424 examined by Delcorno, leaned increasingly toward doctrinal exposition at the expense of biblical narrative. He was impatient with abstruse speakers, declaring clarity the preacher's first duty: '[W]rap not up your speech, speak plain and open. Call a loaf, a loaf: say with your tongue, what you hold in your heart.' His manner of speaking plainly and clearly depended on making high matters accessible through tangible examples, a manner obviously compatible with mnemonics.[37]

Along with these changes are indications that St Bernardino attempted to devise mnemonic techniques for his own use, but even more to inculcate his doctrinal points into the minds of his listeners. In some sermons, he is quite specific about his mnemonic plan. For instance, in a sermon given on 10 April 1424, he relates an exemplum about an illiterate peasant who is taught by a priest to learn the *Pater Noster* by a mnemonic strategy. The peasant is to put the images of twenty debtors in the place of twenty phrases that compose the prayer. He even calls the practice the art of memory.[38]

[35] Bolzoni, 'Oratoria e prediche', p. 1048.

[36] Delcorno, '"Ars praedicandi"', pp. 82–83.

[37] Origo, *World of San Bernardino*, pp. 35, 37.

[38] Delcorno, '"Ars praedicandi"', p. 96; 'Puossi dire che sia l'arte della memoria' (Florence, 1424), pred. XXXIV, in Bernardino da Siena, *Le prediche volgari: Quaresimale del 1424*, ed. by Ciro Cannarozzi, 2 vols (Pistoia: Pacinotti, 1934), II, 93–94). The same story is related in Alan George Ferrers Howell and Julia Mary Cartwright Ady, *S. Bernardino of Siena* (London: Methuen, 1913), pp. 286–87. An English version of the tale was published in 1510 by Wynkyn de Worde. The Italian original evidently passed through a French phase before being translated into English. Eamon Duffy, *The Stripping of the Altars: Traditional Religion in England c. 1400– c. 1580* (New Haven: Yale University Press, 1992), p. 84. As Duffy remarks, the popularity of the story in three languages indicates a common set of European concerns in the late Middle Ages.

We can have some sense of how St Bernardino could have come by his knowledge of the memory techniques. From our examination of Guibert de Tournai's and Francesc Eiximenis's memory advice and Géraud de Pescher's criticisms of current mnemonic practice, it is clear that the Franciscans knew and practised various types of mnemonics. St Bernardino himself knew and used Géraud's sermons.[39] In addition, his confrère in Sienese preaching was Lodovico da Pirano, OFM, who wrote one of the earliest *ars memorativa* treatises in the fifteenth-century enthusiasm for memory arts. Pirano's treatise specifically declares its appropriateness for preachers and furnishes some precepts consistent with his medieval predecessors.[40]

The most distinctive aspects of St Bernardino's mnemonic strategy were his use of imagery and his marriage of that imagery to detailed structure. Though his imagery remained more sober than Holcot's or Ridevall's (he seems to have been of Géraud's mind on the subject of biblical imagery),[41] he was not adverse to using distinctive imagery presented to him by circumstance. In his sermon cycles of 1425–27, he referred to Lorenzetti's fresco in Siena to show the effects of war and peace and the consequences of good and bad government.[42]

Still, most of the imagery he employed to structure his audience's memory was biblical. Bolzoni has studied St Bernardino's use of the Seraph as a mnemonic aid, a symbol previously legitimized by Alain de Lille and Francis of Assisi himself.[43]

[39] Delcorno, '"Ars praedicandi"', pp. 110–11.

[40] For details of Lodovico's life and works, see Vasoli, 'Arte della memoria', pp. 493–96; Yates, 'Lodovico da Pirano's Memory Treatise', p. 22; Yates, *Art of Memory*, pp. 106–07; Baccio Ziliotto, 'Frate Lodovico da Pirano 1390?–1450 e le sue Regulae memorie artificialis', *Atti e memorie della Società istriana di archeologia e storia patria*, 49 (1937), 189–224; and Cesare Cenci, 'Lodovico da Pirano e la sua attività letteraria', in *Storia e cultura al Santo*, ed. by Antonino Poppi, Fonti e studi per la storia del Sancto a Padova, 1 (Vicenza: Pozza, 1976), pp. 265–78. For a revised view of Lodovico's art of memory, see Heimann-Seelbach, *Ars und Scientia*, pp. 20–23, 436–43. Despite her contention that the content of the fifteenth-century art of memory treatises is substantially new, there is evidence of continuity between Lodovico's mnemonic precepts and Francesc Eiximenis's, particularly in the use of lines to structure mnemonic places.

[41] Delcorno, '"Ars praedicandi"', pp. 110–11.

[42] Lina Bolzoni, 'Costruire Immagini: L'Arte della memoria tra letteratura e arti figurativa', in *La Cultura della memoria*, ed. by Lina Bolzoni and Pietro Corsi (Bologna: il Mulino, 1992), pp. 57–97 (pp. 77–78); Bolzoni, 'St Bernardino da Siena', pp. 139–40.

[43] Alain de Lille describes a seraph in enthusiastic detail in *De sex alis cherubim*. Bonaventura's *Legenda minor* relates that a seraph on the cross appeared to Francis of Assisi as part of the stigmata experience, a theme that had a long life in Franciscan literature. Bolzoni, 'Predicazione

During his cycle of Lenten preaching at Florence in 1424, Bernardino wanted to focus his listeners' attention on penance. To achieve this goal, he sketched out from the very beginning of the six-week programme a detailed image of the Seraph. The creature had six wings, each divided into seven parts. The partitions became a series of numbered loci onto which the theme and its divisions could be superimposed. These divisions had a unifying idea to hold them together, although Bolzoni admits that the preacher sometimes had to strain to fit each day's reading into the schema of the wings. Each wing corresponded to a week of Lenten preaching, and each day received an 'illumination' from which additional 'rays' could spring. Thus, the seraph was a foundation piece with room for mnemonic additions.[44] In Holy Week, St Bernardino reserved the last three days to speak of the Resurrection and *Lignum vitae*. The image was also open to other revisions and expansions: sometimes Bernardino added diadems to the head and to the feet.

We cannot easily discover whether St Bernardino's mental constructions really helped the laity to remember his teachings, but we can marvel at the efforts he made to help them. We can also make a few judgements about their likely effectiveness. First, St Bernardino was a popular preacher who drew large crowds to every sermon, despite his tendency to berate sections of his audience. He was not above drawing notice to listeners who let their attention wander during his sermons. On one occasion, he called out, 'I see a woman who, if she were watching me, would not be looking where she is. Listen to me, I say.'[45] His popularity may have stemmed more from the force of his preaching than from structure or contents of his sermons, but at least the latter did not drive people away.

Second, such a canny speaker as Bernardino judged that his methods would be effective. We know that he developed these methods over time, and thus did not grasp at the first available idea. We should not easily dismiss his judgements. Finally, even if the Seraph slipped from his listeners' minds, it almost certainly helped Bernardino himself to keep six weeks of sermons in his own head.

e arte della memoria', pp. 185, 195. Hugh of St Victor also described Isaiah's two seraphim in detail at the beginning of *De arca Noe morali*, PL, CLXXVI, cols 622–26.

[44] Bolzoni, 'Predicazione e arte della memoria', pp. 190–91.

[45] Origo, *World of San Bernardino*, p. 13.

# Conclusion

As we have seen, ancient mnemonic schemes underwent a vital transformation from the time of the *Ad Herennium* (first century BC) to Bernardino da Siena (fifteenth century). Just as the importance of memory and the mechanics of mnemonic techniques were determined by the oratorical and judicial requirements of ancient society, so, too, were the medieval parameters of memory determined by the needs of medieval society. We can see the medieval changes best in the period beginning with the early twelfth century and ending in the early fifteenth. The emergence of the schools and the pastoral duties of the mendicant orders made new demands on the memories of the educated. Mnemonic devices which had previously been used only as mental aids now appeared on the page. In turn, new kinds of ordering schemes that were developed in the schools, such as the seven virtues and vices, the categories, and the four causes, became mnemonic schemes. In addition, the newly discovered books of Aristotelian psychology helped medieval philosophers explain why mnemonic devices, especially Cicero's art, functioned and helped to justify their use. Whether or not either of the two most prominent orders, the Dominicans and the Franciscans, actually revived the *Ad Herennium*'s art of memory, their members no longer shunned the method and promoted it for rhetorical and ethical purposes.

In addition, the Franciscans, at least (and possible the Dominicans as well), continued to employ the kind of meditational techniques used by monks in their own religious development. These methods involved imagery, especially of the virtues and vices. As the Franciscans sought to educate the laity through preaching, they sometimes employed the same kinds of imagery in their sermons. These images served many purposes: they aided the memory of the preachers by giving their sermons a structure; they taught the laity the fundamental beliefs of the Church about the virtues and vices; and they helped the laity to recall what they heard. By the end of the thirteenth century and the beginning of the fourteenth, friars like Robert Holcot, John Ridevall, and the author of the *Fasciculus morum* applied mnemonic imagery to their sermons and exempla collections. The kinds of imagery developed by the English classicizing friars then spread all over Europe.

However, as Heimann-Seelbach points out, it is not until the fifteenth century that we find the fully developed *ars memorativa* treatises studied by Yates. Many of these are written by friars, both Dominican and Franciscan. Though Heimann-Seelbach thinks these treatises have little relation to medieval practice, I am not sure that I agree. Some of them show clear ties to the kinds of practices espoused by Francesc Eiximenis in his *Ars praedicandi*. Some of them also evidence clear interest in the kinds of religious practices practiced in the Middle Ages that Heimann-Seelbach insists were not important to the mnemonic tradition.[1] In any case, the later Middle Ages made mnemonic techniques increasingly available to a wider audience. What was begun in sermons is continued in treatises that are increasingly copied into the vernacular and thus available to a much wider audience than most of the authors studied in this book.

Thus, the study of medieval mnemonic systems is not an esoteric exploration of an arcane subject on the periphery of medieval culture. On the contrary, the use of such techniques by the mendicants, whose activities touched almost every sphere of medieval society, indicate that the friars sought to render their pastoral duties as effectively as possible. First, they had to learn and to remember the relevant authorities, then they had to find a way to help their pastoral charges to learn the essentials of the faith and its practice. Mnemonic imagery and structures seemed an ideal method to many friars — to how many, it is hard to judge as yet. Further study of fourteenth- and fifteenth-century homiletic sources and *ars memorativa* treatises should render that question easier to answer.

[1] Heimann-Seelbach's knowledge of the mnemonic tracts and of ancient and medieval philosophy is phenomenal. Nevertheless, it appears to me that sometimes she is so committed to debunking Frances Yates's main arguments about the relationship of the *ars memorativa* that she misses some clear connections between medieval practice and that of the fifteenth century.

# Bibliography

## *Manuscripts*


### Basel

Universitätsbibliothek, MS A.X. 118

### Bordeaux

Bibliothèque municipale, MS 267

### Cambridge

Corpus Christi, MS 423
Peterhouse, MS 210

### Cologne

Historisches Archiv der Stadt Köln, HAStK 7002 119 (formerly Cod. GB fol. 119)

### Leeds

University Library, Brotherton Collection, MS 102

### London

British Library, MS Additional 30,049
British Library, MS Harley 2316
British Library, MS Harley 7322

British Library, MS Royal 7.C.I
British Library, MS Royal 12.E.xxi.
British Library, MS Sloane 1616

### New York

The Morgan Library and Museum, MS 298

### Oxford

Balliol College, MS 181
Bodleian Library, MS Bodley 649
Bodleian Library, MS Bodley 722 (SC 2648)

### Paris

Bibliothèque Mazarine, MS 271
Bibliothèque nationale de France, codex latinus 590
Bibliothèque nationale de France, codex latinus 15,451

### Prague

Státní knihovna, MS XII.B.20

### Vatican

Biblioteca Apostolica Vaticana, MS Palatinus latinus 1066

### Worcester

Cathedral Library, MS F 154

## *Primary Sources*

Ælred of Rievaulx, *De anima*, in *Opera omnia*, ed. by Anselm Hoste and Charles H. Talbot, CCCM, 1 (Turnhout: Brepols, 1971)
——, *Sermones I–XLVI*, ed. by Gaetano Raciti, CCCM, 2A (Turnhout: Brepols, 1988)
Albertus Magnus, *Commentary* on Aristotle, *On Memory and Recollection*, trans. by Jan M. Ziolkowski, in *Medieval Craft of Memory*, ed. by Carruthers and Ziolkowski, pp. 118–52
—— *De bono*, in *Opera omnia*, XXVIII, ed. by H. Kühle and others (Münster: Aschendorff, 1951)
——, *De memoria et reminiscentia*, in *Opera omnia*, IX, ed. by Borgnet
——, *Liber de apprehensione*, in *Opera omnia*, V, ed. by Borgnet

——, *Opera omnia*, ed. by Auguste Borgnet and others, 38 vols (Paris: Vrin, 1890–99)

Alexander of Hales, *Summa theologica* (Florence: Quaracchi, 1930)

Ambrose, *In Psalmum David CXVIII Expositio*, PL, XV, col. 1289C

Aristotle, *Categoriae vel Praedicamenta, 'Translatio Boethii'*, ed. by Lorenzo Minio-Paluello, Aristoteles latinus, 1.1–5 (Bruges: de Brouwer, 1961)

——, *Metaphysica libri I–IV.4; translatio Iacobi sive 'vetustissima' cum scholiis et translatio composita sive 'vetus'*, ed. by Gudrun Vuillemin-Diem, Aristoteles latinus, 25, 1–1a (Leiden: Brill, 1970)

Armstrong, Regis J., J. A. Wayne Hellman, and William J. Short, eds, *The Francis Trilogy of Thomas of Celano: The Life of Saint Francis, The Remembrance of the Desire of a Soul, The Treatise on the Miracles of Saint Francis* (Hyde Park: New City Press, 1998)

*Ars concionandi*, in St Bonaventura, *Opera omnia*, 10 vols (Ad Claras Aquas [Quaracchi]: Ex Typographia Collegii S. Bonaventurae, 1882–1902), IX, 8–21

Augustine of Hippo, *De civitate Dei*, ed. by Bernhard Dombart and Alfons Kalb, CCSL, 48 (Turnhout: Brepols, 1955)

——, *De Trinitate libri XV*, ed. by William J. Mountain, CCSL, 50–50A, 2 vols (Turnhout: Brepols, 1968)

——, *The Trinity*, trans. by Stephen McKenna, Fathers of the Church, 18 (Washington, DC: Catholic University of America Press, 1963)

Bacon, Roger, *Opera quaedam hactenus inedita*, ed. by John Sherren Brewer, Rolls Series, 15 (London: Longman, 1859)

——, *Opus tertium*, in *Opera quaedam hactenus inedita*, ed. by Brewer, pp. 3–310

Barcelona, Martí de, 'L'Ars praedicandi de Francisco Eixemensis', *Analecta sacra tarraconensia*, 12 (1936), 301–40

Baron, Roger, 'Hugonis de Sancto Victore Epitome Dindimi in philosophiam', *Traditio*, 11 (1955), 91–148

Berlioz, Jacques, and Jean-Luc Eichenlaub, eds, *Stephani de Borbone Tractatus de diversis materiis praedicabilibus: Prologus, Prima Pars De dono timoris*, CCCM, 124 (Turnhout: Brepols, 2002)

St Bernard, *Opera*, ed. by Jean Leclercq and H. M. Rochais, 8 vols (Rome: Editiones Cistercienses, 1957–77)

Bernardino da Siena, *Le prediche volgari: Quaresimale del 1424*, ed. by Ciro Cannarozzi, 2 vols (Pistoia: Pacinotti, 1934)

Berns, Jörg Jochen, ed., *Gedächtnislehren und Gedächtniskünste in Antike und Frühmittelalter* (Tübingen: Niemeyer, 2003)

Bersuire, Pierre, '*The Moral Reduction*, Book XV: *Ovid Moralized*: Prologue and Extracts', in *Medieval Literary Theory and Criticism*, ed. by Minnis and Scott, pp. 366–72

Bode, Georg Heinrich, ed., *Scriptores rerum mythicarum latini tres Romae nuper reperti I–II*, 2 vols (Cellis: Schulze, 1834; repr. Hildesheim: Olms, 1968)

Boethius, *De divisione*, PL, LXIV, cols 875–92

——, *De institutione arithmetica libri duo, De institutione musica libri quinque*, ed. by Godofredus Friedlein (Leipzig: Teubner, 1867)

——, *In topica Ciceronis commentaria*, PL, LXIV, cols 1039–1174

Bonaventura, *Legenda maior S. Francisci*, Analecta franciscana, 10.1 (Florence: Quaracchi, 1941)

——, *Opera omnia*, 10 vols (Ad Claras Aquas [Quaracchi]: Ex Typographia Collegii S. Bonaventurae, 1882–1902)

——, *Opera omnia: Sixti V., pontificis maximi jussu diligentissime emendata*, ed. by Adolpho Carolo Peltier, 15 vols (Paris: Vives, 1864–71)

Boncompagnus, *Rhetorica novissima*, ed. by Augusto Gaudenzi, in *Scripta anecdota antiquissimorum glossatorum*, 3 vols (Bologna: [n. pub.], 1888–1903), II (1892), 251–97

Boynton, Mary Fuertes, ed., 'Simon Alcock on Expanding the Sermon', *Harvard Theological Review*, 34 (1941), 201–16

Bradwardine, Thomas, *On Acquiring a Trained Memory*, trans. by Mary J. Carruthers, in *Medieval Craft of Memory*, ed. by Carruthers and Ziolkowski, pp. 205–14

Callus, Daniel A., *The 'Tabulae super originalia patrum' of Robert Kilwardby, O.P.* (Bruges: De Tempel, 1948)

Carruthers, Mary J., 'Thomas Bradwardine, "De memoria artificiale adquirenda"', *Journal of Medieval Latin*, 2 (1992), 25–43

Carruthers, Mary J., and Jan M. Ziolkowski, eds, *The Medieval Craft of Memory: An Anthology of Texts and Pictures* (Philadelphia: University of Pennsylvania Press, 2002)

Cassiodorus, *Institutiones*, ed. by Roger Aubrey Baskerville Mynors (Oxford: Clarendon Press, 1937)

——, *Institutions of Divine and Secular Learning and on the Soul*, trans. by James W. Halporn, Translated Texts for Historians, 42 (Liverpool: Liverpool University Press, 2004)

Charland, Thomas Marie, ed., *Artes praedicandi: Contribution à l'histoire de la rhétorique au moyen âge* (Ottawa: Institut d'études médiévales, 1936)

[Cicero, Marcus Tullius], *Ad C. Herennium. De ratione dicendi (Rhetorica ad Herennium)*, trans. by Harry Caplan, Loeb Classical Library (Cambridge, MA: Harvard University Press, 1954)

Cicero, Marcus Tullius, *De inventione, De optimo genere oratorum, Topica*, trans. by Harry Mortimer Hubbell, Loeb Classical Library (Cambridge, MA: Harvard University Press, 1960)

——, *M. Tullii Ciceronis Rhetorica*, I: *Libros De oratore tres continens*, ed. by A. S. Wilkins (Oxford: Clarendon Press, 1963)

Corbett, James A., ed., *The De instructione puerorum of William of Tournai, O.P.* (Notre Dame: Medieval Institute, University of Notre Dame, 1955)

Coulton, G. G., ed., *From St. Francis to Dante*, 2nd edn, Sources of Medieval History (Philadelphia: University of Pennsylvania Press, 1972)

David von Augsburg, *De exterioris et interioris hominis compositione secundum triplicem statum incipientium, proficientium et perfectorum*, in Bonaventura, *Opera omnia*, ed. by Peltier, XII, 292–442

——, *Spiritual Life and Progress*, trans. by Dominic Devas, 2 vols (London: Burns, Oates, and Washbourne, 1937)

*De domo interiori*, PL, CLXXXIV, cols 507–52

Delorme, F. M., 'L' "Ars faciendi sermones" de Géraud du Pescher', *Antonianum*, 19 (1944), 169–98

Denifle, Heinrich, and Emile Chatelain, eds, *Chartularium Universitatis Parisiensis*, 4 vols (Paris: Delalain, 1889–97; repr. Brussels: Culture et civilisation, 1964)

Dolce, Lodovico, *Dialogo [...] nelquale si ragiona del modo di accrescere et conservar la memoria* (Venice: Heredi di Marchiò Sessa [Appresso Enea de Alaris], 1575)

Engels, Joseph, and the Instituut voor Laat Latijn of Utrecht, eds, *Petrus Berchorius, Reductorium morale, liber XV: Ovidius moralizatus, cap. i: De formis figurisque deorum*, Werkmateriaal, 3 (Utrecht: Rijksuniversiteit, Instituut voor Laat Latijn, 1966)

Erbe, Theodor, ed., *Mirk's Festial*, EETS, e.s., 96 (London: Paul, Trench, and Trübner, 1905; repr. Millwood, NY: Kraus, 1975)

Faral, Edmond, ed., *Les Arts poétiques du XII^e^ et du XIII^e^*, Bibliothèque de l'école des hautes études, 238 (Paris: Champion, 1924; repr. 1958)

Francesc Eiximenis, '*Ars praedicandi*', ed. by P. Martí de Barcelona, in *Hometage a Antoni Rubió i Lluch: Miscellània d'estudis literaris històricis i lingüistics*, 3 vols (Barcelona: [n. pub.], 1936), pp. 300–40

——, *Lo Crestià: Selecció*, ed. by Albert Hauf (Barcelona: Edicions 62, 1983)

——, *Dotzè llibre del Crestià*, ed. by Curt J. Wittlin (Girona: Col'legi Universitari de Girona, Diputació de Girona, 1986)

——, *On Two Kinds of Order that Aid Understanding and Memory*, trans. by Kimberly A. Rivers, in *Medieval Craft of Memory*, ed. by Carruthers and Ziolkowski, pp. 189–204

——, *Psalterium alias Laudatorium Papae Benedicto XIII dedicatum*, ed. by Curt J. Wittlin (Toronto: Pontifical Institute of Mediaeval Studies, 1988)

Friedman, John Block, ed., *John de Foxton's Liber cosmographiae (1408): An Edition and Codicological Study*, Brill's Studies in Intellectual History, 5 (Leiden: Brill, 1988)

Fulgentius, Fabius Planciades, *Fulgentius the Mythographer*, trans. by George Whitbread (Columbus: Ohio State University Press, 1971)

——, *Opera*, ed. by Rudolph Helm (Leipzig: Teubner, 1898; repr. 1970)

Geoffroi de Vinsauf, *Poetria nova*, in *Les Arts poétiques du XII^e^ et du XIII^e^*, ed. by Faral, pp. 194–262

——, *Poetria nova*, trans. by Mary F. Nims (Toronto: Pontifical Institute of Mediaeval Studies, 1967)

Giovanni da San Gimignano, *Summa de exemplis et rerum similitudinibus locvpletissima Verbi Dei Concionatoribus cunctisque litararum studiosis maximo usui futura* (Lyon: Simphorianum Beraud et Stehanum Michaelem, 1585)

Green, William M., 'Hugo of St. Victor: *De tribus maximis circumstantiis gestorum*', *Speculum*, 18 (1943), 484–93

Gregg, Robert C., trans., *The Life of Antony*, III, in *Athanasius: The Life of Antony and The Letter to Marcellinus* (New York: Paulist, 1980)

Gregory the Great, *Dialogorum libri IV De vita et miraculis patrum italicorum*, PL, LXXVII, cols 149–430

——, 'Dialogues', in *Readings in Medieval History*, ed. by Patrick J. Geary, 3rd edn (Peterborough, ON: Broadview, 2003), pp. 199–220

——, *S. Gregorii Magni registrum epistularum libri VIII–XIV*, ed. by Dag Ludvig Norberg, CCSL, 140A (Turnhout: Brepols, 1982)

Guibert de Tournai, *De modo addiscendi*, ed. by Enrico Bonifacio (Turin: Società editrice internazionale, 1953)

Guilelmus Durandus, *Rationale divinorum officiorum I–VIII*, ed. by Anselme Davril, Timothy M. Thibodeau, and B. G. Guyot, CCCM, 140, 140A, 140B (Turnhout: Brepols, 1995–2000)

Halm, Carolus, ed., *Rhetores Latini minores* (Leipzig: Teubner, 1863)

Hermannus de Runa, *Sermones Festivales*, ed. by Edmundus Mikkers, CCCM, 64 (Turnhout: Brepols, 1986)

Hinnebusch, John Frederick, ed., *The Historia Occidentalis of Jacques de Vitry: A Critical Edition* (Fribourg: University Press, 1972)

Holcot, Robert, *Liber moralizationum historiarum, In Sapientiam* (Basel: [n. pub.], 1586)

——, *Super libros sapientiae* (Haguenau: [n. pub.], 1494; repr. Frankfurt: Minerva, 1974)

Horner, Patrick J., *A Macaronic Sermon Collection from Late Medieval England: Oxford, MS Bodley 649* (Toronto: Pontifical Institute of Mediaeval Studies, 2006)

Hugh of St Victor, *De arca Noe morali*, PL, CLXXVI, cols 649–80

——, *De arca Noe mystica*, PL, CLXXVI, cols 681–704

——, *De meditando*, in *Opera omnia*, PL, CLXXVI, cols 993–98

——, *De modo di<s>cendi et meditandi*, in *Opera omnia*, PL, CLXXVI, cols 875–80

——, *De sacramentis*, PL, CLXXVI, cols 173–618

——, *De scripturis et scriptoribus sacris praenotatiunculae*, in *Opera omnia*, PL, CLXXV, cols 9–28

——, *The Didascalicon of Hugh of St. Victor*, trans. by Jerome Taylor (New York: Columbia University Press, 1961)

——, *Didascalicon: De studio legendi*, ed. by Charles Henry Buttimer (Washington, DC: Catholic University of America Press, 1939)

——, *Hugonis de Sancto Victore, Opera Propaedeutica: Practica geometriae, De grammatica, Epitome Dindimi in Philosophiam*, ed. by Roger Baron (Notre Dame: University of Notre Dame Press, 1966)

——, *In Salomonis Ecclesiasten homiliae I*, PL, CLXXV, cols 115D–133D

Humbert de Romans, *On the Sacraments of the Christian Faith (De Sacramentis)*, trans. by Roy J. Deferrari (Cambridge, MA: Medieval Academy of America, 1951)

——, *Opera de vita regulari*, ed. by Joachim Joseph Berthier, 2 vols (Rome: [n. pub.], 1888)

——, 'Treatise on the Formation of Preachers', in *Early Dominicans: Selected Writings*, ed. by Simon Tugwell, Classics of Western Spirituality, 33 (New York: Paulist, 1982)

Isaac de l'Etoile, *Epistola de anima*, PL, CXCIV, cols 1875–90

Jean de La Rochelle, *Tractatus de divisione multiplici potentiarum animae*, ed. by P. Michaud-Quantin (Paris: Vrin, 1964)

Johannes Scotus Eriugena, *Iohannis Scotia Annotationes in Marcianum*, ed. by Cora E. Lutz (Cambridge, MA: Medieval Academy of America, 1939)

Johannes Trithemius, *Catalogus illustrium virorum*, in *Opera historica*, ed. by Marquard Freher (1601; repr. Frankfurt a.M.: Minerva, 1966)

Johannes von Werden, *Sermones dormi secure de sanctis* (Nuremberg: Anton Koberger, 1494)

——, *Sermones dormi secure de tempore* (Basel: Printer of the Meffreth, 1489)

——, *Sermones dormi secure de tempore* (Nürnberg: Anton Koberger, 1498)

Jourdain, Charles, *Index chronologicus chartarum pertinentium ad historiam Universitatis parisiensis: Ab ejus originibus ad finem decimi sexti saeculi* (Paris: Hachette, 1862; repr. Brussels: Culture et civilisation, 1966)

Kilwardby, Robert, *De natura theologiae*, ed. by Fridericus Stegmüller (Münster: Aschendorff monasterii, 1935)

——, *De ortu scientiarum*, ed. by Albert G. Judy, Auctores britannici medii aevi, 4 (London: British Academy; Toronto: Pontifical Institute of Mediaeval Studies, 1976)

Kulscár, Peter, ed., *Mythographi Vaticani I et II*, CCSL, 91C (Turnhout: Brepols, 1987)

Leclercq, Jean, 'Le "De grammatica" de Hugues de Saint-Victor', *Archives d'histoire doctrinale et littéraire de moyen âge*, 14 (1943–45), 263–322

Lecoy de la Marche, A., ed., *Anecdotes historiques, légendes et apologues tirés du recueil inédit d'Étienne de Bourbon, dominicain du XIIIe siècle* (Paris: Librairie Renouard, 1877)

Liebeschütz, Hans, ed., *Fulgentius metaforalis: Ein Beitrag zur Geschichte der antiken Mythologie im Mittelalter*, Studien der Bibliothek Warburg, 4 (Leipzig: Teubner, 1926)

Luther, Martin, *Selected Writings of Martin Luther, 1529–1546*, ed. by Theodore G. Tappert, 4 vols (Minneapolis: Fortress, 1967)

Martene, Edmundus, and Ursinus Durand, eds, *Thesaurus novus anecdotorum, Tomus primus: Complectens regum ac principum aliorumque virorum illustrium epistolas et diplomata* (Paris: Delaulne [and others], 1717)

Martianus Capella, *De nuptiis Philologiae et Mercurii*, ed. by James Willis (Leipzig: Teubner, 1983)

Marx, Fridericus, ed., *De ratione dicendi Ad C. Herennium libri IV [M. Tulli Ciceronis Ad Herennium libri vi]* (Leipzig: Teubner, 1894)

Matthew, Frederic David, ed., *The English Works of Wyclif Hitherto Unprinted*, 2nd rev. edn, EETS, o.s., 74 (London: Kegan Paul, Trench, Trübner, 1902; repr. Millwood, NY: Kraus, 1973)

McGinn, Bernard, ed., *Three Treatises on Man: A Cistercian Anthropology*, Cistercian Fathers Series, 24 (Kalamazoo: Cistercian, 1977)

McKeon, Richard, ed., *The Basic Works of Aristotle* (New York: Random House, 1941)

Migne, Jacques-Paul, ed., *Patrologiae cursus completus, series latina*, 221 vols (Paris: Garnier, 1844–91)

Nève, Joseph, ed., *Sermons choisis de Michel Menot (1508–1518)*, Bibliothèque du XVe siècle, 25 (Paris: Champion, 1924)

Oesterley, Hermann, ed., *Gesta Romanorum* (Berlin: Weidmännische Buchhandlung, 1872; repr. 1963)

Pack, Roger A., 'An *Ars memorativa* from the Late Middle Ages', *Archives d'histoire doctrinale et littéraire du moyen âge*, 46 (1979), 221–75

——, '*Artes memorativae* in a Venetian Manuscript', *Archives d'histoire doctrinale et littéraire du moyen âge*, 50 (1983), 257–300

Peter of Spain, *Summulae logicales*, ed. by Joseph M. Bochenski ([Turin]: Marietti, [1947])

Petrus Damianus, *Contra inscitiam et incuriam clericorum*, PL, CXLV, cols 497–504

Pico della Mirandola, Gianfrancesco, *On the Imagination*, trans. by Harry Caplan (Westport, CT: Greenwood, 1957)

Pierre de Celles, *Opera omnia*, PL, CCII

——, *Peter of Celle, Selected Works*, trans. by Hugh Feiss, Cistercian Studies Series, 100 (Kalamazoo: Cistercian, 1987)

Porphyry, *Categoriarum supplementa: Porphyrii Isagoge translatio Boethii et anonymi fragmentum vulgo vocatum 'Liber sex principiorum'*, ed. by L. Minio-Paluello and Bernard Geoffrey Dod, Aristoteles Latinus, I, 6–7 (Bruges: de Brouwer, 1966)

Quintilian, *The Institutio Oratoria: With an English Translation by H. E. Butler*, Loeb Classical Library (London: Heinemann, 1921)

——, *Institutionis oratoriae libri duodecim*, ed. by Michael Winterbottom, 2 vols (Oxford: Clarendon Press, 1970)

Rabanus Maurus, *De universo libri viginti duo*, PL, CXI

Remigius of Auxerre, *Commentum in Martianum Capellam*, ed. by Cora E. Lutz, 2 vols (Leiden: Brill, 1965)

Romberch, Johannes, *Congestorium artificiose memorie* (Venice: Melchior Sessa, 1533)

Ross, W. O., 'A Brief *Forma predicandi*', *Modern Philology*, 34 (1936–37), 337–44

Salimbene de Adam, *Cronica*, ed. by Ferdinando Bernini, 2 vols (Bari: Gins, Laterza, and Figli, 1942)

Seneca, *L. Annaei Senecae libri De beneficiis et De clementia*, ed. by Martinus Clarentius Gertz (Berolini: Weidmannos, 1876)

——, *On Benefits* (London: Bell, 1911)

Sorabji, Richard, *Aristotle on Memory* (Providence: Brown University Press, 1972)

Stahl, William Harris, Richard Johnson, and E. L. Burge, *Martianus Capella and the Seven Liberal Arts*, 2 vols (New York: Columbia University Press, 1971–77)

Stump, Eleonore, *Boethius's 'De topicis differentiis'* (Ithaca: Cornell University Press, 1978)

Thomas Aquinas, *Commentary* on Aristotle, *On Memory and Recollection*', trans. by John Burchill, in *Medieval Craft of Memory*, ed. by Carruthers and Ziolkowski, pp. 153–88

——, *In Aristotelis libros de sensu et sensato, De memoria et reminiscentia commentarium*, ed. by P. F. Raymundi M. Spiazzi (Rome: Marietti, 1949)

——, *Summa theologiae*, in *Opera omnia*, III, ed. by E. Fretté and P. Maré (Paris: Vives, 1872)

Thomas of Chobham, *Summa confessorum*, ed. by F. Broomfield, Analecta mediaevalia namurcensia, 25 (Louvain: Nauwelaerts, 1968)

——, *Summa de arte praedicandi*, ed. by Franco Morenzoni, CCCM, 82 (Turnhout: Brepols, 1988)

Thomas Waleys, *De modo componendi sermones*, in *Artes praedicandi: Contribution à l'histoire de la rhétorique au moyen âge*, ed. by Thomas Marie Charland (Ottawa: Institut d'études médiévales, 1936), pp. 325–403

Thomas, Antoine, 'Extraits des Archives du Vatican pour servir à l'histoire littéraire', *Romania*, 11 (1882), 177–87

Thorndike, Lynn, *University Records and Life in the Middle Ages* (New York: Columbia University Press, 1949)

Tommaso da Celano, *Vita prima S. Francisci*, Analecta franciscana, 10.1 (Florence: Quaracchi, 1926)

——, *Vita secunda S. Francisci*, Analecta franciscana, 10.1 (Florence: Quaracchi, 1927)

Tugwell, Simon, ed., *Early Dominicans: Selected Writings* (Ramsey, NJ: Paulist, 1982)

Vincent de Beauvais, *De eruditione filiorum nobilium*, ed. by Arpad Steiner (Cambridge, MA: Medieval Academy of America, 1938)

——, *Speculum quadruplex sive, Speculum maius*, 4 vols (Graz: Akademische Druck- u. Verlagsanstalt, 1964–65)

Webb, Clement Charles Julian, ed., *Ioannis Saresberiensis episcopi carnotensis Metalogicon libri III* (Oxford: Clarendon Press, 1929)

Wenzel, Siegfried, ed., *Fasciculus morum: A Fourteenth-Century Preacher's Handbook* (University Park: Pennsylvania State University Press, 1989)

Wey, Jospeh C., 'The *Sermo finalis* of Robert Holcot', *Mediaeval Studies*, 11 (1949), 219–24

Wibald of Corvey, 'Epistola 147', in *Epistolae*, PL, CLXXXIX, cols 1087–1508

Wilson, Thomas, *The Art of Rhetoric (1560)*, ed. by Peter E. Medine (University Park: Pennsylvania State University Press, 1994)

Wright, Thomas, ed., *Political Poems and Songs Relating to English History*, Rolls Series, 14, 2 vols (London: Longman, Green, Longman, and Roberts, 1861)

Ziliotto, Baccio, 'Frate Lodovico da Pirano 1390–1450 e le sue Regulae memorie artificialis', *Atti e memorie della Società istriana di archeologia e storia patria*, 49 (1937), 189–224

Zorzetti, Nevio, and Jacques Berlioz, eds, *Le Premier mythographie du Vatican* (Paris: Les Belles Lettres, 1995)

## *Secondary Sources*

Akae, Yuichi, 'Between *Artes praedicandi* and Actual Sermons: Robert of Basevorn's *Forma praedicandi* and the Sermons of John Waldeby, OESA', in *Constructing the Medieval Sermon*, ed. by Andersson, pp. 9–31

Alexander, Jonathan James Graham and Margaret T. Gibson, eds, *Medieval Learning and Literature: Essays Presented to Richard William Hunt* (Oxford: Clarendon Press, 1976)

Allen, Judson B., 'Commentary as Criticism: The Text, Influence and Literary Theory of the "Fulgentius Metafored" of John Ridewall', in *Acta Conventus Neo-Latini Amstelodamensis: Proceedings of the Second International Congress of Neo-Latin Studies*, ed. by P. Tuynman, G. C. Kuiper, and Eckhard Kessler (Munich: Fink, 1979), pp. 25–47

——, *The Friar as Critic: Literary Attitudes in the Later Middle Ages* (Nashville: Vanderbilt University Press, 1971)

Amos, Thomas L., Eugene A. Green, and Beverly Mayne Kienzle, eds, *De Ore Domini: Preacher and Word in the Middle Ages*, Studies in Medieval Culture, 27 (Kalamazoo: Medieval Institute Publications, 1989)

Andersson, Roger, ed., *Constructing the Medieval Sermon*, Sermo, 6 (Turnhout: Brepols, 2007)

Antoine, Jean Philippe, 'Ancora sulle Virtù: La "nuova iconografia" et le immagini di memoria', *Prospettiva*, 30 (1982), 13–29

Aston, Margaret, 'Lollards and Images', in Margaret Aston, *Lollards and Reformers: Images and Literacy in Late Medieval Religion* (London: Hambledon, 1984), pp. 135–92

——, *Lollards and Reformers: Images and Literacy in Late Medieval Religion* (London: Hambledon, 1984)

d'Avray, David L., 'Another Friar and Antiquity', in *Modern Questions*, ed. by Bériou and d'Avray, pp. 247–57

——, *Medieval Marriage Sermons: Mass Communication in a Culture Without Print* (Oxford: Oxford University Press, 2001)

——, *Medieval Marriage: Symbolism and Society* (Oxford: Oxford University Press, 2005)

——, 'Portable Vademecum Books Containing Franciscan and Dominican Texts', in *Manuscripts at Oxford: An Exhibition in Memory of Richard William Hunt (1908–1979)*, ed. by Albinia Catherine de la Mare and B. C. Barker-Benfield (Oxford: Bodleian Library, 1980), pp. 60–64

——, *The Preaching of the Friars: Sermons Diffused from Paris before 1300* (Oxford: Oxford University Press, 1985)

——, 'Printing, Mass Communication, and Religious Reformation: The Middle Ages and After', in *The Uses of Script and Print, 1300–1700*, ed. by Julia C. Crick and Alexandra Walsham (Cambridge: Cambridge University Press, 2004), pp. 50–70

——, 'Sermons to the Upper Bourgeoisie by a Thirteenth-Century Franciscan', *Studies in Church History*, 16 (1979), 187–99

——, 'The Wordlists in the "Ars faciendi sermones" of Geraldus de Piscario', *Franciscan Studies*, 16 (1978), 184–93

Baldwin, John W., *Masters, Princes and Merchants: The Social Views of Peter the Chanter and his Circle*, 2 vols (Princeton: Princeton University Press, 1970)

Baron, Roger, 'La Chronique de Hugues de Saint-Victor', *Studia Gratiana*, 12 (1967), 167–80

——, *Science et sagesse chez Hugues de Saint-Victor* (Paris: de Brouwer, 1963)

——, 'Spiritualité médiévale: Le traité de la contemplation et ses espèces', *Revue d'ascétique et de mystique*, 39 (1963), 137–51

Bataillon, Louis-Jacques, 'L'agir humain d'après les distinctions bibliques du XIIIe siècle', in *La prédication*, ed. by d'Avray and Bériou, pp. 776–90

——, *La prédication au XIIIe siècle en France et Italie*, ed. by David d'Avray and Nicole Bériou (Aldershot: Variorum, 1993)

Baudry, Léon, 'Wibert de Tournai', *Revue d'histoire franciscaine*, 5 (1928), 23–61

Baxandall, Michael, *Painting and Experience in Fifteenth-Century Italy: A Primer in the Social History of Pictorial Style*, 2nd edn (Oxford: Oxford University Press, 1988)

Bazàn, Bernardo C., and others, eds, *Les Questions disputées et les questions quodlibétiques dans les facultés de théologie, de droit et de médecine*, Typologie des sources du moyen âge occidental, 44–45 (Turnhout: Brepols, 1985)

Becq, Annie, ed., *L'Encyclopédisme, Actes du Colloque de Caen, 12–16 janvier 1987* (Caen: Éditions aux amateurs de livres, 1987)

Benson, Robert L., and Giles Constable, eds, *Renaissance and Renewal in the Twelfth Century* (Cambridge, MA: Harvard University Press, 1982)

Berg, Kirsten M., 'On the Use of Mnemonic Schemes in Sermon Composition: The *Old Norwegian Homily Book*', in *Constructing the Medieval Sermon*, ed. by Andersson, pp. 221–36

Berger, Carol, 'The Hand and the Art of Memory', *Musica disciplina*, 35 (1981), 87–120

Bériou, Nicole, *L'Avènement des maîtres de la Parole: La Prédication à Paris au XIIIe siècle*, Collection des études augustiniennes, Série moyen âge et temps modernes, 31–32, 2 vols (Paris: Institut d'études augustiniennes, 1998)

——, 'Les Sermons Latins après 1200', in *Sermon*, ed. by Kienzle, pp. 323–447

Bériou, Nicole, and David L. d'Avray, eds, *Modern Questions about Medieval Sermons: Essays on Marriage, Death, History and Sanctity* (Spoleto: Centro italiano di studi sull'alto medioevo, 1994)

Berlière, Ursmer, 'Pierre Bersuire', *Revue bénédictine*, 19 (1902), 317–20

Berlioz, Jacques, 'Comment se souvenir d'un *exemplum*: Marine déguisée en moine', in *Prêcher d'exemples: Récits de prédicateurs du moyen âge*, ed. by Jean-Claude Schmitt (Paris: Stade, 1985), pp. 173–78

——, 'La Mémoire du prédicateur: Recherches sur la mémorisation des récits exemplaires (XIII^e^–XV^e^ siècles)', in *Temps, mémoire, tradition au moyen âge: Actes du XIII^e^ Congrès de la société des historiens médiévistes de l'enseignement supérieur public, Aix-en-Provence, 4–5 Juin 1982* (Aix-en-Provence: Université de Provence, 1983), pp. 157–83

——, '"Quand dire c'est faire dire": Exempla et confession chez Étienne de Bourbon († v. 1261)', in *Faire croire: Modalités de la diffusion et de la réception des messages religieux du XII^e^ au XV^e^ siècle; Table Ronde organisée par l'École française de Rome, en collaboration avec l'Institut d'histoire médiévale de l'Université de Padoue (Rome, 22–23 juin 1979)* (Rome: École française de Rome, 1981), pp. 299–335

Black, Deborah L., 'Estimation (Wahm) in Avicenna: The Logical and Psychological Dimensions', *Dialogue*, 32 (1993), 219–58

Bloomfield, Morton W., *The Seven Deadly Sins: An Introduction to the History of a Religious Concept; With Special Reference to Medieval English Literature* (East Lansing: Michigan State College Press, 1952)

Bloomfield, Morton W., and others, eds, *Incipits of Latin Works on the Virtues and Vices, 1100–1500 A.D.: Including a Series of Incipits of Works on the Pater Noster*, Medieval Academy of America, 88 (Cambridge, MA: Medieval Academy of America, 1979)

Blum, Herwig, *Die Antike Mnemotechnik* (New York: Olms, 1969)

Boese, Helmut, 'John Ridevalle und seine Expositio zu Austins Gottesstaat', in *Xenia medii Aevi historiam illustrantia oblata Thomae Kaepelli O.P.*, ed. by Raymond Creytens and Pius Künzle (Rome: Storia e letteratura, 1978), pp. 371–78

Bohl, Cornelius, *Geistlicher Raum: Räumliche Sprachbilder als Träger spiritueller Erfahrung, dargestellt am Werk De compositione des David von Augsburg*, Franziskanische Forschungen, 42 (Werl: Coelde, 2000)

Bolzoni, Lina, 'Allegories and Memory Images: The *Colloquio Spirituale* and the "Tower of Knowledge Cycle"', in Lina Bolzoni, *Web of Images*, pp. 41–81

——, 'Il *Colloquio spirituale* di Simone da Cascina: Note su allegoria e immagini della memoria', *Rivista di letteratura italiana*, 3 (1985), 9–65

——, 'Costruire immagini: L'Arte della memoria tra letteratura e arti figurativa', in *La Cultura della memoria*, ed. by Bolzoni and Corsi, pp. 57–97

——, *The Gallery of Memory: Literary and Iconographic Models in the Age of the Printing Press*, trans. by Jeremy Parzen (Toronto: University of Toronto Press, 2001)

——, 'Oratoria e prediche', *Letteratura italiana*, 3 (1984), 1041–74

——, 'Predicazione e arte della memoria: Un quaresimale di Bernardino da Siena e l'immagine del Serafino', in *Musagetes: Festschrift für Wolfram Prinz zu seinem 60. Geburtstag am 5. Februar 1989*, ed. by Ronald G. Kecks (Berlin: Mann, 1991), pp. 179–95

——, *La stanza della memoria: Modeli letterari e iconografici nell'éta della stampa* (Turin: Einaudi, 1995)

——, 'St Bernardino da Siena', in Lina Bolzoni, *Web of Images*, pp. 117–95

——, 'Teatralità e tecniche della memoria in Bernardino da Siena', *Intersezioni*, 4 (1984), 271–87

——, 'Trees and Other Schemas: Some Examples of their Use', in Lina Bolzoni, *Web of Images*, pp. 83–117

——, 'The "Triumph of Death Cycle" Frescoes in the Pisan Camposanto and Dominican Preaching', in Lina Bolzoni, *Web of Images*, pp. 11–40

——, *The Web of Images: Vernacular Preaching from its Origins to St Bernardino da Siena* (Aldershot: Ashgate, 2004)

Bolzoni, Lina, and Pietro Corsi, eds, *La Cultura della memoria* (Bologna: Il Mulino, 1992)

'Boncompagno', *Dizionario biografico degli italiani*, 72 vols to date (Rome: Istituto della Enciclopedia italiana, 1960–), XI, 720–25

Bonde, S., ed., *Survival of the Gods: Classical Mythology in Medieval Art; An Exhibition by the Department of Art, Brown University, Bell Gallery, List Art Center* (Providence: Brown University, 1987)

Boyle, Leonard, 'The Date of the *Summa praedicantium* of John of Bromyard', *Speculum*, 48 (1973), 533–37

Boynton, Susan, 'Training for the Liturgy as a Form of Monastic Education', in *Medieval Monastic Education*, ed. by Muessig, pp. 7–20

Brady, I., 'The History of Mental Prayer in the Order of Friars Minor', *Franciscan Studies*, 11 (1951), 317–45

Bremond, Claude and Jacques Le Goff, *L' 'Exemplum'*, Typologie des sources du moyen âge occidental, 40 (Turnhout: Brepols, 1982)

Briscoe, Marianne G., and Barbara H. Jage, *Artes praedicandi and Artes orandi*, Typologie des sources du moyen âge occidental, 61 (Turnhout: Brepols, 1992)

*British Museum Catalogue of Additions to the Manuscripts 1931–35* (London: Trustees of the British Museum, 1967)

Browning, Robert, 'Oratory and Epistolography', in *Cambridge History of Classical Literature*, II: *Latin Literature*, ed. by E. J. Kenney (Cambridge: Cambridge University Press, 1982)

Brundage, James A., *Medieval Canon Law* (London: Longman, 1995)

Buffa, Giuseppa Saccardo del, 'Dalla narrazione alla scena pittorica mediante la tecniche della memoria (Wien, Ö.N.B. 4444)', *Arte lombarda*, 105–07 (1993), 79–84

Bundy, Murray Wright, *The Theory of Imagination in Classical and Medieval Thought* (Urbana: University of Illinois Press, 1927)

Burnett, Charles, 'Give him the White Cow: Notes and Note-Taking in the Universities in the Twelfth and Thirteenth Centuries', *History of Universities*, 14 (1995–96), 1–30

Burnham, Philip Edward, 'Cultural Life at Papal Avignon, 1309–1376' (unpublished doctoral thesis, Tufts University, 1972)

Bynum, Caroline Walker, *Docere verbo et exemplo: An Aspect of Twelfth-century Spirituality*, Harvard Theological Studies, 21 (Missoula, MT: Scholars, 1978)

Camargo, Martin, *Ars dictaminis, Ars dictandi*, Typologie des sources du moyen âge occidental, 60 (Turnhout: Brepols, 1991)

Camille, Michael, 'Seeing and Reading: Some Visual Implications of Medieval Literacy and Illiteracy', *Art History*, 8 (1985), 26–49

Caplan, Harry, *Mediaeval 'Artes praedicandi': A Hand-List*, Cornell Studies in Classical Philology, 24 (Ithaca: Cornell University Press, 1934)

——, *Mediaeval 'Artes praedicandi': A Supplementary Hand-List*, Cornell Studies in Classical Philology, 25 (Ithaca: Cornell University Press, 1936)

Carruthers, Mary J., 'Boncompagno at the Cutting-Edge of Rhetoric: Rhetorical *Memoria* and the Craft of Memory', *Journal of Medieval Latin*, 6 (1996), 44–64

——, *The Book of Memory: A Study of Memory in Medieval Culture* (Cambridge: Cambridge University Press, 1990)

——, *The Book of Memory: A Study of Memory in Medieval Culture*, 2nd edn (New York: Cambridge University Press, 2008)

——, *The Craft of Thought: Meditation, Rhetoric, and the Making of Images, 400–1200* (Cambridge: Cambridge University Press, 1998)

——, 'Late Antique Rhetoric, Early Monasticism, and the Revival of School Rhetoric', in *Latin Grammar and Rhetoric*, ed. by Lanham, pp. 239–57

——, 'The Poet as Master Builder: Composition and Locational Memory in the Middle Ages', *New Literary History*, 24 (1993), 881–904

——, 'Reading with Attitude, Remembering the Book', in *The Book and the Body*, ed. by Dolores Warwick Frese and Katherine O'Brien O'Keefe, University of Notre Dame Ward-Philips Lectures in English Language and Literature, 14 (Notre Dame: University of Notre Dame Press, 1997), pp. 1–33

Cenci, Cesare , 'Lodovico da Pirano e la sua attività letteraria', in *Storia e cultura al Santo*, ed. by Antonino Poppi, Fonti e studi per la storia del Sancto a Padova, 1 (Vicenza: Pozza, 1976), pp. 265–78

Chance, Jane, 'The Medieval "Apology for Poetry": Fabulous Narrative and Stories of the Gods', in *Mythographic Art*, ed. by Chance, pp. 3–44

——, *Medieval Mythography*, I: *From Roman North Africa to the School of Chartres, A.D. 433–1177* (Gainesville: University of Florida Press, 1994)

——, *Medieval Mythography*, II: *From the School of Chartres to the Court at Avignon, 1177–1350* (Gainesville: University of Florida Press, 2000)

——, 'The Origins and Development of Medieval Mythography: From Homer to Dante', in *Mapping the Cosmos*, ed. by Chance and O'Neil Wells, pp. 35–64

——, ed., *The Mythographic Art: Classical Fable and the Rise of the Vernacular in Early France and England* (Gainesville: University of Florida Press, 1990)

Chance, Jane, and Raymond O'Neil Wells, eds, *Mapping the Cosmos* (Houston: Rice University Press, 1985)

Chenu, Marie-Dominique, *La Théologie au douzième siècle*, 3rd edn (Paris: Vrin, 1976)

——, *Nature, Man, and Society in the Twelfth Century*, ed. by Jerome Taylor and Lester K. Little (Chicago: University of Chicago Press, 1968)

Clanchy, M. T., *Abelard: A Medieval Life* (Oxford: Blackwell, 1997)

——, *From Memory to Written Record*, 2nd edn (Oxford: Blackwell, 1993)

Cogan, Marc, 'Rodolphus Agricola and the Semantic Revolutions of the History of Invention', *Rhetorica*, 2 (1984), 163–94

Coleman, Janet, *Ancient and Medieval Memories: Studies in the Reconstruction of the Past* (Cambridge: Cambridge University Press, 1992)

——, 'English Culture in the Fourteenth Century', in *Chaucer and the Italian Trecento*, ed. by Piero Boitani (Cambridge: Cambridge University Press, 1983), pp. 33–63

Colish, Marcia L., 'Another Look at the School of Laon', *Archives d'histoire doctrinale et littéraire de moyen âge*, 53 (1986), 7–22

——, *Medieval Foundations of the Western Intellectual Tradition, 400–1400* (New Haven: Yale University Press, 1997)

——, 'Systematic Theology and Theological Renewal in the Twelfth Century', *Journal of Medieval and Renaissance Studies*, 18 (1988), 135–56

Constable, Giles, 'The Monastic Policy of Peter the Venerable', in *Pierre Abélard, Pierre le Vénérable*, pp. 119–42

Cooke, J. D., 'Euhemerism: A Medieval Interpretation of Classical Paganism', *Speculum*, 2 (1927), 396–410

Copeland, Rita, *Rhetoric, Hermeneutics, and Translation in the Middle Ages: Academic Traditions and Vernacular Texts*, Cambridge Studies in Medieval Literature (Cambridge: Cambridge University Press, 1991)

Coulton, G. G., *Art and the Reformation* (Cambridge: Cambridge University Press, 1953)

Courtenay, William J., *Adam Wodehouse: An Introduction to his Life and Writings* (Leiden: Brill, 1978)

——, 'The Bible in the Fourteenth Century: Some Observations', *Church History*, 54 (1985), 176–87

——, 'The Franciscan studia in Southern Germany in the Fourteenth Century', in *Gesellschaftsgeschichte: Festschrift für Karl Bosl zum 80. Geburtstag*, ed. by Ferdinand Seibt, 2 vols (Munich: Oldenbourg, 1988), II, 81–90

——, 'The Instructional Programme of the Mendicant Convents at Paris in the Early Fourteenth Century', in *The Medieval Church: Universities, Heresy, and Christian Life: Essays in Honour of Gordon Leff*, ed. by Peter Biller and Barrie Dobson, Studies in Church History, Subsidia 11 (Woodbridge: Boydell and Brewer, 1999), pp. 77–92

——, 'The Lost Matthew Commentary of Robert Holcot, OP', *AFP*, 50 (1980), 103–12

——, 'The Role of English Thought in the Transformation of University Education in the Late Middle Ages', in *Rebirth, Reform and Resilience: Universities in Transition 1300–1700*, ed. by James M. Kittelson and Pamela J. Transue (Columbus: Ohio State University Press, 1984), pp. 103–62

——, *Schools and Scholars in Fourteenth-Century England* (Princeton: Princeton University Press, 1987)

——, 'Spanish and Portuguese Scholars at the University of Paris in the Fourteenth and Fifteenth Centuries: The Exchange of Ideas and Texts', in *Medieval Iberia: Changing Societies and Cultures in Contact and Transition*, ed. by Ivy A. Corfis and Ray Harris-Northall (Woodbridge: Tamesis, 2007), pp. 110–19

——, 'Study Abroad: German Students at Bologna, Paris, and Oxford in the Fourteenth Century', in *University and Schooling in Medieval Society*, ed. by William J. Courtenay, Jürgen Miethke, and David B. Priest, Education and Society in the Middle Ages and Renaissance, 10 (Leiden: Brill, 2000), pp. 7–31

Coveney, Dorothy K., 'Johannes Sintram de Herbipoli', *Speculum*, 16 (1941), 336–39

Cruel, Rudolf, *Geschichte der deutschen Predigt im Mittelalter* (Detmold: Mener'sche Hofbuchhandlung, 1879)

Curtius, Ernst Robert, *European Literature and the Latin Middle Ages*, trans. by William R. Trask (New York: Bollingen, 1953)

Dahmus, John W., '*Dormi secure*: The Lazy Preacher's Model of Holiness for his Flock', in *Models of Holiness*, ed. by Kienzle, pp. 301–16

Delcorno, Carlo, 'L'ars praedicandi di Bernardino da Siena', *Lettere italiane*, 32 (1980), 441–75

——, '"Ars praedicandi" e "Ars memorativa" nell'esperienza di San Bernardino da Siena', *Bullettino della deputazione abruzzese di storia patria*, 70 (1980), 77–162

——, *Exemplum e letteratura: Tra medioevo e rinascimento* (Bologna: Il Mulino, 1989)

*Dictionary of National Biography* (Oxford: Oxford University Press, 1909– )

*Dictionnaire d'histoire et de géographie ecclésiastiques*, ed. by Alfred Baudrillart, Albert Vogt, and Urbain Rouziès (Paris: Letouzey et Ané, 1912– )

*Dictionnaire de spiritualité ascétique et mystique: doctrine et histoire*, ed. by Marcel Viller, Ferdinand Cavallera, and J. de Guibert, 17 vols (Paris: Beauchesne, 1932–95)

*Dictionnaire de théologie catholique: Contenant l'exposé des doctrines de la théologie catholique, leurs preuves et leur histoire*, ed. by Alfred Vacant, 15 vols (Paris: Letouzey et Ané, 1899–1950 )

DiLorenzo, Raymond D., 'The Collection Form and the Art of Memory in the "Libellus super ludo schachorum" of Jacobus de Cessolis', *Mediaeval Studies*, 35 (1973), 205–21

Dondaine, Antoine, 'La vie et les oeuvres de Jean de San Gimignano', *AFP*, 9 (1939), 128–83

Duffy, Eamon, *The Stripping of the Altars: Traditional Religion in England, c. 1400–c. 1580* (New Haven: Yale University Press, 1992)

Duggan, Lawrence G., 'Was Art Really the "book of the illiterate"?', *Word and Image*, 5 (1989), 227–51

Ebbesen, Sten, 'Ancient Scholastic Logic as the Source of Medieval Scholastic Logic', in *Cambridge History of Later Medieval Philosophy*, ed. by Kretzmann, Kenny, and Pinborg, pp. 101–27

Ellspermann, Gerard Leo, *The Attitude of the Early Christian Latin Writers Toward Pagan Literature and Learning*, Catholic University of America Patristic Studies, 82 (Washingon, DC: Catholic University of America Press of America, 1949)

Emden, Alfred Brotherston, *A Biographical Register of the University of Oxford to A.D. 1500*, 3 vols (Oxford: Clarendon Press, 1957–59)

Elliot, K. O., and J. P. Elder, 'A Critical Edition of the Vatican Mythographers', *Transactions of the American Philological Association*, 78 (1947), 189–207

Enders, Jody, *The Medieval Theater of Cruelty: Rhetoric, Memory, Violence* (Ithaca: Cornell University Press, 1999)

——, 'Rhetoric, Coercion, and the Memory of Violence', in *Criticism and Dissent in the Middle Ages*, ed. by Rita Copeland (Cambridge: Cambridge University Press, 1996), pp. 24–55

——, 'The Theater of Scholastic Erudition', *Comparative Drama*, 27 (1993), 341–63

Engels, Joseph, 'Berchoriana, I: Notice bibliographique sur Pierre Bersuire', *Vivarium*, 2 (1964), 62–124

Erickson, Carolly, 'The Fourteenth-Century Franciscans and their Critics', *Franciscan Studies*, 35 (1975), 107–35

Espelt, Josep Perarnau, 'Un fragment del Liber sermonum de Francesc Eiximenis', *Arxiu de textos catalans antics*, 10 (1991), 284–92

Evans, Gillian R., 'Two Aspects of *Memoria* in Eleventh and Twelfth Century Writings', *Classica et mediaevalia*, 32 (1971–80), 263–78

Evans, Michael, 'Fictive Painting in Twelfth-Century Paris', in *Sight and Insight*, ed. by John Onians (London: Phaidon, 1994), pp. 73–87

——, 'The Geometry of the Mind', *Architectural Association Quarterly*, 12 (1980), 32–55

Eynde, Damien van den, *Essai sur la succession et la date des écrits de Hugues de St-Victor* (Rome: Apud Pontificium Athenaeum Antonianum, 1960)

Fanger, Claire, ed., *Conjuring Spirits: Texts and Traditions of Medieval Ritual Magic* (University Park: Pennsylvania State University Press, 1998)

Ferruolo, Stephen C., *The Origins of the University: The Schools of Paris and their Critics, 1100–1215* (Stanford: Stanford University Press, 1985)

Ferzoco, George, 'Preaching, Canonization and New Cults of Saints in the Later Middle Ages', in *Prédication et liturgie au moyen âge*, ed. by Nicole Bériou and Franco Morenzoni (Turnhout: Brepols, 2008), pp. 297–312

Fleming, John V., *An Introduction to the Franciscan Literature of the Middle Ages* (Chicago: Franciscan Herald, 1977)

Fletcher, Alan J., 'The Authorship of the *Fasciculus morum*: A Review of the Evidence of MS Barlow 24', *Notes & Queries*, n.s., 30 (1983), 205–07

Folz, Robert, 'Pierre le Vénérable et la liturgie', in *Pierre Abélard, Pierre le Vénérable*, pp. 143–63

Forny, Alberto, 'Giacomo da Vitry, predicatore e "sociologo"', *La Cultura*, 17 (1980), 34–89

Fredborg, Karin Margareta, 'The Scholastic Teaching of Rhetoric in the Middle Ages', *Cahiers de L'Institut du moyen âge grec et latin*, 55 (1987), 85–105

——, 'Twelfth-Century Ciceronian Rhetoric: Its Doctrinal Development and Influences', in *Rhetoric Revalued: Papers from the International Society for the History of Rhetoric*, ed. by Brian Vickers, Medieval and Renaissance Texts and Studies, 19 (Binghamton, NY: Center for Medieval and Renaissance Studies, 1982), pp. 87–97

Freedberg, David, *The Power of Images: Studies in the History and Theory of Response* (Chicago: University of Chicago Press, 1989)

Friedman, John Block, 'Les images mnémotechniques dans les manuscrits de l'époque gothique', in *Jeux de mémoire*, ed. by Roy and Zumthor, pp. 169–83

——, 'John de Foxton's Continuation of Ridewall's *Fulgentius metaforalis*', *Studies in Iconography*, 7–8 (1981–82), 65–79

——, 'John Siferwas and the Mythological Illustrations in the *Liber cosmographiae* of John de Foxton', *Speculum*, 58 (1983), 391–418

Furr, Grover, 'France vs. Italy: French Literary Nationalism in "Petrarch's Last Controversy" and a Humanist Dispute of ca. 1395', *Proceedings of the Patristic, Medieval and Renaissance Conference, Villanova University*, 4 (1979), 115–25 (also available at <http://petrarch.petersadlon.com/submissions/Furr.pdf>)

Gelber, Hester Goodenough, *Exploring the Boundaries of Reason: Three Questions on the Nature of God by Robert Holcot, OP*, Studies and Texts, 62 (Toronto: Pontifical Institute of Mediaeval Studies, 1983)

Georgedes, Kimberly, 'Robert Holcot', in *A Companion to Philosophy in the Middle Ages*, ed. by Jorge J. E. Gracia and Timothy B. Noone, Blackwell Companions to Philosophy, 24 (Malden, MA: Blackwell, 2003), pp. 609–10

Ghisalberti, F., 'L'Ovidius moralizatus di Pierre Bersuire', *Studi Romanzi*, 23 (1933), 5–136

Gieben, Servus, 'Il *Rudimentum doctrinae* di Gilberto di Tournai con l'edizione del suo *Registrum* o tavola della materia', in *Bonaventuriana: miscellanea in onore di Jacques Guy Bougerol*, ed. by Francisco de Asís Chavero Blanco and Jacques Guy Bougerol (Rome: Antonianum, 1988), pp. 621–80

Gill, Miriam, 'Preaching and Image: Sermons and Wall Paintings in Later Medieval England', in *Preacher, Sermon and Audience*, ed. by Muessig, pp. 155–80

Gillmeister, Heiner, 'An Intriguing Fourteenth-Century Document: Thomas Bradwardine's *De arte memorativa*', *Archiv für das Studium der neueren Sprachen und Literature*, 220 (1983), 111–14

Gilson, Étienne, *History of Christian Philosophy in the Middle Ages* (New York: Random House, 1955)

——, 'Michel Menot et la technique du sermon médiéval', *Revue d'histoire franciscaine*, 2 (1925), 301–50

Ginther, James R., 'There is a Text in this Classroom: The Bible and Theology in the Medieval University', in *Essays in Medieval Philosophy and Theology in Memory of Walter H. Principe, CSB: Fortresses and Launching Pads*, ed. by James R. Ginther and Carl N. Still (Aldershot: Ashgate, 2005), pp. 43–73

Glorieux, Palémon, *Répertoire des maîtres en théologie de Paris au* XIIIe *siècle*, 2 vols (Paris: Vrin, 1933–34)

Goering, Joseph, *William de Montibus (c.1140–1213): The Schools and the Literature of Pastoral Care*, Studies and Texts, 108 (Toronto: Pontifical Institute of Mediaeval Studies, 1992)

Gracia, Jorge J. E., 'Francesc Eiximenis' Sources', in *Catalan Studies: Volume in Memory of Josephine de Boer*, ed. by Joseph Gulsoy and Josep M. Sola-Solé (Barcelona: Hispam, 1977), pp. 173–87

Green, Richard Hamilton, 'Classical Fable and English Poetry in the Fourteenth Century', in *Critical Approaches to Medieval Literature*, ed. by Dorothy Bethurum, Selected papers from the English Institute, 1958–59 (New York: Columbia University Press, 1960), pp. 110–33

Gründel, Johannes, *Die Lehre von den Umständen der Menschlichen Handlung im Mittelalter*, Beiträge zur Geschichte der Philosophie und Theologie des Mittelalters, 39 (Münster: Aschendorff, 1963)

Gutsch, Milton, 'A Twelfth-Century Preacher–Fulk of Neuilly', in *Crusades, and Other Historical Essays*, pp. 183–206

Hagen, Susan K., *Allegorical Remembrance: A Study of 'The Pilgrimage of the Life of Man' as a Medieval Treatise on Seeing and Remembering* (Athens: University of Georgia Press, 1990)

Hajdú, Helga, *Das mnemotechnische Schrifttum des Mittelalters* (Vienna: Leo, 1936)

Hamburger, Jeffrey, 'The Visual and the Visionary: The Image in Late-Medieval Monastic Devotions', *Viator*, 20 (1989), 161–82

Hamesse, Jacqueline, and Xavier Hermand, eds, *De l'homélie au sermon: Histoire de la prédication médiévale* (Louvain-la-Neuve: Institut d'études médiévales de l'Université Catholique de Louvain, 1993)

Hammond, Jay M., *Francis of Assisi: History, Hagiography, and Hermeneutics in the Early Documents* (Hyde Park: New City Press, 2004)

Hanska, Jussi, '*Uidens Iesus ciuitatem fleuit super illam*: The *Lachrymae Christi* Topos in Thirteenth-Century Sermon Literature', in *Constructing the Medieval Sermon*, ed. by Andersson, pp. 237–51

Hauf, Albert G., 'El "Ars praedicandi" de Fr. Alfonso d'Alprao, O.F.M.: Aportación al estudio de la teoría de la predicación en la Península Ibérica', *AFH*, 72 (1974), 233–329

Haug, Walter, and Burghart Wachinger, eds, *Exempel und Exempelsammlungen*, Fortuna vitrea, 2 (Tübingen: Niemeyer, 1991)

Head, Thomas, 'Monastic and Scholastic Theology: A Change of Paradigm?', in *Paradigms in Medieval Thought Applications in Medieval Disciplines: A Symposium*, ed. by Nancy Van Deusen and Alvin E. Ford (Lewiston, NY: Edwin Mellen, 1990), pp. 127–42

Hedegård, Gösta, 'Jacobus de Cessolis' Sources: The Case of Valerius Maximus', in *Chess and Allegory in the Middle Ages*, ed. by Olle Ferm and Volker Honemann (Stockholm: Sällskapet Runica et Mediaevalia, 2005), pp. 98–159

Heerinckx, P. Jacques, OFM, 'Influence de l'Epistola ad Fratres de Monte Dei sur la composition de l'homme extérieur et intérieur de David d'Augsbourg', *Études franciscaines*, 45 (1933), 330–47

Heimann-Seelbach, Sabine, *Ars und scientia: Genese, Überlieferung und Funktionen der mnemotechnischen Traktatliteratur im 15. Jahrhundert; mit Edition und Untersuchung dreier deutscher Traktate und ihrer lateinischen Vorlagen*, Frühe Neuzeit, 58 (Tübingen: Niemeyer, 2000)

Hellman, J. A. Wayne, 'Francis of Assisi: Saint, Founder, Prophet', in *Francis of Assisi: History, Hagiography, and Hermeneutics in the Early Documents*, ed. by Jay M. Hammond (Hyde Park: New City Press, 2004), pp. 15–38

Herbert, John Alexander, *Catalogue of Romances in the Department of Manuscripts in the British Museum*, III (London: Trustees of the British Museum, 1910; repr. 1962)

Hillgarth, Jocelyn N., 'Una biblioteca cisterciense medieval: La Real (Mallorca)', *Analecta sacra tarraconensia*, 32 (1960), 89–91

Hinnebusch, William, *The Early English Friars Preachers*, Dissertationes historicae, 14 (Rome: Institutum historicum ff. praedicatorum Romae ad. S. Sabinae, 1951)

——, *The History of the Dominican Order: Origins and Growth to 1500*, 2 vols (New York: Alba House, 1966)

Howell, Alan George Ferrers, and Julia Mary Cartwright Ady, *S. Bernardino of Siena* (London: Methuen, 1913)

Hue, Denis, 'Structures et rhétoriques dans quelques textes encyclopédiques du moyen âge', in *L'Encyclopédisme*, ed. by Becq, pp. 311–18

Hunt, Richard William, 'The Introduction to the "Artes" in the Twelfth Century', in *Studia mediaevalia in honorem admodum Reverendi Patris Raymundi Josephi Martin, Ordinis Praedicatorum s. theologiae magistri LXXum natalem diem agentis* (Bruges: De Tempel, 1948), pp. 85–112

Illich, Ivan, *In the Vineyard of the Text: A Commentary to Hugh's 'Didascalicon'* (Chicago: University of Chicago Press, 1993)

Jaeger, C. Stephen, *The Envy of Angels: Cathedral Schools and Social Ideals in Medieval Europe, 950–1200* (Philadelphia: University of Pennsylvania Press, 1994)

Jeay, Madeleine, 'La Mythologie comme clé de mémorisation: *La Glose des Échecs Amoureux*', in *Jeux de mémoire*, ed. by Roy and Zumthor, pp. 91–122

Jennings, Margaret, 'Tutivillus: The Literary Career of the Recording Demon', *Studies in Philology*, 74 (1977), 1–91

Jerchel, Heinrich, 'Die Bayerische Buchmalerei des 14. Jahrhunderts', *Münchner Jahrbuch der bildenden Kunst*, Neue Folge, 10 (1933), 74–78

Jones, William R., 'Art and Christian Piety: Iconoclasm in Medieval Europe', in *The Image and the Word: Confrontations in Judaism, Christianity and Islam*, ed. by Joseph Gutmann (Missoula, MT: Scholars Press for the American Academy of Religion, 1977), pp. 75–105

Kaeppeli, Tommaso, *Scriptores ordinis praedicatorum medii aevii*, 3 vols (Rome: Santa Sabina, 1970–80)

Katzenellenbogen, Adolf, *Allegories of the Virtues and Vices in Medieval Art from Early Christian Times to the Thirteenth Century*, Medieval Academy Reprints for Teaching, 24 (Toronto: University of Toronto Press, 1989)

Keats-Rohan, Katherine S. B., 'John of Salisbury and Education in Twelfth Century Paris from the Account of his *Metalogicon*', *History of Universities*, 6 (1986–87), 1–45

Kehnel, Annette, 'The Narrative Tradition of the Medieval Franciscan Friars on the British Isles', *Franciscan Studies*, 63 (2005), 461–530

Kelly, Douglas, *The Arts of Poetry and of Prose*, Typologie des sources du moyen âge occidental, 59 (Turnhout: Brepols, 1991)

Ker, Neil Ripley, *Medieval Manuscripts in British Libraries*, 5 vols (Oxford: Clarendon Press, 1969–2002)

Kibre, Pearl, *Scholarly Privileges in the Middle Ages: The Rights, Privileges, and Immunities of Scholars and Universities at Bologna, Padua, Paris, and Oxford* (Cambridge, MA: Mediaeval Academy of America, 1962)

Kieckhefer, Richard, 'Major Currents in Late Medieval Devotion', in *Christian Spirituality*, ed. by Raitt, pp. 75–108

Kienzle, Beverly Mayne, ed., *Models of Holiness in Medieval Sermons: Proceedings of the International Symposium (Kalamazoo, 4–7 May 1995)*, Textes et études du moyen âge, 5 (Louvain-la-Neuve: Fédération internationale des Instituts d'études médiévales, 1996)

——, ed., *The Sermon*, Typologie des sources du moyen âge occidental, 81–83 (Turnhout: Brepols, 2000)

King, Peter, *Western Monasticism: A History of the Monastic Movement in the Latin Church*, Cistercian Studies Series, 185 (Kalamazoo: Cistercian, 1999)

Klaassen, Frank, 'English Manuscripts of Magic, 1300–1500: A Preliminary Survey', in *Conjuring Spirits*, ed. by Fanger, pp. 3–31

Klibansky, Raymond, Erwin Panofsky, and Fritz Saxl, *Saturn and Melancholy: Studies in the History of Natural Philosophy, Religion, and Art* (London: Nelson, 1964)

Knowles, David, *The Religious Orders in England*, II: *The End of the Middle Ages* (Cambridge: Cambridge University Press, 1955)

Kolve, V. A., *Chaucer and the Imagery of Narrative: The First Five Canterbury Tales* (Stanford: Stanford University Press, 1984)

Kraft, Heike, 'Die Bildallegorie der Kreuzigung Christi durch die Tugenden' (unpublished doctoral thesis, Freie Universität, Berlin, 1976)

Kretzmann, Norman, Anthony Kenny, and Jan Pinborg, eds, *The Cambridge History of Later Medieval Philosophy: From the Rediscovery of Aristotle to the Disintegration of Scholasticism, 1100–1600* (Cambridge: Cambridge University Press, 1982)

Krill, Richard M., '"Vatican Mythographers": Their Place in Ancient Mythography', *Manuscripta*, 23 (1979), 173–77

Kristeller, Paul Oskar, 'Philosophy and Rhetoric: The Middle Ages', in *Renaissance Thought and its Sources*, ed. by Michael Mooney (New York: Columbia University Press, 1979), pp. 228–41

Langlois, C.-V., 'Géraud du Pescher', *Histoire littéraire de la France*, 36 (1927), 614–17

Lanham, Carol Dana, ed., *Latin Grammar and Rhetoric: From Classical Theory to Medieval Practice* (London: Continuum, 2002)

Leclercq, Jean, *The Love of Learning and the Desire for God* (New York: Fordham University Press, 1982)

——, 'Le Magistère du prédicateur au XIIIe siècle', *Archives d'histoire doctrinale et littéraire du moyen âge*, 15 (1946), 105–47

Leclercq, Jean, Francois Vandenbrouke, and Louis Bouyer, *The Spirituality of the Middle Ages*, II: *A History of Christian Spirituality* (New York: Seabury, 1968)

Lecoy de la Marche, A., *Le chaire française au moyen âge, specialement au XIIIe siècle* (Paris: Librairie Renouard, 1886)

Leff, Michael C., 'Boethius' *De differentiis topicis*, Book IV', in *Medieval Eloquence*, ed. by Murphy, pp. 3–24

——, 'The Topics of Argumentative Invention in Latin Rhetorical Theory from Cicero to Boethius', *Rhetorica*, 1 (1983), 23–44

Lewis, Charlton Thomas, and Charles Short, *A Latin Dictionary*, 2nd edn (Oxford: Oxford University Press, 1975)

Lewis, Suzanne, 'The English Gothic Illuminated Apocalypse, *lectio divina*, and the Art of Memory', *Word and Image*, 7 (1991), 1–32

Lewry, Patrick Osmund, 'Rhetoric at Paris and Oxford in the Mid-Thirteenth Century', *Rhetorica*, 1 (1983), 45–63

Longère, Jean, *La prédication médiévale* (Paris: Institut d'études augustiniennes, 1983)

Lubac, Henri de, *Exégèse médiévale: Les Quatre sens de l'écriture*, 4 vols (Paris: Aubier, 1959–64)

——, *Medieval Exegesis*, trans. by Mark Sebanc, 4 vols (Grand Rapids: Eerdmans, 1998)

Luttrell, Anthony, 'Jean and Simon de Hesdin: Hospitallers, Theologians, Classicists', *Recherches de théologie ancienne et médiévale*, 31 (1964), 137–40

Lutz, Cora E., 'Martianus Capella', in *Catalogus translationum et commentariorum: Medieval and Renaissance Latin Translations and Commentaries*, ed. by Paul Oskar Kristeller and F. Edward Cranz (Washington, DC: Catholic University of America Press, 1971), pp. 367–81

MacDonald, Alasdair A., Bernhard Ridderbos, and R. M. Schlusemann, eds, *The Broken Body: Passion Devotion in Late Medieval Culture* (Groningen: Forsten, 1998)

Marrou, Henri Irénée, *Saint Augustin et la fin de la culture antique* (Paris: de Boccard, 1938)

Marrow, James H., *Passion Iconography in Northern European Art of the Late Middle Ages and Early Renaissance: A Study in the Transformation of Sacred Metaphor into Descriptive Narrative*, Ars Neerlandica, 1 (Kortrijk: Van Ghemmert, 1979)

Matanic, Athanasius, 'La "hominis compositio" tra la scuola vittorina e la prima scuola francescana', in *L'Antropologia dei maestri spirituali: simposio organizzato dall'Istituto di spiritualità dell'Università gregoriana, Roma, 28 aprile–1 maggio 1989*, ed. by Charles André Bernard and Pontificia Universitá Gregoriana, Istituto di spiritualitá (Cinisello Balsamo: Paoline, 1991), pp. 163–77

McKeon, Richard, 'Rhetoric in the Middle Ages', *Speculum*, 17 (1942), 1–32

McKitterick, Rosamond, *The Carolingians and the Written Word* (Cambridge: Cambridge University Press, 1989)

Meier, P. Ludger, 'Aufzeichnungen aus vernichteten Handschriften des Würzburger Minoritenklosters', *AFH*, 44 (1951), 191–209

Meiss, Millard, *French Painting in the Time of Jean de Berry: The Limbourgs and their Contemporaries*, 2 vols (New York: Braziller, 1974)

Mews, Constant J., 'In Search of a Name and its Significance: A Twelfth-Century Anecdote about Thierry and Peter Abelard', *Traditio*, 44 (1988), 171–200

——, 'Monastic Educational Culture Revisited: The Witness of Zwiefalten and the Hirsau Reform', in *Medieval Monastic Education*, ed. by Muessig, pp. 182–97

——, 'Orality, Literacy, and Authority in the Twelfth-Century Schools', *Exemplaria*, 2 (1990), 475–500

Michaud-Quantin, Pierre, 'La Classification des puissances de l'âme au XIIe siècle', *Revue du moyen âge latin*, 5 (1949), 15–34

Minnis, Alastair J., *Chaucer and Pagan Antiquity* (Totowa, NJ: Rowman and Littlefield, 1982)

——, 'Medieval Imagination and Memory', in *Cambridge History of Literary Criticism*, II: *The Middle Ages*, ed. by Minnis and Johnson, pp. 239–74

——, *Medieval Theory of Authorship: Scholastic Literary Attitudes in the Late Middle Ages*, 2nd edn (Aldershot: Wildewood House, 1988)

Minnis, Alastair J., and Ian Johnson, eds, *The Cambridge History of Literary Criticism*, II: *The Middle Ages* (Cambridge: Cambridge University Press, 2005)

Minnis, Alastair J., and A. Brian Scott, eds, *Medieval Literary Theory and Criticism, c. 1100–c. 1375: The Commentary-Tradition* (Oxford: Clarendon Press, 1988)

Mollat, Guillaume, *The Popes at Avignon, 1305–1378*, trans. by Janet Love (London: Nelson, 1963)

Molsdorf, Wilhelm, *Christliche Symbolik der mittelalterlichen Kunst* (Leipzig: Akademische Druck-u. Verlagsanstalt, 1926)

Moorman, John R. H., *A History of the Franciscan Order from its Origins to the Year 1517* (Oxford: Clarendon Press, 1968)

Morenzoni, Franco, *Des Écoles aux paroisses: Thomas de Chobham et la promotion de la prédication au début du XIIIe siècle*, Collection des études augustiniennes, Série moyen âge et temps modernes, 30 (Paris: Institut d'études augustiniennes, 1995)

Muessig, Carolyn, ed., *Medieval Monastic Education* (London: Leicester University Press, 2001)

——, ed., *Preacher, Sermon and Audience in the Middle Ages* (Leiden: Brill, 2002)

——, 'Sermon, Preacher and Society in the Middle Ages', *Journal of Medieval History*, 28 (2002), 73–91

Mulchahey, M. Michèle, 'The Dominican *Studium*-System and the Universities of Europe in the Thirteenth Century: A Relationship Redefined', in *Manuels, programmes de cours et techniques d'enseignement dans les universités médiévales: Actes du Colloque international de Louvain-la-Neuve (9–11 septembre 1993)*, ed. by Jacqueline Hamesse (Louvain-la-Neuve: Institut d'études médiévales de l'Université Catholique de Louvain, 1994), pp. 277–324

——, *'First the Bow is Bent in Study': Dominican Education Before 1350*, Studies and Texts, 132 (Toronto: Pontifical Institute of Mediaeval Studies, 1998)

Mulchahey, M. Michèle, and Timothy B. Noone, 'Religious Orders', in *A Companion to Philosophy in the Middle Ages*, ed. by Jorge J. E. Gracia and Timothy B. Noone, Blackwell Companions to Philosophy, 24 (Malden, MA: Blackwell, 2003), pp. 45–54

Murdoch, John Emery, *Antiquity and the Middle Ages*, Album of Science (New York: Scribner, 1984)

Murphy, James Jerome, ed., *Medieval Eloquence: Studies in the Theory and Practice of Medieval Rhetoric* (Berkeley and Los Angeles: University of California Press, 1978)

——, *Rhetoric in the Middle Ages: A History of Rhetorical Theory from St. Augustine to the Renaissance* (Berkeley and Los Angeles: University of California Press, 1974)

Mynors, Roger Aubrey Baskerville, *Catalogue of the Manuscripts of Balliol College, Oxford* (Oxford: Clarendon Press, 1963)

Newhauser, Richard G., 'From Treatise to Sermon: Johannes Herolt on the *Novem peccata aliena*', in *De Ore Domini*, ed. by Amos, Green, and Kienzle, pp. 185–209

——, *The Treatise on Vices and Virtues in Latin and the Vernacular*, Typologie des sources du moyen âge occidental, 68 (Turnhout: Brepols, 1993)

Nolhac, Pierre de, *Pétrarque et l'humanisme*, 2 vols (Paris: Champion, 1907)

O'Donnell, James J., 'Augustine's Classical Readings', *Recherches augustiniennes*, 15 (1980), 144–75

Oldoni, Massimo, 'Giovanni da San Gimignano', in *L'enciclopedismo medievale*, ed. by Michelangelo Picone, Memoria del tempo, 1 (Ravenna: Longo, 1994), pp. 213–28

Ong, Walter J., *Ramus, Method and the Decay of Dialogue* (Cambridge, MA: Harvard University Press, 1958)

Origo, Iris, *The World of San Bernardino* (New York: Harcourt, Brace, and World, 1962)

Owens, Joseph, 'Faith, Ideas, Illumination, and Experience', in *Cambridge History of Later Medieval Philosophy*, ed. by Kretzmann, Kenny, and Pinborg, pp. 440–59

Owst, Gerald Robert, *Literature and Pulpit in Medieval England: A Neglected Chapter in the History of English Letters and of the English People*, 2nd edn (Oxford: Blackwell, 1966)

——, *Preaching in Medieval England: An Introduction to Sermon Manuscripts of the Period, c.1350–1450* (Cambridge: Cambridge University Press, 1926)

Pack, Roger A., 'A Life of Saint Marina in an Ars Memorativa', *Classical Folia*, 31 (1977), 78–84

——, 'A Medieval Explicator of Classical Mnemonics', in *Studies in Latin Literature and Roman History: Vol. II*, ed. by Carl Deroux (Brussels: Latomus, 1980), pp. 515–30

Paetow, Louis John, ed., *The Crusades, and Other Historical Essays Presented to Dana C. Munro by his Former Students* (New York: Crofts, 1928)

Palmer, Nigel F., '"Antiquitus depingebatur": The Roman Pictures of Death and Misfortune in the *Ackermann aus Böhmen* and *Tkadlecek*, and in the Writings of the English Classicizing Friars', *Deutsche Vierteljahrsschrift für Literaturwissenschaft und Geistesgeschichte*, 57 (1983), 171–239

——, 'Bacchus und Venus: Mythographische Bilder in der Welt des späten Mittelalters; Mit einem Textanhang', in *Literatur und Wandmalerei*, II: *Konventionalität und Konversation*, ed. by Eckart Conrad Lutz, Johanna Thali, and René Wetzel (Tübingen: Niemeyer, 2005), pp. 189–235

——, 'Das "Exempelwerk" der englischen Bettelmönche: Ein Gegenstück zu den "Gesta Romanorum"', in *Exempel und Exempelsammlungen*, ed. by Haug and Wachinger, pp. 137–72

——, 'Sintram, Johannes OFM', *Die deutsche Literatur des Mittelalters*, ed. by Ruh and others, VIII, 1284

Parkes, Malcolm Beckwith, 'The Influence of the Concepts of *Ordinatio* and *Compilatio* on the Development of the Book', in *Medieval Learning and Literature: Essays Presented to Richard William Hunt*, ed. by Jonathan James Graham Alexander and Margaret T. Gibson (Oxford: Clarendon Press, 1976), pp. 307–52

Parshall, Peter, 'The Art of Memory and the Passion', *Art Bulletin*, 81 (1999), 456–72

Pauly, August Friedrich von, and others, eds, *Paulys Realencyclopädie der classischen Altertumswissenschaft*, 24 vols (Stuttgart: Druckenmüller, 1958)

Petersen, Theodore C., 'Johs. Sintram de Herbipoli in Two of his MSS', *Speculum*, 20 (1945), 73–83

Pfander, Homer G., 'The Popular Sermon of the Medieval Friar in England' (unpublished doctoral dissertation, New York University, 1937)

*Pierre Abélard, Pierre le Vénérable: Les Courants philosophiques, littéraires et artistiques en Occident au milieu du XIIe siècle; [Actes et mémoires du colloque international] Abbaye de Cluny, 2 au 9 juillet 1972*, Colloques internationaux du Centre national de la recherche scientifique, 546 (Paris: Éditions du Centre national de la recherche scientifique, 1975)

Piltz, Anders, ed., *Studium Upsalense: Specimens of the Oldest Lecture Notes Taken in the Mediaeval University of Uppsala* (Uppsala: Uppsala Universitet, 1977)

Poorter, A. de, 'Un traité de pédagogie médiévale: Le *De modo addiscendi* de Guibert de Tournai, O.F.M.', *Revue néo-scolastique*, 24 (1922), 195–228

Post, L. A., 'Ancient Memory Systems', *Classical Weekly*, 25 (1932), 105–10

Powell, Susan, 'Connections between the *Fasciculus morum* and Bodl. MS Barlow 24', *Notes & Queries*, 29 (1982), 10–14

Principe, Walter H., *Introduction to Patristic and Medieval Theology* (Toronto: Pontifical Institute of Mediaeval Studies, 1987)

Quinn, Betty Nye, 'Venus, Chaucer, and Pierre Bersuire', *Speculum*, 38 (1963), 479–80

Quinto, Riccardo, 'Peter the Chanter and the 'Miscellanea del Codice del Tesoro' (Etymology as a Way for Constructing a Sermon)', in *Constructing the Medieval Sermon*, ed. by Andersson, pp. 33–81

Raitt, Jill, ed., *Christian Spirituality*, II: *High Middle Ages and Reformation*, World Spirituality: An Encyclopedic History of the Religious Quest, 17 (New York: Crossroad, 1987)

Rand, Edward Kennard, 'The Classics in the Thirteenth Century', *Speculum*, 4 (1929), 249–69

Rashdall, Hastings, *The Universities in the Middle Ages*, ed. by Frederick Maurice Powicke and Alfred Brotherston Emden, 3 vols (Oxford: Clarendon Press, 1936)

Rathbone, E., 'Master Alberic of London, "Mythographus Tertius Vaticanus"', *Medieval and Renaissance Studies*, 1 (1941), 35–38

Renedo, Xavier, 'Una imatge de la memòria entre les *Moralitates* de Robert Holcot i el *Dotzè* de Francesc Eiximenis', *Annals de l'Institut d'estudis Gironins*, 31 (1990–91), 53–61

Renouard, Yves, *The Avignon Papacy: The Popes in Exile, 1305–1403*, trans. by Denis Bethell (New York: Barnes and Noble, 1970)

Reynolds, Leighton Durham, and Nigel Guy Wilson, *Scribes and Scholars: A Guide to the Transmission of Greek and Latin Literature* (Oxford: Clarendon Press, 1974)

Reynolds, Suzanne, *Medieval Reading: Grammar, Rhetoric and the Classical Text*, Cambridge Studies in Medieval Literature, 27 (Cambridge: Cambridge University Press, 1996)

Reynolds, William D., 'Sources, Nature, and Influence of the *Ovidius Moralizatus* of Pierre Bersuire', in *Mythographic Art*, ed. by Chance, pp. 83–99

Riché, Pierre, *Écoles et enseignement dans le haut moyen âge: Fin du V^e^ siècle–milieu du XI^e^ siècle* (Paris: Picard, 1989)

——, *Education and Culture in the Barbarian West from the Sixth through the Eighth Century*, trans. by John J. Contreni (Columbia, SC: University of South Carolina Press, 1976)

——, 'L'Enfant dans la société monastique', in *Pierre Abélard, Pierre le Vénérable*, pp. 689–701

——, 'Le Rôle de la mémoire dans l'enseignement médiévale', in *Jeux de mémoire*, ed. by Roy and Zumthor, pp. 133–46

Rischpler, Susanne, 'Die Ordnung der Gedächtnisfiguren: Der bebilderte Mnemotechnik-Traktat im Cod. 5393 der Österreichischen Nationalbibliothek', *Codices Manuscripti: Zeitschrift für Handschriftenkunde*, 25 (2004), 73–87

Rivers, Kimberly A., 'Another Look at the Career of Pierre Bersuire, O.S.B.', *Revue bénédictine*, 116 (2006), 92–100

——, 'The Fear of Divine Vengeance: Mnemonic Images as a Guide to Conscience in the Late Middle Ages', in *Fear and its Representations in the Middle Ages and Renaissance*, ed. by Anne Scott and Cynthia Kosso, Arizona Studies in the Middle Ages and Renaissance, 6 (Turnhout: Brepols, 2002), pp. 66–91

——, 'Memory and Medieval Preaching: Mnemonic Advice in the *Ars praedicandi* of Francesc Eiximenis (*c.*1327–1409)', *Viator*, 30 (1999), 253–84

——, 'Memory and the Mendicants in the Later Middle Ages' (unpublished doctoral thesis, University of Toronto, 1995)

——, 'Memory, Division, and the Organization of Knowledge in the Middle Ages', in *Pre-modern Encyclopaedic Texts: Proceedings of the Second COMERS Congress, Groningen, 1–4 July 1996*, ed. by Peter Binkley (Leiden: Brill, 1997), pp. 147–58

——, 'Pictures, Preaching and Memory in Robert Holcot's Commentary on the Twelve Prophets' (M.S.L. thesis, Pontifical Institute of Mediaeval Studies, 1993)

Robertson, D. W., Jr, 'Frequency of Preaching in Thirteenth-Century England', *Speculum*, 24 (1949), 376–88

Roest, Bert, 'Franciscan Educational Perspectives: Reworking Monastic Traditions', in *Medieval Monastic Education*, ed. by Muessig, pp. 168–81

——, *Franciscan Literature of Religious Instruction Before the Council of Trent*, Studies in the History of Christian Traditions, 117 (Leiden: Brill, 2004)

——, *A History of Franciscan Education (c. 1210–1517)* (Leiden: Brill, 2000)

——, 'Reading the Book of History: Intellectual Contexts and Educational Functions of Franciscan Historiography 1226–ca. 1350' (unpublished doctoral thesis, University of Groningen, 1996)

——, '*Scientia* and *sapientia* in Gilbert of Tournai's *(E)rudimentum doctrinae*', in *Le Vocabulaire des écoles des Mendiants au moyen âge: Actes du colloque, Porto, Portugal, 11–12 octobre 1996*, ed. by Maria Cândida Pacheco, Études sur le vocabulaire intellectuel du moyen âge, 9 (Turnhout: Brepols, 1999), pp. 164–79

Rossi, Paolo, *Clavis Universalis: Arti Mnemoniche e logica combinatoria da Lullo a Leibniz* (Milan: Ricciardi, 1960)

——, 'Immagini e memoria locale nei secoli XIV e XV', *Rivista critica di storia della filosofia*, 2 (1958), 149–91

——, 'La costruzione delle immagini nei tratti di memoria artificiale del Rinascimento', in *Umanesimo e Simbolismo*, ed. by Enrico Castelli (Padua: CEDAM, 1958), pp. 161–78

——, *Logic and the Art of Memory*, trans. by Stephen Clucas (Chicago: University of Chicago, 2000)

Rouse, Mary A., and Richard H. Rouse, *Authentic Witnesses: Approaches to Medieval Texts and Manuscripts* (Notre Dame: University of Notre Dame Press, 1991)

——, 'Biblical *Distinctiones* in the Thirteenth Century', *Archives d'histoire doctrinale et littéraire du moyen âge*, 41 (1974), 27–37

——, 'The Book Trade at the University of Paris, ca. 1250–ca. 1350', in Rouse and Rouse, *Authentic Witnesses*, pp. 259–338

——, 'The Development of Research Tools in the Thirteenth Century', in Rouse and Rouse, *Authentic Witnesses*, pp. 221–55

——, *Preachers, Florilegia and Sermons: Studies in the Manipulus Florum of Thomas of Ireland*, Studies and Texts, 47 (Toronto: Pontifical Institute of Mediaeval Studies, 1979)

——, '*Statim invenire*: Schools, Preachers, and New Attitudes to the Page', in Rouse and Rouse, *Authentic Witnesses*, pp. 191–219

——, '*Statim invenire*: Schools, Preachers, and New Attitudes to the Page', in *Renaissance and Renewal in the Twelfth Century*, ed. by Benson and Constable, pp. 201–25

Rowland, Beryl, 'Bishop Bradwardine on the Artificial Memory', *Journal of the Warburg and Courtauld Institutes*, 41 (1978), 307–12

Roy, Bruno, and Paul Zumthor, eds, *Jeux de mémoire: Aspects de la mnémotechnie médiévale* (Montréal: Presses de l'Université de Montréal, 1985)

Ruh, Kurt, 'David von Augsburg', in *Die deutsche Literatur des Mittelalters*, ed. by Ruh and others, II, 47–58

—— and others, eds, *Die deutsche Literatur des Mittelalters: Verfasserlexikon*, 2nd edn (Berlin: de Gruyter, 1977–)

Saenger, Paul, 'Silent Reading: Its Impact on Late Medieval Script and Society', *Viator*, 13 (1982), 367–414

——, *Space Between Words: The Origins of Silent Reading* (Stanford: Stanford University Press, 1997)

Salter, Herbert Edward and Mary Doreen Lobel, eds, *Victoria History of the County of Oxford*, III: *University of Oxford* (London: University of London, Institute of Historical Research, and Oxford University Press, 1954)

Samaran, Charles, and Jacques Monfrin, 'Pierre Bersuire, Prieur de Saint-Éloi de Paris (1290?–1362)', *Histoire littéraire de la France*, 39 (1962), 259–450

Saxl, Fritz, 'Aller Tugenden und Laster Abbildung', in *Festschrift für Julius Schlosser zum 60. Geburtstage*, ed. by Arpad Weixlgärtner and Leo Planiscig (Zurich: Amalthea, 1927), pp. 104–21

——, 'A Spiritual Encyclopaedia of the Later Middle Ages', *Journal of the Warburg and Courtauld Institutes*, 5 (1942), 82–134

Sbaraglia, Giovanni Giacinto, *Supplementum et castigatio ad scriptores trium ordinum S. Francisci a Waddingo, aliisve descriptos*, 3 vols (Rome: Nardecchia, 1908–36)

Schlager, Patricius, *Beiträge zur Geschichte der Kölnischen Franziskaner-Ordensprovinz im Mittelalter* (Cologne: Bachem, 1904)

Schlie, Friedrich, *Die Kunst- und Geschichts-Denkmäler des Grossherzogthums Mecklenburg-Schwerin*, 4 vols (Schwerin i.M.: Bärensprung [u.a.], 1899)

Schneyer, Johann Baptist, *Geschichte der katholischen Predigt* (Freiburg: Seelsorge, 1969)

—, *Repertorium der lateinischen Sermones des Mittelalters für die Zeit von 1150–1350*, Beiträge zur Geschichte der Philosophie und Theologie des Mittelalters, 43, 11 vols (Münster: Aschendorff, 1969)

—, 'Winke für die Sichtung und Zuordnung spätmittelalterlicher Lateinischer Predigtreihen', *Scriptorium*, 32 (1978), 231–48

Scribner, Robert W., 'Elements of Popular Belief', in *Handbook of European History, 1400–1600: Late Middle Ages, Renaissance and Reformation*, I: *Structures and Assertions*, ed. by Thomas A. Brady Jr., Heiko Oberman, and James D. Tracy (Leiden: Brill, 1994), pp. 231–62

Seznec, Jean, *The Survival of the Pagan Gods: The Mythological Tradition and its Place in Renaissance Humanism and Art*, trans. by Barbara F. Sessions, Bollingen Series, 38 (New York: Pantheon, 1953)

Sherman, Claire Richter, *Writing on Hands: Memory and Knowledge in Early Modern Europe* (Carlisle, PA: Trout Gallery, Dickinson College; Washington, DC: Folger Shakespeare Library; Seattle: University of Washington Press, 2000)

Shriver, George H., ed., *Contemporary Reflections on the Medieval Christian Tradition: Essays in Honor of Ray C. Petry* (Durham, NC: Duke University Press, 1974)

Sicard, Patrice, *Diagrammes médiévaux et exégèse visuelle: Le Libellus de formatione arche de Hugues de Saint Victor*, Bibliotheca victoriana, 4 (Turnhout: Brepols, 1993)

Small, Jocelyn Penny, *Wax Tablets of the Mind* (London: Routledge, 1997)

Smalley, Beryl, 'The Bible in the Medieval Schools', in *The Cambridge History of the Bible*, II: *The West from the Fathers to the Reformation*, ed. by Geoffrey William Hugo Lampe (Cambridge: Cambridge University Press, 1967), pp. 197–220

—, *English Friars and Antiquity in the Early Fourteenth Century* (Oxford: Blackwell, 1960)

—, 'Jean de Hesdin O. Hosp. S. Ioh.', *Recherches de théologie ancienne et mediévale*, 28 (1961), 283–330

—, 'John Baconthorpe's Postill on St. Matthew', in *Studies in Medieval Thought and Learning from Abelard to Wycliff*, ed. by Beryl Smalley (London: Hambledon, 1981), pp. 289–343

—, 'Problems of Exegesis in the Fourteenth Century', *Antike und Orient im Mittelalter: Miscellanea Mediaevalia*, 1 (1962), 266–74

—, 'Robert Holcot, O.P.', *AFP*, 26 (1956), 5–97

—, *The Study of the Bible in the Middle Ages*, 3rd edn (Oxford: Blackwell, 1983)

—, 'Thomas Waleys, O.P.', *AFP*, 24 (1954), 50–107

Southern, Richard W., 'Aspects of the European Tradition of Historical Writing: 2. Hugh of St. Victor and the Idea of Historical Development', *Transactions of the Royal Historical Society*, ser. 5, 21 (1971), 159–79

—, *Scholastic Humanism and the Unification of Europe*, II: *The Heroic Age* (Oxford: Blackwell, 2001)

Spencer, H. Leith, *English Preaching in the Late Middle Ages* (Oxford: Clarendon Press, 1993)

Sprandel, Rolf, *Altersschicksal und Altersmoral: Die Geschichte der Einstellungen zum Altern nach der Pariser Bibelexegese des 12.–16. Jahrhunderts* (Stuttgart: Hiersemann, 1981)

Stahl, William, 'To a Better Understanding of Martianus Capella', *Speculum*, 40 (1965), 102–15

Stegmüller, Friedrich, *Repertorium biblicum medii aevi*, 11 vols (Madrid: [n. pub.], 1949–80)

Steneck, Nicholas H., 'The Problem of the Internal Senses in the Fourteenth Century' (unpublished doctoral dissertation, University of Wisconsin, 1970)

Stock, Brian, *After Augustine: The Meditative Reader and the Text* (Philadelphia: University of Pennsylvania Press, 2001)

——, *Augustine the Reader: Meditation, Self-Knowledge, and the Ethics of Interpretation* (Cambridge, MA: Belknap Press of Harvard University Press, 1996)

——, *The Implications of Literacy: Written Language and Models of Interpretation in the Eleventh and Twelfth Centuries* (Princeton: Princeton University Press, 1983)

Swanson, Jenny, 'Childhood and Childrearing in *Ad status* Sermons by Later Thirteenth-Century Friars', *Journal of Medieval History*, 16 (1990), 309–31

——, *John of Wales: A Study of the Works and Ideals of a Thirteenth-Century Friar* (Cambridge: Cambridge University Press, 1989)

Swarzenski, Hanns, *Die lateinischen illuminierten Handschriften des XIII. Jahrhunderts in den Ländern an Rhein, Main und Donau, Denkmäler deutscher Kunst: Die deutsche Buchmalerei des XIII. Jahrhunderts* (Berlin: [Deutscher Verein für Kunstwissenschaft], 1936)

Tachau, Katherine H., *Vision and Certitude in the Age of Ockham: Optics, Epistemology, and the Foundations of Semantics, 1250–1345*, Studien und Texte zur Geistesgeschichte des Mittelalters, 22 (Leiden: Brill, 1988)

Tachau, Katherine H., and Paul A. Streveler, eds, *Seeing the Future Clearly: Questions on Future Contingents by Robert Holcot*, Studies and Texts, 119 (Toronto: Pontifical Institute of Mediaeval Studies, 1995)

Thayer, Anne T., 'Judge and Doctor: Images of the Confessor in Printed Model Sermon Collections, 1450–1520', in *Penitence in the Age of Reformations*, ed. by Katharine Jackson Lualdi and Anne T. Thayer (Aldershot: Ashgate, 2000), pp. 10–29

——, *Penitence, Preaching and the Coming of the Reformation* (Aldershot: Ashgate, 2002)

——, 'Sermon Collections in Print, 1450–1520', *Medieval Sermon Studies*, 36 (1995), 50–63

Thomas, Antoine, 'Extraits des Archives du Vatican pour servir à l'histoire littéraire', *Romania*, 11 (1882), 177–87

Thorndike, Lynn, *History of Magic and Experimental Science*, 8 vols (New York: MacMillan, 1923–58)

Troeyer, Benjamin, *Bio-bibliographica Franciscana Neerlandica ante saeculum XVI*, I: *Pars Biographica, auctores editionum qui scripserunt ante saeculum XVI* (Nieuwkoop: de Graaf, 1974)

Tubach, Frederic C., '*Exempla* in the Decline', *Traditio*, 18 (1962), 407–17

Tunberg, Terence, 'What is Boncompagno's "Newest Rhetoric"?', *Traditio*, 42 (1986), 299–334

Twomey, Michael W., 'Medieval Encyclopedias', in *Medieval Christian Literary Imagery: A Guide to Interpretation*, ed. by Robert Earl Kaske, Arthur Groos, and Michael W. Twomey (Toronto: Toronto University Press, 1988), pp. 182–215

Twycross, Meg, *The Medieval Anadyomene: A Study in Chaucer's Mythography*, Medium Aevum Monographs, n.s., 1 (Oxford: Blackwell, 1972)

Vasoli, Cesare, 'Arte della memoria e predicazione', *Lettere italiane*, 38 (1986), 478–99

Vickers, Brian, *In Defence of Rhetoric* (Oxford: Clarendon Press, 1988)

——, ed., *Rhetoric Revalued: Papers from the International Society for the History of Rhetoric*, Medieval and Renaissance Texts and Studies, 19 (Binghamton, NY: Center for Medieval and Renaissance Studies, 1982)

Viera, David J., *Bibliografia anotada de la vida i obra de Francesc Eiximenis (1340?-1409?)* (Barcelona: Fundació Salvador Vives Casajuana, 1980)

——, *Medieval Catalan Literature: Prose and Drama*, Twayne's World Authors Series, 802 (Boston: Twayne, 1988)

Volkmann, Ludwig, 'Ars memorativa', *Jahrbuch der Kunsthistorischen Sammlungen in Wien*, Neue Folge, 30 (1929), 111–200

Walsh, Katherine, *Richard FitzRalph in Oxford, Avignon, and Armagh: A Fourteenth-Century Scholar and Primate* (Oxford: Oxford University Press, 1981)

Ward, John O., '*Artificiosa eloquentia* in the Middle Ages: The Study of Cicero's *De inventione*, the *Ad Herennium* and Quintilian's *De institutione oratoria* from the Early Middle Ages to the Thirteenth Century with Special Reference to the Schools of Northern France' (unpublished doctoral thesis, University of Toronto, 1972)

——, 'From Antiquity to the Renaissance: Glosses and Commentaries on Cicero's *Rhetorica*', in *Medieval Eloquence*, ed. by Murphy, pp. 26–67

Webster, Jill Rosemary, 'A Critical Edition of *El Regiment de princeps* by Francesc Eiximenis' (unpublished doctoral thesis, University of Toronto, 1969)

Weisheipl, James, 'The Life and Works of St. Albert the Great', in *Albertus Magnus and the Sciences: Commemorative Essays 1980*, ed. by James Weisheipl (Toronto: Pontifical Institute of Mediaeval Studies, 1980), pp. 13–53

Weiske, Brigitte , 'Die "Gesta Romanorum" und das "Solsequium" Hugos von Trimberg', in *Exempel und Exempelsammlungen*, ed. by Haug and Wachinger, pp. 173–207

Welter, Jean Thiébaut, *L'Exemplum dans la littérature religieuse et didactique du moyen âge* (Paris: Guitard, 1927)

Wenzel, Siegfried, 'The Arts of Preaching', in *Cambridge History of Literary Criticism*, II: *The Middle Ages*, ed. by Minnis and Johnson, pp. 84–96

——, 'The Classics in Late-Medieval Preaching', in *Medieval Antiquity*, ed. by Andries Welkenhuysen, Herman Braet, and Werner Verbeke (Leuven: Leuven University Press, 1995), pp. 127–43

——, *Latin Sermon Collections from Later Medieval England: Orthodox Preaching in the Age of Wyclif*, Cambridge Studies in Medieval Literature (Cambridge: Cambridge University Press, 2005)

——, *Macaronic Sermons: Bilingualism and Preaching in Late-Medieval England, Recentiores* (Ann Arbor: University of Michigan Press, 1994)

——, 'The Seven Deadly Sins: Some Problems of Research', *Speculum*, 43 (1968), 9–22

——, *The Sin of Sloth: Acedia in Medieval Thought and Literature* (Chapel Hill: University of North Carolina Press, 1967)

——, *Verses in Sermons: Fasciculus Morum and its Middle English Poems* (Cambridge, MA: Medieval Academy of America, 1978)

——, 'Vices, Virtues, and Popular Preaching', in *Medieval and Renaissance Studies: Proceedings of the Southeastern Institute of Medieval and Renaissance Studies, Summer 1974*, ed. by Dale Randall (Durham, NC: Duke University Press, 1976), pp. 28–54

Whitehead, Christiania, *Castles of the Mind: A Study of Medieval Architectural Allegory*, Religion and Culture in the Middle Ages (Cardiff: University of Wales Press, 2003)

——, 'Making a Cloister of the Soul in Medieval Religious Treatises', *Medium aevum*, 67 (1998), 1–29

Wilkins, Ernest Hatch, 'Descriptions of Pagan Divinities from Petrarch to Chaucer', *Speculum*, 32 (1957), 511–22

——, *Life of Petrarch* (Chicago: University of Chicago Press, 1963)

Willaert, Frank, and others, eds, *Medieval Memory: Image and Text*, Fédération internationale des Instituts d'études médiévales: Textes et études du moyen âge, 27 (Turnhout: Brepols, 2004)

Williams, Arnold, 'Chaucer and the Friars', *Speculum*, 28 (1953), 499–513

Williams, Thomas, 'Transmission and Translation', in *Cambridge Companion to Medieval Philosophy*, ed. by Arthur Stephen McGrade (Cambridge: Cambridge University Press, 2003), pp. 328–43

Witt, Ronald G., 'Boncompagno and the Defense of Rhetoric', *Journal of Medieval and Renaissance Studies*, 16 (1986), 1–31

Wolfson, Henry A., 'The Internal Senses', *Harvard Theological Review*, 28 (1935), 69–133

Worstbrock, Franz Josef, 'Johannes von Werden', in *Die deutsche Literatur des Mittelalters*, ed. by Ruh and others, IV, 811–13

Yates, Frances A., *The Art of Memory* (Chicago: University of Chicago Press, 1966)

——, 'Ciceronian Art of Memory', in *Medioevo e Rinascimento: Studi in onore di Bruno Nardi*, 2 vols (Florence: Sansoni, 1956), II, 873–903

——, 'Lodovico da Pirano's Memory Treatise', in *Cultural Aspects of the Italian Renaissance: Essays in Honour of Paul Oscar Kristeller*, ed. by Cecil A. Clough (New York: Zambelli, 1976), pp. 111–22

Young, Noël Denholm, 'Richard de Bury (1287–1345)', *Transactions of the Royal Historical Society*, ser. 4, 20 (1937), 135–63

Zawart, Anscar, 'The History of Franciscan Preaching and of Franciscan Preachers (1209– 1927): A Bio-bibliographical Study', *Franciscan Educational Conference*, 9 (1927), 242–587

Ziliotto, Baccio, 'Frate Lodovico da Pirano 1390–1450 e le sue Regulae memorie artificialis', *Atti e memorie della Società istriana di archeologia e storia patria*, 49 (1937), 189–224

Zinn, Grover A., Jr, 'Hugh of Saint Victor and the Art of Memory', *Viator*, 5 (1974), 211–34

——, '*Historia fundamentum est* and the Role of History in the Contemplative Life According to Hugh of St. Victor', in *Contemporary Reflections*, ed. by Shriver, pp. 135–58

# General Index

Major concepts as well as medieval and modern authors discussed in the main text are included in the index.

# Sermo: Studies on Patristic, Medieval, and Reformation Sermons and Preaching

All volumes in this series are evaluated by an Editorial Board, strictly on academic grounds, based on reports prepared by referees who have been commissioned by virtue of their specialism in the appropriate field. The Board ensures that the screening is done independently and without conflicts of interest. The definitive texts supplied by authors are also subject to review by the Board before being approved for publication. Further, the volumes are copyedited to conform to the publisher's stylebook and to the best international academic standards in the field.

### Titles in Series

Ruth Horie, *Perceptions of Ecclesia: Church and Soul in Medieval Dedication Sermons* (2006)

Veronica O'Mara and Suzanne Paul, *A Repertorium of Middle English Prose Sermons* (2007)

*Constructing the Medieval Sermon*, ed. by Roger Andersson (2007)

Alan John Fletcher, *Late Medieval Popular Preaching in Britain and Ireland: Texts, Studies, and Interpretations* (2009)

### In Preparation

Holly Johnson, *The Grammar of Good Friday: Macaronic Sermons of Late Medieval England*